The American Synagogue

A Sanctuary Transformed

Edited by
JACK WERTHEIMER

A Centennial Publication of the Jewish Theological Seminary
of America

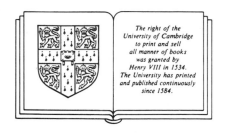

The right of the
University of Cambridge
to print and sell
all manner of books
was granted by
Henry VIII in 1534.
The University has printed
and published continuously
since 1584.

CAMBRIDGE UNIVERSITY PRESS

Cambridge

New York   New Rochelle   Melbourne   Sydney

Published by the Press Syndicate of the University of Cambridge
The Pitt Building, Trumpington Street, Cambridge CB2 1RP
32 East 57th Street, New York, NY 10022, USA
10 Stamford Road, Oakleigh, Melbourne 3166, Australia

First published 1987

Printed in the United States of America

Library of Congress Cataloging-in-Publication Data
The American synagogue: a sanctuary transformed / edited by Jack
Wertheimer.
p.   cm.
"A centennial publication of the Jewish Theological Seminary of America."
Includes index.
ISBN 0 521 33290 7
1. Synagogues - United States - History. I. Wertheimer, Jack.
II. Jewish Theological Seminary of America.
BM655.A48   1987
296'.0973 –dc19
                                                                87 - 20314
British Library Cataloguing in Publication Data   CIP
The American synagogue: a sanctuary transformed.
1. Synagogues - United States - History
I. Wertheimer, Jack   II. Jewish Theological
Seminary of America
296.5'5'0973   BM205
ISBN 0 521 33290 7

The American Synagogue

Contents

v

Preface

Synagogues are the oldest, hardiest, and most participatory institutions maintained by Jews in the United States. Their longevity is attested by the continuous existence of some contemporary congregations since the first half of the eighteenth century – a continuity unmatched by any other Jewish institutions in the United States and few congregations anywhere else in the world. In addition, by the end of the twentieth century, several hundred functioning congregations will have celebrated their centennial milestones. As for the durability of synagogues, we need only note the success of congregations in weathering significant transitions, including fundamental alterations in their demographic bases as neighborhoods and Jewish populations changed, frequent geographic relocations, and thoroughgoing revisions of their programs and practices. All of these developments occasioned disputes among local Jews that directly involved large numbers of members. Although often managed in an oligarchic fashion, synagogues in the aggregate have provided greater opportunities for participation by the Jewish laity than any other institution.

Surprisingly, synagogues are also among the most inadequately studied institutions in American Jewish life. Synagogue histories tend to be written by amateurs who aspire to chronicle key events and express a filiopietistic pride in the achievements of great founders and builders of congregations. Such celebratory accounts provide a foundation for serious scholarly research, but they are generally too parochial in scope to interest readers with no direct connection to the congregation. Insofar as trained historians do write about synagogues, they are apt to do so for the sake of comprehensiveness: They incorporate developments within congregations into larger surveys of communal institutions or histories of denominations. Only rarely do professional historians, in contrast to sociologists and ethnographers, examine congregations as institutions whose histories are inherently of interest.

The synagogue has been absent from the agenda of professional historians for a number of reasons. Most important, the entire subject of Jewish religious history in the United States has until recently stirred little interest in scholarly circles. Instead, American Jewish historiography has focused mainly on the so-called external history of the Jews, on the interaction of Jews with the larger American society. Hence, most writings in American Jewish history have been concerned with legal and political issues, support for Jews abroad, antisemitism, the process of immigrant adaptation, and, of course, "the great Jewish contributions" to American life. If the entire internal experience of Jews has been deemed narrow, how much more so the history of the most parochial and local of all Jewish institutions – the synagogue! Compared to the activities of national Jewish agencies or even local federations of philanthropy, the concerns of synagogue boards appear inconsequential.

Historians have also been discouraged from studying synagogues for pragmatic reasons. Like churches, whose histories are generally not studied by trained scholars either, individual synagogues are both narrow in their demographic bases and widely scattered geographically. As a consequence, research on synagogues may involve a great deal of travel that will yield information on only relatively small populations. Furthermore, it is difficult to conduct research when congregational papers are rarely preserved properly. The sheer logistics of such scholarship are daunting. Matters are further complicated if one seeks to examine how congregational life shapes, as well as reflects, broader social, cultural, and theological trends. Precisely because synagogues are the domain of "average" Jews, their histories raise questions concerning many issues and necessitate wide-ranging research. The religious congregation seems to be an impossibly broad subject of inquiry, even as its concerns appear to be parochial.

The purpose of this book is to illustrate the diversity and richness of synagogue life and suggest ways to approach this complex subject. *The American Synagogue: A Sanctuary Transformed* advances these aims through the discussion of both general and specific topics. The first four essays present broad overviews of the existing literature and sum up the state of the field. The ten essays in Part II each focus on a specific theme in the history of synagogues using an innovative case study approach: They explore thematic issues in depth through developments in a few representative congregations. Taken together, the essays in this volume represent a first attempt to survey the history of American synagogues comprehensively, while illustrating in new ways how the study of congregations sheds light on broader themes in American Jewish history.

Although written by fourteen authors who were trained at different institutions, reside in many localities, and span the spectrum of Jewish religious affiliation, the essays in this volume are predominantly concerned with the social history of the synagogue. This orientation has led to a deliberate decision to examine the synagogue from the "bottom up," from the perspective of the laity. Virtually every essay intentionally downplays the role of the professional leaders such as rabbis, cantors, and educators in order to emphasize the role of synagogue members. For the same reason, ideological issues, liturgical usages, and official pronouncements are not examined in this volume. By approaching the congregation from "the bottom up," this volume does not minimize the contribution of synagogue functionaries, but seeks to break with the prevailing approach to synagogues (and, indeed, all aspects of American Jewish religious life), which focuses almost exclusively on the activities and ideologies of elites. Precisely because synagogues are preeminently the creation of the Jewish laity, they deserve to be studied from the vantage point of nonelites.

The perspective of social history also informs the methods, sources, and analyses employed by contributors. Some essays rely on quantitative techniques; others scrutinize previously untapped primary sources, such as municipal registers and housing maps, court proceedings, newspaper advertisements, oral history interviews, and, of course, the uncatalogued papers of congregations. Furthermore, the themes explored in these essays derive from the interests of social historians in demography, occupational pursuits, patterns of geographic and socioeconomic mobility, ethnicity, and women's history. In fact, the opportunity to analyze congregational life from these perspectives attracted some of the contributors to this project. It is noteworthy that most of the essayists have not written about synagogue life before, but have distinguished themselves in other areas of modern Jewish social history. They were induced to write on topics removed from their earlier research by the opportunity to apply to the study of the synagogue approaches they had previously applied to other subjects.

In its methodological orientation, roster of contributors, and subject matter, this volume reflects some recent trends in American Jewish historiography. As already noted, this volume removes the synagogue from the monopoly of institutional historians and places it squarely within the purview of social historians. This shift mirrors the broader acceptance of social history in the work of American Jewish historians. Moreover, the participation of many scholars who previously have not written on American Jewry or Jewish religious institutions also represents important changes. The earlier work of several of the contributors has been concerned primarily with the history of European Jewries; their participation in this volume bespeaks a growing interest in American Jewish history among specialists in other areas. Finally, this volume also reflects a new concern on the part of American Jewish historians with religious life. With the exception of two senior scholars who have long devoted their work to this area of research, the contributors belong to a younger cohort of scholars trained in the late 1960s and early 1970s who are now exploring the internal history of American Jews. Unlike many of their elders, they are concerned with Jewish particularism, as expressed in the cultural, institutional, and religious lives of Jewish communities.

This historiographic shift is symptomatic of a turning inward that has characterized the American Jewish community during the past decade. Whereas the years between 1945 and 1975 were marked by a continued push toward Americanization and an embrace of social activism, the present-day Jewish community is more inner-directed. Its leaders are preoccupied with questions of Jewish survival and unity, rather than with the general social causes of the day; and many within the laity are probing the spiritual and communal dimensions of Jewish life. One can speculate as to the reasons for this shift: Does it stem from a high level of self-confidence among American Jews, which frees them to explore their own particularity? Or is it caused by insecurity, which propels Jews to withdraw into their own communities in order to withstand the blandishments of assimilation? Or does it mirror the broader trend toward conservatism and quest for community that characterize other sectors of American society? It is not possible to determine yet which factor is paramount, but American Jews are taking a greater interest in their own history and origins. This interest has found tangible expression in the establishment of new research centers and programs designed to preserve the records of American Jewry. Local Jewish communities are supporting central archives, and even many synagogues are organizing their own papers and encouraging research into their own histories. These developments augur well for continued and intensified research on the history of the American synagogue.

It is hoped that, as research goes forward, the present volume will serve as a useful guide to the broad sweep of synagogue history, as well as to important subtopics in the history of congregations. The book opens with Abraham Karp's overview of synagogue history. Karp examines the changing roles assigned to the synagogue in different eras of

American Jewish history. Identifying seven stages in the development of the synagogue, Karp explains how synagogues have reflected the changing needs and aspirations of American Jews. The next three essays examine the synagogue through the prism of denominationalism. The essays by Jeffrey Gurock, Leon Jick, and this editor survey the changing concerns and programs of Orthodox, Reform, and Conservative congregations, respectively – the three dominant denominations among American Jews. These authors have drawn on a broad range of published sources to sum up the existing state of knowledge and develop new interpretive frameworks. Whereas Karp describes how the function of American congregations has differed diachronically, the contributions in Part I discuss the differences and similarities in the responses of contemporaneous congregations to the American environment, and thereby illuminate how ideological and denominational allegiances shaped the Americanization process.

The case studies in Part II are designed to explore broader thematic issues, beginning with the Americanization process. Both Marc Angel and Benny Kraut examine the manner in which immigrant congregations adapted to the American environment and the tensions engendered within congregations by the struggle to Americanize. Although this theme has already been explored in regard to the three major waves of Jewish immigrants – the Sephardim of the colonial era, the German Jews of the mid-nineteenth century, and the East European Jews at the onset of the twentieth century – other populations have received comparatively little attention. The struggles within Ezra Bessaroth of Seattle and New Hope of Cincinnati contribute much-needed details of the history of twentieth-century Jewish immigrants from the Balkans and Germany, respectively. In addition, by drawing attention to subethnic groups within the American Jewish community, such as Sephardim from the Ottoman Empire and Ashkenazic refugees from Nazi Germany, these essays deepen our understanding of the larger American Jewish community, which so often is portrayed as a monolith, whereas it consists of numerous subpopulations that have struggled to retain their identities.

A second aspect of Americanization – namely, the introduction of innovative synagogue forms – is explored by Robert Liberles and Jonathan Sarna. Liberles reanalyzes the history of Beth Elohim in Charleston, the first American congregation that introduced far-reaching reforms. Several historians have already attempted to explain the motives of reformers in Charleston; Liberles challenges earlier works and offers a novel interpretation of developments at Beth Elohim. Sarna examines the development of a particular synagogue innovation – the one that permitted

men and women to pray seated together. Focusing on this specific reform, Sarna studies a distinctive practice in the American synagogue that
has sparked bitter controversies.

Whereas Liberles and Sarna consider innovations within the synagogue
sanctuary, several other contributors trace the development of new programs in other synagogue precincts. Deborah Dash Moore surveys the
diverse activities sponsored by New York's Brooklyn Jewish Center,
one of the most influential synagogue-centers in the first half of the
twentieth century. Her essay describes the emergence of a new style of
rabbinic leadership in the person of Israel H. Levinthal and of new types
of synagogue programs, such as a Hebrew day school, music and art
centers, and educational forums for adults. Although not all of these
models were imitated by other synagogue-centers, the ambitious efforts
of the Brooklyn Jewish Center expressed a particular understanding of
the synagogue that captivated many congregations during the interwar
years. Kay Kaufman Shelemay, Barry Chazan, and Jenna Weissman Joselit concentrate on three aspects of synagogue life that have undergone
extensive revision in American congregations. Focusing on a Reform
temple in Houston, Shelemay describes the multiple uses of music within
congregations. By examining the full spectrum of music activities both
in the sanctuary and in the social hall, Shelemay uses a novel approach
to study the role of music within the synagogue. Barry Chazan studies
the development of educational programs in a Conservative synagogue
in Albany, New York. He traces the rise and decline of a particular
conception of the synagogue's role as an educator of youth, as well as
the opportunities employed by synagogue personnel to teach and socialize
young people. In the process, Chazan examines both formal and informal
channels of education available in congregations. Jenna Weissman Joselit
concentrates on auxiliary organizations that have come to play an important role in the vast majority of American synagogues. Joselit specifically examines the emergence of sisterhoods in three congregations
in New York and the underlying conception of women's roles in the
programs of these women's auxiliaries. By comparing the activities of
sisterhoods in three neighboring congregations of different denominational affiliations, Joselit underscores the similarities among these
institutions.

In addition, two essays in this volume address the socioeconomic and
political dimensions of synagogue life. Marsha Rozenblit analyzes the
demographic characteristics of two congregations in Baltimore in order
to determine what circumstances played a role in the decision of Jews to
join a particular congregation. By comparing the occupational and residential choices of Jews affiliated with an Orthodox synagogue and a

Reform temple, Rozenblit is able to challenge accepted commonplaces about the social bases of Jewish denominationalism. Paula E. Hyman examines the impact of social processes from another perspective: Her analysis of the transplantation of Boston's Mishkan Tefila from an urban to a suburban location sheds light on the impact of changing neighborhoods and Jewish geographic mobility upon congregational life. Hyman also looks at a critical political process within congregations, namely, decision making: How are important decisions, such as relocating a synagogue, taken? And who leads a congregation?

Although this book's contents and structure reflect a desire to examine the synagogue comprehensively, this volume has also been conceived with the understanding that no single volume can do justice to so complex a topic. An effort has been made to study congregations in different geographic regions of this country, but clearly there is a need for additional research on regional variations in synagogue life and for comparative studies of urban and rural, large city and small city, central city and suburban congregations. The essays in this volume are almost equally divided into studies of the three major denominational synagogues, but some of the smaller denominational subtypes deserve extensive research: These include Traditional synagogues, Reconstructionist fellowships, and other variations such as Humanist and Jewish Science congregations. The Americanization experiences of many immigrant synagogues, including *landsmanshaft shuls*, Sephardic congregations, and Hassidic *shtiblach*, warrant attention. There are also serious gaps in our knowledge of how congregations express their architectural preferences, hire and fire professional staffs, select volunteer leaders, raise money, and relate to other local Jewish and non-Jewish institutions. More research is needed on the changing roles of professional leaders, such as rabbis, cantors, and educators. And much research is needed on recent trends in synagogue life, such as the movement to form intimate fellowships (*Havurot*), the drive for greater women's participation, and the impact of intensified religious controversies on the life of synagogues. Finally, we need to develop methods for studying the spiritual and communal meaning Jews find in their synagogues. It is the aim of this volume to spur research on these and other unstudied issues in the history of the American synagogue.

Acknowledgments

This book owes much to individuals and institutions whose names do not appear in the list of contributors. It was the vision of Dr. Robert Lynn, senior vice-president at the Lilly Endowment, and Chancellor Gerson D. Cohen of the Jewish Theological Seminary of America, that inspired this project. Together, they launched a program to study the future of the synagogue in America, which was funded by the Lilly Endowment and conducted under the auspices of the Seminary. Headed by Prof. Neil Gillman of the Seminary and organized by a planning committee consisting of academicians, pulpit rabbis, and lay leaders of the Conservative Movement, this program eventually incorporated a component on the history of the American synagogue. I wish to thank the members of this committee for entrusting me with the coordination of a historical study, the fruits of which appear in this book. I particularly wish to thank Robert Lynn, Gerson Cohen, and Neil Gillman for their ongoing interest and support. In the light of the Seminary's direct role in sponsoring this project, as well as its century of active leadership in American Jewish religious activities, it is fitting that this volume appears as a centennial publication of the Jewish Theological Seminary of America.

A second group of advisors helped shape this volume. In thinking through the book's conception and structure, I was advised by a working editorial board consisting of Profs. Jeffrey Gurock, Yeshiva University; Leon Jick, Brandeis University; Gillian Lindt, Columbia University; Michael A. Meyer, Hebrew Union College – Jewish Institute of Religion, Cincinnati; and Ismar Schorsch, the Jewish Theological Seminary of America. These scholars met collectively to plan the volume and thereafter aided me when I needed to call on them for their individual expertise. As the commissioned manuscripts were submitted by contributors, Jeffrey Gurock and Michael Meyer served as referees. Their thoughtful and constructive criticism helped all the contributors improve their essays. In the final stages of preparing this volume for publication, I have been aided by John Ruskay, vice-chancellor for public affairs at the Seminary, and Jean Highland, the Seminary's consultant on publications. Janis Bolster, David Emblidge, Emily Loose, Vicki Macintyre, and Deborah Menzell, my editors at Cambridge University Press, have acted in an exemplary fashion as patient and helpful editors. And Moshe Zabari, artist-in-residence at the Jewish Museum and good friend, graciously aided in the process of selecting an appropriate design for the dust jacket. Last, but most important, I thank the thirteen colleagues whose names do appear in the table of contents for joining me in this collaborative effort to explore the history of the American synagogue.

Contributors

Marc D. Angel is Rabbi of Congregation Shearith Israel, the historic Spanish-Portuguese Synagogue in New York City. His scholarly interests are in the fields of Jewish law and Sephardic history and culture. He is the author of *The Jews of Rhodes: The History of a Sephardic Community, La America: The Sephardic Experience in the United States, The Rhythms of Jewish Living: A Sephardic Approach,* and *The Orphaned Adult: Confronting the Death of a Parent.*

Barry Chazan is on the faculty of the School of Education at the Hebrew University, where he has served as Director of the Melton Center for Jewish Education in the Diaspora. His books on ethnic, moral, and religious education include *Contemporary Approaches to Moral Education, Studies in Jewish Education, The Language of Jewish Education,* and *Moral Education.*

Jeffrey S. Gurock is Libby Klaperman Professor of Jewish History at the Bernard Revel Graduate School of Yeshiva University. His research interests include the history of New York Jewry and the history of Judaism in America. He is the author of *When Harlem Was Jewish* and *The Men and Women of Yeshiva and the Changing Face of American Orthodoxy.*

Paula E. Hyman is Lucy Moses Professor of Modern Jewish History at Yale University. She has particular interests in West European and American Jewish history as well as Jewish women's history. The author of *From Dreyfus to Vichy: The Remaking of French Jewry* and co-author of *The Jewish Woman in America,* she has recently co-edited *The Jewish Family: Images and Reality.*

Leon A. Jick is Helen and Irving Schneider Professor of American Jewish Studies and Chairman of the Department of Near Eastern and Judaic

xvi

Studies at Brandeis University. He is the author of *The Americanization of the Synagogue, 1820–1870* and editor of *The Teaching of Judaica at American Universities.*

Jenna Weissman Joselit, a Research Associate in History at the YIVO Institute for Jewish Research, is the author of *Our Gang: Jewish Crime and the New York Jewish Community, 1900–1940.* She is currently completing a book on the history of Orthodox Jews in New York.

Abraham J. Karp is a Professor of History and Religion and the Philip S. Bernstein Professor of Jewish Studies at the University of Rochester. He is a past president of the American Jewish Historical Society. His latest books are *Haven and Home, A History of the Jews in America* and *Haye Ha-Ruach shel Yahadut America* (Hebrew).

Benny Kraut is Professor and Director of the Judaic Studies Program at the University of Cincinnati. He has published essays on American Judaism and Jewish-Christian relations and is the author of *From Reform Judaism to Ethical Culture: The Religious Education of Felix Adler.*

Robert Liberles is Senior Lecturer in Modern Jewish History at Ben Gurion University in Beersheva, Israel, where he currently serves as head of Jewish History. His fields of research are German Jewish history, modern Jewish religious movements, and the controversy over emancipation in Western Europe. His book *Religious Conflict in Social Context: The Resurgence of Orthodox Judaism in Frankfurt am Main, 1838–1877* was awarded the 1986 National Jewish Book Award in History.

Deborah Dash Moore teaches Jewish Studies and American Culture at Vassar College, where she is an Associate Professor of Religion. She is the author of *At Home in America: Second Generation New York Jews* and *B'nai B'rith and the Challenge of Ethnic Leadership.* She is currently researching a study of Jewish migration and communities in the sunbelt.

Marsha L. Rozenblit is an Associate Professor of Modern Jewish History at the University of Maryland, College Park. She specializes in Jewish social history, focusing in particular on the modernization of Central European Jewry in the nineteenth century. She has written articles on Jewish religious reform and Jewish nationalism in Vienna and is the author of *The Jews of Vienna, 1867–1914: Assimilation and Identity.*

Jonathan D. Sarna is Associate Professor of American Jewish History at the Hebrew Union College – Jewish Institute of Religion (Cincinnati) and Director of its Center for the Study of the American Jewish Experience. He specializes in nineteenth- and twentieth-century American

Jewish History and has written or edited five books, including *The American Jewish Experience, Jacksonian Jew: The Two Worlds of Mordechai Noah,* and *People Walk on Their Heads: Moses Weinberger's Jews and Judaism in New York.* He is currently completing a history of the Jewish Publication Society.

Kay Kaufman Shelemay is Associate Professor of Music and Coordinator of the Urban Ethnomusicology Program at New York University. She has done extensive research on Ethiopian liturgical traditions, as well as Jewish music in the United States. She is the author of *Music, Ritual and Falasha History.*

Jack Wertheimer is the Joseph and Martha Mendelson Associate Professor of American Jewish History and Director of the Archives of Conservative Judaism at the Jewish Theological Seminary of America. He has written essays on modern European and American Jewry, and is the author of *Unwelcome Strangers: East European Jews in Imperial Germany.*

1

Overview: The Synagogue in America – A Historical Typology

ABRAHAM J. KARP

Little more than half a year after the first Jews arrived in New Amsterdam, the Reverend Johann Megapolensis of the Reformed Dutch Church wrote to his superiors in Amsterdam, on March 18, 1655: "Last summer some Jews came here from Holland. . . . Now again, in the spring some have come . . . and report that a great many of that lot would yet follow and then build here their synagogue."[1] The Reverend's apprehensions that the handful of immigrant Jews, the first of their people on the North American continent, planned to form a congregation, were well founded. Governor Peter Stuyvesant complained to the directors of the Dutch West India Company, owners of the colony, on June 10, 1656, that "the Jewish nation . . . have many times requested of us free and public exercise of their abominable religion." He urged that this not be granted, for "giving them liberty, we cannot refuse the Lutherans and the Papists."[2] A year earlier, in July 1655, in reply to a petition by the recently arrived Jews to "purchase a burying place for their nation," the council of the colony noted, "that inasmuch as they did not wish to bury their dead in the common burying ground, there would be granted them when the need and occasion thereof arose, some place elsewhere of the free land belonging to the Company,"[3] and on February 22, 1656, two members of the council were "authorized to point out to the petitioners a little hook of land situate outside of this city for a burial place."[4]

Within the year of their arrival, the Jews of New Amsterdam had already joined together for their common religious needs, the first of which was consecrated ground for burial. Congregation Shearith Israel, mother synagogue of American Israel, may well be right in dating its inception to the year of arrival, 1654. The first congregation's initial holding, as in the case of many of the congregations that followed, was a cemetery.

1

As the Reverend Mr. Megapolensis feared, many were to follow the first arrivals and "did build here their synagogue" for the transmission of Jewish knowledge and for the retention and fostering of Jewish loyalties. The establishment of a congregation was not always an expression of piety, nor was the building of a synagogue evidence of a desire to worship. For many, the act represented no more than a profession of Jewish identity or a response to what was believed to be an American "demand." Said Dr. Jacob De La Motta in an address at the consecration of the newly built synagogue of Congregation Mikve Israel of Savannah, Georgia, June 21, 1820: "Were we not influenced by religious zeal, a decent respect to the custom of the community, in which we live, should actuate us to observe public worship."[5]

The definition and function of the American synagogue were forged within the parameters of Jewish needs and American demands, changing in response to the changing religious needs of the American Jew and in conformity both to the possibilities for public expression of corporate Jewish religious life that America afforded and to the perceived limitation upon it that America imposed.

Synagogue Community

In colonial America, synagogue and community were synonymous, and the congregation served all communal needs. "No colonial American Jewish community ever sheltered more than one permanent synagogue," Jacob R. Marcus has noted, "and the local synagogue virtually exercised a monopolistic control over every Jew within its ambit."[6] It was able to do so because it alone provided for the basic needs of the recently arrived or native Jew: companionship with fellow Jews, a place to worship when piety or other sentiments demanded it, circumcision for a son and a wedding service for a daughter, kosher meat for the table and a proper burial in consecrated ground, and the opportunity to give or to receive charity. Hannah, the widow of Moses Louzanda, remained on the pension rolls of Shearith Israel for some twenty years from 1756 through 1774, and Levi Michaels petitioned "the President and Elders of the Synagoga in the City of New York" in 1764 for "a sum of money, upon loan, as you in your wisdom shall see meet" to enable him to return to Montreal. In 1762 Abraham I. Abrahams was engaged by the congregation "to keep a publick school . . . to teach the Hebrew language and translate the same into English, also to teach English, reading, writing, and cyphering." Seven years later he described his tenure as "having served this congregation in the capacity of a Ribbi [*sic*]"[7] (the term designates teacher, for there were no ordained rabbis in America until the middle of the nineteenth century). The chief religious functionary was the *hazzan*, who led the services, officiated at religious ceremonies (although permission to officiate at a marriage had to be granted by the lay leaders), and on occasion would be permitted to preach. The governance of the congregation in all its aspects was firmly in the hands of lay leaders, who kept a tight rein.

For the immigrant Jew, the synagogue provided the comforting continuity of familiar liturgy and ritual and the security of the company of fellow Jews who would care and provide for one's family in time of need or loss. In a society that was splintering into a religious pluralism, the synagogue was becoming part of the religious landscape, its adherents clothed with an identity coherent and acceptable to the host community. Marcus suggests that "in its hegemonic aspect the colonial American synagogue did parallel contemporary Protestantism" as it moved "toward the integration of [its] communicants into one rounded-out religious, social, and eleemosynary whole."[8] What permitted the local synagogue to exert "monopolistic control" was the place and power of the church in colonial America. Franklin Hamlin Littell notes that the major religious factor in colonial America was the established church and that even in the early years of the Republic, the great Virginians, Washington, Jefferson, et al., "were all committed to the cause of organized religion . . . the large majority as taxpayers and patrons of the state church."[9] The Jews, seeking acceptance, laboring at integration, took instruction and example from their Protestant neighbors, choosing the synogogue as the institution that would establish their community; indeed, they regarded congregation and community as synonymous.

No more than a half dozen congregations served colonial Jewry. They were small and far apart. Almost one hundred miles separated the nearest two, New York's Shearith Israel and Philadelphia's Mikveh Israel. Although separated by distance, they were united by their shared Jewish identity, by a similar Sephardi synagogue rite, and by family and business ties. One congregation could freely turn to another in time of need, whether it was for aid in building a synagogue, for the loan of a Torah or other ritual objects, or for guidance in religious matters. This unity found symbolic expression when four of the six – the Hebrew congregations in the cities of Philadelphia, New York, Richmond, and Charleston – united in an "Address . . . to the President of the United States," George Washington, in 1790. Only the most northern congregation in Newport, Rhode Island, and the most southern, in Savannah, Georgia, framed their own letters. The Jewish communities spoke through their congregations, which were the sole communal institutions.

The mother congregation, as we have noted, was Shearith Israel, New

York. The earliest extant minute books disclose that by 1728 it was a fully functioning organization presided over by a "Parnaz and Two Hatanim" and served by three functionaries:

> The Hazzan Mosses Lopez de fonseca shall be obliged to attend at the Sinogog at the customary hours twice every weekday, and three times on the Sabbath and feasts . . . Semuel Bar Meyr a Cohen of this Kahall shall be obliged to kill at severall places and Sufficiently for the whole Congregation. . . . Valentin Campanall Shamaz shall be obliged to atend at the Sinogog and shall call the Yehidimz that they may assemble togeathere at the usual hours . . . he shall keep the Synagog candlesticks & lamp clean and make the candles also shall keep the sestern supplyed with watter.[10]

The *hazzan, bodek* (ritual inspector), and *shamash* (beadle) were paid £50, £20, and £16, respectively, and were supplied with firewood and *matzot* (unleavened Passover bread). The congregation met in a house on Mill Street, "commonly known by the name of the Jews' synagogue."[11]

Dr. Alexander Hamilton, of Annapolis, Maryland, on a visit to the New York synagogue on Rosh Hashanah, 1744, wrote:

> I went in the morning with Mr. Hog to the Jews' sinagogue where was an assembly of about 50 of the seed of Abraham chanting and singing their doleful hymns, dressed in robes of white silk. Before the rabbi, who was elevated above the rest, in a kind of desk, stood the seven golden candlesticks transformed into silver gilt. They were all slipshod. The men wore their hats . . . and had a veil of some white stuff which they sometimes threw over their heads in their devotion; the women, of whom some were very pritty, stood up in a gallery like a hen coop. They sometimes paused or rested a little from singing and talked about business.[12]

The colonial synagogue represented continuity. It replicated in form and function the Jewish houses of worship on the European continent – adopting the same prayers, garb, melodies, and decorum, or lack thereof. It was that, and more. Already in colonial days it was part of the American religious landscape. When Rabbi Haim Isaac Carigal, emissary from Hebron, preached in the Newport, Rhode Island, synagogue on Shavuot, 1773, the twenty-five Jewish families were joined at the service, Ezra Stiles reports, by Governor Joseph Wantan and judges Oliver and Auchmuty. The dedication of a new synagogue in Charleston, South Carolina,

on September 19, 1774, was attended by Governor William Moultrie
and civil and military officers of the state and city. The *South Carolina
State Gazette* noted: "From the style of the building and the splendor of
its ornaments, we can perceive that, that injured people . . . have realized
their promised land . . . in the blessed climes of America. The shackles
of religious distinctions are now no more . . . they are permitted to the
full privileges of citizenship, and bid fair to flourish and be happy.[13]

The Jews perceived that in America "religious distinctions" expressed
by the synagogue were not bars to "privileges of citizenship." To the
contrary, the synagogue served as a symbol of the Jews' at-homeness in
America. In 1788 the Jews of Philadelphia solicited contributions for
building a synagogue from "worthy fellow Citizens of every religious
Denomination . . . flattering themselves that their worshipping Almighty
God in a way and manner different from other religious societies will
never deter the enlightened citizens of Philadelphia, from generously
subscribing."[14] They were correct in their surmise. Benjamin Franklin
was the first to respond with a generous £5, and he was joined by a
who's who of the community.

The small size of the Jewish communities in colonial America permitted
only single congregations, all following the Sephardic rite. As established
churches became prevalent, community and congregation were seen as
identical. Functionally, the total needs of Jewish life were provided for
by the congregation, which in turn exerted considerable discipline over
its membership. The synagogue as an institution of religion afforded the
immigrant community an accepted and respected vehicle for its integration into the larger society.

Rite Congregations

During the first half of the nineteenth century, while the Jewish
population of the world doubled in size, that of the United States increased twenty-five fold, from some two thousand to fifty thousand.
Migration from central and western Europe provided the numbers and
helped diversify the rapidly growing network of Ashkenazi synagogues.
By midcentury, the ten synagogues of the early 1800s had grown to
almost ninety. New York City alone could boast of twenty, Philadelphia,
five. Their rite varied with country of origin, as noted in the Lyons-De
Sola *Jewish Calendar of 1854*.[15] New York's synagogues ranged from the
Portuguese *minhag* (rite) Shearith Israel to seven following the Polish
minhag, seven the German, and one the Bohemian; in addition, one was
described as a Netherlandish congregation. As identified by their *minhag*,
the five synagogues of Philadelphia were Portuguese, German (two),

Polish, and Netherlandish. The *Calendar* also discloses that communal function was becoming diversified. No fewer than forty-four societies served the charitable and educational needs of New York Jewry; Philadelphia listed seventeen; and Cincinnati, served by two Polish and two German congregations, supported eleven societies and schools.

Factors external and internal to Jewish life were responsible for the proliferation and diversification of synagogues. In the 1830s Francis Grund described the role of religion in America: "Religion has been the basis of the most important American settlements; religion kept their little community together, religion assisted them in their revolutionary struggle. . . . The Americans look upon religion as a promoter of civil and political liberty; and have, therefore, transferred to it a large portion of the affection which they cherish for the institutions of their country."[16]

The immigrant Jew quickly perceived that religion and religious institutions were highly esteemed in America, that those associated with these institutions were respected as "good citizens," and that religious diversity was viewed as a mandate of democracy. Thomas Jefferson stated to Jacob De La Motta that in religion the maxim is "divided we stand, united, we fall."[17] The diversity that the synagogue brought to the religious scene was a service to democracy. Hence, to build and maintain a synagogue was a response to the American as well as to the Jewish call to duty. Wherever Jewish and American interests fortified each other, American Jews responded with complete enthusiasm.

American church bodies, whether Episcopalian, Presbyterian, Lutheran, Methodist, or Baptist, reflected differences not only in religious ideology but also in European national origins. The immigrant Jews took example and did the same. The rite synagogues afforded the immigrant the needed comfort and security of the known, the habitual. Continuity of ritual and familiar liturgical melodies sung by *landsleit* (fellow immigrants from the same town or region) eased the trauma of migration and resettlement. The first Ashkenazi congregation, Rodef Shalom of Philadelphia, came about naturally, when in 1795 a group of Jews felt more comfortable praying "according to the German and Dutch rules" than the Sephardi rite of Mikveh Israel. The older congregation accepted this division as natural and right.[18] This was not the case in New York's first Ashkenazi synagogue, B'nai Jeshurun. In May 1825, fifteen members of Shearith Israel requested that they be permitted to conduct their own services in the synagogue. The request was summarily turned down by the trustees, who stated that they could not "recognize any society or association for religious worship distinct from Congregation Shearith Israel." Nonetheless, the petitioners were determined to found a new congregation, explaining: "We have a large portion of our brethren who have been educated in the German and Polish minhag, who find it difficult to accustom themselves to what is commonly called the Portuguese minhag."[19] They also argued that increasing immigration and dispersal of places of residence would soon make another synagogue necessary. The leaders of the mother congregation never replied to the seceders; unhappy with the defection, they would not wish them well, but, recognizing the inevitable, they knew that to protest would be useless.

Once begun, the process of congregation building, aided by growing immigration, continued. In 1828, a group of German, Dutch, and Polish Jews left B'nai Jeshurun, which styled itself as an English synagogue recognizing the authority of London's Great Synagogue and its rabbi, to found Anshe Chesed. Eleven years later, a group of Polish Jews left both synagogues to form Shaarey Zedek, which in turn was abandoned by a group of its congregants who organized Beth Israel in 1843.

The professional traveler I. J. Benjamin II describes the situation well:

> The Portuguese claimed a sort of patronage – over the immigrants. . . . Accordingly, the immigrants founded a new synagogue. Those of English origin . . . introduced the London *minhag* with a sermon and discussion of congregational matters in English. The Germans . . . could not endure the English; the Poles could not endure the Germans; so there was soon division and separation in all directions. New York spread ever more rapidly; distances became too great, the synagogues too small.[20]

Most separations were acrimonious, occasioned by disagreement on a point of ritual or liturgical usage, social distinctions, ethnic loyalties, or personal peeves. What made possible this volatility and viability of the new congregations was the congregationalism that marked American religious life, legitimizing secession, and a constantly increasing immigration from numerous countries.

The same group that had left Shearith Israel to found B'nai Jeshurun in 1825, twenty years later left it to form Shaaray Tefilah. The immediate cause of the rupture was a contested election of trustees, which reached the state supreme court. On leaving, the dissidents were accompanied by the Reverend Samuel M. Isaacs, *Hazzan* of B'nai Jeshurun and its *shammas* B. M. Davis. The religious rites, rituals, liturgy, and order of services remained identical in both congregations. Like its parent congregation, it remained fully Orthodox, worshiping "according to the rites of the Polish and German Jews."[21]

Isaac Leeser described Jewish religious life in 1844:

> We have no ecclesiastical authorities in America, other than the congregations themselves. Each congregation makes its own

rules for its government, and elects its own minister, who is appointed without any ordination, induction in office being made through his election.... As yet we have no colleges or public schools of any kind, with the exception of one in New York... one in Baltimore and another in Cincinnati, and Sunday schools... in New York, Philadelphia, Richmond, Charleston, Columbia, S.C., Savannah, and Cincinnati.... In all our congregations where the necessity demands it, there are ample provisions made for the support of the poor.[22]

Leeser anticipated an expansion of educational endeavors "as soon as we become more numerous," and his optimism was bolstered by the fact that, although "in the southern and western states the arrival of Israelites [was] but recent," there were already congregations in Mobile, New Orleans, Louisville, Cincinnati, Cleveland, and St. Louis.[23] The Israelites were becoming more numerous; they were settling in the cities and towns of the south and west and establishing congregations to answer their communal needs.

In the smaller communities, one congregation served the needs of all. Since the great majority of the Jews in these communities were immigrants from Germany, the congregational articles of incorporation often provided, as did those of Congregation Beth El of Detroit, that the "Divine... services shall be held according to the German Ritual (Minhag) and not be changed." The congregation had been organized in 1850 at the urging of a pious woman, Sarah Cozens. That year twelve Jews founded the Beth El Society and brought Samuel Marcus from New York to serve as rabbi, cantor, teacher, *shohet* (ritual slaughterer), and *mohel* (circumciser) at an annual salary of $200.00. He instituted services, opened a Hebrew-German-English day school and organized the Hebra Bikur Cholim to care for the sick and the dying. In 1854 he was succeeded by Dr. Liebman Adler, who had arrived from Germany and to whose duties was added preaching in German, all for a salary of $360.00. Dr. Isaac M. Wise, who had recommended Dr. Adler, was pleased to publish in *The Israelite* extracts of Beth El's constitution and bylaws adopted in 1856, translated from the original German:

1. ... An Israelitish congregation... should be one great family.
3. [It] is obliged to establish and support regular and public divine worship... by warm, earnest and cordial participation....
4. The education of the young in all its branches, especially in religion, is a duty involving the whole congregation....

5. An appropriate, dignified and religious treatment of the dead is likewise a duty of the congregation.
6. [as is] The support of the poor co-religionists . . . .
7. The congregation shall, in all its religious institutions, pay due attention to the progress of the age, and maintain the respect due to customs or laws handed down to us by our pious fathers. In case of innovation, this congregation shall attempt to remain in unity with the majority of the American congregations, and shall always attempt to produce uniformity in the American synagogue.[24]

Wise hails this permission for modest reform as "fairly opening the way to the *Minhag America* [the American rite]," a uniform prayerbook for American synagogues, and sees in article 7 an expression of commitment to a united synagogue body, synod, and college.[25]

The Reform Temple

In the second half of the nineteenth century the Reform Movement began to make serious inroads. Within three decades it had enlisted the great majority of the leading congregations and grew ever more radical with each triumph. "The number of reform congregations prior to the Civil War was small," Leon A. Jick notes, but "by 1870, there were few congregations in America in which substantial reforms had *not* been introduced and in which an accelerating program of radical revision was *not* in process." The war had brought to a virtual end the large-scale immigration from Germany, which had trebled the Jewish population from 50,000 in 1850 to 150,000 in 1860. Few immigrants "who might have reinforced the ranks of traditionalism" arrived in the 1860s and 1870s; those who had arrived earlier were caught up in an assimilatory process that the "nationalist fervor generated by the war" had accelerated, and that expressed itself through religious reform. "Respectability and Americanization were the goals; decorum, reform of ritual, and English were the means."[26]

Reform as a product of Americanization had already been noted by Joseph Krauskopf in 1887. "From the moment that the American-born element began to make itself felt," he wrote, "it could not reconcile its mode of thought and its higher aspirations with the musty ghetto religious practices."[27]

In 1824, forty-seven members of the Charleston, South Carolina, Beth Elohim congregation petitioned for synagogal reforms. Rebuffed, they founded the Reformed Society of Israelites a year later, adopted articles of faith, worshiped from their own prayerbook, with heads uncovered, to the accompaniment of instrumental music. The society lasted only eight years, but when Beth Elohim built a new synagogue, it voted "that an organ be erected in the Synagogue to assist in the vocal parts of the service." At the synagogue's dedication, the Reverend Gustav Poznanski advocated "the reformed practice of conducting certain portions of the service in the vernacular."[28]

American Reform Judaism was, however, an imported product. Thus in 1842 in Baltimore, a group of German immigrants, influenced by the Hamburg (Germany) Reform Temple, protested the Orthodoxy of the existing congregation and formed the *Har Sinai Verein*, "the first American synagogue founded *ab initio* on a Reform basis."[29] On Shavvot of that year, following refusal of the loan of a Torah scroll by the mother congregation, the Torah portion was read from a printed Bible. The new congregation used the Hamburg temple prayerbook at its Rosh Hashanah services, singing hymns from its hymnal to the accompaniment of a parlor organ. Its "most learned member," Max Sutro, "reader, preacher and teacher of the congregation," questioned whether it should observe the Tisha B'Av day of mourning for the destruction of the temple in Jerusalem for fear that "Christian fellow-citizens . . . [seeing us] mourning the destruction of Jerusalem, [would conclude] that we are longing to return there and that our patriotism for our present homeland cannot be a true, genuine and fervent one."[30]

A dozen years later, the now radical Reform congregation did hold a service on the "Anniversary of the Destruction of Jerusalem," but it was not a service of lamentation – it was one of commemoration and celebration. As its rabbi David Einhorn explained in his prayerbook *Olath Tamid*, "The one temple in Jerusalem sank into the dust, in order that countless temples might arise to thy honor and glory."[31]

One such temple was Har Sinai in Baltimore, another, Emanu-El in New York, founded in 1845. Its road to reform was gradual. In its first prayer room, "the front seats were set apart for use of men, and those at the back for use of the women," and a volunteer choir was established. Leo Merzbacher (called "Mr." in the early minutes) was engaged as rabbi and G. M. Cohen as cantor at salaries of two hundred dollars per annum. The rabbi's discourse was central to the service. The congregation took offense when he failed to preach and requested that he give notice in advance if circumstances prevented him from speaking. He was also asked to introduce hymns in German at the services and to supply the board with a list of the prayers to be said on the forthcoming High Holidays. In the spring the board inquired of the rabbi how the Purim service might be conducted *mit kirchliche Hinsicht* (with becoming churchly respect). At the first annual meeting a committee was appointed to assist the Reverend Dr. Merzbacher with liturgical reforms.

Two and a half years after its founding, having purchased a church building, Emanu-El began its program of reform: it introduced an organ to accompany the choir, the triennial cycle of Torah reading, and a confirmation service for boys and girls; at the same time, it abolished "old- fashioned, useless ceremonies, such as reading a portion of the Law by a so-called Bar Mitzvah boy, making a *mi-sheberach* for one called to hear the Law read, and eventually the calling up to the reading of the Law."[32] The weekday elementary school was replaced by a religious school that met on Saturday and Sunday. In 1849, the rabbi was directed to prepare a ritual for services in German and English. Five years later, the rabbi and a committee prepared a revised prayerbook, and this was followed by the abolition of the wearing of a *talith* (prayer shawl) and the second-day observance of the festivals. Americanization also prompted the adoption of English as the language of the pulpit. "Patriotic in all things," the chronicler of Emanu-El explains, "they desired that the language of the land should be heard in their shrine, and Dr. Merzbacher was asked to speak in English at times . . . and a committee was appointed to secure an English lecturer."[33] Mr. R. J. De Cordova, a popular professional lecturer, was engaged to deliver lectures every other Saturday, "the topics to be selected after consultation with the minister." Although there was sentiment in the congregation that "the lecturer ought to be a theologian," De Cordova's tenure extended from 1856 through 1864. When Merzbacher's successor, Dr. Samuel Adler, permitted the uncovering of the head during the English lecture that was delivered after the Sabbath service, the congregation decided to do away with wearing a hat at the service as well.

Har Sinai and Emanu-El had been founded as Reform congregations, but more typical were those that began as traditional congregations and subsequently moved toward reform, as was the case of Congregation B'rith Kodesh in Rochester, New York. Founded in 1848 by German Jews, mainly from Bavaria, it remained fully traditional until 1862, when an organ and choir music were introduced. Family pews followed in 1869. A year later, some of the more radical members succeeded in having the minister of the Unitarian church lecture at the temple. In 1873, Unitarian lecturer Dr. N. M. Mann and Rabbi Max Landsberg brought their congregations together for a Union Thanksgiving Service.

In 1879, David Rosenberg was elected president on the promise that he would remove his hat at services when occupying his official seat. He did so, bringing "down upon his unprotected head a storm of indignation and abuse from the older members."[34] Nevertheless, during his administration the wearing of hats was abolished. In 1883, the temple introduced a new ritual that "practically excluded the use of Hebrew from the services, the English language being substituted. It was the first Jewish congregation in the United States, and probably in the world to take this step."[35] In the prayerbook that Dr. Landsberg published two years later he notes that "he cannot find adequate terms to express my admiration to my dear friend Rev. N. M. Mann, Pastor of Unity Church, for the kind interest he has taken in the preparation of this Ritual, and the valuable services he has rendered in making the English more idiomatic and perfect."[36] Dr. Landsberg also notes that "the desire for English prayers is growing everywhere, and will soon become universal in this country," and welcomes "the recent attempt to introduce an English Service for Friday night at the largest temple in Cincinnati."

The Cincinnati temple was Isaac M. Wise's B'nai Jeshurun. Wise favored the use of Hebrew in public worship for, "dispersed as the house of Israel is in all lands, we must have a vehicle to understand each other in the house of God, so that no brother be a stranger therein."[37] The prayerbook he edited, *Minhag America*, read from right to left. It was an abridged, altered text of the liturgy, retaining the traditional order and rubrics, with either an English or German translation facing the Hebrew text. The main service of worship was held on Friday evening. Dr. David Einhorn produced his radical Reform *Olat Tamid* prayerbook, a completely altered liturgy in German with Hebrew selections reading from left to right, for Sunday morning services. Comprising scriptural readings, prayers, and hymns in the vernacular, the service was conducted by the rabbi and featured the sermon. In 1894, when the official prayerbook of the Reform Movement, the *Union Prayerbook*, was published, it was modeled on the radical Reform *Olat Tamid* rather than the moderate Reform *Minhag America*. The Reform temple had become a religiously radical institution.

The service of worship was rabbi centered, but governance and authority in the temple were in lay hands. Thus, at the annual meeting of the Chicago Sinai Congregation on March 26, 1885, the president reported that questions on such matters as the rite of circumcision, the language of prayer, and the observance of a holiday on the Sunday nearest to it had been presented to the rabbi, Dr. Emil G. Hirsch, for his opinions, which were then circulated to the congregation. Thereupon the congregation decided through a vote what its policy would be. The rabbi had voiced his position, but the decision was in the hands of the laity.

The Reform temple served its congregants as a bond to Judaism and a portal to America. Beyond that, its leaders saw its purpose to be the creation of a new Judaism, suited to the new age and their new homeland. As the president of the Sinai congregation expressed it:

> We have discarded many obsolete rites . . . . Our work will not be completed until we have removed every unnecessary vestige, until we have built on the old foundation a new structure, in keeping with the modern style of religious architecture. . . . [For] the observance of certain obsolete customs is inconsistent with true religion. . . . When darkness gives way to light, Sinai congregation will have the proud satisfaction of having served in the front ranks among the founders of a religion, broad enough for all humanity to stand on.[38]

The Reform temple was the product of the confrontation of the immigrant German Jews already undergoing cultural assimilation with an America that welcomed such integration and valued religious institutionalization, denominationalism, and experimentation.

The Orthodox *Shul*

In the last decades of the nineteenth century, when the great majority of American synagogues were turning to Reform Judaism, a new kind of congregation appeared on the American scene, the East European Orthodox *shul* (synagogue). The first "Russian-American Jewish Congregation" (as its chronicler J. D. Eisenstein calls it) was organized on June 4, 1852, by East European immigrants and "several non-Russian Jews who were dissatisfied with the reform movement of their congregations."[39] It took the name Beth Hamedrash. A growing membership caused it to move to larger quarters twice in the first year of its existence. Among the organizers was Abraham Joseph Ash, who served as its rabbi. In 1856 it dedicated the former Welsh Chapel on Allen Street as its synagogue. Three "Portuguese" Jews provided almost three-fourths of the down payment of $4,000, leaving a mortgage indebtedness of $3,500. Rabbi Ash, having succeeded in eliciting support from wealthy nonmembers, enlarged his field of solicitation through a letter in the *Occident*. The appeal is prefaced by a description of the congregation: "Its founders were few . . . [but] one by one, daily, men of Israel united with them . . . and now it is supported by about eighty men. . . . Our members are poor in money . . . they labor hard for their daily bread, yet set aside from their limited means a portion for the holy offering."[40]

Ash also describes its activities: daily services, morning and evening; open all day for study; every evening "a portion of the law is expounded publicly . . . and there are persons who study the law for themselves, either in pairs or singly"; on Sabbaths and festivals "the house is full to overflowing"; "it is filled with all sorts of holy books, several sets of Babylonian and Jerusalem Talmuds, the Turim, Rambam, Rif, Schulchan Aruch, Rabbinical Opinions, Bibles, commentaries, Midrashim, Kabbalah." The rabbi sounds the challenging note that marked East European American Orthodoxy:

> It is the only institution in the land, that is otherwise a waste, as regards religious knowledge, which laughs to scorn every scorner, him who goes astray . . . it bids defiance to every unbeliever and infidel . . . devoid of knowledge and devoid of faith . . . [who] makes lighter the yoke of the service of the Lord and his commandments . . . in the eyes of the blinded Hebrews . . . in order that they may be snared and caught in the net of the times.[41]

According to Leeser in his introduction to the Ash letter, the function of the Orthodox *shul* was to promote "Talmudical knowledge and meetings for prayer"; in Ash's view, it was to wage the battle of the Lord for the true faith, against the infidel shepherds who were leading God's flock astray. Its more immediate and mundane mandate was to serve the needs of its immigrant congregants. This was no easy task, for their needs went beyond religious ministrations to like-minded communicants. Coming from different sections of the European continent, they brought with them diverse customs, and, feeling the need for the familiar, they felt impelled to transplant religious usage as they had known it in the Old World. It was not until later, however, that mass immigration permitted such diversification, and that Jews coming from Russia, Poland, Romania, Hungary, Lithuania, Galicia, and Bohemia would form their own *landsmanshaft* congregations.

The diversity of ethnic origin of the congregants made synagogue membership volatile. It was the usual and the accepted thing for congregations to splinter, sometimes in vying for power or even out of personal pique. Thus, after the dedication of the new synagogue of the Beth Hamidrash, a conflict between Rabbi Ash and the congregational president over the question of official authority and "honor" led to synagogue disturbances, contested elections, a court suit, and a split in the congregation. In 1858, a group led by Rabbi Ash formed a new congregation, the Beth Hamidrash Hagadol. Three years later, a split took place in the new congregation, this time over liturgical rite when a "musical cantor" was engaged for the High Holidays.

With the rapid increase in immigration, synagogues on New York's

Lower East Side proliferated, and the competition between them became keen. It expressed itself in ever "grander" synagogues and ever more costly imported "star hazzanim," climaxed by the importation of the world-renowned cantor Pinchos Minkowsky from Odessa at "the enormous salary of $5,000 per annum." The strain imposed on the resources of the congregations, Eisenstein reports, soon brought the inevitable crisis, and this expensive luxury had to be discontinued.[42]

Moshe Weinberger, in his *Jews and Judaism in New York*, estimates that there were 130 Orthodox congregations on the Lower East Side in 1887. Their function was "to gather twice daily, or on the Sabbath to worship together, to visit the sick, to provide a proper and honorable burial for the dead, and to help a brother member in time of need. But the highest ambition [was] to build an imposing synagogue edifice."[43]

It is, of course, not surprising that an immigrant community would transplant the institutions that had served its needs in the "old country." Oscar Handlin notes this about Christian immigrants to America. "The immigrants thought it important to bring their churches to the United States, to reconstitute in their new homes the old forms of worship."[44] The East European Jewish immigrant transplanting his synagogue, his *hevrah*-congregation, to America, was engaging in an American immigrant experience. What role and function it served him in his life, we can discern from a glimpse at some congregational constitutions and from a study of the minute books of the early years of one such congregation. The constitution and bylaws of the Beth Hamidrash Hagadol, New York, adopted in 1887 provide that the Ritual of the Congregation shall be conducted in accordance with the *Shulchan Aruch* (the Code of Jewish Law), that *Nussach Ashkenaz* be the only prayerbook used for services, and that the Beth Hamidrash shall be open morning and evening for the holding of services and the study of Jewish texts. One who openly violates the Sabbath is ineligible for membership, as is one who is married "otherwise than in accordance with the law of Moses and Israel." If taken ill, the member will be visited daily by two brother members; if deathly ill, a person will be sent "to watch at the death bed, and to perform the religious rites." If a member, his wife, or children should die, the congregation will not only defray all funeral expenses, but will provide ten members to accompany the funeral to the cemetery, four of whom shall perform the burial ceremonies and rites; it will send a *minyan* (a quorum of ten men necessary for public worship) to the house of mourning, and a committee of five will "call and tender the sympathy of themselves and in behalf of the congregation."[45] Absent the extended family, the greatest benefits the congregation could provide were concern and brotherly care in case of sickness or death. The minutes of the congregation record a resolution that extends to a member the benefit of paying only one-half the pledge he publicly made at the reading of the Torah – no small inducement for membership to an immigrant for whom the best way to attain status would be through a display of generosity.

Although the salaried officers listed are "Rabbi, Chazan, Sexton and Secretary," only the duties of the latter three are described. The rabbi was considered a communal, not a congregational functionary, in accordance with the usage in European communities. The governance of the congregation was American: president, vice-president, treasurer, and trustees. The title "president" was already a product of Americanization, the earlier incumbents in the 1850s and 1860s having borne the title *Parnas*. The Orthodox *shul* was further Americanized by incorporating the rabbi as a congregational functionary, in recognition of the American practice of making the congregation, not the community, the functional corporate body. Thus the constitution of sister congregation Kahal Adas Jeshurun adopted in 1913 devotes Article XII to the rabbi or *magid*. "No Rabbi or *Magid* can be accepted by this Congregation, who is not in possession of bona fide certificates (*smichot*) of at least three celebrated authorities on theology of Russia and Poland."[46] The benefits provided are similar to those of the Beth Hamidrash, as is the case in other congregational constitutions. The constitution of the Anshei Sefarad Synagogue of Manchester, New Hampshire, before listing benefits, states: "All brothers must keep the synagogue holy. It is forbidden to talk or to walk about during services. It is forbidden to smoke in the synagogue. One must wear clean clothes and clean shoes . . . and to refrain from spitting on the floor."[47]

The history, form, and function of one Orthodox *shul*, Beth Israel, Rochester, New York, is typical.[48] From 1848 to 1870 Congregation Berith Kodesh had served the entire Rochester Jewish community, "German, Englishmen and Poles, all acting in harmony."[49] In the late 1860s it began veering toward Reform Judaism, and the East European Jews, mainly of Lithuanian origin, formed congregations of their own, one in 1870 and another in 1873. A year later these joined together to form Beth Israel, which in all aspects was an Old World institution transplanted on new soil.

The time from the founding of the new congregation in 1874 to the building of its synagogue in 1886 was marked by congregational growth and division, by the acquisition of improved synagogal facilities, and by the professionalization of religious functionaries. Determined to retain its primacy in the face of growing competition from the new congregations produced by dramatically increasing immigration, it undertook the building of a grand synagogue. The cornerstone was laid with appropriate pomp and ceremony on June 27, 1886, and three months later the local press was able to report: "Yesterday. was a memorable day to members of the Beth Israel Congregation. Shortly after 3 o'clock they moved from their old church on Chatham street, in which they had worshipped for years, into their new synagogue on Leopold street."[50] Only a dozen years earlier it had been a small, struggling *hevra*, meeting in a rented hall for Sabbath services; now it would be worshiping in a new brick building seating 800.

The congregation was run by four officers – a president, vice-president, secretary, and treasurer – and four trustees. The only prerequisite for the presidential office was the ability to sign one's name. The first salaried functionary of the congregation was a *shamas*-collector responsible for maintaining the facilities and ritual objects, for arranging the burials on the congregational cemetery, and for directing (though not leading) the services. The first *hazzan*, Kalman Bardin, was a *shochet*, in keeping with the European tradition. He had the scholarly competence to serve as *hazzan*, but apparently lacked the voice, and from 1879 on the congregation was served by a succession of professional cantors. Tension between lay leaders and professionals was generally high and tenure was precarious.

Time and again the question was raised whether a congregation needed a rabbi. East European Jewry knew a communal not a congregational rabbi. The West European and American Reform practice of using congregational rabbis as preachers, leaders of worship, and ambassadors to the world outside was strange to them. When in 1895 a conflict with a rabbi developed into a public scandal, the congregational president offered this defense in the public press: "A rabbi is not a minister. He does not belong to one congregation, but to the city. His duties, only to a very small extent, resemble the duties of a Christian minister. He is an interpreter of the law, not a spiritual advisor."[51]

The congregation was primarily concerned with its cemetery, on which it depended for its functioning and financing, whereas its involvement with the education of the young was intermittent. Now and again schools were organized and then dissolved. In the European community, education was a private or communal concern, not a province of congregational responsibility. Parents sent their sons to a *heder* or engaged a tutor. The community maintained a school for the children of the poor. For Beth Israel to have an educational program was an accommodation to the "American way," an accommodation it was ready to make only when forced to do so by the demands of congregants. In the first decade of the twentieth century, the congregation took the lead in organizing and supporting a communal Talmud Torah, and in response to the demands of younger members, conducted a weekday school for the sons of members and a Sunday school for their daughters.

The congregation served as an arena for acting out interpersonal relationships and provided members with a safe place in which to release their hostility. Strong words could be exchanged, charges brought, fines levied, sanctions imposed – and then reconciliations arranged, fines rescinded, peace restored. For the German Jewish immigrant, his temple served as a portal to America. For the East European immigrant, his *shul* served as a sanctuary and haven – a sanctuary in an America that threatened his faith, a haven to which one could return to join cronies in worship or meetings, after days of peddling in the countryside or laboring in the not-too-friendly city.

Among the chief characteristics of the Orthodox *shul* retained in the twentieth century were the use of Yiddish, the *landsmanshaft* composition of its membership, and the centrality of the cantor.

In many congregations Yiddish was constitutionally mandated as the language of "all transactions." But with time and acculturation, English was grudgingly permitted to intrude. The constitution of two of the newer Rochester congregations, Agudas Achim (1911)[52] and Vaad Hakolel (1913),[53] mandated that all congregational business be conducted in Yiddish only. Beth Israel's constitution adopted in 1906 retained Yiddish as its language, but added that "speaking in the English language may be permitted."[54] In 1913, the long-established Khal Adas Jeshurun of New York City, although retaining "Juedish-Deutsch," gave its members the "liberty to avail themselves of the English language during proceedings."[55] Congregation Reidfei Zedek Anshe Ritove, organized in 1885, adopted bilingualism only in 1930, accepting "both the Yiddish and English languages."

Newark's Congregation Anshe Russia was its leading Orthodox synagogue. Similarly, congregations in many American cities bore the name of a European country, city, or town. The Warsaw and Byalistok synagogues of New York, for example, were composed of members who had come from these large cities, but small towns also gave congregations their names, as for example, Anshe Janover, Anshe Balshovtza, Anshei Lebovner Wohliner.[56]

The star cantor continued to reign in the *shul* in the first decades of this century, which became known as the Golden Age of the American cantorate. The weal and woe of a congregation often depended on its ability to obtain and retain such a star. He could pack the synagogue and fill its coffers through the sale of tickets for High Holiday services.

All three of the characteristics described above came in for criticism. With English excluded from the services and governance, it was pointed out, the sons of immigrants could not participate in synagogal affairs and were discouraged from attending services. The *landsmanshaft* designation marked the *shul* as an Old World institution to a generation of young Jews seeking acceptance by the new. The centrality of the cantor shunted to the side gifted rabbis who might have made a more telling contribution to the solution of what Dr. Judah Magnes saw as the main problem of the synagogue, "not so much an economic question or one of organization, as it is spiritual . . . the revival of religious enthusiasm."[57]

A solution was attempted by members of the second generation, the Young Israel Movement. Organized in 1912 by a group of young men on the lower East Side, its goal was to transform the *shul* into an Americanized synagogue that offered decorous services and a program of educational, cultural, and social activities using the English language, but that remained fully Orthodox. The Young Israel Movement announced that the days of the transplanted East European *shul* were coming to an end and that America's Jews, even the Orthodox, were in need of a new type of synagogue that would serve traditional Jewish needs, but in a manner that would be attractive and meaningful to a generation undergoing rapid integration into the American scene.

The Synagogue-Center: In Its Urban Setting

Mordecai M. Kaplan, who helped found the Young Israel, viewed with alarm the condition of the synagogue in 1918. Noting that it owed its existence "more to the momentum of the past, than to any new forces created in this country," he warned that only the concentration of "all possible material and moral resources" might save "the synagogue from impending doom."[58] He proposed that a new type of synagogue be created, a Jewish center whose purpose would be to afford its users "pleasures of a social, intellectual, and spiritual character."[59] Such a synagogue-center, a *bet am* (house of the people) should provide: "Jewish elementary school facilities; recreational facilities such as gymnasia, showers, bowling alleys, pool tables and game rooms; adult study and art groups; communal activities; religious services and festival pageants and plays; informal meetings of friends and associates."[60] Kaplan saw social togetherness rather than religious worship as "the primary purpose of congregational organizations."[61] He was the founding rabbi of the Jewish Center (on Manhattan's West Side), which incorporated a synagogue, an assembly hall, a gymnasium, a swimming pool, meeting rooms, and classrooms.

The evolution of the synagogue from a worship-centered institution, as were both the Reform temple and the Orthodox *shul*, into a multi-

faceted entity serving the social, cultural, and spiritual needs of the community, as Kaplan advocated, began in the postwar years. The change
was due in part to the new needs of a rapidly Americanizing community,
in part to the response to a new conceptualization of America and the
role of a minority culture within it, and in part to forces that had brought
about a similar development in the American church. Henry Kalloch
Rowe, in *The History of Religion in the United States*, notes that "up to
1890 most churches seemed to thrive . . . [then] conditions began to
change. A shifting population drifted into the churches and out again."
In the twentieth century, the change in conditions of life brought about
the institutional church. "The principle on which it was organized was
the obligation of the church to minister to all the highest needs of the
human personality, . . . The institutional church opened its door every
day. It equipped a gymnasium and baths. It provided a reading room
and library. It organized classes for mental improvement. It provided
wholesome recreation and the social opportunity of clubs."[62] The institutional church was created to retain the urban masses for Christianity;
the synagogue-center had a similar purpose, to win the adherence to
Judaism of the sons and daughters of the immigrant generation, a Judaism
now more broadly defined as a civilization rather than a faith.[63]

The synagogue-center drew its ideological justification as an American
institution from cultural pluralism, whose proponents argued that a minority group has both the right and the duty to retain and develop its
culture. Indeed, such adherence and creativity were not only in the best
interests of the individual and his group, but were a singular contribution
to the strengthening of democracy and the flourishing of American civilization.[64] A synagogue so conceived and so fashioned had a great appeal
for a generation of American Jews who were the children of East European immigrants and wanted to maintain their Jewish identity but who
were also intent on becoming fully integrated into the American scene.

The Reform temples, Marshall Sklare states, "hesitated to expand their
activities and to gain too many new adherents. . . . They were suspicious
of too much nonreligious activity on synagogue premises," which would
be an expression of "racial consciousness." They did not want to attract
and serve "the unaffiliated," who were of a lower social and economic
class.[65] The Orthodox *shul* viewed expansion as change, and resisted it
because any change, in its view, imperiled the faith.[66] The new expanded
synagogue was the creation of the new emerging religious movement,
Conservative Judaism, conforming to its definition of Judaism as an
"evolving religious civilization." In some instances, it was established
by seceding members of an Orthodox synagogue; more often it resulted

from the transformation of an existing synagogue from Orthodoxy to Conservatism.

Rochester's Beth Israel did not appoint an English-speaking "teacher and preacher" until the fourth decade of its existence. In 1911, seminary-ordained Rabbi Paul Chertoff was elected "to deliver lectures and teach in daily school at a salary of $1,200, for one year trial." He was designated preacher or reverend, not rabbi; that title was reserved for the communal Orthodox *Rov*. The young preacher reorganized the weekday school for boys and the Sunday schools for girls, and organized Young Judea clubs for boys and girls and the Emma Lazarus Club for young ladies.[67] The synagogue building was alive with activity, but the congregation remained ambivalent about the role of a congregational rabbi and the scope and nature of congregational activities. In 1915, a group of younger members, apparently encouraged by Rabbi Chertoff, began to confront the issue. By the fall of the year they published their conclusion and solicited participation: "Recognizing that it is our duty as Jews to bear witness to the truths of our Faith in our days and generation as our Fathers did in theirs . . . we hereby constitute ourselves a Jewish congregation for the purpose of conserving Judaism."[68]

Their fathers had established an Orthodox *shul*; now, in response to their needs, they were organizing a Conservative synagogue, Beth El, which would have family pews for men and women; prayers in Hebrew and English, conducted by the rabbi, cantor, and choir; congregational singing and music with an organ; the choir, composed of Jews; a congregation wearing hat and *talith*; daily services; special services on Friday evening, Saturday morning, and holidays; daily and Sunday school to be supported by the congregation.[69] The first three provisions separated them from the Orthodox Movement, the next two from the Reform. Special emphasis was placed on education. The congregational constitution stipulated that the rabbi would "supervise the Sunday School and Hebrew School" and "establish . . . classes for adolescents and study circles of adults," in addition to attending all services and officiating at "all religious ceremonies." The rabbi was made the central congregational functionary, and the cantor his associate and assistant. Within a year the group purchased and adopted for synagogue use the Park Avenue Baptist Church, and by 1922 it could boast of the largest congregational school in the city, with 270 pupils to Reform B'rith Kodesh's 175 and Orthodox Beth Israel's 100. In the 1920s and 1930s its Sisterhood, Men's Club, Junior Congregation, Boy Scout Troop, youth clubs, and athletic teams made it "respected as an established coequal" of Temple B'rith Kodesh.[70]

Congregation Rodef Sholom, Johnstown, Pennsylvania, was established in 1885 as an Orthodox synagogue. In the 1930s, fearing that unless the synagogue was modernized the next generation would join the Reform temple, the board invited a Conservative rabbi, Ralph Simon, to "modernize" it. Rabbi Simon recalled:

> Very few changes [were made] in the Sabbath and holidays Synagogue service. It was only in Friday evening late service that changes could be made . . . sermons in English . . . decorum and interpretation of the liturgy. The major area of change was in the cultural and social programs. All the activities envisioned in the synagogue-center program of Dr. Kaplan were introduced. Adult education classes were organized. A good Hebrew school was conducted. There was an active Men's Club, Sisterhood and Youth Group. There were frequent programs of music, a new choir, dramatic presentations and guest speakers.[71]

Across the state in Scranton, Temple Israel was proud to report what a newly established synagogue could accomplish in but a year and a half:

1. *Education.* A Hebrew School . . . over 100 children attending daily. . . . The religious school meets every Sunday morning and the children are taught the elements of Jewish ethics, ceremonies and Jewish history.
2. *Social and Communal Activities.* Boy Scout Troop . . . second leading troop in the city . . . Girl Scout Troop . . . carried away all the prizes for scout work.
3. *The Ham-Zam-Rini* Society . . . the musical glee club of the Junior congregation . . . only boys of musical and vocal talents are accepted.
4. The *Zadik-Zadik* Club of the Junior Auxiliary looks after the social programs.
5. *Junior Menorah Society* for high school boys and girls meets weekly for discussion . . . and papers are read by members.
6. *The Progress Club*, consists of older sons and daughters of members.[72]

The emphasis of synagogal concern and activities was clearly on the youth. For the adult membership there were services, thrice daily, Sabbaths, and holidays; and "visiting speakers from New York were delighted to find such a large turn-out . . . at the late Friday night Services . . . considering the location of the Temple, being in the non-Jewish section of the city."[73]

Few congregations, of course, could have full programs of religious, cultural, social, and athletic activities – "a shul with a pool," as Rabbi

Joel Blau described it. Most contented themselves with a synagogue-center that served the religious and cultural needs of the majority of their congregants, its function being threefold: to act as a *beth hatefilah* (house of worship), a *beth hamidrash* (house of study), and a *beth hakenesseth* (house of assembly). Initially descriptive of the Conservative synagogues, this began to apply as well to a growing number of Orthodox and Reform congregations.

Orthodox Rabbi David de Sola Pool saw the synagogue-center, as "one of the most promising features in American Jewish life. . . . The synagogue is tending to become once more a focus for Jewish needs and causes. In this lies a strong hope of a Jewish life once more integrated in and around the synagogue."[74] Others, however, felt some misgivings about the synagogue-center, as Reform Rabbi Abraham J. Feldman pointed out: "In actual practice, the Synagogue Center too often becomes a substitute for the Synagogue. . . . [Its] recreational and social attractions are primary, while the religious functions are little more than a concession to the proprieties. . . . Synagogue Centers have tended to detract from the centrality of religion in Jewish life."[75]

Conservative Rabbi Israel H. Levinthal, whose Brooklyn Jewish Center represented the synagogue-center at its best, was not unaware of its shortcomings, but nonetheless spoke of its potential contribution with satisfaction and optimism in 1936, when his congregation was at its height of activity and influence.

> If the Synagogue as a *Beth Hatefilah* has lost its hold upon the masses, some institution would have to be created that could and would attract the people so that the group consciousness of the Jew might be maintained. The name center seems to work this magic with thousands who would not be attracted to the place if we simply called it Synagogue or Temple. . . . The Center is a seven-day synagogue. From early morning to late at night its doors should be open. It is true that many will come for other purposes than to meet God. But let them come.[76]

The Synagogue-Center: In Suburbia

In the years between the wars, the synagogue-center replaced the classic Reform temple and the insular Orthodox *shul* as the prototypical American synagogue. In post–World War II America, the synagogue became the central institution of the Jewish community.

During the 1920s and 1930s the synagogue had grown dramatically. The Jewish population had increased by 40 percent, but the number of synagogues had almost doubled, rising from 1,901 in 1916 to 3,118 in

1926, to 3,738 in 1937.[77] What makes this growth all the more noteworthy is that the 1930s were the years of economic depression and a time of difficulty for religious institutions, which were burdened with heavy mortgage obligations inherited from the synagogue building boom of the 1920s. The programs of expansion that had been undertaken in the years of prosperity and optimism had to be curtailed, and staffs pared. Through it all, however, synagogues displayed a remarkable resilience. All were hard-pressed and a few faltered, but almost none failed. In a time of testing, American Jewry did not abandon its synagogues.

The war years witnessed an upsurge in the general influence of religion and the status of its institutions, which continued in postwar America. The postwar suburbanization of America greatly affected the country's Jewish population, which before 1945 had been concentrated in urban areas. As Jews moved to the suburbs, the need to secure their status led them to establish congregations and erect synagogues. The Jews became part of their new community through their religious institution, which was accepted by the "natives" as part of the suburban landscape.

The *American Jewish Yearbook* reported in 1954 that "the movement of the Jewish population to suburban areas continued to gain momentum," and "that the Conservative and Reform groups had been pioneers in establishing new synagogue centers in suburban areas."[78] It noted further that the new synagogues being built "laid special stress on original art forms" and had commissioned the work of leading artists. All three religious movements were directing resources to the new suburban communities. The Union of Orthodox Jewish Congregations launched a $300,000 campaign for a program to establish Orthodox congregations in the suburbs. The New York Federation of Reform Synagogues placed a pre–High Holidays ad in New York newspapers listing its congregations in the metropolitan area: There were thirty-three serving the 200,000 Jews in suburban Nassau and Westchester counties, and fourteen serving the 1,345,000 Jews in the Bronx and Brooklyn. The architectural consultant for the Conservative United Synagogue claimed that in 1954–1955 alone 150 Conservative synagogues were being planned or constructed.[79]

Each movement claimed rapidly growing numbers of affiliated synagogues. All suburban synagogues boasted of increasing membership. The growth of synagogues and their status in the community was most pronounced in the area of education. Jewish school enrollment had risen from 231,028 in 1946 to 488,432 in 1956; that is, it more than doubled in the first decade after the war. Of that number, over 85 percent were in schools under congregational auspices.[80] In 1959, the *New York Times* reported that since the war fifty-seven Reform, sixty-eight Conservative, and thirty-five Orthodox congregations had been established in New York City's suburbs: "Congregations have sprung up in firehouses, banks and even Protestant churches. . . . The congregation in Harrison was organized as a Conservative temple, with an assist from a Protestant Episcopal minister."[81]

According to U.S. Bureau of Labor statistics, about 2,517 rabbis were serving congregations, and officials projected that "a sufficient supply of rabbis . . . is not likely to be available during the 1960 decade . . . to fill the openings which will be created by the formation of new congregations."[82] By the middle of the decade, however, it became obvious to observers of Jewish life that the Bureau's projection had been too optimistic. Morris N. Kertzer noted that 1962–1963 "was the year of consolidation rather than expansion for the American synagogue,"[83] and Sefton D. Temkin wrote two years later that the same was true for the years 1964 and 1965. Although he noted "no decline in Jewish religious life . . . the force of the upsurge, which characterized the American Jewish community immediately after World War II, has abated."[84]

The "upsurge" of Jewish religious life made the synagogue "suburbia's nuclear and most important Jewish institution."[85] Like its neighboring Protestant church, it emphasized "the ethical, moral and social values associated with religion, and the needs of living people."[86] Albert I. Gordon in his study *Jews in Suburbia* attributed the preeminence of the synagogue in suburbia in the mid–1950s not so much to its religious function, as to its having been "usually the first organized body to provide a physical structure in which Jews can meet as Jews within the community . . . [because] it provides for the formal Jewish education of the children . . . and [because it] helps Jews feel Jewish even when there is little Jewish symbolism in the home."[87] He describes the process of founding a suburban synagogue as beginning with the need for fellowship and friendship felt by the young couples newly arrived in a suburb. "A Jewish community center does not suffice, for they also need a religious school for their children, so they quickly conclude that a synagogue-center with a rabbi and teachers will provide what they seek," an institution that will provide for their children's religious needs, as well as for their own social and fellowship interests. They soon find that the rabbi is available for counseling in the many personal and family problems that dislocation from extended family and integration into a new community and way of life may bring. They also find that the same rabbi who has become their counselor and friend is the recognized leader of the Jewish community as its esteemed representative to the general community.

Why did people affiliate? "Reasons vary," states Gordon, "because people vary":

> We want to give our children some kind of Jewish education, and we wish to be part of the Jewish community.
>
> The temple represents us to the Gentile world. They know through it that there is such a thing as a Jewish community. . . . In that way the Temple helps me and my family live as respected people.
>
> I belong to the synagogue because I have friends there. . . . It is true that we could get along without any synagogue . . . – but our own non-Jewish neighbors cannot understand that . . . so we are building one which will be a source of pride to all Jews and the whole community.
>
> We joined the temple to try to live a fuller life as a Jewish family unit.
>
> We want our children to know and appreciate their heritage.[88]

The great majority (83 percent), reports Gordon, thought their congregations were "doing a good job," but only 1.8 percent had cited "I am religious" as the reason for affiliation. Although most congregants were satisfied with the role and program of the postwar synagogue, sharp criticism was voiced for synagogues in which religious services played an auxiliary role to fellowship functions. Rabbi Eugene Borowitz spoke the sentiments of many of his colleagues:

> The average synagogue member . . . comes . . . to join the synagogue because there are few if any socially acceptable alternatives to synagogue affiliation for one who wants to maintain his Jewish identity and wants his children to be Jewish, in some sense, after him. Though this is not the only motive or level of concern to be found within the synagogue today, the Jew who does not rise above such folk-feeling unquestionably and increasingly represents the synagogue's majority mood. More than that, however, it must be said that he also represents the synagogue's greatest threat. . . . No one wishes to lose Jews for Judaism, but the time has come when the synagogue must be saved for the religious Jew . . . [from] the indifferent and the apathetic who control it for their own non-religious purposes.[89]

Rabbi Gordon, came to the defense of suburbia's synagogues:

> The synagogue is not now and never was *only* a house of worship. It is also a center of fellowship for young and old. It provides leisure-time and recreational activities, as well as Jewish educational facilities, for young and old. It is the primary means by which identification as a Jew is currently achieved. Suburban synagogues are, in fact, synagogue-centers. They offer each Jew the opportunity to come to know his own rich heritage and to live his life as an American Jew.[90]

The American Jew in the postwar decades chose to live a largely secular life, free of religious discipline, but at the same time demanded that American Jewry maintain a communal religious identity. For him this was the American way of life – to esteem established religion and its institutions, but to live free of its restraints. The synagogue-center was the institution that served him well in this choice. To the world outside, it was a synagogue, a religious institution. For him it was a center for Jewish fellowship; even the religious services and the cultural and educational activities served that function for the great majority of synagogue members.

In the postwar years, America accepted Will Herberg's image of America as the land of the three great faiths – Protestant, Catholic, and Jewish. That is to say, American Jewry was no longer considered one of many minority groups, but had risen to a prominent position among the leading religious and cultural groups of the nation. The tripartite status was expressed symbolically in a whole network of interfaith activities: joint church–synagogue visitations; teams of minister–priest–rabbi that made joint platform appearances at civic functions and college campuses and offered prayers at state occasions, including the presidential inaugural – activities that accorded Judaism parity and the Jew equal status. Because the synagogue was the vehicle through which this was accomplished, it established itself as the unchallenged central institution in American Jewish life.

The status of the synagogue was elevated in the 1950s and early 1960s through its participation with the church in spearheading the Civil Rights movement. The nation approved of organized religion fulfilling its mandate for social justice, and none more so than America's Jews. For them, the synagogue was acting in the best prophetic tradition by helping to unfold the American dream. Through the synagogue, American Israel had entered the mainstream of progressive American enterprise. It seemed wise and rewarding for American Jewry to maintain a religious posture in a country in which religion was esteemed and its influence growing, as a Gallup poll conducted in 1957 indicated. Only 14 percent

thought that the influence of religion was decreasing, whereas 69 percent
believed that it was increasing.

The Contemporary Synagogue: In Service of the Individual

The change in the cultural climate and the status of organized
religion that took place in the late 1960s was as precipitous as it was
dramatic. Americans turned their attention and concern from social betterment to personal satisfaction. The church as savior of society gave
way to churches as servants of their communicants. The mainline Protestant denominations that had been in the forefront of civil rights activities suffered a loss of membership and influence. Fundamentalist groups,
with their disdain for formalism, staid dignity, and impersonal authority
and their emphasis on emotional expression, community, and charismatic
leadership, grew in numbers. The privatization of religion eroded its
influence. In 1970 a Gallup poll asked the same question as it had in 1957:
"At the present time do you think religion as a whole is increasing its
influence on American life or losing its influence?" Fourteen percent
responded "increasing," whereas 75 percent stated "losing!"

The synagogue, which had benefited from its association with the
church in the "glory days" of American organized religion immediately
after World War II, now was affected by the decline in status and influence
of mainline Protestantism. However, to a degree unmatched by the major
church denominations, the synagogues were able to retain their membership by becoming service synagogues ready to provide, as called upon,
specific, discrete services: education; life passage rites for birth and Bar
and Bat Mitzvah; wedding ceremony and celebrations; burial, mourning,
and *yahrzeit* (anniversary of death) services; and various ministrations in
the realm of spiritual social work.

The synagogue of the 1970s and 1980s, the "decades of the ethnics,"
has maintained its primacy because it continues to provide a spiritual and
cultural nourishment that can be termed both religious and ethnic, and
American Jews continue to prefer to live ethnically under a religious
identity. Moreover, the synagogue has remained willing to adopt and
adapt. In this era of pluralism and diversity, the synagogue has diversified
itself into a mosaic of distinct and differing congregations, and individual
congregations have effected inner diversification. A wide variety of synagogues serve a widely varied constituency. They range from a Hassidic
shtibl in Brooklyn's Williamsburg or Borough Park, a prayer room presided over by a dynastic *rebbe*, to the Stephen S. Wise Temple across the

continent in Los Angeles, with its staff of rabbis, cantors, educators, social workers, and executives administrating day care centers, schools, social service bureaus, and a fleet of busses.

Congregations grown large in the 1960s are attempting to answer the needs of the 1980s for the humanization and personalization of the synagogue. The *havurah*, a product of the Jewish students' counterculture movement, has been embraced by a large number of synagogues. In 1973, Rabbi Harold M. Schulweis, who pioneered with *havurot* in his Congregation Valley Beth Shalom, Encino, California, shared his philosophy and experiences with his colleagues of the Rabbinical Assembly:

> We are challenged to decentralize the synagogue and deprofessionalize Jewish living so that the individual Jew is brought back into the circle of shared Jewish experience. . . . In our congregation, a *havurah* is comprised of a minyan of families who have agreed to meet together at least once a month to learn together, to celebrate together and hopefully to form some surrogate for the eroded extended family. . . . Cerebration must not eclipse celebration. . . . I know what it means for children to see ten Jewish males with hammers and saws helping to build a sukkah. . . . The *havurot* plan their own *Sedarim* . . . they wrestle with the Haggadah and the decision to add and delete. . . . There was a death in the havurah. The widow had few members of the family around her . . . I saw who was at the funeral, who took care of the children during the black week of the *shivah*. . . . The *havurah* offers the synagogue member a community small enough to enable personal relationships to develop. It enables families to express their Jewishness. . . . Hopefully the synagogue itself will gradually be transformed into . . . a Jewish assembly [of] *havurot*. . . . My grandfather came to the synagogue because he was a Jew. His grandchildren come to the synagogue to become Jewish.[91]

The Young Israel Movement is meeting the challenge that suburbanization poses to the Orthodox way of life by making synagogues the hubs about which a Jewish community will be built. It views the synagogue as one of the quintessential Jewish communal institutions, the central institution that will give coherence and coordination to the rest. Advertisements in the *Young Israel Viewpoint*, inviting young families to move to the community served by a Young Israel synagogue, list these other institutions and services:

A Young Growing Orthodox Community
Young Israel of New Rochelle

Day Schools; New Completed Community Eruv; Yeshiva High School; Community Mikvah; Kosher Take-out Butchers; Kosher Bakeries; Good Access to Parkways; Easy Commute – 25 minutes from Manhattan, Queens, N.J.[92]

The Young Israel of East Northport, New York, "near Nassau line in booming Suffolk county," "where the Accent is always on Torah education for all," promises "6 classes a week for adults," a day school "under the direction of Yeshivah Chofetz Chaim musmachim," and "luxurious, suburban living in modern, spacious homes."[93]

The American synagogue, coextensive with the entire historic experience of the Jews in America, has been remarkably sensitive to the changing needs of America's Jews and has responded by reordering its priorities and programs to meet these needs. It continues to retain its resilience and adaptability, but the problems besetting it are substantial. The power of the local Jewish community federations has grown as vast sums from campaigns for overseas needs are now placed in their hands to allocate. More than half these sums are apportioned for national and local needs, and, as a general rule, federations choose the Jewish community centers to be their institutional counterparts in the community and allocate increasing subsidies to them. In the 1970s and 1980s, when synagogue building has all but ceased, multimillion-dollar centers continue to rise. Their new facilities and communal subventions enable them to compete successfully with the synagogues in cultural and fellowship activities – activities generally of lesser Jewish content than those provided by the synagogues. With the federations and centers attracting the more affluent and able lay leaders, the financial burdens of the synagogues are becoming all the more difficult to bear. Adding to these problems is the changing nature and the high mobility of the Jewish community. As fewer Jews enter business and more become salaried professionals, the burden of maintaining the synagogues built by the businessmen – as a rule, generous and enterprising – will fall upon the shoulders of professionals, who tend to be more conservative in giving and timid in venture. The increasing mobility of American Jewry, making for a generation of consumers rather than supporters of institutional services, the diminishing status of synagogue and rabbi both within and outside Jewish communities, and its effect on the quality of future staffs are causes of concern to the synagogue.

Although the synagogue is experiencing a decline in membership and influence, it continues to be the preeminent institution in American Jewish life. Many agree with the view of Mordecai M. Kaplan, expressed in 1917: "In this country, as well as in all other countries where the Jews have been emancipated, the synagogue is the principal means of keeping alive the Jewish consciousness. . . . [It] is the only institution which can define our aims to a world that would otherwise be at a loss to understand why we persist in retaining our corporate individuality."[94]

NOTES

1   Samuel Oppenheim, "The Early History of the Jews in New York," *Publications of the American Jewish Historical Society*, 19 (1909), pp. 73–74.

2   Ibid., p. 21.

3   Ibid., p. 75.

4   Ibid., p. 76.

5   Joseph L. Blau and Salo W. Baron, *The Jews of the United States 1790–1840 A Documentary History*, vol. 2 (New York and London, 1963), p. 576.

6   Jacob R. Marcus, *The Colonial American Jew 1492–1776*, vol. 2, (Detroit, 1970), p. 857.

7   Jacob R. Marcus, *American Jewry–Documents* (Cincinnati, 1959), pp. 88–92.

8   Ibid., pp. 859, 856.

9   Franklin Hamlin Littell, *From State Church to Pluralism* (New York, 1962), pp. 13, 14.

10 *Publications of the American Jewish Historical Society* (hereafter, *PAJHS*), no. 21 (n.p., 1913), p. 4.

11 David and Tamar De Sola Pool, *An Old Faith in the New World* (New York, 1955), p. 39.

12 *PAJHS*, 39, no. 2 (December 1949), p. 194.

13 Charles Reznikoff and Uriah Z. Engelman, *The Jews of Charleston* (Philadelphia, 1950), p. 56.

14 Edwin Wolf, 2nd and Maxwell Whiteman, *The History of the Jews of Philadelphia* (Philadelphia, 1957), pp. 143–144.

15 Jacques J. Lyons and Abraham De Sola, *A Jewish Calendar for Fifty Years* (Montreal, 1854).

16 Cited in *The Voluntary Church*, ed. Milton Powell (New York and London, 1967), p. 81.

17 Blau and Baron, *Jews of the United States*, vol. 1, p. 13.

18 Wolf and Whiteman, *History of the Jews of Philadelphia*, p. 225ff.

19 Israel Goldstein, *A Century of Judaism in New York* (New York, 1930), p. 52.

20 [I. J.] Benjamin, *Three Years in America*, trans. Charles Reznikoff (Philadelphia, 1956), pp. 76–77.

21 Simon Cohen, *Shaaray Tefila* (New York, 1945), pp. 1–14.

22 Isaac Lesser, "The Jews and Their Religion," in *An Original History of the Religious Denomination in the U.S.*, ed. I. Daniel Rupp (Philadelphia, 1844), p. 368.

23. Ibid.

24 *The Israelite*, 3 (December 26, 1856), p. 196.

25 Ibid.

26 Leon A. Jick, *The Americanization of the Synagogue, 1820–1870* (Hanover, N.H., 1976), pp. 174, 193.

27 Joseph Krauskoff, "Half a Century of Judaism in the United States," *The American Jews' Annual for 5648 A.M.* (New York, Cincinnati, Chicago, 1888), p. 72.

28 Reznikoff and Engelman, *Jews of Charleston*, pp. 139–140.

29 W. Gunther Plaut, *The Growth of Reform Judaism* (New York, 1965), p. 9.

30 Isaac M. Fein, *The Making of an American Jewish Community* (Philadelphia, 1971), p. 65.

31 [Olath Tamid] *Gebetbuch für Israelitische Reform – Gemeinden*, 2d ed. (Baltimore, 1862), pp. 396–397.

32 Myer Stern, *The Rise and Progress of Reform Judaism* (New York, 1895), pp. 28–29.

33 Ibid., p. 41.

34 Isaac A. Wile, *The Jews of Rochester* (Rochester, N.Y., 1912), p. 12.

35 Ibid.

36 *Ritual for Jewish Worship* (Rochester, N.Y., 1885), pp. v–vi.

37 Isaac M. Wise and others, *Hymns, Psalms and Prayers* (Cincinnati, 1866), p. 3.

38 *Extracts from Proceedings of Chicago Sinai Congregation at Its Annual Meeting, March 26, 1885 and Special Meeting, April 9, 1885* (Chicago, 1885), pp. 2–7.

39 J. D. Eisenstein, "The History of the First Russian-American Jewish Congregation," *PAJHS*, no. 9 (n.p., 1901), p. 64.

40 Abraham Joseph Ash, "The Beth Hamidrash, New York," *The Occident*, 15, no. 12 (March 1857), p. 600.

41 Ibid.

42 Eisenstein, "History of the First Russian-American Jewish Congregation," p. 74.

43 Moshe Weinberger, *Jews and Judaism in New York* (New York, 1887), p. 2.

44 Oscar Handlin, *The Uprooted* (Boston, 1951), p. 124.

45 *Constitution and By-Laws of the Beth Hamidrash Hagadol of the City of New York*, revised and adopted at a special meeting, March 20, 1887 (New York, 1887).

46 *Constitution of the Congregation Kahal Adas Jeshurun with Anshe Lubtz* (New York, 1913), p. 15.

47 *Constitution Fun Shul Anshei Sefarad* (Yiddish) (n.p., 1918).

48 See Abraham J. Karp, "An East European Congregation on American Soil," in *A Bicentennial Festschrift for Jacob Rader Marcus*, ed. Bertram W. Korn (New York, 1976), pp. 263–302.

49 *Occident*, 13, no. 9 (December 1855), p. 467.

50 *Rochester Democrat and Chronicle*, September 20, 1886.

51 *Rochester Union-Advertiser*, April 5, 1895.

52 *Constitution of Agudas Achim Nusach Ari* (Yiddish) (Rochester, N.Y.), art. 3, p. 3.

53 *Congregation Vaad Hakolel, Constitution and By-Laws* (Yiddish) (Rochester, 1915), art. 2, p. 4.

54 *Constitution and By-Laws of the Congregation of Beth Israel* (Rochester, N.Y., 1906), art. 3, p. 1.

55 *Constitution of the Congregation Khal Adas Jesshurun with Anshe Lubtz* (New York, 1913), sec. 5, p. 3.

56 See *The Jewish Community Register of New York City, 1917–1918* (New York, 1918), pp. 111–285.

57 Ibid., pp. 111–112.

58 Ibid., pp. 121–22.

59 *The American Hebrew*, March 22, 1918.

60 Mordecai M. Kaplan, *Judaism as a Civilization* (New York, 1934), p. 428.

61 Mordecai M. Kaplan, "The Way I Have Come," in *Mordecai M. Kaplan: An Evaluation*, ed. Ira Eisenstein and Eugene Kohn (New York, 1952), p. 311.

62 Henry Kalloch Rowe, *The History of Religion in the United States* (New York, 1924), pp. 142, 152.

63 Herbert S. Goldstein, a graduate of the Jewish Theological Seminary, but an orthodox rabbi, founded the *Institutional Synagogue* in Harlem, then a place of residence of economically and socially upwardly mobile Jews, provided full facilities for religious, cultural, and social activities, including athletics and day camp.

64 See Abraham J. Karp, "Ideology and Identity in Jewish Group Survival in America," *American Jewish Historical Quarterly*, 65, no. 4 (June, 1976), pp. 310–334.

65 Marshall Sklare, *Conservative Judaism* (New York, 1972), p. 131.

66 It must be noted, however, that two of the most prominent "synagogue centers" were Orthodox, the Jewish Center and the Institutional Synagogue. The former was founded by Mordecai M. Kaplan, on the faculty of the Conservative Jewish Theological Seminary, and the latter was organized by a graduate of that school.

67 Rabbi Chertoff's Congregation Beth Israel Hebrew School and Sunday School ledger records thirty students (twenty-seven boys and three girls) in the Hebrew school; and thirty in the Sunday school (twenty-six girls and four boys). He lists himself as "Rabbi and Principal of the School," and he taught the advanced classes. Among the subjects listed were, "Hebrew Translation and Writing," "Abbreviated Humash," and "Jewish Biblical History and Religion." Ledger in possession of author.

68 *Minute Book of Temple Beth El*, n.p. Beth El Archives.

69 Ibid.

70 Stuart E. Rosenberg, *The Jewish Community of Rochester, 1843–1925* (New York, 1954), p. 179.

71 Cited in Abraham J. Karp, "The Conservative Rabbi – 'Dissatisfied but Not Unhappy,' " in *The American Rabbinate*, ed. Jacob Rader Marcus and Abraham J. Peck (Hoboken, 1985).

72   *United Synagogue Recorder*, 3, no. 5 (April, 1923), p. 14. Conservative con-
      gregations in the East generally called themselves temple, in the Midwest,
      synagogue.
73   Ibid.
74   David de Sola Pool, "Judaism and the Synagogue," in *The American Jew*,
      ed. Oscar I. Janowsky (New York and London, 1942), p. 54.
75   Abraham J. Feldman, "The Changing Functions of the Synagogue and the
      Rabbi," in *Reform Judaism, Essays by Hebrew Union College Alumni*, ed. Ber-
      nard J. Bamberger (Cincinnati, 1949), p. 212.
76   Cited by Marshall Sklare, *Conservative Judaism*, p. 136, from the *United
      Synagogue Recorder*, 6, no. 4 (October, 1936).
77   *American Jewish Yearbook* (hereafter *AJYB*), 5699 (Philadelphia, 1938), p. 61;
      AJYB 5701 (Philadelphia, 1940), p. 217.
78   *AJYB*, 55 (Philadelphia, 1954), p. 81.
79   *AJYB*, 57 (Philadelphia, 1956), p. 191.
80   *AJYB*, 59 (Philadelphia, 1958), pp. 125, 131.
81   *New York Times*, April 6, 1959.
82   Cited in *AJYB*, 62 (Philadelphia, 1961), p. 130.
83   *AJYB*, 65 (Philadelphia, 1964), p. 75.
84   *AJYB*, 67 (Philadelphia, 1966), p. 176.
85   Albert I. Gordon, *Jews in Suburbia* (Boston, 1959), p. 85.
86   Ibid., p. 88.
87   Ibid., pp. 96, 97.
88   Ibid., pp. 116–119.
89   Eugene Borowitz, *A New Jewish Theology in the Making* (Philadelphia, 1968),
      pp. 45, 46, 53, 54.
90   Gordon, *Jews in Suburbia*, p. 127.
91   Harold M. Schulweis, "Restructuring the Synagogue," *Conservative Judaism*,
      27, no. 4 (Summer, 1973), pp. 19–23.
92   *Young Israel Viewpoint*, 24, no. 5 (January 1984), p. 13.
93   *Young Israel Viewpoint*, 24, no. 7 (March, 1984), p. 19.
94   *The Jewish Community Register of New York*, p. 122.

I
The Denominational Perspective

2

The Orthodox Synagogue

JEFFREY S. GUROCK

Introduction: Exclusion and Inclusion in the Orthodox Synagogue

In March 1847, New York's Congregation Shearith Israel, America's oldest congregation, adopted a position on one of this country's most enduring Jewish communal problems. In an amendment to organizational bylaws, congregational trustees ruled that "no seat in our holy place of worship shall hereafter be leased to any person married contrary to our religious law and no person married contrary to our religious law shall be interred in any of the burial places belonging to this Congregation." Religious legislators hoped that the fear of exclusion from the faith's most basic privileges would deter young Jewish men from intermarriage. Such, however, proved not to be the case. Jews continued to marry non-Jews out of love, the unavailability within the severely limited Jewish marriage pool of suitable spouses, or the desire for socioeconomic advancement through familial linkage with society's dominant culture. This American synagogue, lacking its medieval European counterpart's communal power of prior restraint through effective excommunication (*herem*), could not legally or forcibly prohibit a co-religionist in a free society from doing what he pleased. It could only punish after the fact, imposing sanctions that may or may not have troubled the resolute intermarrying Jew. This piece of modern ecclesiastical legislation did, of course, assure that a Jew who intermarried – still a member of that faith community in the eyes of its own religious law – would be immediately and permanently lost to his people.[1]

Ostracism, however, was not the only possible organizational response to rampant exogamy. Indeed, prior to 1847, the synagogue had had a long history of official disinterest in members' marital choices and was tacitly accepting the intermarried Jew as both a seat-holder and even as a congregational elector. This latter policy was informed by the understanding that no matter what one's deviation from accepted religious norms, an offending Jew remained a member of the synagogue. There were, however, congregational critics of this early "lenient attitude," which was designed, as one historian of this synagogue has characterized it, "as a means of keeping those intermarried in the fold." Trustee Jacob Abrahams, for one, demurred: "To give such a person the rights of a member will have a baneful influence on the welfare of the congregation . . . by encouraging the young men of our persuasion to marry those of another faith."[2]

This episode in nineteenth-century congregational history points to a dilemma that has confronted Orthodox[3] rabbinic and lay leaders of synagogues throughout this country's history: What stance should their religious institution take toward the majority of American Jews, who, owing to the open and secular nature of general society, lead lives clearly in variance with Orthodox rendering of traditional law? In general, Orthodox synagogue spokesmen and functionaries have adopted two opposing views on this question: Some have argued that the Orthodox synagogue must neither accept nor accommodate those who do not recognize and obey the past traditions. This exclusionary policy, found mainly in the early phases of American Jewish history, prescribed formal "reading out" through the denial of synagogue rights and honors to those publicly known to be less observant than the rule setters. Later on, these same excluders often chose – when they were not forced to do so –to remove themselves from their own indigenous congregations. When some congregations began to overlook violations by worshipers and when in the mid-nineteenth century many synagogues voted to abandon, officially, Orthodox ritual, those who wished to maintain the old standards separated themselves from institutional life and established competing Orthodox institutions. More frequently, particularly during the period of Jewish immigration from Eastern Europe, the reluctance or inability to modify, update, or Americanize synagogue ways to satisfy worshiper demands led Jewish masses to voluntarily abandon Orthodoxy, at least the form transplanted from Russia or Poland.

Others within the American Orthodox camp have traditionally turned a blind eye to the heterodoxy of potential communicants. These includers have attempted, particularly in the twentieth century, to attract the largest number of Jews to their fold. They have often purposefully instituted novel – but to their minds religiously permitted – liturgical, sermonic, and ancillary synagogue activities.

The excluders have often deemed that the includers' efforts to make the Orthodox synagogue more appealing to the less, or no longer observant, were at best a major sociological blunder and at worst a fundamental theological deviation. At the same time, the includers have characterized their opponents as unknowingly consigning traditional Judaism to oblivion in an American Jewish world of rampant nonobservance. To a great extent, these positions have been crystallized and strengthened by the postures taken by America's more liberal denominations. But this division within Orthodoxy, as is already apparent, preceded the rise of the Reform and Conservative movements. In many instances, this difference of approach has had little to do with what other organized Jewish groups have said or done.

The Era before the Rise of Reform Judaism (circa 1800–1850)[4]

Shearith Israel was not the only American congregation in the first half of the nineteenth century to vacillate between exclusionary and inclusionary policies toward its religiously nonconforming congregants. Beginning in 1798, Philadelphia's Congregation Mikve Israel officially withheld membership and "religious rights and privileges" from any Jew who intermarried. But twenty-eight years later, it voted down a similar motion to deny intermarrieds "all synagogue honors and privileges." Its sister congregation in Philadelphia, Rodeph Shalom, behaved similarly when it first ruled in 1826 that "no member married to a non-Jew could share in honors and privileges." Three years later, the synagogue backed off and decided that exogamists who pledged to raise their children as Jews would not be expelled.[5]

In the 1840s exclusionary forces in Baltimore led by Abraham Rice, the first ordained rabbi to serve in the United States, articulated a more stringent set of requirements for synagogue integration. Here the Rabbi ruled that known Sabbath violators should be denied Torah *aliyot*. But Rice and his backers too were quickly forced to backtrack. In the late 1840s, Sabbath violators were granted *aliyot*, but congregants were instructed by clergy not to recite "amen" to the nonconformist's blessing. But in 1853, this practice was effectively quashed. No congregation was willing to maintain a law that would effectively destroy their institution by reading the majority of its worshipers out of the synagogue.[6]

This perspective also motivated New Orleans's first congregation, Shanarai-Chasset, to legislate in its original bylaws that not only intermarried Jews, but also their "strange women" (non-Jewish spouses), could be buried in the Jewish cemeteries, albeit in a special section. This very lenient position arose from the recognition that over one-half of the Jews then marrying in the Bayou chose Gentile mates. "Congregational leaders," historian Bertram Korn has suggested, "tried to keep these men from feeling alienated from their ancestral faith and how profoundly they hoped that the children of these marriages might be saved for Judaism."[7]

Still, even these most lenient synagogue leaders did not adapt customs and practices to counteract the broader alienation felt by nineteenth-century American Jews. In the most celebrated instance of intrasynagogal strife of that era, the request of congregational insurgents that certain synagogue procedures be modified "to bring back under your immediate protection and influence [a number of Israelites] whom are now wandering gradually from the true God and . . . the faith of their fathers," was met with a resounding no.[8]

In 1824, forty-seven memorialists submitted their now famous petition to the president and adjunta of Charleston, South Carolina's K. K. Beth Elohim, calling for changes in the synagogue's life within Orthodox tradition.[9] Although they were aware that much of what they were suggesting closely resembled the demands of members of the early German Reform Movement, they nonetheless averred that they wished "not to abandon the institutions of Moses, but to understand and observe them."[10]

These petitioners probably could not have chosen to convince a more unyielding group of synagogue leaders. Beth Elohim was on record in the 1820s as denying membership to both intermarrieds and Sabbath violators. Furthermore, it had sought to control congregants' behavior through the levying of fines for innumerable offenses both within and without synagogue precincts. Thus, in a move totally consistent with the policies of their then most exclusionary American synagogue,[11] "the miscreated front among our people," as one trustee characterized the memorialists, were denied even a hearing on their submission. Asserting that Jewish tradition "prescribed a certain fixed mode of service, established at the destruction of the second Temple," the *Parnassim* (trustees) held out no hope that innovations would be considered by this Orthodox congregation.[12]

Outright rejection did not prevent the insurgents from leaving the synagogue altogether and establishing their own Reformed Society of Israelites. This early experiment in Reform Judaism, as it has been frequently called, lasted but nine years. In 1833, the combined forces of familial and social pressure (the last informal, modern, remnants of medieval Jewry's once official power of excommunication), the absence of trained liberal Jewish functionaries, and the removal from Charleston of the Reformed Society's foremost spokesman brought the offending minority back into the Beth Elohim fold. The victory of the unbending exclusionists was short-lived. When, a decade or so later, a new Beth Elohim majority under the direction of Hazzan Gustav Poznanski ruled that an organ was admissible for use in synagogue services, its now minority of Orthodox members decided to secede from their no-longer traditional congregation. This remnant founded Congregation Shearith Israel, which was open to those who still adhered to Orthodox teachings and procedures.[13]

Charleston's Shearith Israel was the only early nineteenth-century Orthodox congregation founded by those unwilling to acquiesce to their home synagogue's liberal drift. It was not, however, the only congregation of this period to have been formed by exclusionist minorities who were uncomfortable with the heterodox religious practices of fellow congregants and displeased with inclusionary policies of the synagogue leaders. In New York, Shearith Israel's reign of more than a hundred years as that city's sole congregation came to an end, in part, because it was unwilling to control, beyond periodic anti-intermarriage legislation, the religious deportment of congregants. In striking out on their own, B'nai Jeshurun's founders moved that their synagogue would enroll as a member only "he [who] adheres to our religion as regards the observance of our holy Sabbaths and Holidays."[14] However, in New York, unlike Charleston, exclusionary sentiments were not expressed by long-standing members demanding liberalization. Rather, they were voiced by new immigrants who felt uncomfortable with the processes and practices of this American synagogue.

Although to this day Shearith Israel proudly proclaims itself the Spanish-Portuguese synagogue, long before the nineteenth century it housed a mixed Sephardic-Ashkenazic constituency. Only its liturgy remained uniquely Sephardic.[15] The arrival of a new, large contingent of German-Polish Jews beginning in the 1820s upset this unified or homogeneous synagogue-community.[16] Displaying an attitude that would characterize the response of Jewish immigrants for the next 125 years, the new Americans, coming from lands where religion pervaded every Jew's life, were struck by the marginality of the synagogue. As another historian has aptly put it, "the established burghers" that the immigrant encountered "wanted an orderly and undemanding Jewish church which would affirm their respectability without interfering with their life style." This type of religion, which consisted of Judaism in the synagogue and Americanism at home and in the streets, was unacceptable to the new arrivals. For these still unacculturated Jews, exclusionary policies grew out of a program for recreating on these shores a familiar and encompassing synagogue life. Liturgy, synagogue governance, and social controls were all to be reconstituted according to the norms of homelands where obeisance to Jewish law was, or had been, legally mandated.[17]

But once having ordained that prayers in B'nai Jeshurun should follow a particular variant of the Ashkenazic *minhag*, the new congregation soon discovered elements within their own mixed Dutch, Polish, and German constituency partial to an alternate rendering of the liturgy. In this case, although the congregation was prepared to *include* these ritually observant Jews as members, they could not change their services to meet every individual's liturgical tastes. Consequently, unaccommodated congregants chose to *exclude* themselves from New York's second synagogue to form newer congregations that practiced one or another version of the Orthodox rite. Thus in 1828, some Dutch, Polish, and German Jews left B'nai Jeshurun to form Anshe Chesed. In 1839, other Polish Jews from B'nai Jeshurun and Anshe Chesed left to organize Shaarey Zedek. Divisions over rites and disagreements over the distribution of synagogue rights and honors continued through the 1840s until there were no fewer than fifteen types of Polish, Bohemian, Dutch, English, German, and, of course, Sephardic-Ashkenazic synagogues in New York City by 1850.[18]

The propensity of new immigrants to follow their own Orthodox liturgy, which was based on their European country of origin, led to the proliferation of synagogues in other American cities: In 1841 a German congregation, Beth Ahabah, was established in Richmond, Virginia; in 1842 K.K. B'nai Jeshurun was established in Cincinnati by members who believed that "the mode of worship in the established synagogue of our beloved brethren K. B. Israel is not in accordance with the rites and customs of the German Jews"; and in 1847 Baltimore's Bavarian Nidhei Israel (also known as the Baltimore Hebrew Congregation) joined another German congregation, Oheb Israel, in meeting the needs of Orthodox Jews. All in all, by 1850, six American cities housed multi-congregational communities, split along national lines.[19]

But for all the ethnic-cum-liturgical differences that splintered congregations, and despite significant differences of opinion over how much control synagogues should exert over those who sought their precincts, American congregations were united in one basic, overriding approach to institutional life. No congregation sought to recruit that large segment of American and Americanizing Jews who, disaffected from synagogues, cared little for the demands of synagogue discipline. For the German immigrant groups, comfortable only with transplanted Old World ways, their inactivity was largely preordained by their lack of understanding of this new country. In the Sephardic synagogues, a combination of

Hidalgo Jewish pride coupled with organizational resistance to change precluded experimentation with service revision.[20]

This era of complacency ended in the 1850s, for within their own organizations, voices arose urging reforms that would accommodate Judaism to American society. Orthodoxy's monopoly over synagogues ended. From then on, Jews possessed more than just the option of following established procedures or abandoning synagogue life. The Orthodox synagogue now had to determine to what extent its definition of Jewish law permitted ritual change to counter Reform Judaism. As might be expected, significant differences in opinion emerged.

Orthodox Institutions (circa 1850–1880)

In 1848, New York's Emanu-El Congregation took its first hesitant steps on the road toward becoming one of America's flagship Reform synagogues. A German hymnal was introduced to supplement the traditional *Siddur* used by the two-year-old congregation. In so doing, Emanu-El joined Baltimore's Har Sinai Congregation, formed just a few years earlier by members of the city's Hebrew congregation, which had been unhappy with its Orthodox rabbi's leadership. However, it was not until the 1850s that this first "self-declared Reform congregation in America" abandoned all Orthodox forms and practices. Nor did reform come overnight to the initially Orthodox congregations in Buffalo, Chicago, and St. Louis. Important Orthodox traditions remained even as synagogues adopted mixed choirs, organs, and abridged services. Most significantly, even when reforms were initiated, they were justified as attempts "to preserve and advance in the path of Orthodox Judaism."[21]

Although slow and sometimes unsteady, American Judaism's drift toward liturgical and procedural liberalism continued unabated throughout the years 1850–1880 and affected both immigrant German and indigenous Sephardic congregations. By 1880, America's Orthodox congregations – which had numbered 13 in 1840 and which grew to some 200 by 1860 when liturgical liberalism had just begun to gain mass popularity – were reduced to a mere handful of the some 275 synagogues serving this country's acculturated Jews in the years immediately preceding the period of Jewish immigration from Eastern Europe.[22]

The Americanization of synagogue laity, as one path-breaking historian has taught us, motivated liturgical and structural liberalism. As large numbers of German immigrants acculturated, adopting the work habits, dress, language, and overall life-styles of their fellow citizens, they desired to see their houses of worship adopt American norms. It was widely recognized that the Orthodox synagogue, rooted in European customs and prevented from change by archaic laws and practices, could not help Jews remain Jewish while integrating more and more with American culture. Or, to paraphrase another historian's earlier conceptualization, when nineteenth-century American Jews were asked whether it was possible for them to become part of a land that accepted them and still adhere to the 3,000-year Jewish tradition, they answered with a resounding no! Accordingly, the overwhelming response of initially Orthodox synagogues to calls for change from within their congregation was to accede. They tacitly agreed that Jewish law and Orthodox practice could not coexist with Americanization. Clearly, the moment of acquiescence differed from synagogue to synagogue, in accordance with the level of acculturation achieved by those affiliated, but the end result was the same.[23]

Still not all Orthodox congregations, or Orthodox minorities within changing synagogues, capitulated to the drive for liturgical liberalization. For example, in any number of American cities, Orthodox institutions were established by worshipers disaffected by their home congregation's adoption of mixed seating, an organ, or some other innovation. Sometimes protesters against synagogue reforms attempted to utilize America's civil courts to bolster their position. The disaffected obtained court injunctions barring reforms, arguing that reforms violated publicly filed articles of incorporation that services be conducted along Orthodox lines. Out-of-court settlements often provided traditionalists with financial assistance to establish new congregations.[24]

The survival rate of these breakaway Orthodox synagogues was not particularly high. Few remained Orthodox through the 1870s. Some were drawn into the Reform orbit. Others came to be comfortable with a hydrid religious ceremonial. They abandoned the Orthodox policy of separate seating, but did not adopt the Reform practices of mixed choir and organ music. Nor did they show interest in abridging the service and in utilizing a modern prayerbook, customs then characteristic of the nascent group of synagogues later to be categorized as Conservative.[25] All of these congregations were caught within the maelstrom of Americanization currents that so energized the Reform Movement. Thus, although they perceived Reform teachings and customs as too extreme for their liking, they were also uncommitted to Orthodoxy's personal demands. Although they may not have been attuned to Conservative liturgical departures, they still wanted to pray like good Americans, seated next to their wives and children even as they recited the traditional services.[26]

Breakaway synagogues that remained permanently within the Orthodox camp sometimes had to resort to extraordinary exclusionary policies to ensure that, no matter how small the Orthodox constituency might possibly become, the congregation's ritual would remain Orthodox. Such was the case for Baltimore's Chizuk Amuno. Its constitution boldly announced that "no change or alteration" could be made in divine services without the unanimous approval of all members. Moreover, "should any member offer a motion or resolution to change . . . , he shall ipso facto forfeit his membership."[27] Still, Chizuk Amuno, and for that matter all other American Orthodox institutional remnants of this period, did move to accommodate, within the framework of Jewish law, the sociological wants of synagogue-goers. Like their Reform opponents, they, too, Americanized. By the 1880s, the German vernacular had been widely replaced by English in prayer and discourse. The need to maintain decorum in services was strongly emphasized and in many places the often-riotous and always unsightly sale of synagogue honors was curtailed or abolished. What is most significant, in 1876 Chizuk Amuno called to its pulpit Henry W. Schneeberger, the first American-born Jew of any denomination to be trained as a rabbi. A definite statement was thus made that an acculturated German immigrant and his children could behave as Americans within the more up-to-date Orthodox synagogue.[28]

Orthodox synagogues of long standing, like New York's Shearith Israel, looked to strict exclusionary controls in synagogue governance to protect their denominational integrity. The Manhattan-based congregation, to ensure that its Orthodox majority would not be easily outvoted by any newly affiliating insurgents who might neither share their religious sentiments nor their sense of history, created a committee to investigate the religious opinions of potential members. Subsequently, a rule was passed that members had to be affiliated three years before they could be considered synagogue electors; and only electors could enact ritual changes.[29]

Baltimore's Shearith Israel, for its part, placed its hopes for survival on even stricter exclusionary policies. It officially denied membership to Jews known to be Sabbath violators and persisted with these policies well into the twentieth century. Richmond's Beth Shalom, too, resisted pressure to accommodate calls for synagogue modification, but its refusal to change its practices effectively led to institutional suicide. Slowly but surely, the synagogue's inertia toward religious liberalism induced congregants to move toward the Reform Beth Ahabah. In 1898, with nary a soul left to serve, Richmond's oldest congregation closed.[30]

Alone among its sister congregations, Philadelphia's Mikveh Israel consistently tried to do more than simply survive institutionally with its traditional liturgy intact. Not content to merely endure as an Orthodox remnant in a Reform-dominated country, it sought to fight back, to develop nationally acceptable programs, and to seek out alliances linking all those opposed to the denationalized, deritualized denominational foe. To do otherwise, reasoned its two famous nineteenth-century leaders, Hazzan Isaac Leeser (served 1829–1850) and Rabbi Sabato Morais (served 1851–1897), would be to abandon all but a handful of American Jews to a faith system so attuned to American ways that it threatened Jewish group continuity. Believing that even if Jews did not practice all of Orthodoxy's teachings they had to be kept away from Reform, these nineteenth-century Orthodox includers par excellence accepted as colleagues in the struggle to control the Americanization of the synagogue gone wild, individuals and groups that had themselves broken with Orthodoxy to some extent, either ritually or ideologically; these were predominantly the men and institutions that would later be credited with founding or inspiring the Conservative Movement.

Cooperation to combat a larger threat was evident as early as 1840 and soon thereafter, in 1855, when Mikveh Israel's Leeser joined with Isaac M. Wise and others in developing schemes for national religious unity.[31] The resultant Cleveland Conference of 1855 dealt programmatically with the quest for a universally acceptable *Minhag America* (American ritual) but also directly addressed the radical reforms advanced by David Einhorn. Some thirty years later, Mikveh Israel and Sabato Morais were instrumental in bringing together another coalition. This one was dedicated to combat the antinationalistic, antitraditional ritual, and nonceremonial postures assumed by the Reform Movement in its 1885 Pittsburgh Platform. On January 31, 1886, Morais led Chizuk Amuno's Schneeberger, H. P. Mendes of Shearith Israel (New York), Bernard Drachman of the newly established Zichron Ephraim,[32] and other Orthodox synagogue spokesmen into a meeting with, among others, Rabbis Marcus Jastrow of Philadelphia's Rodef Shalom, Alexander Kohut of Ahawath Chesed (New York), and Aaron Bettelheim of San Francisco's Ohabei Shalom – soon to be rabbi of Baltimore's Hebrew Congregation –all leaders of congregations that had adopted some reforms. These Orthodox and Conservative representatives pooled their energies to create the Jewish Theological Seminary of America, an institutional bulwark against the unfettered growth of Reform.[33]

Mikveh Israel was also there as a guiding spirit in 1898 when some fifty congregations founded the Union of Orthodox Jewish Congregations of America. This national congregational association – an institutional alternative to the Reform Union of American Hebrew Congregations – was mandated to "protest against the declarations of Reform rabbis not in accordance with the teachers of our Torah."[34]

But for all these efforts to attract individuals and groups away from Reform, the ultimate reality remained that neither they nor their ideological opponents were particularly successful in halting defection from Judaism. Whatever its institutional strength in the 1880s and 1890s, Orthodoxy, like American Judaism in general, had a weak constituency. And even when acculturated Jews did attend the most traditional synagogues, they did not see those institutions as central to their lives. Lewis N. Dembitz, a founder of the Orthodox Union, probably said it best when he characterized most of his fellow Orthodox Jews as "persons who do not lead a Jewish life, but read the olden prayers." Fortunately for American Orthodoxy and ultimately for the faith's survival in general in this country, their ranks were more than refilled by a new migration of Jews who brought a new vitality to that denomination. But then again, it would be years before these new arrivals would recognize their counterparts in the Orthodox Union as colleagues in battles against both assimilation and Reform Judaism.[35]

From *Shtibl* and *Landsmanshaft* to Young Israel and Synagogue-Center (1850–1920)

Distinctively East European synagogues began in the United States in the 1850s. Although numbers of Jews from the Czarist empire, Romania, Hungary, and their environs had found their way to America long before the mid-nineteenth century, it was only with the founding of New York's Beth Hamidrash in 1852[36] that this Jewish ethnic minority expressed its religious and cultural individuality by founding institutions. Prior to that time, "Russian" Jews, if they chose to affiliate, prayed and associated with co-religionists in congregations run along Central European, though increasingly Americanized, Orthodox lines.[37]

The circumstances surrounding the founding of the Beth Hamidrash and its successors were highly reminiscent of those that fostered their sister congregation in New York, B'nai Jeshurun, almost thirty years earlier. Newly arriving immigrants found synagogue practices in America foreign to them. Liturgical variations and modernizations were only part of the problem. Like all Jewish immigrants before and after them, these East Europeans recognized that their Americanized brethren viewed the synagogue as little more than a ceremonial center of minor significance in their lives. For them, the synagogue was central to the civilization they possessed in Eastern Europe.

Beth Hamidrash Hagadol provided its worshipers, in the words of its long-time member, historian Judah David Eisenstein, with a "socially religious [atmosphere]." Jews who affiliated there, he explained, "combine[d] piety with pleasure; they call[ed] their *shule* a *shtibl* or prayer-club-room; they desire[d] to be on familiar terms with the Almighty and abhor[red] decorum; they want[ed] everyone present to join and chant the prayers; above all they scorn[ed] a regularly ordained cantor." Although devotionals looked informal, the commitment of members to Judaism's traditions was quite serious. The religious reliability of the *shohet* (ritual slaughterer) employed by the synagogue was scrupulously monitored. And the congregation's baking of *matzot* was also overseen with strict care. "As an extra precaution," Eisenstein tells us, "every member personally supervise[d] the baking of the *matzot* for his own family use." Their *Hebrah Mishnayot* and a *Hebra Shas* (Talmud study classes) also reflected staunch allegiance to tradition. Founded in the 1870s, they were maintained by the congregation every morning and evening. In all events and for all occasions, the synagogue endeavored to recreate for its members the world they had left behind.[38]

Four years later, the Romanian[39] Kehal Adath Jeshurun of New York's Allen Street joined the quest to transplant East European religious culture to America. Over the next two and a half decades, the period immediately preceding the mass migration of Russian Jews to these shores, a vanguard of more than twenty similarly mandated synagogues was established both in downtown New York and in at least six other American cities.[40] They ranged from Chicago's famous Beth Hamidrash Hagadol U'Bnai Jacob (established 1867) and New York's renowned First Hungarian Congregation Ohab Zedek (established 1873) to Philadelphia's Chevrah Bikur Cholim (established 1861) and Boston's long-forgotten Congregation Shomre Shabbos (established in the early 1870s).[41] Each of these congregations offered their worshipers a comfortable sense of belonging as the immigrants slowly made their way in a new American world. In return, the synagogue requested – when it did not demand – that members continue to observe Judaism's teachings as brought over from Europe. The requirement, for example, that "every member... attend services on Sabbath and Holidays, and if found violating the Sabbath is to be expelled" was a common feature of these congregations' bylaws.[42]

It soon became abundantly clear that many immigrants were not living up to their end of the bargain. Although they needed and wanted the ethnoreligious camaraderie that came with synagogue associations, they were uncertain how strongly or for how long they could continue to follow traditional behavior patterns when commandments conflicted with their drive for advancement in this country. So stated Rabbi Hirsch Falk Vidaver in his 1875 description of Boston's first East European congregation. Congregation Shomre Shabbos, he observed, was "founded by Russian Jews who observed the Sabbath and study the

Talmud. Yet many of its members, though faithful to other Orthodox regulations nevertheless break the Sabbath."[43]

America's pressures threatened the very holding of services at New York's Ohab Zedek. In the late 1870s, synagogue leaders reported that "although the number of members was slowly increasing, the attendance at services kept dwindling. Ten men, therefore, were appointed each week to attend services under penality." Inevitably also, Americanization played a significant role in the actual structuring of synagogue life. Like the Germans before them, the East European Jews desired to see their houses of worship reflect their new-found comfort. As soon as finances permitted, congregations looked to move from storefront *shtibls* to renovated former churches, newly built synagogue edifices or to buildings previously occupied by German congregations.[44]

In 1885, for example, Beth Hamidrash Hagadol, which began in an attic on Bayard Street and which later called "an old Welsh chapel" its home, purchased the Norfolk Street Baptist Church and moved into this Gothic Revival building. Two years later, Kehal Adath Jeshurun, born on Allen Street, engaged the Herter Brothers, a Christian architectural firm, to build a Moorish-style sanctuary-center. During that same time period, Ohab Zedek took over the Norfolk Street Synagogue, which had previously been occupied by two West European congregations, Anshe Chesed and Shaarey Rachamim.[45]

Although services in these new precincts were conducted largely as they had been in the past, the demeanor of worshipers underwent a significant transformation. Men still sat separately from their wives; the *siddur* was followed without abridgement; and the time of prayers was not altered. However, gone now was the "prayer club room" intimacy that had earlier characterized synagogue life. Decorum, always the first demand of acculturating groups in making their religious regimen more intelligible and respectable to the world around them, was strongly emphasized. The maintenance of order was furthered by the assignment of seats or pews. This new formality was intensified further in the 1880s, when four of New York's landmark East European synagogues embarked upon what one historian has aptly described as "the chazan craze."[46]

As newly arrived immigrants, worshipers at Beth Hamidrash Hagadol had "scorn[ed] a regularly ordained cantor . . . [with] his foreign melodies." A generation later, in 1877, now as Americanized Jews, the congregants of this same synagogue hired Rev. Judah Oberman for $500 per year. Three years later, Simhe Samuelson replaced him and was paid an annual fee of a thousand dollars. Not to be outdone, and also fearful of losing members to their Norfolk Street competitors, the Suvwalker

Congregation and the Kalvarier quickly hired their own cantorial vir-
tuosi. In 1886, Kehal Adath Jeshurun shocked downtown society by
engaging Rev. P. Minkowsky for the then-staggering sum of five thousand dollars per annum. But Beth Hamidrash Hagadol remained competitive by bringing "over the well-known cantor, Israel Michaelowsky
. . . paying him a large salary."[47]

To the Americanizing immigrants – Eisenstein called them "the young
reformers" – these cantors were well worth the investment. They
brought a certain elegance to the services and created an aura of respectability. Contemporaries must have reasoned that a man who contributed
beyond his means to support a famous cantor would certainly remain
silent during the prayers. For synagogue leaders, failure to acquiesce to
this new trend was tantamount to institutional suicide. Immigrants on
the way up socially and economically would not pray in synagogues
beneath their station.[48]

Although there was nothing in this new synagogue style that ran
counter to Orthodoxy's teachings and traditions – who could object to
quiet during services or fail to remember that renowned cantors were a
fixture in the Orthodox synagogues of Europe long before the phenomenon hit America – the rise of congregational formalism did not receive
universal, communal approbation. Downtown, Rabbi Moses Weinberger spoke for the chorus of critics when he argued that although no one
"can deny that a sweet-singing *chazan* is pleasing to the ear . . . , the lust
for great *chazanim* and larger and more magnificent synagogues . . . has
taken our people ten steps backwards." Weinberger was explicitly troubled by the sight of Jews violating the Sabbath by carrying admission
tickets to their packed-house prayer extravaganzas. Implicitly, he was
disturbed by the changing attitudes toward synagogue life that departed
from European modes. Jews were no longer attending services primarily
to face God. Rather, they were there first and foremost to see and to be
seen by other Jews and by society around them. But in his heart, Weinberger also probably understood that this synagogal accommodation to
the acculturating immigrant's proclivity for conspicuous consumption,
even in religion, was the price that was to be paid to maintain the Jews'
loyalty to Orthodox ritual in the synagogue and allegiance to Judaism
as they adjusted to this country.[49]

Besides, there is much evidence to suggest that only a small fraction
of the rapidly Americanizing immigrants remained long enough within
synagogue life to care about decorum, "edifice complexes," cantors, and
the like. More frequently, the acculturating immigrant in his quest for
greater mobility and social acceptance perceived the synagogue as an
antiquated embarrassment and chose to break completely with the syn-

agogue. He either assimilated or expressed his Jewishness through continued geographical propinquity to other Jews or through identification with any one of the myriad of modern Jewish ideological movements that made up ghetto civilization.[50]

America's East European Jewish congregations first faced up to the disaffection with synagogue life in 1879 when representatives of some twenty-four immigrant *shuls* from New York and other cities organized the Board of Delegates of United Hebrew Orthodox Congregations. In their "Call to Israel," these spokesmen complained that "while our material prosperity has been increased to a marvelous extent, . . . the disintegration process in our religious system . . . is appalling beyond description." "All the glare and glamour of costly synagogues and temples," they declared, "cannot conceal [this] from our view." The association fervently believed that the way to counteract inroads against traditional commitments and observances was to recreate an enduring East European civilization on American soil. For them, that reestablishment began with the appointment of a powerful "Chief Rabbi . . . for all the congregations in the United States," who would guide, advise, and above all, rule over his community. An offer was soon tendered to Rabbi Meir Loeb ben Jehiel Michael Malbim, a famous East European scholar. Malbim accepted this call, but to the dismay of all concerned, Rabbi Michael passed away en route to this country and with him died this first attempt to bring drifting Jews back into the religious fold.[51]

Eight years later, in 1887, with the religious conditions of immigrant Jewry far from improved, a second initiative was undertaken. The arrival, beginning in 1881, of tens of thousands of refugees from Czarist pogroms and legislation, multiplied by ten- to twentyfold the number of congregations in this country. Even so, this mass migration neither substantially nor permanently increased the numbers of unwavering, practicing Orthodox Jews. To be sure, by the mid–1880s, the interested worshiper, searching for a socially religious atmosphere that would remind him of home, had the option of praying not only in an East European–style synagogue but in a *landsmanshaft* congregation that perpetuated the particular customs of the ancestral home. An intricate *landsmanshaft* network grew out of this drive, as the synagogue succored the immigrant and provided a myriad of social and economic services.[52]

But, as already mentioned, the affinity of worshipers for the fidelity to Orthodox ritual in this type of religious setting, more often than not did not carry over into personal religious behavior. Simply put, immigrant Jews went to *shul* Friday night to be among friends and to pray to God, but they went to work Saturday morning to advance themselves in America. And as European memories began to recede, as they made their way in America, social attachments to the *landsmanshaft* system inevitably loosened. Still, when they went to *shul*, they expected services to be authentically Orthodox as carried over from Europe.[53]

This form of religiously inconsistent behavior, based on nostalgia and the communal elements of synagogue life, was incomprehensible to the immigrants' children born in America, who were imbued early on with the quest for economic mobility and social acceptance. This was the dilemma that the Association of the American Orthodox Hebrew Congregations confronted when in 1887 it called to New York Rabbi Jacob Joseph of Vilna to serve as chief rabbi of the city.[54]

Although Rabbi Joseph survived his trip to America, his career on these shores was a disaster. He possessed authority and expertise, but he had no power in this country. Although his East European–style oratory packed Beth Hamidrash Hagadol, the seat of his administration, he could not stop his audiences from desecrating the Sabbath. In addition, his Yiddish-language message said nothing to the next generation of Jews. It soon became clear to elements within the Orthodox community that transplanted institutional forms, which took no cognizance of the centrality of Americanization within the immigrants' consciousness, would not save Judaism. These new Orthodox spokesmen also understood that they could not alone successfully refashion synagogue life to recapture for the faith "the rising generation in Israel."[55]

So disposed, the lay, and a portion of the rabbinic, leadership of some of the earliest established East European synagogues cooperated with their Central European Orthodox brethren by founding the Orthodox Union (OU) in 1897. Even as Eisenstein of Beth Hamidrash Hagadol, Yiddish newspaper editor Kasriel Sarasohn of Kehal Adath Jeshurun,[56] and Ohab Zedek's Rabbi Philip Hillel Klein[57] still supported the declining Rabbi Joseph, they also led a downtown contingent ready to talk with the officialdom of New York's Shearith Israel, Baltimore's Chizuk Amuno, and so on, with respect to establishing a united Orthodox front.[58]

All of these men had been in this country long enough before the founding of the Orthodox Union to understand the promises and pitfalls of Americanization. Significantly, they had themselves achieved a noticeable degree of acculturation without abandoning ancestral teachings and they wanted the same for their brethren. Thus, although the original mandate of the Orthodox Union said much about challenging "the declarations of Reform rabbis not in accord with the teachings of our Torah," it was clear from almost the very start, that the organization's focus would be more on helping immigrants balance their allegiance to Judaism with the drive to Americanize than on striking out against another denomination.[59]

The banker Sender Jarmulowsky and businessman Jonas Weil of upper Manhattan's Zichron Ephraim shared their co-ethnics' and religionists' sentiments. These immigrants of long standing in this country had also arrived in the decades before 1881, so that, by the time the Orthodox Union was established, they had achieved not only a high degree of Americanization, but had also reached a remarkable level of affluence. They were able to move their families from the Lower East Side to residential Yorkville, and there established a decorous, architecturally beautiful Orthodox synagogue. The plans of the Orthodox Union, as we shall presently see, fit well their understanding of Judaism's requirements in America. In 1889, Zichron Ephraim engaged Bernard Drachman, an American-born, university-trained rabbi. A man destined to be a major force in the Orthodox Union, he already possessed the linguistic and cultural capabilities to appeal to Americanized children of immigrants.[60]

This major personnel decision was soon emulated by Zichron Ephraim's Yorkville sister congregation, Kehilath Jeshurun, an affiliate of the Orthodox Union that had been founded in 1871 by economically advanced East Europeans. In 1904, this congregation replaced its Yiddish-speaking rabbi with a Columbia University graduate, Rev. Mordecai Kaplan, a Drachman student and a recent ordainee of the early Jewish Theological Seminary of America.[61] When in 1906 Ohab Zedek moved uptown, they began to share Drachman with the Zichron Ephraim synagogue. The English-speaking rabbi shared a Harlem pulpit with the foreign language–speaking, but American thinking, Rabbi Philip Klein.[62]

Twelve other East European congregations from nine other American and Canadian cities joined in the founding of the Orthodox Union. Their participation in and cooperation with the Union testifies that East European groups outside the metropolis also recognized that immigrant disaffection from Judaism had to be solved along American lines.[63]

The Orthodox Union moved upon its self-imposed mandate to "take action of a more positive nature to conserve the true intentions of Judaism" when, beginning in 1901, it tacitly adopted the Jewish Endeavor Society (JES) as its "youth division." The union believed that "congregations must have ministers and ministers to hold the young men and women must be acceptable." The JES, founded by the early students and first rabbis produced by the early Jewish Theological Seminary of America, was considered by the Union to be more than equal to the challenge.[64]

The Endeavor Society offered Jewish educational, social, and cultural programs to Americanizing immigrants on the Lower East Side, and later on in Harlem and in Philadelphia, and conducted "dignified services" dedicated to "recall indifferent Jewry back to their ancestral faith." They understood that if Judaism was to remain, or become once again, vital in the immigrants' life, the Orthodox synagogue had to recognize Americanization's pressures upon potential communicants. Accordingly, the "young people's synagogues" established under JES auspices generally held their Sabbath and holiday services in the late afternoons to attract individuals who had been working until evening. Society leaders, to be sure, characterized their services as Orthodox and buttressed their assertion by using the traditional prayerbook and insisting upon the separation of the sexes. But in many other ways, these services differed dramatically from those in the *landsmanshaft* synagogues. The Endeavorers sought to admit America into the Orthodox service as much as Jewish law would permit and to exorcise those customs that would embarrass and disillusion acculturating worshipers. Recognizing the growing unfamiliarity of Jews with Hebrew, they instituted supplementary English-language prayers and considered the substitution of English translations for standard prayers. A weekly English sermon on topics related to the American Jewish experience became standard, and Yiddish played no role in rabbinic discourse or lay discussion. In addition, of course, all overt signs of commercialism were eliminated from synagogue life.[65]

The Union also supported a number of other independent youth synagogue initiatives. In 1902, reacting to the reported need for a "large well-constructed Orthodox synagogue" for acculturating Jews in Harlem, Mendes and Drachman assisted local leaders in establishing Congregation Shomre Emunah. Like the Endeavor Society, the organizers of this synagogue promised to conduct services loyal "to Orthodox ritual in an impressive, decorous manner." This up-to-date Orthodox synagogue sought to spare worshipers the unseeming distractions of noise, commotion, and blatant commercialism.[66]

Three years later, in 1905, Henry S. Morais, son of Seminary founder Sabato Morais and a leader himself of the OU, organized Congregation Mikve Israel in Harlem. This synagogue took the Americanization of the cantor's role a significant step further. Morais and his followers rejected outright the *landsmanshaft*-style, untrained functionary who droned on as Jews prayed noisily at their own rate. But they also recognized that many young people were not comfortable in congregations where cantors sang solos, even in a quiet sanctuary. Instead, Mikveh Israel leaders became the earliest advocates of congregational singing in the Orthodox service. Morais instructed his cantor to be a true "servant of the community" by chanting simple tunes that could be easily followed by worshipers. Lay people were encouraged to join in singing the prayers, so that traditional forms of prayer would become more meaningful. Congregational singing also helped synagogue leaders to maintain decorum; lay people who were actively participating had little time for idle gossip.[67]

Mikve Israel was also way ahead of its time in addressing the role and status of women within an Orthodox context. Although most congregations across all denominations kept women from synagogue office, relegating them to the women's auxiliary or sisterhood, two women were members of its original twelve-member board of trustees. Here, although females were precluded from leadership in prayer, they had an important voice in all other congregational activities.[68]

These groups' ambitious attempts to draw those disaffected from Judaism into the Orthodox synagogue were neither quickly nor universally accepted. Rabbi Jacob Willowski (Ridbaz), the so-called Slutska Rav, a leader of the immigrant Agudath Ha-Rabbonim (Union of Orthodox Rabbis of the United States and Canada), was probably the most outspoken ideological critic of these changes. He was keenly aware of the difficulties transplanted East European synagogues were experiencing, but for him modifications in the sociology of synagogue life, if not tantamount to deviation from the faith's theological teachings, were the first step toward that eventuality. In his view, the ways of the past had to be better promoted and not abandoned, and no accommodation would be accorded those breaking with ancestral beliefs. The Ridbaz was particularly angry at congregational adoption of English-language sermons. If such practices persisted, he declared, there would be "no hope for the continuance of the Jewish religion."[69]

Willowski publicly punctuated his point of view in 1904 by demanding to deliver a Yiddish-language sermon at the High Holiday services of Yorkville's Congregation Kehilath Jeshurun, a leading synagogue in the modernization movement. This affront to the synagogue's English-speaking spiritual leader, Mordecai Kaplan, prompted one unimpressed contemporary to characterize the Slutska Rav's action as an "insult to honest Orthodoxy."[70]

The Endeavorers and their cohorts also had difficulties with less respected elements in the immigrant Orthodox community who opposed their initiatives on more practical grounds. Saturday and holiday afternoons were a time often reserved in downtown synagogues for popular rabbinic discourses given by *magidim*. These ghetto preachers sold tickets, before and sometimes during Jewish holidays, to their histrionic performances and did not appreciate the competition for synagogue space. They often succeeded in influencing synagogue leaders to refuse rentals to these young interlopers. As one Endeavorer regretfully put it: "Services were successful but unfortunately a *magid* usually appeared on the scene followed by his hosts and naturally the services had to make room for the Yiddish preacher."[71]

The Endeavorers and early youth synagogues ultimately did not survive the decade.[72] But it was not the Ridbaz's fulminations nor the *magidim*'s competition that defeated them.[73] Rather, Americanization, the lures of secularized society, effectively undermined these, as it would undercut all later Jewish reclamation efforts. Many second-generation Jews were simply unmoved by Endeavorer appeals, as they followed the road toward assimilation. These early youth-oriented Orthodox synagogues did, however, leave an important legacy: They were the forerunners of the enduring Young Israel and Institutional Synagogue movements that began after 1910.[74]

In 1913, with the problem of youth disaffection from Judaism unsolved, a new institutional initiative to "bring about a revival of Judaism among the thousands of Jews and Jewesses . . . whose Judaism is at present dormant" was inaugurated on the Lower East Side. Like the Endeavorers before them, the founders of this new Young Israel (YI) movement were students at the Jewish Theological Seminary. Not surprisingly, Moses Rosenthal and Samuel Sachs looked to their teachers Rabbi Mordecai M. Kaplan and Israel Friedlander for advice in developing programming "to awaken Jewish young men and women to their responsibilities as Jews in whatever form these responsibilities are conceived." Their appeal was directed to "all . . . whatever be their views of Judaism, whatever be their social or economic status." Their activities were to consist of a balance of classes, educational forums and lectures, and Americanized Orthodox religious services.[75]

For the Seminary leadership, the Young Israel movement fit well the mandate set for that rabbinic institution by its president, Solomon Schechter. In his reorganization efforts, Schechter focused the Seminary's goals on training a new generation of American rabbis of East European heritage who would recapture their brethren for the faith. Although Kaplan and Friedlaender's own personal and institutional understandings of Judaism clearly deviated from that of Orthodoxy, they understood that their American-style services and activities would have to be strictly Orthodox if they hoped to receive the approbation of downtown society. Their sensitivity to the attitudes of potential downtown critics was so acute that when Rabbi Joseph Hertz (a pre-Schechter Seminary graduate and later chief rabbi of Great Britain) spoke at YI sabbath services, he lectured Friday night in English and Saturday morning in Yiddish.[76]

This careful approach had its rewards. Four downtown synagogues – including, not surprisingly, the Orthodox Union–affiliate Kalvarier and Kehal Adath Jeshurun, who had backed earlier Endeavorer efforts – trusted the Orthodoxy of the Young Israel and opened their doors to their activities. More significantly, the Orthodox *Morgen Zhurnal*, the downtown organ slowest to accept harmonization schemes of any kind, stamped its approval upon their initiatives.[77]

Whatever its Seminary connection, the strength of the early YI resided in its lay constituency of "young businessmen and professional people" who attempted "to arouse and intensify the Jewish consciousness of our young men and women and thus to close up the gap now existing between young and old." It was they who helped the YI grow beyond its original balance of educational and strictly religious programming toward the synagogue-center it became.[78] It was this objective that moved a contingent of YI men in 1915 to establish the first permanent Young Israel (Model) Synagogue. Layman Harry G. Fromberg explained the goals of this endeavor:

> [a model synagogue is to be created] where every atom of our time honored traditions could be observed and at the same time prove an attraction particularly to the young men and women; a synagogue where, with the exception of prayer, English would be spoken in delivering sermons and otherwise, complete congregational singing instituted, *schnoddering* eliminated and decorum to an extent of almost 100 percent maintained.[79]

Lay leaders of Young Israel also knew that modern, decorous services alone could not ensure institutional survival under the pressures of assimilation. Early on, the Young Israel linked itself with Drachman's Jewish Sabbath Observers Association, which had sought to find jobs for those loyal to Sabbath observers. It thereby hoped to undermine the economics of assimilation. Equally important, the YI defined its synagogue as a Jewish social center, where young men and women could meet. Dancing, boat rides, and athletics such as were standard at non-sectarian or Christian settlement houses were included as part of synagogue life. Fromberg, speaking for his organization in 1918, argued that:

> The time has come when the man and woman in America must be taught to feel that he or she need not be deprived of the

innocent social pleasures so long as it is done in accord with
Jewish rites and principles, it is the aim of the synagogue to make
the young people feel that being Jews need not deprive them of
their social activities and pleasure.[80]

Rabbi Herbert S. Goldstein could not have agreed more. His Institutional Synagogue in Harlem, even more than the YI movement, constituted the most consciously articulated attempt to approximate within
the Orthodox synagogue the activities available in other Americanizing
social settings. Goldstein came to this post with both an impressive
rabbinic pedigree and with important early career experience. He was
twice ordained; first by Rabbi S. E. Jaffee of Beth Hamidrash Hagadol,
a stalwart defender of downtown religious society, and later by the JTS,
from which he was graduated as a rabbi in 1913. He thus knew both
traditional ways and modern American Jewish plans.

While at the Seminary, Goldstein had been exposed to Kaplan's teachings that the synagogue had to offer the second-generation Jew more
than modern services if it hoped to compete with assimilation. Settlement
house and Young Men's Hebrew Association (YMHA) social programs
had to be brought into the Orthodox synagogue. Synagogue life could
now be entered through any number of portals. Ultimately, it was hoped,
they would find their way toward religious dedication and identification.[81]

Goldstein first acted upon these ideas during his tenure as English-
speaking rabbi of Yorkville's Kehilath Jeshurun. There, with Kaplan's
assistance, he was instrumental in the founding of the Central Jewish
Institute (CJI), a prototype of the envisioned religious center. CJI became
the institutional mecca for all social, recreational, and educational programs ancillary to Kehilath Jeshurun's Americanized Orthodox services.
Still, its critics claimed that it possessed "all the elements of the synagogue
center but only externally so. The three departments have no close contact
because the synagogue element is not bold enough. The synagogue has
not developed its full capacity and its influence is small." By 1917, convinced that he had taken that model as far as it could go, Goldstein
severed his connection with the Yorkville congregation, brought together a group of fledgling Harlem youth organizations, and established
his own Institutional Synagogue. There he was free to develop and to
integrate all aspects of synagogue life. A year later, Kaplan followed his
student's lead and created the Jewish Center of New York's West Side,
which would also serve as a prototype for hundreds of Jewish synagogue
centers organized around the country over the next decades.[82]

By the close of the First World War, youth-oriented Orthodox synagogues had come of age. The Young Israel and the Institutional Synagogue both boasted of several thousand members and followers. Both were economically stable and each would influence the establishment of similar initiatives in cities throughout the United States. But this was only a partial victory. As Kaplan pointed out in 1917,

> The synagogue has lost hold on more than one-half of the largest Jewish community in the world. . . . It is evident that the density of population, economic conditions and length of stay in this country have so rapid an effect upon synagogue affiliation that we cannot but infer that the synagogue owes its existence more to the momentum of the past than to any new forces created in this country for its conservation and development.[83]

What was true of New York was apparent in other smaller, and less ambitious and creative Jewish communities. In truth, none of the institutional forms of Orthodoxy – whether *landsmanshaft* synagogue, affiliating first-generation Orthodox Union congregation, Young Israel, or Institutional Synagogue/Jewish Center – succeeded in retarding assimilation. With the battle unfinished, the 1920s opened under a new threat to the Orthodox synagogue. Conservative and Reform Judaism began to seriously challenge Orthodoxy for the allegiances of those Jews of East European heritage who still wanted to adhere to some version of their faith as they advanced in America.

In Competition with Conservative and Reform Judaism (circa 1920–1945)

Reform and Conservative interest in East European constituencies began long before the 1920s. But neither the Reform-leaning People's Synagogue, founded in the 1890s, nor Reform Rabbi Stephen S. Wise's Free Synagogue, established in 1908 out of Clinton Hall, a part of Lillian Wald's Henry Street Settlement, captured the imagination of downtown Jewry. The immigrant generation, which was often ambivalent when not downright antagonistic toward Americanized Orthodox youth services, had no interest whatsoever in these foreign conceptions and expressions of Judaism. And the second-generation Jews, who could be attracted to services with an American flavor, perceived the Reform ritual and practice as too extreme a break with the faith of the fathers.[84]

Early twentieth-century Conservatives fared only slightly better. In fact, its United Synagogue of America (USA), founded in 1913, first demonstrated its potential strength only in the last years of the 1910s. At the same time that the Young Israel, Institutional Synagogue, and Jewish Center initiatives emerged within American Orthodoxy, less traditional congregations catering to the second-generation constituency appeared coast to coast. However, not all of its member synagogues were Conservative in practice. New York's and Kaplan's Jewish Center, the West Side's Pincus Elijah, and Young Israel of Brooklyn were just three that had retained strict Orthodox ritual and seating patterns, even as they joined this congregational association.[85]

Denominational competition for the allegiances of affiliating second-generation Jews began in earnest in the 1920s. The battlegrounds were the clean streets and fresh meadows of the outer boroughs, city limits, and early suburban neighborhoods of America's immigrant metropolises. The now-grown children of Jewish immigrants flocked to these areas in search of improved living conditions and as a reflection of their intensifying American identification. For some, the physical removal from their parents' transplanted East European environment facilitated their ongoing assimilation. Now on their own, making their way in American economy and society, they had no use for the synagogue, be it unreconstructed European, American Orthodox, Conservative, or Reform. For others, however, suburbia was the site of their continued efforts to harmonize Judaism with their newer cultural heritage, and there they found that the Conservative and Reform synagogues, possibly even more than American Orthodox, presented reasonable solutions to their religious dilemmas.[86]

Orthodox synagogues and their leaders were of several minds in their response to Reform and Conservative competition. For East European–born rabbis serving immigrant inner-city congregations, the answer was a consistent categorical condemnation of liberal ritual practices. These clergymen also lent moral support outside their neighborhoods to Orthodox Jews who were within congregations moving toward Conservativism. In one celebrated case, the Agudath Ha-Rabbonim went to court to stall a Cleveland synagogue's efforts to install family pews and to change the starting time of prayers. Then again, these rabbinic authorities also had difficulties with the halachically innocuous goings-on in Young Israel and other American-style Orthodox congregations. These critics followed Willowski's old exclusionary tradition when they expressed grave reservations over Orthodox synagogues holding Friday night lectures on "secular" topics to attract the uncommitted because it seemingly emulated other denominations' practices.[87]

Old-line synagogue leaders could easily express their belief that modifications in the sociology of synagogue life were tantamount to theo-

logical deviations because they were, more often than not, geographically, linguistically, and culturally removed from the battle for the second-generation allegiances. Not so the Young Israel and the Orthodox
Union Synagogue, which defined itself as American, for they presented
themselves as attuned to the identity problems of the acculturated. For
some of these congregations, the answer was acquiescence to the burgeoning Conservative Movement. Not all newly affiliating United Synagogue congregations began de novo in the 1920s. Some, like the
Cleveland Jewish Center noted above, started out as Orthodox congregations and, with Seminary men at the helm, moved slowly from the
Orthodox Union to the United Synagogue. Other American-style
Orthodox congregations disdained capitulation and chose instead to compete with their liberal brethren. In their search for followers, however,
they understood that most potential communicants were not only moving from Orthodoxy in personal practice, as had already been the case
twenty years earlier, but that there were other denominations that accepted their heterodoxy without question.[88]

The answer of interwar Americanized Orthodox synagogues was a
two-pronged plan of modernization in the service and conscious inclusion
in congregational life of all Jews regardless of their personal religious
deportment. Synagogues made concerted efforts to push Orthodox ritual
practice to its halachic limits. A member's activities at home and in the
streets were overlooked as long as he upheld Orthodoxy in the sanctuary.
Most important, university-trained, English-speaking rabbis ordained
primarily at the Rabbi Isaac Elchanan Theological Seminary (RIETS),
later and better known as the rabbinical-training branch of Yeshiva University, were called upon to implement these policies.[89]

These American rabbis entered the field just in time. RIETS frequently
received appeals from Orthodox Jews when synagogues contemplated
adopting Conservative practices. They requested a capable Yeshiva graduate to hold the line. In 1929, a communal leader in Massachusetts wrote:

> If we do not get a Yeshiva man, I am quite sure that there will
> be a Seminary man. I am not saying this in the nature of a threat
> but I feel that the spirit aroused among the younger men is such
> that they feel the need for an English speaking rabbi and they
> will want it satisfied.[90]

Once installed in the pulpit, RIETS men endeavored to make Orthodoxy as acceptable and as inclusive as the liberal denominations. Some
rabbis were highly successful. In the 1920s, men like Joseph H. Lookstein
and Leo Jung came to Manhattan's Kehilath Jeshurun and the West Side's
Jewish Center, respectively. There they led flagship Orthodox Union

congregations, continued the traditions of Drachman, Goldstein, and early Kaplan and raised decorum and the Orthodox sermon to its highest level. They made, according to one historian, "Orthodoxy respectable" within their affluent, second-generation, albeit inner-borough, Jewish communities.[91]

Orthodox rabbis placed in outer-borough and suburban locales were as culturally refined as Jung and as homiletically proficient as Lookstein, but did not have the political sagacity to keep the liberalizing elements at bay. And they could do nothing about their synagogue's location away both from urban work areas and sometimes from members' homes. Clerical and lay synagogue leadership was faced with the same questions that had troubled Orthodox congregational officials a century earlier: Can a mixed-seating synagogue remain in the Orthodox fold? Should membership or synagogue honors be bestowed upon individuals known to be Sabbath violators? The evidence was, of course, right there. Members drove their cars from home to Orthodox service. Ultimately (here the question echoed Orthodox difficulties over two centuries), should a man married to a Christian be allowed to join the congregation?[92]

Many congregations responded affirmatively to some of these questions, creating, beginning in the 1920s, the so-called traditional-Orthodox congregation. These hybrid synagogues were most prevalent in Midwestern and Southern Jewish communities far removed from Orthodoxy's New York hub, the home of the OU, YI, and, in 1935, the Rabbinical Council of America (RCA), which linked RIETS and other English-preaching Orthodox rabbis. This "Orthodoxy on the Periphery," as one Danville, Virginia, RIETS man described it, served those whose "practical observance (of mitzvoth) may have vanished from their lives to an alarming extent. Yet they want an Orthodox shul with Orthodox leadership." These Jews, in the words of a St. Louis-based rabbi, were "at best a half-baked laity with a confused and distorted version of Judaism." They deported themselves as Orthodox only insofar as their ritual practices within synagogue precincts were closer to the old ways than the Conservatives in town.[93]

Still, the Orthodox Union and the RCA tacitly and even formally accepted these congregations as bona fide Orthodox synagogues. To do otherwise would have been be to drive their rabbinic colleagues and lay constitutents into the arms of the USA and the Conservative Rabbinical Assembly (RA). The RCA, for example, voted in 1942 to admit to its membership all men ordained by RIETS or by any other Orthodox institution or authority. They did, however, reserve national officeholding for rabbis officiating at synagogues with separate seating. The Orthodox Union, for its part, never publicly defined its admission criteria.

Still, many congregations with several hundred members, both within and outside New York, had mixed-pew synagogues.[94]

These heterodox synagogues battled for second-generation allegiances against both the liberal denominations and the threat of assimilation. In the former encounter, the American Orthodox synagogue (defined here as including YI and OU congregations of both mixed- and separate-seat orientations) more than held its own. It survived American Jewry's move toward suburbia and offered an alternative to USA congregations. Indeed, in the 1920s and 1930s, YI and OU congregations in New York City's outer boroughs of the Bronx, Queens, and Brooklyn and suburban Long Island may well have outnumbered their Conservative counterparts. Just as eleven USA synagogues served Queens and Long Island during the 1930s, so did an estimated nineteen OU affiliates. Both offered potential communicants socioreligious attractions ancillary to the divine services. In the Bronx, eleven Conservative temples were matched by at least as many Orthodox synagogues. In Brooklyn's new Flatbush, Bensonhurst, and Borough Park neighborhoods, the Brooklyn Jewish Center and sixteen other Conservative congregations competed with fourteen Young Israel affiliates.[95]

Outside of New York, the Orthodox Union was not as popular, and the Young Israel was almost nonexistent.[96] In other American cities, Orthodox institutions were overwhelmed by liberal denominational power and influence. In Newport News, Virginia, for example, an Orthodox rabbi publicly deplored "the spiritual plight of the adolescent girls lured away from traditional Judaism by the confirmation ceremonies in Reformed and Conservative congregations." His New Orleans–based colleague understood his predicament quite well. The latter's report on "Orthodoxy in the South" indicated that "Orthodoxy does not seem to be in style. . . . There are a number of Orthodox congregations, which, in the interest of harmony, have no Sunday School of their own, but send their children to the Reform school." And from California came the news that "while Orthodox groups . . . do not feel qualified as yet to do constructive work, the Conservatives and their Reform colleagues are taking full advantage of their inactivity." Nonetheless, in 1938, the OU made the claim that it represented 900 U.S. congregations in at least 150 cities in an estimated 27 states (coast to coast), and constituted "the largest Jewish religious group numerically in the United States."[97] Whatever their success in battling the Conservatives and the less pervasive Neo-Reformers, it is clear that American Orthodoxy – and, indeed, Conservatism and Reform – did not accomplish its ultimate goal of recapturing assimilating Jewry back to the faith. The "one-half baked" congregants, about whom the St. Louis rabbi complained, were at least affiliated with synagogue life. Many others were simply uninterested. So great was the problem that in 1935 the OU willingly joined with its USA and Union of American Hebrew Congregations rivals in a "Back to the Synagogue" endeavor to reclaim Jews to religious life, whatever their denominational expression. However, even this cooperative effort was minimally successful.[98]

In 1940 American Orthodoxy was congregationally large but the practice of Orthodoxy beyond synagogue precincts was weak. Like their counterparts of the 1880s, even when most second-generation Jews attended the most traditional of American synagogues, they did not view that involvement as central to their lives. However, once again a new Jewish migration hit America's shores during and after World War II and quickly revitalized and transformed Orthodoxy's strength and orientation.

The American Orthodox Synagogue – Postwar and Beyond

A breed of Orthodox Jews, previously unseen in America, settled here beginning in 1933. Refugees first from Hitler's terror and later from Stalin's tanks sought this country because their European home communities had been, or were in the process of being, destroyed. During the period from 1880 to 1920 these Jews had harkened to the Chofetz Chaim's (Rabbi Israel Meir HaKohen Kagan) admonition: "Whoever wishes to live properly before God must not settle in that country." Brought to America by tragic fate, they set out to make the best of an unwanted situation. They approached the reconstitution of the synagogue life and the religious civilization they had seen burned before their eyes with uncompromised zeal. Far more than any prior wave of migrants, they remained true to the ideal of excluding America from their community's life.[99]

Their success in perpetuating European modes of worship and behavior, and in keeping the impulse to Americanize off their *shtibl's* agenda, is owed to a temporal power that for them is greater than America, that of their *rebbes*, or transplanted religious leaders.

Chief rabbis did predate the postwar period, but men like poor Rabbi Jacob Joseph were given the unenviable task by their lay employers of recapturing or luring immigrants and their children back to Orthodox Judaism after Americanization had severely affected their potential constituencies. Postwar religious leaders, ranging from the German community's Joseph Breuer to the Hasidic rebbes to the *roshei yeshiva* of transplanted Lithuanian yeshivas, gained and maintained powers that Rabbi Joseph never possessed. Their followers were immigrants who came to Washington Heights or to Williamsburg or to Lakewood, New Jersey, precisely to be with them and together to live the good Jewish life at a distance from this country.[100]

This intense, exclusionary orientation has, with only one noteworthy exception, not been exported to the wider American Jewish community. The proselytizing Lubavitcher Hasidim alone have attempted to extend their formal suzerainty beyond the community of true believers and toward third- and fourth-generation co-religionists disaffected with acculturated, middle-class life-styles. All other refugee communities have not been actively concerned with the assimilated. Indeed, in a most poignant commentary on his group's attitude toward Orthodox outreach, one Lakewood Yeshiva student told a contemporary sociologist that the best thing that he could do to bring other Jews closer to the Torah was to intensify his own study of the sacred texts: "We do not know what God's motives are and how he works. It is entirely possible that my keeping my *Gemora* [Talmud] open five minutes longer will result in God influencing someone to become a little more interested in religion."[101]

Although staying behind their own fences, these staunchly Orthodox elements have made a tremendous impact upon the indigenous American Orthodox synagogue movements. Those who have borne witness to the faith that traditional Judaism could progress in this country without accommodation to the host environment have, for example, undermined the original assumptions and redirected the priorities of the contemporary Young Israel movement. These youth synagogues of two generations ago were built by Jews unhappy with *landsmanshaft* Judaism and convinced that their parents' European rabbis could contribute little to the maintenance of their religious identity. Indeed, many early Young Israel congregations prided themselves on their ability to survive and conduct services without the benefit of professional clergy, rabbinic or cantorial. Finally, for the acculturated these synagogues were most comfortable conducting dances and mixed socials. They reasoned that it was far better for their generation to congregate under American Orthodox auspices than at competing events sponsored by the Young Peoples Socialist League (YPSL) or Christian settlement houses.

The postwar YI synagogues have been influenced by refugees who reject such an inclusionary approach. These synagogues are today almost always headed by a pulpit rabbi; pay more than nominal obeisance to transplanted East European authorities, even if their own spiritual leaders are American-born and English-speaking; and widely disdain ancillary synagogue activities. One sociologist has suggested that the watershed in the YI's drift toward the orientation of refugee Orthodoxy took place in 1963, when its national director – significantly a graduate of a transplanted European-style yeshiva – "urged a united Orthodox front which would turn to the '*Gedoley Torah*' (leading Orthodox sages in America) . . . and be bound not only by their decisions on purely halachic matters, but also by their point of view on non-legal matters." In essence, this scholar contends, the YI was now turning for advice and direction to the same type of rabbis against whom their predecessors had tacitly rebelled. In recent years, when Young Israels have looked to reach out beyond their synagogue precincts, it has been in the promotion of kosher kitchens for Orthodox students at American universities or to the development of their movement's presence in the State of Israel.[102]

The rightward shift of Young Israel and other liked-minded OU synagogues has been spurred on by two other significant sociological developments: the growth of Jewish day schools and the limited acculturation of the refugee's children and grandchildren. During the interwar period, even the most traditionally observant members of YI or strictly Orthodox OU congregations attended American public schools and after-school Talmud Torah programs. Immigrant parents, with few exceptions, sent their children to the public schools and expressed their residual Jewish commitment by directing these pupils to afternoon congregational and communal schools. Those second-generation Jews, positively influenced by supplementary Jewish education, filled the rows of American Orthodox synagogues between 1920 and 1945.[103]

The proliferation of Jewish day schools after 1945, a result of the disenchantment of middle-class parents with the educational program offered at public schools coupled with increased confidence in their dual identities as Americans and as Jews, has changed Orthodox synagogue life. Third- and fourth-generation children generally know more of Jewish traditional teachings and practices than do their elders. Day school youth, many of whom by the time of this writing have themselves reached middle age, look at a rabbi not so much as a senatorial, homiletically proficient figure, but as a teacher who can help them expand their familiarity with tradition beyond the years of their formal education. Equally important, their social expectations of synagogue life are different from those of their parents. Younger worshipers do not check the synagogue calendar for socials and dances. They see the *shul* reestablishing its traditional role as house of assembly, study, and prayer.[104]

For the acculturated, these synagogues also have attracted some members of refugee Orthodoxy's second and third generation. American economics, technology, and higher education have today facilitated the emergence of affluent, scientifically trained, and sophisticated American-born Jews who are unimpressed, if not relatively untouched, by American societal values. These doctors, lawyers, accountants, computer scientists, and engineers feel more at home in their transplanted European *yeshivot* even as they seek higher general training at colleges, which, ironically, had been off limits to even their most assimilated of co-religionists a generation earlier. American universities, for their part, have permitted individuals to graduate from their schools without exposure to the assimilatory liberal arts – most even give some transfer credit for yeshiva talmud study – not only because the business of education has changed, but because cold war America is trying to train its best and brightest. Americanization, consequently, is no longer a requirement for advancement in American society.

Accordingly, the children and grandchildren of refugees have emerged from ghetto poverty to fashionable middle- and upper-class status in urban and suburban neighborhoods without a concomitant break with immigrant culture and religion. There they have linked arms with and have significantly influenced their co-religionists trained in day schools in creating a contemporary synagogue life that is committed to the study and maintenance of traditional law. When these Jews talk about issues ancillary to the synagogue, their concerns are with *eruvim* (enclosures) permitting observant parents to wheel baby carriages to services on the Sabbath. Thus they ensure that the Orthodox family living in suburbia stays together, albeit on opposite sides of the synagogue's partition.[105]

Not all of the Orthodox Union's 1,000 congregations look to European-trained *gedolim* for inspiration. Nor are they led by day school graduates or products of the yeshiva world. For the majority of congregations, particularly those situated away from large metropolises and suburbias (still the homes of refugee Orthodoxy and its cultural epicenters), advanced-level Talmud class programming and *eruv* installation and maintenance are the least of their problems. They are, rather, concerned with continuing their struggle for institutional survival against both assimilation and the now very powerful liberal denominations.[106]

In the postwar battle for affiliates, the Conservative and Neo-Reform approaches to synagogue life were well suited to the demography and sociology of the Jewish move to suburbia. However, for all the strength of liberal Judaism within these most contemporary Jewish frontiers, Orthodox synagogues for the not particularly observant have survived. (Indeed, the OU claimed as late as 1965 that it spoke for three million Jews and for 3,600 synagogues; an inflated figure.) Ironically, these synagogues, whatever their true numbers, have been successful with third- and fourth-generation Jews for some of the same reasons that *landsman-*

shaft synagogues were popular with their immigrant ancestors. "Non-observant Orthodox," as one sociologist has described them, opt for the more traditional congregations because they feel that Conservative or Reform synagogue-centers are "too cold, too large, or too formal" for their tastes. These somewhat nonconformist suburbanites seek the same familiarity with other Jews and with the Almighty that fueled the faith of their parents.[107]

American Orthodox synagogues are divided more than ever between those accepting and accommodating Jews who do not privately follow traditional practices and those that are founded and maintained by individuals who, more than any previous generation in American Jewish history, observe the Orthodox understandings of tradition. Yet, with religious lines clearly drawn, a new sociological force, that of women's rights and religious privileges, has entered the Jewish world and augurs to redefine again the terms *inclusion* and *exclusion* as applied to the Orthodox synagogue.

The rise of the feminist movement clearly has not made an impact upon Orthodoxy as it has upon other Jewish denominations. Women have not appeared at Yeshiva University's portals demanding admission to RIETS, as they have at the JTS Rabbinical School. Nor have women served as cantors in even the most liberal Orthodox synagogues, as they do in Reform temples. Yet American Orthodoxy, too, has not been immune to currents of change. To date, the majority of Orthodox synagogues – across the denomination's spectrum – exclude their women from formal ritual and organizational leadership. However, an increasing number of congregations now include women on lay boards of trustees and some even permit female membership on synagogue ritual committees. What is most striking, a few let their women carry *sifrei Torah* (Torah scrolls) around the synagogues as a regular, accepted part of the ritual. Moreover, these same congregations have placed their imprimatur upon separate women's *tefillot* (prayer groups) within their organization's precinct. Time will tell whether the Orthodox women so involved in these services will remain content with the changed but still limited access to the divine now accorded them. In all events, a history of the Orthodox synagogue in America written fifty years from now will undeniably begin with the fate of this social development within and outside Orthodoxy.[108]

NOTES

1   Hyman B. Grinstein, *The Rise of the Jewish Community of New York* (Philadelphia, 1946), pp. 377–378. For important discussions of the phenomenon

of intermarriage in the nineteenth century that notes the role synagogue legislation played in the decline of Jewish numbers, see Moshe Davis, "Mixed Marriage in Western Jewry," *Jewish Journal of Sociology*, 15, no. 2 (1968), pp. 180–181; Malcolm H. Stern, "The Function of Genealogy in American Jewish History," in *Essays in American Jewish History* (Cincinnati, 1958), pp. 83–84.

2   Grinstein, *Rise of the Jewish Community*, pp. 375–381.
3   The use of the term "Orthodox" to describe the synagogue practices of early nineteenth-century congregations is, of course, somewhat anachronistic. One can only begin speaking accurately of Orthodox congregations when there are Reform and Conservative congregations to which they can be compared. Until the rise of *the liberal* denominations in American Judaism, all synagogues observed the base-level, later to be called Orthodox, practices of separate seating, unabridged or unmodified services as prescribed in the *Siddur*, services unaccompanied on the Sabbath and holidays by instrumental music, and the staging of services at times corresponding to Judaism's traditional clock and not America's time schedule. For the purposes of this study, nineteenth-century congregations truly begin to be called Orthodox when they manifest, into *the rise of liberal denominations*, an adherence to these fundamentally important ritual practices. These basic liturgical elements also can be effective, if somewhat imperfect, criteria, for designating late nineteenth- to twentieth-century synagogues as Orthodox. For us, a synagogue will be called Orthodox in the later era if it follows these practices, or failing on one or more characteristics, does not self-consciously or formally see itself as part of the more liberal denominational camps. It should be remembered that not until 1913 and the founding of the United Synagogue of America (Conservative) did there exist three national bodies to which congregations could belong. Of course, even after 1913 not all congregations in the United States affiliated with one or another of these groups. We will also see later that not all self-declared Orthodox congregations accept these elements as a strict enough basis for defining denominational life. Nor have all Orthodox leaders accepted as Orthodox those groups that deviate somewhat from these norms, but that have not joined the Conservatives or Reformers.
4   In 1820, there were but six U.S. congregations; all were Orthodox and all but one practiced the Sephardic ritual. Thirty years later, there were approximately thirty-seven American synagogues situated in eleven states. Almost all of these synagogues were founded as Orthodox German or Polish congregations and the vast majority of them had yet to break with Orthodoxy, hence the periodization for the first, pre-Reform stage of our study. The date of 1800 was chosen on the assumption that for a comparative study of exclusionary and inclusionary policies, one needs a critical mass of congregations, which simply did not exist before the nineteenth century.
5   Edwin Wolf II and Maxwell Whiteman, *The History of the Jews of Philadelphia from Colonial Times to the Age of Jackson* (Philadelphia, 1975), pp. 224,

234–235, 240–241, 45a. In its decision of 1829, Rodeph Shalom went beyond the limits of inclusionary policies. If indeed a pledge to "raise children as Jews" stopped short of their formal conversion – a rare phenomenon to be sure in early nineteenth-century America – the synagogue seemingly admitted to its larger fold the legally non-Jewish children of intermarrieds.

6   Isaac M. Fein, *The Making of an American Jewish Community: The History of Baltimore Jewry from 1773–1920* (Philadelphia, 1971), pp. 55–56. Buffalo Jewry's first congregation, Beth El, also attempted in its earliest years to impose "church discipline" through a system of fines. See Selig Adler and Thomas Connolly, *From Ararat to Suburbia: The History of the Jewish Community of Buffalo* (Philadelphia, 1960), p. 60.

7   Bertram W. Korn, *The Early Jews of New Orleans* (Waltham, 1969), pp. 196–197. A similar policy of leniency seems also to have characterized the history of Richmond's Beth Shalome, and probably for the same reason. Richmond Jewry's historian has noted "that unlike the earlier Sephardic congregations established in the New World, Beth Shalom did not compel religious observance by their members. See Myron Berman, *Richmond Jewry, 1769–1976, Shabbat in Shockoe* (Charlottesville, Va., 1979), pp. 38–39. It should be noted, however, that the New Orleans congregation's very lenient approach lasted only until 1841 when, in part as a result of the influx of German Jewish immigrants, who seemingly broadened the community's Jewish marriage base, regulations were passed denying membership to intermarrieds. See Korn, p. 248.

8   Morris U. Schappes, *A Documentary History of the Jews in the United States 1654–1875* (New York, 1950), p. 175.

9   Questions may be raised concerning the designation of the reforms suggested initially by those who would found the Reformed Society of Israelites as still "within Orthodox Judaism." Clearly, their group's later activities, when on their own, cast doubt on whether their original idea of not "abandoning the institution of Moses" meant the maintenance of Orthodox teachings and core practices. But were their original demands outside Orthodoxy's widest pale? Indeed, with the possible exception of the shortening of the service proposal, these amendments were almost exactly the same as those, which we will see later, were offered in the early twentieth century by, among others, the Jewish Endeavor Society and the Young Israel within that era's Orthodoxy. Of course, as we will also see, not all Orthodox Jews of those days accepted these opinions as legitimate. In other words, this initial petition belongs as much within the history of the modernization or Americanization of Orthodoxy as to the beginning of Reform.

10 Schappes, *A Documentary History*, p. 175.

11 To be fair, other pre-1850 congregations had exclusionary policies toward intermarrieds on their books. However, questions must always be asked about how scrupulously they were enforced. For example, Cincinnati's earliest congregation, K. K. Bnai Israel (1824), also disqualified intermarrieds from synagogue membership. See James G. Heller, *As Yesterday When*

It Is Past: A History of Isaac M. Wise Temple – K.K. B'nai Yeshurun – of Cincinnati (Cincinnati, 1946), pp. 26–28. As we will soon see, splits took place in congregations over laxity in enforcing religious behavior. However, Beth Elohim was designated the most exclusionary congregation of its time by virtue of the welter of regulations that governed the lives of those who accepted its leadership.

12 Charles Reznikoff and Uriah Z. Engleman, The Jews of Charleston: A History of an American Jewish Community (Philadelphia, 1930), p. 115–128; Barnett A. Elzas, The Jews of South Carolina (Philadelphia, 1905), pp. 147–159. On the Charleston experiment in reform, see also Lou H. Silberman, American Impact: Judaism in the United States in the Early 19th Century, R. G. Rudolf Lecture in Jewish Studies, Syracuse University (29 March 1964).

13 Allan Tarshish, "The Charleston Organ Case" American Jewish Historical Quarterly (hereafter AJHQ), 54, no. 4 (June 1965), pp. 411–449.

14 Grinstein, Rise of the Jewish Community of New York, p. 43.

15 Ibid., p. 40. On the quick end of Sephardic hegemony in America and continued institutional primacy into the nineteenth century, see Stern, Function of Genealogy, pp. 74–75.

16 Grinstein and Jick differ as to the degree of amalgamation and muting of ethnic differences that took place in New York among Sephardim and Ashkenazim before the 1820s. The former speaks of the united community, whereas Jick describes New York Jewry as "a small, relatively homogeneous group." See Leon Jick, The Americanization of the Synagogue, 1820–1870 (Hanover, N.H., 1976), p. 26, Grinstein, Rise of the Jewish Community of New York, p. 49.

17 Jick, Americanization of the Synagogue, p. 24. Clearly the controversy over religious laxity was part of a broader list of complaints the recently arrived immigrants had with the American synagogue. Other significant complaints included the immigrants' disapproval of costly, obligatory synagogue offerings – which probably the poorer element could not afford – the unequal distribution of honors, poor educational services, the increased significance of the Hazzan as religious functionary, etc. See the entire list of particulars in Grinstein, Rise of the Jewish Community of New York, pp. 40–44.

18 Grinstein, Rise of the Jewish Community of New York, pp. 49–53.

19 Berman, Richmond Jewry, pp. 139–140; Heller, As Yesterday When It Is Past, p. 25; Fein, Making of an American Jewish Community, p. 55; Jick, Americanization of the Synagogue, p. 43.

20 To be entirely accurate, Philadelphia's Mikve Israel, alone among its sister Sephardic congregations, did take small, faltering, and clearly unenthusiastic steps toward Americanizing its services when in 1843 it finally officially permitted its Hazzan, Isaac Leeser, to deliver a weekly sermon in English. Leeser had introduced this practice more than ten years earlier and did not get much congregational support. His move toward modernization was reportedly "frowned upon with disdain." See Jick, Americanization of

the Synagogue, pp. 60–61, as quoted from Maxwell Whiteman, "Isaac Leeser and the Jews of Philadelphia," *Publications of the American Jewish Historical Society* (hereafter *PAJHS*) (1959), 48, no. 4, 213. See the discussion later in the chapter on Leeser and his efforts to develop a more responsive American Orthodox synagogue during the era of Reform.

Among the Ashkenazim of Baltimore Hebrew Congregation before 1850, we note, as did Jick, the somewhat strange behavior of congregants opposing Rabbi Rice when he attempted to control their Sabbath observance patterns, clearly an indication of lay permissiveness. At the same time, they also opposed Rice's attempt to Americanize the service by eliminating *piyutim*. See Jick, *Americanization of the Synagogue*, p. 72, as derived from Adolph Guttmacher, *A History of the Baltimore Hebrew Congregation* (Baltimore, 1905), p. 27.

21 Jick, *Americanization of the Synagogue*, pp. 86–88, 90–94; Grinstein, *Rise of the Jewish Community of New York*, pp. 355–356; Fein, *Making of an American Jewish Community*, pp. 56, 62–63; Adler and Connolly, *From Ararat to Suburbia*, p. 67; Hyman L. Meites, *History of the Jews in Chicago* (Chicago, 1924), p. 40; Morris A. Gutstein, *A Priceless Heritage: The Epic Growth of 19th Century Chicago Jewry* (New York, 1953), pp. 164–166. Bylaws of the United Hebrew Congregation of St. Louis (1843) quoted in Jick, p. 50. *Minutes of United Hebrew Congregation of St. Louis* (15 April 1855, 17 July 1859), quoted in Jick, *Americanization of the Synogogue*, pp. 151–152.

22 The statistics on synagogues discussed here are derived from Jick, *Americanization of the Synagogue*, who in turn obtained his information from Engleman, "Jewish Statistics in the U.S. Census of Religious Bodies (1850–1936)," *Jewish Social Studies*, 9, no. 2 (April, 1947), pp. 54–64, and from three nineteenth-century sources: Jacques I. Lyons and Abraham De Sola's *A Jewish Calendar for Fifty Years* (Montreal, 1984); Israel Joseph Benjamin, *Three Years in America, 1859–1862*, vol. 1, trans. Charles Reznikoff (Philadelphia, 1956), p. 82, which records highly impressionistic statistics; and *Statistics of the Jews in the United States* (Philadelphia, 1880).

23 That the stages in the rise of Reform in America followed closely the Americanization of German Jews in the nineteenth century is central to Jick's thesis in *The Americanization*. For an earlier discussion of the problems of nineteenth-century Judaism in this country, see Moshe Davis, *The Emergence of Conservative Judaism: The Historical School in 19th Century America* (Philadelphia, 1965), pp. 6–7.

24 Adler and Connolly, *From Ararat to Suburbia*, pp. 94–95; B. G. Rudolph, *From a Minyan to a Community: A History of the Jews of Syracuse* (Syracuse, 1970), p. 72; Stuart E. Rosenberg, *The Jewish Community in Rochester, 1843–1925* (New York, 1954), p. 87; Fred Rosenbaum, *Architects of Reform: Congressional and Community Leadership: Emanu-El of San Francisco, 1844–1980* (Berkeley, 1980), p. 28; Fein, *Making of an American Jewish Community*, pp. 114–118; Israel Goldstein, *A Century of Judaism in New York: B'nai*

Jeshurun, 1825–1925, New York's Oldest Ashkenazic Congregation (New York, 1930), pp. 158–160.

25 A continuum existed among nineteenth-century Americanized synagogues that ranged from the Orthodox, who permitted English-language sermons and emphasized decorum, through the most radical of Reform temples. Within that continuum there could also be found – among innumerable other phenomena and variations – synagogues whose ritual was totally Orthodox except that mixed seating was permitted; I have characterized this as a hybrid type of religious behavior. Conservative Jewish congregations, according to this definition, were more liberal still. They could be characterized as those permitting instrumental music in an abridged service, conducted according to the modern prayerbooks edited by nineteenth-century authors. But they were less liberal than their contemporary reform counterpart, by virtue of their continued observance of second days of holidays and the custom of men wearing hats during services – ceremonials that characterize Orthodoxy. Clearly, these denominations are not easily defined in the abstract; they are best identified by comparison. We have noted here and earlier some of the variables.

26 Adler and Connolly, *From Ararat to Suburbia*, pp. 94–95; Rosenberg, *Jewish Community in Rochester*, pp. 87–98; Rosenbaum, *Architects of Reform*, p. 28. The behavior patterns of these hybrid congregations closely adumbrates the activities of twentieth-century so-called traditional Orthodox congregations, situated particularly in the Midwest, which permit mixed seating but maintain all other Orthodox procedures and practices. These synagogues are discussed later in the chapter.

27 Fein, *Making of an American Jewish Community*, pp. 110–118.

28 Israel M. Goldman, "Henry W. Schneeberger: His Role in American Judaism," *AJHQ*, (December 1967), 179–190. The dozen or so German congregations that stayed Orthodox were not the only such institutions in the United States before 1880. In Cincinnati, for example, in the very heart of the Reform center, Congregation Shearith Israel founded in 1855 sustained its Orthodoxy until 1885, when a graduate of Hebrew Union College, Dr. David Davidson, assumed the pulpit. In the 1860s, Rabbi Bernard Illowy, an Orthodox rabbi late of Baltimore, New Orleans, and four other American cities, served as the rabbi. Although Heller, *As Yesterday When It Is Past*, pp. 199–200, notes its existence, nothing has yet been published on Shearith Israel, a topic for future consideration. Furthermore, when the Union of Orthodox Jewish Congregations – to be discussed shortly – was founded in 1898, some fifty-one congregations sent representatives to the inaugural meetings. The congregations attending could be described as including Conservative, traditional, and strictly Orthodox – although to what proportions remains to be determined. On the founding of the Orthodox Union (OU), see *American Hebrew* (henceforth *AH*), 10 June 1979, p. 173.

29 Adler and Connolly, *From Ararat to Suburbia*, pp. 96, 100, 103; David and

Tamar De Sola Pool, *An Old Faith in the New World: Portrait of Shearith Israel, 1654–1954* (New York, 1955), pp. 99–101, 112; Grinstein, *Rise of the Jewish Community of New York*, p. 366.

30 Fein, *Making of an American Jewish Community*, p. 118; Berman, *Richmond Jewry*, pp. 41, 61–63; Herbert T. Ezekiel and Gaston Lichtenstein, *The History of the Jews of Richmond from 1769–1917* (Richmond, 1917).

31 To be accurate, Leeser's first foray toward achieving a union of congregations to offset rampant disaffection from Judaism took place in 1841, when in the wake of the Damascus Blood Libel and several years before Wise's arrival, his proposal was offered. In 1849, Leeser's fears of "the threat an unrestrained Reform movement posed to the character of American Judaism" seemingly coincided with Wise's ambition for a unified American Jewry under his sway. See Jick, *Americanization of the Synagogue*, pp. 105; Moshe Davis, *The Emergence of Conservative Judaism: The Historical School in Nineteenth Century America* (Philadelphia, 1953), pp. 119–120, 128–129, 133.

32 Zichron Ephraim, although a nineteenth-century American Orthodox synagogue, was of a different ethnic kind. It was one of the first congregations made up primarily of East European and not German Jews. Sender Jarmulowsky, the founder of the first bank run by East European Jews, was a member. This congregation adumbrated a larger tradition, which came to the fore in the first decade of the twentieth century.

33 Davis, *Emergence of Conservative Judaism*, p. 237; Bernard Drachman, *The Unfailing Light: Memories of an American Rabbi* (New York, 1948), pp. 177–182; Henry Pereira Mendes, "The Beginning of the Seminary," in Cyrus Adler, ed., *The Jewish Theological Seminary of America: Semi-Centennial Volume* (New York, 1939), pp. 35–41.

34 *AH*, 10 June 1889, p. 172; 4 January 1901, pp. 231–234. More work needs to be done on the respective ritual and ideological positions and the ethnic orientations of the some fifty-odd congregations that founded the Orthodox Union. A preliminary examination reveals a mixture of American Orthodox of German extraction, typified by Chizuk Amuno and Shearith Israel of Baltimore; East European ethnic Orthodox with clearly some Americanized leanings – adumbrations of the future – exemplified by Zichron Ephraim, Sephardic synagogues led by New York's Shearith Israel; and, significantly, a number of synagogues "where organ and pews were in vogue." I would estimate that more than one-half of the congregations noted were Orthodox synagogues composed of German-American Jews.

35 *AH*, 20 June 1898, p. 172.

36 The Beth Hamidrash established in 1852 is the antecedent of the more famous Beth Hamidrash Hagadol, founded in 1859 and still existing (1986) on Norfolk Street. The Congregation Beth Hamidrash Livne Yisrael Yelide Polin, established in 1853 and characterized by Grinstein as a mixed Russian-Polish congregation, also drew members from the original Russian Jewish

synagogue. See Grinstein, *Rise of the Jewish Community of New York*, pp. 474, 477–478.

37 A differentiation is being made here among varieties of so-called Polish Jews arriving in this country. The Russo-Polish Jews arriving before and after 1852 were clearly less acculturated in the ways of the West than, say, Polish Jews from Posen, who were Central European in their attitudes and outlook. They constituted the beginnings of a new migration, which, of course, reached tremendous proportions after 1881. They, along with Jews from other parts of the Russian Empire, Romania, and Hungary, made up the new immigration of East European Jews.

38 Judah David Eisenstein, "The History of the First Russian-American Jewish Congregation: The Beth Hamedrosh Hagodol," *PAJHS*, 9 (1901), pp. 64–72.

39 The official name of that synagogue is Congregation Kehal Adath Jeshurun M'Yassy (Jassy of Romania). This synagogue has been frequently mislabeled a Polish or Russian congregation. For more on this synagogue's chequered history, see the author's manuscript "A Case of Synagogue 'Imperialism': The Kehal Adath Jeshurun Incident."

40 It is impossible to determine how many East European congregations existed in the United States before the era of mass migration. The early Union of American Hebrew Congregation pamphlet, *Statistics of the Jews in the United States* (Philadelphia, 1880), upon which Jick based his assertion that there were some 275 synagogues then in the United States, lists nary an East European institution. Eisenstein in his memoir, *Ozar Zichronothai* (New York, 1929), p. 31, states that there were 152 congregations in this country. How many of these were East European is not indicated. My cursory survey of extant communal histories has indicated to me that at least twenty East European congregations existed in America before 1880.

41 In counting the number of East European synagogues that existed in America before 1880, I have omitted the most ephemeral of synagogues, later to be called "mushroom synagogues," which sprang up under sometimes unethical auspices every Jewish High Holiday season. In Milwaukee, for example, the first East European congregations were these "sporadic congregations" characterized by one contemporary as "Shaarey Harevach (Gates of Profit) to whose establishment the smartest preparations were being made." See Louis J. Switchkow and Lloyd P. Gartner, *The History of the Jews of Milwaukee* (Philadelphia, 1963), p. 192. Attempts to deal with this nefarious trafficking in religion in the twentieth century are discussed later in the chapter.

42 Gutstein, *A Priceless Heritage*, p. 35. Some congregations went even further in their theoretical requirements for membership. To be a member of Chicago's Congregation Ohave Sholom Mariampoler Chevrah Kadisha (burial society) or Chevrah Mishno U'Gmoro (Talmud society), candidates

not only had to be Sabbath observers, but were expected to refrain from shaving their beards. See Gutstein, p. 203.

43 Rabbi Hirsch Falk Vidaver Levy quoted in Albert Ehrenfried, *A Chronicle of Boston Jewry from the Colonial Period to 1900*, (n.p., 1963), p. 430.

44 Congregation Ohab Zedek, *Golden Jubilee, 1873–1923* (New York, 1923), n.p.

45 Gerard Wolfe and Jo Renee Fine, *The Synagogues of New York's Lower East Side* (New York, 1978), pp. 25, 43, 52, 96.

46 Wolfe and Fine, *Synagogues of New York's Lower East Side*, pp. 43–97; Jonathan D. Sarna, trans. and ed., *People Walk on Their Heads: Moses Weinberger's Jews and Judaism in New York* (New York, 1982), pp. 13–14. Sarna aptly describes this change toward greater formality as a "shift from participation toward performance." Although much has been written about the sociological implications of mixed seating, work needs to be done on the adoption of pews or assigned seats.

47 Eisenstein, "History of the First Russian-American Congregation," pp. 69, 73–74.

48 Ibid., p. 73.

49 Sarna, *People Walk on Their Heads*, pp. 105–106. Weinberger's sentiments were undoubtedly seconded by the Beth Hamidrash Hagadol group identified by Eisenstein as *hasidim* who as early as 1861 opposed "the reformed element [in that congregation who] wanted to introduce decorum and a musical cantor." See Eisenstein, "History of the First Russian-American Congregation," p. 69. Divisions over the necessity of hiring a cantor led to a temporary split in that congregation long before the cantor craze of the 1880s.

50 For the best primer on the subjects noted here, see Moses Rischin's classic, *The Promised City-New York's Jews, 1870–1914* (Cambridge, 1963), especially the chapters entitled "Tradition at Half-Mast" and "The Great Awakening."

51 Abraham J. Karp, "New York Chooses a Chief Rabbi," *PAJHS* 44, no. 3 (March 1954), pp. 129–198. The public announcement of the selection of the *Malbim* was published in the *Jewish Record* (Philadelphia). It noted that twenty-four synagogues signed the call and twenty-five others were prepared to cooperate.

52 The proliferation of *landsmanshaft* synagogues continued unabated up to World War I and the effective end of immigration. So great was the splintering of worshiping New York Jewry into this myriad of regional and local congregations that by 1917 the New York Kehillah could estimate that there were approximately 730 Orthodox synagogues in New York alone, the vast majority East European. What is also significant, the Kehillah noted that one-half of the Jewish population was unsynagogued totally, and that included the thousands who were hoodwinked yearly by unscrupulous mushroom-synagogue operators. There were plenty of seats for "interested worshipers" but most of these seats went unused throughout

the year. See *Jewish Communal Register* (henceforth *JCR*), pp. 117–121. For a short treatment of the complex history of the social, cultural, and religious role played by the *landsmanshaft* synagogue, see *Di Yiddishe Landsmanshaften fun New York* (New York, 1938).

53   This continued affinity for the old style of services even as Jews broke with the social-religious system that supported the immigrant synagogue came to the fore primarily in the form of opposition to innovation within Orthodoxy.

54   The attitude of second-generation Jews toward old-style religion is documented by their reaction to the post–1900 innovations sponsored by, among other groups, the Jewish Endeavor Society and the Young Israel.

55   Karp, "New York Chooses a Chief Rabbi," pp. 129–198.

56   Sarasohn's devotion to the harmonization of Judaism with Americanization through his newspaper was expressed through his development of the first English-language page in the *Yiddishes Tageblatt*. It was expressly dedicated to second-generation Jews and was full of information of a communal nature. It was in these pages that American Orthodox synagogues would, after 1897, get their message across to their acculturated potential members. On this and other Yiddish newspaper, see Mordecai Soltes, "The Yiddish Press: An Americanization Agent," *American Jewish Yearbook* 26 (hereafter *AJYB*) (1924–25), pp. 165–372.

57   For a biographical treatment of Klein and his affinity for Americanization, see Jeffrey S. Gurock, "Resisters and Accommodators: Varieties of Orthodox Rabbis in America, 1886–1983," *American Jewish Archives* (hereafter *AJA*) 35, no. 2 (October 1983), 120–130.

58   The downtown contingent was actually made up of some six congregations. They included Mishkan Israel, Chebra Kadisha Talmud Torah, Chebrah Kadusha Talmud Torah, Emuno Israel, B'nai Jacob, and Zichron Torath Moshe. Also included in the New York Orthodox camp were a small number of recent German immigrant Orthodox congregations, such as Adas Israel and immigrant Sephardic congregation Nefuzoth Israel. More needs to be done on these varieties of immigrant Orthodox synagogues, which are often left unnoticed. See *AH*, 10 June 1898, p. 172.

59   In 1901, Rabbi H. P. Mendes, president of the Orthodox Union, reviewed his organization's first three years of activities. Although Mendes reiterated that the Union was born to fight against Reform Jewish teachings and activities, it is clear that most of the organization's time – as noted by Mendes – was spent acting "in the interest of Orthodox Judaism whenever occurrences arose in civil or social matters as well as religious affairs." See *AH*, 4 January 1901, pp. 231–234.

60   Bernard Drachman, *The Unfailing Light: Memories of an American Rabbi* (New York, 1948), pp. 213.

61   Joseph H. Lookstein, "Seventy-Five Yesteryears: A Historical Sketch of Kehilath Jeshurun," *Congregation Kehilath Jeshurun, Diamond Jubilee Yearbook* (New York, 1946), pp. 58. For a more complete discussion of the

nature of the American Orthodoxy espoused by the Jewish Theological Seminary in its pre-Solomon Schechter days, see Gurock, "Resisters and Accommodators," pp. 100–109.

62 Jeffrey S. Gurock, *When Harlem Was Jewish, 1870–1930* (New York, 1979), pp. 23, 25, 26, 92–93, 95. Ohab Zedek also maintained the upgraded role of the cantor in the Americanized congregation when it hired Rev. Joseph (Yosele) Rosenblatt as its chazan. See Samuel Rosenblatt, *Yosele Rosenblatt: The Story of My Life as Told to His Son* (New York, 1954). Joining the three congregations noted above were two other East European uptown synagogues, Ateres Zwie and Nachlath Zwie, early arrivals in what would become Jewish East Harlem.

63 *AH*, 10 June 1898, p. 172.

64 *AH*, 4 January 1901, p. 233.

65 *Hebrew Standard* (hereafter *HS*), 18 October 1901, p. 4; *AH*, 18 January, 8 February, 5 March 1901, pp. 284, 379; 596; Drachman, *Unfailing Light*, pp. 225ff.

66 *Yiddishes Tageblatt* (hereafter *YT*), 13 March 1902, p. 2; *HS*, 21 March 1902, p. 4; *AH*, 24 June 1904, p. 160, as described in Gurock, *When Harlem Was Jewish*, p. 117.

67 *HS*, 23 April, 26 May 1905, pp. 4, 4; also 14 April 1905, p. 4, as described in and quoted from Gurock, *When Harlem Was Jewish*, p. 118.

68 *YT*, 25 March 1906, p. 8. See the "Incorporation Papers of Congregation Mikve Israel" on file in the Office of the New York County Clerk, as described in Gurock, *When Harlem Was Jewish*, p. 118.

69 Aaron Rothkoff, "The American Sojourns of Ridbaz: Religious Problems within the Immigrant Community," *HJHQ*, 57, no. 4 (June, 1968), pp. 561–562. For an on-the-scene look at the attitudes of the Aguath Ha-Rabbanim (of which the Ridbaz was a member) toward Americanization efforts, see its major publication, *Sefer Ha-Yovel shel Agudath ha-Rabbanim ha-Ortodoksim de-Artsot ha-Brit v-Canada* (New York, 1928). See also Gurock, "Resisters and Accommodators," pp. 114–122. I note there the difficulties the Agudat Ha-Rabbonim had with the Endeavorers' willingness to cooperate with Reform leaders who were then initiating their own style of youth services downtown.

70 *AH*, 30 September 1904, p. 516; *HS*, 7 October 1904, p. 7, as derived from Jenna Weissman Joselit, "What Happened to New York's Jewish Jews: Moses Rischin's *The Promised City Revisited*," *American Jewish History* (hereafter *AJH*) 73, no. 2 (December 1983), pp. 163–172.

71 *AH*, 16 January 1903, p. 295. Ironically, it should be observed that the JES stood for one of the causes that most troubled the most traditional of downtown religious authorities – namely, the battle to stop the proliferation of mushroom synagogues. See *AH*, 17 October 1902, p. 608, for the Endeavorers' view of this dilemma.

72 *HS*, 29 June 1906, p. 4; Drachman, *Unfailing Light*, pp. 276–277, as described in Gurock, *When Harlem Was Jewish*, pp. 118–119. Endeavorers

faced the institutional headaches of the graduation and migration out of New York of their early seminary student leaders, who seemed not to be replaced until the rise of the Young Israel several years later and by Drachman's removal from the Seminary during that same period.

73 Not all East European groups or rabbis opposed these efforts. Rabbi Shmarya Leib Hurwitz, for example, in an article entitled "The Necessity to Found Synagogues for Youths Here in America," *YT*, 15 April 1912, p. 7, declared that as long as *landsmanshaft*-style synagogue services remained disorganized too long, were held in physically unattractive structures, and featured rabbis or preachers who offered discourses on esoteric Talmudic topics, young people would stand apart from the synagogue. See also *YT*, 7 March 1910, p. 5, for a similar type of critique of the old-time synagogue within downtown society.

74 Youth-oriented synagogues under Orthodox auspices did not disappear totally during the hiatus between the JES and YI-institutional Synagogues era. Modern Talmud Torahs ran youth services and the Kehillah itself toyed with the idea of inaugurating "model synagogue" programs. Indeed, in 1911, they set up eight provisional synagogues during the High Holidays to attract youngsters. On those post-JES and pre-YI activities, see Shulamith Berger, "Youth Synagogues in New York, 1910–1913" (unpublished seminar paper, TS, Bernard Revel Graduate School, Yeshiva University, 1981).

75 *AH*, 10 January 1913, p. 303; *HS*, 12 January 1913, p. 9. Rosenthal, the YI's first president was in the JTS class of 1913. See *Jewish Theological Seminary Student Annual*, 1914, pp. 50–51, (1915), pp. 51–52, all quoted from and utilized by Shulamith Berger "The Early History of the Young Israel Movement" (seminar paper, TS, YIVO Institute, Fall 1982).

76 Davis, *Emergence of Conservative Judaism*, pp. 324–326; Herbert Parzen, *Architects of Conservative Judaism* (New York, 1964), pp. 26–29ff; *HS*, 30 January 1913, p. 12.

77 *AH*, 10 January 1913, p. 303 and *HS*, 12 January 1912, p. 9; *Morgen Zhurnal*, 10 January 1913, p. 4, all derived from Berger, "Early History." The *Morgen Zhurnal*, for example, was a harsh critic of the contemporaneous New York Kehillah. See Arthur A. Goren, *New York Jews and the Quest for Community: The Kehillah Experiment, 1908–1922* (New York, 1970), pp. 127–128 and *passim*.

78 *AH*, 10 January, p. 303. One source suggests that the YI idea did not originate with Seminary students at all, but with a troika of downtown youths who wanted more than their parents' *landsmanshaft* Judaism, but who were unimpressed by initiatives like Rabbi Stephen S. Wise's ghetto-based Free Synagogue. Soon thereafter, they linked arms with the Seminary students and leaders. Interestingly, they contacted Rabbi Judah L. Magnes for assistance. Two years earlier the Kehillah leader had called for a "presentation of Judaism which shall overcome the formalism and sterility of old-time Orthodoxy and shall yet avoid the extremes and extravagances of

Reform. See David Warsaw, "A History of the Young Israel Movement, 1912–1937" (Master's thesis, Bernard Revel Graduate School, Yeshiva University, 1974), p. 9ff.

79   *HS*, 29 September 1916, p. 11.

80   *HS*, 18 January 1918, p. 9; Benjamin Kline Hunnicut, "The Jewish Sabbath Movement in the Early Twentieth Century," *AJH*, 69, no. 2 (December 1979), pp. 196–225.

81   Gurock, *When Harlem Was Jewish*, pp. 135ff. *YT*, 19, 27 July 1915, p. 8; Ira Eisenstein and Ira Kohn, ed., *Mordecai Kaplan: An Evaluation* (New York, 1952), passim as discussed, by Gurock, *When Harlem Was Jewish*, pp. 124–125.

82   Gurock, *When Harlem Was Jewish*, pp. 127–133.

83   Mordecai M. Kaplan, "Affiliation with the Synagogue," *JCR*, pp. 120–121.

84   *AH*, 5 February 1904, pp. 378, 384; *HS*, 31 January 1902, p. 8. Rischin, *Promised City*, p. 102, 242; Carl Hermann Voss, ed., *Stephen S. Wise: Servant of the People* (Philadelphia, 1970), p. 34.

85   Of the twenty-four charter-member congregations in the United Synagogue at the time of its founding in 1913, no more than two can be characterized as both Conservative in ritual – mixed seating etc. – composed of East European Jews and attractive to them. Some thirteen were nineteenth-century, formerly Orthodox or Conservative congregations composed of German Jews. Two others were headed by Seminary rabbis and attracted East European constituents, but like the Endeavorers and the YI, did not break ritually from American styles of Orthodoxy. See the analysis of the early U.S. congregations, The United Synagogue of America, "Report of the Second Annual Meeting (1914)," pp. 17–20. Parenthetically, it should be noted that a number of the once-Orthodox Union congregations moved on to the United Synagogue in the late 1910s. Why and how they moved has yet to be considered.

86   For extensive discussions of the rise of Conservative Judaism and the emergence of Neo-Reform, see chapters 3 and 4.

87   It is suggested here – as well as in most historical accounts – that the locus of East European rabbis and their congregations was the inner city. One must note, however, that *landsmanshaft*-style synagogues did survive the pre-World War I migration to satellite ghettos such as New York's Harlem or Brownsville. See Gurock, *When Harlem was Jewish*, and Alter Landesman *Brownsville: The Birth, Growth and Passing of a Jewish Community in New York* (New York, 1969), for examples of that phenomenon. How far beyond these areas and for how much longer than 1880–1920 immigrant religious civilization did survive remains to be studied. In all events and from whatever location, East European rabbis were outspoken in their condemnation of Conservative activities. See *Ha-Pardes*, June 1930, p. 26; December 1930, p. 6; June 1931, p. 25; May 1934, p. 2; June 1935, pp. 2–5. See also, Agudat Ha-Rabbonim deArtzot ha-Brit ve-Canada, *Le-Dor*

Aharon (New York, 1936). The battle against Conservative Judaism in Cleveland is discussed in Aaron Rakeffet-Rothkoff, *The Silver Era in American Jewish Orthodoxy* (Jerusalem and New York, 1981), pp. 112–114, 326–347. For the Conservative rabbi's side of the story, see Solomon Goldman, *A Rabbi Takes Stock* (New York, 1931).

88 It remains to be determined how many Conservative congregations in the period from 1920 to 1940 were formerly Orthodox.

89 Gilbert Klaperman, *The Story of Yeshiva University: The First Jewish University in America* (London, 1969); Aaron Rothkoff, *Bernard Revel: Builder of American Jewish Orthodoxy* (Philadelphia, 1972), pp. 43–71; *The Rabbi Isaac Elchanan Theological Seminary Register 5685 (1924–1925)* (New York, 1925).

90 Rothkoff, *Bernard Revel*, p. 169.

91 See Gurock, "Resisters and Accommodators." See also Bernard Sheintag, "Rabbi Joseph H. Lookstein: A Character Study by a Congregant," in *Congregation Kehilath Jeshurun*, pp. 53–57; and Leo Jung, *The Path of a Pioneer: The Authobiography of Leo Jung* (London and New York, 1980). The very useful term "respectable Orthodoxy" was coined by my colleague Jenna Weisman Joselit, who is working on an important biography of Lookstein. Finally, it may be suggested that the Yorkville and West Side adherence to Orthodoxy might be due to a combination of the geographical proximity to their work and to the congregants' socioeconomic status. As upper middle-class congregations, members there may have been able to more easily adjust their work and life schedules to remain consistent with ancestral traditions. Of course, more investigation needs to be done to explain their attitudes toward nonegalitarian synagogue seating patterns.

92 That each of these problems and others posed real problems for American Orthodox synagogues and their rabbis is indicated by the fact that between 1935 and the 1950s questions on each of these concerns were submitted by members of the Rabbinical Council of America (the organization of Americanized, English-speaking rabbis, founded in 1935) to their Standards and Rituals Committee or to their Halacha Commission. See Louis Bernstein, *Challenge and Mission: The Emergence of The English Speaking Orthodox Rabbinate* (New York, 1982), pp. 39–51 and *passim*.

93 *OU*, April 1943, p. 5; February 1945, p. 11.

94 Bernstein, *Challenge and Mission*, pp. 14–15.

95 OU figures are derived from the organizations noted as members published in their organ, the *Orthodox Union*, which ran from 1933 to 1946. In 1935, for example, the paper noted that a convention of Orthodox synagogues at the Far Rockaway Jewish Center on Long Island (which included Queens) was attended by the center's nineteen member congregations; hence that number. See *OU* October 1935, p. 7. The *Orthodox Union*, a major untapped source for the social history of this period, also highlights two other issues for consideration in making such calculations. A number of U.S. synagogues in 1929 appear as members of the OU in the 1930s. That means

that either synagogues drifted back and forth between movements or held dual memberships. In addition, it appears that the term "Jewish Center" applied both to American Orthodox and to Conservative congregations of that era. Statistics on the New York–based Young Israel Movement are derived from a pamphlet, *Young Israel: Its Aims and Activities*, published by its National Council circa 1935.

96   In 1925 the YI had thirty-two affiliates, twenty-four situated in New York City proper.

97   *OU*, July 1937, p. 2; December 1942, p. 5; April 1944, p. 6. Significantly, each of these writers contrasted the strength of Orthodoxy in New York with their own powerlessness in the country. Some made the point that all New York wanted from the hinterlands was money and never gave any logistical support for the growth of the movement elsewhere. I derived the unofficial statistics on the OU from synagogues listed as members in the Orthodox Union.

98   *OU*, January 1941, p. 12; January 1935, p. 1.

99   Israel Maier Ha Kohen Kagan, *Niddehei Yisrael* (Warsaw, 1884), pp. 129–130, quoted in Rothkoff, *Bernard Revel*, p. 18.

100 For interesting, albeit hagiographic, biographical sketches of the transplanted Yeshiva rabbis and of Dr. Breuer, see Nisson Wolpin, ed., *The Torah World: A Treasury of Biographical Sketches* (New York, 1982). This volume is a collection of articles culled from the pages of the *Jewish Observer*, the organ of the Agudath Israel. In particular see the discussion on Rabbi Aaron Kotler in Shaul Kagan, "From Kletzk to Lakewood," pp. 184–205; and on Rabbi Bloch of Cleveland's Telshe Yeshiva in "He Brought Telshe to Cleveland," pp. 262–276. For information on Dr. Breuer, see Ernst J. Bodenheimer with Nosson Scherman, "The Rav of Frankfurt, U.S.A.," pp. 223–238. On the settlement patterns and sociology of the Hasidic groups, see Israel Rubin, *Satmar: Island in the City* (New York, 1972). The Breuer and the Lithuanian Yeshiva groups were placed with the Hasidim because they, too, viewed their religious leaders as true chief rabbis. However, the influence of each rabbi on daily lives varies greatly from group to group.

101 William Helmreich, *The World of the Yeshiva: An Intimate Portrait of Orthodox Jewry* (New York and London, 1982), p. 284.

102 Shubert Spero, "Orthodox Judaism," in *Movements and Issues in American Judaism: An Analysis and Source Book of Developments since 1945*, ed. Bernard Martin (Westport, Conn., 1978), p. 88; Charles Liebman, "Orthodoxy in American Jewish Life," *AJYB* 66 (1965), pp. 58–61.

103 Rabbi Moses Scherer, president of the Agudath Israel, summed up best the changed educational orientation of Orthodox Jews from interwar days to today when he said: "When I was a youngster, it was very possible for someone to be an Orthodox Jew without continuing (intensive Jewish education) beyond elementary school. . . . Today it is unthinkable that one can really be an Orthodox Jew unless he had at least graduate Yeshiva high

school." See this statement in William Helmreich's "Old Wine in New Bottles: Advanced Yeshivot in the United States," *AJH*, 69, no. 2 (December 1979).

104 Alvin I. Schiff, *The Jewish Day School in America* (New York, 1966), pp. 48–86; Samuel Heilman, *Synagogue Life: A Study in Symbolic Interaction* (Chicago, 1973); and Heilman, *The People of the Book: Drama, Fellowship and Religion* (Chicago, 1983).

105 See Helmreich, *The World of the Yeshiva*, pp. 220–238, for his important discussion of college education and the yeshiva world students. Also see pp. 272–275, for a description of the economic and demographic patterns. Interesingly enough, although the new-era Orthodox see themselves as resisting if not being merely unimpressed with American societal phenomena and change, they have been consciously, or unconsciulsy, affected by American social patterns. The *eruv* issue is a graphic example. The idea that families and not just grown men should go as a unit to services is an American religious phenomenon. The role and status of women in the Orthodox synagogue are discussed later in the chapter.

106 The estimate of 1,000 present day synagogues has been offered by my colleague, Marc Lee Raphael, in *Profiles in Faith: American Judaism* (New York, 1984). This work is based on his close examination of synagogue lists extant in the New York offices of the Orthodox Union and is thus to be considered highly reliable. Less reliable statistics that magnify the numbers of synagogues and constituents by the OU are published without revision yearly in *AJYB*. For an important discussion of the reliability of earlier estimates, see Liebman, "Orthodoxy in American Jewish Life," pp. 22–26.

107 Bernard Martin, "Conservative Judaism and Reconstructionism," in *Movements and Issues in American Judaism: An Analysis and Source Book of Developments since 1945*, ed. Bernard Martin (Westport, Conn., 1978), p. 102. The relative strengths of Conservatism, Reform, and Orthodoxy in three cities are discussed in Morris Axelrod, Floyd S. Fowler, and Arnold Gurin's *A Community Study for Long Range Planning* (Boston, 1967); these authors found that 44 percent of the synagogues in Boston at the time were Conservative affiliates, as opposed to 27 percent Reform and 14 percent Orthodox. Sidney Goldstein and Calvin Goldscheider, *Jewish Americans: Three Generations in a Jewish Community* (Englewood Cliffs, N.J., 1968), found that in Providence 54 percent were Conservative, 21 percent Reform, and 20 percent Orthodox. See also Michael Meyer, "Reform Judaism," in *Movements and Issues*, p. 159; Spero, "Orthodox Judaism," p. 85; Liebman, "Orthodoxy in American Jewish Life," pp. 34–36.

108 Anne Lapidus Lerner, "Who Has Not Made Me a Man: The Movement for Equal Rights for Women in American Jewry," *AJH* (1977), pp. 3–38; Charlotte Baum, Paula Hyman, and Sonya Michel, *The Jewish Women in America* (New York, 1976). The debate within American Orthodoxy can be followed to some extent through the pages of *Tradition*, an RCA publication. See for ex-

ample, Saul Berman, "The Status of Women in Halachic Judaism," *Tradition*, 14, no. 2 (Fall 1973), pp. 5–28; Michael Chernick, "The Halachic Process – Growth and Change," *Sh'ma*, 6, no. 112 (April 1976), pp. 92–94; A. M. Silver, "May Women be Taught Bible, Mishna and Talmud," *Tradition*, 16, no. 2 (Summer 1978), pp. 74–83; Avraham Weiss, "Women & Sifrei Torah," *Tradition*, 20, no. 2 (Summer, 1982), pp. 106–118: Saul Berman and Shulamith Magnus, "Orthodoxy Responds to Feminist Ferment," *Response*, 12, no. 2 (Spring, 1981), pp. 5–18. See also the *Jewish Press*, 10 December 1982, p. 3, for the Agudat-Ha-Rabbonim's condemnation of women's services within Orthodox synagogues.

3

The Reform Synagogue

LEON A. JICK

The Triumph of Reform: 1830–1885

Prior to 1820 seven Jewish congregations existed in the United States, all of them on the Atlantic seaboard.[1] All but one of these followed the Sephardic ritual, and the lone exception – Rodeph Sholom of Philadelphia – barely sustained a precarious existence. The Jewish population was numerically small (in 1818 a contemporary observer estimated the number as three thousand) and religiously stagnant. In the decades that followed, tens of thousands of Jewish immigrants from the German-speaking provinces arrived and founded scores of congregations throughout the length and breadth of the land.[2] By 1850, there were at least 76 formally organized synagogues and by 1877, 277.[3] Given the informality of synagogue organization and the absence of any hierarchical structure or network of communication, it is likely that the number was even larger and that additional congregations whose existence was unknown in the major urban centers were not recorded.

With less than a handful of exceptions, all of the new congregations were established as traditional synagogues in which the patterns of worship of Central European Jewry were observed – either *minhag Ashkenaz* (German rite) or *minhag Polin* (Polish rite). For the impoverished struggling immigrants, the synagogue initially served as a comforting link with home and past in the midst of a strange and often bewildering new world.[4] The newcomers were predominantly simple folk from hamlets and villages who had not been affected by the stirrings of religious reform that had unsettled their urban brethren in Europe. In the words of a contemporary observer: "They all had brought with them a strong love for the religious customs which prevailed in the lands of their nativity. . . . Every one of them desired to have such a mode of worship established

85

in the synagogue as would remind him of his own youth."[5] When they had established themselves sufficiently in America to be able to think beyond mere subsistence, they organized congregations that were unequivocally traditional. As Isaac Leeser wrote in 1848: "From the newly gotten Sante Fe to the confines of New Brunswick and from the Atlantic to the shores of the western sea, synagogues are springing up as if by magic despite the fact that our people are poor and many of them are laboring hard for their daily bread."[6]

Of all of these new congregations only two designated themselves as reformed at the time they were established. Har Sinai of Baltimore (founded in 1842) and Emanu-El of New York (founded in 1843) were founded by upwardly mobile immigrants who were already well along on the road to acculturation and economic stability. Even these congregations remained substantially traditional in their ritual practices in their early years. Men and women were seated separately, heads were covered, the Sabbath and dietary laws were "strictly observed." Initial changes even in these reformist congregations were minimal and related to decorum and image rather than to substance or ideology.[7]

In the early years of the Central European immigration, the quarrels and schisms that frequently arose dealt not with reforms but with nuances of differences in ritual or music between Jews from various European provinces – Bayers (Bavarians) versus Pollacks (immigrants from Posen) – or with distinctions in style and piety between earlier immigrants and newcomers who invariably found their partially acculturated brethren not sufficiently observant for their tastes. The constitutions and bylaws adopted by newly formed congregations stipulated the form of worship and often included injunctions designed to forestall any attempts to introduce changes. Bene Israel in Cincinnati was described as "a congregation for the purpose of glorifying our God and observing the fundamental principles of our faith as developed in the Laws of Moses." Its charter obtained in 1828 provided that the service be conducted "according to the form and mode of worship of the Polish and German Jews."[8] The constitution of the United Hebrew Congregation founded in St. Louis in 1838 is more stringent. It specifies that "the prayers shall never be performed otherwise than according to Minhag Polin [the Polish rite]. This section shall never be altered or amended under any pretense whatsoever."[9]

Services were traditional, facilities modest – usually rented halls – and ritual functions were conducted by laymen or by poorly qualified paraprofessionals who, in addition to their religious duties, performed a variety of menial tasks. A typical contract drawn in Congregation Brith Sholom of Easton, Pennsylvania, in 1848 provided for a *hazan* (cantor) who would also "fulfill the duties of shochet [ritual slaughterer], conduct school daily for six hours; supervise the mikveh [ritual bath] and provide a substitute at his own expense during illness or absence." The constitution of this congregation had earlier stated that "no person shall be elected to administer the affairs of this Congregation who shall publicly profane the Sabbath by attending at his place of business on that sacred day."[10]

In one significant respect all of these synagogues were different from their European antecedents. All were voluntary membership organizations unrelated to any communal structure or authority and were dependent upon and responsive to those individuals who freely chose to affiliate with them. As a result, congregational practices, whether traditional or reformist, were determined by the tastes and desires of the members rather than by decisions of authoritative interpreters of tradition. As Isaac Leeser wrote in an 1844 volume on the religious denominations in the United States: "We have no ecclesiastical authority in America other than the congregations themselves. Each congregation makes its own rules for its government and elects its own ministry, who is appointed without any ordination, induction in office being made through his election."[11] As a consequence, autonomous congregations, governed by laymen who were pragmatic in their concerns, blundered along seeking to maintain the old ways while adapting to the requirements of a new kind of society.

Initial changes were unsystematic and were related to decorum rather than ideology. In the 1840s Rodeph Sholom of Philadelphia instituted a schedule of fines for members "who do not behalf [sic] orderly."[12] Bnai Jeshurun of Cincinnati passed a proposal "to prevent disorder." It was decreed that only the president might call for order, and he was constrained to do so "in a quiet fashion."[13] Knesseth Israel of Philadelphia passed a series of regulations requiring "orderly dress" and requiring members to enter the synagogue "with decency and without noise."[14] The precursor of the desire for reform was the concern for respectability.

The first rabbis arrived in America uninvited in the early 1840s. Their reception was less than enthusiastic and their impact on synagogue practices was modest. Abraham Rice, a traditionalist, was unable to assert his authority over his congregation in Baltimore. He wrote to his teacher in Germany: "The religious life in this land is on the lowest level. . . . I wonder whether it is even permissible for a Jew to live in this land."[15] In 1849 he resigned his position and opened a dry goods store. Max Lilienthal, who arrived in 1845, failed in an attempt to establish a *bet din* (a rabbinic court to render "beneficial service to the Jewish congregations of America"). He soon left his post as rabbi of three German congregations and established a private Jewish day school.[16] Even the most successful of the immigrant rabbis, the pragmatic Isaac Mayer Wise, who arrived in 1846, was assaulted by the president of his Albany congregation on the pulpit on Rosh Hashanah (the Jewish New Year).[17] In the American setting, not only the authority but even the person of the rabbi was not secure from attack by laymen.

In 1855, David Einhorn was called to be the rabbi of Har Sinai in Baltimore. He was the first bona fide rabbi to be invited to America. Einhorn had had a distinguished career in Europe and was noted for his intellect as well as his personality. Yet even he had little success in imposing his commitment to the German language or his insistence on systematic principled reform on his congregation.[18] America, he concluded, was a "land of humbug." As for his "reform" congregants – "there is nothing more loathsome than this riffraff of bacon reformers."[19] Even Einhorn was unable to change the American pattern in which "the ultimate decision in all matters of reform was not in the hands of the minister."[20]

In 1861, the German Jewish traveler I. J. Benjamin completed his three-year tour of America. He reported that "in a land that numbers more than two hundred orthodox congregations, the reform congregations number eight." Among these eight were a number that would, by twentieth-century standards, be considered conservative. Indeed, as Benjamin reports, even in Isaac Mayer Wise's congregation men and women were still seated separately, and on the New Year and the Day of Atonement, the traditional prayerbook was still in use. "Perhaps," he wrote, "they were afraid that God was awake on those days and they might be the worse for it in God's judgement."[21] At this time no congregation had as yet begun to worship with uncovered head.

The social, economic, and intellectual changes that followed in the wake of the Civil War gave rise to a new progressive vision and to unprecedented prosperity that American Jewry enthusiastically shared with the society at large. The inhibitions against a radical break with tradition that had prevailed before the war disappeared. In the postwar years, economic advance, accelerating acculturation, and pervasive optimism nourished the rising tide of reform that suffused the American synagogue.

By 1880, the synagogue had undergone a radical transformation in style and substance. In that year the Union of American Hebrew Congregations (established in 1873) published the first report ever issued dealing with "Statistics of the Jews in the United States."[22] The Union was the only national Jewish organization of consequence and its affiliates included all but a handful of the well-established congregations in the

United States. Although some of these still maintained vestiges of traditional Jewish observances, all were well along the road to thorough-going reform and the Union could plausibly claim to represent American Judaism. Even the conservative among the rabbis who remained outside the Union – like Sabato Morais of Sephardic Mikveh Israel in Philadelphia – agreed on the need for an "American Judaism more conformable to our changed condition."[23]

By 1880, most congregations had built or were in the process of building grand and opulent edifices whose size and style reflected the tastes of prosperous, upwardly mobile burghers. The experience of Congregation Adath Israel of Boston was typical. "Adath Israel soon to be known as Temple Adath Israel now found the narrow wooden yellow-painted building on Pleasant Street unworthy of the aspirations of its members."[24] Changes in synagogue structure corresponded to those in non-Jewish religious institutions. "Everywhere there were signs of expansion and prosperity in the churches. Where once there was a simple frame meeting house there now stood a majestic edifice testifying to the affluence of its congregation."[25]

The elegant new structures of Jewish congregations invariably included organs, and the "orientalism" of traditional Hebrew chants was replaced with the measured cadences of German hymns. In synagogues, as in churches "robed choirs strengthened by professional singers, marched in dignity to their stations."[26] Men and women sat together in "family pews." Perhaps the most radical (certainly the most visible) reform was the removal of head covering during worship. The covering of heads is not an important issue in Jewish law, but the practice had long been of symbolic importance and served as a visible distinction between Jewish and Christian practice. Its abrogation became a sign of a decisive break with the past. The first congregation to take this decisive action was Emanu-El in New York in 1864.[27] Isaac Mayer Wise's congregation in Cincinnati followed suit in 1874.[28] By 1880, the practice was well on the way to becoming the norm in Reformist congregations. Increasingly, visitors desiring to keep their heads covered during worship were denied entry or asked to leave. These were more observant Jews, usually recent immigrants whose attendance was thereby discouraged.

By this time, the synagogue was generally referred to as "temple." The new terminology betokened a change in mood and mode. In his sermon at the dedication of the new Plum Street Temple, Isaac Mayer Wise explained that the distinction between "synagogue" and "temple" lay in the fact that worship in a temple was to be "conducted in gladness and not in perpetual mourning."[29] This contrast between the atmosphere of "mourning" attributed to the old European style of Judaism and the "gladness" of the optimistic new American mode was typical of the attitude of reformers and their constituents. Even a Conservative like Rabbi Benjamin Szold of Baltimore transformed the Fast of the Ninth of Av from a day of lamentation to a day of affirmation of Israel's universal mission. "We do not unduly lament over the Temple that is destroyed," he wrote. "We mourn not despairingly over the downfall of Jerusalem. . . . Thou has given us another home in place of that which we lost in the Land of our Fathers."[30] The Jewish house of worship had been transformed into an emblem of prosperity and integration.

In addition to elegant edifices and decorous worship, prestigious congregations of all denominations sought the services of clergymen whose eloquence and bearing would reflect the recently acquired status of their constituents. Students of American Protestantism have described them as "princes of the pulpit."[31] Jewish temples were no less eager than Protestant churches to secure the services of such star preachers. They resembled the traditional rabbi no more than the temple in which they served resembled the traditional synagogue. Initially, prosperous congregations sought Reformist rabbis from the German-speaking areas of Europe. However, the pressure for use of the English language in service and in sermon increased rapidly and the conflict between German-speaking rabbi and congregation intensified. Not even David Einhorn, the apostle of the German language as the "carrying case of reform," could withstand the tide. In his farewell sermon in 1879, he still maintained that "where the German language is eliminated, there reform of Judaism is nothing more than a glittering veneer." The sermon concluded with his wistful acknowledgment: "Henceforth you will hear the word of God expounded alternately one week in English and one week in German."[32]

In 1882 Benjamin Szold of Oheb Shalom in Baltimore was asked to deliver one lecture each month in English "for the benefit of the younger members of the congregation." By 1886, Szold was delivering his sermon in English every other week and "portions of the service formerly read in German were read in English on the weeks of the English sermons."[33] In that same year, Adath Israel in Boston adopted the English language sermon. In 1883, the Hebrew Union College (established in 1875 in Cincinnati) graduated its first class and the transition to English-speaking, American-born and trained rabbis was inevitable.

The reformation was rapid and thoroughgoing. However, it was pragmatic and piecemeal without any ideological framework or intellectual coherence. Each congregation acted according to its own pace and tastes. Attempts to rectify the anarchy and to organize a "synod" had proven unsuccessful. Neither Isaac Mayer Wise in 1855 nor David Einhorn in 1869 could mobilize widespread support for the platforms that were proposed by the conferences they had convened. When Wise finally succeeded in forming the Union of American Hebrew Congregations in 1873, it represented the triumph of organization over ideology. No platform was adopted or even proposed.

A conference of rabbis was convened in Pittsburgh by Rabbi Kaufman Kohler in 1885 to address the ideological haphazardness. Nineteen rabbis attended, including three of the four graduates of the first class of the Hebrew Union College. The platform that was agreed upon provided an intellectual justification for the changes in ritual and practice that had already taken place or were in process. It provided a principled rationale for rejecting all ceremonies "not adapted to the views and habits of modern civilization" and dismissing laws regulating diet, priestly purity, and dress as "altogether foreign to our present mental and spiritual state." Judaism was redefined as "a progressive religion ever striving to be in accord with the postulates of reason," and the quest for social adjustment was invested with religious significance. The platform heralded "the approaching of the realization of Israel's great Messianic hope for the establishment of the kingdom of truth, justice and peace among all men."[34] David Philipson, writing his autobiography fifty years later, reminisced: "What halcyon days the closing decades of the nineteenth century were compared with the confusing and confounding years in which we are now living."[35]

In addition to the eight-point "declaration of principles," the Pittsburgh conference also passed a resolution declaring that "there is nothing in the spirit of Judaism or its law to prevent the introduction of Sunday services in localities where the necessity for such services appears or is felt."[36] The resolution did not propose to transfer the Sabbath to Sunday and indeed affirmed "the importance of maintaining the historical Sabbath as a bond with our great past and the symbol of the unity of Judaism the world over." At the same time, it sanctioned the proliferating practice of holding Sunday services that invariably overshadowed the traditional Saturday morning service in attendance and attention.

The problem of Sabbath observance, and especially that of synagogue attendance on the Sabbath, had troubled every congregation from the time of its establishment. Isaac Mayer Wise, a vigorous advocate of Sabbath observance, had responded to the problem in 1866 by introducing the "late service with lecture on Sabbath eve." The "more drastic remedy" of a Sunday morning service was inaugurated in 1874 by Temple Sinai in Chicago.[37] In the 1880s many other congregations began to follow this example. Har Sinai of Baltimore introduced the Sunday service in 1883;[38] Adath Israel of Boston took "the so much dreaded step" in 1885;[39] Beth El of Detroit in 1889.[40] In 1888 Joseph Krauskopf of

Knesseth Israel in Philadelphia produced a "Service Ritual with appropriate materials for Sunday morning." The publication contained thirty different services and was "entirely in English except for a single Hebrew sentence to give it as he said 'a distinctly Jewish tone.' "[41]

By this time, the service as well as the general ambience of the Reform temple had been substantially Protestantized. A normative pattern had emerged in which Bar Mitzvah was replaced by confirmation of boys and girls, the wearing of the *talit* (prayer shawl) had been eliminated (except in a few instances for the officiating rabbi), and the cantor had been replaced by a choir of mixed sexes and religious affiliations. An abbreviated portion of the Torah was read – not chanted – and the practice of calling members of the congregation for *aliyot* and of offering special petitionary prayers during the Torah reading was eliminated. The prophetic portion (*Haphtarah*) was read in English. In the view of the leaders of the movement "the service in reform congregations [was] decorous, uplifting, and reverential."[42]

From Mainstream to Margin – The East European Influx: 1880–1920

One unresolved issue remained: the prayerbook. Abbreviated and modified prayerbooks had been issued by numerous individual rabbis. Among them were Leo Merzbacher's *Seder Tephillah* in 1855; I. M. Wise's *Minhag America* in 1857; David Einhorn's *Olath Tamid* in 1858; Benjamin Szold's *Kodesh Hillulim* in 1862; and Marcus Jastrow's revision of the Szold prayerbook in 1870. In the absence of any coordinating body, it was impossible to achieve any degree of uniformity in synagogue practice. This problem was addressed in 1889 when Isaac Mayer Wise brought together twenty graduates of his Hebrew Union College and formed the Central Conference of American Rabbis. The conference undertook the task of preparing a standard prayerbook that would reconcile linguistic and ideological differences, most of which had become moot by this time. In 1896 the two-volume *Union Prayer Book* containing little Hebrew and no German was published and immediately gained wide acceptance. By 1905, the *Union Prayer Book* had been adopted by 183 congregations. By 1907, the number was reported to have reached 234.[43] The Reform temple had achieved a normative style and content. A member of a Reform congregation could enter any other such institution and feel quite at home.

During these years of institutional and ideological consolidation, a total transformation of American Jewry was taking place. The mass immigration of East European Jews that began in 1881 had changed the size and character of the American Jewish community. Estimates suggest that the Jewish population of the United States had grown from 230,000 in 1880 to 400,000 in 1888 to 937,800 in 1897.[44] By 1914, the estimated number was 2,933,374.[45] The old German Jewish community was swamped by the influx of newcomers who were separated from it by social, cultural, and economic, as well as religious, differences.

The religion of most of the immigrants was Old World Orthodoxy. A substantial element was not religious at all, being secularist and socialist. In either event, they found little attractive or even intelligible in the temples of the prosperous assimilated "Yahudim," as the German Jews were dubbed. "The newcomers were in training and background wholly unable and quite unwilling to comprehend or endure Reform's program."[46] The Reform congregations, which for a brief time had considered that they represented the totality of American Jewry and the future of American Judaism, found themselves a minority on the margins of communal life. In his presidential address to the Central Conference of American Rabbis in 1897, Isaac Mayer Wise could still assert that "this conference does represent the sentiment of American Judaism minus the idiosyncracies of late immigrants."[47] The historian of Oheb Shalom in Baltimore is more sanguine in reporting that "the older community felt itself engulfed."[48] By 1907, David Philipson in his history of the Reform Movement acknowledged: "The past fifteen years have witnessed remarkable changes in Jewish religious life in the United States. The reform group which at one time was in the majority has become a minority."[49] In 1908, 181 congregations were affiliated with the union; by 1920, despite the enormous increase in population, the number of affiliates was 206.[50]

Reform congregations were ambivalent toward the new immigrants, but no more so than the established community at large. Almost every congregation established some kind of committee to provide assistance to immigrants while at the same time distancing itself from them. In Bnai Jehudah in Kansas City it was a Hebrew Men's Relief Society in 1882.[51] Beth El in Detroit established a Hebrew Ladies Relief Society in the same year and a Committee for the Relief of Russian Refugees in 1890.[52] EmanuEl of San Francisco established a relief committee and an employment bureau in the mid–1890s at the same time that its Rabbi Voorsanger opposed the settlement of Eastern European refugees in the West.[53]

In all, the congregational efforts were marginal and the initiative for dealing with problems of the immigrants passed to communal agencies with no congregational affiliation. Prominent individual members of Reform congregations often took the initiative in establishing charitable agencies and institutions, but the temples themselves were largely by-passed in the work of "helping them [the immigrants] to become respected and reputable citizens."[54]

The waning years of the nineteenth century saw the birth of the Zionist movement, whose nationalist outlook and program were antithetical to the universalism of Reform. In 1897, the year when the first Zionist Congress was convened, the Central Conference of American Rabbis unanimously passed a resolution stating that "we totally disapprove of any attempt for the establishment of a Jewish state."[55] The following year a resolution of the Union of American Hebrew Congregations declared that "we are unalterably opposed to political Zionism." Rabbi Gustave Gottheil of Temple Emanu-El in New York, one of the handful of Reform rabbis sympathetic to Zionism, was forbidden to discuss the subject from the pulpit. "Only in his later years could he mention it at all and then only in the basement vestry rooms."[56] The temples remained free of Zionist indoctrination.

The early years of the twentieth century found the prosperous and acculturated Reform temples faced with the question of Jewish continuity. Their increasingly tenuous link to historic Judaism had been stretched to its limit. Felix Adler, son of Rabbi Samuel Adler of Temple Emanu-El in New York, had left Judaism and founded the Ethical Culture Society. In 1911, Charles Fleischer, rabbi of Temple Israel in Boston abandoned Judaism for "free religion" and founded the Community Church of Boston. His congregation was shaken, but few followed his example. In 1912 Fleischer's successor, Harry Levi, restored Saturday services – alongside the Sunday morning service. The following year Levi introduced a congregational Passover seder.[57] The Reform temple had faced the prospect of a break from the Jewish fold and had drawn back. "The disquieting feeling had set in that their earlier breaks had been too abrupt and that they must proceed more temperately if they were not to relinquish their essential industry. . . . They began to qualify the damaging extremes of their earlier excisions."[58]

At its thirteenth conference in 1902, the Central Conference of American Rabbis adopted a resolution declaring itself in favor of "maintaining the historical Sabbath as a fundamental institution of Judaism and exerting every effort to improve its observance." The discussion on this issue stressed concern over the widespread neglect of the Sabbath in all congregations. However, the proposal for transferring the Sabbath to Sunday was decisively rejected. Joseph Krauskopf, who had instituted an additional Sunday service as early as 1887 declared, "The gravest mistake ever made by the Conference was the confusion of the traditional Sabbath with the proposition of a service of an entirely weekday character on the first day of the week." Even Emil G. Hirsch, the most radical of reformers, admitted that Sunday "has an anti-Jewish connotation."[59] Kaufman Kohler summed up the debate some years later when he wrote: "The conviction has become well-established that the continuity of our great past must be upheld and the general feeling is that the historical Sabbath should under no condition be entirely given up."[60]

In 1909 the Central Conference of American Rabbis by an overwhelming vote adopted a resolution declaring that "mixed marriages are contrary to the tradition of the Jewish religion and should therefore be discouraged by the American Rabbinate." This resolution was interpreted by Beryl Levy in his analysis of the movement as a sign that Reform "had lost its early triumphant and militant ardor." A more cogent comment is that of Rabbi C. Levi, who observed that whereas the question facing the movement was once, "How shall we make Americans of Jews?" it was now, "How shall we make Jews of Americans?"[61]

Perhaps the most significant stimulus for a reassertion of the link with the Jewish people resulted not from any ideological reassessment, but rather from response to the intensifying persecution of Jews in Eastern Europe. Following the Kishineff pogroms of 1903, Samuel Silverman, the president of the Central Conference of American Rabbis, called for the establishment of "a central authoritative body that in crises and emergencies shall have the indisputable right to speak and act for all Israel."[62] Silverman felt that the Central Conference should take the initiative in "uniting the scattered forces." At the meeting of the Union of American Hebrew Congregations in that year a resolution was adopted calling upon the Union Executive Board to invite "organizations of a national character to appoint delegates to an American Jewish Congress to be held under the auspices of the Union of American Hebrew Congregations."[63] The lack of vigor and influence of the movement at that time is reflected in the fact that no action was taken in response to this resolution.

In 1906 Rabbi Joseph Stoltz, president of the Central Conference of American Rabbis, observed that the "lamentable persecutions in Russia" had a positive effect in unifying the Jews in the countries of the dispersion. He called on the conference to concentrate its efforts "on laying the foundation of a union of the forces of American Israel."[64] By this time the task of representing American Jewry had been undertaken by a group of prominent Reform laymen who formed the American Jewish Committee and bypassed the Reform movement and its institutions.

Within the synagogue, women were assuming more significant roles. Although women possessed theoretical equality from the earliest days of reform, practice had lagged behind theory. In 1900 Mt. Zion Congregation had allowed women to join the congregation in their own

names.[65] A year later a Women's Auxiliary Association was founded at
Beth El in Detroit.[66] The Current Topics Club founded in Congregation
Shaarey Shamayim, Lancaster, Pennsylvania, included men and women.[67]
In the ensuing years temple sisterhoods and women's auxiliaries were
established everywhere. The Kansas City Sisterhood, organized with
seventy-five members in 1906, had a membership of 260 by 1908.[68] In
1913 the National Federation of Temple Sisterhoods was organized with
seventy-one affiliated societies. The enfranchisement of women in congregational life suffered occasional setbacks, as in Congregation Shaarey
Tephilla of New York, where in 1908 a motion to permit women to
vote at a congregational meeting was defeated by a vote of forty to
thirty-nine. This setback was temporary. Subsequently women not only
voted, but by 1929 a woman was elected to serve on the board of trustees
even of this congregation.[69] Five years earlier, two women had been
appointed to the board of trustees of Temple Israel in Boston.[70] Slowly
but surely women assumed an ever more prominent role in congregational affairs. In 1925 an amendment to the bylaws of Beth-El in Detroit
provided that the wife of a member of the congregation become a member in her own right with "voting and full membership privileges."[71]

Religion as Respectability: 1920–1933

The coming of the First World War brought an end to the flood
of immigration and a period of sustained prosperity to the United States.
In Reform congregations, the period was one of relative stability, perhaps
even stagnation. Ideological issues had been largely resolved; fiscal obstacles had been overcome. The temples were comfortable, decorous
strongholds of prosperous middle- and upper-class burghers of German
ancestry who were content with a none-too-disturbing, none-too-
demanding Judaism. Only a stormy petrel dissenter like Judah Magnes
raised fundamental objections. In his final sermon prior to resigning as
assistant rabbi of Temple Emanu-El of New York on April 24, 1910,
Magnes declared:

> Just as the parasite may at times have more outward beauty than
> the parent tree, so have the richer Reformed congregations an
> outward appeal in the beauty of their buildings, their glorious
> music and their perfect decorum. But these outward trappings
> have not been able to hide from me the emptiness and shallow-
> ness of your Jewish life. . . . You cannot remain as you are. The
> retention of the status quo means a gradual sinking into decay.[72]

Magnes left the congregation and the movement. The prevailing mood was closer to the report of Har Sinai in Baltimore in 1918: "Nothing of signal importance has happened with the Congregation in recent years."[73] In Temple Israel of Boston, "the happy optimism of the American middle class" prevailed.[74]

When the Balfour Declaration affirming British support for a Jewish National Home in Palestine was issued in 1917, the Central Conference of American Rabbis adopted a resolution reiterating that "we are opposed to the idea that Palestine should be considered *the home-land* of the Jews. . . . The ideal of the Jew is not the establishment of a Jewish state – not the reassertion of a Jewish nationality which has long been outgrown."[75] Three years later, the president of the Central Conference of American Rabbis declined to send a delegation to participate in a meeting convened to celebrate the issuance of the mandate for Palestine to Great Britain. Nevertheless, throughout the 1920s Zionist sentiment grew in Reform congregations among the rabbinate and the laity. Men like Abba Hillel Silver (1915), James Heller (1916), and Barnett Brickner (1917) conducted their Zionist activities outside their congregations, but their influence and example were felt. Maurice Samuel, the Zionist polemicist, wrote in 1927: "A gradual semi-furtive spiritual interest in the reconstruction of a Jewish Palestine has spread through the Reform world."[76]

The organization of the National Federation of Temple Brotherhoods in 1923 was more a token of "embourgeoisment" than of increasing religious fervor. The men's clubs stressed sociability rather than piety. Their programs bore a greater resemblance to fraternal orders and lodges than to religious organizations. Their emergence in the 1920s betokens an attempt to find new ways to strengthen institutional loyalty in the face of waning spiritual commitment.

A more significant development was the modest increase in attention given to religious education. In 1924, after years of bickering and "benign neglect," the Union of American Hebrew Congregations and the Central Conference of American Rabbis established a Joint Commission on Jewish Education. Dr. Emanuel Gamoran, described as a "trained educational expert of fine ability and untiring energy" was hired as executive director.[77] A curriculum for religious schools was adopted and a program of publication of textbooks was undertaken. A survey of religious schools affiliated with the union found the quality and quantity of schooling to be meager. Of 121 schools reporting, 103 met for only one session per week. Sixteen met for two sessions and only two for three sessions. Eighty-one of the schools claimed to offer Hebrew instruction, but in half of these, the instruction was "optional." Of the 42 schools that answered the question as to when Hebrew was introduced into the curriculum, 28 had begun the instruction within the last six years. This statistic was taken to indicate that "there is a tendency in our congregations to provide a more intensive Jewish education for our children than they have received in the past."[78]

The commission issued an "urgent recommendation of the desirability, nay, the necessity of an additional session [of religious school] on some week day." However, 80 percent of the congregations responding to the survey stated that "no steps are taken at present to increase the hours for Jewish religious instruction"[79] The commission resigned itself to the reality: "We understand fully that so radical a departure can be realized only gradually." In the meantime, 50 percent of the children of members of Temple Emanu-El of San Francisco were not enrolled in religious school at all.

The following year (1925), a subcommittee of the Commission on Youth Education recommended that the curriculum of schools "be supplemented by the organization of our youth through a system of clubs in connection with the various congregations."[80] Over the years, various congregations had sponsored youth programs: Shaarey Tephilla of New York had its Young Folks League and Sub-Debs; Emanu-El of San Francisco had its Pathfinders for young men and Reviewers for young women; Boy Scout troops under synagogue sponsorship were to be found almost everywhere. Such groups of varying degrees of seriousness regularly appeared and disappeared. Now, the Youth Education subcommittee called for a coordinated effort to infuse all "organizations for youth now existing in connection with congregations and all such that are created are to be inspired by a very definite goal and ideal, namely that of consecrating themselves to the moral and spiritual heritage of Israel and making it a power in the lives of our young people."[81] The subcommittee was apparently responding to Mordecai Kaplan's contemporary proposals for the creation of synagogue-centers and was recommending the "club idea," which it said "is the natural expression of the social instincts of youth." Despite such fulsome endorsement, action did not live up to rhetoric and resolutions. The National Federation of Temple Youth was not organized until 1939.

One of the changes that marked congregational life in the 1920s was the introduction of broadcasts in the new medium of radio, especially in the large metropolitan congregations whose pulpits were filled by distinguished preachers. Beginning in 1924, Harry Levi's Sunday morning sermons in Temple Israel were broadcast throughout New England.[82] The following year broadcasts were instituted at Beth El in Detroit[83] and in 1926 at Mt. Zion in St. Paul.[84] The broadcasts were seen primarily as a means of outreach to non-Jews, but they also served as a means of

contact with unaffiliated Jews, especially the growing number of acculturated Jews of East European origin and their children. Increasing numbers of these began to affiliate with Reform temples.

The extent of the change in the character of the Reform constituency
became clear in a survey published in 1931. A discussion on the perpetuation of Judaism at the Union of American Hebrew Congregations
convention of 1927 had resulted in the establishment of a Commission
on Research. In 1931 the commission published its report, entitled "Reform Judaism in the Large Cities." By that time it found that "about
equal proportions of Temple members were of German parentage and
of East European parentage."[85] This surprising statistic revealed the extent of the change that had taken place over the previous decade. This
change in background undoubtedly helped prepare the way for the modifications of Reform ideology and practice in subsequent years.

In the Valley of the Shadow: 1933–1948

Perhaps even more significant than the diversification of ethnic
origin was the transformation of political and economic circumstances
and the drastic alteration of expectations that came to pass in the 1930s.
The rise of fascism, the onset of a disastrous depression, the spread of
antisemitism even before the rise to power of Hitler "served notice upon
the Jew that the Emancipation program of complete assimilation except
for religious observance required reconsideration."[86] Whereas an unreconstructed "universalist" like David Philipson of the Rockdale Avenue
Temple in Cincinnati might denounce "a retreat into a ghetto" and cling
to the notion that "the forces of light and love, of brotherhood and peace
shall yet conquer,"[87] more credence was being given to Stephen Wise's
critique of "the Temple fixation of Reform Judaism." "Today," Wise
declared, "we Jews must no longer be ready to be liberalized into a
Semitic version of Unitarianism, nor yet to be Humanists with a Jewish
accent."[88]

One of the signs of the change in atmosphere in Reform congregations
was an infusion of egalitarianism. In 1922 Temple Israel in Boston had
abolished assigned pews.[89] Rabbi Martin Meyer of Emanu-El in San
Francisco conducted an extended campaign decrying segregation within
the congregation on the basis of economic class. His efforts led to an
increase in availability of High Holiday tickets for the less affluent.[90]
Rabbi Mayerberg of Kansas City failed in an attempt to abolish membership categories but succeeded in persuading the congregation to rent
a large hall so that the congregation would not be split into differing

categories of contributors.[91] In Temple Bnai Zion of St. Paul, the practice of blackballing potential members was abrogated.[92]

The advance of democratization and openness in congregational life was accelerated by the onset of the depression and the impact of the Hitler era. The Brotherhood Board of Temple Bnai Jehuda in Kansas City, committed itself to find signers of affidavits of sponsorship to enable German and Austrian Jews to enter the United States. German refugees were invited to join the congregation free of charge, and classes in English were conducted for immigrants.[93] Shaarey Tephilla in New York formed a refugee committee and offered free High Holiday services.[94] Emanu-El of San Francisco assisted in the resettlement of refugees and in finding employment for them. Refugee children were enrolled in religious school without charge, and High Holiday services in German were conducted.[95] The sense of Jewish peoplehood, negated in the days of facile optimism, was regenerated by the experience of sharing in common destiny in times of trial.

By the mid–1930s, the mood and character of the Reform temple had clearly changed. Graduates of Stephen Wise's seminary, the Jewish Institute of Religion (founded in 1923), were unabashedly pro–Zionist, pro–Jewish peoplehood, and pro–traditional practice. Graduates of the Hebrew Union College with Zionist sympathies assumed leading roles in the Reform Movement as well as the Zionist Movement. The new reality led to a reassessment of ideology and practice.

In most congregations, a reassessment of ritual and practice was already under way. In 1933 Bar Mitzvah was reintroduced in Shaarey Shamayim in Lancaster, Pennsylvania.[96] In 1934, Mt. Zion in St. Paul celebrated its first Bar Mitzvah in fifty years, soon to be followed by the introduction of chanting of the Kiddush and cantorial singing.[97] Joshua Liebman, a pro–Zionist, was elected rabbi of Temple Israel in Boston. He replaced the Sunday morning service with a Friday evening service and reinstituted Bar Mitzvah. Hebrew content in prayer and in the religious school was increased. Temple Israel of Boston established an afternoon Hebrew school.[98] The Reform temple was reclaiming its place in the mainstream of American Jewish life.

At the meeting of the Central Conference of American Rabbis in 1936, Felix Levy, president of the conference declared: "A supposed criticism is often leveled at us that we are now indistinguishable from Conservatism. To my mind this is the highest compliment for it proves we are not a sect of a schism but an integral and I hope necessary part of 'catholic Israel.' "[99] That year, a commission that had been appointed to reexamine the guiding principles of Reform Judaism presented its report. The statement began with an acknowledgement of "the changes that have taken place in the modern world and the need of stating anew the teaching of Reform Judaism."

In a sharp break with earlier Reform deemphasis of "peoplehood," Judaism was now redefined as "the historical religious experience of the Jewish people." The once uncompromising rejection of Zionism was replaced by the affirmation of the "obligation of all Jewry to aid in the upbuilding of Palestine as a Jewish homeland, not only as a haven for the oppressed but also as a center for Jewish cultural and spiritual life." The importance of ceremonies in home and synagogue is reaffirmed together with an emphasis on "greater use of Hebrew . . . in our teaching and worship."[100] In the debate that followed the presentation of the document, Samuel Cohon, chairman of the commission, acknowledged the "radical shift [which] has taken place in thought" since the adoption of the Pittsburgh Platform. "We cannot guide our people by convictions which we have outgrown," he declared. Even David Philipson, the preeminent exponent of "classical reform," supported the new formulation "for the sake of peace." In order to give members of the conference an opportunity to suggest emendations, approval of the declaration was deferred until the next year, when it was accepted with minor emendations. The change in direction of the Reform temple was sanctioned and endorsed by the rabbinic leadership of the movement.

In 1940 a revised version of the *Union Prayer Book* was issued. It was not radically different from the older version, but all of the changes were in the direction of restored traditional practices, increased use of Hebrew, and away from the extreme assimilationism of earlier reform. Among the prayers that now found their way back into the service was one endorsing the restoration of Zion.

The onset of the Second World War and the unfolding of the Nazi holocaust occasioned a final conflict over the issue of Zionism. Although many rabbis and their congregations had by this time become Zionist supporters and most were at the very least sympathizers, a vocal minority remained anti-Zionist. At the Central Conference of American Rabbis convention of 1942, the conflict came to a head over a resolution calling for the establishment of a Jewish army. The passage of the resolution by a vote of sixty-four to thirty-eight signified the definitive success of the Zionist majority.[101] A minority of rabbis threatened to withdraw from the conference and establish a separate organization. The split was averted but a new anti-Zionist organization called the American Council for Judaism was formed by dissident Reform rabbis and laymen. For a brief time the issue of Zionism continued to be a source of contention in congregational life, and a handful of congregations split over the issue. In Houston, Texas, congregants sympathetic to Zionism left Temple

Beth El, a stronghold of the Council for Judaism, and formed Temple
Emanu-El. In Glencoe, Illinois, supporters of the Council for Judaism
left the North Shore Israel Temple and formed Am Sholom. By 1948,
only an insignificant minority of rabbis and laymen continued to support
the council.

The Postwar Years – Growth and Consolidation: 1948–1968

When Temple Oheb Shalom of Baltimore celebrated its centennial in 1953, its historian observed that the wartime and postwar years
were "so crowded with world shaking events that drastic changes taking
place in congregational life have not received the attention they would
have been accorded in more peaceful times."[102] During these turbulent
years of change, Reform congregations experienced unprecedented
growth in membership, in school population, in scope of activities, and
in size of budgets. Oheb Shalom grew from 800 families in 1936 to 1,100
in 1953, and its religious school enrollment increased from 300 to 665.
Beth El in Detroit grew from 1,013 families in 1940 to 1,663 in 1954.[103]
Old established congregations expanded. New congregations sprang up
like mushrooms in suburban areas to which Jews – along with most other
Americans – flocked. Suburban Jews, like their Christian neighbors,
affiliated with religious institutions as never before. In the *American Jewish
Yearbook* of 1937–1938, the Union of American Hebrew Congregations
had reported 290 temples with 50,000 family members. By 1956, the
number of congregations had increased to 520 and the number of member
families to 255,000. By 1975, 700 congregations were enrolled in the
Union.[104]

In the immediate postwar years, the move to the suburbs and the
accompanying social and economic changes made Jews, many of whom
had been secular or simply unaffiliated, "self-conscious about religion."[105] The Union of American Hebrew Congregations made a decision to recruit the masses of the unaffiliated and to repudiate the
remaining vestiges of social exclusivism that attached to the movement.
As a token of an "active dynamic program of leadership," the Union of
American Hebrew Congregations decided to move from provincial Cincinnati to cosmopolitan, Jewishly intense New York, and in 1951 the
enlarged union staff took up residence in the House of Living Judaism
on Fifth Avenue. Ideological purity ceased to be of much consequence
and the "modified American standard of piety" was easily accommodated
in the suburban Reform congregation.[106] A variety of congregational
modes found their place in the Reform family, including some that re-

quired head covering and others that made it optional. Worshiping with a covered head was no longer forbidden anywhere. In many new congregations, the distinction between Reform and Conservative virtually disappeared. Terminology and image were almost interchangeable. In Mt. Vernon, New York, the Conservative congregation was known as *Temple* Emanuel, whereas the Reform congregation was the Free *Synagogue*. Even where the distinction between Reform and Conservative congregations was still discernible, the distinction between congregants had blurred almost to the vanishing point.

Increasingly, the Reform congregation became a social center with a large proportion of child-centered activities and programs of all kinds, from nursery school to golden age groups. The religious school became an increasingly important factor in attracting membership, and enrollment in religious schools increased even more rapidly than temple membership. A survey of 1959 estimated the school population of Reform congregations to be 150,000.[107] In a 1958 survey, 207 of 317 congregations responding conducted midweek Hebrew classes and were adding higher levels to their Hebrew instruction.[108] Classes at the high school level were conducted in almost all congregations and a substantial number continued schooling through the twelfth grade. Increasingly, full-time professional educators were engaged to supervise congregational schools. The congregational building boom of the 1950s invariably included a new, enlarged school building.[109]

Youth programming emerged as a prominent feature of congregational life. In 1958, the membership of the National Federation of Temple Youth was estimated at 15,100 – a 20 percent increase over the previous year. Camping emerged as an important component of youth programming. A few congregations – Emanuel of Denver, Temple Israel in Minneapolis, Wilshire Boulevard in Los Angeles – operated camps of their own in which "Jewish content and spirit pervade[d] every aspect."[110] Most congregations sent their youth to the growing network of camps sponsored by the Union of American Hebrew Congregations. Youth programs in Israel in the form of summer institutes and semester-long high school exchanges grew in number and educational intensity. In 1965, Bnai Jehuda of Kansas City, once a stronghold of anti-Zionism, began sending all of its high school seniors to Israel for a summer study program. In 1970, Emanu-El of San Francisco, whose rabbi until 1947 was a leader of the American Council for Judaism, inaugurated a program of sending its entire confirmation class to Israel.

No constituency was neglected in the expansion of congregational services and activities. Nursery schools became a feature of many congregational programs.[111] The union survey of 1958 reported that 84 of

317 congregations sponsored young married couples clubs and 36 of 317 included unmarried adult clubs – these in addition to brotherhoods and sisterhoods present everywhere. Senior citizens' groups were less common, but the number of these organized under temple auspices was growing.

Theology remained a concern of some rabbis, but the emphasis in most congregational activities was on Jewish peoplehood. The rituals observed by Reform Jews, especially in their homes, increased considerably. When compared to the survey of 1931, the statistics of the 1950s show a substantial continuing increase in traditional observance.[112] A survey conducted in 1971 indicated that 93 percent of all respondents took part in a Passover seder, 90 percent reported owning a Hannukah menorah, and 50 percent reported that they lit Sabbath candles.[113] As for the ritual in the congregation, "Services today are likely to include a generous quantity of Hebrew and have the musical portions rendered by a cantor. . . . More commonly today rabbis, cantors, and in some instances laymen wear a prayer shawl and/or a head covering."[114]

The experience of Congregation Bnai Jehuda of Kansas City, an old-line, midwestern congregation, is typical. In 1953, the *shofar* (ram's horn) replaced the trumpet in the Rosh Hashanah service after a sixty-year absence. Six years later the chanting of Kiddush and the Hakafot (procession of the Torah scrolls on Simchat Torah) were restored and a cantor was hired.[115] The reemphasis of traditional rituals was virtually universal.

At the same time, one of the distinctive emphases of Reform congregations in the 1950s and 1960s was the stress on social action. The Union of American Hebrew Congregations had taken the initiative in 1940 in establishing the Commission on Social Action and in 1961 in opening the Social Action Center in Washington, D.C. Throughout this period and especially in the heyday of the Civil Rights Movement in the early 1960s, Reform congregations participated actively in the drive for racial desegregation on the local as well as the national level. The balance between particularism and universalism, between being good Jews and becoming involved in the burdens of society, seemed to have been achieved. A mood of confidence and optimism suffused the Reform synagogue.

New Moods and Modes: 1968–1986

By the late 1960s, the so-called return to religion in America had waned and the "death of God" was being proclaimed in some theological circles. A series of sharp and unanticipated shocks unsettled American society in general and American Jewry in particular: assassinations, urban riots, an endless war in Vietnam, the Six-Day War in Israel. As Eugene Borowitz has written: "The crisis in American society, the peril to the state of Israel, the new appreciation of ethnicity all seemed to call for a reexamination of Reform Jewish principles. . . . The style of synagogue life which seemed so fresh a few years previous, seemed somewhat stale and in need of invigoration."[116] In addition, the temples lost some of the preeminence that they had assumed within the Jewish community. Federations and fund raising – particularly focused around support of Israel – assumed an increasingly important place. "By 1975 the upward curve [of synagogue growth] had begun to level off."[117]

As early as 1963, Jacob Shankman, in a volume commemorating the seventy-fifth anniversary of the Central Conference of American Rabbis, had asked: "Should the size of congregations be limited? Must bigness follow its own momentum?" He observed that, "in 1937, our largest congregations boasted memberships of 500–800 families; only a half dozen had passed the 1,000 family mark. In 1963 a score had passed the 1,400 family mark and some had exceeded 2,500 families." Now, Shankman asked, "can the runaway development of overswollen congregations and programs be prevented?"[118] "Runaway development" was *not* prevented and the congregational crisis of the 1970s was intensified by the sense of impersonality that characterized more and more "overswollen" Reform temples. It became clear that where the quality of religious life was concerned, bigger was not necessarily better.

In responding to the new circumstances, the Reform Movement in general and Reform synagogues in particular demonstrated a considerable degree of vitality and initiative. When a study in 1971 revealed the dissatisfaction of congregants with the failure of the temple to satisfy the "need for community," many congregations responded by organizing *havurot*, intimate groups within the congregation to share in worship, celebration, study, or other religious experiences.[119] Everywhere, attempts to add warmth and intimacy to the congregational experience were undertaken. Communal singing – sometimes accompanied by guitar – supplemented or replaced the formal, austere "contrapuntal singing of a professional choir" of former times. Pulpit conversations and informal discussions supplemented or replaced the "exhortatory" sermon. These developments were most obvious in smaller, newer suburban congregations. However, even the large old-line "cathedral" temples were affected. The quest for dignity and decorum, the "ethereal atmosphere of a worshipful largely passive congregation" has given way to the desire for participation and involvement. Even synagogue architecture has been affected. Congregations now build "more intimate sanctuaries out of a desire to stress intimacy rather than awe in worship."[120]

At the same time, the restoration of traditional observances in the home was encouraged. In 1972, the Central Conference of American Rabbis published a *Tadrikh le-Shabbat, A Sabbath Manual* that provided guidance for enriching the celebration of the Sabbath in the home. Since then the conference has issued *Gates of the House* in 1977, *Gates of Mitzvah –A Guide to the Jewish Life Cycle* in 1979 and *Gates of the Seasons – A Guide to the Jewish Year* in 1983. Not only do these publications confirm the "undeniable trend toward the reinstitution of traditional practices in Reform Judaism,"[121] they demonstrate that the traditional balance in Judaism between home and synagogue, which had been radically disrupted by reform, is being increasingly redressed.

An additional development of recent decades has been the growing prominence of women in the Reform synagogue. Although theoretical equality had always prevailed in Reform, the participation of women on synagogue boards increased markedly in the 1960s and the tempo of participation accelerated in the 1970s. In 1971 the first woman was ordained as a rabbi. By 1986, women constituted almost one-half of the student body of the Hebrew Union College–Jewish Institute of Religion.

In 1975 the first new prayerbook to be published since 1940 was issued. The new volume, like the *Centenary Perspective* adopted by the Central Conference a year later, reflected both the diversity of Reform congregations and the growing traditionalism of a significant segment of the movement. It offered a variety of options from the strongly traditional to the explicitly humanist. It included prayers not only for putting the *tallit* on but even *tefillin* (phylacteries). Whether or not there are actually Reform congregations in which significant numbers of members don *tefillin* is doubtful. However, the concept of what constitutes a Reform synagogue (or temple) has clearly been broadened to accommodate such practices when and if they should be revived.

In the decade of the 1980s the Reform Movement seems to have reached a balance in which a variety of styles and modes of liberal Judaism coexist in relative harmony and stability. Congregations are not experiencing rapid growth; neither are they suffering from massive defections. This conservative decade is not an era of radical new departures in any social realm. It is a period of reassessment of the value of traditional ideas and institutions in religion, as in many aspects of life.

At its biennial convention in 1983, the Union of American Hebrew Congregations adopted a resolution affirming that "a variety of authentic Jewish styles, practices, rituals, and religious meanings are expressed within our ranks and congregations." The resolution called for the development of "sound strategies for congregations to deal with change ... and ensure the stability and creativity of Reform Judaism."[122] The

Reform synagogue, true to its tradition, remains liberal, tolerant, un-dogmatic, open to change, but committed to the essential unity of the Jewish tradition and the Jewish people. As a historian of the movement concluded: "With all of its diversity, it [Reform Judaism] offered a religious expression of Judaism both intellectually attractive and emotionally satisfying."[123]

NOTES

1 Joseph Krauskopf, "Half a Century of Judaism in the United States," *American Jewish Annual*, 4 (1888), pp. 70–71.

2 *The Occident and American Jewish Advocate*, 6 (1848), p. 317. In describing the growth of American Jewry, Isaac Lesser wrote: "The country is fast filling up with Jews; from the newly gotten Santa Fe to the confines of New Brunswick and from the Atlantic to the shores of the western sea, the wandering sons of Israel are seeking homes and freedom."

3 Uriah Z. Engelman, "Jewish Statistics in the United States Census of Religious Bodies, 1850–1936," *Jewish Social Studies*, 9 (1947), pp. 5–64.

4 Leon A. Jick, *The Americanization of the Synagogue* (Hanover, N.H., 1976), pp. 88, 91.

5 Solomon Schindler, *Israelites in Boston* (Boston, 1889), chap. 2, n.p.

6 *The Occident* 6 (1848), pp. 317, 366.

7 Jick, *Americanization of Synagogue*, pp. 86–96.

8 David Philipson, *The Oldest Jewish Congregation in the West* (Cincinnati, 1894), p. 14.

9 *Constitution of the United Hebrew Congregation of St. Louis* (1841).

10 Joshua Trachtenberg, *Consider the Years: The Story of the Jewish Community of Easton (1752–1942)* (Easton, Pa., 1844), pp. 145–146, 237–241.

11 Daniel I. Rupp, *An Original History of the Religious Denominations at Present Existing in the United States* (Philadelphia, 1844), p. 368.

12 Minutes of Congregation Rodeph Sholom of Philadelphia, (25 May 1840).

13 Minutes of Congregation Bnai Jeshurun of Cincinnati, 27 February 1848. During this same period some members of the congregation were still "staying up Shebuos Night for reading and learning according to our wholly [sic] Law of Germany." Minutes, 2 June 1848.

14 Minutes of Congregation Knesseth Israel of Philadelphia, 3 October 1852.

15 Isaac M. Fein, *The Making of an American Jewish Community* (Philadelphia, 1971), pp. 56–57.

16 David Philipson, *Max Lilienthal, American Rabbi: His Life and Writings* (New York, 1915), pp. 1–45.

17 Isaac Mayer Wise, *Reminiscences* (Cincinnati, 1901), p. 155.

18 *Sinai*, 2 (1857), p. 443.

19 Correspondence of Einhorn and Ruben Oppenheimer, August 12, 1861, cited in Fein, *Making of an American Jewish Community*, p. 98.

20   Hyman B. Grinstein, *The Rise of the Jewish Community of New York, 1654–1860* (Philadelphia, 1945), p. 365.

21   Israel Joseph Benjamin, *Three Years in America, 1859–1862*, vol. 1 (Philadelphia, 1956), p. 310.

22   Union of American Hebrew Congregations, *Statistics of Jews in the United States* (Philadelphia, 1880).

23   Moshe Davis, *The Emergence of Conservative Judaism* (Philadelphia, 1965), p. 163.

24   Arthur Mann, ed., *Growth and Achievement: Temple Israel 1854–1954* (Cambridge, Mass., 1954), p. 31.

25   Clifton E. Olmstead, *History of Religion in the United States* (Englewood Cliffs, N.J., 1960), p. 447.

26   Ibid.

27   Minutes of Congregation Emanuel of New York, 1 May 1864.

28   Minutes of Congregation Bnai Jeshurun of Cincinnati, 19 August 1874.

29   James Heller, *As Yesterday When It Is Past* (Cincinnati, 1942), p. 106.

30   Benjamin Szold, *Abodoth Israel* (Baltimore, 1873), p. 589.

31   Sidney Ahlstrom, *A Religious History of the American People* (New Haven, Conn., 1972), p. 738.

32   Bernhard N. Cohen, "Early German Preaching in America," *Historia Judaica*, 15 (1953), p. 105.

33   Louis F. Cahn, *The History of Oheb Shalom* (Baltimore, 1953), pp. 35, 37.

34   Walter Jacob, ed., *The Pittsburgh Platform in Retrospect* (Pittsburgh, 1985), pp. 108–109.

35   David Philipson, *My Life as an American Jew* (Cincinnati, 1941), p. 39.

36   Jacob, *Pittsburgh Platform*, p. 119.

37   David Philipson, *The Reform Movement in Judaism*, rev. ed. (Cincinnati, 1931), pp. 373–374.

38   C. A. Rubenstein, *History of the Har Sinai Congregation* (Baltimore, 1918), n.p.

39   Mann, *Growth and Achievement*, p. 51.

40   Irving Katz, *The Beth El Story* (Detroit, 1955), p. 92.

41   Beryl Levy, *Reform Judaism in America* (New York, 1933), p. 10.

42   Philipson, *Reform Movement in Judaism*, p. 377.

43   Levy, *Reform Judaism in America*, p. 12.

44   *American Jewish Yearbook 5665*, (Philadelphia, 1904), p. 306.

45   *American Jewish Yearbook 5665* (Philadelphia, 1904), p. 32.

46   Levy, *Reform Judaism in America*, p. 11.

47   *Central Conference of American Rabbis*, vol. 9 (1897), p. 12.

48   Cahn, *History of Oheb Shalom*, p. 46.

49   Philipson, *Reform Movement in Judaism*, p. 379.

50   *American Jewish Yearbook 5669*, (Philadelphia 1908–09), p. 39.

51   Frank J. Adler, *Roots in a Moving Stream: The Centennial History of Congregation Bnai Jehuda of Kansas City 1870–1970* (Kansas City, 1972), p. 49.

52   Katz, *Beth El Story*, p. 89.

53 Fred Rosenbaum, *Architects of Reform: Congregational and Community Leadership, EmanuEl of San Francisco, 1849–1980* (Berkeley, Calif., 1980), p. 51.
54 Mann, *Growth and Achievement*, p. 33.
55 *Central Conference of American Rabbis*, 7 (1898), p. xli.
56 Levy, *Reform Judaism in America*, p. 132.
57 Mann, *Growth and Achievement*, p. 33.
58 Levy, *Reform Judaism in America*, p. 132.
59 *Central Conference of American Rabbis*, vol. 13 (1902).
60 Kaufmann Kohler, *Jewish Theology* (New York, 1918), p. 459.
61 Levy, *Reform Judaism in America*, pp. 88, 117.
62 Ibid., p. 10.
63 Philipson, *My Life as an American Jew*, p. 163.
64 Levy, *Reform Judaism in America*, p. 121.
65 Gunther W. Plaut, *Mount Zion 1856–1956: The First Hundred Years* (St. Paul), p. 73.
66 Katz, *Beth El Story*, p. 97.
67 David Brener, *The Jews of Lancaster, Pennsylvania: A Story with Two Beginnings* (Lancaster, 1979), p. 122.
68 Adler, *Roots in a Moving Stream*, p. 115.
69 Simon Cohen, *Shaarey Tephilla: A History of Its Hundred Years 1845–1945* (New York, 1945), pp. 43, 50.
70 Mann, *Growth and Achievement*, p. 37.
71 Katz, *Beth El Story*, p. 108.
72 Arthur Goren, ed., *Dissenter in Zion* (Cambridge, Mass., 1982), pp. 108, 111.
73 Rubenstein, *History of Har Sinai*.
74 Mann, *Growth and Achievement*, p. 89.
75 *Central Conference of American Rabbis Yearbook*, 37 (1924), p. 133.
76 Maurice Samuel, *I, The Jew* (New York, 1927), p. 240.
77 *Central Conference of American Rabbis Yearbook*, 34, (1924), p. 117.
78 Ibid., pp. 352–370.
79 Ibid., p. 368.
80 *Central Conference of American Rabbis Yearbook*, 35, (1925), p. 170.
81 Ibid.
82 Mann, *Growth and Achievement*, p. 88.
83 Katz, *Beth El Story*, p. 108.
84 Plaut, *Mount Zion 1856–1956*, p. 97.
85 Union of American Hebrew Congregations, *Reform Judaism in the Large Cities* (1931), p. 10.
86 Levy, *Reform Judaism in America*, p. 133.
87 Philipson, *My Life as an American Jew*, p. 315.
88 Stephen Wise, *As I See It* (New York, 1944), p. 26, Wise's comment is taken from an essay entitled "A Tragic Blunder" written in 1933.
89 Mann, *Growth and Achievement*, p. 36.
90 Rosenbaum, *Architects of Reform*, p. 83.

91　Adler, *Roots in a Moving Stream*, p. 162.
92　Plaut, *Mount Zion 1856–1956*, p. 89.
93　Adler, *Roots in a Moving Stream*, p. 181.
94　Cohen, *Shaarey Tephilla*, pp. 57–58.
95　Rosenbaum, *Architects of Reform*, p. 132.
96　Brener, *The Jews of Lancaster*, p. 140.
97　Plaut, *Mount Zion 1856–1956*, pp. 93, 100, 103.
98　Mann, *Growth and Achievement*, pp. 39, 102.
99　*Central Conference of American Rabbis Yearbook*, 46 (1936), p. 163.
100　Ibid., pp. 89, 91.
101　*Central Conference of American Rabbis Yearbook*, 52 (1942), 169–170.
102　Cohen, *Shaarey Tephillah*, p. 61.
103　Katz, *Beth El Story*, p. 229.
104　*American Jewish Yearbook*, vols. 39, 58, 77.
105　Nathan Glazer, *American Judaism* (Chicago, 1972), p. 119.
106　Ibid., p. 113.
107　*Congregational Survey, Union of American Hebrew Congregations (1958–59)*, vol. 2 (New York, 1959), p. 36.
109　For examples, see reports in congregations histories of Detroit, Miami, Kansas City, Lancaster, and San Francisco.
110　Max Shapiro, *Here Am I: Send Me* (Minneapolis, 1980), p. 164.
111　Ibid., p. 165.
112　Marshall Sklare and Joseph Greenblaum, *Jewish Identity on the Suburban Frontier, A Study of Group Survival in the Open Society* (New York, 1967), pp. 83–85.
113　Leonard Fein, *Reform Is a Verb*, Union of American Hebrew Congregation, (New York, 1972), p. 27.
114　Michael Meyer, "Reform Judaism," in *Trends and Issues in American Judaism*, ed. Bernard Martin, (Westport, Conn., 1978), p. 164.
115　Adler, *Roots in a Moving Stream*, p. 242.
116　Eugene Borowitz, *Reform Judaism Today – Reform in the Process of Change* (New York, 1978), p. xii.
117　Meyer, *Trends and Issues*, p. 160.
118　Jacob Shankman, "The Changing Role of the Rabbi," in *Retrospect and Prospect*, ed. Bertram Korn (New York, 1965), pp. 246, 248.
119　Fein, *Reform Is a Verb*, p. 146.
120　Meyer, *Trends and Issues*, p. 164.
121　*Gates of the Seasons* (New York, 1983), p. vii.
122　Ronald Ashkenaz and Todd Jick, *Coping with Change: The Reform Synagogues and Trends in Worship* (New York, 1984), p. 2.
123　Meyer, *Trends and Issues*, p. 169.

4

The Conservative Synagogue

JACK WERTHEIMER

The Conservative synagogue is a twentieth-century creation of American Jews. Although other Jewries also founded synagogues that charted a course between the extremes of Orthodoxy and Reform, the particular mixture of religious and social activities that characterize the Conservative synagogue first emerged in the United States.[1] The earliest versions of the Conservative synagogue were intially established by dissatisfied members of either Reform or Orthodox congregations seeking alternative worship services and synagogue programs. Led mainly by rabbis trained at the Jewish Theological Seminary of America and guided by the then fledgling congregational organization known as the United Synagogue of America, these congregations gradually developed a distinctive Conservative style and identity by the early 1920s. Thereafter, Conservative synagogues experienced a dramatic rate of growth so that by midcentury the United Synagogue of America numbered over 850 affiliates whose members constituted the plurality of American Jews identified with any Jewish religious movement.

This chapter is about the historical evolution of the Conservative synagogue. In particular, it examines the programmatic development and numerical growth of congregations from one era to the next. Because the concerns of such synagogues have varied over the course of time and because even within the same era there was no uniformity among contemporaneous congregations, the Conservative synagogue is given an institutional definition here: The congregations of interest are those that affiliated with the United Synagogue of America or in other ways identified themselves as Conservative.[2]

Origins

The first Conservative synagogues emerged in response to the increasing polarization of American synagogue life during the late nineteenth century. Following the Civil War, older congregations were swept by a seemingly irreversible tide of Reform Judaism. By 1870, notes historian Leon Jick, "there were few congregations in America in which substantial reforms had *not* been introduced and in which an accelerating program of radical revision was *not* in process. Even some of the surviving old-line Sephardic congregations had succumbed."[3] However, just when the triumph of the Reform Movement appeared inevitable, a countervailing trend began: Hundreds of traditional congregations mushroomed across the American landscape as newly arriving East European immigrants transplanted their synagogues to the New World.

The older American congregations were quite different from the recently founded immigrant synagogues. The former, serving Jews who had arrived in America prior to the onset of the mass migration from Eastern Europe, were frequently housed in ornate cathedrals that had been erected during the synagogue building boom of the post–Civil War era. Prayer services were characterized by Reform innovations: The liturgy included English readings and eliminated many traditional prayers; organ music and the voices of mixed choirs accompanied worship services; rabbis wore black robes and preached sermons either in English or German; and their flock sat in family pews and adhered to western norms of decorum. In contrast, East European *shuls* generally were housed in modest surroundings, since most immigrants could ill afford to subvent a lavish building program. Because many such congregations were formed by *landsleit* (fellow immigrants from the same area of Eastern Europe) services followed the liturgical and musical practices of the Old Country. Immigrant congregations catered primarily to men; if women attended, they were relegated to a separate gallery, as was customary in the traditional synagogue. Those congregations that could afford to hire a rabbi were served by Yiddish-speaking leaders. Thus, by the turn of the century, the great majority of American synagogues either had adopted radical reforms or adhered steadfastly to Old World patterns.[4]

Within both types of congregations, however, bitter struggles erupted between reformers and traditionalists. In the older, so-called Sephardic and German congregations, the tide of reform was powerful, but not uncontainable. Innovations were adopted piecemeal, and, in some cases, congregations blocked the introduction of what then were regarded as more radical reforms. New York's Shaarey Tefilah, for example, voted in 1880 to introduce mixed pews, an organ, a mixed choir, and English prayers; but it also rejected proposals to read the Torah according to a triennial cycle, to censor prayers that "we would not dare to put into the hands of our young daughters and sisters," and to abridge the holiday services. Only decades later, did Shaarey Tefilah fully embrace Reform Judaism. Other congregations introduced moderate innovations, but refused to join the burgeoning Reform Movement. In Ohab Sholom of Newark, a Bohemian congregation, mixed seating was already permitted during the mid–1880s, but, according to its rabbi of that period, Bernard Drachman, it otherwise adhered to the "Orthodox religious code." During the same decade, Beth El in Buffalo, New York, introduced an array of innovations, including mixed seating at Friday evening services and confirmation of both boys and girls; however, traditionalists fought off more radical reforms. To cite an additional case, B'nai Jeshurun in Cleveland sanctioned family pews and late Friday evening services before the turn of the century, but continued to adhere to the traditional prayerbook and Torah readings.[5]

The behavior of these congregations illustrates that, among older congregations, reform was indeed in full swing during the last decades of the nineteenth century. As Herbert Parzen has noted, "The only established American congregations that did not succumb to the current fashion to reform the ritual were the Sephardic congregations in New York and Philadelphia." Such was the pervasiveness of reform that contemporaries questioned whether New York's B'nai Jeshurun would "resist the influence of the Reform movement by which it will be, so to say, surrounded." Yet, B'nai Jeshurun and other congregations did resist the tide; even as they introduced moderate innovations, they rejected the radical program of the Reform Movement. Significantly, these moderately reformed congregations were all of the so-called German variety, consisting of Jews from Central Europe. Their role in the emergence of the Conservative synagogue deserves to be noted, for in time some of these German congregations banded together with comparable East European synagogues to constitute the founding nucleus of the United Synagogue of America, the Conservative synagogue organization.[6]

Controversies over reforms flared in East European congregations as well. In general, moderate reformers were drawn from the ranks of immigrants who were among the first to arrive from Eastern Europe in the 1870s and 1880s. By the turn of the century, they and their children had climbed to the middle rungs of the socioeconomic ladder after having weathered exposure to American life for several decades, so that they were no longer satisfied with the Old World practices of immigrant synagogues. Under the prodding of reformers, congregations gradually

innovated. In some cases, such synagogues simply introduced a few
American practices: Chicago's Rodfei Zedek already permitted mixed
seating in 1905 and shortly thereafter adopted norms of decorum that
were enforced by ushers; the first innovation of Kansas City's Keneseth
Israel was to abolish the auctioning of synagogue honors, and then it
gradually adopted other reforms.[7]

Perhaps the major catalyst for change was the decision of a congregation to relocate to new housing. Once such a decision was taken,
members were forced to consider questions of design, such as whether
to build a separate women's gallery. Equally important, the act of moving
to a new geographic locale symbolized the congregation's break with
immigrant life. The transplantation of Beth Israel Bikkur Cholim from
New York's Lower East Side to its new uptown location in 1887
prompted this thoroughly traditional congregation to introduce mixed
seating. Similarly, when Beth El of Buffalo, a predominantly East European congregation by the turn of the century, relocated in 1910, even
the inclusion of mixed pews and an organ in its new structure did not
satisfy reformers, who, over the next years, agitated for additional innovations. By the first decade of the new century, the more affluent and
Americanized sector of the immigrant population was rapidly abandoning its original areas of urban settlement and finding housing in more
prosperous neighborhoods. In these new quarters, generally areas of
second settlement, they introduced American innovations. Even when
such new congregations formally defined themselves as Orthodox, they
now insisted that English must be the language of public discourse and
some prayers. In time, such congregations voted to introduce mixed
pews, organ music, late Friday evening services, western aesthetic norms,
and special programs for young people. By the onset of World War I,
dozens of such moderately reformed congregations had been established
outside the ghetto areas by first- and second-generation East European
Jews.[8]

The efforts of local Jews to steer both German and East European
congregations on a course of moderate innovation were significantly
abetted by the emergence of the Jewish Theological Seminary as the
rallying point and organizing force for Conservative Judaism. During
the last decades of the nineteenth century, the Sephardic and Central
European rabbis who had founded the Jewish Theological Seminary
Association in 1886 served as spokesmen for Jews dismayed over the
radicalism of American Reform. But it was not until the early twentieth
century that the reorganized seminary wielded sufficient influence to
affect local synagogue life. Its initial contribution was to provide a growing cadre of rabbis to lead congregations that desired a traditional yet

Americanized service. As congregations floundered between traditionalism and reform, they turned to Seminary-trained rabbis (and even rabbinical students) for leadership. In the decade before World War I, early graduates of the Seminary such as Paul Chertoff in Rochester, Max Drob in Buffalo, Charles Hoffman in Newark, C. Hillel Kauvar in Denver, Eugene Kohn in Baltimore, and Marvin Nathan in Philadelphia decisively shaped the programs and practices of their congregations.[9]

Seminary graduates also assumed pulpits in traditional synagogues and gradually nudged their immigrant congregants toward Americanized practices. In such congregations the movement toward moderate reform was slow and frought with danger for young rabbis. At Boston's Mishkan Tefila, for example, Herman Rubenovitz labored for years to convince his board to introduce a mixed choir and organ music. His colleague, Louis Egelson, managed to introduce a few innovations at Washington's Adas Israel, only to be fired when traditionalists gained the upper hand. Despite such setbacks, Seminary-trained rabbis gradually steered traditional congregations toward innovations.[10]

The Seminary assumed more direct leadership in synagogue affairs when it organized the United Synagogue of America in 1913. To be sure, the founders of this body did not share a common vision of its purpose: Some were primarily concerned with establishing a financial base for the Seminary; others saw the new agency as a force for unifying all traditional Jews in a common struggle against Reform; still others viewed it as an instrument for forging a third religious movement between Orthodoxy and Reform. In fact, at the founding convention Solomon Schechter, the first president of the United Synagogue, promised "not to create a new party, but to consolidate an old one." Once established, however, the United Synagogue developed its own momentum. Its very existence made it possible for member congregations to develop a sense of unity as well as a clearly defined identity distinct from the Union of American Hebrew Congregations (Reform) and the Union of Orthodox Jewish Congregations of America. Congregations unwilling to join either body now could rally to the United Synagogue. Moreover, when Jews wanted to establish a new synagogue or revamp the programs of existing congregations, the United Synagogue could offer its support and guidance. By serving as a rallying point and central address for congregations seeking a course of moderate innovation, the United Synagogue helped spur the growth of a new synagogue movement, the Conservative Movement.[11]

The founding of the United Synagogue of America therefore represents the beginning of an new era in the history of the Conservative synagogue. During the three decades prior to 1913, congregations had struggled on their own to define an alternative to Reform and Orthodoxy. It had been, as Joel Blau wrote in 1909, a period of "gropings and wanderings and even of disorder and chaos." The new agency did not immediately bring order out of chaos. Its original mandate from Solomon Schechter to "appeal to all such congregations as have not accepted the [Reform] Union prayer-book nor performed their religious devotions with uncovered heads" was far too vague. In the coming decade, however, the United Synagogue and its affiliated congregations, along with the Seminary and its alumni, gradually crystallized a new synagogue program, a program that was increasingly identified as Conservative Judaism.[12]

The Era of Urban Expansion, 1913–1929

The Conservative synagogue entered its first era of sustained growth and consolidation during the second and third decades of the twentieth century. The extent of this expansion was tangibly evident in the dramatic increase of congregations that joined the United Synagogue. A decade after it had been launched by merely 22 congregations, the new body boasted a membership of over 150 affiliates. By 1929 congregational strength leaped to 229 affiliates, thereby almost matching the 281-member Union of American Hebrew Congregations, which had been in existence since 1873.[13]

One of the more noteworthy features of this stunning expansion was the disparity between patterns of affiliation with the United Synagogue and the population distribution of America's Jews. In 1917, for example, there were an equal number of United Synagogue affiliates in Chicago and in the combined boroughs of Brooklyn and Manhattan, even though close to five times as many Jews resided in these two sections of New York City as lived in Chicago. Figures for 1929 reveal an even greater imbalance between patterns of affiliation and Jewish population density. Why was there only one affiliate in Los Angeles and five in Newark, New Jersey, when both cities contained approximately the same number of Jews? Why did Detroit's 75,000 Jews establish only one Conservative synagogue, whereas Pittsburgh's 53,000 Jews maintained five? Why were there fourteen United Synagogue congregations in Philadelphia and only nine in the Bronx, even though the latter was populated by 150,000 more Jews? And why did Maryland contribute one affiliate and adjacent West Virginia three, when the Jewish population of the former was nearly ten times the size of the latter?[14]

These disparities suggest that a variety of circumstances – aside from population density – accounted for the establishment of Conservative synagogues in particular locations. Perhaps the most universal factor was the upward mobility and Americanization of East European Jews: As immigrants and their children achieved a measure of economic success and moved away from ghetto neighborhoods, they established a new type of synagogue to reflect their current achievements and aspirations.[15] The pace and quality of this upward mobility, however, differed from one locality to the next since they depended upon the health of the local economy, the possibility for economic advancement, and the availability of housing. In addition, two other local peculiarities played a role: whether East European Jews had settled in a particular city during the early years of mass migration (and therefore had experienced decades of exposure to American life by the 1920s); and whether local immigrant culture was sufficiently developed to retard the process of Americanization or so attenuated that it had little hold on the newcomers.

Although these impersonal processes were important, the initiative of key individuals often was the decisive factor in the establishment of a Conservative synagogue in a particular locality. Congregational histories are replete with oral traditions about the determination and forcefulness of a few strong-willed and wealthy laymen who convinced others of the need to modernize a traditional synagogue or establish a new congregation that would better serve the needs of the community. Rabbinic leadership was equally crucial. Even though rabbis rarely founded Conservative congregations, but generally assumed leadership of synagogues that already had decided to introduce some innovations, they nonetheless played a critical role in providing a coherent program of congregational practices for a laity that possessed only an ill-defined agenda for change. For this reason, synagogue historians routinely credit Seminary-trained rabbis with introducing new religious rituals, educational programs, and social activities. These rabbis did not create their synagogues, but they did transform their congregants' vague impulse for change into specific new programs. Furthermore, they fostered institutional allegiance to the national bodies of the Conservative Movement, thereby shaping their congregations' identities and legitimizing the adoption of more uniform Conservative practices. Thus the presence of lay and rabbinic leadership committed to a particular program was crucial in the formation of Conservative synagogues.[16]

A final factor in the growth of Conservative synagogues was the success of the United Synagogue in promoting its programs to local congregations. Shortly after its founding, the synagogue body established new means to win adherents: It organized several district offices around the country to publicize United Synagogue activities; it published a newsletter that advertised and coordinated the activities of affiliates; and it established a women's auxiliary, the Women's League of the United

Synagogue, to widen its appeal and programs. With the appointment in 1917 of Rabbi Samuel Cohen as director of activities, the United Synagogue embarked on an aggressive campaign to attract new affiliates. Cohen offered guidance to congregations that had no clear denominational allegiances in the hope of winning them to the Conservative cause. Moreover, he approached lay leaders in communities where there was no Conservative presence and tried to convince them of the need to establish a congregation affiliated with the United Synagogue.[17]

Although affiliates of the United Synagogue were hardly identical during this period, they shared several common concerns and features. Perhaps most important, these synagogues consciously strove to attract the Americanized children of immigrants from Eastern Europe. Philip Joslin, the lay leader most responsible for the founding of Providence's Temple Emanu-el, expressed an oft-repeated sentiment when he warned: "Unless something is done to check the indifference and apathy which is on the daily increase, particularly among our growing children and young folks, numberless of our people will be estranged and forever lost to the faith of their ancestry. I have the firm conviction that an appeal in a tongue and under conditions which are more tasteful to our modern American life, yet not forgetting the fundamentals, the traditions and the ideals of Judaism, is the way to the solution to the problem."[18] In the opinion of lay leaders such as Philip Joslin, neither the foreign ways of Orthodox immigrant congregations nor the radical departures from traditionalism in American Reform temples could attract the second generation.

In the light of their concern over the apathy of young people, it is not surprising that Conservative leaders oriented their congregations to meet the needs of youth. Characteristically, when a Conservative congregation was formed, it swiftly organized a Hebrew School. (Some congregations even developed schools before they could arrange for regular religious services.) Indeed, the general growth of Jewish congregational schools in America coincided with the expansion of Conservative synagogues. In New York, for example, enrollments in congregational schools leaped by 150 percent between 1917 and 1927, a pattern closely paralleled in the rest of the country. Although they hardly held a monopoly on congregational schools, Conservative synagogues accounted for much of this growth. Moreover, it was already in the decades of the 1920s that Conservative congregations struggled to shift Jewish education from the Sunday school (one day a week) format common in Reform temples to the thrice-weekly program of the Hebrew school. At first, they offered members a choice of sending their children to Sunday school or Hebrew school; but then gradually some congregations began to require several years of Hebrew school education as a prerequisite for the celebration of a Bar Mitzvah.[19]

Congregational programs focused on the needs of youth in other ways, as well. According to Rabbinical Assembly surveys taken in 1933 and 1936, close to three-quarters of rabbinic respondents claimed that their congregations organized special children's services and 65 percent celebrated the educational achievements of young people at special confirmation or consecration services, programs that simply did not exist in traditional synagogues. Efforts were also made to attract young adults to the synagogue by orienting late Friday evening services to their interests; such services were capped by lectures and discussions on topics of particular interest to younger American-born Jews. Congregations also founded special young people's clubs, which in 1921 were organized nationally in the United Synagogue's Young Folk's League.[20]

A second area of concern to founders of Conservative synagogues was the development of religious services that balanced traditional Jewish and modern American values. The ten-point program put forth in 1922 by founders of the Jamaica Jewish Center both illustrates how this was done and adumbrates much of the Conservative synagogue's religious program to the present day: "I. Family pews; II. Conservative services in Hebrew and English; III. English preaching; IV. A Mixed Choir consisting of boys and girls; V. Congregational singing; VI. Two services on Fridays: the first at Sundown all year round, and the second at 8:00 o'clock for the fall and winter seasons only; VII. Confirmation exercises on Shevuoth; VIII. Observing the first and last two days of each and every holiday; IX. Eliminating all auctioneering of *aliyot* and excessive *mi-Sheberachs* on High Holidays; X. Daily services, mornings and evenings when a permanent house of worship is established."[21] On the one hand, traditional observances such as the Sabbath, all holidays, and daily worship services were affirmed; on the other hand, western church norms such as English preaching, congregational singing, and a choir were introduced, and undecorous practices such as the auctioning of honors were eliminated. It was symptomatic of the tension that the congregation offered two Friday evening services – one at the traditional time and another at an hour more convenient for working people.

A survey on ritual undertaken by Rabbi Morris Silverman in 1933 provides some limited quantitative information on the uniformity of particular religious practices in Conservative synagogues around the country. On the basis of 110 responses from Rabbinical Assembly members (a better than 50 percent rate of return), Silverman reported the following: (1) approximately 70 percent of congregations conducted daily services; (2) late Friday evening services were almost universal (95 percent of the respondents officiated at such services) and included many English readings and supplementary selections that were not based on the traditional liturgy; (3) Saturday morning services conformed to the traditional liturgy and Torah readings (only two respondents used the triennial cycle and five more abridged the Torah portion); (4) approximately 20 percent of congregations had organs, but only half of these allowed them to be played on the Sabbath or holidays; (5) Bat Mitzvah ceremonies for girls were virtually nonexistent in this period (many rabbis did not even know what they were); (6) fewer than one-fifth of congregations held special Friday evening services on the eve of American holidays; (7) in the absence of a uniform prayerbook, at least seven different *Siddurim* were in use for daily services and several *Maḥzorim* were employed on the High Holidays, whereas for festivals the prayerbook recently compiled under the United Synagogue's auspices was gaining a small following; (8) over one-third of rabbis preached sermons both on Friday evenings and Saturday mornings.[22] (The survey provides no information on the presence of mixed pews, a practice that apparently was taken for granted in United Synagogue congregations by the 1920s and 1930s.)

Attendance figures for this period are sketchy, but several patterns were frequently discussed in contemporary journals. In general, synagogue services were poorly attended, except on the High Holidays. Counts of actual synagogue attendance in several small Jewish communities around the country in 1928 indicate that fewer than 20 percent of Jews attended *any* synagogue on a regular Sabbath, a figure that also held true for members of Conservative synagogues. The demographic profile of those who did attend Conservative synagogues, however, differed sharply from the population that frequented Orthodox immigrant congregations. Whereas adult men virtually monopolized the latter, they were underrepresented in Conservative synagogues on the average Sabbath. Reporting on his congregation in Wilkes-Barre, Pennsylvania, Rabbi Louis Levitsky noted in 1936 that only a half-dozen men out of a membership of 250 did *not* go to work on Saturday. Although the Great Depression may have accounted in part for this stunning statistic, articles written in the early 1920s already noted the emptiness of Conservative synagogues on the Sabbath because men were away at work. As a consequence, noted Rabbi Alter Landesman, "in many Conservative congregations and in practically all of the Reform congregations the proportion of women and children is very large on Saturday mornings."[23]

It is in this context that the activities of women in the Conservative synagogue must be understood. Writing in the *United Synagogue Recorder* in 1921, Deborah Melamed urged Jewish women to participate more in religious services by filling the pews left vacant by men and by learning to join in congregational prayers and singing. Significantly, Melamed entitled her essay "Woman's Opportunity in the Synagogue." By their sheer presence, women could no longer be relegated to passive and minor roles: If they were to constitute the majority of worshipers at prayer services, they could not be segregated in a separate gallery; and if they were to organize fund-raising events, bazaars, school programs, and social activities, they would have to be given places on congregational boards. Thus, out of practical necessity as much as personal taste and ideology, women assumed a more active role in congregational life virtually from the inception of the Conservative synagogue.[24]

The low level of attendance also occasioned a far-reaching rethinking of the structure and purpose of synagogues. As Rabbi Israel Levinthal of the Brooklyn Jewish Center noted during this period, "The Synagogue as a *Beth Hatefilah* has lost its hold upon the masses . . . ; [therefore] some institution would have to be created that could and would attract the people so that the group consciousness of the Jew might be maintained." That new institution was the synagogue-center. Originally conceived by Professor Mordecai Kaplan of the Jewish Theological Seminary as a "deliberate and conscious . . . experiment to help us solve the problem of Jewish life and religion," the center was to serve as a setting for prayer, education, physical recreation, and social action. Such an environment could best foster a vibrant Jewish life. The synagogue-center, contended the president of the Brooklyn Jewish Center, "will show the world the ideal that you can be a Jew and enjoy life, and will express in every thing you do that the same thing can be done in a Jewish way." Not coincidentally, the center's manifold programs also served as a magnet to bring Jews back to the synagogue. To quote a gushing contemporary description of another synagogue-center in New York, B'nai Jeshurun serves "every member of every family affiliated with our congregation. The center building is used every afternoon and every evening of the week by our own groups who come here for educational, philanthropic, social, and athletic activities. Our synagogue is fast becoming the real center of the whole of Jewish life for all the week 'round."[25]

Convinced that the synagogue-center could become such a communal center, Conservative congregations embarked on a frenzied building program during the 1920s. New congregations founded in second and third areas of settlement hastily drafted ambitious plans for mammoth edifices to house a panoply of recreational and social programs, while existing congregations, under pressure to compete, poured considerable resources into programs for expansion. By the late 1920s, when construction was in full swing, over thirty new structures were dedicated in a one-year period (most were Conservative). A survey of fourteen Conservative congregations scattered across the country found that construction expenses ranged from $35,000 to one million dollars, with the average synagogue shouldering costs of nearly a quarter of a million dollars. Much of this construction was undertaken in the anticipation of expanded membership, but, whereas some congregations in fact grew within a few years from a few score members to over one thousand families, others struggled under staggering mortgage debts when their optimistic expectations of increased membership proved erroneous. Despite the dangers of overexpansion, lavish synagogue-centers proliferated. They served both as a testament to the new middle-class attainments of their members, upwardly mobile East European Jews, as well as a means to remedy the decline of the synagogue as a house of prayer.[26]

Some dissenting voices, however, questioned the wisdom of burdening congregations with the responsibility of supporting elaborate social and recreational programs. In an address to his rabbinic colleagues, Rabbi Israel Goldstein lamented the failure of centers to live up to expectations:

> Whereas the hope of the Synagogue Center was to Synagogize the tone of the secular activities of the family, the effect has been the secularization of the place of the Synagogue. . . . If the Synagogue Center has had the effect of easing the distinction between the sacred and the secular, it has been at the expense of the sacred. The Synagogue as a week-end institution may have seemed aloof and ineffective. As a week-day institution, functioning through the Center, it has become banal, and even vulgar.

It could be demonstrated easily that the popularity of social and recreational functions did not translate into impressive attendance figures at worship services. Still, proponents of the synagogue-center rejoiced at the numbers of people who were now flocking to the synagogue, arguing that "many will come for other purposes than to meet God. But let them come."[27]

These debates came to a halt when new fiscal circumstances severely curtailed synagogue construction during the 1930s. With the onset of the Great Depression, synagogues were hard-pressed to maintain, let alone expand, their facilities. Most congregations sustained a severe loss of membership so that existing facilities went underutilized. At Sinai Congregation in Los Angeles, for example, 350 member families struggled to keep afloat a synagogue that had been built for a far larger membership (its sanctuary alone seated over 1,200 people). The problem was not simply caused by a halt in membership growth, but by the loss of members who felt they could not afford to pay dues or other synagogue-related expenses. The experience of Chicago's Rodfei Zedek is illustrative: In 1929 the congregation had 234 member families and 350 children enrolled in its religious school; four years later, membership stood at 113 families and enrollments at 62 pupils. Under such circumstances, additional synagogue expansion was neither warranted nor feasible.[28]

However, the problem went far beyond a moratorium on new construction. Most Conservative congregations struggled to provide services while paying off their enormous mortgage debts. Not surprisingly, synagogues cut their programs, and when that failed, they released their personnel. The experience of Temple Emanuel in Bayonne was particularly depressing, though not atypical: Unable to cover its expenses, the congregation first released its senior rabbi in order to hire a younger and less expensive spiritual leader; not long thereafter, the new rabbi was let go and replaced by a rabbinical student who only officiated at High Holiday services. (Temple Emanuel's cantor also departed in frustration with the congregation owing him close to $1,700 in back pay.) Given these difficult financial problems, Conservative synagogues, like most American religious institutions, endured a decade of stagnation and depression during the 1930s.[29]

The Era of Suburban Growth, 1940–1965

As America emerged from the Great Depression and entered an era of sustained prosperity, the Conservative synagogue experienced its second era of explosive numerical growth. Already during the war years there was evidence of a rebound from the decline of the 1930s: New congregations were formed, existing ones revived, and the United Synagogue found the resources to hire new personnel and establish several new publications. Such growth, however, paled in comparison with the dynamic expansion of the postwar era. United Synagogue membership, which stood at approximately 350 affiliated congregations at the end of the war, leaped to 800 congregations within two decades. Particularly during the 1950s, it seemed that Conservative synagogues were being formed in unending succession. The United Synagogue inducted 131 new congregations from 1955 to 1957, another 58 during the next two years, and 80 additional affiliates from 1959 to 1961.[30] It is little wonder that when rabbis and students of religious life surveyed the contemporary scene at midcentury, they heralded the Conservative synagogue as the paramount institution of American Judaism, one that had much to teach to both Reform and Orthodox congregations.[31]

In contrast to the Conservative synagogues of 1900–1930, which were primarily located in urban centers, the new affiliates were concentrated in suburbia. They were founded by the masses of Jews who joined the larger American population shift from urban to suburban areas. Initially, the greatest growth occurred in the suburbs of New York City, where dozens of new congregations mushroomed in Queens, Nassau, Westchester, and the suburbs of cities in New Jersey. (In Queens and Nassau counties, alone, some fifty new Conservative synagogues were established in the decade after the conclusion of World War II.) Once these areas reached their level of saturation, the greatest growth occurred outside of the New York metropolitan area. This movement profoundly affected the fortunes of existing urban synagogues, which were forced to choose between staying put (and thereby risking eventual abandonment) and transplanting themselves in the surburbs and leaving behind the huge physical facilities they had struggled so hard to build. Congregations that waited too long to decide frequently found their membership base eroded by the inexorable movement of congregants to the new suburban areas.[32]

Although the movement of Jews to the suburbs accounts for the synagogue boom of the postwar era, it does not explain why so many of the new congregations chose to identify as Conservative. In part, the decision was motivated by pragmatic, rather than ideological concerns. Since founders of synagogues could not anticipate how large a Jewish population would eventually concentrate in a particular suburban community, they created middle-of-the-road congregations that would appeal to the broadest spectrum of Jews. As one synagogue organizer told Rabbi Albert Gordon, a Conservative rabbi who wrote several books on the suburbanization of American Jews, "We figured that the Conservative [synagogue] was 'middle of the road' and would not offend any group in the community. So we called it a Conservative congregation." Later, after the Jewish population had grown sufficiently to support additional congregations, Reform and Orthodox synagogues were established as well.[33]

Although such pragmatic considerations undoubtedly were crucial, some additional factors accounted for the astounding growth of Conservative synagogues. A great many congregations were founded by Jews who had previously attended Orthodox synagogues but were no longer satisfied with either the religious practices or social programs of immigrant or American Orthodox congregations. Often housed in delapidated ghettos or unfashionable areas of second settlement and offering congregants only limited programs aside from worship services, such congregations held little appeal to Jews who no longer adhered to Orthodox practices and had Americanized. As a result, some of these congregations moved to the suburbs and merged with new Conservative synagogues. Others tried to accommodate to their congregants' needs by instituting changes in traditional practices. As a consequence, the 1950s were punctuated by a series of bitter controversies between traditionalists and reformers as previously Orthodox congregations began to introduce American innovations. The removal of physical barriers separating men and women in the synagogue and the introduction of mixed pews came to symbolize a congregation's defection from the Orthodox to the Conservative camp.[34]

Perhaps most important, Conservative synagogues mushroomed in the postwar era because they appealed to a specific generational cohort of American Jews. The Jews who joined Conservative synagogues during the 1940s and 1950s were primarily children of East European immigrants who had arrived after the turn of the century (the era of most massive Jewish migration to America). Born in the years between 1900 and 1940, this huge generational cohort came of age in the postwar era and constituted the preponderant majority of Jews who moved to suburbia after World War II. Like the larger population of Americans that participated in this geographic shift, young Jews abandoned urban centers in search of spacious, yet more affordable housing outside of large cities. Many became the first members of their families to own homes. As a consequence of their mobility, however, these Jews were forced to sever their ties to the ethnic communities that had sustained them in urban areas. Having been raised in densely populated Jewish enclaves where identification with Jewishness, if not necessarily Judaism, was taken for granted, they now found themselves in far more integrated neighborhoods that provided no natural outlet for Jewish identification.

Conservative synagogues attracted these young suburban Jews precisely because they were structured as synagogue-centers. Although Rabbi Leo Spitz may have exaggerated somewhat when he declared the synagogue-center a "Conservative patent," the overwhelming majority of Conservative congregations were organized as centers. They did not necessarily boast swimming and gymnasium facilities, but they offered a broad range of social and recreational programs, including men's and women's auxiliaries, dances and entertainment, adult education, fundraising for synagogue and other causes, and sports programs. By offering these activities, suburban Conservative synagogues helped to diminish the loneliness of transplanted urban Jews living on the suburban frontier. They provided a communal setting for Jews who shared common generational experiences, as well as the trials and tribulations of geographic and socioeconomic mobility in postwar America.[35]

Equally important, Conservative synagogues appealed to this generation because, in the words of a contemporary observer, they offered families "a new adventure in Jewishness, expressing itself in formal af-

filiation for the first time in their lives with a Jewish community institution." Sociologist Marshall Sklare has explained why this particular
population was especially in need of Jewish affiliation: "Suburbanization
brought with it the problem of the maintenance of identity, and it was
to the synagogue that the new Jewish suburbanite tended to look for
identity-maintenance. The result was that the synagogue emerged in the
1950s and 1960s as the crucial institution in Jewish life. And Conservatism
exemplified that which was most appealing to the new suburban Jew."
As already noted, Conservative congregations contributed to the maintenance of Jewish identity by offering second-generation Jews a center
for communal activities. Moreover, they appealed to parents who wanted
their children to acquire a measure of Hebraic and Judaic literacy and
also wanted their children to socialize with other young Jews. In the
words of a contemporary promotional leaflet: "The community needs a
place for our children and we adults need some place to carry on our
social lives. What better place can there be than our synagogues?"[36]

All of these factors came into play during the founding of the Israel
Community Center of Levittown, a congregation that was regarded in
the 1950s as the quintessential Conservative synagogue in the model
suburban community. Established in 1948 by World War II veterans and
their wives, the congregation produced a brochure to advertise its programs. The pamphlet begins with the question, "What is the Israel Community Center?" and responds that, as its name implies, it "combines
the functions of a Synagogue with those of a Community Center." This
means that "our members look upon the Center not merely in terms of
'seats for the observance of the three holy days,' but rather do they and
their families look to the Center for 'all-year-round Congregational activity,' social as well as cultural and religious." The pamphlet then pro-
ceeds to announce that its "accent is on youth," not only because it was
founded recently, but because its membership consists of young people.
Finally, it candidly explains what brought its founders to the center:
"Most of our people have had little previous contact with synagogue
life, having hitherto regarded the synagogue as the province of their
elders. Many have not seen the inside of a 'shule' since their Bar Mitzvah.
Now, however, they feel it is time that they 'grow up'. . . . The responsibilities of parenthood have led many to rethink their position with
regard to the Jewish heritage which they now seek to maintain in order
to be able to transmit it to their children." Although the pamphlet briefly
refers to the synagogue as a Conservative congregation affiliated with
the United Synagogue and "dedicated to the advancement of Traditional
Judaism by revitalizing the tradition and making it more inspiring and
more meaningful to the modern American Jew," it nowhere explains its

ritual program or religious services. We need only compare this brochure to the above-mentioned ten-point program of the Jamaica Jewish Center to discover how the concerns and emphases of the Conservative synagogue had changed between 1922 and 1948.[37]

During the postwar decades, the process of achieving a uniform and cohesive program for Conservative synagogues continued. The United Synagogue grew into an extensive bureaucracy that strove to shape the practices of its affiliates. Separate offices developed curricula for synagogue schools, plans for congregational budgeting, and guidelines for synagogue ritual practices. (The United Synagogue even offered architectural blueprints to congregations planning to construct new facilities). Auxiliaries such as the Women's League for Conservative Judaism, the Federation of Men's Clubs, and the United Synagogue Youth vastly expanded their programs and publications to bring a measure of national cohesiveness to local synagogue branches. And all of these groups cooperated with other Conservative agencies to produce uniform synagogue materials – most notably, prayerbooks and other liturgical texts. Although it is not possible to measure the extent of influence these national bodies exerted over local congregations, it is evident that they managed, through regional and national conventions, publications, and direct advisory programs, to bring a degree of conformity to affiliated congregations.[38]

One of the central features of Conservative synagogues during this period was their massive investment in congregational schools. According to a survey conducted in the mid-1960s, over 25 percent of synagogue budgets were spent on school programs, an allocation second only to the cost of salaries for synagogue personnel. Certainly, this arrangement of budgetary priorities was in part dictated by the fact that a significant percentage of synagogue members consisted of parents with school-age children. But it also signified the emphasis of Conservative synagogues on youth during the baby boom era. It was widely recognized that a significant number of synagogue members joined congregations primarily in order to provide their children with a Jewish education. Hence congregations used their schools as a means to develop a larger membership: They required parents to become synagogue members if they wished to enroll their children in the congregational school. (According to a 1950 survey, 40 percent of Conservative synagogues did not even charge tuition, but rather financed their schools exclusively through membership dues.) In this manner, congregations attracted new members who were otherwise indifferent to synagogue programs and involved them in the life of the synagogue through PTA activities.[39]

From the perspective of synagogue lay leaders and especially rabbis, there was an additional reason to develop strong school programs: to teach synagogue skills to the coming generation. As early as 1928, Max Arzt, a leading pulpit rabbi who later assumed national positions in the Conservative Movement, warned that Sunday schools were not only inadequate, but actually posed a danger to Conservative congregations.

> From the view of the synagogue which has the traditional prayerbook and which conducts most of the service in Hebrew, the Sunday School is an enigma. It surely does not and cannot train its pupils for participation in a traditional service and at best it can graduate them into a reform temple where Hebrew is limited to the *Borchu* and the *Shema*. Most of our congregations have now come to realize that a good Hebrew School with an intensive course of instruction and with Hebrew as the vehicle of that instruction, is indispensable to their own future – for when a Jew ceases to tolerate Hebrew he clamors for a translated service and eventually emerges as a Jew of the reform persuasion.

Thus, in order to ensure that young people would develop sufficient Hebrew skills to follow Conservative services, it became imperative for congregations to develop their school programs. It was simply impossible to foster language skills, let alone teach children about ritual practices, the Bible, Jewish history, and other areas of Judaica, within the time constraints of a Sunday school program.[40]

As a consequence of these concerns, a remarkably forceful movement developed within the Conservative Movement to eliminate Sunday schools and replace them with three-day-a-week Hebrew schools. As noted above, a few congregations had already introduced such programs during the 1920s, but it was not until the 1940s and 1950s that this became a movement-wide trend. It began with congregations imposing a requirement upon boys that they attend Hebrew school three days a week for a minimum of three years prior to their Bar Mitzvah. But gradually, the number of mandatory years of Hebrew school was extended and girls, too, were pushed into these schools. According to a survey conducted by the United Synagogue during the 1950s, 74 percent of responding Conservative congregations did not permit their students to attend school only on Sundays. In addition, 7.5 percent required weekday school attendance by ages six and seven, 50 percent by age eight, and another 38 percent by age nine.[41]

There were several consequences to this heavy investment in Hebrew school education. First, Conservative supplementary schools were partly responsible for the demise of communal schools. Whereas in the 1920s the majority of children in the United States who were enrolled in Jewish schools were still educated under communal auspices, by the end of the 1920s most were enrolled in congregational schools, a trend that continued to accelerate in subsequent decades. Second, Conservative efforts ensured the rapid growth of Hebrew schools: Outside New York, almost half the students enrolled in three-day-a-week schools were Conservative in comparison with 34 percent of Jewish children in Sunday schools; in the New York metropolitan area, Hebrew school enrollment was even higher, accounting for nearly three-quarters of all Conservative children.[42] Third, Hebrew school enrollment occurred at the expense of Conservative day schools: Although a few congregations actually founded their own day schools and thereby helped develop the Solomon Schechter Day School movement, most Conservative synagogues promoted Hebrew schools as the preferred setting for Jewish education. As a result, fewer than 5 percent of children enrolled in day schools outside New York during the 1950s were Conservative (in New York this figure was higher).[43] Finally, Conservative congregations paid a price for their insistence upon Hebrew school education. A leading Conservative rabbinic leader has directly attributed the growth of Reform temples in suburbia to the educational demands imposed by Conservative synagogues on prospective Bar Mitzvah boys. Although an exaggeration, this view is supported by the testimony of some local rabbis. In the late 1940s, for example, a rabbi in Youngstown, Ohio, reported that his congregation lost ninety families within two years after it began to require three-day-a-week school attendance; all of these families joined the local Reform temple, whose rabbi proclaimed, "come one day a week to us and they will be just as good Jews."[44]

Given their strong emphasis upon children, it is noteworthy that Conservative synagogues did not invest heavily in extracurricular programs for youth. As of the mid-1960s, merely 2½ percent of synagogue budgets were spent on youth programs.[45] Although many congregations ran programs for children, they often did not bother to hire professional youth directors; in the early 1950s, for example, fewer than one-quarter of surveyed Conservative synagogues employed a youth director, whereas close to 50 percent relied upon volunteers. Synagogue youth programs varied widely: A larger congregation such as Philadelphia's Har Zion, boasted a range of activities for nursery school children to college age youth, which served some 1,500 young people; other congregations even developed summer camping programs that eventually provided the nucleus for the Ramah Camping movement; but others, in contrast, offered few activities for children other than special youth services.[46]

The greatest degree of uniformity achieved by Conservative synagogues during this period was in the area of public religious and ritual life. One of the most universally accepted practices was the celebration of late Friday evening services. According to a 1941 survey, 97 percent of rabbinic respondents indicated that they conducted such services (70 percent also provided early Friday evening services). As noted by Rabbi Samuel Cohen, these services developed because of the "difficulty of securing an adequate attendance on the Sabbath morning"; it was felt that "a great deal of the Sabbath spirit is saved when the congregation establishes a late Friday evening service." Rabbis strove to make these services even more popular by dedicating Friday evening services to the celebration of special occasions – Balfour Day, Mother's Day, Thanksgiving, and so on – and to honor specific synagogue or other Jewish groups – men's clubs, Sisterhood, Hadassah, the Jewish War Veterans, Hebrew school students, and the like. It is difficult to ascertain how successful these "special occasion" Sabbaths, as they were then called, proved in attracting more worshipers.[47]

On the whole, at least during the 1940s and 1950s, Conservative synagogues adhered to the traditional service on Sabbath mornings. On the basis of a survey conducted for the Rabbinical Assembly in 1941, Rabbi Max Routtenberg claimed that "in the overwhelming majority of cases, the traditional *Shacharis* is conducted with almost no modification or change" and virtually no supplementary readings were used. Similarly, 81 percent of rabbis surveyed reported that Torah readings still accorded with the annual cycle and with the traditional number of men called to the Torah. In the preponderant majority of congregations, the traditional *Haphtorah* portion continued to be chanted in the original Hebrew. Surprisingly, it was still common in the vast majority of congregations of this period for each recipient of a Torah honor to receive a separate benediction (*mi-Sheberach*). In time, a great deal of experimentation developed in several areas as congregations adopted the triennial cycle, eliminated the *mi-Sheberach*, and omitted parts of the traditional liturgy.[48]

A major breakthrough toward liturgical uniformity occurred when the Rabbinical Assembly and the United Synagogue agreed to adopt a Conservative prayerbook that had been prepared by Rabbi Morris Silverman. Introduced in the late 1940s, the *Sabbath and Festival Prayerbook* was widely employed by Conservative congregations. Within two years of its official adoption, it was already in use in 185 congregations. Silverman's *High Holiday Prayerbook* also won official sanction and by the mid-1960s was employed in over 85 percent of Conservative synagogues. With these texts, Conservative synagogues were able to achieve two long-desired goals. First, they now possessed a flexible liturgical work that contained a variety of poems and prayers suitable for special occasions. Equally important, they now had a common liturgical text deemed acceptable by the vast majority of United Synagogue affiliates. The Silverman prayerbooks brought a new-found uniformity of religious worship to Conservative synagogues.[49]

Several other innovations gradually gained wide usage. By 1948, for example, a "Synagogue Ritual Survey" found unanimous acceptance of mixed pews (although some congregations still maintained both mixed pews and special sections for men and women who preferred to sit separately). According to this survey, two-thirds of congregations also employed a mixed choir. The vast majority also held confirmation ceremonies for both boys and girls. Only 20 percent, however, permitted the playing of an organ at Friday evening or Sabbath services and only one-third celebrated the Bat Mitzvah of girls who had come of age. The latter practice, however, spread rapidly during the next decade.[50]

Despite the growing clarity and uniformity of religious practices, Conservative synagogues continued to suffer from a major gap between official policies and the practices of members. Thus, although the United Synagogue adopted a set of "Standards for Synagogue Practice" that required all affiliates to observe the Sabbath and traditional dietary restrictions on synagogue-owned property, the vast majority of synagogue members observed neither. Similarly, when congregations pledged to accept the rabbi as the "authority on all matters of Jewish law and practices and as the interpreter of the decisions rendered and principles established by the Committee on Jewish Law and Standards of the Rabbinical Assembly," they were affirming a public policy that had little relevance to the private lives of individual synagogue members. The contrast between official religious policy and private behavior was made painfully clear in a "National Survey of Synagogue Leadership" conducted by the United Synagogue in the early 1950s. On the basis of questionnaires sent both to congregations and synagogue leaders, the survey found that: (1) two-thirds of members did not attend even late Friday evening services with any regularity, and attendance at Sabbath morning and holiday services was negligible; (2) even among synagogue leaders, 85 percent stated that they did not say daily prayers either at home or in the synagogue; (3) only 35 percent of such leaders claimed they could follow the Hebrew services and comprehend "all" or "a lot" of the liturgy, whereas barely half claimed they could "follow the Hebrew but can understand very little of it"; (4) only slightly more than one-third of leaders kept Jewish dietary laws at home; (5) more than half of the leadership in Conservative congregations could "boast any satisfactory acquaintance with the aims, tendencies and practices of the Conservative movement;" (6) only a small minority of synagogue members involved themselves in administrative work or accepted positions of leadership. Reporting on these findings, Dr. Emil Lehman, executive director of the United Synagogue, noted that the survey takes "us behind the scenes into the living rooms where the game of congregational politics is played with great fervor . . . and [turns] the spotlight on stately synagogues filled often with the heavy emptiness of empty pews."[51]

In an attempt to remedy this situation, synagogues and especially their rabbis launched a variety of programs to educate congregants and woo them to worship services. The Conservative rabbinate especially focused on intensifying the level of congregants' Sabbath observance with a special campaign launched during the 1950s. At least one pulpit rabbi administered an oath on the Day of Atonement in which his congregants pledged to observe every Sabbath "by kindling the Sabbath candles and reciting the Kiddush at home and by attending the Synagogue with my family." Although it is impossible to determine the success of these efforts, it is clear that low levels of synagogue attendance continued to plague congregations. Whereas synagogue programs for recreation, socializing, and especially education continued to attract impressive numbers of people, religious services were sparsely attended, a trend that deeply disturbed rabbinic and lay leaders who scrutinized the Conservative synagogue during its era of most dynamic growth and robust expansion.[52]

Recent Trends

Although it is not yet possible to characterize the nature of Conservative synagogues in the last third of the twentieth century, several new trends are apparent. For one thing, the demographic decline of American Jewry has brought a halt to the frenetic pace of synagogue growth that was characteristic of the two postwar decades. During the years from 1965 to 1971, for example, not one new Conservative synagogue was founded.[53] Moreover, the needs and interests of synagogue members shifted substantially during the 1960s and 1970s in response to changing American norms as well as new developments in Jewish communal life. As a consequence, Conservative synagogues have innovated and experimented in order to better serve the needs of their members and involve unaffiliated Jews in synagogue life.

Already during the mid-1960s, Conservative leaders took note of the decline in synagogue membership. Not only was it more difficult to recruit new members, but existing congregants slowly began to drift away from the synagogue. One of the major factors responsible for this decline in membership was the decision of some parents to drop their synagogue membership after their youngest child had celebrated the Bar or Bat Mitzvah. A 1965 United Synagogue survey found that during the previous three years, the primary reason members left a congregation other than death or geographic relocation was that a "son had completed Bar Mitzvah or Hebrew School." Whereas young parents flocked to Conservative congregations during the postwar baby-boom years in order to provide a Jewish education for their children, now that those children had completed their studies, some parents no longer felt compelled to retain their membership. Not surprisingly, congregational schools suffered a decline in enrollments and were forced to curtail or eliminate their programs; more generally, the 1970s witnessed numerous mergers between Conservative schools and even synagogues because individual congregations could no longer sustain their own programs.[54]

Most congregations, however, were less affected by declining membership than by the aging of their congregational population. This pattern was made particularly evident in a 1979 study conducted by Charles Liebman and Saul Shapiro that found the greatest number of Conservative synagogue members in the age cohorts from forty-six to sixty. By contrast, there were far fewer members in the age cohorts from twenty-six to forty-five. The authors concluded that although American Jewry, in general, is aging, the membership of Conservative synagogues is aging even more rapidly. Put differently, Conservative synagogues were simply not retaining the allegiance of their younger people. Instead, they were populated mainly by Jews who had come of age during the great postwar expansion, a cohort that had reached late middle age by the end of the 1970s. Liebman stated matters bluntly:

> The data suggested that the Conservative movement of the 1970s resembled Orthodoxy of fifty years ago – an appearance of numerical strength but the absence of a strong infrastructure. Orthodoxy's mass strength was confined to first generation American Jews. It never made significant inroads among second generation American Jews. It appeared that Conservative Judaism as the mass movement of American Jews might be a peculiarly second generation American Jewish phenomenon. However, unlike Orthodoxy, it was not clear that Conservative Judaism had a "hard core" membership around whom it might seek to rebuild itself. On the other hand, the data were not clear that such a group was absent.

The question, therefore, was whether Conservative synagogues could replenish themselves by attracting sufficient numbers of third- and fourth-generation Jews.[55]

In recent years it appears that greater numbers of young families *are* joining Conservative congregations. Members of the 1960s generation who deferred marriage and child rearing (as well as joining a synagogue) are belatedly starting families and seeking congregations in which to raise and educate their children. Although conclusive data are not available, there is evidence that Conservative congregations are gradually attracting younger people. In some cases, congregations located in new sunbelt communities or in recently constructed suburban subdivisions are attracting primarily young families, much as the Levittown type of congregations did that were founded during the postwar suburban boom. In other cases, existing congregations have developed programs to attract singles and young couples. Among the most dynamic Conservative congregations in the early 1980s are urban synagogues that were eclipsed during the suburban era and have suddenly experienced rejuvenation because of the gentrification of their urban environment.[56] Although these developments attest to the vitality of some congregations, they cannot entirely forestall the numerical decline of Conservative synagogues during the last decades of the twentieth century.

In order to broaden their appeal, as well as meet the changing concerns of their members, Conservative synagogues have developed new kinds of programs in recent years. To begin with, efforts have been made to foster a less formal atmosphere in the synagogue and to return to more traditional concepts of Jewish worship. Symptomatic of such efforts were innovations adopted by Congregation B'nai Jeshurun in New York, the oldest continuously functioning Conservative synagogue in the United States: During the 1970s, the synagogue ceased to employ an organ and "encouraged Jews to *daven* rather than worship." In many congregations, rabbis opted for a less formal role, both by ceasing to dress in black robes and by using their time at the pulpit to teach, rather than deliver a sermon. In addition, a perceptible shift occurred in the focus of Sabbath programs, with congregations downplaying late Friday evening services and emphasizing Sabbath morning services instead.[57] All of these trends indicate a return to traditionalism and a rejection of churchlike behavior, patterns that are evident in other denominational synagogues as well. They may indicate that Jews, like other Americans, are returning to tradition; or that Jews feel so at home in America that they are willing to reinstate rituals regarded as too old-fashioned and alien by earlier generations.

A more comprehensive attempt to break down the formality of large congregations found expression in the formation of *Havurot* within Conservative synagogues. Originating on college campuses during the 1960s, the *Havurot* were increasingly embraced by synagogues as a means of reducing the levels of alienation felt by members of huge and impersonal congregations. The *Havurah* was defined by Bernard Reisman, a Brandeis University sociologist, as "a small community of like-minded individuals and families who form together as a Jewish fellowship to offer one another social support and to support and pursue self-directed programs of Jewish study, celebration, and community service."[58] *Havurot* serve as a means of dividing the membership of large, impersonal congregations into smaller, more intimate units. *Havurot*, in brief, seek to create a sense of community among congregants.

Synagogue *Havurot* focus their activities principally on study, communal meals, and holiday celebrations; in some cases, they also hold prayer services and retreats away from the main congregation. Not surprisingly, such separatist activities cause concern among both rabbis and lay leaders who fear that *Havurot* will destroy the unity of congregations. Despite such fears, *Havurot* continue to proliferate in synagogues. According to a recent study, synagogue *Havurot* are most apt to be found in "large, non-Orthodox, suburban [congregations] founded after the Second World War, and with a predominant membership of adults aged between 40 and 59 years." Synagogues in the American West are most likely to sponsor *Havurot*.[59] Although it is not yet possible to assess the long-term importance of such fellowships, in Conservative congregations they clearly represent a departure from the trend toward ever larger synagogues. It remains to be seen whether the quest for fellowship will collide with the very different agenda of synagogue-centers, for whereas the *Havurah* thrives on the intimacy possible only in small groups, the synagogue-center cannot function without a large, critical mass of financial supporters and participants.

Undoubtedly, the most far-reaching changes in Conservative congregations during the past decade have focused on the changing role of women in the synagogue. Although women have participated to a greater extent in Conservative synagogues than in traditional Orthodox congregations, it was only during the 1970s that congregations moved toward granting women total equality in synagogue life. The first step in this direction, of course, was to eliminate women's galleries, which had separated women not only from men, but also from the focal points of the service – the *bimah* (when the cantor stands and the Torah is read), the ark housing Torah scrolls, and the pulpit. Mixed seating did not, however, result in equal participation in the service. Only gradually could women play any role in the service and then, as Marshall Sklare noted still in the 1950s, they were excluded from "the ritual surrounding the handling and reading of the Torah scrolls." Yet even this varied, Sklare observed, "according to the sanctity of the service. During the High Holidays the exclusion of females from the pulpit is almost complete. The procedure is modified at times during the less awesome Sabbath morning service. Women are frequently allowed considerable freedom at Friday evening worship, for the Torah scrolls are not particularly important in this service." For the most part, women were only allowed to recite special liturgical poems – especially English prayers – and to open and close the ark; they could not lead the services, be counted as part of the prayer quorum (*minyan*), or enjoy a Torah honor.[60]

The most important breakthrough for women during the middle decades of the century was the adoption of Bat Mitzvah rituals. As noted above, such programs were virtually unknown until the post–World War II era, despite the fact that the Society for the Advancement of Judaism, an innovative United Synagogue congregation led by Rabbi Mordecai Kaplan and guided by his Reconstructionist philosophy, had already instituted Bat Mitzvah services during the 1920s. Matters changed dramatically in the 1950s and 1960s however, as increasing numbers of Conservative congregations introduced Bat Mitzvah ceremonies on Friday evenings or Sabbath mornings.[61] During the course of these services, girls who had come of age chanted from the prophetic works and sometimes even from the Torah scrolls – honors that were not granted to their mothers. The activities of Bat Mitzvah girls pioneered the way for adult women: First, by their participation in Torah and prayer-related rituals, Bat Mitzvah girls began the process of legitimizing the involvement of all females in such rites. Second, when they grew to adulthood, women who had at an earlier age participated more in synagogue services during their Bat Mitzvah ceremonies, refused to accept their present exclusion from prayer and Torah rites; they thus formed an important body for change in the status of women in the synagogue.

Changes also occurred in the participation of women in synagogue administration, albeit at a slow pace. Two surveys conducted during the mid-1970s illustrate the dimensions of this change. In a survey of Midwestern congregations conducted by the United Synagogue, 100 percent of the responding synagogues indicated that women could serve on the congregational board and could chair committees, and 87 percent permitted women to serve as president or chairman of the board. In practice, however, not one congregation had ever elected a woman to the last two positions. A national survey conducted by the Women's League for Conservative Judaism based on responses by 437 Sisterhoods (a better than 50 percent return) discovered that twenty-one Conservative congregations had elected women to preside over them, and over two-thirds had elected women to chair committees or serve on their boards. Thus, by the 1970s women had made considerable progress in assuming administrative positions, but they rarely were elected to their congregations' highest offices, a circumstance all the more remarkable when we consider that women may well constitute the majority of worshipers in Conservative synagogues.[62]

The status of women in Conservative ritual and administrative life has undergone rapid and sweeping changes during the 1970s and early 1980s. To recognize the dimensions of change, we need only refer to a survey of some 250 Conservative rabbis conducted in 1962 by Rabbi Aaron Blumenthal, the author of a responsum that permitted women to receive Torah honors. Blumenthal's survey found that only 7 percent of congregations granted women Torah honors (*aliyot*) on a regular basis and 17 percent on special occasions; only 6 percent allowed women to be counted in the prayer quorum; and 11 percent allowed women to read from the Torah and 33 percent from the prophets (*Haphtorah*). Surveys conducted in the mid-1970s, present a dramatically different situation: The majority of congregations surveyed permitted women to speak from the pulpit; and one-third to one-half of congregations counted women in the quorum, granted them *aliyot*, and permitted them to chant part of the service. According to the most recent survey, well over 50 percent of Conservative congregations now grant *aliyot* to women at least on some occasions. Concluding their survey of "Women in the Synagogue Today," Daniel Elazar and Rela Monson contend that urban and small town congregations, particularly on the East Coast, have retained more traditional roles for women, whereas Conservative congregations on the West Coast, in suburban areas, and with a predominant membership under forty years of age are most likely to permit women to participate with full equality.[63] It seems likely that such policies will gain wider acceptance as women enter the Conservative rabbinate and cantorate in the late 1980s.

In the preceding historical survey, Conservative synagogues have been defined in institutional terms – as affiliates of the United Synagogue of America. Beyond such institutional loyalties, what shared rituals, programs, and points of view are held in common by member congregations of the United Synagogue of America? To begin with, there are commonalities in the balance of traditional and innovative rituals practiced in Conservative congregations. From their inception, Conservative synagogues have endeavored to conduct thrice-daily prayer services according to the hallowed liturgy and mainly in Hebrew. But they also have instituted reforms in the ritual such as the inclusion of

English prayers, the adoption of the triennial cycle of Torah readings, and the elimination or modification of prayers relating to the sacrificial worship of ancient Israel. Also in keeping with tradition, men (and often women) cover their heads during prayer and don prayer shawls; but men and women also sit together, a practice long identified solely with American Reform synagogues. These commonalities should not obscure the significant differences in worship that have appeared in Conservative synagogues: Throughout the century, there has never been a uniform prayerbook adopted by all congregations; and in our own time, congregations vary greatly in the roles assigned to women during the worship service.

Conservative synagogues therefore are not united by a series of uniform practices, but by common concerns and patterns of behavior. In the realm of synagogue ritual there has always been a concern with hewing to a centrist course between the extremes of Orthodoxy and Reform. Conservative congregations have amalgamated traditional usages and prayers with some of the innovations pioneered by Reform. This approach has often been derided as a compromise, and Conservative synagogues have suffered criticism for their inconsistency. If consistency is not defined solely as adherence to a code or fixed ideology, but rather as adherence to a pattern of choices, Conservative congregations have been remarkably consistent in eschewing the extremes of synagogue conduct prevalent in Orthodox and Reform congregations. Instead, they have adopted elements of both. Within a given locality, Conservative synagogues characteristically include more traditional customs than Reform temples and more innovations than Orthodox congregations.

A second historical pattern characteristic of Conservative congregations is found in their broad conception of the synagogue's proper function. Reports on affiliates of the United Synagogue from 1910 to 1920 and during the 1920s consistently highlight the broad range of programs offered, including adult education forums, congregational schools, recreational events, social activities, and auxiliaries for men, women, young adults, and children. Conservative synagogues have not monopolized the concept of the synagogue-center, but they have played a major role in winning wide acceptance for this model of the synagogue.

Without doubt, the central feature of the synagogue-center has been its emphasis upon congregational schooling. Already at the turn of the century, Conservative synagogues pioneered new forms of congregational education. We have seen that in the 1920s and again in the post–World War II era, much of the growth of congregational schools was directly attributable to the efforts of Conservative synagogues. The Hebrew school was especially promoted by United Synagogue congregations, in direct contrast to the investment of Reform temples in Sunday schools and of Orthodox congregations first in communal heder schools and later in day schools. Conservative congregations clearly were not alone in offering Hebrew school education, but they chose thrice-weekly supplementary schools as their preferred vehicle for Jewish education. Moreover, most Conservative congregations not only invested a significant part of their budgets in Hebrew schools, but also risked alienating members by requiring minimum school attendance of all their Bar and Bat Mitzvah children. Clearly, congregational schooling has been a central concern of Conservative synagogues.

Such concern derives not only from the professional leadership of congregations, but also from the membership. Conservative synagogue members characteristically want their children to have a Judaic and Hebraic education. In fact, it may be possible to identify Conservative congregants by their commitment to a more intensive Jewish education than that offered by Reform temples. For better or worse, a great many people join Conservative synagogues primarily in order to place their children in a setting they deem conducive to the formation of a strong Jewish identity.

In the light of this motive, it is easier to understand the ongoing attendance problems of Conservative synagogues. From their inception to the present day, such congregations have never attracted more than a scant minority of members to prayer services on a regular, weekly basis. This was the case during the periods of greatest expansion, and it remains so to the present day. The overwhelming majority (75 percent) of Conservative rabbis responding to a 1975 survey reported that fewer than one-quarter of their congregants attend late Friday evening services on a regular basis, and almost half reported an attendance of less than 10 percent of their total membership on the average Sabbath morning service.[64] Although these figures may be somewhat lower than in earlier eras and the population attending services may be somewhat older than in previous decades, sparse synagogue attendance is a characteristic of the Conservative synagogue.

A related characteristic is the proportionally high percentage of women who have traditionally attended services. In marked contrast to Orthodox synagogues – particularly of the immigrant variety – Conservative synagogues attract fewer men than women to prayer services. There is substantial evidence that this pattern obtained during the first decades of the century when men routinely worked on the Sabbath, and it has persisted to the present. During the mid-1950s, women constituted between 50 and 74 percent of worshipers at the majority of Conservative services on Friday evenings. As Marshall Sklare noted in citing these figures, "Women in the Conservative synagogue are taking up the slack produced by the male whose decrease in attendance may well represent his acceptance of the general American pattern in the field of religious behavior. The sex distribution during worship in Conservative synagogues may soon approach Western standards; . . . [i.e.,] much concern on the part of women for religion – an interest for which they are presumed to have a special affinity."[65] Given these demographic realities, it is understandable that women have consistently played a greater role in the ritual and organizational life of Conservative, as opposed to Orthodox, synagogues. It is also not surprising that women's roles have constantly expanded.

In sum, the history of the Conservative synagogue is marked by a cluster of patterns and emphases present in congregations affiliated with the United Synagogue. The Conservative synagogue is characterized by a centrist orientation that amalgamates Orthodox and Reform practices, a particular pattern of attendance and membership involvement, a heavy investment in congregational schooling, and a broad definition of the proper role of the synagogue within the Jewish community. Although particular practices and rituals have changed over time, the Conservative synagogue has developed its own orientation to the three classical functions of the synagogue and therefore represents a peculiarly twentieth-century American version of the Jewish house of prayer, study, and assembly.

NOTES

1   This is not to suggest that Conservative synagogues exist only in the United States. In fact, such congregations may be found throughout the world and are even joined together in the World Council of Synagogues. Member congregations of this international organizaton are located in Canada, South America, several European countries, Israel, and New Zealand, in addition to the United States. However, with the exception of Canadian affiliates (whose development was coterminous with their counterparts in the United States), other congregations borrowed heavily from the American Conservative synagogue and frequently were even founded by Americans. It is also not my intention to suggest that there were no similarities in ideology or ritual practices between American Conservative congregations and nineteenth-century Liberal synagogues in Europe. Nonetheless, the Conservative synagogue is a uniquely American institution, both in its internal structure and function and in the role it plays in the Jewish community.

2   I employ an institutional rather than descriptive definition of the Conservative synagogue for two reasons: first, because the practices of synagogues that have identified themselves as Conservative have varied over the course

of time and from one community to the next; and second, because it enables us to rely upon the data collected by the major agencies of the Conservative Movement about their own institutional affiliates. The reader should note, however, that membership in the United Synagogue did not always signify that a congregation identified itself as Conservative. Especially during the first deacdes of this century, some modern Orthodox congregations joined the United synagogue – including several Young Israel congregations. On the other hand, not all congregations that identify themselves as Conservative or that adopt Conservative conventions necessarily affiliate themselves with the United Synagogue: Some do not join because they are led by rabbis who feel no allegiance to the institutions of the Conservative Movement or because they wish to remain independent, whereas others are stripped of their affiliation for failing to pay dues to the United States. With the exception of the depression years, when many congregations could not afford to support a national organization, the United Synagogue won the allegiance of the preponderant majority of Conservative synagogues. Maurice J. Karpf estimated in 1937 that only 50 percent of Conservative congreations belonged to the United Synagogue; see *Jewish Community Organization in the United States: An Outline of Types of Organizations, Activities, and Problems* (New York, 1937), p. 70.

By adopting an institutional definition of the Conservative synagogue, this chapter eschews the ongoing, often highly partisan, debate about the antiquity of the various Jewish denominations in the United States. Certainly, twentieth-century Conservative synagogues have drawn upon ideological and institutional models developed by nineteenth-century American congregations. However, it was only in the first decades of the twentieth century that distinctive and identifiable Conservative synagogues fully emerged.

3 Leon Jick, *The Americanization of the Synagogue 1820–1870* (Hanover, N.H., 1976), p. 174.
4 For descriptions of reforms introduced during this period, see Jick, *Americanization of the Synagogue*, pp. 174–191, as well as Jick's essay in the present volume. On immigrant congregations, see Irving Howe, *The World of Our Fathers* (New York, 1976), pp. 183–200. Herman and Mignon Rubenovitz describe the traditional practices of Boston's Mishkan Tefila in *The Waking Heart* (Cambridge, Mass., 1967), pp. 31–34. In his essay, "Orthodoxy in American Jewish Life," Charles Liebman has questioned the "Orthodoxy" of most East European immigrants on the grounds that they displayed scant interest in some traditional institutions – e.g., the Mikva and Yeshiva. Although this line of inquiry raises important questions about the historical origins of what today is labeled as Orthodoxy, Liebman does not deny that immigrant congregations essentially followed the practices of their East European counterparts. Liebman's essay appears in *The American Jewish Yearbook*, 1965; see especially pp. 27–30.
5 Simon Cohen, *Shaaray Tephilla: A History of Its Hundred Years, 1845–1945*

(New York, 1945), pp. 31–34; Bernard Drachman, *The Unfailing Light: Memoirs of An American Rabbi* (New York, 1948), p. 175; Selig Adler and Thomas E. Connolly, *From Ararat to Suburbia: The History of the Jewish Community of Buffalo* (Philadelphia, 1960), pp. 266–272; Lloyd P. Gartner, *History of the Jews of Cleveland* (Cleveland, 1978), pp. 166–170.

6   Herbert Parzen, "The Early Development of Conservative Judaism," *Conservative Judaism*, July 1947, p. 11; Israel Goldstein, *A Century of Judaism in New York: Bnai Jeshurun 1825–1925* (New York, 1930), p. 200. There is no question that East European immigrants and their children played the dominant role in synagogues affiliated with the United Synagogue. Nevertheless, the role of so-called German congregations should not be overlooked. Central European Jews who arrived in America during the 1860s and 1870s only slowly introduced reforms, and even German immigrants who arrived in earlier decades did not all succumb to radical reform.

7   Carole Kruckoff, *Rodfei Zedek: The First Hundred Years* (Chicago, 1976), p. 17ff; Joseph P. Schultz, ed., *Mid-America's Promise: A Profile of Kansas City Jewry* (Kansas City, 1982), pp. 18–19.

8   Drachman, *The Unfailing Light*, pp. 197–204, describes his unsuccessful struggle to stave off the introduction of mixed pews at Beth Israel Bikkur Cholim. On developments in Buffalo, see Adler and Connolly, *From Ararat to Suburbia*, pp. 266–272. For some examples of immigrant congregations that insisted on English discourse, see Henry S. Schnitzer, *Thy Goodly Tent: The First Fifty years of Temple Emanuel, Bayonne, N.J.* (Bayonne, 1961), p. 3; and Allen duPont Breck, *The Centennial History of the Jews of Colorado 1859–1959* (Denver, 1960), pp. 88–89, 218–220. The latter work describes the founding of Beth Ha midrash Hagidol as "an English-speaking Orthodox congregation." On congregations established outside of the immigrant ghettos that gradually introduced American innovations, see W. G. Plaut, *The Jews of Minnesota: The First Seventy-Five Years* (New York, 1959), pp. 196–198; *Rededication Journal: Temple Beth El* (Springfield, Mass., 1968), p. 18; Lloyd P. Gartner and Max Vorspan, *History of the Jews of Los Angeles* (New York, 1970), p. 162. These examples refer only to developments prior to 1913; during the next decades, hundreds of congregations would follow this pattern.

The present analysis departs from Marshall Sklare's pioneering study of Conservative Judaism, which traces the development of the Conservative synagogue to areas of third settlement. See *Conservative Judaism: An American Religious Movement* (New York, 1954), chaps. 2 and 3. That clearly was the pattern in the era after World War II, but during the first decades of the century, many Conservative synagogues arose in areas of second settlement. For more on this issue, see my essay "The Conservative Synagogue Revisited," *American Jewish History*, December 1984, pp. 120–121.

9   On the efforts of rabbis associated with the Jewish Theological Seminary Association to challenge Reform and define a traditional, yet American alternative, see Moshe Davis, *The Emergence of Conservative Judaism* (New

York, 1964); Abraham Karp, "The Origins of Conservative Judaism," *Conservative Judaism*, Summer 1965; and Herbert Rosenblum, "The Founding of the United Synagogue of America, 1913" (Ph.D. diss. Brandeis University, 1970). For a study of the emerging Conservative rabbinate, see Abraham Karp, "The Conservative Rabbi," *American Jewish Archives*, October 1983. See the references in notes 5–8 on the experiences of early Seminary graduates.

10　Rubenovitz and Rubenovitz, *The Waking Heart*, pp. 31–34; on the difficulties encountered by Egelson and others, see Rosenblum, "Founding of the United Synagogue," pp. 133–134.

11　Herbert Rosenblum's dissertation provides a first-rate history of the circumstances and deliberations leading up to the founding of the United Synagogue. Schechter's speech at the founding convention appears in *The United Synagogue Report*, 1913, pp. 14–23. Schechter urged the new agency to "be in constant communication with our congregations" and to send "out Rabbis and preachers for the purpose of propaganda, not only to enlist new congregations, but to help such outlying communities in the various states as are in need of advice and counsel" (p. 21).

12　Joel Blau, "Conservative Judasim," *The American Hebrew*, 1 October 1909, p. 547.

13　To obtain United Synagogue membership figures, I counted affiliates listed in the *Annual Reports of the United Synagogue* (New York, 1917, 1922, 1929). For the membership of the Union of American Hebrew Congregations, see *American Jewish Yearbook*, 1929, p. 285.

14　Figures on affiliates are based on my compilations from the *Annual Reports of the United Synagogue*. For Jewish populations in various American cities and states, see Harry S. Linfield, *The Jews in the United States, 1927* (New York, 1929), especially pp. 10–11, 18–19, 83ff.

15　This analysis of the growth of Conservative synagogues has been put forth most explicitly by Marshall Sklare, in *Conservative Judaism*, chaps. 3 and 4.

16　For a few of the numerous communal and congregational histories that credit the initiative of Seminary-trained rabbis for steering congregations toward Conservative practices and allegiance, see the references in note 7, as well as S. Joshua Kohn, *The Jewish Community of Utica, N.Y. 1847–1948* (New York, 1959), pp. 63–77; Lloyd P. Gartner and Louis Swichkow, *The Jews of Milwaukee* (Philadelphia, 1963), p. 213ff.; Joseph Gale, ed., *Eastern Union: The Development of a Jewish Community* (Elizabeth, N.J., 1958), pp. 42–43; Marc Lee Raphael, *Jews and Judaism in a Mid-Western Community* (Columbus, Ohio, 1979), pp. 185–186; and I. A. Melnick, ed., *Bnai Israel Congregation, Pittsburgh 1904–1929* (Pittsburgh, 1929), p. 17ff.

　　One of the as yet unexamined aspects of Jewish denominational history in America concerns the competitive efforts of the major rabbinical seminaries to place their graduates in pulpit positions. In the period from 1918 to 1927, the Jewish Theological Seminary graduated 95 students, whereas Yeshiva graduated only 55. Moreover, Seminary students took pulpits throughout the country, whereas Yeshiva graduates remained in a few key cities. One wonders how these placement patterns affected the growth of Conservative and modern Orthodox synagogues. It is also worth speculating on the impact of immigrant rabbis on the careers of American-trained Orthodox colleagues. It seems that a strong rabbi such as Bernard Levinthal in Philadelphia played an important role in keeping modern Orthodox rabbis out of his city, thereby paving the way for success of Seminary-trained rabbis in Philadelphia. For some reflections on this theme, see Jeffrey Gurock, "Resisters and Accommodators: Varieties of Orthodox Rabbis in America, 1886–1983," *American Jewish Archives*, Fall 1983, especially p. 172, n. 64.

17   On these activities, see *The United Synagogue Recorder, 1921–29*, especially vol. 2, no. 1 (1922), p. 10. On Cohen's instrumental role in the founding of a Conservative congregation in Providence, see *Temple Emanu-El: The First Fifty Years* (Providence, 1976), pp. 28–29.

18   *Temple Emanu-El*, p. 29.

19   For a good analysis of these developments, see Sidney Solomon, "The Conservative Congregational School as a Response to the American Scene" (DHL diss., The Jewish Theological Seminary of America, 1982), especially chap. 3. Solomon cites some statistics on school growth on p. 66ff. For two examples of congregations that required Hebrew school attendance for aspiring Bar Mitzvah boys, see Schnitzer, *Thy Goodly Tent*, p. 41ff; and Louis Levitsky, "The Story of an Awakened Community," *The Reconstructionist*, 7 February 1936, p. 12ff. Levitsky describes how, from its founding in 1923, Temple Israel of Wilkes-Barre, Pennsylvania, contained a group of members determined not to permit the establishment of a Sunday school; already during the 1920s, the congregation required attendance at three-day-a-week Hebrew schools of potential *Bnai Mitzvah*. For an example of a congregation that established its Hebrew school several years prior to its organization of regular prayer services, see Israel A. Allen, *History of the Baldwin Jewish Center, 1928–1948* (Baldwin, L.I., 1948), p. 8.

20   Morris Silverman, "Report of Survey on Ritual," *Proceedings of the Rabbinical Assembly*, 1933, p. 335; Leon S. Lang, "What Have We Done with Confirmation," *Proceedings of the Rabbinical Assembly*, 1936, p. 289. On the Young Folk's League, see *United Synagogue Recorder* vol. 1, no. 2 (1921), p. 3.

21   Isidoro Aizenberg, "The Early History of Two Conservative Synagogues in Queens – The Jamaica Jewish Center and The Jamaica Estates Hebrew Center," TS, p. 4. I thank Rabbi Aizenberg for making this unpublished history available to me.

22   Silverman, "Report of Survey on Ritual," pp. 328–335.

23   Alter Landesman, "Synagogue Attendance," *Proceedings of the Rabbinical Assembly*, 1928, p. 41ff; Levitsky, "Story of an Awakened Community," p. 9. On the emptiness of synagogues, see Deborah Melamed, "Women's Opportunity in the Synagogue," *The United Synagogue Recorder*, vol. 1, no. 2 (1921), pp. 12–13.

24   Melamed, "Women's Opportunity," p. 12ff. On the activities of women

in Conservative congregations early in the century, see the reports in *The United Synagogue Recorder*, especially vol. V, no. 2 (1925). According to Marc Lee Raphael, women generally did not serve on the boards of Conservative synagogues during this period or even into the 1940s; Raphael, *Jews and Judaism*, p. 267. See the subsequent discussion for more on the changing role of women in Conservative synagogues.

25 Levinthal and the president of the Brooklyn Jewish Center are quoted in Deborah Dash Moore, *At Home in America: Second Generation Jews in New York* (New York, 1981), pp. 130–131. Chapter 5 of Moore's study contains an important analysis of the development of synagogue-centers in New York City. Kaplan is quoted in Harry L. Glucksman, "The Synagogue Center," *Proceedings of the Rabbinical Assembly*, 1933, pp. 268–269. The description of Bnai Jeshurun appears in the *United Synagogue Recorder*, vol. 2, no. 2 (1921), p. 15.

26 On the synagogue construction boom, see *Census of Religious Bodies, 1936 – Jewish Congregations: Statistics, History, Doctrine, and Organization* (Washington, 1940), especially pp. 1–7; and the *American Hebrew*, 17 May 1929, p. 6ff. On mortgage costs, see S. Joshua Kohn, "The Rabbi and the Congregational Budget," *Proceedings of the Rabbinical Assembly*, 1932, p. 220.

27 Goldstein is quoted in Glucksman, "The Synagogue Center," p. 271; the latter quotation is from Moore, *At Home in America*, pp. 144–146 and represents the views of Israel Levinthal.

28 Gartner and Vorspan, *History of the Jews*, p. 210; Kruckoff, *Rodfei Zedek*, p. 38.

29 Schnitzer discusses the impact of the Great Depression in *Thy Goodly Tent*, chap. 4. The economic crisis also forced the United Synagogue to curtail many of its programs and suspend publication of its annual reports and *Recorder*.

On the general depression that characterized American religious life in this era, see Robert T. Handy, "The American Religious Depression, 1925–35," *Church History*, vol. 29, no. 1 (March, 1960), pp. 3–16. The "spiritual lethargy" described by Handy applied primarily to mainline Protestant denominations; as Handy notes, "both Judaism and Roman Catholicism were deeply affected by economic depression." Further research is needed to determine whether American Judaism also suffered from a spiritual malaise during this era.

30 Congregational histories report on an easing of financial problems toward the end of the 1930s and certainly by the time of World War II. By 1941, the United Synagogue could afford to resume publishing newsletters and even launched *The Torch* for its Federation of Men's Clubs and *The Synagogue Center* to guide boards of synagogues.

For data on congregational growth, see the *Biennial Convention Reports of the United Synagogue of America* 1952, p. 52; 1957, p. 97; 1959, p. 140; 1961, p. 3; 1963, pp. 184–185; and 1965, p. 6, which reports the induction of the 800th affiliate. There are no published statistics on affiliates during the 1940s, but Albert I. Gordon, a key United Synagogue official, claimed that in 1949 there were 365 congregations in the United Synagogue. See *Jews in Suburbia*, (Boston, 1959), p. 97.

The membership of congregations also increased during this period: In 1957, Eli Ginzburg reported that of United Synagogue congregations, half numbered 250 families or less, a quarter between 250 and 400 families, and another quarter over 400 families, with 20 synagogues numbering over 1,000 members. *Proceedings of the Rabbinical Assembly*, 1960. p. 23.

31   For some cautious, yet celebratory assessments of the Conservative Movement's success, see Morris Freedman, "A New Jewish Community in Formation," *Commentary*, January 1955, pp. 36–47; and Sklare, *Conservative Judaism*, chap. 8. Partisans of Conservatism were less restrained in advertising the seemingly endless opportunities of the movement to lead American Jewry.

32   See *Biennial Report to the Convention* (a report prepared by the United Synagogue in 1950) on the geographic distribution of affiliates; it reported the most dense concentration (182 congregations) in the New York metropolitan region (pp. 12–13). See also the Biennial Convention proceedings cited in note 30 for the geographic locations of newly inducted affiliates. On the dramatic growth of Conservatism on Long Island, see Freedman, "A New Jewish Community in Formation," p. 36. For an example of one of many congregations eclipsed by the move to suburbia, see Adler and Connolly, *From Ararat to Suburbia*, pp. 324–326.

33   Gordon, *Jews in Suburbia*, chap. 4, and especially, p. 97.

34   It was not uncommon for such controversies over synagogue innovations to be brought before American courts of law. For documents submitted to courts, see Baruch Litvin, ed., *The Sanctity of the Synagogue* (New York, 1959), pp. 49–77. For more on these court cases, see Louis Bernstein, "The Emergence of the English Speaking Orthodox Rabbinate" (Ph.D. diss., Yeshiva University, 1977), pp. 289–297. Also see *Conservative Judaism*, Fall 1956; and Herman Landau, *Adath Louisville: The Story of a Jewish Community* (Louisville, 1981). It should be noted that the introduction of mixed pews in this period, as well as in earlier eras, did not necessarily mean that a congregation identified itself as Conservative. In some cases, congregations that introduced mixed seating described themselves as traditional and identified with modern Orthodoxy. In other cases, congregations decided not to affiliate with any national religious movement.

35   See Leo Spitz, "The Synagogue Center Marches On," *Jubilee Volume of the Brooklyn Jewish Center* (New York, 1946), p. 60. Spitz quotes Rabbi Stanley Rabinowitz, then director of field activities for the United Synagogue, to the effect that three-quarters of affiliates "may be regarded as Synagogue Centers" (p. 63). See also, Marshall Sklare's contention that the Conservative movement pioneered in creating synagogue-centers, in "The Conservative Movement/Achievements and Problems," *The Jewish Community in America* (New York, 1974), p. 179.

One highly visible manifestation of this group's desire to advertise its socioeconomic attainments was its lavish investment in synagogue art and architecture. For two congregations that hired noted artists and architects, see Freedman, "A New Jewish Community in Formation," pp. 37ff and especially Patricia Talbot Davis, *Together They Built A Mountain* (Lititz, Pa., 1974), on Frank Lloyd Wright's achievement in Elkins Park, Pa.

36　Freedman, "A New Jewish Community in Formation," p. 36; Sklare, *Conservative Judaism*, p. 256; and Gordon, *Jews in Suburbia*, chap. 4, and the quotation on p. 98.

37　Gordon, *Jews in Suburbia*, pp. 98–99. Wolfe Kelman, executive director of the Rabbinical Assembly, has suggested that wartime encounters between Jewish soldiers and Seminary-trained chaplains fostered a positive attitude toward Conservatism that bore fruit in the postwar era. Interview, 12 March 1984.

38　See the *Biennial Convention Reports* and *The Synagogue Center* for information on the departments and programs of the United Synagogue during the postwar era. For material on the Department for Synagogue Architecture, see especially *The Synagogue Center*, October 1943, p. 13.

39　On synagogue budgets, see the Department of Synagogue Administration of the United Synagogue of America, "Survey of Synagogue Finances," November 1963, p. 21. I thank Mr. Jack Mittelman of the United Synagogue for graciously supplying me with these survey data and other information gathered by his office during the 1960s.

　　On the financing of schools, see the *Biennial Convention Report of the United Synagogue*, 1950, pp. 96–97. See also, Sklare, p. 77ff. on the importance of schools in attracting members. Sidney Solomon provides a good analysis of why Conservatism embraced Hebrew schools as their preferred vehicle for Jewish education rather than day schools (p. 92). Some congregations, however, did support their own foundation and day schools. See Walter Ackerman, "The Day School in the Conservative Movement," *Conservative Judaism*, Winter 1961, p. 50ff.

40　Arzt is quoted in Solomon, "Conservative Congregational School," p. 94.

41　The United Synagogue, in fact, founded a publication entitled *The Synagogue School* in order to encourage the development of Hebrew schools. Many issues of the late 1940s approvingly described the efforts of Conservative congregations to eliminate Sunday schools and replace them with thrice-weekly programs. See especially the September 1948 issue, pp. 26–27, on developments in Philadelphia; and the harsh report on Sunday schools issued by the United Synagogue Commission on Jewish Education and prepared by Stanley Rabinowitz and Gershon Winer, "The Objectives and Standards for the Congregational School," *The Synagogue School*, January 1951. For the results of a survey conducted in the 1950s by the American Association for Jewish Education, see Alexander Dushkin and U. Z. Engelman, *Jewish Education in the United States*, vol. 1 (New York, 1959) pp. 57, 100.

42 For a good analysis of how congregational schools replaced communal schools, see Solomon, "Conservative Congregational School," pp. 67–74.

43 On day school attendance by Conservative children, see Dushkin and Engleman, *Jewish Education*, pp. 57–58.

44 Wolfe Kelman, interview, 12 March 1984. For some corroboration, see Karp, "Conservative Rabbi," p. 226.

45 "Survey on Synagogue Finances," p. 21.

46 For data on youth activities and services, see the *Biennial Convention Report* of the United Synagogue, 1950, pp. 96, 97, 104. On Har Zion, see Rose Goldstein, "The Youth Program in a Large-Sized Congregation," *Conservative Judaism*, Winter 1961, p. 33ff. On Junior Congregations, see Elliot Schwartz, "The Junior Congregation Program," *The Synagogue School*, September 1951, p. 3. On pioneering efforts of congregations in Chicago to found the first Ramah camp in Wisconsin, see Kurckoff, *Rodfei Zedek*, p. 49, and Shuly Schwartz, "Ramah – The Early Years, 1947–1952" (Master's thesis, Jewish Theological Seminary, 1976).

47 Morris S. Goodblatt, "Synagogue Ritual Survey," *Proceedings of the Rabbinical Assembly*, 1948, pp. 105–109; Samuel M. Cohen, "Friday Night Services," *The Synagogue Center*, March 1944, p. 7.

48 Max J. Routtenberg, "Report of the Prayer Book Commission, "*Proceedings of the Rabbinical Assembly*, 1942, pp. 147–156.

49 For some of the background to this venture, see Routtenberg, "Report of the Prayer Book Commission," p. 150; and Robert Gordis, "A Jewish Prayerbook for the Modern Age," *Conservative Judaism*, October 1954, pp. 7–9. Data on usage appears in Goodblatt, "Synagogue Ritual Survey," p. 108; and "High Holiday Practices in Conservative Congregations," Department of Synagogue Administration of the United Synagogue, July 1967, p. 6.

50 Goodblatt, "Synagogue Ritual Survey," pp. 105–109.

51 "Standards for Synagogue Practice," *United Synagogue Biennial Report*, 1957, p. 49; Emil Lehman, "National Survey on Synagogue Leadership," (New York: United Synagogue and the Bureau of Applied Social Research, Columbia University, 1953), pp. 6–8, 12–14, 28. Lehman's comments appear in the *Biennial Convention Report*, 1953, pp. 36–37.

52 On the Sabbath revitalization plan, see *Proceedings of the Rabbinical Assembly*, 1950, pp. 117–125; on the Yom Kippur oath, see *Bulletin of the Rabbinical Assembly*, December 1949, p. 7. The decision of the United Synagogue to publish *The Torch* for laymen was in part motivated by a concern over the poor attendance at synagogue services. See especially Joel S. Geffen, "A Challenge to the American-Jewish Laity," *The Torch*, November 1944, pp. 23–25.

53 Wolfe Kelman, "The American Synagogue: Present Prospects," *Conservative Judaism* Fall 1971, p. 13.

54 "Survey on Synagogue Membership," p. 8. On mergers, see Kelman, "American Synagogue," p. 13.

55 Charles S. Liebman and Saul Shapiro, "A Survey of the Conservative Movement and Some of Its Religious Attitudes" pp. 1, 22 (unpublished). For a critique of this study, see Harold Schulweis, "Surveys, Statistics and Sectarian Salvation," *Conservative Judaism*, Winter 1980, pp. 65–69.

56 For evidence of the growth of the Conservative movement in sunbelt communities, see the report on new United Synagogue affiliates in *The United Synagogue Review*, Fall 1984, p. 12. Two urban congregations that have developed extensive programs for young Jewish gentrifiers are Anshe Chesed on Manhattan's West Side and Adas Israel in Washington, D. C. On the latter, see *Proceedings of the Rabbinical Assembly*, 1981, p. 128.

57 For reports on some of these developments, see the *Biennial Convention Reports of the United Synagogue*, 1975, p. 75, and 1977, p. 19.

58 Reisman is quoted in Daniel Elazar and Rela Geffen Monson, "The Synagogue *Havurah* – An Experiment in Restoring Adult Fellowship to the Jewish Community," *The Jewish Journal of Sociology*, June 1979, p. 67.

59 See Elazar and Monson, "The Synagogue Havurah," p. 74 for data on synagogue *Havurot*. See also, Gerald B. Bubis, *Synagogue Havurot: A Comparative Study*, (Washington, 1983) on several Reform and Conservative synagogue *Havurot* in Los Angeles; Dov Peretz Elkins, *Humanizing Jewish Life* (South Brunswick and New York, 1976), chaps. 5–8 on the activities of *Havurot* in a Rochester congregation; and "*Havurah* Failures and Successes," *Proceedings of the Rabbinical Assembly* 1979, pp. 55–75.

60 Sklare, *Conservative Judaism*, p. 89.

61 On the pioneering efforts of the Society for the Advancement of Judaism, see "Sex Equality in the Synagogue," *The Reconstructionist*, 6 March 1953, pp. 17–19. See above for surveys that included questions about Bat Mitzvah ceremonies.

62 For some data on the role of women in synagogue leadership, see "Midwest Regional Survey on the 'Role of Women' within our Conservative Congregations," March, 1974 (an unpublished survey conducted by the United Synagogue); and especially, Zelda Dick, "Light from Our Poll on Women's Role," *Women's League Outlook*, Summer 1975, pp. 14–15.

63 Several surveys were conducted during the mid-1970s to measure the degree of women's participation in the religious services of Conservative synagogues. Unfortunately, they contain wildly disparate findings, a possible consequence of the self-selection of respondents who knew of the sympathies of the surveyors. See Dick's survey of sisterhoods; and also Daniel Elazar and Rela Geffen Monson, "Women in the Synagogue Today," *Midstream*, April 1979, especially p. 25 on the Blumenthal survey and p. 27 for their conclusions; also Anne Lapidus Lerner and Stephen C. Lerner, "Lerners Report Survey Results," *Rabbinical Assembly News*, February 1984, pp. 1, 8 (the latter surveyed rabbis).

64 See Rela Geffen Monson's address in *Convention Report of the United Synagogue*, 1977, p. 43.

65 Sklare, *Conservative Judaism*, p. 89.

II
The Thematic Perspective

5

The American Experience of a Sephardic Synagogue

MARC D. ANGEL

Much has been written about the experience of Ashkenazim in the United States – their neighborhoods, communities, synagogues, and their adaptation to American life over the past several generations. Far less has been written about the Sephardim. This chapter focuses on one Sephardic synagogue, Congregation Ezra Bessaroth of Seattle, Washington. As a tightly knit congregation, Ezra Bessaroth has successfully maintained many of its traditions; at the same time, it has been profoundly influenced by its American environment. By studying the experience of Congregation Ezra Bessaroth, we gain insight into the adaptation of Judeo-Spanish-speaking Sephardim to American life.

The Settlement of Sephardim in Seattle

The first quarter of this century found thousands of Sephardim leaving their native towns and villages in Turkey, Greece, the Balkan countries, and Syria. Many went to Israel, Europe, South America, and Africa. However, the vast majority of emigrants came to the United States and settled primarily on the Lower East Side of New York City. A variety of factors contributed to the migration. For one thing, western educational methods were making deep inroads into the traditional Sephardic communities. The schools operated by the Alliance Israélite Universelle throughout the Levant, for example, had introduced young Sephardim to French culture and western civilization. In addition, traditionalism was gradually giving way to modernism. Young people began to dream of the economic and social advancement that would be available to them in the West, and the United States had the most attractive reputation as a land of promise.

Migration from Turkey and the Balkan countries was stimulated by

153

political and military developments. In 1908, the revolt of the Young Turks led to a variety of changes, including compulsory military service for all men. Wealthy people were able to buy their way out of military service so that the burden of responsibility fell upon the poor. Moreover, life was disrupted by revolution, the Turko-Italian War, as well as natural disasters that damaged major cities. During the Balkan War against Turkey (1912–1913), Sephardic communities in the belligerent countries were ravaged. Then came World War I with all its misery. It is not surprising that many Sephardim decided to emigrate.

One of the most significant Sephardic communities outside New York City during the early twentieth century was to be found in Seattle, Washington. Sephardim came to Seattle from the Island of Rhodes, and the Marmara littoral, from such places as Istanbul, Tekirdag, Bursa, Corlu, and the Island of Marmara. In 1912, *La America*, the leading American Sephardic newspaper, reported that the Sephardic community of Seattle numbered more than 800 people. Dr. David de Sola Pool, writing in 1914, estimated the Sephardic population of Seattle at 600. Although these numbers were approximations, they indicate that the largest Sephardic community outside New York at that time resided in Seattle. Additional migrants continued to settle in Seattle until 1924, when new American quota laws practically cut off immigration from the countries where most Sephardim lived.

The first Sephardim to settle in Seattle arrived with non-Jewish Turks and Greeks. Once they began to prosper, they sent for their wives and other family members. When a nucleus of Sephardim had been established, others in the home countries also began to consider the possibility of emigrating to Seattle. Moreover, in 1907 the Industrial Removal Office, a Jewish organization begun as part of the Jewish Agricultural and Industrial Aid Society, sent small numbers of Sephardim away from New York to a variety of places, including Seattle. The theory behind this project was that Jews would have a better chance to prosper in a city not as congested as New York. The physical beauty of Seattle and its impressive bodies of water – such as Lake Washington, Lake Union, and Puget Sound – may also have attracted Sephardim who were born, raised, and had worked on the shores of the Sea of Marmara and the Aegean Sea.

The Sephardim of Seattle were not a united community. Although they had much in common, Jews from Rhodes and from the Marmara littoral differed somewhat in their liturgical traditions, their pronunciation of Judeo-Spanish, and some customs. In the fall of 1908, all the Sephardim in Seattle attempted to overlook these differences and unite to hold services for the High Holy days. They rented a hall at Ninth and

Yesler, but the services proved to be unsatisfactory since each group wished to have its particular melodies and customs prevail and each vied for control of the service. That experiment convinced both groups that they each needed to have a separate congregation. The two congregations that emerged in those early years still flourish today; they are the Sephardic Bikur Holim, which consists mostly of Turkish Jews, and Congregation Ezra Bessaroth, which consists of Jews from Rhodes.

Ezra Bessaroth Synagogue in the Early Days

The Ezra Bessaroth Synagogue was established in order to maintain the synagogue and religious traditions of the Jews from the Island of Rhodes, as well as their social togetherness. In the early years, services were conducted by Haim De Leon, who was a shoemaker by trade. He was born and raised in Rhodes, and was about thirty years old when he arrived in Seattle in 1909. He knew the traditions well and was the man most responsible for transplanting the synagogue traditions of Rhodes to Seattle.

By 1912, the Rhodes Jews had officially united under the name of Koupa Ezra Bessaroth of Rhodes. Articles of incorporation were filed on June 19, 1914. In 1915, two lots were purchased on the corner of Fifteenth and East Fir Street, in the hope of building a synagogue there. However, the small community was hard-pressed to come up with the money needed to construct the synagogue. For the High Holy Days the congregation rented Washington Hall. Late in the afternoon of Yom Kippur, before the services had concluded, the worshipers were forced to vacate the hall in order to make room for another group that had hired it for a dance that evening. The Jews were outraged by this disruption and determined once and for all to have their own synagogue building by the next Yom Kippur. Leaders such as Dr. Harry S. Tarica, Solomon Alhadeff, and Sadick Angel saw to it that the funds were raised, and the building was built.

In 1917 David J. Behar arrived in Seattle from Rhodes. A tailor by trade, Mr. Behar was well versed in synagogue traditions. Haim De Leon and others prevailed upon Mr. Behar to accept the post of *hazzan* of Ezra Bessaroth. He agreed to accept the post temporarily, until a permanent *hazzan* could be found. As things turned out, Mr. Behar remained in this position almost sixty years. During that long stretch of time he conducted almost all the services, with the assistance of a number of knowledgeable laymen. Not only did he read the daily services, but also the Sabbath and holiday services, including the reading of the Torah portions.

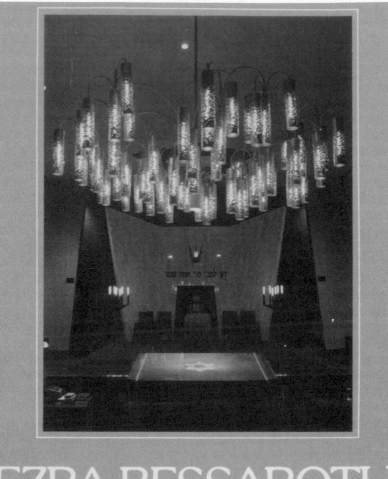

The cover of a souvenir album celebrating the congregation's Sephardic heritage. Courtesy of Congregation Ezra Bessaroth, Seattle.

During the early years of Ezra Bessaroth, the synagogue services largely resembled those conducted in the synagogues on the Island of Rhodes. They were conducted entirely in Hebrew and were chanted aloud by the *hazzan* as the congregants read along in low voices. The synagogue music had a definite Oriental flavor that reflected the influence of Turkish music.

By western standards, synagogue services were not formal and dignified. Rather, congregants interspersed their prayers with conversation with their neighbors, and the women – most of whom could not read Hebrew – enjoyed chatting together during services. Shabbat morning services would begin and end early, so that congregants would be out by 10:30 or 11:00 A.M. There were no sermons, since there were no rabbis. Prior to Shabbat afternoon services, Mr. Behar would conduct a class in Judeo-Spanish, generally expounding on midrashic texts.

Although the Sephardic immigrants had a reverence for tradition and a strong sense of loyalty to their community in Rhodes, American life made its inroads on their patterns of living. Many were forced to work on the Sabbath, something that would have been abhorrent to them had they still been living in Rhodes. With many men working on the Sabbath, attendance at synagogue services declined. Once parents began to break Sabbath rules, children followed suit. If the immigrants remembered the community in Rhodes where the Sabbath was widely observed and where the synagogues were the center of religious life, their children grew up without these memories. This fact affected, and continues to affect, the function of the synagogue in the lives of its congregants.

Like members of many other immigrant groups, not many of the Sephardim had received extensive formal education or training in skills in the old country. But they were ambitious and industrious. In Seattle, Sephardim found work in the fishing industry, the shoe repair business, the produce business, and other types of business. During the early years, most struggled to earn enough to support themselves and their families, and also to send money to their relatives still living in Rhodes. These men and women, so vitally concerned with their livelihoods, had relatively little time and inclination to develop a strong synagogue administration, a viable religious school, or elaborate religious and cultural projects. The operation of the synagogue was left to a few dedicated leaders and to the *hazzan*. Rev. Behar, for example, not only conducted services for the synagogue, but also operated a religious school for the young.

The immigrant generation did not fully realize how different America was from Rhodes. In Rhodes, the Jewish quarter was a powerful social influence. Children grew up as Jews; no one assumed that any other possibility existed. But Seattle was not Rhodes. Although the Jews tended to live together in the central district, a vast number of non-Jews also lived there. Because their children attended public schools, Jewish influence on the younger generation was significantly lessened. Religious education was inadequate, so that most children learned to read Hebrew only by rote and had little or no comprehension of the language.

The Americanization of the immigrants and of their children could not help but affect the synagogue in many ways, some subtle and others obvious. By the early 1930s, a period of challenges and transitions was under way.

Challenges and Responses

By 1930, the Rhodes Jews of Seattle had succeeded in forming their own congregation, had built a lovely synagogue, gained the services of a competent *hazzan*, arranged for many of the social needs of the community, and provided at least some religious education for their children. In spite of these accomplishments, Congregation Ezra Bessaroth still had a great many problems. In the early 1930s members of the younger generation, together with some of the progressive individuals of the immigrant generation, began to pressure the synagogue for changes. For example, Jacob Almeleh, born in Rhodes, was a fiery critic of the status quo and an avid advocate of modernization of the synagogue service. He edited an English language monthly newsletter known as *Progress*, which appeared during 1934–1935. Other Sephardim collaborated with him to make *Progress* an important, if controversial, cultural organ for the Sephardim of Seattle. Its pages reflected pride in the achievements of this group, but also the frustrations and failures of the community.

In one issue of *Progress* (January, 1935), Morris B. Hanan, president of Ezra Bessaroth, wrote with pride of the success of his community.

> To me and numerous pioneers, it is amazing to note the transformation that took place in the last 25 years from a group of uneducated, untrained young people, unaccustomed to the ways of American life and ideals into a progressive virile community, cognizant of its responsibilities, awake to the realization of its higher aims and ambitions to raise their level to the highest peak of progress and to the highest standard of community life.

Hanan rejoiced at the modernization and Americanization of the Sephardim in Seattle. He was proud of the beautiful synagogue, the Hebrew schools, the charity organizations of his community. However, another article in the same issue of *Progress* called for serious reforms. The article lamented that, since the executive committees of the congregations were so concerned with financial matters, little time was left to devote to "purely progressive and constructive innovations." Noting that "very little was done to improve our communal status or our religious services through much-needed reforms," it called upon the congregation to abridge the service and include more melodious tunes; prepare and integrate fitting English translations into portions of the liturgy; incorporate the preachings of effective sermons; adopt uniform prayerbooks for both men and women; inculcate a feeling of respect and reverence for Jewish institutions; display more order and decorum within the synagogue; attract the younger element to its bosom; found a choir to add the enchantment of music to prayer; and blend the beautiful, age-old traditional Oriental music with modern Occidental compositions. These recommendations indicate strong dissatisfaction with the old ways. There was a clear desire to make the synagogue services less Oriental and more Westernized, to introduce English into the service, and to make the service more aesthetically pleasing, in accordance with Western standards by insisting on decorum and instituting a choir.

This critique reflected the growing turmoil within the synagogue. Opposition to the old style of services was on the increase, and public debate and discussion were widespread. In the spring of 1935, the executive committee of Ezra Bessaroth sent a letter to its young members asking that they participate in congregational activities. The committee appealed to the young generation to attend services and become more involved in synagogue affairs. In response, two of the young people – Isaac Israel and Sarah Israel – wrote an open letter that was published in the August 1935 issue of *Progress*. Addressing themselves to Morris Hanan, the young people began, "After receiving your letter and hearing your plea for a closer union between the younger element of the Sephardic community and Judaism, we were prompted to write informing you of our own ideas on this problem. Have things become so deplorable that you, an officer of the congregation, must ask US JEWS to attend our own services? Have these services become so meaningless to us that we have no desire to attend them?" The letter went on to complain that the method of religious instruction available in the community was antiquated and inadequate. The writers asked the synagogue to sponsor a Bible class for older Sephardic boys and girls, where they could receive a rational, intelligent, and understandable foundation for their religion.

The rising discontent within Ezra Bessaroth was symptomatic of conditions in many Sephardic congregations throughout the country. The new generation, together with progressive members of the older generation, were engaged in a struggle to modernize and Americanize their synagogues. On Friday, September 14, 1934, the Judeo-Spanish newspaper *La Vara* printed an article by Dr. Vitali Negri entitled "A Temple of God or an Auction House?" In it, Dr. Negri lambasted Sephardic synagogues for being devoid of true worship and religiosity. He expressed outrage at the widespread custom, observed also at Ezra Bessaroth, that various honors such as opening the Ark and carrying the Torah were auctioned off to the highest bidder during services on Sabbath and holiday mornings. He complained that Hebrew was not understood by the young, by the women, or by 90 percent of the older men. "The services," he claimed, "were 'intoned' in peculiar sing-song accents in an unconvincing and ineffectual effort to stimulate piety." Negri called on the young Sephardim to eliminate the "intolerable hypocrisy" of the synagogues and to bring about needed reforms, to restore the honor of their people.

Rabbi David de Sola Pool of Congregation Shearith Israel in New York responded to Dr. Negri's article in a letter that appeared in *La Vara* on September 28, 1934. Although sharply critical of Dr. Negri's vituperative language and exaggerated criticism, Dr. Pool still found himself largely in agreement with Dr. Negri's criticisms. Dr. Pool considered the auction of mitzvoth in the synagogue "a disgrace to the synagogue." He agreed that Sephardic services should be graceful, inspirational, and appealing to the young. "The status of most Sephardic synagogues in this country is indeed deplorable. But what is called for is not a radical condemnation of the synagogue as an institution, but an enlightened community of Sephardim which shall abolish the undignified auctioning of mitzvoth and which shall remove the reproach of ignorance of Hebrew." Services should be aesthetically, reverently, and beautifully conducted, and

> the teaching of Judaism shall be expounded in the language of the country by qualified rabbis. What is demanded is that the Sephardim of this country realize that the synagogue in America cannot remain as it was in the old Turkish Empire. . . . A synagogue which exists only for occasional prayers and for burying the dead is a travesty of what the synagogue can be and very often is in America.

These two articles were read, discussed, and debated within the Sephardic community of Seattle. Even the champion of Sephardic tradition–Rabbi de Sola Pool–admitted that the old-style Sephardic synagogue maintained outmoded customs and practices. It was inevitable, then, that changes would be introduced.

An early expression of Americanization: the Ezra Bessaroth choir, c. 1930s. Courtesy of Congregation Ezra Bessaroth, Seattle.

During the early 1930s Jacob Almeleh became chairman of a committee whose goal was to establish a choir for Ezra Bessaroth. Samuel Goldfarb, choir director of the Reform Temple de Hirsch, was hired by Ezra Bessaroth to train a choir to perform for the High Holy Days. Rev. Behar, Mr. Almeleh and Mr. Goldfarb selected a group of seventeen boys from the Talmud Torah, who were trained for approximately eight months. Some of the women in the congregation made robes for the choir members. Mr. Goldfarb taught the young people a number of pieces, some of his own composition; others were traditional Ashkenazic selections, and still others were adaptations of Sephardic music to a choral setting.

Mr. Almeleh recalled: "The holidays came, and the choir was ready for its first performance. All of our congregation sat amazed and spellbound at hearing the angelic voices of their own children." The choir was generally considered to be a rousing success. The choir is still in existence and participates in the services of all holidays.

With the introduction of the choir came a number of significant innovations. Most of the choir's music was not Sephardic, and the pieces were sung according to western harmonies, rather than the traditional Sephardic musical style. Putting the choir members in special uniforms was an attempt to make the service more dignified and formal. Also, the fact that Ezra Bessaroth turned to the choir director of the leading Reform temple in Seattle demonstrates in itself an attempt was made to emulate the practices of the Americanized Reform Movement.

The choir symbolized the possibility of change within the synagogue service. It directly involved young men, and the congregation at large was favorably disposed to this new element in their services. The voices for Americanization gained more confidence with this success.

As indicated earlier, the language of the immigrants was Judeo-Spanish. Since the young people who attended public schools in Seattle spoke English as well as Judeo-Spanish, there was a rising sentiment for the introduction of at least some English readings during services and for a sermon in English. Previously the congregation had been addressed only in Judeo-Spanish.

In the early 1930s, the Union of Sephardic Congregations began to issue Sephardic prayerbooks with an English translation by Rabbi David de Sola Pool. These books served to standardize services in Ezra Bessaroth, as in many other congregations. Formerly, the individual congregants owned a variety of prayerbooks, none of which carried an English translation. Since various editions were being used, it was impossible to announce pages. With the introduction of Dr. Pool's books, page numbers could be announced and a fine English translation was available. However, English readings had not yet been introduced into the service in this early period.

Until 1939, Ezra Bessaroth did not have a formally trained rabbi. Rev. Behar carried the burden of spiritual leadership of the congregation. In 1939, Rabbi Isidore Kahan, an Ashkenazi, was brought to Seattle from the Island of Rhodes to serve as the rabbi of the two Sephardic congregations. However, this arrangement soon proved unsatisfactory, and Rabbi Kahan then served as the rabbi of Ezra Bessaroth alone. He was a fine rabbinic scholar who had been on the faculty of the highly respected rabbinical college of Rhodes. During his tenure as rabbi, he followed Rev. Behar's lead in maintaining the synagogue traditions of the Jews of Rhodes.

With the arrival of Rabbi Kahan, the synagogue witnessed a number of changes. For one thing, Rabbi Kahan preached sermons in English each Shabbat morning. He also initiated various attempts to attract young people to the synagogue, such as upgrading the Bar Mitzvah ceremony. In earlier years the Bar Mitzvah was celebrated at a weekday morning service. Sweets would be served following this service, and on the following Shabbat the boy would be called to the *Sefer* (Torah). A small party in honor of the occasion might be held on a Sunday morning or afternoon when the men did not have to work. Rabbi Kahan instituted the practice of celebrating the Bar Mitzvah on a Shabbat. The Bar Mitzvah boy would lead the congregation in the Friday evening service. On the following morning he would be called to the *Sefer*. The boy would wear a special gown for this occasion. (This practice was discontinued with Rabbi Kahan's retirement in 1958. The Bar Mitzvah now reads his Torah portion on Shabbat morning and delivers a short address to the congregation as well.)

Recognizing that many of the younger members of the congregation could not even read Hebrew, let alone understand it, Rabbi Kahan prepared a pamphlet for the service of the Eve of Rosh Hashanah that included major portions of the service in English transliteration. Thus, even if one could not read Hebrew, one could still follow the service by means of the transliterated text. In his foreword to this pamphlet, Rabbi Kahan wrote: "It is regrettable that a great percentage of our youth today are unable to follow the Hazzan in rapid reading of Hebrew prayers, which must remain the basis of our very existence as a united people. However, we recognize that they have not been able to continue their studies for one reason or another, and for these young people this booklet has been prepared." He ends with the hope that "our young people will be enabled to follow the service with understanding and zeal and that through this means they will be drawn closer to a religious life, and therefore will participate more actively in our congregational activities."

Changing Neighborhoods

By the mid-1950s many members of Ezra Bessaroth had moved away from the old neighborhood. After much discussion, the synagogue building was sold to a Baptist church in 1956. Plans were made to build a social hall in the Seward Park District where a number of congregants lived. It was completed in 1958. For a little more than a year Ezra Bessaroth was in transition, without a synagogue building of its own. Some members attended services at the Sephardic Bikur Holim on Twentieth Street and East Fir. For the holiday services, Ezra Bessaroth rented space in the Seattle Hebrew Day School.

During this period of transition, a new battle erupted over the question of mixed seating in the synagogue. Ezra Bessaroth, as a traditional Sephardic congregation, had always maintained separate seating for men and women. But since a new building was to be constructed, some individuals argued that the congregation should adopt mixed seating and not bother with putting up a balcony or a women's section. This question did not arise in a vacuum. For many years members of Ezra Bessaroth had been eager to adapt to American ways. The Reform Temple de Hirsch was seen as a model, and ties between it and Ezra Bessaroth were long-standing. Even as far back as the days when the members of Ezra Bessaroth had tried to raise funds for their first building, members of the Reform temple had helped organize a bazaar for the benefit of the Ezra Bessaroth building fund. Moreover, some individuals of Rhodes background – especially those who had achieved financial success – had become members of Temple de Hirsch.

Those who wanted to institute mixed seating in the new synagogue believed that this innovation would help the congregation maintain its membership. Since many of the members were no longer Orthodox in their religious practice, a synagogue with mixed seating would be more appealing to the younger generation. Why should the synagogue continue to lose members to the Reform temple when a simple innovation would keep the members within Ezra Bessaroth?

The traditionalists argued that Ezra Bessaroth must maintain its historic traditions. To institute mixed seating would be a betrayal of what the congregation stood for. It would be a repudiation of the traditions held sacred by the Jews of Rhodes, going back many centuries. Rev. David Behar strongly favored separate seating. He, the members of his family, and his devoted followers contended that it was important to keep the sexes separated in the synagogue as a sign of faithfulness to the Sephardic tradition. Interestingly, he did not argue his case in the name of traditional Orthodoxy, but appealed to the congregants' feelings for Sephardic tradition.

Rabbi Kahan also wanted to retain Orthodox Sephardic tradition, and most members of the congregation were satisfied to maintain the status quo. Thus, the traditionalists won the debate, and the new synagogue was built with separate sections for men and women, which are still in use at present.

However, this victory was not complete. A number of congregants left the synagogue and joined the local Reform temple or Conservative synagogue. There were bitter feelings in the community as a result of the ongoing debate. Although the battle to maintain separate seating had been won, the new challenge was to keep the remaining members within the congregation and attract new members, lest the victory be hollow.

Shortly after the congregation was reestablished in Seward Park in 1958, Rabbi Kahan retired. He had been an erudite and soft-spoken man, and the congregation now wanted to hire an energetic rabbi who could relate well with the younger people. It selected Rabbi Abraham Shalem, an outstanding rabbinic scholar. Rabbi Shalem faced enormous problems in the few years he spent with the congregation. Not American-born, he spoke English with a Spanish accent, and his short beard was disliked by individuals who thought a modern rabbi should have no beard.

Rabbi Shalem was intense and active; he started classes both in his home and at the synagogue, and a number of congregants became his devoted students. He tried to establish a youth choir, but that project did not succeed. He was instrumental in getting young men to participate in the synagogue services, not only during regular Shabbat services, but also on holidays. Although Rabbi Shalem was quite Orthodox, he was willing to experiment with late Friday night services, to be held at 8:00 p.m. in order to accommodate congregants who worked. Although these late services must have been very much against Rabbi Shalem's inner conviction, he conducted them himself and encouraged people to attend. Nonetheless, these services enjoyed only modest success and were discontinued after his departure from the congregation.

In searching for a rabbi to replace Rabbi Shalem, the congregation was unable to find a qualified American–born Sephardic leader. There was a strong sentiment to hire an American rabbi, on the assumption that he could relate better to the young people, and in September of 1962 Ezra Bessaroth engaged Rabbi William Greenberg, an Ashkenazic Orthodox rabbi who had learned the Sephardic customs and style of service from his previous congregation.

Over the years he has introduced a number of changes into the service. For example, Shabbat morning services now feature English liturgical readings prior to the returning of the Torah to the Ark, and the congregation reads the Psalms in English preceding evening services on the Festivals. On weekday evenings, Psalms 49, 134, and 121 are read in English, especially at the service commemorating the anniversary of a death. On *Rosh Hodesh* (the first of the month), Psalm 104 is read in English.

Rabbi Greenberg also introduced several Ashkenazic melodies into the service, such as the *Bei Ana Rahets*, which is sung just before the Torah is taken from the Ark, and the *Aleinu*, which concludes the service. Although these melodies were initially resisted by some members, they have now become a standard part of the service at Ezra Bessaroth.

Rabbi Greenberg was also a major force in establishing a summer camp for the children of Ezra Bessaroth. The camp generally lasts up to two weeks and gives the children an opportunity to have a good time and also to learn many Sephardic customs and traditions. The camp experience has strengthened the religious feelings of many young people who have participated as campers and counselors. In fact, there has been a spillover from the camp experience into the synagogue, so that the Shabbat services now attract a larger number of young people.

Hazzan Isaac Azose, who began his association with Ezra Bessaroth in 1965, brought yet another dimension to the synagogue services by introducing a number of Israeli melodies into the services. It is not unusual to hear the melodies of "Erev shel Shoshanim" or "Jerusalem of

Gold" worked into the *Musaf Kedusha*. Mr. Azose has also taken melodies from traditional Judeo-Spanish songs and has adapted them to the synagogue liturgy. Interestingly, he has brought to Ezra Bessaroth a number of melodies sung in the Sephardic Bikur Holim, the rival Seattle Sephardic congregation in which he was raised.

Then and Now

Elazar Behar, the son of Rev. David Behar, has served as volunteer *gabbai* (sexton) of Ezra Bessaroth for many years. In reminiscing about the changes within the synagogue over the years, he has offered several important observations.

In the early years, Judeo-Spanish was a vital element in the religious life of the community. Many of the *piyutim* (hymns) of the High Holy Days were sung in Judeo-Spanish, especially in the translation of Rabbi Reuben Eliyahu Israel of the Island of Rhodes. Today a number of these *piyutim* are still sung in Judeo-Spanish, but fewer than formerly. Similarly, the service of the Ninth of Ab used to include many dirges sung in Judeo-Spanish. Today several are still sung in Judeo-Spanish, out of a reverence for tradition. Mr. Behar recalls that on Purim eve the Megillah was read in Hebrew, but it was read in Judeo-Spanish the next evening, for the benefit of the women. This practice stopped many years ago.

Judeo-Spanish songs were sung when the father of a newborn child was called to the *Sefer* (Torah). Similarly, special songs were sung in honor of a bridegroom and at the naming of a baby girl. These practices have been discontinued since Judeo-Spanish is no longer spoken much, certainly not by the younger generation.

Mr. Behar recalls other customs that have fallen into disuse. On the evening of the thirty-third day of the Omer, congregants would gather in the synagogue and light candles, singing songs and staying late into the evening. On the day preceding Yom Kippur a table would be set up in a corner of the synagogue and on it would be placed bowls filled with oil. During the day women came into the synagogue and lit the wicks in these bowls so that, by the time services began on Yom Kippur Eve, the synagogue would be filled with the fragrance of the burning oil.

All these customs are no longer observed, However, Judeo-Spanish is making a comeback in the synagogue services. Although there is considerably less in the liturgy than in the 1920s, more Judeo-Spanish is now used than was the case ten years ago. Perhaps as part of their search for roots and a return to tradition, the young people in particular have been eager to reestablish Judeo-Spanish as a feature of the synagogue services. There seems to be greater interest now in the old melodies and the old language of the Sephardim. For example, each Shabbat morning *Ein Kelohenu* is sung in both Hebrew and Judeo-Spanish. A Judeo-Spanish passage is chanted after the Grace After Meals at all synagogue events. Pamphlets containing the Judeo-Spanish translation of *piyutim* for the High Holy Days have been prepared with an English transliteration, so that these songs may be sung and enjoyed by the entire congregation, even those who do not understand Judeo-Spanish.

Several ritual observances have been changed as well. Formerly, *meldados*, services held on the anniversary of a loved one's death, took place in the family's home. The service would be chanted and followed by refreshments and socializing. Now very few congregants retain this custom, preferring to observe *meldados* at the synagogue. Moreover, there has been a growing tendency to observe the *meldados* on a convenient night rather than on the actual anniversary date. Similarly, services during the week of mourning have been largely transferred to the synagogue from the home. Some traditional families in the congregation still insist on holding these services in the home, but they are few in number.

In recent years, the congregation has instituted a Bat Mitzvah service based on that developed in Congregation Shearith Israel in New York. It is held on Sunday, rather than Shabbat, and involves the recitation of a number of Psalms, a speech by the Bat Mitzvah, and a short address by the rabbi, followed by a blessing.

The demographic character of the congregation is changing, too. The congregation has enjoyed an increase in membership among Ashkenazic Jews. Many of the Ashkenazim are married to Sephardic spouses, but others simply wish to join the congregation to enjoy its services and warm community spirit. Ashkenazim are readily accepted in the community and have positions on the board of trustees and in the various synagogue committees. Ashkenazic members are likely to increase in number, and this may ultimately lead to other changes in the synagogue service.

Members of Ezra Bessaroth tend to agree that the services of the synagogue today are very much like the services in its early years. Gordon de Leon, son of Haim de Leon, who had served as *hazzan* in the early years, wrote to tell me that the tunes of Ezra Bessaroth are the same now as in the old days. Except for a few Ashkenazic pieces, "all the melodies that are sung are those that were used in Rhodes." Rabbi William Greenberg indicated to me that he suspects that "the service (order and melody) would be almost identical." Elazar Behar also told me that the Shabbat and holiday services at Ezra Bessaroth are not much different today from what they were more than a half-century ago. This sentiment is echoed by many members of the congregation.

All the same, quite a number of changes have taken place in the service: English has been introduced; the use of Judeo-Spanish has declined; Israeli melodies have been added. A number of services formerly observed in the synagogue have been discontinued, and the *meldados* that had formerly been observed in the home are now largely observed in the synagogue. The service today, in spite of a happy sense of informality, is conducted with more order and decorum than in the early years. If one of the pioneers of Ezra Bessaroth were to return to the synagogue after a hiatus of fifty years, he would recognize the service – but he would also notice many differences in style, language, and melodies. The service in Ezra Bessaroth today is not identical with that performed on the Island of Rhodes early this century.

What is extraordinary, however, is that the congregation has remained quite faithful to its Sephardic traditions. In spite of adaptations and changes, the services continue to be Sephardic in essence and substance. The innovations have not taken anything away from the congregation's basic liturgical style. Any challenge to the primary Sephardic identity of the services would be sharply repulsed. An Ashkenazic melody here and there – fine. An Israeli melody in the *kedushah* – that, too, is fine, but the basic service must remain intact.

It is not easy for a religious institution to be receptive to change while retaining faithfulness to tradition. The members of Ezra Bessaroth have managed to keep a balance – incorporating changes, but retaining the basic traditions. The proof of the congregation's success is that most congregants feel the service today is about the same as it was when the congregation was founded early in this century.

NOTES

The early history of Sephardim in Seattle may be studied in an unpublished master's thesis by Albert Adatto, "Sephardim and the Seattle Sephardic Community" (University of Washington, 1939). See also my article, "Notes on the Early History of Seattle's Sephardic Community," *Western States Jewish Historical Quarterly*, October 1974, pp. 22–30; and my book, *La America: The Sephardic Experience in the United States* (Philadelphia, 1982), pp. 158–162.

Information on the history of Ezra Bessaroth is available in an article by William Greenberg, which appeared in the dedication program of Ezra Bessaroth, Seattle, 1970.

For a general picture of the Americanization of Sephardim, see my article, "The Sephardim of the United States: An Exploratory Study," *American Jewish Year Book* (New York and Philadelphia, 1973). See also my book, *La America*.

For a history of the Jews of Rhodes, see my book, *The Jews of Rhodes* (New York, 1978).

Issues of the *Progress* were given to me by Jacob Almeleh, together with his reminiscences of that era. See my article, "Progress – Seattle's Sephardic Monthly 1934–5," *American Sephardi*, Autumn 1971, pp. 90–95.

The articles in *La Vara* dealing with the Sephardic synagogue were dated September 14, 1934, and September 28, 1934. The English translation of these articles is found in Adatto, "Sephardim and the Seattle Sephardic Community," pp. 171–182.

Rabbi Kahan's pamphlet for the Eve of Rosh Hashanah, now out of print and not in use, was published by the Congregation in 1947.

The formation of the first choir of Ezra Bessaroth was described by Jacob Almeleh in a short article that appeared in the souvenir journal of Ezra Bessaroth on the occasion of the congregation's sixty-seventh anniversary.

Although I was a young boy at the time, I distinctly remember the turmoil in the community concerning the question of establishing mixed seating in the new synagogue building. Rabbi Greenberg informed me that Rev. Behar told him that the issue of separate seating "should be approached not as a religious requirement but as the Sephardic way of doing things."

Information about changes within the services over the years has been derived from my memory as well as my personal observation. I was born and raised in Congregation Ezra Bessaroth. In 1963 I left Seattle to attend Yeshiva College in New York. I have been living in New York ever since, but I and my family have returned to Seattle almost every summer. I suppose a number of the changes are more obvious to me, coming to the synagogue at yearly intervals, than to the members who attend regularly.

I extend gratitude to my father, Victor Angel, for the information he provided me. A special word of thanks is owed to Rabbi William Greenberg, Gordon de Leon, and Elazar Behar. Rabbi Greenberg and Mr. de Leon sent me written answers to a questionnaire I had sent them about the service. Mr. Behar tape-recorded his comments.

6

Education in the Synagogue: The Transformation of the Supplementary School

BARRY CHAZAN

The story of the synagogue supplementary school is a fascinating chapter in the saga of twentieth-century American Jewry. Numerically, supplementary schools have been the dominant form of Jewish education for most of the century.[1] Such schools have been the major preoccupation of most central agencies of Jewish education throughout their existence. Some of the most illustrious American Jewish educators have been employed in synagogue schools. Indeed, the synagogue school is a striking barometer and mirror of twentieth-century American Jewish life.

The history of the institution can be divided into three distinct periods.[2] The first phase, from the 1920s to the 1940s, was the era of creation and formation. This was the time in which some basic parameters were established and the institution struggled to survive. The second period in the history of the synagogue schools, from the early 1950s to the late 1960s, was an era of growth, expansion, and legitimization. In these years, synagogue schools became respectable educational institutions, which engendered excitement, dynamism, and hope. The third period in the history of the synagogue school, from the 1970s to the present, is an era of retrenchment and defense. The current mood within these schools is one of questioning and concern.[3]

The problems that confront today's supplementary schools include the most basic issues of Jewish education: (1) personnel; (2) the curriculum; (3) professional leadership; (4) parental support; (5) student motivation; (6) time; and (7) their ultimate goal and direction. The profession of full-time teaching for the supplementary school apparently no longer exists.[4] Many supplementary school principals have opted for headmasterships of day schools. The immediate demands of the part-time school have effectively paralyzed long-term curriculum development. Professional, parental, and student discontent has led many people to begin to question the viability of such schools.

Nevertheless, the supplementary school remains the dominant form of American Jewish education, encompassing approximately 72–75 percent of all school-age children in the United States who receive any form of Jewish education. Moreover, all indicators point to the likelihood that the afternoon supplementary school will continue to be prominent. Hence it would be instructive to identify some of the archetypical characteristics of the supplementary school during its great age of fruition. This discussion will better enable us to recognize the critical breakdown and dissolution of the midcentury synagogue supplementary school in the past quarter-century and its re-creation in two new forms: the elementary day school and a new model of the afternoon supplementary school.

Characteristics of the Synagogue Supplementary School

During its evolution, the supplementary type of American Jewish school developed six prominent characteristics. First, by their very structure and name, such schools were secondary to the general educational world of the American Jewish child. Education in the synagogue meant that Jewish schooling was "in addition to" a child's regular education, and as such it was one of several extracurricular activities (i.e., dance, sports, music, Hebrew school). Like sports, music, and dance lessons, however, it normally was not thought to carry the same weight for advancement and achievement in life as one's general education.

Second, such schools have been mainly elementary educational institutions. There are some noteworthy examples of pre- and postelementary supplementary Jewish education (indeed, they may be among the best instances of American Jewish education), but they are exceptions rather than the norm. The supplementary school world is typically populated by American Jews of the primary age level.

Third, such schools were generally attached to synagogues of specific religious movements (e.g., Orthodox, Conservative, Reform). Consequently, they have been utilized to promulgate specific denominational conceptions of Judaism. In contrast to such other forms of American Jewish education as the Jewish community center, the community school, and even the day school, the supplementary synagogue school was a unique product of and vehicle for Jewish religious denominationalism.

Fourth, the curriculum of the synagogue school was defined by the need to transmit a complex body of religious knowledge, ritual skills, and behaviors in a severely limited amount of time (two to six hours). Consequently, there was an ongoing – and frustrating – struggle to develop a curriculum that would be both intellectually and behaviorally comprehensive and that could be effected within the given time limits of the part-time school. The result was a series of curricula defined by the principle of random selectivity; that is, a select number of topics, skills, and contents were introduced in no particularly systematic order. The acceptance of this principle implied the rejection of other curricular approaches, for example, textual mastery, self-realization, or social reconstruction.[5] What in practice emerged in the supplementary school was a host of eclectic courses of study that encompassed an ambiguous collection of facts, skills, and attitudes.

Fifth, the professional population of the supplementary school included a broad range of educators, including immigrant *maskilim* and Hebraists, American-born professional educators affiliated with specific denominations, part-time professionals (often housewives), visiting or emigrant Israelis conversant in Hebrew, religious Jews concerned with perpetuating Jewish observance, and skilled public school educators with little or no Jewish education.[6]

Finally, three goals characterized synagogue supplementary schools. First, almost all schools of this genre were concerned with socializing young Jews into basic norms and rituals of a synagogue-oriented Judaism. Such norms and rituals included prayer skills, holiday and Shabbat skills (kiddush, the blessings over the candles, the four questions at the Passover *seder*, Bar and Bat Mitzvah rites), and some key facts and concepts of Jewish history and thought. Second, some schools of this genre were concerned with the larger aim of preparing young American Jews for a comfortable and compatible coexistence as Jews in American society. In this case, the concern was not specifically Jewish rituals, but attitudes and skills that would help young people feel at home in their Jewish and non-Jewish worlds. Third, a small number of American Jewish supplementary schools were concerned with the development and perpetuation of an intensive involvement in Jewish life. Such schools saw their mission as extending beyond both synagogue skills and cultural accommodation, and rather as aimed at the promotion of an intensive Jewish life-style within the fabric of contemporary American Jewry.

These six parameters constitute the framework within which the supplementary school developed. Many different versions of supplementary schools emerged as a result of alternative combinations of these characteristics (therefore it is misleading to talk about "the supplementary school" as a monolithic phenomenon). The various emergent models of supplementary Jewish schooling in the 1950s and 1960s were the precursors of the Jewish educational forms that became prevalent in the 1970s and 1980s, and it may well be argued that the roots of the current dynamics and dilemmas of Jewish education are to be found in the world of the midcentury supplementary school.

To demonstrate how the supplementary school was a crucible of the contemporary Jewish educational world, I will sketch a brief portrait of one such institution, the Temple Israel Educational Center of Albany, New York, during the 1950s and 1960s.[7] This portrait shows how the six factors cited above interacted in one school and how new forms of Jewish education emerged.

Temple Israel

The Albany Jewish community was significantly shaped by the influx of Eastern European Jewish migration early in the twentieth century.[8] Albany's proximity to New York City made it a convenient way station and then permanent home for many newcomers. Temple Israel was established in 1949 as a result of the merger of two smaller Conservative congregations,[9] and it was to develop into a large suburban congregation of nearly 1,000 families in the 1950s and 1960s.[10]

The School

Structure

The Temple Israel Educational Center (as it was formally known) comprised the following divisions: (1) a five-day-a week nursery school, (2) a five-year elementary school, (3) a one- and a three-day-a week junior high school, (4) a one- and a three-day-a-week high school, and (5) an adult education division. Most of the students in the school (70–85 percent)[11] were in the elementary division, and Bar and Bat Mitzvah served as the dropout point for the majority of the school's population. This was the general structural and demographic pattern of most of the three-day-a-week supplementary schools in this period (the percentage of high school students in this school was somewhat above the national average of the time). Gradually, the Temple Israel school began to add additional divisions to this basic structure, including (6) a junior college program, (7) a summer camp, (8) a winter vacation camp, (9) a youth department, and (10) a day school.[12]

Thus, the basic components of the standard supplementary school were present, in this institution, along with a number of educational programs that reflected the attempt to extend the boundaries of the school beyond the confines of the normal six–hour–a–week supplementary school. This school reflected a form of Jewish educational expansionism, in which steadily increasing elements of synagogue and communal life would be "conquered" for Jewish education:

> What framework is needed to provide this kind of *emotional relevance*? The traditional concept of "school" cannot do because we are faced with homes that are indifferent and sometimes even hostile to our cause. . . . What we need is an all-season Ramah – a self-contained community, a "ghetto" if you will. . . .
> Although we believe that the Day School, time-wise, offers the best opportunity to create this environment, we are convinced that, with vision and careful planning, it can be introduced into the six hour a week afternoon Hebrew school. . . . Our synagogues must expand from narrow houses of religion into socio-cultural religious complexes with all the elements of our Jewish civilization . . . they must be *environments* of total Jewish experience.[13]

Such expansionism was neither smooth nor unanimously received. There was perpetual opposition to each attempt to extend into new areas, and lengthy debate and even subterfuge were often required to implement the plans (for example, at one point a small group of concerned laymen purchased the campsite to be used for a Hebrew-speaking summer camp in order to circumvent the opposition of the majority synagogue board.)[14] This tension does not simply reflect local synagogue politics; rather, it represents the confrontation of two conceptions of Judaism within the synagogue supplementary school. In the minimalist conception, Jewish education was expected to occupy clearly defined places and moments (three days a week for five years, September through June) that were structurally defined as the formal parameters of the supplementary school. In the expansionist conception, Jewish education was limited by neither time nor space, and instead, attempted to break down existing boundaries. The tension between these two views is one of the most prominent dimensions of midcentury supplementary Jewish education.

Staff

The staff of this school consisted of a principal, teachers, the professional synagogue leadership (rabbi, cantor, and ritual director), and office staff. Early in its existence, the congregation established the position of a full-time educational director who was entrusted with responsibility for all facets of the school program. Not all supplementary schools followed this pattern; some schools were headed by either the rabbi, an assistant rabbi, a head teacher, a qualified public school teacher, or an administrator. The principal of this school from 1955 to 1971 was the late Shraga (Philip) Arian, a young, American-born educator who had recently completed studies at the Jewish Theological Seminary. Arian was a charismatic educational personality, committed to the belief that both Judaism and education must be all-encompassing and organic: "He conceived of [Judaism] as a whole approach to life; he urged Jews to let Judaism impinge on every aspect of their existence and to interpret life through knowledgeable Jewish experience."[15] Indeed, his own style of leadership transcended the boundaries of what was regarded as appropriate for a synagogue-based professional in the mid-1950s. On Purim he appeared in the main sanctuary dressed in red tights; for many years he was part of a theater troupe at the local university; he once led a group of teenagers in picketing a performance of the Bolshoi Ballet at a newly renovated downtown theater (much to the chagrin and anger of many congregational members). Indeed, his educational theory and practice were total and nonsupplementary in nature, and in many instances were inconsistent with the supplementary world in which he was functioning.

The majority of the teaching staff of Temple Israel consisted of individuals who had lived in Albany for many years or who had come to Albany for reasons other than to teach in the school. Some were housewives, others were local professionals or businessmen who were knowledgeable about Judaism but were not trained educators; still others were students at the numerous professional schools located in Albany. Very few of the teaching staff of this school were full-time professional teachers who had moved to Albany for the specific purpose of teaching in a Jewish school.

Although most of the teaching staff had basic credentials in Judaica or education, the portrait that emerges from an analysis of school documents, school board minutes, and interviews is of fairly conventional and mainstream teaching. There is no evidence of particularly original pedagogic style or unusual academic excellence. Three qualities, however, are prominent in this staff – personal commitment, self-growth, and ideological diversity. The personal Jewish lives of these teachers were apparently important educational factors. Mrs. M. taught Hebrew school during the afternoon, conducted evening classes for adults on "the Jewish home," and accompanied her husband to services every Shabbat. Mr. F. was a young and attractive lawyer who continued to teach first and second grades even as he developed a growing law practice. Mrs. I. was a sophisticated European intellectual whom one met in class, at concerts, at services, at adult education classes, and at local art movies. The overt

Jewish life-style of these teachers was as much of an educative factor as their classroom teaching.

In addition, the records reveal an intensive in-service training program. The principal regularly visited classes and discussed pedagogic issues with staff. Monthly teachers' meetings dealt exclusively with educational issues. Subsidies were provided for special courses. Great demands were placed on this staff, which far exceeded the limited number of hours for which they were hired or the comparatively modest salaries that they earned.[16]

Finally, this staff provided a broad range of models of Jewish commitment. Mr. A. was a nonreligious Hebraist; Rev. M was a pious Orthodox Jew; Mrs. I. was an ideological Reconstructionist; Miss R. was an Israeli. This staff reflected the panorama of Jewish ideologies that characterizes twentieth-century Jewish life. Interestingly, this school (like many of the supplementary schools of the Conservative movement) was not populated mainly by professionals who had been trained in the synagogue's denominational ideology. Few of these teachers were trained Conservative educators; rather, they were a potpourri of committed individuals who gravitated to teaching in this school.

In contrast to many synagogues of this period, the professional leadership of the institution played an active educational role. The rabbi taught high school classes, led the elite youth group (Leadership Training Fellowship), taught adult education classes, and conducted classes for teachers. The cantor led youth choir, taught Bar and Bat Mitzvah classes, and led youth groups. The ritual advisor conducted a tallis and tefillin club, prepared Bar Mitzvah boys and taught school classes. The synagogue's professional staff functioned as an integral part of the school faculty.

The Curriculum

There were two curricula in this school: (1) the course of study used to guide the six hours and twelve grades of classroom teaching and (2) the program of Jewish living that encompassed the entire year (Shabbat, holidays, winter vacation, and summer). The formal curriculum covered the conventional list of major subject areas (Bible, history, Hebrew, customs, and ceremonies) and used standard textbooks (Pessin's Jewish history texts, Schortstein's version of the *Humash*, the *Hasefer* Hebrew primer). In general, it paralleled the standard curriculum of the United Synagogue Commission on Jewish Education, first developed in the late 1940s and published in the late 1950s.[17] However, there were some innovations in the Temple Israel curriculum: the introduction of

Holocaust and Eretz Yisrael studies almost a decade before these subjects began to assume prominence in American Jewish schools, emphasis on spoken Hebrew, and a commitment to formal textual study rather than the use of secondary sources. Overall, however, this curriculum reflects the major problem of all supplementary Jewish education: the need to distill a huge culture into severely delimited subject areas and time blocks.

The second curriculum refers to a series of educational programs and interventions that took place beyond the normal classroom hours. (Arian rejected the phrase 'co-curricular,' arguing that "no activity is co-curricular since *all* activities form the essence of the curriculum.")[18] It included the following activities: a five-day winter camp revolving around a Jewish theme, weekend teenage retreats to other communities, one-day bus trips to Jewish sites in New York City, all-night study sessions on *Shavuot,*a *Tashlich* ceremony on Rosh Hashanah, and a summer Hebrew-speaking day camp that encompassed prayer, study, sports, arts and crafts, and swimming. The objective of this second curriculum was to expose students to authentic Jewish experiences and to teach them Jewish skills and behaviors related to such experiences. It was a response to the classic problem of part-time Jewish education: namely, it had neither enough time nor the right time for introducing children to the comprehensive spirit and practice of Jewish experience.

The Peer Culture

Any discussion of American Jewish education is incomplete if it does not refer to the youth culture in which the young American lives. Baseball, ballet, bicycles, and braces constitute the milieu in which Judaism and Jewish education occur. In Albany, afternoon Hebrew school classes had to compete with Little League practice; Friday night services coincided with dances at the neighborhood school; and weekday evening Hebrew high school classes conflicted with meetings of the high school debating and literary society.

For most of the young people in this community, the general culture predominated: baseball, dances, public school activities, and college board preparation. For a much smaller group of young people, an intense Jewish-centered peer culture developed. This group consisted mainly of achievers or overachievers in the general world who were at the same time intensely involved with Jewish activities. Bob A. was a star back of the local high school team, at the top of his class academically, and president of the elite synagogue youth group and regularly attended Camp Ramah in the summer. Bob C. was valedictorian of the local high school, president of the debating society, and a regular participant in services on Shabbat morning. Perry R. was an attractive and popular teenage personality and he and his family were stalwarts of synagogue life. When these people made choices about their college years, they considered options that would enable them to pursue both general and Jewish studies; and many of them were to choose undergraduate and graduate programs in New York City, where they could continue their Jewish studies.

Consequently, there developed in this community a viable, intense Jewish subculture, predicated on the assumption that a teenager could exist in the worlds of both Judaism and the general culture. This subculture had a strong impact on those who were part of it, as well as on the brothers, sisters, cousins, and younger peers who observed it. In part, this culture was to develop naturally, and in part it was the result of sustained and persistent efforts by the synagogue educational staff. Indeed, a great deal of time and energy were invested in an extremely small and not representative group of young people; this investment represented a conscious educational and philosophic choice.

The Synagogue

In general, supplementary schools have been part of larger synagogue complexes, and the nature of the relationship between school and synagogue has had important implications for the work of the school. The Temple Israel school was housed in a separate school wing that included classrooms and school offices. However, this wing also included the rabbi's office, the synagogue office, and the synagogue library. School events took place throughout the synagogue building, rather than being restricted to the school wing. Thus, the life of the school was physically an intimate part of the regular daily life of the synagogue.

The program of the synagogue encompassed the broad panorama of activities that characterized many midcentury synagogue-centers: religious services, a men's club, sisterhood, socials, lecture series, burial society, pastoral counseling, adult institute. This congregation seemed to emphasize cultural and educational programs, and a typical year included sermons on educational issues, weekend study sessions with visiting scholars, a series of lectures by prominent guests, and a homecoming Shabbat for congregational young people studying at the Jewish Theological Seminary.[19]

This congregation, like others of its genre, was governed by an elected lay board that worked together with the professional leadership to plan and implement synagogue policy. Many different conceptions of Judaism, Jewish education, and the synagogue were reflected in the lay leadership. A mainstream group of lay leaders was committed to an efficiently functioning congregation that would provide basic religious and educational programs. This group believed in the minimalist approach to Jewish supplementary education. A smaller group of lay leaders (successors to a generation of ardent supporters of Jewish education in this community) continually fought for additional Jewish educational opportunities. It raised money for scholarships to Camp Ramah; it fought for the establishment of a Hebrew speaking summer day camp; and it struggled to create a day school in Albany. A clear alliance between this small group and the professional leadership of the congregation emerged. The fundamental position of this group was that *the* purpose of the synagogue was Jewish education: "One thing we are NOT prepared to do or become: 'social directors,' 'recreation workers' or 'entertainers'– ... THESE ARE NOT THE BUSINESS OF THE SYNAGOGUE!... We want people who are looking for the kind of Jewish life and *mentschlichkeit* which we try to achieve within the guidelines of the Conservative movement... we are not a supermarket of activities".[20] The position of this group was generally not the majority view in the congregation and usually not the popular one. It represented an alternative conception of American Jewish education that eventually would not be able to find full expression within the confines of the part-time school and would have to look elsewhere.

This school, then, reflects several prominent motifs of the midcentury synagogue supplementary school: it was part-time, elementary, synagogue-oriented, and aimed at harmonizing Jewishness and Americanism. At the same time, it was committed to perpetual educational expansionism, the subservience of the synagogue to the school, and a disproportional investment in a small group of young people.

The Transformation of the Supplementary School

What happened to the two "schools" that were housed in the same building on New Scotland Avenue in Albany, New York? The story of Jewish education from the 1960s until today is ultimately about the dismantling of the midcentury supplementary school and its recreation in two new forms: the new supplementary school and the new day school.

The ever-expanding supplementary school that was continually looking for new walls to break down was frustrated by the confines of the synagogue-sponsored part-time school. However one might try to stretch it, the part-time school, meeting in late afternoons and on Sunday mornings, simply did not provide enough time nor the right time to do effective Jewish education. The hours were too few, the times of the day (4:00–6:00 p.m. and Sunday 9:00–11:00 a.m. or 11:00 a.m. to 1:00 p.m.) were too tiring, and the days were too spread out. Moreover, the Jewish educational maximalists became frustrated with the endless battles within the synagogue structure for increased Jewish education. Finally, there was increasing frustration with what were regarded as unsatisfactory results in knowledge, skills, and attitudes from a typical supplementary school education.

This changing mood occurred at a time when American public education was undergoing a profound metamorphosis, described by some as "the collapse of public education".[21] Parents who had been brought up on the ethos of state-sponsored general education and privately sponsored supplementary religious education now became more receptive to the idea of private general education in a Jewish context. The result has been the remarkable growth in the past two decades of a network of private Jewish elementary day schools that provide high-quality general and Jewish education in one setting.[22] The new day schools are the contemporary manifestation of the expansionist supplementary schools of the 1950s–1960s. The new day school is able to offer more hours of Judaic learning as well as greater flexibility and creativity in the use of time. Moreover, all this can be done within a totally controlled Jewish setting. Such day schools are not outgrowths of either the classical Eastern European *yeshiva* or of the modern Orthodox day schools.[23] Rather, the new Conservative, Reform, and community elementary day schools are really transformed versions of the midcentury intensive supplementary schools.

The expansionist synagogue supplementary school was to be reborn as the contemporary non-orthodox day school; the minimalist supplementary school was also destined to change. Originally the agenda of the synagogue school consisted of three items: (1) synagogue skills, (2) the coexistence of Jewishness and Americanism, and (3) an intensive Jewish life-style. Those concerned with the third objective eventually moved to the day school. The transmission of synagogue – particularly Bar Mitzvah – skills became more technically efficient and less dependent on five years in a Hebrew school (through the use of tapes or records, trips to Israel, and more experience in how to train American youngsters in such skills). More important, the agenda of American Jewish life changed in this period; the challenge of accommodating Jewishness and Americanism was no longer the issue – instead the struggle now was for Jewish identity and consciousness. By midcentury, the possibility of adapting to America was confirmed; now the challenge was whether

Jews could retain and transmit Jewishness to their young. Thus, the phrase "Jewish identity" entered the lexicon of Jewish education and by the 1970s had become the prominent emphasis of Jewish education.[24]

This shift in priorities was to have a profound effect on the existing supplementary school. Its original task of transmission, training, and accommodation was replaced by a new function, to make young people "feel more Jewish." The new supplementary school increasingly shifted its attention to issues of contemporary importance and interest (Israel, Russian Jewry, intermarriage) and to techniques and programs that would increase Jewish concern and consciousness (values clarification, retreats, classroom discussion). In many ways, the new supplementary school was asked to serve more as a community center in which young Jews could meet and less as a formal school. This implied major shifts in content and staff, and many of the earlier knowledge- or skill-oriented curricula and teachers became less appropriate. Thus, many new curricula and teacher-training programs emerged in the 1970s that reflected entirely new conceptions of the aims of American supplementary Jewish education.[25]

Yesterday, Today, and Tomorrow

The part-time synagogue supplementary school was a unique American Jewish educational form. It was created in the twentieth century to respond to the needs and directions of the emergent American Jewish society and it became a remarkable barometer of the dynamics and diversity of that society. The supplementary school reached its zenith at midcentury, at which point it began to be confronted with internal and external pressures. The classic midcentury supplementary school contained within it the seeds of the new forms of Jewish education that have emerged in our days. The origins of American Jewish education lie in the early twentieth century, but its critical and formative period was the era of the synagogue supplementary school. The story is not yet over; today's part-time school will not be like its predecessor. Thus far, it has proven to be an adaptive form, which may only now be entering a new and even more creative age.

NOTES

1   See the following studies of the American Jewish supplementary school: Sidney Solomon, "The Conservative Congregational School as a Response to the American Scene" (DHL diss., Jewish Theological Seminary, 1982); L. Hamburger, "A Study of the Failures and Dilemmas of Part-Time American Jewish Education" (Ph.D. diss., University of Maryland, 1971).

2 Judah Pilch, ed., *A History of Jewish Education in America* (New York, 1969); Lloyd Gartner, ed., *Jewish Education in the U.S.* (New York, 1965).

3 See, for example, "Prospect: The Jewish Supplementary School in the 1980's," *Jewish Education*, 50, no. 4 (Winter 1982).

4 Susan Shevitz, *The Deterioration of the Profession of Jewish Supplementary School Teaching: An Analysis of the Effects of Communal Myths on Policy and Program* (Cambridge, Mass., 1983).

5 See the discussion of alternative conceptions of curriculum in education in Daniel Tanner and Laurel Tanner, *Curriculum Development: Theory into Practice* (New York, 1980), chap. 1.

6 See the discussions of personnel in the part-time school in: O. Janowsky, ed., *The Education of American Jewish Teachers* (Boston, 1967); Shevitz, *Deterioration of the Profession*; Barry Chazan, *Personnel in Jewish Education* (Jerusalem, 1984).

7 The "portrait" method is an increasingly popular approach to the analysis of educational institutions. See Sara Lawrence Lightfoot, *The Good High School* (New York, 1983).

8 William Kennedy, *O Albany: An Urban Tapestry* (New York, 1984), pp. 215–233.

9 "Temple Israel: Fifteen Years of Progress," in *Temple Israel 15th Annual Purim Festival Journal* (Albany, N.Y., 1964).

10 I would like to acknowledge the following people for making data and files available to me and for sharing their knowledge of the subject: Juday Arian, Morris Eson, Susie Isser, Rabbi Hayim Kieval, Mollie Konikoff, Leo Phaff, Ruth Phaff, Stephen Phaff, Hayim Picker, Rabbi Paul Silton, and the office staff at Temple Israel.

11 *Temple Israel School Enrollment Figures, 1957–1961*

	1957	1958	1959	1960	1961
Nursery	14	20	23	15	20
Primary	176	169	148	155	148
Elementary	324	327	327	326	340
Junior high and high school	65	105	126	115	147
Citizenship	23	20	15	36	84
Junior college	3	2	3	3	1
Special	—	5	3	3	5
Total	605	648	661	691	745

Report of Temple Israel Educational Center School Board, 1961.

12 Originally, the day school in Albany was officially housed in the Temple Israel congregation, but was not sponsored by the synagogue (for various

political and strategic reasons). However, the core of the professional leadership, lay support, and student population initially came from this congregation.

13 Shraga Arian, "The Environment School: A New Format," in *He Kindled a Light: A Philosophy of Jewish Education* (from the Speeches and Writings of Shraga Arian), ed. Chaim Picker (New York, 1976), pp. 117–122.

14 Minutes of School Board, 1 March, 1955, 19 March, 1955; Rabbi's 4th Annual Report, 13 May, 1958.

15 Picker, *He Kindled a Light,* pp. xi–xx.

16 The following table compares teachers' salaries in several U.S. synagogue supplementary schools in 1957: *Minutes, Temple Israel Educational Center School Board,* 1957:

Teacher's salaries in some supplementary schools, 1957

School	Salary range ($)	Teacher cost per weekly pupil hour
Rodef Zedek (Chicago)	4,600–7,000	14.48
Beth Shalom (Kansas City)	3,500–6,000	15.59
Shaaray Zedek (Detroit)	4,600–9,000	16.20
Park Synagogue (Cleveland)	3,750–7,000	9.71
Beth El (South Orange)	3,850–5,250	18.85
Forest Hills Jewish Center	3,800–6,000	21.69
Shaar Hashamayim (Montreal)	n.a.	18.75
East Midwood (Brooklyn)	3,200–5,200	18.71
Beth David (Miami)	3,600–6,000	18.04
Beth Tzedec (Toronto)	3,500–6,500	19.18
Beth El (Utica)	6,000–7,350	23.26
Germantown (Philadelphia)	1,500–3,600	11.55
Beth El (Rochester)	n.a.	18.09
Temple Israel (Albany)	5,300–6,500	17.33

Note: n.a. = not available.

Source: Minutes, Temple Israel Educational Center School Board, 1957.

17 Louis Ruffman, *Curriculum Outline for the Congregational School* (New York, 1959).

18 Arian, "Environmental School," p. 113.

19 *Temple Israelight,* vol. 8, 1956.

20 Rabbi's Annual Address, 14 May 1963, p. 4; 20 May 1968, p. 13.

21 James Coleman, Thomas Hoffer, and Sally Kilgore, *High School Achievement: Public, Catholic, and Private Schools Compared.* (New York, 1982); Samuel Bowles and Herbert Gintis, *Schooling in Capitalist America: Educational Reform and the Contradictions of Economic Life* (New York, 1976); Susan Abromowitz and Ann Stackhouse, *The Private High School Today* (Washington, D.C.,1980).

184   *Barry Chazan*

22   In the 1960s, approximately 10 percent of all school-aged children in the United States who received Jewish education, did so in a day school; in the 1970s the figure was 16 percent, and in the 1980s, approximately 27 percent. Alvin Schiff, *The Jewish Day School in America* (New York, 1966); I. Fried, "Trends and Issues in Hebrew Day School Education" (Ph.D. diss., Ohio State University, 1973); Sergio Dellapergola and Nitza Genuth, *Jewish Education Attained in Diaspora Communities: Data for 1970's* (Jerusalem, 1983); Nitza Genuth, Sergio Dellapergola, and Allie Dubb, *First Census of Jewish Schools in the Diaspora 1981/2–1982/3* (Jerusalem, 1985); *Jewish School Census* (New York, 1985).
23   For discussions of these types of Jewish day schools, see William Helmreich, *The World of the Yeshiva* (New York, 1979); Daniel Kramer, *The History and Impact of Torah Umesorah and Hebrew Day Schools in America* (Ph.D. diss., Yeshiva University, 1976).
24   Barry Chazan, "Theories of Jewish Nationalism," *Forum* (Spring-Summer, 1984), pp. 40–55.
25   An interesting reaction to this metamorphosis is the curriculum produced by the United Synagogue Commission on Jewish Education, which was an attempt to return to the more knowledge- and skill-oriented notion of the midcentury supplementary school. See United Synagogue Commission on Jewish Education, *A Curriculum for the Afternoon School* (New York, 1978).

7

From City to Suburb: Temple Mishkan Tefila of Boston

PAULA E. HYMAN

The social and ideological development of the American synagogue in the twentieth century has been linked to changing Jewish
residential patterns and levels of acculturation. Although the first areas
of settlement housed only East European immigrant Orthodox synagogues, modest in size and appearance, the middle-class second and
third areas of settlement within cities saw the proliferation of imposing
modern Orthodox and Conservative synagogues and Jewish centers. As
suburbanization proceeded, Conservative and Reform temples, designed
in accordance with the regnant tastes of modern American architecture,
became the dominant form of synagogue in the suburban landscape. This
transition from immigrant *shul* to suburban temple has been characterized
as a virtually automatic process accompanying geographic, social, and
cultural mobility.[1] Although the schematic nature of first, second, and
third areas of settlement has recently been challenged,[2] the connection
between neighborhood, generation, and synagogue type remains the
prevailing sociological model.

Within this broad framework of synagogue development as a response
to population movement and acculturation, there occurs the special case
of the uprooting of an urban synagogue situated in a declining neighborhood and its relocation to a more desirable suburban community.
Since a move of this sort is conscious and deliberate, rather than automatic
and reactive, it provides an opportunity to study a number of central
issues.

Most important, the relocation of a synagogue brings to the fore the
decision-making process of the synagogue administration. What moti-
vates the move? Who are the crucial personalities in determining the
timing of the move and the area chosen for relocation? What provisions
are made for the synagogue members left behind in the old neighbor-

185

hood? How do other institutions, either in the original community or in prospective areas of relocation, influence the outcome of the decision?

Since a suburban community differs substantially in spatial arrangement and class composition from a declining inner-city neighborhood, relocation is likely to affect the temple itself: the style of its architecture, the makeup of its membership, the norms of religious behavior. If the transition from one area of settlement to another is part of acculturation, is that acculturation reflected in the synagogue itself? Although there exists a considerable literature on the demographic and social characteristics as well as identification of suburban Jews, less attention has been paid to the specific nature and function of the suburban synagogue.[3]

When a major communal institution leaves a community, its decision has an effect upon the local population. Does the relocation of the synagogue follow, or precipitate, the decline of a once-thriving Jewish neighborhood? Are any efforts made to stabilize the neighborhood so that its Jewish residents will continue to feel comfortable there?

Studying the relocation process enables us to test the sociological model of synagogue development and to examine the impact of neighborhood and community upon the synagogue, the nature of synagogue governance, and the function of the synagogue within the community.

November 1955, a ground-breaking ceremony was held on Hammond Pond Parkway in Chestnut Hill, Massachusetts, for the construction of a new building for Temple Mishkan Tefila of Boston. Founded in 1858 by immigrants from East Prussia, Mishkan Tefila was the oldest Conservative congregation in New England. Since 1895 it had been located in Roxbury and in 1925 had dedicated a magnificent white neoclassical building at the corner of Seaver Street and Elm Hill Avenue, overlooking the expanses of Franklin Park.

Roxbury was a middle-class Boston neighborhood that had grown in size with the expansion of streetcar transportation in the last third of the nineteenth century.[4] Within easy commuting distance of downtown Boston, it attracted lower-middle-class families to its three-decker houses and inexpensive single and two-family homes constructed on small lots in the section closest to the industrial and commercial heart of Boston. Middle-class households chose to locate in the more distant corner of outer Roxbury near Franklin Park, where larger and more luxurious homes occupied ample lots on hilly streets. By the 1890s upwardly mobile Russian Jewish immigrants, eager to escape the wretched and crowded housing of the working-class North and West End slums, made their first appearance. In the 1920s an influx of second-generation Jewish families into outer Roxbury spurred the construction of apartment houses

Temple Mishkan Tefila in its urban setting. Courtesy of Congregation Mishkan Tefila, Boston.

and transformed the neighborhood into a major area of Jewish settlement. By the late 1930s, the Jewish population of Roxbury and neighboring Dorchester had reached more than 70,000, forming, in the words of one observer, "a significant ethnic enclave."[5]

It was in outer Roxbury that Temple Mishkan Tefila found its home and became a major religio–cultural institution. Under the leadership of Rabbi Herman Rubenovitz, a graduate of the Jewish Theological Seminary, who served the congregation from 1910 to 1946, Mishkan Tefila affiliated with the Conservative Movement and grew to a membership of more than 700 families. As early as 1910 it had defined itself as a Jewish center, seeking to expand the legitimate expressions of congregational life and to appeal to Jews across the generations and stages of the life cycle.[6] It also saw itself as a *stadt shul*, that is, as the predominant synagogue of the metropolitan community whose appeal transcended its own membership as well as neighborhood boundaries.[7] Indeed, the prominence of its rabbi, the high intellectual caliber of its cultural activities, and its proximity to public transportation combined to attract large numbers of nonneighborhood residents to its events. Its building served as a meeting center for more than a dozen Zionist and Jewish philanthropic and fraternal organizations.

With the conclusion of World War II, Mishkan Tefila entered a decisive phase. A change of leadership coincided with a period of population movement, setting the stage for consideration of the future of the institution and making possible its removal within less than a decade to the western suburb of Newton.

In 1945 Rabbi Rubenovitz announced his intention to retire. His successor, hired in 1946, was Israel Kazis, a young Conservative rabbi with a Ph.D. from Harvard University, who was deemed by the Search Committee to demonstrate "the qualities of leadership, oratory, scholastic ability, and the energy to carry on the work of Temple Mishkan Tefila."[8] Indeed, the new rabbi was to play a central role in the decision to relocate the temple.

Kazis assumed his post at a time when the class composition of the Jewish community of outer Roxbury was changing. In the 1940s many of the wealthiest lay leaders of the congregation no longer lived in the vicinity of the temple, having moved to the western suburbs of Brookline and Newton. By 1953 the suburban members of Mishkan Tefila, who accounted for 49 percent of the membership, provided 53 percent of the congregation's income.[9] Roxbury's Jewish population remained substantial, however, for lower-middle-class Jews had thronged to the area. Even in the early 1950s sisterhood and brotherhood officers as well as the members of the School Committee, the Youth Commission, and the Young People's League still lived, for the most part, in Roxbury and Dorchester. Moreover, Mishkan Tefila's Hebrew school population was increasingly drawn from less affluent local Jews who chose not to join the temple.[10] Because tuition fees were modest, the Hebrew school produced a sizable deficit and did not yet serve the children of the wealthy laity.

Roxbury had also begun to attract a considerable black population, particularly in its interior sections, which had the oldest and cheapest housing stock. Thus, by 1950, the two census tracts contiguous to the area where Mishkan Tefila was located were 56 percent and 25 percent nonwhite, although the population of the immediate vicinity of the temple remained more than 98 percent white.[11]

Interested in the long-term survival of the temple and its suitability as the locus of his own rabbinate, Kazis quickly expressed his concern about the membership level of Mishkan Tefila. With approximately 700 member families, Mishkan Tefila did not compare favorably with such major congregations as Kehilath Israel and Ohabei Shalom of Brookline and Temple Israel of Boston, despite the fact that Mishkan Tefila was reputed to attract the largest Friday night attendance of any synagogue in the metropolitan area.[12] On September 15, 1948, Kazis recommended that the board take "a radical step to stop the loss of outstanding members and sons of members because of geographical reasons." He suggested that "social center facilities in other localities in Greater Boston" be created to meet the needs of nonresident members and to ensure the survival of the temple.[13] A year later, at his recommendation, the board approved a different tactic, the provision of bus transportation to the children and grandchildren of members living in Brookline, Newton, and other areas to enable them to attend Hebrew school at Mishkan Tefila.[14]

Kazis continued his campaign to retain the loyalty of members living outside the neighborhood of Roxbury and its adjacent community, Dorchester. In April 1950 Kazis informed the board of directors that, if the temple were to thrive, it was necessary to establish a synagogue center and Hebrew school in the Brookline–Brighton–Newton area.[15] The next month the executive committee recommended and the annual meeting authorized the establishment of such facilities.[16] By June a committee had been established to undertake the project and to meet with representatives of the Young People's Committee, who were younger member couples living in the suburban areas.[17] Throughout the year Kazis took every opportunity to urge the officers of the temple to "give immediate attention to the proposed branch of Mishkan Tefila in the Brookline–Brighton–Newton area."[18] By December 1950 the committee was able to report that it was actively seeking both temporary facilities and a permanent location, the preferred area for the latter being in the Hammond Pond Parkway sector of Chestnut Hill, Newton.[19]

Early in 1951 Bernard Short, chairman of the Suburban Branch Committee and a former president of the congregation, reported that the group numbered seventy-five members and was meeting regularly.[20] In March the executive committee allocated $5,000 to obtain school facilities for the 1951–1952 academic year, and the board of directors unanimously endorsed the appropriation. At the board's meeting Rabbi Kazis noted that "the migration towards Newton was an inevitable geographical phenomenon and that it would be an act of foresighted religious statemanship that would decide the continued existence of Temple Mishkan Tefila as the great religious center of Greater Boston."[21]

Whereas Kazis hailed the wisdom of the temple's proposed move to the suburbs, the three Conservative congregations already located in South Brookline and Newton – Temples Emanuel, Reyim, and Emeth – were less than welcoming. In the fall of 1950 Temple Emanuel of Newton had made overtures to Mishkan Tefila, suggesting possible consolidation of the two congregations. However, the negotiations were not successful.[22] As Mishkan Tefila proceeded in the spring of 1951 with its plans to open a suburban branch school, the three Conservative temples lodged a protest with the Jewish Theological Seminary. Informed that the conference of the four rabbis with an arbitrator from the seminary had been postponed, the Mishkan Tefila Executive Committee urged that the establishment of the school facility in the Newton area "be implemented without delay" and recommended "ascertain[ing] the interest" of Jewish Theological Seminary officials in this project.[23]

Since Mishkan Tefila did not succeed in finding appropriate facilities in Newton, no further action took place until the spring of 1953, when the temple once again began to look in earnest for a site in Newton. Thereupon, Temple Reyim of Newton protested to the United Synagogue of America, the constituent organization of Conservative congregations. After Temples Emeth and Emanuel joined in the protest, charging that Mishkan Tefila would injure their congregations by competing for membership and financial support and hence was violating the principle of *hasagat gvul* (encroachment), an arbitration under the auspices of the Rabbinical Assembly of the Conservative Movement was held on December 14, 1953.

Kazis prepared and presented Mishkan Tefila's case well, providing the arbitrators with information on the vitality of the opposing synagogues, the unaffiliated Jewish population of Newton and Brookline, the presence of Mishkan Tefila members in those areas, the changing Roxbury neighborhood, and the precedents found both in Europe and in other American cities for the location of several synagogues in close proximity to each other.[24] In their decision, which was favorable to Mishkan Tefila, the rabbinic arbitrators, headed by Simon Greenberg, drew freely upon this material. Although urging the leaders of Mishkan Tefila "to find a site at a maximum distance from the existing congregations in order to avoid even the appearance of competition and rivalry," it permitted Mishkan Tefila to proceed with its plans.[25] In good Conservative fashion the arbitrators based their decision upon the determination of the facts, Jewish tradition on the subject, and "the present situation which may serve to modify the traditional attitude."[26] Given the continued and potential growth of the Jewish population of Newton and the inability of the existing synagogues to serve that population, the arbitrators found that Mishkan Tefila would not threaten the functioning of those institutions, but that its own survival in Roxbury was precarious because of the changing nature of the neighborhood and the exodus of the financial backbone of the congregation. It is interesting that only in the material prepared for the rabbinic arbitration and in the decision handed down is any explicit reference made to the influx of blacks into Roxbury. Mishkan Tefila's information sheet includes the statement "Temple surrounded by negroes [*sic*]", and the decision euphemistically notes that "the neighborhood in which Mishkan Tefila is located is rapidly changing its character."[27] There was no public discussion of the future prospects of the neighborhood, no suggestion, public or private, that means be found to encourage whites to continue to live in an integrated neighborhood.

The renewed proposal to expand Mishkan Tefila in the suburbs, first raised at a small meeting held in a private home on April 13, 1953, changed the nature of the discussion. Whereas earlier proposals had focused upon providing school facilities, now Kazis made explicit his goal in opening a branch of the Hebrew school. "It must lead to the establishment of Temple Mishkan Tefila into the Newton area," he stated. Kazis presented this move not only as a self-interested step to ensure the survival of the temple, but also as an altruistic mission to promote Conservative Judaism in Newton and prevent "the possibility of losing our younger men to reform temples."[28] The meeting resulted in the establishment of two committees, one to find a site and the other to raise the funds necessary for the project.[29]

By December 1953, when Kazis presented his expectation of a favorable ruling by the rabbinic arbitration board, the Location Committee had selected three possible sites available in Newton, one of which was the Hammond Pond Parkway parcel owned by the Metropolitan District Commission.[30] As the temple negotiated with the commission, rumors spread throughout the congregation. In April 1954, at Kazis's request, the board of directors voted to postpone the annual meeting of the temple for two months in the hope that the land would then be available for purchase. One member, however, suggested that a general meeting be held soon, "to clear the air about the status of the Temple – i.e., that it hasn't been sold, etc."[31] Instead, the board decided to appoint a committee, composed equally of local members and suburbanites, "to study the best methods of . . . insuring the perpetuation of Congregation Mishkan Tefila."[32]

The minutes of the meeting of that joint committee on June 9, 1954, reported the conclusions of the Newton group at length and the concerns of the Roxbury group in brief. The Newtonites had determined that "Temple Mishkan Tefila cannot exist for any length of time in Roxbury" and that "there must always be *only one* Temple Mishkan Tefila." It therefore proposed "to move all of Temple Mishkan Tefila to Newton" and "to operate the school in Roxbury this Fall by a Roxbury group with its own support." It had even selected an architect for the new synagogue building – Percival Goodman. The Roxbury group was reported to "have an open mind except for the closing of the Roxbury school" and was determined "that the school must operate and the people of Roxbury must take on the burden of operating it." The committee then suggested that the congregation meet to vote on its proposals and appointed another committee "to obtain title of land in Newton."[33]

Within a month the temple leadership hired an executive director to conduct the building fund campaign as well as to direct current operations and administer the cemetery.[34] In July, too, the board of directors voted to purchase 23 acres of land offered by the Metropolitan District Commission at $400 per acre.[35]

The decision to relocate the temple had been made, to all intents and purposes, by a small group of temple leaders, at meetings that often took place off the temple premises and before the entire membership was consulted. By the early 1950s the temple leadership consisted almost entirely of prosperous businessmen and professionals who no longer lived in Roxbury or Dorchester. In 1954, for example, the thirty-member executive committee counted only two members residing in proximity to Mishkan Tefila; the rest lived in Newton (thirteen), Brookline (twelve), and downtown Boston (three).[36] These lay leaders considered themselves to be Temple Mishkan Tefila, and Rabbi Kazis agreed. Their style of operation was to inform the congregational membership only after key decisions had been made and to keep pertinent data limited to a select group. Like most American synagogues, Mishkan Tefila was a hierarchical, oligarchic institution. Its core leadership, however, was both wealthy and generous: Two-thirds of the $695,000 pledged to the Mishkan Tefila building fund by December 1956 came from fifty-six members, and a full 40 percent of the total from thirteen individuals.[37]

As the decision to relocate became known, the membership of the temple declined, and its deficit grew accordingly. To close the deficit, minimum dues were set, for both suburban and Roxbury members, at $100 per family.[38] After several months' discussion, provisions were made to enable Roxbury members to pay annual dues of $60 with High Holiday seating in the schoolhouse rather than in the main sanctuary.[39] Despite this concession, the change in the dues structure made membership difficult for lower-middle-class community residents. Indeed, one member of the finance committee, comparing Mishkan Tefila's fees with those of four large Conservative and Reform temples in the Boston area, argued that Mishkan Tefila's dues schedule was too high.[40]

In April 1955, in his annual report to the congregation, the president, Nathan Yamins, a lawyer, reported on the purchase of the land in Newton and the rental of temporary quarters there, the hiring of "the outstanding synagogue architect in America," and the preparation of a brochure describing the projected new temple. He then raised the issue that had not previously been addressed in an open congregational meeting:

> The question has been asked, "What is going to happen to Mish-kan Tefila when the Newton Temple is built?" Unfortunately, a lot of rumors have been circulated that the Temple and School-house will be sold, and that the Newton Temple will be available only to Newton residents. I want to take this opportunity of stating emphatically that the present administration has no thought of selling or otherwise disposing of the existing Temple and schoolhouse building. . . . It must be obvious to everyone that when Mishkan Tefila in Newton is completed, a realistic readjustment will be necessary in the operation of the Roxbury Temple, and while each temple will enjoy complete autonomy, I am certain help will be forthcoming on an individual basis from those living in the Newtons. As for membership in the new Mishkan Tefila, it will be open to everyone who wants to become affiliated. Naturally, the present members of Mishkan Tefila in Roxbury or elsewhere will be particularly welcome, but it is only fair to expect that everyone joining in this wonderful venture will be expected to contribute to the cost of its erection in accordance with his means.[41]

The president's remarks did not mollify the Roxbury membership. At an executive board meeting in September 1954, they had expressed their feeling that the Newton residents were kidnapping the temple.[42] After the 1955 annual meeting, thirty-one Roxbury members gathered in June to give vent to their anxiety about the survival of their synagogue. They discussed the feasibility of bringing legal action against the move and of retaining the assets of the temple – the building was no longer mortgaged. In response to a question about the temple's assets, the chairman re-marked that "if no members remain in Roxbury, Newton Temple takes all. If Roxbury organizes as [a] new organization, Newton Temple still takes all." Those in attendance retorted that it was Newton that should organize as a new congregation. Finally, they complained that "members could not join Newton because of $1,000 minimum pledge to building fund." The meeting concluded with the formation of a committee "for the sole purpose of perpetuating the Roxbury Temple," and a subcom-mittee to enter into discussions with the temple leadership.[43]

That leadership did not consider the opposition on the part of Roxbury members a major obstacle to the relocation plans. At the next executive committee meeting they were assured that the temple had the legal right to relocate anywhere within the state of Massachusetts. The executive committee then delegated representatives to meet with the Roxbury committee without being "empowered to make any committments [*sic*]."[44] In fact, the leaders had come to the conclusion that it was necessary to break immediately with Roxbury.[45]

The needs of the Roxbury community were to be met through the formation of the Combined Roxbury Hebrew School, a consolidation of several schools, including Mishkan Tefila's. Subsidized by the Associated Jewish Philanthropies of Boston, it would meet in the Mishkan Tefila building.[46]

The local Roxbury leadership was not sufficiently strong to organize the Jewish population of the neighborhood to maintain the Seaver Street property of Mishkan Tefila. With the temple leadership preoccupied solely with funding and constructing the new building, it became clear that the future of Mishkan Tefila lay elsewhere. Moreover, the imposing Roxbury temple was expensive to maintain. By 1955–1956 the Roxbury membership had fallen to 203 from 361 in 1951–1952.[47] Mishkan Tefila's president publicly doubted whether there was sufficient interest among the Roxbury population in supporting the institution. Although the leadership offered the Roxbury members access to the buildings "for religious and educational purposes providing that they can maintain the buildings properly,"[48] it made available no assistance of any kind. To meet a proposed annual budget of $50,000, Roxbury would need a total of 500 members. With only 135 Roxbury members remaining in the fall of 1956, the local committee faced the daunting task of recruiting 365 new members for what would be defined as a new congregation.[49] Their failure to do so resulted in a decision by the temple leadership to sell the Roxbury property. In April 1958 the congregation voted, in a meeting that lasted fifteen minutes and took place at the Newton temple, to sell the Seaver Street buildings to the Lubavitz Yeshivah.[50] The Combined Roxbury Hebrew School had previously been absorbed by the Beth-El Hebrew School of Dorchester.[51]

Although the opposition of Roxbury members to the removal of the temple proved easy to surmount, temple leaders now confronted another problem – the need for adequate financing of the new building – which had a profound impact upon the shape of the Newton congregation. In order to cover the projected cost ($1,500,000) of the new building and its furnishings, the minimum pledge to the building fund was set at $1,000, which was to be paid over a period of three years.[52] The initial fund-raising campaign, however, raised pledges totaling only $325,000.[53] Although a second campaign brought the total to $695,000, the original plans for the Newton temple had to be scaled down and a temporary bank loan secured. Only the willingness of a dozen men to guarantee the loan with personal notes enabled the temple to secure a mortgage.[54] Because of this pressing financial need, only in extremely rare instances were members accepted who could not afford the minimum pledge.

In December 1958 Temple Mishkan Tefila celebrated its centennial in its new quarters in Newton with a whirlwind weekend of activities, including a centennial ball and an open house.[55] Among those sending messages of congratulations to the congregation were President Dwight D. Eisenhower and Governor Foster Furcolo.[56]

Mishkan Tefila leaders, lay and rabbinic, used the centennial as an occasion to congratulate themselves on the success of their move to suburbia. In articles in the *Jewish Advocate*, Boston's Anglo-Jewish weekly, they explained the relocation of the temple as evidence of loyalty of the membership to the institution. Even after moving from the old neighborhood, Mishkan Tefila members refused to sever their ties with the old *shul*. Both Bernard Garber, chairman of the Centennial Committee, and Nathan Yamins, president of the temple, presented the temple's response to the population shift as "inevitable." Garber depicted the relocation as a grass-roots movement rather than a project promoted by the rabbi and the highest echelons of the lay leadership. "The inevitable happened, and folks in the Temple began to plan a meeting house and school . . . somewhere in Brookline or Newton," wrote Garber.[57] Yamins, for his part, dubbed the transformation of Mishkan Tefila "the miracle that happened in Newton," for the temple had prevailed over such obstacles as bitter opposition from Roxbury members and insufficient funding. Only with the leadership of Rabbi Kazis and of "a small group of dedicated men" was the Newton temple built.[58]

Rabbi Kazis presented a historical overview of the temple's recent past. He observed that Mishkan Tefila's leaders were motivated to move the temple because of a need to serve "the families which had been affiliated with the Temple for many years" as well as the failure to recruit new members from the Roxbury community.[59] He pointed with pride to the temple's decision to sell its Roxbury property to a Jewish educational institution even though higher bids had been received from commercial interests. And he commended "the deep-rooted loyalty of a small group of members for whom the religious service at Mishkan Tefila was a source of so much inspiration that they were determined to preserve it for themselves and their descendants. It was the motive power of this spiritual experience which was responsible for the miraculous rebirth of the oldest Conservative congregation in New England.[60] Thus, Kazis acknowledged the central role of a handful of lay leaders in the relocation of the temple, attributed their philanthropy and dedication to religious motives, and endowed both with religious significance. Finally, he linked the renewal of Mishkan Tefila to the transcendent transmission of Judaism from generation to generation. In his article he highlighted five-generation member families, the loyalty of sons and daughters of members to the temple, and the dedication ceremony in which lay leaders walked down the "center aisle of the Sanctuary, each one with a Torah in his arms and with his son by his side" and then physically handed the Torah scrolls to their sons.[61] Kazis concluded by placing the relocation of Mishkan Tefila within the broadest historical context, comparing the move to Newton with the cyclical development of Jewish centers in the Diaspora: "When one center of Jewish life began to decline another arose to take its place and to continue the heritage."[62] In Kazis's view, then, by responding to demographic facts Mishkan Tefila was able to survive the decline of its urban base and preserve its historical role.

After defusing the opposition and clearing away the obstacles to the purchase of the land, Mishkan Tefila leaders outlined their vision of the purpose and design of a preeminent Conservative temple. The move from city to suburbs impelled Mishkan Tefila leaders to reflect self-consciously upon the aims of the temple, as stationary synagogues were unlikely to do. In a fund-raising brief they described the temple's mission, resources, and self-definition. Although it is not clear that they defined the temple's functions differently now that it had moved to the suburbs, their self-definition was consonant with the self-confidence and optimism characteristic of an upper-middle-class midcentury American suburban community. Their depiction of the temple's purpose reflected the newly popular acceptance of psychology as well as a conception of religious institutions as integrative elements in American life.[63] The temple appears in the brief as a therapeutic institution. "The primary objective of Temple Mishkan Tefila," begins the statement, "is to help develop the human being's total personality. In the opinion not only of clergymen but also of psychologists, the cultivation and strengthening of man's faith in God represents a vital factor in the emergence of a philosophy which enables the individual to confront life positively and to cope with its many problems in a spirit of confidence, courage, and hope."[64]

Not only does the temple produce well-adjusted individuals, it also serves the larger society. As the statement puts it, "The emphasis on ethical values and standards, which occupies a very prominent place in the religious teachings of Judaism as well as in the sermons of the Rabbi, makes for a deeper... appreciation of man's obligations... to his fellowmen. This... results in... more responsible citizenship. Thus, the achievement of the spiritual goals projected by Temple Mishkan Tefila represents a contribution not only to Judaism and to the Jewish people but to Americanism and to the entire community."[65] In seeking to borrow money, Mishkan Tefila's leaders presumed that presenting the temple in the least parochial and most civic-minded terms would appeal to bank directors who controlled loan funds. The temple may have also appeared to its own leaders in these terms. Certainly Marshall Sklare found that Lakeville Jews defined the "good Jew" as the "good American" and the "good human being."[66]

The psychological and civic motifs reappear in the descriptions of three of the four major activities of the temple: religious services, religious education, cultural programming, and fellowship. According to the brief, the sermon occupies a central role in religious services and the rabbi utilizes his preaching "to fortify the individual with greater confidence in his own internal resources . . . so that he may encounter the challenges . . . of life effectively . . . and practice steadfastly the basic moral virtues." Because "the foundation of an individual's personality is laid in his childhood," the temple saw as its primary educative function, "the formation of sound moral character in children." Moreover, it promoted a civic role in religious education as well as a moral one: "The religious education of our children is a basic prerequisite for any effective solution of the problem of juvenile delinquency which has assumed such staggering proportions in our day." Just as religious education conferred benefits upon the larger society, the cultural program of the temple was explicitly "designed to serve . . . the community as a whole. Distinguished lecturers . . . enlighten their audience on many of the great issues which confront our world today." Only in reference to adult education does the brief cite a specifically Jewish tenet that study is equivalent to worship–and emphasize the Judaic content of the courses.[67]

If the relocation offered an opportunity for Temple Mishkan Tefila to reflect upon and formulate its program in terms acceptable to mid-twentieth-century upper-middle-class suburbanites, it also provided a chance to design a model house of worship for a suburban community. The emphasis fell upon the aesthetic component of the new building. In their fund-raising brief, Temple Mishkan Tefila leaders had described religious services as "a moving aesthetic experience." To enhance the experience, they envisioned a "sanctuary of simple and noble proportions."[68]

A new theme emerging from the suburban setting was the linking of Jewish religious expression with the appreciation of nature. In a brochure lavishly illustrated with drawings of the proposed structure that the temple had prepared for its membership, the natural setting appears as an integral part of the new building: "In our new Temple, windows open

Mishkan Tefila after its move to the suburbs. Courtesy of Congregation
Mishkan Tefila, Boston.

on nature and the soul finds repose through a long vista of trees and sky.
Here the child, while learning the book lesson, lifts his eyes to see the
living fact of the Creator's design in every leaf and blade of grass or
snow-clad knoll."[69] Or again, in describing the sanctuary, the brochure
stresses the interpenetration of the building with the outdoors: "The
bright white glitter of stars shine through the glass windows at the top
opening up to the natural beauty of the surrounding forest."[70] An account
of the ground-breaking ceremony appearing in the *Jewish Advocate* also
commended the site chosen for the temple for "affording a natural screen
of trees to seclude the spiritual center from the roadway and furnish an
atmosphere appropriate to prayer and study."[71] This is a striking reversal
of a traditional Jewish attitude that saw the beauty of nature as a seductive
force, diverting the pious Jew from study.[72]

The effect of the temple would derive not only from its comfortable
communion with nature but also from its artful combination of tradition
with modernity. As a Conservative synagogue, Mishkan Tefila sought
to articulate the possibility of adapting Judaism to the American environment while remaining true to Jewish tradition. As its fund-raising
brief phrased it, "Temple Mishkan Tefila has endeavored to bring the

Jewish religious and cultural heritage into consonance with modern thought and culture."[73] The temple's brochure, citing "the dramatic impact of glass and stone" in the entrance, expressed the view that the building embodied the tenets of Conservative Judaism: "Here the initial effect gives a vivid impression of functional modernity without sacrificing the beauty and dignity of the traditional synagogue. Tradition is exemplified in the view of the Chapel . . . – a unique and original design – yet brilliantly crowned with the shining Mogen David." The architect chosen to design the building, Percival Goodman, was also found appropriate to the task, not only because he was "the foremost designer of Synagogue buildings in the nation" but also because he "appreciat[ed] . . . Jewish values and . . . [understood] the relationship of these to the contemporary American scene."[74] Descriptions of a school facility designed for 800 children and a social hall seating 700 for dinner and 1,200 for a lecture completed the proposed suburban synagogue-center, which was meant to meet the needs of the modern American Jewish family.

Testimony to the social reality of the suburbs and the relatively isolated location of the temple was the brochure's assumption of the need to drive to the synagogue, which was, happily, accessible "through uncongested thoroughfares."[75] Indeed, whereas the Seaver Street temple had been located on a busy main artery in the heart of Jewish Roxbury, the Newton site was in an undeveloped area. Although the new building was imposing, it did not define or symbolize a particular Jewish neighborhood as the Roxbury temple had done even while serving as a self-styled *stadt shul*. Its isolation and seclusion transformed it from a public expression of Jewish presence into a semiprivate Jewish institution partly hidden from public view. With Jewish residence in the suburbs far more diffused than in urban communities, it was appropriate for the suburban temple to shelter itself from the street and to have a far less intimate relationship with its surroundings than did its urban predecessor.

Although the architecture of the new Mishkan Tefila differed dramatically from its Roxbury forebear, the religious, social, and cultural programming of the temple remained virtually unchanged. After the move to Newton, the sisterhood, brotherhood, and United Synagogue Youth were reconstituted.[76] The Young People's League, which did not survive the move, in large part because young singles did not live in the suburbs, was replaced by the Temple Forum, a project of the young couples who had originally organized in Newton and Brookline, in sponsoring lectures and other programs of cultural interest.[77] As a synagogue-center, Mishkan Tefila had aimed for more than a generation to serve the entire family in Roxbury and to provide social and cultural as well as religious activities. New social realities and new aesthetic values had led to the introduction of late Friday-night services in Roxbury and to the abandonment of the open appeal for contributions and public pledges during the Kol Nidre service on Yom Kippur Eve.[78] These innovations, now easily accepted, were continued in Newton.

What changed was the composition of the temple membership. The Roxbury temple had been heterogeneous in terms of class; its members represented a range of social levels. Moreover, the Mishkan Tefila community in Roxbury was far broader than its membership. The Hebrew school enrolled the children of local residents who could not afford even the most modest of membership dues. In addition, many members of the brotherhood and the Young People's League were not members of the temple, a practice discontinued in Newton.[79] Finally, as we have noted, the accessibility of Mishkan Tefila made its activities available to large segments of the neighborhood and city. The Newton temple membership, on the other hand, was virtually exclusively upper middle class, not only because of the demography of Newton but also because of the temple's dues structure. Dues were set at a minimum of $100, and the $1,000 minimum pledge to the building fund demanded of members intimidated all but the affluent. Although one stated reason for moving was that a *stadt shul* like Mishkan Tefila should aim for a membership larger than the 700 families it claimed in 1950 in Roxbury, it did not grow appreciably in Newton. The rebuilt temple closed its membership when it reached the 800 mark, for its facilities could not easily accommodate a larger population.[80] However, 800 member families in Newton generated far more income than a membership of like size in Roxbury.

In choosing to relocate in Newton, Mishkan Tefila thus chose to serve a population different from its clientele in Roxbury and Dorchester. Whereas the wealthiest lay leaders of the congregation had moved to the western suburbs, the majority of Jews who left Roxbury and Dorchester in the 1950s and 1960s settled in Mattapan (a Boston neighborhood contiguous to Dorchester) or in the adjacent suburbs south of Boston. The 1965 Combined Jewish Philanthropies survey of Greater Boston Jews found that only 9 percent of Dorchester–Mattapan Jewish residents who moved within the Boston area in the years 1960–1965 relocated in Newton-Wellesley and 14 percent in Brookline-Brighton. On the other hand, 20 percent of those who picked up stakes found another home in the neighborhood, 29 percent headed for the south suburbs, and 18 percent to central Boston.[81] Newcomers from Roxbury and Dorchester were only a small minority of those thronging to Newton, Boston's largest suburb. For example, of 353 new Jewish families purchasing homes in Newton between July 1, 1954, and December 31, 1955 – the period during which Mishkan Tefila bought its property in Newton and publicly announced its relocation plans – 27 came from Roxbury and 38 from Dorchester.[82] The temple, not surprisingly, followed its leadership rather than the masses of its membership in its move.

It is difficult to assess the impact of Mishkan Tefila's relocation upon the Jewish population of Roxbury and Dorchester. Between 1945 and 1955 Roxbury's Jewish population declined dramatically, from 15,500 to 8,574, whereas in the same years Dorchester's Jewish community experienced a modest reduction, from 32,161 to 29,698.[83] Yet there is no clear causal connection between these demographic facts and Mishkan Tefila's move to the suburbs, except for the obvious conclusion that perception of the demographic shift inspired the temple's relocation. The influx of blacks into Roxbury, and later Dorchester and Mattapan, as well as the upward social mobility of the area's second-generation Jews and their desire to realize the American dream of owning a single-family home were the primary causes of the geographic mobility of the area's Jewish population. Yet Mishkan Tefila's *decision* to relocate in the suburbs seems to have occurred *before* the mass exodus of Jews from Roxbury. Not only did the temple's removal deprive Roxbury's Jews of their preeminent and most impressive synagogue and the religious and cultural services it offered, but it may have signaled to many Jews in both Roxbury and Dorchester that the time to move was imminent. By 1965 Roxbury was no longer considered an area of Jewish residence for purposes of the Combined Jewish Philanthropies' Community Survey; and Dorchester-Mattapan was described as a declining Jewish community whose size had shrunk in one decade from nearly 50,000 to only 14,000 Jews.[84]

Mishkan Tefila's relocation from deteriorating urban neighborhood to thriving suburb preserved the temple as a viable institution even as it changed the nature of its membership base. The move was accomplished with relative ease and speed because of the forcefulness of the rabbi and lay leaders and the prior suburbanization of the latter. In 1950 only the minor offices within the temple – in the brotherhood, sisterhood, Young People's League, and Youth Commission – were in the hands of local residents. The key positions in the temple hierarchy – on the board of directors and the executive committee – were filled by wealthy suburbanites. Their loyalty was not to neighborhood or geographic community but to the temple itself, in part because of its reputation as a *stadt shul*. The Mishkan Tefila story indicates that determined leaders, even when in the minority, can shape the destiny of an institution.

Mishkan Tefila's relocation also suggests that the model linking geographic mobility and acculturation to synagogue structure and function is not adequate for understanding the fourth area of settlement and its religious institutions. Although geographic mobility is a necessary pre-condition for the development of the suburban synagogue, class is a far more important factor than acculturation in analyzing the synagogue's operation. The limits of Mishkan Tefila's size and opulence in Newton were set by the availability of financial resources; its style reflected the prevailing currents of mid-twentieth-century American modernism as the Roxbury temple had reflected the tastes of an earlier era. Further, the type of lay leadership that characterized the officers of Mishkan Tefila – primarily independent businessmen – remained stable in city and suburb alike. Evidence of the continuity in levels of acculturation of the urban and suburban membership is the fact that the programming of Mishkan Tefila – religious, social, cultural, and educational – did not change in any significant way with its transformation from "urban neoclassical" to "suburban contemporary" temple. Level of affiliation, architectural style, diversity of membership, and site utilization differed in suburb and city, but the move to the suburbs appears to have produced few sub-stantive developments in the content of synagogue life.

NOTES

1   See, for example, Marshall Sklare, *Conservative Judaism*, 2d ed. (New York, 1972), pp. 25–28, 47–48, 66–74; Nathan Glazer, *American Judaism*, rev. ed. (Chicago, 1972). Both built upon Louis Wirth's classic study, *The Ghetto* (Chicago, 1928).

2   Jeffrey Gurock, *When Harlem Was Jewish* (New York, 1979), pp. 27–85, 159–165.

3   For discussions of the suburban synagogue, see Marshall Sklare, *Jewish Identity on the Suburban Frontier* (New York, 1967); Albert I. Gordon, *Jews in Suburbia* (Boston, 1959); and Samuel Klausner, "Synagogues in Transition," *Conservative Judaism*, 25, no. 1 (Fall 1970), pp. 42–54.

4   Sam B. Warner, Jr., *Streetcar Suburbs* (Cambridge, Mass., 1962), pp. 39–45.

5   Ibid., pp. 114–115; John F. Stack, Jr., "The City as a Symbol of International Conflict: Boston's Irish, Italians, and Jews, 1935–44" (Ph.D. diss., University of Denver, 1977), pp. 136–137.

6   P. Israeli, "The American Congregation, the Center of Religious Activities," *Golden Jubilee Booklet*, 1910. See, also, Herman Rubenovitz, "The Synagogue as a Community Center," *The Jewish Advocate*, 12 March 1923, p. 2. On the development of the concept of the synagogue center, see Deborah Dash Moore, *At Home in America* (New York, 1980), pp. 124–147.

7   Mishkan Tefila leaders often referred to the synagogue as a *stadt shul*. See, for example, the Annual Meeting Report, 23 May 1950, and the 1950 Executive Committee Report, as well as the report of the Young People's League, 13 May 1954, Mishkan Tefila Archives (hereafter, MTA). See also Editorial, *Jewish Advocate*, 11 December 1958, section 2,

p. 2; and Bernard Garber, "Reflections on Going to Shul," *Jewish Advocate*, 11 December 1958.

8　Report of Committee on Rabbis, 23 June 1946, Board Minutes, MT, American Jewish Archives (hereafter, AJA), 1072.

9　Membership analysis, 28 May 1953, MTA.

10　Membership lists of School Committee, Youth Commission, Young People's League, Youth Committee, Brotherhood, Sisterhood, 1952–1954, MTA.

11　U.S. Bureau of the Census, *Census Tracts, 1950*, vol. 3, Tracts 1–16, Bulletin 6, Boston, Mass., p. 46.

12　Membership Committee Report, 6 January 1948; Board Minutes, MT, AJA, 1072.

13　Board Minutes, 15 September 1948, AJA, 1072.

14　Board Minutes, 15 September 1949, AJA, 1072.

15　Meeting of Board of Directors, 30 April 1950, MTA.

16　Executive Committee meeting, 23 May 1950; annual meeting of congregation, 23 May 1950, AJA, 1072.

17　Meeting of Board of Directors, 7 June 1950, AJA, 1072.

18　E.g., Executive Committee meeting, 29 October 1950, 7 December 1950, MTA.

19　Executive Committee meeting, 7 December 1950, MTA.

20　Meeting of Board of Directors, 25 February 1951, MTA.

21　Executive Committee meeting, 11 March 1951; meeting of Board of Directors, 27 March 1951, MTA.

22　Meeting of Board of Directors, 7 September 1950, AJA, 1072; B. Leonard Kolovson, president of Mishkan Tefila, to Peter Groper, president of Temple Emanuel, 16 October 1950, MTA.

23　Executive Committee meeting, 3 May 1951, MTA.

24　Information sheets, 9 December 1953, MTA.

25　"Report of the Rabbinical Assembly Committee involving the Differences That Arose as a Result of the Intention of Congregation Mishkan Tefila to Build a School and Eventually a Synagogue in the Newton Area," 18 January 1954, MTA.

26　Ibid., p. 2.

27　Information sheets and Report of the Rabbinical Assembly, MTA.

28　Meeting at Home of Henry G. Cohen, Brookline, 13 April 1953, MTA.

29　Ibid., and follow-up meeting at Hampton Court Hotel, 21 April 1953, MTA.

30　Meeting of Board of Directors, 20 December 1953, MTA.

31　Meeting of Board of Directors, 28 April 1954, MTA.

32　Ibid.

33　Land Site Committee meeting, Parker House, 9 June 1954, MTA.

34　Meeting at Hotel Statler, 1 July 1954; conference with Joseph Abrahams, proposed executive director, MTA.

35　Meeting of Board of Directors, 16 July 1954, MTA.

36　Executive Committee membership list, 7 May 1954, MTA.

37 Analyses of building fund pledges, 15 December 1956, MTA.
38 Notes on combined meeting of Ways and Means and Membership committees, 30 November 1954, MTA.
39 Meeting of Special Committee from Suburban and Local Areas regarding temple finances, 10 February 1955; meeting of Special Finance Committee, 10 March 1955, MTA.
40 Meeting of Special Finance Committee, 10 March 1955, MTA.
41 President's Annual Report, 28 April 1955, MTA.
42 Cited in unpublished paper of Fay Yudkin, from tape recording of 8 September 1954 Executive Committee meeting, MTA.
43 Report of Roxbury meeting, 22 June 1955, by Executive Director at Executive Committee meeting, 26 June 1955, MTA.
44 Executive Committee meeting, 26 June 1955, MTA.
45 Notes on meeting of the Building Fund Steering Committee, 14 July 1955, MTA.
46 Report regarding Community Hebrew School, March 1955; Leslie Pike, president of Combined Roxbury Hebrew School to Nathan Yamins, president of Mishkan Tefila, 24 October 1955, MTA; *Jewish Advocate*, 23 June 1955, section 2, p. 7.
47 "Membership and School," 26 November 1951; President's Annual Report, 30 April 1956, MTA.
48 President's Annual Report, 30 April 1956, MTA.
49 President's Annual Report, 30 April 1957, MTA.
50 Minutes of a special congregational meeting, 15 April 1958, MTA.
51 *Jewish Advocate*, 29 August 1957, p. 1.
52 President's Annual Report, 30 April 1958; Executive Committee meeting, 12 June 1958, MTA.
53 President's Annual Report, 30 April 1956.
54 Ibid., and analysis of building fund pledges, 15 December 1956, MTA; Nathan Yamins, "The Miracle That Happened in Newton," *Jewish Advocate*, 11 December 1958, Centennial Supplement.
55 *Jewish Advocate*, 27 November 1958, section 2, p. 11.
56 *Ibid.*, 4 December 1958, p. 3.
57 Bernard Garber, "Reflections on Going to Shul," *Jewish Advocate*, 11 December 1958, Centennial Supplement.
58 Nathan Yamins, *Jewish Advocate*, 11 December 1958, Centennial Supplement.
59 Israel Kazis, "Temple Mishkan Tefila – 1910–1958," Part II, *Jewish Advocate*, 11 December 1958, Centennial Supplement, p. 4.
60 Ibid., pp. 4–5.
61 Ibid., p. 5.
62 Ibid.
63 Brief, "Obtaining Finances for New Temple on Hammond Pond Parkway: The Objectives of Temple Mishkan Tefila," p. 1, MTA. Internal evidence dates the brief from late 1956 or early 1957. The arguments about the civic

benefits of religious affiliation reflect the point of view expressed most vividly by Will Herberg in his classic *Protestant, Catholic, Jew* (Garden City,
N.Y., 1955). For contemporary descriptions by psychologists and psychi-
atrists speaking under various synagogue auspices and praising the psychological benefits of religion, see the *Jewish Advocate*, 25 October 1956, section
2, p. 8, and 21 February 1957, section 1, p. 7.

64 Brief, p. 1.
65 Ibid.
66 Sklare, *Jewish Identity on the Suburban Frontier*, pp. 324–326.
67 Brief, pp. 2–3.
68 Ibid., p. 1.
69 Brochure, no date, n.p., MTA.
70 Ibid.
71 *Jewish Advocate*, 10 November 1955, section 1, p. 1.
72 See, for example, *Ethics of the Fathers*, chap. 3, Mishnah 7.
73 Brief, p. 1.
74 Brochure. The building plan was subsequently modified and scaled down
    owing to the high cost of the original plan.
75 Ibid.
76 United Synagogue Youth was functioning in Newton by 1957. The broth-
    erhood and sisterhood did not resume operations until the fall of 1958. *Jewish
    Advocate*, 9 May 1957, p. 14. Brotherhood and Sisterhood Reports, annual
    meeting, 27 April 1959, MTA.
77 *Jewish Advocate*, 11 December 1958, Centennial Supplement; Report of the
    Temple Mishkan Tefila Forum, 27 April 1959, MTA.
78 Letter to congregants, 20 September 1944, MTA.
79 President's Annual Report, 30 April 1958, MTA.
80 President's Annual Report, 1963, MTA.
81 Morris Axelrod et al., *A Community Survey for Long-Range Planning* (Boston,
    1967), pp. 63, 65.
82 Gordon, *Jews in Suburbia*, p. 27.
83 National Jewish Welfare Board Survey for the Hecht House, cited in ibid.,
    p. 27.
84 Axelrod, *A Community Survey*, p. 20. On the decline of Mattapan as a Jewish
    neighborhood, see Yona Ginsberg, *Jews in a Changing Neighborhood* (New
    York, 1975). The disparity between the National Jewish Welfare Board's
    1955 population estimate and the Long-Range Planning Survey's figures can
    be attributed to the fact that the former refers to the Jewish population of
    Dorchester and the latter to the Jewish population of Dorchester-Mattapan.
    In neither case are the precise geographical boundaries of the neighborhoods
    made clear.

8

The Special Sphere of the Middle-Class American Jewish Woman: The Synagogue Sisterhood, 1890–1940

JENNA WEISSMAN JOSELIT

Sisterhood is the rabbi's best friend.
—*The American Hebrew*, January 6, 1928

I

In the winter of 1897, the *Reform Advocate* held a symposium entitled "Woman in the Synagogue." Noting that with growing modernization, the "bars were falling" to the Jewish woman's participation in the synagogue, the influential weekly wondered in what ways the American Jewish woman should become involved in organized religious affairs. Should she devote herself to charity, take an active part in the administration of the synagogue, or perhaps even assume a pulpit, asked the paper, putting these questions to a dozen prominent American Jewish women. Although the respondents differed among themselves, some advocating that women be trained as rabbis and others favoring a more carefully delimited role of synagogue volunteer, each of the women polled maintained proudly that the American Jewish woman was, above all else, a deeply religious personality, one whose "spiritual insight" was far "keener" than that of the American Jewish male.[1]

That American Jewish women and religiosity were "interchangeable terms" dominated the community's thinking on the matter throughout the nineteenth century and well into the mid-twentieth.[2] From the pulpit and the printed page, American Jewish women were extolled as inherently religious beings whom "nature, itself... has designated... as the upholder of religion."[3] Where man was rational and clinical, woman was an emotional creature, easily "susceptible" to religious sentiment. Taking his cues from Emerson, Rabbi David Philipson observed that "a woman without religion is like a flower without perfume," adding, in his own

206

words, that "a prerequisite of the Jewish woman is religion."[4] The Jewish woman, it was widely believed, was uniquely equipped by temperament and heredity not only to be inherently religious but also to express that sensibility in concrete ways. "Priestess of the Jewish ideal, Prophetess of Purity and Refinement,"[5] the Jewish woman, by her actions, safeguarded the future of Judaism, as she upheld its standards and promoted its ritual. "It is through them [the Jewish woman]," explained Solomon Schechter to the members of the United Synagogue in 1913, "that we reach the children . . . that we can save a great part of the Sabbath . . . and that the dietary laws will be observed in our homes."[6]

Priestesses and prophetesses, Jewish women may have been; more realistically perhaps, they were also wives and mothers. In fact, it was as wife and mother that the Jewish woman was most esteemed. Of all the ideals of womanhood, the Jewish community most preferred that of the "Mother in Israel, the *Aym B'Yisroel*. For the American Jewish woman or, for that matter, her European sister, the heroic and virginal Joan of Arc or the beauteous Cleopatra were inappropriate models. "The Jewish ideal of womanhood," one of its students observed, "was not the entrancing beauty of the queen of a knightly tournament nor the ascetic life of a virgin saint but wifehood and motherhood."[7] "The ideal Jewess," the *United Synagogue Recorder* stated rather categorically, "is a homemaker."[8] It followed, then, that the American Jewish woman most fully realized herself within her home; it and not the synagogue or the wider American Jewish community was her "religious domain," the natural staging ground for the "essential work of the Jewish woman."[9] Using language derived from the sanctuary, both male and female American Jewish leaders compared Jewish housework to "service at the altar," and enjoined of the American Jewish woman "to make of her home a miniature Temple" by consecrating it to religion.[10] As "queens of the home," a much favored phrase of the *American Jewess*, the middle-class American Jewish woman was to ensure the continuity of traditional Jewish life and to bring about the "reign of religion."[11] Thus, it was up to the American Jewish woman to see to it that the Sabbath and the dietary laws were observed, the children educated Jewishly, and that the family attended religious services and participated in all manner of Jewish communal activity. "An energetic propaganda of the mothers," the *American Jewess* explained, "would speedily reinstate the Sabbath to its old glory. We must begin at the beginning – in the Home. It is for the Jewish women . . . to set the religious ball rolling and inaugurate the observance of the Sabbath in the home."[12]

While the Jewish male built and financed American Jewry's communal institutions, it devolved upon the Jewish woman to nurture religious sentiment both within and without the home. "To make Jewish life function regularly," exhorted Louis Ginzberg in 1918, "methodical work must be done by man and women, each in his or her SPHERE."[13] Enumerating the various avenues by which Jewish women could develop and maintain American Jewish life, Mrs. Abraham Simon, an active Jewish communal leader, ranked the home as the most central and preeminent of the Jewish woman's "SPECIAL SPHERES," for the home, she explained, "is the fountain source [of Judaism]."[14]

Despite their professed and shared allegiance to that "special sphere," the Jewish home, American Jewish middle-class women began increasingly, toward the latter part of the nineteenth century, to participate in social and cultural activities outside of its sacred precincts. Much like their non-Jewish counterparts who, in the years following the Civil War, "laid down the broomstick to pick up the club," middle-class Jewish women formed hundreds of voluntary associations between the 1870s and the new century.[15] No sizable American Jewish community at that time was without its own Ladies Temple Aid Society, Ladies Auxiliary, Ladies Fuel Society, Passover Relief Fund, Toechter, Deborah and Leah lodges, and, in some cities, an all-women "Chevra Kadusha."[16] In creating a Toechter or Deborah lodge, middle-class American Jewish women drew on prevailing American models of confraternity.[17] They did not look to Europe but to their own communities for institutions to emulate; all around them women's cultural, social, and charitable organizations were flourishing as labor-saving devices increasingly freed the housewife from time-consuming household tasks, allowing her to use her newly discovered leisure time inventively.[18] "Jewish women in this country first began meeting in groups, following the prevailing club movement," recounted Mrs. Mayer Sulzberger to a National Federation of Temple Sisterhoods convention in 1923. "I am sure that we did not discuss the preserving of our traditions then as much as the preserving of our fruit." "For those were the days," she added facetiously, "when we lived up to Heine's flattering observation that the Jewish religion had an excellent kitchen."[19] Perhaps unduly harsh in some ways, Sulzberger's comment was not without its elements of truth: Many Jewish women's associations, like those of their non-Jewish confreres, were often little more than glorified kaffeeklatsches where women honed their verbal skills and cultivated their aesthetic senses amidst "the aroma of fragrant coffee and fresh cake."[20]

All the same, an increasing number of Jewish women began at this time to apply their compassion and sensitivity to the ordering of society, extending the boundaries of their Jewish homes to embrace those of society at large or, more commonly, those of Jewish immigrant society.

In the days before professional social workers, middle-class women volunteers attended personally to the distressed and the needy. "Friendly visitors," they would descend to the slums to clothe the poor, tend the sick, and rehabilitate the delinquent. "Women's clubs," writes Sheila Miller Rothman, "best exemplified the effort to popularize and fulfil the principles of Victorian womanhood . . . through these associations, female fellowship would work to elevate the moral character of society."[21] Jewish women threw themselves with great fervor into what has been called moral, municipal, or social housekeeping. "We do not wait until the poor comes to our house but by means of our society we go out to meet the poor," explained the members of Ahawath Chesed Shaar Hashomayim's Sisterhood in 1896, as they distributed 575 pounds of matzoh and 109 pairs of shoes in that one year.[22] Jewish women felt that tradition and temperament equipped them to be friendly visitors to the Jewish poor for, as Rosa Sonnenschein proclaimed, the Jewish women's "real realm, her sceptre and her crown is in the sphere of charity."[23]

Those Jewish women's groups that applied themselves with particular fervor and diligence to moral caretaking were most often associated with a synagogue. Called sisterhoods, ladies' auxiliaries, or ladies' benevolent societies, groups of middle-class Jewish women banded together under the umbrella of the synagogue to do good works. The nineteenth-century American synagogue was most hospitable to these associations. For one thing, *gemilus chesed*, or what later became known in more secular circles as "applied religion," was a central tenet of American Judaism, especially that formulated by Reform Jewish leaders. For another, the synagogue made possible the coming together of Jewish women. With the congregation as the basic unit of nineteenth-century American Jewish life and religion as the only socially acceptable basis of association, Jewish women seeking to fraternize with one another *as Jews* could do so comfortably only under the aegis of the synagogue.

New York's Jewish congregations took the lead, it seems, in organizing, sponsoring, and hosting these charitably inclined Sisterhoods of Personal Service; by 1900, there were sixteen such groups with a combined membership of several thousand.[24] Temple Emanu-El, Temple Israel, Rodeph Shalom – each of the city's major synagogues could boast an active and dedicated core of charity workers. As thousands of immigrants pressed into the Empire City, the need for systematic charitable and relief work became acute. At the urging of the United Hebrew Charities, the existing sisterhoods in 1900 federated to form the New York Federation of Sisterhoods. Assigned a district – the Lower East Side south of Houston, the Lower East Side east of Rivington, Harlem, and Yorkville – "corps of visiting Jewesses" would act, in effect, as agents of the United Hebrew Charities, visiting the poor and bringing them cheer, food, clothing, and, on occasion, money.[25]

Making over the immigrant into a member of America's middle class by teaching him appropriate middle-class forms of behavior was an especially valued aspect of sisterhood activities. Jewish women, urged Henry Rice, president of the United Hebrew Charities, "should teach the laws of ventilation, the art of preparing a wholesome, inexpensive meal, how to ply the needle and how to use the broom."[26] Thus sisterhoods with several thousand dollar budgets conducted cooking and sewing classes, maintained vocational schools, recreational clubs, and employment bureaus as well. They also sought energetically to instill in the Jewish poor what they believed to be appropriate middle-class habits: "The elevation of their morals, the inculcation of thrift and industry, the recognition of the value of cleanliness and of neatness" was a pivot of sisterhood programming.[27]

Ultimately, the growing professionalization of social work and with it, the emergence of the "professional altruist," rendered obsolete the work of and need for dedicated but untrained friendly visitors.[28] By World War I, the United Hebrew Charities had disbanded its federation of sisterhoods, claiming that its work was "not organized on a professional basis."[29] Sisterhood members, the organization explained, were not trained social workers nor were their methods sufficiently scientific.[30] The Sisterhoods of Personal Service were asked, therefore, "to relinquish their responsibility for the care of families" which, according to the United Hebrew Charities' historian, they did "amicably" enough.[31]

II

In the years following the dissolution of the New York Federation of Sisterhoods, the synagogue sisterhood assumed what has come to be its characteristic structure and identity as its members transferred their energies and allegiance from the larger Jewish community to that centered around the congregation per se. Still perceived as innately religious beings, a perception that would go unchallenged well into the post–World War II period, Jewish women needed a new venue for their talents. Prompted by their rabbis, they turned to the synagogue. Years before, the *American Jewess* had scolded its female readers for not applying their skills to the synagogue. "There is no reason why she [the Jewish woman] should not have the same opportunities for activity and power in regard to . . . religion, that she had in her charitable work," the paper stated. "Has not woman's, Jewish woman's, charity amply justified the freedom of action she enjoys in that field?"[32] A generation later, American

Jewish women began to heed and to implement the *American Jewess*'s call.

In its second stage of development, the sisterhood more directly harnessed the allegedly natural religious inclinations and proven organizational talents of the modern American Jewish woman to the synagogue. Institutionalizing her religious sensibilities once opportunities for "personal service" were no longer possible and providing an outlet for communal involvement, the synagogue sisterhood also reflected the fact that, in many congregations, women made up a majority of the worshipers. "When women in the gallery were admitted to the main floor of the synagogue," quipped Israel Zangwill, "the men disappeared from the services."[33] Reform rabbis and their Conservative colleagues as well had to admit that Zangwill's observation was right on the mark: As the most "enthusiastic of shuel-goers," women filled the American synagogue; without them, one observer related, "the spacious and luxurious temple would be almost empty."[34]

It was no wonder, then, that middle-class American Jewish women on the eve of World War I took to American synagogue life, making religion their "fortunate cause."[35] "Rally 'round the synagogue! is our slogan," pronounced one advocate of the reconstituted sisterhood, urging American Jewish women to devote themselves fully to synagogue affairs.[36] "Fundamentally religious organizations," the twentieth-century sisterhood pressed for the observance of the Sabbath and holidays and set an example for other American Jews by attending the synagogue.[37] "We pledge ourselves to urge all our members to realize that it is one of our solemn duties as Jewish women to abstain from shopping, diversions and secular preoccupations that interfere with our religious duties; to attend divine worship and to advance in every way possible the holy cause of Judaism," resolved the members of Reform synagogue sisterhoods.[38] Their colleagues in Conservative and Orthodox sisterhoods likewise affirmed that "if women are interested in disseminating the teachings and ideals of Judaism, they must emphasize regular synagogue attendance for themselves and their families."[39]

Encouraging the "temple-going habit" was only one area in which the sisterhood was expected to play an active role.[40] More important still, the sisterhood was to render the American synagogue a warm and accessible institution, to transform it into the hub of American Jewish social, cultural, and communal life. "We need the Jewish woman in the congregation to lift it out of . . . formalism . . . to make membership . . . more real," insisted leading Reform rabbi, Louis Grossman. "Woman must help restore the historic feeling of communion."[41] In much the same way that the modern American Jewish woman had made of her home a miniature temple, she was now to make of her temple a miniature home, applying her domestic sensibilities to the task. Assigned the "inner life, the housewivery," of the synagogue, sisterhood women were to act as its "housekeepers," tending to that institution's needs.[42] Like those of the Jewish homemaker, the responsibilities of the sisterhood were many and varied: from buying *tallesim* and *tefillin* to hiring and firing the janitor; from supporting the Talmud Torah to equipping the synagogue kitchen. They were also extensions of her duties within the home. Supporting the congregation's educational activities grew naturally out of the Jewish woman's role as the primary educator within the home; equipping the synagogue kitchen likewise grew out of the Jewish woman's essential talents as homemaker, as did decorating the synagogue, a task that she appeared to relish. Festooning the altar with flowers, decorating the Sukkah, designing Torah covers and wedding canopies, even operating a synagogue gift shop where members could easily purchase Jewish ritual objects – each was an application of the aesthetic sensibility and taste of the Jewish woman to synagogue life. Above all, it behooved the sisterhood woman "to cultivate a spirit of good feeling and of hospitality" within the synagogue much as she did within her own home.[43] "Before and after the services," advised one sisterhood guidebook, "the ladies of the sisterhood should not hurry to and from the services with barely a word or smile to their neighbors . . . they should encourage by their own example the exchange of 'Gut Shabbes' greetings and pleasant conversations."[44] Sponsoring afternoon Bible classes or holding regular meetings opened by a prayer and followed by light refreshments were additional ways of "cultivating good feeling." In sum, American sisterhoods were not designed initially as the fund-raising apparatus they ultimately came to resemble. "It is not the primal business of the sisterhood to raise money," one of its leading members insisted, "but TO RAISE JEWS."[45]

For all the discussion accompanying the transformation of the sisterhood into a vehicle for "raising Jews," the home remained the lodestar of the American Jewish woman's existence. No one, not even the most ardent champion of the sisterhood, so much as suggested that the synagogue supplant the home. Rather, appealing exclusively to the "Jewish mother," the sisterhood bridged the complementary spheres of home and synagogue, serving as the "medium" between the two.[46] Through the sisterhood, the home and the synagogue would work in concert, fostering Jewish life: The teachings of the synagogue would be implemented in the home while the sensibilities of the well-ordered home would be applied to the synagogue. The sisterhood, then, was designed not so much to free the American Jewish woman from the confines of her home as it was to be a leavening agent for "put[ting] Judaism back into the home."[47] Inspired by participating in synagogue affairs, the Jewish woman, sisterhood members believed, would bring into her own home a renewed sense of Jewish purpose, a heightened conviction to "revive Jewish religious home observance."[48] Taken with the beauty and the sweetness of the Sabbath service, Jewish women would be eager to make their own Sabbath, and studying the dietary laws in depth with the rabbi would help the modern Jewish woman to realize their importance. A sisterhood guidebook put it this way: "The dietary laws must find their first expression in the home and the Jewish woman must be their exponent. . . . In a Jewish home, a perfectly prepared meal, daintily served, is not enough. It may satisfy the physical desires and the esthetic sense, but to be perfect, IT MUST BE KOSHER."[49]

Hundreds of synagogue sisterhoods developed between the First and Second World Wars. No modern American synagogue – Reform, Conservative, or Orthodox – was without one. What is more, synagogue sisterhoods proliferated so rapidly during the interwar years that umbrella organizations developed "to nationalize and to mobilize the forces of Jewish womanhood . . . for religion."[50] Thus, the National Federation of Temple Sisterhoods, a coalition of Reform sisterhoods, was established in 1913; within a decade, its membership had grown to 45,000, making it, at the time, the "largest army of women organized for religious purposes."[51] Conservative women followed suit five years later with the formation of the Women's League of the United Synagogue of America; their Orthodox sisters formed a similar organization, the Women's Branch of the Union of Orthodox Jewish Congregations of America, in 1926. Representing the coming of age of the modern American Jewish woman, or what has elsewhere been called her "de-orientalization," the sisterhood distinguished the modern synagogue from its pre-modern predecessor by allowing Jewish women the opportunity to participate actively in some of its affairs.[52] "Our Jewish women," one writer observed perceptively in 1925, "are not catering to a fad in assuming the burdens of congregational activity no more than Vassar, Smith, Barnard and Radcliffe coddle a whimsicality in granting women academic degrees."[53]

III

The history of three denominationally distinct New York City sisterhoods – the Reform Rodeph Shalom, the Conservative Park Avenue Synagogue, and the modern Orthodox congregation Kehilath Jeshurun – illustrate the general trends discussed earlier. Composed of affluent, well acculturated American Jews, each of the three sisterhoods serves as a case study of American Jewish sisterhood life on the local level.[54]

Of the three, the Rodeph Shalom Sisterhood was the oldest, dating back to the 1890s. One of New York's leading Reform congregations, Rodeph Shalom was first organized in 1842 as an orthodox synagogue and remained so for thirty years. But in 1874, with the election of Aaron Wise, Stephen Wise's father, as rabbi, the congregation began somewhat gingerly to throw off some of its more traditional trappings by making what Wise himself called "a few concessions to the reform spirit": the installation of an organ and mixed seating.[55] Moving uptown, in 1897, to Lexington Avenue and 63rd Street, Rodeph Shalom wholeheartedly threw in its lot with Reform Judaism as "a new spirit," Wise observed, "has awakened in our Temple."[56] A new prayerbook was introduced, Friday evening services were moved from sundown to a later, more convenient, hour, and hats were removed during divine worship.

Shortly before its relocation uptown, in 1891, the congregation established The Rodeph Shalom Sisterhood of Personal Service. Encouraged by Reverend Wise, 100 women formed an organization to perform "some charitable work in a systematic manner."[57] Within the decade, over 350 women were involved, at least once and sometimes several times a week, with what they themselves liked to call "practical philanthropy.[58] Visiting the poor, first on the Lower East Side and then later in the Yorkville section of the city assigned to them by the United Hebrew Charities, the Rodeph Shalom Sisterhood tended to the needs of close to four hundred families and disbursed several thousand dollars in relief aid. As the need for its social services grew, the sisterhood leased and then purchased its own sisterhood house on East 94th Street. "A center for [the sisterhood's] very busy and many-sided charitable activities," the building also served as a school and clubhouse.[59] There, young Jewish boys and girls attended afternoon Hebrew school, and had their choice of three social clubs – the Hawthorne Literary Society, the Ivy Club, or the Teller Social Club – while their mothers sought counseling on matters of hygiene and parenting from the members of the Mothers Club. What's more, shortly after the death of Reverend Wise, the Sisterhood honored his memory with the establishment of the Aaron Wise Industrial School. Located on the Lower East Side, it provided vocational training to those area youngsters "sadly unskilled in the arts of sewing and mending."[60]

Despite its apparent success in the field of social welfare, the Rodeph Shalom Sisterhood of Personal Service discontinued such efforts in 1918, shortly after the Federation of Jewish Philanthropies came into being, superseding the United Hebrew Charities. Holding repeated meetings to decide whether or not "Federation has a right to take away our identity," the sisterhood's executive reluctantly gave in, noting with some discomfort that with the disbanding of its charity work, a "new era" had begun.[61] In the years that followed, the sisterhood floundered in search of a raison d'être and an objective. For a time, it concentrated on providing Rodeph Shalom's Talmud Torah students with books and an occasional outing; it then turned its considerable energies to rolling bandages for the Red Cross and sponsoring Americanization classes for those Yorkville Jewish women unable to speak English. None of these activities provided the Rodeph Shalom Sisterhood with a suitable identity.

After a decade of unsystematic and unsatisfying activity, the sisterhood merged with another of the congregation's voluntary societies, the Rodeph Shalom's Women's Association. Established in 1914, it had grown out of the Mothers Club developed years before by the sisterhood to provide impoverished and beleaguered immigrant mothers with recreational activities. Over the years, it had assumed more and more of the social responsibilities characteristic of the twentieth-century sisterhood: holding monthly lectures, maintaining a flower fund, and a membership committee. Fittingly, it now joined with the Rodeph Shalom Sisterhood (under that very name) "to draw the women of our congregation closer to the Temple and its causes."[62] To that end, the newly "amalgamated" sisterhood concentrated on developing and retaining social ties among synagogue members by sponsoring a congregational *seder* (in Delmonico's, no less), having sisterhood women greet worshipers – especially strangers – cordially at services, and sending members "cheery messages" when they were ill or bereaved.[63] Like their colleagues throughout the country, the Rodeph Shalom Sisterhood also attended to the congregation's religious needs. "To make women . . . realize their obligation to the Temple and . . . ceremonial observance in the home," the sisterhood inaugurated a Temple Attendance Committee and weekly Bible classes, and even assembled a songbook of melodies sung regularly at the temple service.[64] Furthermore, the sisterhood was especially vocal in its call for more congregational singing and responsive readings to involve Rodeph Shalom members more actively and directly in devotion.[65]

Shortly after the merger of the two groups, Rodeph Shalom entered what must have been its most exciting era. For one thing, the congregation moved for the third time in its history: to the rapidly developing Upper West Side – 83rd street off Central Park West, where it remains today. For another, the congregation hired young Louis I. Newman, a disciple of Stephen S. Wise and himself an unusual combination of Classical Reformer and ardent Zionist Revisionist. With these two events, the congregation was revitalized and "a new spirit" once again "awak-

ened in our Temple." Newman very consciously sought to make the
sisterhood his ally in the development of that new spirit and pressed its
members into service in a number of ways. In its new domicile, the
sisterhood continued, as it had in the past, to visit the sick, welcome
new members, and sponsor social events, but it did so with heightened
enthusiasm and zeal. Making congregational affairs "more sociable" took
on all the earmarks of a religious crusade as sisterhood women promoted
a dizzying round of social and communal activities.

Making the congregation more attentive to things religious was another one of the sisterhood's explicit objectives. Under Newman's direction, the sisterhood developed into a vehicle for enhanced religious
observance, even choosing as its logo the figure of a young, attractive
woman lighting the Sabbath candles. "The Sisterhood is cooperating
with Rabbi Newman in encouraging the observance of the Kiddush in
the homes of Rodeph Shalom congregants," observed the Temple *Chronicle* (another one of Newman's innovations). "There are now available
copies of the Kiddush Service Card, beautifully illustrated and printed."[66]
Similarly, the sisterhood hosted special Sukkoth services and, as the
Sisterhood Singsters, met monthly to rehearse hymns, chants, and responsive readings used in the Rodeph Shalom Shabbat service.[67]

With the onset of the Depression and the growing threat of a Second
World War, the sisterhood took time out from its constant round of teas,
bridge games, classes, and meetings to sew and distribute "beautiful
garments" for the city's poor and those of European Jewry.[68] Having
come full circle, from a social welfare agency to a purely congregational
one, the Rodeph Shalom Sisterhood entered the World War II era confident that, through all of its activities, it would "foster . . . a deeper
attachment" to American Jewish life.[69]

Like Rodeph Shalom for much of its history, the Park Avenue
Synagogue, an amalgam of three congregations, was located on the Upper East Side of Manhattan.[70] Established in 1882 as the Gates of Hope
and affiliated at the time with the Union of American Hebrew Congregations of America, the congregation was housed in a refurbished church
on 86th Street, where it was variously known as the Little Temple,
Agudath Jeshurun, or the 86th Street shuel. Over the course of the next
half-century, the Little Temple merged with several other local congregations, the most prominent being Congregation Bikur Holim-Beth Israel, which, prior to joining with the Little Temple, had occupied
majestic quarters on Lexington Avenue and 72nd Street, down the block
from Rodeph Shalom. In 1923, as the growing congregation contemplated the purchase of property further uptown – on 87th street, between

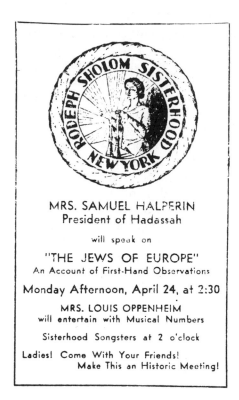

MRS. SAMUEL HALPERIN
President of Hadassah

will speak on

"THE JEWS OF EUROPE"
An Account of First-Hand Observations

Monday Afternoon, April 24, at 2:30

MRS. LOUIS OPPENHEIM
will entertain with Musical Numbers

Sisterhood Songsters at 2 o'clock

Ladies! Come With Your Friends!
Make This an Historic Meeting!

The model sisterhood woman. Reprinted with permission from the *Rodeph Sholom Chronicle*, c. 1930.

Madison and Park Avenues – it changed its name from the awkward-sounding Agudath Jeshurun to the smoother Park Avenue Synagogue. Petitioning the New York State government to change its corporate name, the congregation explained that most of its members were uncomfortable with the original Hebrew name, unable either to pronounce or to remember it.[71]

During these years, the congregation quietly prospered, drawing its approximately 150–200 members from the affluent, middle class, merchants and manufacturers of the neighborhood.[72] A cross between liberal Reform and what would, in later years, be called left-wing Conservative Judaism, the synagogue followed the Reform liturgy and eschewed the donning of hats during the Sabbath and holiday service; it stopped short, however, of adopting all of that movement's ritual and ideology. Not until the ascension of Milton Steinberg, a graduate of the Jewish The-

218   *Jenna Weissman Joselit*

ological Seminary, to the pulpit in 1933 did the congregation grow into its own as a leading Conservative synagogue with over seven hundred members.[73]

Like so much else associated with the Park Avenue Synagogue during Steinberg's tenure, its sisterhood was also revitalized. At precisely what point the sisterhood first came into being is not known; the first extant record of its activities dates to 1920. Still, like so many other nineteenth-century American Reform synagogues, this one, too, probably maintained a ladies auxiliary of some sort or, at the very least, inherited that of Congregation Bikur Holim-Beth Israel. As the congregation developed during the nineteenth century, its sisterhood, like that of other modern sisterhoods, tended more and more to the congregation's social needs than to those of the larger Jewish community: increasing the number of Sabbath worshippers and the congregation's "social standing and its finances."[74] With bimonthly meetings, musicales, Purim luncheons, bridge parties, and sewing circles, the sisterhood "created the social atmosphere in the community," providing the congregation's middle-class members with full and well-rounded leisure activities.[75] Not that all of its efforts were frivolous. When it came to raising money for the congregation's building fund campaign, the sisterhood raised over $5000 in one year, all of the proceeds derived from a bazaar![76] The president of the congregation between 1917 and 1937 was frequently taken with the abilities of the sisterhood and "its splendid women" and occasionally suggested to his fellow officers that "one or two of these splendid women" join the synagogue's board. Nothing seems to have come of his suggestion.[77]

With Steinberg as the Park Avenue synagogue's rabbi, the sisterhood continued actively as the congregation's "pace-maker," through its sponsorship of teas, luncheons, theater parties, book clubs, and dinner dances; its objective, throughout, was to create what Steinberg called "a sense of at-homeness" within an expanding and increasingly popular synagogue.[78] More dramatically still, the sisterhood took on the added responsibility of becoming that "moral force for religion" of which national sisterhood leaders often spoke. The members of the Park Avenue Synagogue, it seems, were not as exacting in their observance of Jewish ritual as Steinberg would have liked. Accordingly, he enlisted the sisterhood's assistance. Urging every household "to make certain that it has a menorah which is aesthetically appealing," the rabbi convinced the sisterhood to open a gift shop where menorahs, *mezzuzahs, tallesim, tefillin, havdalah* candles and spice boxes would be beautifully exhibited and for sale.[79] With the sisterhood's backing and imprimatur, Steinberg reasoned, the purchase and use of Judaica would become socially acceptable and thus of interest to his exceedingly affluent and Americanized congregants.

With Steinberg's encouragement, the sisterhood developed into a potent feature of Park Avenue Synagogue life. How the sisterhood perceived itself and its role in the congregation is best illustrated by a scene from a 1939 sisterhood skit in which the board, faced with a mounting deficit, decides to turn over the running of the congregation to the sisterhood. The following discussion ensues: "Splendid. They're the only ones who have any money. They're the only ones who know how to raise money. They're the only ones who use the Synagogue anyway. . . . Well then, why should we worry – let's vote to give the shuel to the sisterhood."[80]

Congregation Kehilath Jeshurun, established in 1872, was the grandfather of modern Orthodox synagogues in New York.[81] Originally a *landsmanshaft* or *chevra*-type congregation known as Anshe Jeshurun, it developed into what contemporaries called "the most modern and beautiful orthodox synagogue in New York" with the erection, in 1902, of an "architecturally ambitious," Romanesque structure on East 85th Street, between Park and Lexington avenues.[82]

Changing its name to the more modern-sounding Congregation Kehilath Jeshurun (congregants called their synagogue "KJ"), the synagogue was composed of what was perhaps the first generation of "alrightniks": "the highest economic class among the Russian Jewry of New York City, the bourgeoisie, the well-to-do and the distinctly conservative."[83] Manufacturers and real estate entrepreneurs, KJ's members – especially its young guard – lobbied for internal changes in the traditional form of the Orthodox services, changes that would correspond to their synagogue's handsome, contemporary exterior. "They no sooner found themselves in that spacious building," one eyewitness later recalled, "than their rising next generation began demanding sermons."[84] To retain the interest of that "rising next generation," KJ hired Mordecai M. Kaplan, a graduate of the Jewish Theological Seminary, to deliver occasional English sermons and to conduct a modern Talmud Torah. To retain the allegiance of the congregation's old guard, the board also hired Rabbi Moses Z. Margolies (the Ramaz), a Yiddish-speaking *rav* of the old school, to *pasken*, deliver *divrei Torah* (especially at *Shalosh Seudos*) and, in a very real sense, to legitimate by his presence the more liberal activities of his younger colleague. After Kaplan left KJ in 1910 (allegedly for personal reasons), some of the rising stars of the American rabbinate succeeded him. They included Herbert S. Goldstein and Elias Solomon, both of whom later enjoyed considerable success as the rabbi of the Institutional Synagogue and Shaare Zedek, respectively.

In 1923, the congregation hired Joseph H. Lookstein, a recent RIETs graduate, as its English-speaking rabbi. Occupying KJ's pulpit for over

half a century, Lookstein defined modern Orthodox practice, style, and
ideology for his congregants and, in turn, for what emerged during the
interwar years as modern Orthodox Jewry. As Lookstein saw it, most
American Jews were "resistant" to orthodox synagogues because the
latter lacked decorum and an English-language sermon and were, in most
things, uncompliant "with the aesthetic standards of our day."[85] Lookstein's congregation, that "cathedral of orthodoxy," made decorum and
dignity the linchpin, indeed the hallmark, of its service.[86] Decorous and
dignified – replete with ushers, top-hatted and frock-coated clergy, an
English-language sermon, responsive readings, English interpolations,
and a uniform prayerbook – KJ's services sought to draw the modern,
acculturated American Jew to traditional Jewish life. "Sad and inescapable
is the grim reality that not a halakhic question on the Rambam but an
attractive . . . service concerns most congregations," Lookstein observed
in an address before his more traditionally minded colleagues, as he urged
them to make an "attractive service" their concern as well.[87]

As Lookstein's innovations met up with success, he broadened the base
of KJ's activities. Where once the congregation had come alive only on
the Sabbath and holidays, it now developed a "healthy social spirit."
With its sisterhood, men's club, boys and girls scouts, Hebrew school,
Friday-night lectures, and American holiday celebrations, the expanded
KJ served not only as a revitalized and Americanized Orthodox synagogue but, perhaps even more to the point, as the basis for a modern,
sophisticated Orthodox community. In this particular respect, the KJ
Sisterhood was pivotal.

KJ established a sisterhood in 1886, calling it the Ladies Auxiliary
Society. Virtually nothing is known about the activities of this group
apart from its having donated a *Sefer Torah* to the young congregation
and its sponsorship of an apparently successful strawberry festival.[88] With
the congregation's move to 85th Street and its acquisition of even more
American notions of social and cultural behavior, the sisterhood was
rejuvenated. At the prompting of Mordecai Kaplan who felt keenly the
"necessity" of a women's association, the sisterhood was reorganized in
1908 to help run KJ's religious school.[89] Kaplan, it seems, was exhilarated
by the prospect of working together with the "congregation's ladies,"
for shortly after the group's reestablishment, he told the board that the
"Sisterhood will be discharging its task in a way far beyond our expectations."[90] Kaplan's expectations notwithstanding, the sisterhood remained more or less dormant and ineffectual for a good twenty years.

A new revitalized KJ Sisterhood emerged during Lookstein's tenure.
Shortly after taking up his new post, Joseph Lookstein asked, and received permission from, the board to "use our best efforts" in forming

a sisterhood that would serve as the cultural and social arm of the congregation.[91] "A congregation without a sisterhood," the rabbi explained, "is like a home without a mother. It is the Sisterhood that brings in a spirit of hospitality, friendship, sociability and warmth into a congregation."[92] KJ's Sisterhood rose to the challenge, sponsoring a full complement of activities – teas, dinner dances, theater parties, and Sabbath luncheons – cultivating all the while a sense of community and of belonging to the extended "KJ family." The sisterhood went even a step further in its efforts to weld together the members of KJ. "Consistent with the tradition of motherhood," the president of the KJ Sisterhood explained, its members provided holiday souvenirs and eatables for the congregation's youngsters on Purim and Simchat Torah, presented a prayerbook as a gift to each Bar Mitzvah, and maintained handsome scholarships to KJ's afternoon school and later, to the Ramaz Academy (School), one of America's first all-Jewish day schools, a school linked organically by staff, student body, and finances to KJ itself.[93] The sisterhood also took care to see to it that the congregation was physically, no less than socially, an extension of their homes by making it a "beautiful place."[94] Sisterhood women decorated the sanctuary with flowers, provided cushions for the synagogue's pews and "beautiful velvet portieres over the Holy Ark"; thanks to their largesse, the social hall was bedecked with curtains, drapes, and a modern kitchen.[95]

Like their counterparts elsewhere throughout the city, the women of the KJ Sisterhood saw in their group an opportunity to learn more about Judaism and to apply that knowledge to Jewish home life. Thus, the sisterhood sponsored classes in Hebrew, Bible, Jewish history, and Jewish religious practices and cooperated with the Women's Branch of the Union of Orthodox Jewish Congregations in advocating the observance of the dietary laws, family purity, the Sabbath, and the holidays.[96]

To these various activities, KJ's women applied their special feminine skills. "Women's creativeness," the sisterhood's president explained in 1939 in a brief essay entitled "The Woman's Place Is In – – –," "should not be limited merely to the culinary arts nor should her destiny be circumscribed by mere biological function."[97] Instead, KJ's women were encouraged to attend to and participate in that area of American Jewish synagogue life open to them: the sisterhood, that "higher calling of womanhood and motherhood." Whatever its expression – tea or dinner dance, Bible class or decorations – the sisterhood was designed, as Lookstein once wrote, to help American Jews realize that traditional Judaism "is and should be a religion of gladness and of joy."[98] Perhaps in the long run, what was true of the KJ Sisterhood was true as well of the American Jewish sisterhood in all of its manifestations.

"WOMAN'S PLACE IS IN ---"

BY

MRS. JACOB H. ALPERT

President of Sisterhood

In a democracy such as ours, woman's place is in every area of human activity. Possessed of intuition, intelligence, and spiritual sensitiveness, woman's creativeness should not be limited merely to the culinary arts nor should her destiny be circumscribed by mere biological function.

Jewish tradition has always glorified womanhood. Mistress in her home, which was her castle, she was also considered the pillar of the community and the soul of society. Her participation in the affairs of the world was welcomed and her contributions to the advancement of Jewish and human welfare were gratefully acknowledged.

Mindful of this tradition, Kehilath Jeshurun Sisterhood has won an honored place in the life of our synagogue and in the larger community about us. If our affections seem to be lavished principally upon the Ramaz Academy, it is because of our conviction that an integrated Jewish education is the primary need of the growing Jewish child. We are happy that we can afford, through our Scholarship Fund, an opportunity to deserving children to receive the best that a progressive education can offer. It is the understanding instinct of motherhood that makes our primary interest the children — their religious services, their holiday gifts, and their special celebrations that cumulatively mean so much to their development into ideal men and women.

To this higher calling of womanhood and motherhood do we invite the women of our community. Our Sisterhood can become for them the finest medium of service and self-enrichment.

A sisterhood credo. Reprinted with permission from the Souvenir Journal of Congregation Kehilath Jeshurun, New York, 1939.

IV

Providing an opportunity for middle-class Jewish women to participate in American synagogue life, the sisterhood did not challenge prevailing assumptions about either the allegedly unique nature of the American Jewish woman or her "separate spheres" of Jewish communal activity. Instead, the sisterhood made these assumptions an intrinsic part of its vocabulary and ideology. Nowhere in the voluminous writings of the National Federation of Temple Sisterhoods, the detailed handbooks of the Women's League of the United Synagogue, or the guidebooks of the Women's Branch of the Orthodox Union does one find even a hint of implied criticism or demurral.[99] The synagogue sisterhood of the interwar years fully internalized the larger community's notions about Jewish womanhood – and actualized them. Surely it is no coincidence that Mathilde Schechter, founder of the Women's League, was affectionately described by each one of her eulogizers (among them Henrietta Szold) as a woman whose chief characteristic was that of "homemaker" and whose overriding objective in life was "to beautify the Jewish home."[100]

Occasionally, some sisterhood women spoke proudly of the increased power that came their way via the sisterhood, of being propelled into the synagogue boardroom through the sisterhood kitchen. Writing about the National Federation of Temple Sisterhoods, one of its representatives allowed that "the development of the power of the American Jewess in the life of the congregation has been experienced through Sisterhood experience."[101] Such comments and the realities they purportedly represented were far and few: As forces for change within the American Jewish community, the sisterhoods were negligible factors. In every case, the sisterhood left untouched the basic social structure of the synagogue and, by extension, that of the larger Jewish community.

Although the sisterhood as a social and religious institution did not lobby for change or for increased opportunities for Jewish women within the American Jewish community as a whole, it can be seen perhaps as an example of a "social feminist" organization. Able to reconcile the often conflicting demands of home and society, the sisterhood was "feminist in a larger sense," for it met the needs of its middle-class members, enhancing their own personal sense of involvement and of self-worth.[102] The sisterhood realized, and concretized the realization, that the Jewish woman needed an outlet outside of her home lest, as one keen observer put it, "her outlook would be narrow and her temper sharpened."[103] Ultimately, the American Jewish sisterhood provided a viable and fulfilling outlet for thousands of middle-class American Jewish women, one that was contained, delimited, and within the acceptable bounds of community.

NOTES

1 *Reform Advocate*, 20 February 1897, pp. 1, 7; 27 February 1897, p. 24. What follows relates exclusively to middle-class American Jewish women. The experience of their immigrant and lower-middle-class counterparts, the available literature suggests, was entirely different. See, for example, Paula Hyman, "Culture and Gender: Women in the Immigrant Jewish Community," in *The Legacy of Migration: 1881 and Its Impact*, ed. David Berger (New York, 1983), pp. 157–168.

2 David Philipson, "The Ideal Jewess," *American Jewess* (hereafter *AJ*), March 1897, p. 257.

3 David Goldberg, "Woman's Part in Religion's Decline," *Jewish Forum*, 4, no. 4 (May 1921), p. 871.

4 Philipson, "The Ideal Jewess."

5 Emil Hirsch, "The Modern Jewess, *AJ*, 1, no. 1 (April 1895), p. 11; Betty F. Goldstein, "The Women's Branch of the UOJCA," in *The Jewish Library*, 3d ser. (New York, 1934), p. 108.

6 Solomon Schechter, "Address Delivered at the 1913 Convention," in *First Annual Report, The United Synagogue*, 1913, p. 22.

7 David Philipson, "Woman and the Congregation," *Proceedings*, National Federation of Temple Sisterhoods (hereafter NFTS), 1913, p. 16.

8 *United Synagogue Recorder*, 5, no. 1 (January 1925), p. 37.

9 "Save the Sabbath," *AJ*, 7 no. 2 (May 1898), p. 97; Irene Wolff, "The Jewish Woman in the Home," *The Jewish Library*, pp. 93–103, especially pp. 100, 103. See also Goldberg, "Woman's Part."

10 Betty Greenberg and Althea O. Silverman, *The Jewish Home Beautiful* (New York, 1941), p. 17; Goldberg, "Woman's Part," p. 824; Philipson, "The Ideal Jewess."

11 "Save the Sabbath," *AJ*, 7, no. 2 (May 1898), p. 97.

12 Ibid.

13 "Address of Louis Ginzberg," *6th Annual Report of the United Synagogue*, 1918–1919, p. 23.

14 Mrs. Abraham Simon, "Woman's Influence in the Development of American Judaism," *41st Annual Report, Union of American Hebrew Congregations* (hereafter *UAHC*), 1915, p. 7690. American Jews were ardent devotees of the so-called cult of true womanhood, adding to it their own special Judaic gloss. See, for example, Barbara Welter, "The Cult of True Womanhood, 1820–1860," *American Quarterly*, 18 (Summer 1966), pp. 151–174.

15 Quoted in Karen Blair, *The Clubwoman as Feminist: True Womanhood Redefined, 1868–1914* (New York, 1980), p. 24.

16 "Directory of Local Organizations," *American Jewish Yearbook* (hereafter

AJYB), 1900, especially pp. 120, 198; Rebecca Kohut, "Jewish Women's Organizations," *AJYB*, 1931, pp. 165–201; Rudolph Glanz, *The Jewish Woman in America: Two Female Immigrant Generations, 1820–1929* (New York, 1976), pp. 125–132.

17 In creating their own voluntary associations, American Jewish women could easily have drawn on the model of European Jewish women's groups. That they did not do so suggests the pull of the larger American culture on them. See, for example, Marion A. Kaplan, *The Jewish Feminist Movement in Germany: The Campaigns of the Judischer Frauenbund, 1904–1938* (New York, 1979).

18 See, for example, Louis Auchincloss, *The Book Class* (New York, 1984); Blair, *The Clubwoman as Feminist*; Robert Lynd and Helen Merrell Lynd, *Middletown: A Study in American Culture* (New York, 1929), pp. 276–304; Mary Ryan, *Cradle of the Middle Class: The Family in Oneida County, New York, 1790–1865* (Cambridge, 1981); Helen Hoover Santmyer, ... *And Ladies of the Club* (New York, 1984); Welter, "Cult of True Womanhood"; Gwendolyn Wright, *Building the Dream: A Social History of Housing in America* (Cambridge, 1983), pp. 158–176.

19 Mrs. Mayer Sulzberger, "The Jewish Problem in the Larger World," *Proceedings of the 5th Biennial Association, NFTS*, 1923, p. 138.

20 Annual Report, Sisterhood of Personal Service of Congregation Ahawath Chesed Shaar Hashomayim, 1896–1897, p. 15.

21 Sheila Miller Rothman, *Woman's Proper Place: A History of Changing Ideals and Practices, 1870 to the Present* (New York, 1978), p. 64.

22 Annual Report, Sisterhood of Personal Service of Congregation Ahawath Chesed Shaar Hashomayim, pp. 5, 23.

23 Rosa Sonnenschein, "The American Jewess," *AJ*, 6, no. 5 (February 1898), p. 207.

24 "Directory of Local Organizations," *AJYB*, p. 359; *The Jewish Messenger*, 27 March 1891, p. 1; *The American Hebrew*, 20 March 1891, p. 130. For parallels with Christian women's organizations, see Keith Melder, "Ladies Bountiful: Organized Women's Benevolence in Early 19th Century America," *New York History*, 48, no. 3 (July 1967), pp. 231–254.

25 *Fifty Years of Social Service: The History of the United Hebrew Charities of the City of New York* (New York, 1926), pp. 18, 38.

26 Ibid., p. 38.

27 Annual Report, Sisterhood of Personal Service of Congregation Ahawath Chesed..., pp. 8–9; Annual Report of the Temple Emanu-El Sisterhood of Personal Service, 1905.

28 Roy Lubove, *The Professional Altruist: The Emergence of Social Work as a Career, 1880–1930* (Cambridge, 1965).

29 *Fifty Years*, p. 92.

30 Ibid. A few sisterhoods like that of Congregation Shearith Israel of New York continued charitable activities. Serving as a "major guardian of

those Jewish women out on probation," the sisterhood looked after the interests of Jewish women criminals, making sure that they had decent paying jobs, lived in respectable neighborhoods, and attended the synagogue. On the Shearith Israel Sisterhood, see my "Dark Shadows: New York Jews and Crime" (Ph.D. diss., Columbia University, 1981), pp. 79–82.

31   *Fifty Years*, p. 92.

32   *AJ*, 1, no. 3 (June 1895); 5, no. 2 (May 1897), pp. 96–97; 4, no. 2 (November 1896), p. 94; *23rd Annual Proceedings, UAHC*, 1913, p. 7081.

33   Israel Zangwill quoted in the *Proceedings of the First Convention, NFTS, 1913*, p. 27.

34   Rabbi Jacob Mielziner, "Remarks," *Proceedings of the First Convention, NFTS*, 1913, pp. 27–28; Alter Landesman, "Synagogue Attendance: A Statistical Survey," *Proceedings of the Rabbinical Assembly of America*, 2 (1928), p. 50; Rosa Sonnenschein, "The American Jewess," p. 207; "Report of the National Committee on Religion," *13th Annual Report, NFTS*, 1925.

35   See Benjamin Kline Hunnicutt, "The Jewish Sabbath Movement in the Early 20th Century," *American Jewish History*, 69, no. 2 (December 1979), pp. 196–215. The transformation of what had once been a communally oriented association into one that was far more locally and privately centered may well reflect what Arthur Goren has defined as the move from "communalism to privatism." See his unpublished article, "Traditional Institutions Transplanted: The Chevra Kadisha," 1983, p. 10.

In this, as in so many other respects, American Jewish women strongly resembled their nineteenth-century non-Jewish counterparts. Religion, explains Barbara Welter in her analysis of the nineteenth-century American woman's involvement with church affairs, "became the property of the ladies." Barbara Welter, "The Feminization of American Religion, 1800–1860," in Mary Hartman and Lois Banner, eds., *Clio's Consciousness Raised* (New York, 1973), pp. 137–155, especially p. 138. See, as well, Richard Stiels, "The Feminization of American Congregationalism, 1730–1835," *American Quarterly*, 33, no. 1 (Spring 1981), pp. 44–62; and Melder, "Ladies Bountiful," passim.

36   Simon, "Woman's Influence," p. 7691.

37   "Report of the National Committee on Religion," *Proceedings of the Third Biennial Meeting, NFTS*, 1919, p. 45.

38   *Proceedings of the Fourth Biennial Meeting, NFTS*, 1921, p. 72.

39   "Women and the Sabbath," *United Synagogue Recorder*, 4, no. 4 (October 1924), p. 26; The Women's League of the United Synagogue, *Handbook for Jewish Women's Organizations* (New York, 1924), pp. 8–10; Stella Burstein, *Manual for Sisterhoods* (Women's Branch, Union of Orthodox Jewish Congregations of America, 1947), pp. 1–2, 35.

40   *24th Annual Report, NFTS*, 1937, p. 103; "Report of the President," *15th Annual Report, NFTS*, 1927, p. 15.

41 Rabbi Louis Grossman, "The American Jewess," *Proceedings of the First Convention of the NFTS*, 1913, p. 22.
42 *Reform Advocate*, 13, no. 1 (20 February 1897), p. 17; 13, no. 4 (13 March 1897), p. 60.
43 "Report of the National Committee on Religion," p. 45.
44 Ibid.
45 Simon, "Woman's Role," p. 7689. See also *The Constitution of the Women's League of the United Synagogue*, 1930.
46 Goldstein, "Women's Branch," p. 108; *Reform Advocate*, 13, no. 1 (20 February 1897), p. 10.
47 Grossman, "American Jewess," p. 23; Simon, "Woman's Influence," pp. 7688–7689.
48 Mathilde Schechter, "Aims and Ideals of the Women's League," May 1918, p. 3; "Address of Mrs. Charles Hoffman," *7th and 8th Annual Reports of the United Synagogue*, 1920–1921, pp. 65, 68; "President's Annual Message," *Proceedings of the 2nd Biennial Meeting, NFTS*, 1917, p. 30; Nima Adlerblum, "The Elan Vital of the Jewish Woman," *The Jewish Library*, 3d ser. (New York, 1934), p. 474; Goldberg, "Woman's Part," p. 875.
49 Deborah Melamed, *The Three Pillars: Thought, Practice and Worship for Jewish Women* (New York, 1927), pp. 40–41.
50 Simon, "Woman's Influence," p. 7688.
51 *Proceedings of the 5th Annual Meeting, NFTS*, 1923, p. 102.
52 Kohut, "Jewish Women's Organizations," *AJYB*, p. 165; *Proceedings of the 23rd Council of the UAHC*, 1913, p. 7081; Philipson, "Women and the Congregation," p. 17.
53 Joseph Leiser, *American Judaism* (New York, 1925), pp. 174–203, especially pp. 191, 193.
54 If synagogues are notoriously poor record keepers, synagogue sisterhoods are worse still: Their extant records are few, arbitrarily preserved, and woefully incomplete. The section on the history of the Rodeph Shalom Sisterhood is drawn from the following sources: the Rodeph Shalom Archives, which consist of assorted notebooks, minute books, and memorabilia; the Rodeph Shalom bulletin, *The Temple Chronicle*, 1930–1934; Rev. Aaron Wise, "The History of Congregation Rodeph Shalom of New York – In Commemoration of the 50th Anniversary of Its Incorporation" (New York, 1892); and the galleys of Louis I. Newman's unpublished manuscript, "The History of the Congregation of Rodeph Shalom from the Date of Its Organization – In Commemoration of Its 115th Anniversary" (hereafter cited as the Newman manuscript).
55 Wise, "The History of Congregation Rodeph Shalom," p. 14.
56 Ibid., pp. 15–16.
57 Ibid., pp. 24–25; *American Hebrew*, 27 March 1891, p. 151.
58 Newman manuscript, "The Year 1902," p. 34;
59 "The Rodeph Shalom Sisterhood," pp. 34–38; Newman manuscript, "Outline and Notes," vol. 1, p. 122.

60   Ibid.
61   Rodeph Shalom Sisterhood Minutes, 6 June, 5 December 1918; 3 February, 1 May 1919; 4 October 1920.
62   Minute books of the Rodeph Shalom Women's Association, 13 December 1920, 8 October 1923; Newman manuscript, pp. 78–79.
63   Minute books of the Rodeph Shalom Women's Association, 16 May 1920.
64   Minute books of the Rodeph Shalom Women's Association, 20 October, 16 May 1920.
65   Minute books of the Rodeph Shalom Women's Association, 11 April 1921, 8 October 1923, 16 November 1925.
66   *The Temple Chronicle of Rodeph Shalom*, 28 November 1930, p. 2; 21 November 1930, p. 3.
67   *Temple Chronicle*, 7 October 1932, 6 January 1933, 4 October 1933.
68   *Temple Chronicle*, 27 April 1933.
69   Newman manuscript, p. 80.
70   The material in this section is drawn from the archives of the Park Avenue Synagogue, which include minute books and assorted ephemera; private conversations with Rabbi Harlan Wechsler, Associate Rabbi of the Park Avenue Synagogue were also conducted. Of special value was the "Park Avenue Synagogue Golden Jubilee Program," August 1923, and an interview, in the files, with Milton and Irma Heller, 5 November 1979.
71   "In the Matter of the Application of Congregation Agudath Jeshurun, A Domestic Religious Corporation, to Change Its Corporate Name to Park Avenue Synagogue," 6 January 1923. Rabbi Steinberg strongly disliked his congregation's English name. It is, he once wrote, "literally inaccurate as well as snobbish." *Park Avenue Synagogue Bulletin*, 14 April 1947.
72   Annual Report of the President of Congregation Agudath Jeshurun, 1920–1927; Rabbi Judah Nadich to Jack Maltz, 27 February 1958.
73   Personal communication with Rabbi Wechsler; Simon Noveck, *Milton Steinberg: Portrait of a Rabbi* (New York, 1978), p. 327.
74   Annual Report of the President of Congregation Agudath Jeshurun, 1920, p. 5.
75   Annual Report of the President, 1921, p. 5; 1922, pp. 4–5; 1924, p. 5.; 1926, p. 5.
76   Annual Report of the President, 1923, p. 5.
77   Annual Report of the President, 1929, p. 8.
78   Steinberg quoted in Noveck, *Milton Steinberg*, p. 327.
79   *Park Avenue Synagogue Scroll*, 3 December 1940, 8 December 1941; personal communication with Rabbi Wechsler.
80   "Park Avenue Sillygags," 1939.
81   The material in this section is derived from the minute books, souvenir dinner-dance journals, and bulletins of Congregation Kehilath Jeshurun.
82   Joseph H. Lookstein, "75 Yesteryears – A Historical Sketch of Kehilath Jeshurun," *Congregation Kehilath Jeshurun Diamond Jubilee 1946 Yearbook*,

pp. 17–32; "Rabbi Moses Z. Margolies – High Priest of Kehilath Jeshurun," pp. 48–51; Shirley Levittan to Dr. David de Sola Pool, 7 May 1947; *The Hebrew Standard*, 9 May 1902; *American Hebrew*, 12 September 1902.

83 Isaac Berkson, *Theories of Americanization: A Critical Study* (New York, 1920), p. 183.

84 Unpublished diaries of Mordecai M. Kaplan, 7 February 1959, Jewish Theological Seminary Archives.

85 "Digest of Rabbi Lookstein's Address on Practical Rabbinics," n.d., p. 1.

86 Personal communication with a KJ congregant who preferred to remain anonymous; see also "Kehilath Jeshurun: A Congregational Portrait," in *Diamond Jubilee*, pp. 93–94; *Kehilath Jeshurun Bulletin*, 18 November 1938.

87 Joseph H. Lookstein, "Problems of the Orthodox Rabbinate," n.d., p. 3.

88 Mrs. Harry Etra, "Jewish Womanhood in Action – A History of the Kehilath Jeshurun Sisterhood," *Diamond Jubilee*, p. 39; "What Our Synagogue Offers," *Bulletin*, 20 January 1939.

89 KJ minutes, 1 October 1908.

90 KJ minutes, 18 October 1908.

91 KJ minutes, 10 February 1925; Etra, "Jewish Womanhood," p. 40.

92 Quoted in Etra, "Jewish Womanhood," p. 40.

93 *KJ 1945 Yearbook*, pp. 12, 42; Etra, "Jewish Womanhood," pp. 41–42; *KJ 1948–49 Yearbook*.

94 Etra, "Jewish Womanhood."

95 Ibid.

96 "Women's Page," *The Orthodox Union*, 5, no. 5 (1938), p. 12; Etra, "Jewish Womanhood," p. 42; *The Orthodox Union*, 6, no. 2 (1939), p. 1.

97 Mrs. Jacob Alpert, "Woman's Place Is in – – –," *KJ Souvenir Journal*, 1939.

98 *KJ 1945 Yearbook*, p. 12.

99 In this, and in other respects, Reform, Conservative, and Orthodox sisterhoods were strikingly similar; differences between the three were few. The basic structure of the American synagogue sisterhood – indeed its overall objectives – remained constant in all three denominations. Constructed along similar, if not identical, lines, the Reform, Conservative, and Orthodox sisterhoods shared the same ideology, resorted to the same rhetoric, and engaged in the selfsame activities: holding luncheons, equipping the synagogue kitchen, conducting Bible classes, decorating the sanctuary, and publishing manuals and guidebooks on how best to run a sisterhood and have a "Jewish Home Beautiful." Each, in its own denominational way, sought to promote Jewish ritual observance both within and without the home; to be sure, each differed from the other on how best to accomplish that objective. See, for example, Betty Greenberg and Althea O. Silverman, *The Jewish Home Beautiful* (New York, 1941), pp. 13, 14, 72; *The Orthodox Union*, 8, no. 1 (September-October), 1940.

100 *Services in Memory of Mrs. Solomon Schechter* (New York, 1925), passim; see especially, Henrietta Szold, "The Lineaments of Mathilde Roth Schechter," pp. 13–14.
101 Felicia Lee, "From a Small Group to 55,000 in Fourteen Years – A Splendid Record," *American Hebrew*, 6 January 1928, p. 33; Report of the President, NFTS, 4 January 1924, p. 114.
102 Paula Hyman, "The Volunteer Organizations: Vanguard or Rearguard," *Lilith*, 5 (1978), p. 17.
103 Wolff, "The Jewish Woman in the Home," pp. 102–103.

9

Ethnic–Religious Ambiguities in an Immigrant Synagogue: The Case of New Hope Congregation

BENNY KRAUT

Introduction

The phenomenon of Jewish immigrants to America establishing their own synagogues has been a recurring motif in the American Jewish experience. With few exceptions, the discrete ethnic or national waves[1] of Jewish newcomers to American shores – the Sephardim of the Colonial era, the German Ashkenazim of the mid-nineteenth century, the East Europeans of the nineteenth and early twentieth centuries, the Sephardim of the early twentieth century, and the German Jewish refugees of the 1930s – all established their own congregations. These congregations constituted vital ethnic-religious enterprises in at least two respects. They reinforced or created feelings of Jewish ethnic solidarity, and they provided the immigrants with outlets for socialization, mutual support, and cultural activities.[2] In addition, immigrant synagogues embodied the attempt to replicate the distinctive congregational atmosphere, liturgical rite, and nuanced religious traditions of the ancestral region from which their founders came. It was not merely Judaism or Jewish worship that these synagogues fostered, but a particular ethnic or territorial form of Judaism and of Jewish worship, with a particular congregational *minhag* (liturgical rite) and a particular ethos.[3]

Cincinnati's German Orthodox Tikwoh Chadaschah,[4] or New Hope Congregation as it is more often called, typifies this congregational pattern. Its founding in the late 1930s reflected a national trend of congregation building by German Jewish refugees[5] who came to America around this time. Between 1933 and 1943, approximately 130,000 German Jews arrived in the United States. The majority settled in New York (75,000), but others ventured principally to the urban areas of Chicago, Philadelphia, Los Angeles, Cleveland, Baltimore, Detroit, St. Louis, and

231

Washington. Approximately one thousand reached Cincinnati.[6] Although the immigrants' adjustment was aided by the benevolent activities of American Jewish agencies, both national and local, German Jews, with considerable initiative, created a number of self-help organizations and social institutions to ease their own transition. Among the more significant of these were the German synagogues that sought to meet not only religious and ritual requirements, but also social, cultural, and educational needs, not unlike the East European *landsmanshaft* synagogues of the previous generation. Dozens of German immigrant congregations were founded in the late 1930s and during the 1940s; understandably, New York featured the largest number of them – about thirty – mostly concentrated in the Washington Heights area of Manhattan (sometimes dubbed in rather questionable taste, the "Fourth Reich"). Active German Jewish synagogues, however, were organized in almost every city with a significant German-Jewish refugee population.[7]

Although New Hope is hardly the most significant of these, either in size, prestige, or impact, its history does clearly illustrate continuities and discontinuities arising in any immigrant congregation that tries to re-create an ethnic-religious framework in the New World modeled after the religious traditions and institutional structures of the Old. In this respect, little New Hope sheds light on a phenomenon far larger than itself. The central focus of this chapter is the synagogue's struggle within itself and within the singular Cincinnati Jewish community to preserve its special ethnic-religious character and style. Yet the New Hope saga may also serve as a useful paradigm for understanding the dialectical and ambiguous forces of ethnicity and religion at work in American immigrant congregations in other historical periods and circumstances.

The Founding of New Hope

On July 16, 1939, fourteen recently arrived German Jews – thirteen men and one woman – virtually all from South and Southwest Germany, met at the behest of Dr. Leo Teitz, born in Fuerth, Bavaria, and a doctor by profession, and decided formally to establish a congregational union to be known as Chewrat Tikwoh Chadaschah.[8] The name – New Hope – was deemed appropriate for the new enterprise as it reflected the cautious optimism of the immigrant community. Disenchanted with the religious services at several of the existing East European congregations, the founding New Hope members had been encouraged by Rabbi Eliezer Silver, the predominant Orthodox rabbi in Cincinnati and *Rav* of its Vaad Hoir, (the central Orthodox agency overseeing kosher supervision and other religious institutions) to initiate separate services according to their own German *minhag*. Within two years, the synagogue was incorporated in the State of Ohio and by 1944, it boasted a *chevra kadisha* (burial society), a sisterhood auxiliary, and an afternoon school for the religious instruction of the congregants' children. Membership over the next thirty years fluctuated between 100 and 180 individual and family memberships.[9]

Like almost all new German Jewish synagogues, New Hope's first services were housed in makeshift rooms either donated or rented from other synagogues or institutions.[10] This imposed innumerable hardships on the congregation. Understandably, therefore, like other German synagogues, New Hope confronted the decision as to whether or not to obtain or build a permanent edifice.[11] This act not only entailed considerable funds and financial commitments – no small issue for recent immigrants – but also was of utmost symbolic significance: It represented a conscious choice on the part of the members to continue to affirm their own ethnic-religious identity through allegiance to a German Jewish institution. Certainly, most members agreed that not only would a permanent home solve the severe logistical problems, give a sense of stability and identity to the congregation, and help beautify the services, but also it might prove attractive to other German Jews not yet affiliated and win greater respect for German Jews in the wider Jewish community. After much deliberation in the course of the 1940s, New Hope inaugurated its first permanent place of worship – a renovated house on 615 Prospect Place in the South Avondale section of the city – on March 19, 1950, amid much pomp and ceremony. Its stay there was relatively brief; faced with a changing neighborhood and periodic vandalism, the New Hope board agonized for four years before deciding to move further north to the Roselawn neighborhood. On November 29, 1959, it dedicated its newly built home at 1625 Crest Hill Avenue, where it is situated to this day.[12]

Unlike most other German Jewish synagogues established in this period, New Hope never had a permanent rabbi. New Hope was an egalitarian lay association, reminiscent of the innumerable small-town congregations in Southern Germany that were run by laymen in the absence of a permanent resident rabbi. The New Hope laymen who took charge of services all had other full-time jobs.

With the death of Leo Teitz on July 11, 1951, however, members gradually looked to Manfred Rabenstein as "spiritual leader" of the congregation, a title that first appeared linked to his name in 1952. A graduate of the Cologne Jewish Teachers Seminary with a diploma as *Religionslehrer*, *hazan*, and *shohet*, Rev. Rabenstein was employed full-time as a *shohet* by E. Kahn's slaughterhouse in Cincinnati. Having been in charge

PUBLIC DEDICATION PROGRAM

SUNDAY . . . 2:00 p. m.

Vocal Selection . . . . New Hope Choir
Arnold Schatz at the Piano

Opening Remarks . . . . { Fred S. Mott
{ President of the Congregation

Invocation . . . . Rev. Manfred Rabenstein

Presentation of the United States Flag (Rabbi Michael Aaronsohn
) Max Middleman
American Legion Wittstein-Middleman Post) Stanley Silverstein
(Albert A. Rogoff, Commander

Response . . . . Eugene J. Hilb

G-d Bless America . . . . Congregation

Presentation of the Jewish Flag . . { Maurice A. Chase
{ Chairman of the Zionist Council
(of Cincinnati

Response . . . . Sigfried Kugelman

Hatikvah . . . . Congregation
Arnold Schatz at the Piano

The Story of the New Hope Congregation . . . . { Alfred Segal
{ Member of the
(Cincinnati Press

Vocal Selection . . . . Manfr. Rabenstein, Soloist
Arnold Schatz at the Piano

Greetings:
Hon. Albert D. Cash . . . . . . Mayor, City of Cincinnati
Rabbi James G. Heller . . . . Jewish Community Council
Hon. Dennis J. Ryan . . . Judge of Court of Common Pleas,
Hamilton County
Rabbi Fishel Goldfeder . Board of Jewish Ministers of Cincinnati
Sol Goodman . . . . B'nai B'rith
Charles Heiman . . . Gate Club and Chairman of Building
Committee of the Congregation

Vocal Selection . . . . New Hope Choir
Arnold Schatz Conducting

Address . . . . { Rabbi Leo Baeck
{ Formerly of Berlin, Germany

Vocal Selection . . . . Congregation

Floral Decoration by Courtesy of Kyrk Flower Shop

Noteworthy in this program for the dedication of New Hope's building in 1950 is the broad spectrum of communal participation, the stress on American symbols, the synagogue choir, and of course the keynote address of Liberal Rabbi Leo Baeck. Courtesy of New Hope Synagogue, Cincinnati.

of New Hope's Hebrew school from its inception and possessing exceptional liturgical skills, a fine voice, total familiarity with the German *minhag*, and a much better Jewish education than virtually any other member, Rev. Rabenstein became the logical and, perhaps, only choice to fill the religious leadership vacuum. And yet, interestingly, his leadership evolved over time; he was never formally invited to serve as spiritual leader, but was always paid by the board for specific services rendered. By the 1950s, these duties included a weekly sermon, leading of the services, reading of the Torah, and teaching in the Hebrew school. Only in 1966 did the board attempt to elevate him to the position of full-time "rabbi" – which would have meant leaving his job at Kahn's – but the financial terms offered him did not make the proposal sufficiently enticing, and he declined. Hence, since the early 1950s, New Hope has been served by Rev. Rabenstein as a part-time "rabbi," an educated layman who nonetheless, as most New Hopers readily attest, kept the synagogue together and the German liturgical character intact.[13]

By conscious design and articulated clearly in its initial constitution, the congregation defined itself as Orthodox, but Orthodox according to the *minhag Ashkenaz* of southern Germany.[14] New Hope was devoted to a specific brand of ethnic religion that reflected the regional origins not only of its founders but of the overwhelming majority of its growing membership over the years. The actual prayer rite adopted was primarily that of Fuerth, whence Teitz came, with occasional emendations from the customs of Fulda and Frankfurt am Main. These synagogue *minhagim* are followed by and large to this day. As was the custom with so many synagogue communities in Germany, New Hope – or more precisely, Dr. Teitz – drafted a *minhag* book outlining in specific detail all the practices to be observed on all ritual and prayer occasions during the course of the Jewish calendrial year. These included not only the order and content of prayers during the services, but also such items as the sequence of honors distributed, *aliyot* for designated individuals, the order of priority of those required to say *kaddish*, and the like.[15]

Adopting the synagogue *minhag* was by no means a smooth process, and there was endless bickering over customs.[16] This was typical of many synagogues established in America in the nineteenth and twentieth centuries.[17] New Hope members discovered that coming from the same general Southwest German region, but not from the same town, did not guarantee total uniformity in liturgical practice.[18] Common national origins and American-German-Jewish ethnic identity that on the one hand drew people together did not always promote social unity and religious cohesion in this immigrant congregation; indeed, they often served as a springboard for many internal divisions as individuals recalled different local customs they wished to make the norm. When disputes could not be settled, letters were sent to Rabbi Joseph Breuer, grandson of Samson Raphael Hirsch and founder of the German Orthodox *kehillah* (community) in Washington Heights, New York, requesting that he adjudicate as to what the authoritative and appropriate *minhag Ashkenaz* was in a given circumstance.[19]

Although formally and unambiguously Orthodox from the outset, New Hope united under its wing individuals of various religious leanings, from the small number of staunchly pious and strictly observant, to the more religiously liberal and even religiously indifferent. Most of the founding members were either totally Orthodox in their practice, or at least very traditional in religious orientation. But the potential pool of such members was not large, and, as more Germans joined, the socio-religious composition of the synagogue changed dramatically. The strictly observant never constituted more than 20 percent of the membership after the first few years. That figure dropped even further with the passage of time.

By trying to embrace as many German immigrants as possible, Teitz attempted in modified form to recreate on American soil the spirit, if not the institutional framework, of the German communal synagogue model of the *Einheitsgemeinde*. The *Einheitsgemeinde* refers to a peculiar sociocommunal structure regnant in Germany in the nineteenth and twentieth centuries that incorporated all Jews and the institutions of their religious and social life into one structurally unified community. This structure developed in response to the demands of most German states during this period that mandated Jewish affiliation to a state-recognized, corporate Jewish communal body in each locale in which Jews lived. This body, the *Gemeinde*, whose characteristic centralization and unity saw it commonly referred to by German Jews as the *Einheitsgemeinde*, was legally empowered to levy taxes on its members in order to support its various institutions, including schools, synagogues, old age homes, hospitals, and the like. Usually the tax procedure saw collected taxes forwarded to the state with a percentage of the money disbursed to the community for its needs. In large Jewish communities, the *Einheitsgemeinde* board had under its jurisdiction synagogues of different rites, and it supported synagogues of both religiously liberal (right-wing Conservative by American standards) and conservative (Orthodox in American terms) tendencies. Individuals then had the opportunity to attend the synagogue of their choice. But in smaller provincial areas and towns often only one synagogue existed, and the *Einheitsgemeinde* leadership usually steered that synagogue to a religious point of view closer to one or the other of the two possibilities, thus determining whether the one available community congregation was to follow the liberal or conservative approach. As much as religiously possible, however, the one *Einheitsgemeinde* synagogue in small towns often attempted to satisfy all its congregants, and sometimes it even compromised on certain matters, such as the extent of German language used in the service.[20]

In establishing a modified, voluntary *Einheitsgemeinde* synagogue based on traditional Judaism, Teitz did not heed the advice of Rabbi Joseph Breuer with whom he had consulted on New Hope matters. Rabbi Breuer strongly advised him to establish a synagogue only for *yereim* – the truly pious or God fearers – and not to try to appeal to all German Jews. Coming from a man who was at that very time rebuilding a separatist and completely self-contained Orthodox *kehillah* in Washington Heights in the Frankfurt tradition of the *Israelitische Religionsgesellschaft* of his separatist grandfather, Samson Raphael Hirsch, this advice was not at all surprising. Nevertheless, Teitz chose to do otherwise, quite cognizant of the danger that "accepting a great number of people whose religious opinions differ from ours" could change the nature of his community. Yet this apprehension was overcome by his desire to include all, and not to cause "a split of our [German Jewish] strength." With this fateful decision, knowingly or not, Teitz helped found an immigrant synagogue steeped in ethnic-religious ambiguity with concomitant religious tensions that would erupt over the coming decades.[21]

Synagogue Ambiguities

Self-definition

The first of these ambiguities emerged from the need to articulate the synagogue's self-definition and goals and to clarify the congregation's ostensible meaning for its members. Constitutional declarations aside, two divergent attitudes on the issue of synagogue identity and purpose that manifested themselves illustrated clearly the different weight of religion and ethnicity as factors attracting immigrants to New Hope.

For the smaller number of members who were exacting in their Orthodox observance, the true merit and meaning of the congregation lay in its replication of the particular German religious pattern of worship to which they were accustomed; for these Jews, maintaining this distinctive religious service constituted the fundamental raison d'être of New Hope and constituted the preeminent reason for their affiliation with it. To them, New Hope represented an institution in which ethnicity and religion were integrally and symbiotically linked: Its specific ethnic makeup molded its unique brand of Orthodox Judaism with its distinctive *minhag*, while the synagogue's special form of religious service was the keynote of the pride these pious Jews felt for their ethnic congregation. New Hope existed to perpetuate a certain kind of ethnic religion, just as the first constitution had stipulated. As Leo Teitz put it in his Rosh Hashana sermon of 1942: "Cincinnati shall be our Hamburg and Köln and Frankfurt and Fulda and Halberstadt. We want to continue what over there is no longer possible . . . and we want to continue and re-establish to a new glory the centuries-old fame of the great and the devotion of the small German Jewish congregations."

But already in New Hope's earliest years there existed a second type of member who became the majority in the congregation, someone of traditional or nominally traditional religious background, liberal or lax in religious purposes, for whom loyalty to parents or memories of past observances in Germany, distinctive holiday services, and of crucial import, a special religious style including decorum, dignity, and the particular German musical liturgy, were still sources of abiding inspiration. To this individual, New Hope, especially in its early decades, represented a significant ethnic-religious association that drew on deep-seated emotional feelings linking him to the German-Jewish past; it was a monument to what was destroyed, a religious framework that legitimated and fostered ethnic-social fraternization.[22] Although, to be sure, this kind of member periodically expressed religious feelings as well – coming to the synagogue on High Holidays, to a lesser extent on holidays, and very infrequently on a Sabbath, or to recite *kaddish* – his membership primarily reflected ethnic sentiment. The fundamental meaning of New Hope for him lay in its cementing a sense of extended German Jewish family in which religion played a part – perhaps important, perhaps not, depending on each person – but not the preeminent part that it assumed for the strictly Orthodox. As Max Feder, a religious liberal, declared in his after-dinner speech, "From Avondale to Amberley," at the congregational banquet of 1966, although he had "been troubled by the fact of . . . being a Jew," and had not "always been very comfortable with it [Judaism]," he joined New Hope and "as a member . . . found in time of stress a haven in New Hope, a refuge, a place to belong."[23]

Consequently, over the years, as some of the more religiously liberal members called for constitutional revisions or innovations in the synagogue ritual, or as they organized social activities such as New Year's Eve parties, which were frowned upon by the more traditional, religious tension between the two sides was heightened and sometimes exploded dramatically at congregational board meetings.

Interestingly, religious tensions were mitigated within New Hope's highly organized and socially effective sisterhood, in which ethnic sociability transcended religious differences. For the women, the various sisterhood activities – organizational and planning meetings, card parties, Chanukah parties, *Kaffee und Kuchen* afternoons, social action projects, and fund-raising functions – fostered a marvelous atmosphere of ethnic solidarity, fellowship, and *Gemuetlichkeit*, even if different levels of religious observance separated many from each other outside the synagogue. Moreover, since the overwhelming majority of the young women did not go to college, the sisterhood provided a meaningful social framework for its members' maturation and their growing up together. Repeatedly, when asked to reflect upon the sisterhood, members stress the sense of family, of mutual concern, and aid that the organization spawned. A large part of this harmony must be attributed, no doubt, to the fact that "religion" was the domain of the men in New Hope, that the sisterhood was not involved in the formulation of religious policy in the congregation, and that apart from the women's *hevra*, it functioned strictly as a sociocultural group. Although certainly not oblivious to religious dissension, the New Hope Sisterhood generally kept itself removed from the fray.[24]

Among the men, however, the differences over the meaning and religious direction of the synagogue and over the latitude for religious innovation consistent with ethnic-religious custom from time to time fractured congregational harmony, generated considerable ill-will, and in more than one instance almost split the congregation irrevocably. Without question, the idiosyncratic nature of the New Hope constituency contributed to the sometimes vociferous congregational bickering and turmoil that frequently revolved around perceived personal slights as much as genuine religious differences. Although a number of refined, cultured, but mostly Jewishly uneducated, German Jews had joined the congregation, the majority consisted of former shopkeepers, salesmen, small businessmen, plus a few small town cattle dealers, some considered by others rather uncouth and a few definitely "hotheaded."[25] Indeed, a few of the latter, beneficiaries of significant sums of German reparations money, *Wiedergutmachung* – as was virtually every New Hope member – just became more aggressive and picayune; their new socioeconomic station was not matched by any refinement in social graces. Nonetheless, the inner religious strife and ethnic-religious problematics of this *Einheitsgemeinde* synagogue were built into its organizational structure from the start. The New Hope experience thus underscored the profoundly ambiguous and even dialectical functions of ethnicity and religion in an immigrant congregational setting: Both ethnicity and religion simultaneously served as unifying and divisive forces. Whereas the ethnic factor brought together the more religious and less religious element under the

History of Our Congregation

By DR. LEO TEITZ, Past President

It happened in February 1939. A small number of new-comers had been in Cincinnati for about one year. On the high holidays 1938, they had to attend services in various synagogues. Rabbi Eliezer Silver was approached by these men, who then upon his suggestion founded our congregation in August 1939. Among those were the following: Moritz Engel, Justin Frankel, Henry Holzinger, Simon Gutmann, Sigfried Kugelman, Manfred Rabenstein, Emanuel Silbermann, Theo Pauly, Sol Wollenreich, Dr. Leo Teitz, Emil Zieler, the late Lazarus Appel, Theodore Appel, Joseph Leva.

The name New Hope (Tikvoh Chodoshoh) was selected for our congregation and Dr. Leo Teitz was elected as its first president.

The first high holiday services were held on Rosh Hashono 1939 in the Bureau of Jewish Education attended by approximately fifty persons. From 1940 to 1942 our services were conducted in the hall of the American Legion and later in the Jewish Center.

In 1942, the congregation became incorporated. The charter members were Mr. Bernhard Seelig, Mr. Richard Wise and Mr. Sigfried Lowenstein. Shortly thereafter, the cemetery was acquired. Twenty-five members subscribed the amount of $700.00 which was needed to purchase it.

In the years to follow we continued in our efforts to preserve unity among our members: liberal, conservative, and orthodox. All worked harmoniously together.

I pray that this spirit of unity may prevail in our midst for a long time to come. May our new synagogue always be filled with the blessings of G-d and may the light of the Tauroh burn in it forever.

A brief history by New Hope's first president, Leo Teitz. This message, asserting congregational harmony among the religious factions, was more optimistic than realistic. Courtesy of New Hope Synagogue, Cincinnati.

same roof for social fraternization, conflicts over the precise ethnic liturgical rite to be adopted led to early disagreements as we have seen; and whereas religion united ethnic liberals and traditionalists in prayer at least a few times a year, it still worked to separate them as the different religious factions promoted their discrete perceptions of the meaning of the synagogue and their antithetical conceptions of permissible religious change.

The ethnic-religious pull of New Hope is highlighted by the explanations offered by some German immigrant Jews for *not* joining New Hope. Some, from German liberal religious backgrounds, found New Hope too Orthodox; for them, the need for ethnic sociability did not overshadow their perception of New Hope's religious rigidity. And if they had such a need, they fulfilled it by membership in the Gate Club, a social-cultural club for German refugees founded in 1935 that gradually petered out in the 1950s. They fulfilled their spiritual wants, if extant, with membership in Reform temples such as Rockdale or Wise or in Conservative Adath Israel.[26] Some of more traditional background – potential New Hope members – married spouses of liberal religious orientation and followed them into more liberal religious frameworks.[27] Others avoided New Hope because they consciously sought to end as quickly as possible their separate German Jewish identification. As a matter of principle, they eagerly desired to assimilate into the broader, more homogenized American Jewish community; that is, they longed to identify as *American* Jews rather than as *American German* Jews. Hence, the religiously conservative among them gravitated to Adath Israel (which had separate seating until the early 1950s),[28] willingly forfeiting the particular German service they had been used to, whereas the religious liberals among them joined Reform temples. Both religious options were viewed as more American than German New Hope.[29] In some cases, parents followed their children's wishes and joined the temples in which their children's friends attended Sunday school. Then, too, religious and social motivations for not joining New Hope for a number of the upwardly mobile German Jews were supplemented by considerations of class. Some Germans declined to join New Hope or left once they returned to their previous class standing, viewing the congregation as a lower-middle-class association, which, with a few notable exceptions, it was. To these Jews, ethnic togetherness was not sufficiently attractive to transcend class distinction.[30] Finally, in Cincinnati, as elsewhere, those German Jews who had neither German ethnic nor religious needs tended either to involve themselves in secular Jewish communal affairs, to assimilate out of the Jewish community altogether, or to remain at its margins.[31] In contradistinction to all these types of German immigrants, those who joined New Hope and stayed with it tolerated its religious divisions and the ambiguity of its congregational character. The Orthodox took pride in participating and perpetuating German Orthodox Judaism; the liberals found satisfaction in a socially gratifying German Jewish ambience, which also provided an occasional German-style religious outlet when needed.

Transplanting a previously state-legitimated and compulsory institutional framework into the voluntaristic and pluralistic settings of the American and American Jewish communities could not but be frought with complex challenges. On the heels of the dislocating immigrant experience, Jewish newcomers understandably sought mutual support from a German congregation that recalled past national religious associations. And yet, their exposure to a more mobile society that encouraged freedom of expression and to a far more religiously differentiated Jewish society that gave religious options if one was dissatisfied with existing religious attachments necessarily tested the viability of an Old World institution in the new land.

German New Hope and Cincinnati's Reform Judaism

In the gradual process of coming to terms with its identity as a German traditional congregation, New Hope discovered the inner complexities and contrary forces at work in an immigrant religious association. But like other immigrant synagogues of its generation and of previous generations, it had to articulate its relationship to the outer Jewish community as well, if for no other reason than to justify its separateness, both to its members and to outsiders.[32]

The Jewish community of Cincinnati during the 1930s was decisively split along German and East European Jewish lines.[33] The Germans, many of whose ancestors arrived at Cincinnati in the mid-nineteenth century, comprised a Jewish patriciate. Wealth, social prestige, Jewish communal and institutional governance were their hallmarks, as were a highly developed social conscience, civic involvement, and sense of belongingness to the city. By the 1930s, German Jews and their descendants had made outstanding contributions to Cincinnati's philanthropic agencies, politics, medical science, culture, and the arts and had pioneered models of social service. Their religious orientation was strictly Reform Judaism and was generally channeled by membership in one of two historic temples, the aristocratic classical Reform Rockdale Temple (Bene Israel) led by David Philipson and the somewhat more moderately Reform and slightly less elegant Isaac M. Wise Temple (Bene Yeshurun) led by James G. Heller. The presence in the city of the national Reform seminary, Hebrew Union College, only heightened the sense of religious preeminence that Reformers felt.

Socially, culturally, and religiously, German Jews from the nineteenth century through the first forty years of the twentieth century had very little to do with the East Europeans who, by and large, began arriving in significant numbers during the 1880s.[34] The native German Jews did organize relief and social assistance for the immigrants, many of whom started their new lives as peddlers, tailors, and petty businessmen.[35] But charity was not camaraderie: East European Jews "were given food, but not asked to dinner."[36] Cleavages between the the subcommunities were reinforced by religious and ethnic-national differences. Religious traditionalists from Eastern Europe and German Jewish Reformers (or more precisely, the American Reform descendants of the original German immigrants) did not cross religious lines. Wise Temple was not entirely closed to East European membership when desired in a small number of cases, but Rockdale Temple, in effect, was; for their part, Germans did not join the East European synagogues. Moreover, the issue of Zionism also helped exacerbate the split between the two groups. East Europeans like Rabbi Louis Feinberg of Adath Israel were supportive of Jewish nationalism, if not outspoken advocates, whereas most Reformers were either outrightly opposed to it or waffled.[37]

New Hope therefore provided Cincinnati Jewry with a new and intermediate religious model: Ethnically related to Germans who were identified with Reform Judaism, it was separated from them by its Orthodox religious tradition; ethnically distinct from East European Jews, it was tied to them by virtue of its formal Orthodox religious character, although with an admittedly distinctive ethnic flavor. But precisely because of its own particular ethnic-religious character, New Hope experienced extremely ambiguous relationships with Cincinnati's Reform Jews and Reform Judaism on the one hand and with its East European Jews and their religious Orthodoxy on the other. Viewing the evolution of New Hope from a historical perspective, one is struck by the extent to which the delicate interplay between ethnic and religious forces in the Cincinnati Jewish community at large promoted unity yet also provoked dissension within the congregation. The specific character of the Cincinnati Jewish community in large measure helped shape New Hope's future.

Established as a German Orthodox synagogue, New Hope and its religious posture were channeled especially under Teitz in a decided and conscious anti-Reform direction. This institutional repudiation of Reform Judaism in its first decade was demonstrated compellingly in the summer and fall of 1946 over an incident that almost destroyed the congregation. Article VII of the New Hope constitution dealing with membership eligibility stipulated that anyone over the age of eighteen could become a member and that this membership passed automatically to children of members upon their eighteenth birthday. Membership, however, was "revoked in a case of a marriage with a gentile or marriage without *kiduschin*," and an individual who was married without *kiduschin* (the ritual ceremonies of Jewish marriage) could not become a member. As a result, when a son of one of the members was married by a Reform rabbi – hence without proper *kiduschin* – his formal request to have his personal membership acknowledged was rejected, much to the consternation not only of his family but some of the more liberal members of the congregation. Demands were made to change the constitution and numerous official and unofficial meetings were held to avert a full-scale crisis.[38] Ultimately a compromise between liberal and Orthodox members was reached. By a board resolution, the constitution was left intact, but a note was appended to it that stated that every applicant for membership had to be recommended by an existing member, that a committee of six, "consisting of three orthodox and three liberal members has to decide on all membership applications" (a tie vote denoted rejection of the application), and that it was "expected in the future that all members will not let themselves be married by a Reform rabbi." Apparently, even liberal New Hope members, indicative of their acceptance of the primacy of the synagogue's Orthodox traditions and constraints, were willing at this time to go on record against granting religious legitimacy to Reform marriages. The compromise footnote was dropped in the revised constitution of 1955, although the original article revoking membership of those married without *kiduschin* was retained. The 1968 constitution, reflective of the sentiment of some of New Hope's more vocal religious liberals and of the liberalizing of New Hope (in outward form at least), dropped even that requirement and simply declared that any Jewish person over age eighteen upon written application to the board was eligible to become a member.

To Teitz, maintaining New Hope as a traditional German Jewish synagogue with explicit repudiation of Reform imposed a historic challenge to its membership, replete with social and ethnic-religious significance. By successfully assuming the mantle of German Orthodoxy in America, New Hope was to prove that contemporary German Jewish immigrants could be traditional and modern, that unlike those of previous generations, they need not become Reform in order to become American. Neither Reform Jews nor Reform Judaism, Teitz proclaimed, were to be models for New Hope Jews:

My friends, when you go among the crowds here, the Jewish crowds, I mean, you will often hear them refer to the Reformed Jews as "Germans." It always hurt my soul when I heard that all Jews of German background were generally considered Reformers. We have to atone for the sins of those who came here 80 and 100 years ago, who blackened the name of German Jewishness in the midst of others. In their time they acquired riches, in their time they did their share as eager citizens of the new country, but as *Jews* they should not be considered models for us. There is no need for us to throw overboard all what [*sic*] we experienced over there, what was passed down to us by our fathers and mothers, just to become good citizens. Don't let anyone tell you that you have to join a Reformed congregation, that you have to take part in their "services," "social events," and their religious instruction to become Americanized. Did not Traditional synagogues bring forth equally brave soldiers as Reformed congregations? Our specific task now must be to prove to our Jewish fellow citizens that not all Jews coming from Germany are Reformed, that there still exists another circle – and not even so small a flock – of those who are willing to lead their lives according to the rules. It shall be the task of this congregation to gather all those who consider Traditional Judaism to be the right one [BK: even if they don't personally practice all or most of its *mitzvot*] in order to form an honorable link in the chain of the older *kehilos* in the city of Cincinnati.[39]

By conveying the message of radical religious opposition to Reform Judaism, New Hope was theoretically putting itself beyond the sphere of influence of Reform; in practice, this was not at all the case. Ties with Reform Jews and Judaism persisted, and they manifested themselves in diverse social and religious ways, both during Teitz's administration and certainly after it. First, despite Teitz, Reformers of German background did serve as models of successful integration and Americanization. The temples and their Sunday schools continued to attract some New Hope parents and particularly their children, especially as the latter entered high school age. If the children were at all active Jewishly, they wanted to join the Jewish temple activities of their Jewish peers whom they befriended in public school.[40]

More significantly, ties with Reformers were cemented by personal family relationships. Having come to Cincinnati by virtue of the letters of affidavits sent to them by family members residing in the city, a

number of New Hopers found their families to be socially and economically successful and, in some cases, very influential members of the
community; in virtually all cases, the temple affiliation of these Jews, if
they had any, was to a Reform congregation. And sometimes these local
relatives informed their newly arrived families in no uncertain terms that
if they expected additional assistance, they would have to conform to
American and American Jewish standards, that is, to speak English, to
work on Saturday, and not to cover their heads when entering a synagogue or, in other words, to attend a Reform temple.[41]

Beyond the pragmatic, familial-ethnic bonds drawing New Hopers to
Reform, Reform Judaism and certain individuals associated with it held
significant cultural attraction to some of the younger, more religiously
liberal and Americanizing New Hope members. On the other hand,
Reform and its proponents were perceived as grave threats to the integrity
of the synagogue by the more traditional membership. Over the years,
therefore, the built-in cleavage between the small number of vocal liberals
and the minority traditionalists within New Hope assumed the guise of
a quasi-ideological battle as each side, according to its differing religious
inclinations, aligned itself with respect to Reform Judaism and to some
of its spokesmen. Reform Judaism served as a consistent consensus-
breaker within New Hope, especially in the light of its omnipresence
and the dominating Jewish cultural role of Hebrew Union College in
Cincinnati.

Thus, the lecturer at the first New Hope Young Couples Club activity
was a young ordained rabbi from Hebrew Union College, Robert Katz,
today a professor at the college.[42] The German liberal Rabbi Albert
Friedlander spoke at the joint New Hope–Gate Club *Kristallnacht* services
in November 1950. In the fall of 1966, one member of the New Hope
Sisterhood proposed that the group attend Wise Temple's lecture and
culture series, a proposal that was judged inappropriate and that was
ultimately set aside. More important, to inaugurate New Hope's new
building in March 1950, the featured guest speaker amid all the festivities
was none other than Rabbi Leo Baeck, the heroic national and cultural
symbol of German Jewish spiritual resistance under the Nazis and, at the
time, Efroymson Visiting Professor at the Hebrew Union College in
Cincinnati.[43] Yet the invitation to Baeck, a German liberal rabbi intimately associated with the premier Reform seminary in America, infuriated Leo Teitz.[44] Not only had he not been party to the organizing
committee of New Hope's dedication ceremonies, but he deemed it
inexcusable to initiate a new Orthodox congregation with a Reform
rabbi, notwithstanding Baeck's uniquely relevant background to New

Hope. Common national origins, even those additionally charged by a common, tragic fate – if most New Hopers luckily escaped what Baeck had personally experienced, some of their relatives had not – was not a sufficient factor to transcend religious differences within the ethnic group, at least to Teitz and to a few of his supporters.

Similarly, the Reformer Jakob J. Petuchowski and his family played an ambiguous religious role in New Hope's history. Despite being a faculty member at Hebrew Union College, Professor Petuchowski was a guest speaker at New Hope's annual banquet in 1960, 1963, 1965, and 1973, and he lectured to the congregation on other occasions as well. Cultured, learned, and German, Petuchowski appealed to a select number of the more culturally oriented religious liberals of New Hope who found in him a welcome model of refined and modern religiosity. From his side, Petuchowski was drawn to New Hope by the superb Torah reading of Rev. Rabenstein, the melodies of Lewandowski, which reminded him of the religious services he had attended as a Berlin youth, and the distinctive German flavor and atmosphere of the congregation. He truly hoped that New Hope could recreate the *Einheitsgemeinde* of his native land. On more than one occasion, he – the Reform rabbi – called on New Hope to live up to the traditions of German Orthodoxy and of Samson R. Hirsch of which it was heir. This irony is explicable only within the context of the peculiar ethnic–religious *Einheitsgemeinde* that New Hope represented.[45]

Petuchowski's active involvement with New Hope, from 1965 until his resignation from the board in 1975, came at a time of aroused agitation for change within the synagogue that eventually spilled over into the most serious religious *Kulturkampf* in its history. Although he was by no means directly responsible for it, he was nevertheless not an insignificant or passive figure in the events as they unfolded. In fact, his presence and actions helped sharpen the contours of opposing religious views within the congregation and underscored the destabilizing impact that Reform Judaism had on Orthodox New Hope. To understand this phenomenon properly, some background information is essential.

Upon becoming president of the congregation in 1964, Ernst Kahn set about to revitalize it. He felt that a definite malaise had gripped New Hope: There was "something wrong with the congregation." Under his administration, the most significant and intense attempts were made to broaden the synagogue culturally and socially, to appeal to the youth, and to satisfy the more liberal constituency of the congregation. His five-year presidency saw the introduction of a Purim ball, dinner dances, New Year's Eve parties, a communal *seder* on the second night of Passover, periodic lectures, *ongei shabbat* programs, a recharged youth group, and a bimonthly breakfast *minyan* for teenagers – in short, many of the activities often associated with the "Americanization of the synagogue."[46]

In a sense, Kahn was the perfect kind of person to try to mediate the gap between the two religious poles of the congregation. Son of Moritz Kahn, who, although not a founder, was one of the earliest members of New Hope, Ernst grew up in the synagogue as one of its native sons; moreover, religiously, he was "middle of the road," or, in German terms, he represented one type of an Americanized version of South German "popular Orthodoxy." Personally more observant than most New Hopers and deeply attached to German Jewish traditions, he was not, however, fully observant, and did not hide the fact. While consciously seeking to attract the liberals and the young – announcing that the 1967 congregational dinner would be a dinner dance because the younger members wanted it, he invited those who did not believe in that kind of activity to leave after supper[47] – he was also the initiator of the New Hope daily *minyan* (prayer quorum) in 1964 and was intimately familiar with German *nusach* (liturgy). He served as one of the main *hazanim* during the High Holidays. Although supportive of the liberal thrust within the synagogue, Ernst Kahn was nonetheless sympathetic to the traditionalists.

By encouraging the more active participation in New Hope of the more religiously liberal members, however, Kahn opened the door for their subsequent attempts to alter the synagogue service itself. During his five-year term in office, especially between late 1966 and 1969, a minority of the younger (fortyish) religious liberals like Werner Coppel and Lothar Haas led almost a house revolt to introduce English readings in the High Holiday services, to delete some of the mostly incomprehensible medieval *piyutim* on holidays, High Holidays, and special *Shabbatot* like *parshat shekalim*, *parshat zakhor* endemic to the South German Ashkenazic rite, to allow the youth a greater role in the services, and to permit Bat Mitzvah celebrations for those girls and their families who wanted them. Although some of these requests were bitterly contested by the traditionalists, especially Rev. Rabenstein, as being contrary to the German Orthodox tradition, all of them were actually instituted, however briefly. None of these changes took lasting effect, however, because of the unwavering opposition of the religious leadership and because, fundamentally, they were inconsequential; they really did not resolve the religious dissatisfaction that the vocal liberal critics felt for prayers they could not understand and the extended period of time it took to say them. The experiment with English readings, in particular, failed because of the poor readings done by the young and the stilted English translations that were used.[48]

Although Professor Petuchowski did not spark this latest round of internal religious strife and the tempestuous board meetings that ensued, the presence and willing participation of this native German Reform rabbi in a German Orthodox congregation at this juncture severely exacerbated the liberal-traditional tension. Some of the liberals in New Hope looked to him almost as an unofficial patron and religious advisor who could religiously validate their desire for liturgical changes.[49]

The simmering tension between the vociferous minority of liberals who demanded changes in the religious service and the synagogue traditionalists exploded in the wake of a speech delivered by Petuchowski in the spring of 1973 at the annual congregational dinner. In this speech, Professor Petuchowski called into question an interpretation of Judaism's attitude to autopsies that Rev. Rabenstein had circulated to the entire congregation; he offered an alternate point of view. Aside from the content of the speech, its public context appeared to challenge and compromise Rev. Rabenstein's religious authority in his own congregation. Certainly the Rabenstein family and its supporters interpreted the implications of the speech in that way and were deeply insulted. Professor Petuchowski felt constrained to apologize in a personal letter to Rev. Rabenstein. Although he saw no reason for taking "ideological disagreements as personal insults," he nonetheless assured Rev. Rabenstein that "no offense was intended!" He noted that although they were separated by "a difference in emphasis" and different religious perspectives, his "respect and admiration" for Rev. Rabenstein were such that he "should never dream of wanting to offend" him.[50]

Hurt feelings notwithstanding, the incident might have blown over had not passions been inflamed by a stinging polemical letter, humorously entitled "An Autopsy of a Speech," sent to members of the board by Bernard Rabenstein, son of Rev. Rabenstein.[51] The younger Rabenstein defended his father's views, repudiated Petuchowski's authority as an arbitrater of *Halacha* (Jewish law), and provocatively baited the board.

> Do you think that Jewish law and the Judaism that Orthodoxy maintains harms you? Why torture yourself? Join others who have gone to temples. (Cincinnati gives you a variety of choices in temples and conservative synagogues) . . . Besides, these well-established temples have much more to offer you in (so-called) spiritual guidance.

The ensuing reactions came swiftly and furiously and the letter was a conversation piece for weeks. But in the aftermath of this furor, it became obvious to the half-dozen or so disenchanted liberals that the rest of the congregation, even the majority of those non-Orthodox in observance, did not agree with their urging for fundamental religious change and did not wish to rock the religious boat. The majority of them came to New Hope but a few times a year for services or social functions. They had no interest in changing the traditional liturgy or in seeing more synagogue-sponsored cultural activities. Most were content with New Hope as it was, or found it sufficient to "attend services, burials, and visit bereaved families," as president Ernst Kahn sarcastically lamented in a March 1968 letter to the congregation.[52] Although these individuals had varying relations with Rev. Rabenstein – some were personal and intimate friends, others found him too aloof and religiously dogmatic – they realized that without him, New Hope as a German ethnic synagogue was impossible. Hence, loyal to the congregation, the "silent majority" of New Hope – the nonobservant orthodox – did not mobilize behind the radicals to force the traditionalist's hand. Consequently, rather than starting a breakaway congregation, as was so customary in the nineteenth century under similar circumstances, the small number of religious liberals who had fought for change either left New Hope and joined a temple, just as Bernard Rabenstein had suggested, or stayed on in New Hope as totally marginal, disinterested members, more out of vestigial loyalty to parents or to keep their cemetery privileges or perhaps inertia than anything else. On July 2, 1975, Jakob Petuchowski also resigned as a member of the board.[53]

This entire period of Jakob Petuchowski's intensive involvement in the synagogue (1965–1975) underlined the ambiguous relationship of New Hope to Reform Jewry, despite its founders' intentions, and allows for the drawing of certain historical conclusions on the subject. First, not only were Reform Jews the ethnically and socially "significant other" to many younger members and their children growing up in the late 1950s, 1960s, and early 1970s, but Reform Judaism personified by Petuchowski was the culturally and religiously "significant other" as well. Not surprisingly, most non-Orthodox members – including the nonradicals – came to services only on the first day of two-day Jewish holidays, following Reform custom, although not necessarily for ideological reasons.[54] Second, Petuchowski's participation in New Hope affairs pointed to the innately problematic character of this reconstituted German immigrant *Einheitsgemeinde* synagogue. It challenged the limits of New Hope's ethnic-religious consensus and confronted it with fundamental questions: What were the limits of religious tolerance and pluralism that this ethnic-Orthodox association could countenance? Could it safely allow a native German Reform rabbi to preach his understanding of Jewish religious change and legal evolution if it did not conform to that of the official religious leadership? Petuchowski himself opined that indeed this might have been possible with a more open and forthcoming leadership, but there is much room to doubt this.[55] Although the larger portion of members may ultimately have been indifferent to the clashes over religious forms, the Orthodox members who preserved the religious character of the synagogue felt genuinely threatened as the strong-minded liberals demanding changes rallied round Petuchowski as both a catalyst and justifier of their views. This situation was inherently unstable and problematic because of the differing perceptions of what the fundamental synagogue goal was to be. That it was ultimately to prove religiously untenable could have been anticipated. It is arguable whether the *Einheitsgemeinde* had to have been religiously or theologically monolithic to succeed as Rabbi Breuer had cautioned Leo Teitz. Certainly, however, its officially Orthodox orientation dictated some limits to its religious consensus and to the expressions of religious norms, even though it was open to all who cared to join.

The Reform Jewish ambience in Cincinnati in general and the affiliation with New Hope of Jakob Petuchowski in particular also significantly colored the debate between traditionalists and liberals over liturgical changes in the service. Traditionalists saw themselves in an Orthodox–Reform struggle, and they were determined to thwart the encroachments of Reform Judaism. On the other hand, the liberals who fought to remove the *piyutim*, insert English readings or translations of prayers into the High Holiday services, and to hold Bat Mitzvah ceremonies viewed these changes as legitimate means of Americanizing the synagogue, or better put, of integrating New Hope into a broader, more uniform brand of mainstream *American* Judaism. To them, the German American synagogue could do what other American synagogues were doing, even some Orthodox ones. The traditionalists, however, perceived all such attempts at "Americanization" as reforms inspired by a few individuals seeking to transform New Hope into a Reform temple or at least a Conservative synagogue. The specter of Reform Judaism and the thoroughly Americanized descendants of native German Jews who supported it hovered in the background, and this reconstituted Orthodox German *Einheitsgemeinde* could not help but enjoy a deeply ambiguous relationship to them.

New Hope and Cincinnati's East European Orthodoxy

If New Hope's relationship to Cincinnati Reform Jewry was steeped in ambiguity, its interaction with the city's East European Jewish community was no less so. In a sense, the congregation's relationship with the East Europeans was simply the reverse of the one with the city's

Reformers: Here, religion was the factor fostering unity, whereas ethnic or national differentiation was the force of separatism. Indeed, contrary forces of religion and ethnicity served simultaneously to attract New Hope to and repel it from the orbit of East European Jews. The congregation's constitutional commitment to religious orthodoxy in a formal sense bound it in common cause to the East Europeans, virtually the only proponents of Orthodox Judaism in the city.[56] Mutual German–East European ethnic stereotypes and prejudices, however, militated against the emergence of intimate solidarity and communal fraternity between the two groups.

New Hope's ambivalent interaction with East European Orthodoxy is graphically and best illustrated in its unusual and highly sensitive relationship to Rabbi Eliezer Silver, the preeminent Orthodox figure in the city,[57] prime exponent of the Eastern European Orthodox tradition.

Silver was the inspiration and, in a sense, patron of New Hope Congregation. He helped many German Orthodox immigrants find jobs, and he prodded some of the Orthodox German Jews attending his Knesset Israel (Washington Avenue) congregation "to found some organization to hold together the German newcomers who would otherwise get lost in Jewish life." No doubt, Silver's feelings of religious triumphalism and disdain for non-Orthodox forms of Judaism actuated his desire to steer the German Jews away from the religious competition.

From the time of the first *minyan* to the period of the formal founding of New Hope Congregation in the summer of 1939 and on through the first decade or more of its existence, Eliezer Silver was intimately involved with New Hope affairs, and he was the recognized spiritual authority over New Hope. He delivered periodic sermons in the congregation, officiated at marriages of some of the New Hope members, established the fiscal season of New Hope from April to April (Nisan to Nisan, according to ancient practices of the Judean Kings and as practiced in contemporary Israel), served as New Hope's *halachic posek*, intervened when internal disputes over congregational duties disrupted New Hope congregational life, and did not hesitate to advise New Hopers on practical matters, such as whether or not to erect their own building.[58] Not only was Eliezer Silver the de facto rabbi of New Hope, but technically he was its rabbi de jure. The constitution of the Vaad Hoier declared that its *Rav* – currently, Eliezer Silver – was to serve as the legally recognized rabbi of any congregation that formally joined the organization. Hence, when New Hope did so, uniting in the umbrella organization with most of the city's East European Orthodox synagogues and the Sephardic congregation, Rabbi Silver in effect became its rabbinic leader.[59]

Ironically, he ministered to it much like a city or district rabbi of Southwest Germany, a *Kreisrabbiner*, might have served the multiple congregations under his supervision. Furthermore, Silver's authority over New Hope was actually drafted into the congregation's first constitution of 1939, which he was instrumental in formulating. As a sign of deference, Rev. Rabenstein did not sit in the rabbi's seat in the synagogue or apply for an Ohio license to perform marriage ceremonies, or represent New Hope on a dais in which Reformers sat as long as Silver lived.

Notwithstanding feelings of gratitude and respect for Silver on the part of a few New Hopers,[60] some of the more traditional members, not to mention the religious liberals, shared a profound ambivalence toward him. Mindful of their indebtedness to him as synagogue patron, and, in numerous cases, as personal benefactor, the majority of the congregants could not mask their feelings of discomfort and unhappiness over his continuing influence in New Hope. Silver personified so many of the tangible and intangible characteristics they disliked about East European Jews, and his position as rabbi of almost all the Orthodox East European congregations that they found so distasteful further elicited the latent prejudices toward East European Jews they had harbored still in Europe. Silver, to some, seemed pushy and aggressive; certainly his dedicated followers tried to raise money for him often enough with testimonial tributes on occasions of significant anniversaries or birthdays.[61] New Hope participated in most, though not all, of these fund drives and not always with great eagerness.[62] Silver's personal manner, appearance, and most disconcerting – his incomprehensible Yiddish sermons – especially disturbed the congregation. One can only try to imagine the impression Silver's Yiddish sermons made on German immigrants whose quest to create a German synagogue service in an American context were entirely antipathetic to an event that, symbolically and in actual atmosphere, reminded them of an East European ghetto! So galling were his Yiddish sermons that on occasions when Silver's appearance was anticipated, New Hope members simply stayed away, prompting special appeals to the congregants by the leadership – such as that of Leo Teitz who reminded New Hopers of the "delicate nature of their relationship" to Silver[63] – exhorting them to attend the services. At the congregants' urging, president Fred Mott in the mid-1950s successfully prevailed upon Silver to deliver his sermons at New Hope in English, which he did not deign to do in his own home synagogue of Knesset Israel.

Silver's rabbinic authority and ability to take control of the congregation at will also rankled some of the liberal members. They saw this as outside interference in their own affairs and an affront to congregational independence. The revised constitution of 1955 removed from the 1939 draft every one of the carefully inserted stipulations Silver had earlier written in giving him decisive authority in the congregation. Not surprisingly, therefore, the sometimes strained or tense relationship between the *Rav* and the congregation – representatives of two discrete Jewish subethnic cultures, religious *minhag*, and style – were plainly felt in New Hope, especially during its first two decades.

Beyond the relationship of Eliezer Silver to New Hope, the distance between the German congregation and East European Orthodox Jewry of Cincinnati – despite Orthodox religious commonalities – persisted both inside and outside the New Hope framework. Old world Jewish prejudices continued to manifest themselves.[64] Many East European Jews looked askance at the New Hopers as "Daitscher" or *yekkes*, pejorative epithets mocking the alleged stuffiness, excessive concern for order and formality, and superciliousness of German Jews. For their part, some New Hope congregants still harbored their stereotypes of East European Jews as dirty, uncouth *shnorrers* who spoke the bastardized German jargon of Yiddish. Some even used this characterization of them as a justifying rationale for not sending their children to the Orthodox Chofetz Chaim Day School (today, Cincinnati Hebrew Day School), which was administered by Jews of East European origin. Furthermore, negative images of East European Jews sometimes served as metaphors for internal criticism of New Hope when German members protested what they took to be "un-German" behavior. Hence, reacting to the noise made by children during services, one German member remonstrated that this was not a *Judenschule*, a German Jewish pejorative for an East European congregation or *shtibl* where disorder and uncivility were thought to be the norm.[65]

The discomfort experienced by the older, traditional-minded German Jews in East European synagogues like Knesset Israel and Ohav Shalom, moreover, was matched by the sense of alienation East Europeans felt when participating in the New Hope services. The *nusach* and atmosphere, let alone the social-ethnic group were foreign to them. Consequently, over the years, New Hope retained its remarkably homogeneous German-Jewish ethnic character. Of the more than two hundred members it has attracted since its founding, only seven were born in Eastern Europe; another eleven were American-born and of East European extraction, but most of these joined only in the mid-1970s. These few memberships, moreover, rather than resulting from any special attraction to the unique *minhag* of the services, were motivated by other considerations, such as living in close proximity to New Hope, the desire for an Orthodox-sponsored afternoon school (relevant only until 1973 when the school closed), and, in some cases, disaffection with some of the other neighborhood synagogues and their rabbis.[66]

Some of the strains of East European–German Jewish tensions ironically stemmed from the Rabenstein family itself. On the one hand, Rev. Rabenstein had been and continues to be the unequaled standard bearer of New Hope's German Orthodoxy. And yet, simultaneously, within the congregation he and his family have served as a bridge to East European Jewish culture. From the earliest days, Rev. Rabenstein had been an ardent supporter of Rabbi Silver, personally abiding by his *halachic* (legal) rulings, and insisting that Rabbi Silver was New Hope's *mara d'atra* (communal leader). The Rabensteins sent all their children to the Chofetz Chaim Day School; their eldest son Aaron (Arno) later attended Telshe Yeshiva in Cleveland and their son Jacob attended Telshe as well as Ner Israel in Baltimore. When Aaron returned from Telshe in 1958, he studied daily with Rabbi Silver and subsequently received a personal *smicha* (ordination) from him in 1961, *yoreh yoreh, yadin yadin* (the highest level of ordination).[67] Much to the chagrin of the New Hope membership, Aaron began to incorporate some East European *yeshiva* customs, melodies, and style of prayer into New Hope as his father began to delegate increasing liturgical responsibilities to his three sons. For example, Aaron's introduction of dancing – some say, rowdiness – on the festival of *Simchat Torah* was equated with East European chaos and infuriated the staid congregation, as did his putting his *tallit* (prayer shawl) over his head when he prayed. And when he began to deliver sermons from the pulpit at the prodding of Fed Mott, and he chose to talk on such standard *yeshiva* topics as *batel beshishim* (the declared nullification of an object in a mixture of which it is less that 1/60), most of the congregants just looked on in uncomprehending astonishment at what they took to be arrant nonsense. Aaron and his wife Lois took over many of the duties of the New Hope Talmud Torah in the mid-1960s through 1972, and generally they were extremely well liked and appreciated by the youth of the school. Aaron was acknowledged as a fine *baal tefillah* and, together with Lois, was in charge of the biannual synagogue bulletins. Despite his work on behalf of the congregation and despite having toned down what was considered "excessive *yeshiva* characteristics," his request that the board declare him assistant rabbi of New Hope in 1971 was rejected. The liberal board members feared a Rabenstein dynasty, but they also expressed concern that Aaron, protégé and ordinee of Elizer Silver and allied to the East European *yeshiva* world, might prove too Orthodox for New Hope and would deflect its ethnic-religious character to a more "East European style."[68] In 1972, Aaron and his family moved to Beersheva, Israel, where they currently reside.

One of the more interesting sagas illustrating the problematic inter-action between New Hope and Jews of East European descent unfolded from the mid-1970s to the spring of 1983. During this time, a handful of young American and Canadian families of East European background joined the synagogue. They chose New Hope either because it was the nearest synagogue to their homes, or because of disenchantment with their previous places of worship. Consisting entirely of academicians or doctors, this group brought a number of things to the congregation: (1) a highly visible minority – comprising anywhere from 20 to 75 percent of the *minyan*, depending on the occasion – dedicated to Orthodox Ju-daism and favoring the East European liturgy;[69] (2) youth, and a sense of vibrancy – the group lowered the median age to below fifty; (3) young children – to the great consternation of some of the Germans who con-stantly hushed them; and (4) a certain measure of prestige because of academic and medical status. The group, which in 1975–1976 was fairly cohesive, also brought to New Hope new religious tensions and ambi-guities. In order to make themselves feel more comfortable in the syn-agogue, they lobbied to institute liturgical changes in the service, such as removing or reducing the number of *piyutim*, introducing melodies of the East European *nusach*, and permitting others beside Rev. Raben-stein and his sons to conduct the service. If Jakob Petuchowski sometimes set himself up as New Hope's *German* religious conscience, some indi-viduals in this group stood up as its *Orthodox* conscience. Unfettered by German ethnic considerations, they frequently challenged the religious legitimacy of a non-Orthodox German Jew conducting services on the High Holidays just because of his acquaintance with the German *nusach*.

In 1975–1977, a few meetings were held between president Jerry Schot-tenfels and a few of the more vocal critics within this younger, non-German group in an effort to reach some accommodations. Although no drastic changes were implemented as a result of these meetings, in subsequent years certain concessions were made and some changes in-troduced such as greater merriment on *Simchat Torah*. The synagogue was in decline, and badly needed the presence of these younger families to support the *minyan*, to prepare *divrei torah* (sermons), and to lead *Pirke Avot* study sessions, and in general to infuse some life into the congre-gation. New Hope, therefore, was prepared to make concessions, and from its point of view, it did.

Ultimately, however, the main liturgical grievance – excessively lengthy services on the special instances when the *piyyutim* were recited – was not worked out to the satisfaction of these younger individuals. High Holiday and other holiday services sometimes found them ven-turing to other Orthodox congregations in the city. On the seventh day of Passover, 1983, the pent-up impatience finally erupted. After a terribly lengthy morning service because of the *piyutim,* some of these families walked out prior to the *musaf* service when it became obvious that, despite the late hour, a sermon was still to be delivered. Those who walked out did not return the next day. Three of these families have now left the congregation, two permanently, and the other family attends services less frequently.

In analyzing the sequence of events that led to the breach between New Hope and its younger members of East European origins, one should note the irony of Orthodox Jews leaving New Hope because they took a position advocated by Reformers: reduction or elimination of the *piyutim.* In taking this stance, however, one must emphasize equally that the Orthodox group lacked all historical perspective of the congregation and had no appreciation of the intricacies and ambiguities of its ethnic-religious identity. They did not realize that their request to excise the *piyutim* merely rehashed an all too familiar refrain of a more turbulent New Hope past. Although the context was now radically different – ten to fifteen years ago, this proposal was interpreted by the Orthodox leadership as an attempt by liberals to reform the congregation, a charge not applicable to this group of Orthodox stalwarts – the final congregational response, reflecting stiff resistance to the demand, remained the same: Such moves would alter the fundamental liturgy of the German *minhag* – the legacy of German Orthodoxy – which New Hope was charged with preserving. Regardless of the religious quarter from which these demands for change emanated, they could under no circumstances be permitted.

The relationship between German New Hope and its members of East European origin – in fact, to Cincinnati's Orthodox East Europeans in general – illuminates a simple but profound observation so readily apparent in the millenial history of the Jewish people, and highlighted especially, although not exclusively, in contemporary Israel: The specific coloration of distinctively Jewish ethnic religious tradition contributes significantly to the separation of one group of Jews from another. The persistence of a subethnic religious consciousness and *minhag* within Judaism, supplemented by subethnic stereotypes, separates Jew from Jew, so that even denominational kinship, such as exists between the Orthodox of different groups, often cannot break through the barriers erected by centuries-old ethnic customs and liturgical rites. Clearly, common religious ideology is all too often ineffective in overcoming deeply felt Old World divisions within Jewry. Only when the affirmation of Jewish subethnic religion and stereotypical cultural myths fade can religious denominational unity begin to take place.

Although theoretically the common commitment to Orthodox religious tradition might have brought together many of Cincinnati's East European Jews and their German New Hope counterparts, in practice their different forms of subethnic religious *minhagim*, sometimes reinforced by latent and not-so-latent subethnic prejudices, worked to keep them apart. Only those Germans who were devotedly Orthodox yet prepared to dismiss the ethnic component of their religious attachment as secondary – for religious or social reasons – could find an Americanized East European Orthodox congregational setting appealing.[70] To be sure, over the years New Hope cooperated with East European congregations in joint ventures. Rabbi David Indich of the Agudas Israel (Golf Manor) Congregation initiated a Tri-Synagogue Council in 1971, which included Agudas Achim (Roselawn), New Hope, and his own synagogue, to promote Orthodox Judaism in the city through joint efforts in youth work, adult education, and sisterhood programming. Its modest achievements aside, this congregational umbrella did not forge a real sense of Orthodox unity nor did it break the ethnic-religious barriers that separated New Hope from the other Orthodox synagogues in the city.

Conclusion

The story of New Hope provides a special and enlightening example of the dynamic yet problematic process of immigrants transplanting an Old World communal-congregational framework to America. In its struggle to preserve its distinctive German ethnic-religious character in the face of a gradually Americanizing and religiously diverse membership, the New Hope *Einheitsgemeinde* found that its fragile consensus abounded with internal tensions and ethnic-religious ambiguities. New Hope learned that however potent the appeal of ethnic religion to an immigrant congregation at the outset, both the factors of ethnicity and religion can be as divisive as they are unifying. Moreover, New Hope discovered the significant impact of a host community on an immigrant population. The ethnic and religious divisions between East European and German Jews in Cincinnati, as well as the direct involvement in New Hope affairs of radically divergent ethnic-religious personalities, certainly made their mark on the congregational experience.

Starting as it did in the late 1930s and reaching its most fulfilling years in the 1950s and early 1960s, New Hope, in reconstituting its brand of *minhag Ashkenaz*, was confronted with a powerful countervailing American Jewish social and religious trend that had gradually evolved over decades: the ethnicization of American Jewry into a broader *American* Jewish ethnic group transcending Jewish subethnic identification such as

German, Polish, Hungarian, Romanian, and Russian Jews.[71] This collective ethnicization brought with it a large degree of religious homogenization in which American Jewish religious denominationalism rather than subethnic religious attachments constituted the primary locus of religious identification and self-definition, and in which the quest for "an American form of religious tradition" was the fundamental religious and cultural leitmotif.[72] As the importance of Jewish subethnic origins waned, as more East European Jews and their descendants entered Reform congregations, as an American-style Orthodoxy was emerging, and as a nascent American movement of Conservative Judaism was taking shape, by the mid-twentieth century, with a few possible exceptions, Jewish subethnic religion within the context of American Judaism inevitably declined.[73]

Therefore, during the decades when New Hope was carving out its particular German Jewish religious identity, the phenomenon of Jewish subethnic religion and subethnic feeling was diminishing, even in Cincinnati, however gradually; and by affirming its German-Orthodox *minhag*, New Hope was out of sync with prevailing American Jewish religious and ethnic trends. Those of its members who sought to introduce religious changes in the congregation were undoubtedly influenced by this religious homogenization of American Jewry. They tried to superimpose *American* Jewish religious *minhagim* onto the New Hope *Einheitsgemeinde* in order to incorporate it into the framework of American Judaism irrespective of its unique ethnic liturgical style. Ultimately, their attempt failed; their proposed changes were deemed too radical a departure from the *minhag Ashkenaz* rite. Unlike the nineteenth-century pattern, however, when synagogue schisms over religious reforms in emerging communities led to the creation of breakaway congregations, the disgruntled New Hopers living in the twentieth century and in an established Jewish community simply joined other existing synagogues more to their liking.

Admittedly rooted in a unique Cincinnati setting, the New Hope experience nevertheless points to larger historical questions and observations concerning ethnic religion that should at least be crystallized here. What factors in American and American Jewish life promote or hinder the preservation of Jewish subethnic religion? Why do some forms persist, for example, those of the Syrian Jewish community in Brooklyn, New York, or the Persian Jews of Kew Gardens, New York, or the diverse forms of Hasidism originating in different parts of Europe, whereas other forms of ethnic religion such as the scores of Polish, Romanian, Russian, and Hungarian *landsleit* synagogues founded at the turn of the century and most German synagogues of the 1930s did not?

What does this suggest about the nature of the ethnic groups themselves
and of their relationship to the process of American Jewish ethnicization?
If in some sense they resisted this trend, how and why? To what extent
did their very distinctive forms of ethnic religion contribute to this ethnic
separation? A good deal of Jewish cross-cultural analysis remains to be
done to illuminate these issues. These last questions, moreover, suggest
others. How important is the factor of religion in fostering immigrant
Jewish ethnic life, in comparison with the importance of language and
general group culture? How important is religion in promoting Jewish
subethnic attachments for the second and third generations? Finally, if
ethnicity and ethnic religion for many non-Jewish groups are still vital
forces, do those forms of Jewish subethnicity and subethnic religion that
still persist similarly have much of a future in America?[74]

NOTES

I would like to thank the members of New Hope Congregation for their
wonderful cooperation, which made this study both exciting and a pleasure
to undertake. I am very grateful to the University of Cincinnati Taft Council for a grant-in-aid, which facilitated the research and writing of this
essay. My thanks go as well to Professors Steven Bowman, Lloyd P.
Gartner, Stephen J. Whitfield, and to my wife Penny for their perceptive
comments on earlier drafts. I am indebted to Professor Jonathan D. Sarna
who was instrumental in helping me reduce the text from its much larger,
comprehensive form to the present length. All New Hope material such
as congregational minutes, bulletins, correspondence, sisterhood and *chevra
kadisha* minutes are located in the congregation's office, with the exception
of some items such as plays and some correspondence that are in the hands
of various individuals. Material of any consequence of this latter group has
been xeroxed and is now in my possession. In addition to written material,
this chapter draws on two types of oral material: taped interviews of New
Hope members, which I personally conducted and which are in my possession; and taped interviews of ninety Cincinnati Jews of German and
Austrian origin, most of whom arrived in the city during the 1930s, which
were conducted by volunteers of the National Council of Jewish Women
(NCJW) for their jointly sponsored oral history project with the American
Jewish Archives entitled "The Survivors of Hitler's Germany: An Oral
History." Approximately one-third of those interviewed were or are members of New Hope. The Archives (AJA) is the depository of these tapes
and of the typed transcripts. I am indebted to Abraham J. Peck, Associate
Director of the AJA, and Mrs. Toni Lyons, president of the NCJW, for
permission to peruse and cite from this important collection. Because all
primary oral and written sources pertaining to New Hope and Cincinnati's

German Jewish refugees of the 1930s are only locally available, to save space for this volume I have deposited a copy of the complete original manuscript at the AJA, and all references in this text, especially to the oral interviews, will simply refer the reader to the expansive notes of the original version, hereafter designated as AJA, MS. The fuller and more complete text will be published as a separate volume by Markus Wiener Publishing.

1   In preparing this manuscript, I have been struck by the apparent looseness in sociological and historical references to "ethnicity." What precisely is the difference between an ethnic group and a nationality; at what point in the immigration procedure should people of different nationalities coming to the United States become identified as ethnics? Moreover, is this a historical question or a historiographical question; that is, did historians in a certain period, say post–World War II, begin to label former nationals as ethnics? If so, why? The practical ramifications of these questions for my study are simply these: Should German Jewish immigrants of the 1930s be classified as "ethnics" and the German Jewish religious culture they established be limned as "ethnic-Judaism," or as Jews of German nationality and their culture as a form of "national Judaism?" The terminological difficulty is compounded when one thinks of the contemporary reference to American Jews as an ethnic group; how then does one label Syrian Jews, Persian Jews, Sephardic Jews, German Jews, Israeli Jews, and any group of Jews from a different nation and nationality still preserving their regional Jewish culture – "subethnics?" These questions should be asked even if this chapter is not the place to answer them. For the sake of convention, I have adopted "ethnic" as the adjective for German Jews and later in the essay even resort to subethnic when talking of German Jews and other distinct nationality-based Jewish cultural subunits of the supposedly integrated American Jewish ethnic community.

    Those espousing the views of Daniel J. Elazar on this whole terminological issue certainly would disapprove of this approach. See Daniel J. Elazar, "Sephardim and Ashkenazim: The Classic and Romantic Traditions in Jewish Civilization," *Judaism*, 33 (1984), pp. 146–159, esp. p. 152, n. 2. Helpful historical studies on ethnic groups include Leonard Dinnerstein and David M. Reimers, *Ethnic Americans: A History of Immigration and Assimilation* (New York, 1975); Victor Greene, *For God and Country: The Rise of Polish and Lithuanian Consciousness* (Madison, 1975); Humbert S. Nelli, *From Immigrants to Ethnics: The Italian Americans* (New York, 1983). Useful conceptual essays on some of the broad issues identified include James H. Dormon, "Ethnic Groups and 'Ethnicity': Some Theoretical Considerations," *Journal of Ethnic Studies*, 7 (1979), pp. 23–36; Jonathan D. Sarna, "From Immigrants to Ethnics: Towards a New Theory of 'Ethnicization,' " *Ethnicity*, 5 (1978), pp. 370–378; Rudolph J. Vecoli, "European Immigrants: From Immigrants to Ethnics," *International Migration Review*, 6 (1972), pp. 403–434.

2   The importance of religion to the formation of immigrant ethnic commu-

nities and to a sense of a group's ethnic differentiation and the ethnic function of churches have begun to be appreciated only in recent years. See J. P. Dolan, *The Immigrant Church: New York's Irish and German Catholics, 1815–1865* (Baltimore, 1975); Randall M. Miller and Thomas D. Marzik, *Immigrants and Religion in Urban America* (Philadelphia, 1977); Andrew M. Greeley, *The Denominational Society: A Sociological Approach to Religion in America* (Glenview, 1972); and *Ethnicity in the United States: A Preliminary Reconnaissance* (New York, 1974); Timothy Smith, "Religious Denominations as Ethnic Communities: A Regional Case Study," *Church History*, 35 (1966), pp. 207–226; and "Religion and Ethnicity in America," *American Historical Review*, 83 (1978), pp. 1155–1185, esp. pp. 1169, 1174–1185. For constructive examples of how the synagogue and Jewish religion promoted ethnicity, see Deborah Dash Moore, *At Home in America: Second Generation New York Jews* (New York, 1981), pp. 123–147; and Marshall Sklare, *Conservative Judaism* (New York, 1972), esp. pp. 35–37.

3   See, for example, Lloyd P. Gartner, *History of the Jews of Cleveland* (Cleveland, 1978), p. 165; Nathan M. Kaganoff, "An Orthodox Rabbinate in the South: Tobias Geffen, 1870–1970," *American Jewish History* 73 (1983), pp. 56–70, esp. p. 70; Leon Jick, *The Americanization of the Synagogue, 1820–1870* (Hanover, 1976), pp. 46–47.

4   The transliteration of the Hebrew name finds innumerable variations, including: Tikwah Chadoschoh, Tikwa Chadoscho, Tikwah Chadascha, Tikvoh Chodoschoh, and the one preferred in recent years, Tikvah Chadoshoh. The spelling in the text is that found in the first synagogue constitution.

5   Although German Jews preferred to be called emigrés or immigrants, they were nevertheless officially designated "refugees" in public literature. The American government and the League of Nations High Commissioner for Refugees employed the term "political refugees." See Herbert A. Strauss, "Social and Communal Acculturation of German-Jewish Immigrants of the Nazi Period in the United States," in *Ethnicity, Identity and History*, ed. Joseph B. Maier and Chaim I. Waxman (New Brunswick, 1983), p. 230.

6   Maurice Davie, *Refugees in America* (New York, 1947), p. 80; Alexander Carlebach, "The German-Jewish Immigration and Its Influence on Synagogue Life in the United States," *Leo Baeck Institute Year Book*, 9 (1964), p. 351.

7   The literature is replete – and growing – with material on the German Jewish refugees of the 1930s. During their arrival and shortly thereafter, the major concerns of sympathizers were to have them understood and to defend them. See, for example, Samuel Joseph, "Survey of Jewish Immigration to the United States," *Jewish Social Science Quarterly*, 15 (1939), pp. 299–304; Gerhart Saenger, "The Psychology of the Refugee," *Contemporary Jewish Record*, 3 (1941), pp. 332–344; Saenger, *Today's Refugees, Tomorrow's Citizens: A Story of Americanization* (New York, 1941); Willi Schlamm, "Cultural Dilemma of the Refugee," *Jewish Frontier*, 6 (1939), pp. 6–9; Davie, *Refugees in America*. Other useful sources include Werner Rosenstock, "Exodus 1933–

1939: A Survey of Jewish Immigration from Germany," *Leo Baeck Institute Year Book* 1 (1956), pp. 373–390; Albert H. Friedlander, "Cultural Contributions of the German Jew in America," in *Jews from Germany in the United States*, ed. Eric E. Hirshler (New York, 1969); Werner G. Cahnman, "Die deutschen Juden und die jüdische Gemeinschaft in Amerika: Ein Kommentar," *Emuna* 6 (1971), pp. 240–248; *Ten Years: American Federation of Jews from Central Europe, Inc. 1941–1951* (New York, 1951); *Twenty Years: American Federation of Jews of Central Europe, Inc. 1940–1960* (New York, 1961); see also the works of Herbert A. Strauss, "The Immigration and Acculturation of the German Jews in the United States of America," *Leo Baeck Institute Year Book*, 16 (1971), pp. 63–74; "Jewish Emigration from Germany: Nazi Policies and Jewish Responses," 1, *Leo Baeck Institute Year Book*, 25 (1980), pp. 313–358; part II in *Leo Baeck Institute Year Book*, 26 (1981), pp. 343–404; "Changing Images of the Immigrant in the U.S.A.," *Amerikanstudien*, 21 (1978), pp. 119–138; and the bibliographical works that he has edited, *Jewish Immigrants of the Nazi Period in the U.S.A.*, 1 (New York, 1978), and 2 (1981). Also, Kurt R. Grossman, *Die Deutsche Emigration in die U.S.A., 1933–1942* (Düsseldorf, 1972); Leo Grebler, "German-Jewish Immigrants to the United States during the Hitler Period," unpublished personal reminiscences, 1976.

On German Jewish congregations specifically, see Strauss, *Jewish Immigrants*, 1, p. xxvi; Carlebach, "German-Jewish Immigration"; Michael N. Dobkowski, "The 'Fourth Reich' – German Jewish Religious Life in America Today," *Judaism*, 27 (1978), pp. 80–95; Gertrude Hirschler, *To Love Mercy: The Story of Chevra Ahavas Chesed of Baltimore* (Baltimore, 1972); Ernest Stock, "Washington Heights' 'Fourth Reich,' " *Commentary*, 2 (1951), pp. 581–588.

8　On Leo Teitz, see his own writings, including sermons on Rosh Hashana 1942 and at New Hope's dedication weekend 18 March 1950, editorials in New Hope Bulletins, 1945–1948, a satirical play – "Aufführenganlässlich der Chanukafeier der Chewro Tikwo Chadoscho-Dezember, 1940." See also the eulogy of Teitz by Max Feder, "In Memoriam, Leo Teitz," New Hope Bulletin, September 1952. See AJA, MS, n. 13.

9　See AJA, MS, nn. 14, 15.

10　See for example, Carlebach, "German-Jewish Immigration," pp. 366ff.

11　Hirschler's *Story of Chevra Ahavas Chesed of Baltimore* depicts one situation in which a group of German Jews, on the verge of becoming a permanent congregation through the purchase of a building, changed course dramatically and transformed itself into a *chevra kadisha* on the occasion of the death of one of its members. See the "Minute Book of New Hope Congregation," 31 October 1943 (hereafter cited as MB).

12　On the Prospect Place building, see *American Israelite*, 16 March 1950; also, the *Program Book of the Dedication of New Hope Synagogue*, 19 March 1950. On the extended discussions to move New Hope to Roselawn, see MB, 24 October 1954; 24 April, 17 May, 13 December 1955; 10 May 1956; 24 March,

31 March, 9 April 1957. See also letter of the board to the congregation, December 1958. Also, correspondence file, 15 July 1956, for a copy of the letter New Hope sent to United Help, an agency supported by the American Federation of Jews from Central Europe, requesting financial assistance for the building of a new synagogue. The request was denied, MB, 19 July 1956. See, too, the letter of the board to George Auman, a former Cincinnati German Jewish immigrant then residing in New York, asking that he intercede with United Help on the congregation's behalf, correspondence file, 29 August 1956. On United Help, see Strauss, "Social and Communal Acculturation," p. 243. On the 1959 dedication ceremony, see *Every Friday*, 27 November 1959. See AJA, MS, n. 19.

13   On Rev. Manfred Rabenstein, see *American Israelite*, 27 February 1969; *Cincinnati Post and Times Star*, 1 March 1969; also, the tribute to him by Max Feder, undated, but probably written in 1961, extolling his sense of duty and his sermons, and Fred Mott's laudatory play about him put on by the sisterhood in 1969. See AJA, MS, nn. 20, 21.

14   In 1945, 80 percent of New Hope's membership, 86 of 107 members, were from Southern Germany.

15   See "Minhogim der K'hilo tikwoh Chadoscho in Cincinnati, Ohio, 1940" by Leo Teitz. Teitz was heavily influenced by the venerable *Sefer minhagim* of Fuerth, *Sefer Minhagim d'Kehillatenu Fiorda* [Fuerth], arranged and collected by the brothers Israel and Koppel, sons of Gumpel, Fuerth, 1767. Another example of the scores of collected German municipal *minhagim* is Solomon Geiger, *Sefer Divrei Kehillot Hamodia Minhagei Tefillot K.K. Frankfurt al Ha-Mein* (F.a.M., 1862); see, too, a recently published abbreviated English version, *Minhagei Frankfurt* (New York, 1982), according to the customs of K'hal Adath Jeshurun, arranged and collected by Zvi Yehoshua Leitner.

16   A few selected examples can be found in the MB, 16 July, 6 August 1939; 5 May, 27 July, 7 September 1941; 25 April, 2 May 1943. The *minhag* book of New Hope has a few references to "*minhag* Rabenstein" and "*takanos* Koplowitz" (Dr. Ernst Koplowitz) referring to such instances in which each man successfully argued for the inclusion of certain *minhagim* that Teitz had not initially inserted. See, too, AJA, MS, n. 24.

17   See, for example, Jick, *Americanization of the Synagogue*.

18   On the fierce loyalty to and scrupulous observance of communal *minhagim* that was so characteristic of – in Leo Baeck's words – the *Milieufrömmigkeit* of South German Jews, see Yeshayahu Wolfsberg, "Popular Orthodoxy," *Leo Baeck Institute Year Book*, 1 (1956), pp. 237–254, esp. pp. 248–249; Werner J. Cahnman, "The Three Regions of German Jewish History," in *American Federation of Jews from Central Europe Jubilee Volume*, ed. Herbert A. Strauss and Hans G. Riessner (New York, 1969), p. 11; Kurt Wilhelm, "The Jewish Community in the Post-Emancipation Period," *Leo Baeck Institute Year Book*, 2 (1957), p. 56; Jacob Picard, "Childhood in the Village," *Leo Baeck Institute Year Book*, 4 (1959); pp. 273–293, esp. p. 277.

19   Examples include questions as to whether or not *minhag Ashkenaz* mandates

the priestly *duchening* on Yom Kippur if it falls on a Sabbath; or, which *yotzrot* to read on a special Sabbath; or, the appropriate order of steps in the procedure of *taharat ha-met*. See extant letters of Rabbi Breuer to Rev. Rabenstein responding to such questions, October 1948, December 1951, August 1952, 16 October 1955, June 1968, and May 1963. See, too, AJA, MS, n. 27. On Joseph Breuer, see Marc and Jacob Breuer, eds., *Ateret Zvi Jubilee Volume in Honor of the Eightieth Birthday of Rabbi Dr. Joseph Breuer* (New York, 1962); Nosson Scherman, "Rabbi Joseph Breuer," *Jewish Observer*, 5 (1981), pp. 3–12; Ernst J. Bodenheimer with Nosson Scherman, "The Rav of Frankfurt, U.S.A.," in *The Torah World: A Treasury of Biographical Sketches*, ed. Nisson Wolpin (New York, 1982), pp. 223–228. On the Breuer Community, see Steven M. Lowenstein, *Frankfurt on the Hudson: The German Jewish Community of Washington Heights, 1933–1983* (Wayne State University Press, forthcoming).

20 A good discussion of the German Jewish communal structure can be found in Kurt Wilhelm, "Jewish Community in the Post-Emancipation Period," pp. 47–75. See also "Gemeinde," *Jüdisches Lexikon*, 2 (Berlin, 1927), col. 967 f., 971–972. Leo Baeck is reported to have considered *Einheitsgemeinden* as one of the three pillars of German Jewry; see Ismar Elbogen and Eleonore Sterling, *Die Geschichte der Juden in Deutschland: Eine Einführung* (Frankfurt am Main, 1966), p. 293. I am grateful to Professor Elizabeth Petuchowski for this reference and others on the issue of *Einheitsgemeinden* in letters to me of 26 April and 10 May 1983. Very illuminating on the subject also is Alexander Altmann, "The German Rabbi: 1910–1939," *Leo Baeck Institute Year Book*, 19 (1974), pp. 31–61, esp. p. 40. See, too, Joseph Walk, "The Torah va' Avodah Movement in Germany," *Leo Baeck Institute Year Book*, 6 (1961), pp. 236–239. The *Gemeinde* structure still prevailed for the most part after World War I, even though the 1876 *Austrittsgesetz* legally permitted secession from the Jewish community on the grounds of religious conscience without requiring conversion. In practice, this law led some Orthodox in some cities, not wishing to support liberal institutions within a total community framework, to withdraw from the official *Gemeinde* and to establish their own. The leader of this separatist movement was Samson Raphael Hirsch in Frankfurt am Main, but other separatist communities sprang up in Darmstadt, Koenigsberg, Wiesbaden, Cologne, and Giessen. Rabbi Seligmann Baer-Bamberger of Würzburg opposed this trend, which precipitated a major dispute with his Orthodox colleague, Samson R. Hirsch. Most Orthodox Jews remained within the original *Gemeinden*, as long as their religious needs were provided for; indeed, the threat of separation made *Gemeinde* liberals more sensitive and forthcoming to Orthodox needs.

The actual religious compromises liberal or conservative *Einheitsgemeinde* synagogues instituted in small towns to please almost everybody varied considerably. See, for instance, Werner Weinberg, "To Be a Jüdischer Lehrer," in *Israelitische Lehrerbildungsanstalt Würzburg* ed. Max Ottensoser and Alex Robey (Detroit, 1982), p. 199, in which he describes his liberal congregation. It did not shorten services, it did include *piyutim*, and the only German recited was the first part of the *Aleinu* prayer. On the other hand, the congregation was not as meticulous about having a *minyan* for services as was Weinberg. Some valuable material on small-town congregations in Germany can be gleaned from some of the taped interviews in the AJA. It is clear from these memoirs that many Southern German Jews who belonged to a Conservative-Orthodox synagogue attended only on holidays.

21 See AJA, MS, n. 49. Abraham Karp's description of the Orthodox East European, Beth Israel Congregation in Rochester, New York, which he labeled a *hevra*, aptly characterizes the German New Hope *Einheitsgemeinde*. "It was in concept a congregation but in function a mini-community. As such it was a European institution transplanted in American soil." In many though not in all ways, the *hevra* and the *Einheitsgemeinde* functioned in similar fashion. See Abraham J. Karp, "An East European Congregation on American Soil: Beth Israel, Rochester, New York, 1874–1886," in *A Bicentennial Festschrift for Jacob Rader Marcus*, ed. Bertran W. Korn (Waltham, 1976), pp. 265–302, esp. pp. 264–265, 300.

22 German sermons were delivered through the 1940s and into the 1950s, although English became increasingly used in the 1950s owing to the dissatisfaction of some of the younger members with the German language. See MB, 13 October 1949. The Minutes of the Board were kept in German until 1946, whereupon the language of record changed to English. It should also be noted that New Hope started as a relatively aged congregation. The "Family Records" of New Hope compiled by Ruth Koplowitz in 1964 indicate that approximately 25 percent of its membership during the 1940s were in their fifties or sixties, 62 percent in their thirties and forties, and only 13 percent in their teens and twenties. With such an age distribution, it is no wonder that memories of past German Jewish experiences and the desire to recall them remained strong.

23 His speech was given to me by his widow, Marion Feder, who in a taped interview elaborated about her husband Max's reasons for joining. See AJA, MS, n. 53.

24 On the New Hope Sisterhood, see the Minutes of the Sisterhood from 1941 to the present. See also AJA, MS, n. 56.

25 New Hope's "Family Records" lists among other details the members' professions in Germany and in America, thus providing a portrait of the socioeconomic class of many of the members. The bickering over petty personal matters and alleged insults was often very intense, so much so that one reads of threats or actual acts of resignations of people in positions such as congregation president, sisterhood president, cemetery warden, and *gabbai*. Of the four most important presidents in New Hope history, three – Leo Teitz, Fred Mott, and Ernst Kahn – all threatened to resign and wrote resignation letters in the course of their administrations. On one occasion, Leo Teitz was so incensed by some members' quests for *kavod*, honor, that

he wrote a blistering rebuke of such concerns in the Bulletin of September 1945 couched in terms German Jews would have understood only too well: "Did you forget, you Jews of Germany, what happened in 1933? Did you feel less honorable when each hoodlum dared to yell at you, spit on you, sometimes to beat you and more? Do you believe the *kedoshim*, who gave their lives in the gas chambers, etc. had for one minute the feeling they did not have *kovoud* because the other did not give him *kovoud*?"

26 See AJA, MS, n. 58.

27 See AJA, MS, n. 59.

28 The transition to mixed seating at the Adath Israel caused a major local and national uproar. See *Opinion in Kahila Kodesh Adath Israel Congregation Matter* (Cincinnati, 1954) and the article by Jonathan D. Sarna in this volume on synagogue seating.

29 See AJA, MS, n. 61.

30 See AJA, MS, n. 62.

31 See AJA, MS, n. 63.

32 A marvelous example of the type of communal opposition with which ethnic congregations were faced is found in the comments of the nineteenth-century Cleveland Reform Rabbi Michael Machol of Ansche Chesed cited by Gartner, *History of the Jews of Cleveland*, p. 164: "Wherein lies the justification in establishing German congregations, Hungarian congregations, Bohemian congregations, Polish congregations, and Russian congregations . . . when we all take pride in being called Americans?"

33 Regrettably, to date there is no comprehensive and good study of the Cincinnati Jewish community, which most assuredly merits one. On aspects of nineteenth-century Cincinnati Jewry, see Steven G. Mostov, "A 'Jerusalem' on the Ohio: The Social and Economic History of Cincinnati's Jewish Community, 1840–1875" (Ph.D. diss., Brandeis University, 1981); also see Barnett R. Brickner, "The Jewish Community of Cincinnati, Historical and Descriptive" (Ph.D. diss., University of Cincinnati, 1935); David Philipson, "Cincinnati," *Universal Jewish Encyclopedia*, 3 (1941), pp. 205–211; Stanley F. Chyet, "Cincinnati," *Encyclopedia Judaica*, 5 (1971), pp. 562–566. For a revealing journalistic assessment of the East European and German Jewish divisions in the city, see Polk Laffoon IV, "Cincinnati's Jewish Community," *Cincinnati*, April 1977, pp. 46–55. For informative autobiographical accounts, see Boris D. Bogen, *Born a Jew* (New York, 1930), pp. 72–83; David Philipson, *My Life as an American Jew* (Cincinnati, 1941); James G. Heller, *As Yesterday When It Is Past* (Cincinnati, 1942); and Morris S. Schulzinger, *The Tale of a Litvak* (New York, 1985).

34 Some East European Jews found their way to Cincinnati already in the 1840s and the decades preceding the 1880s. See Bogen, *Born a Jew*, p. 73. The Adath Israel Congregation of today was founded in 1847 and was known as the "Polishe Shul."

35 Bogen, *Born a Jew*, p. 72.

36 Laffoon, "Cincinnati's Jewish Community," p. 47.

37   See Heller, *Yesterday*; and Laffoon, "Cincinnati's Jewish Community," p. 48.
38   MB, 4 August, 18 August, 24 August, and 26 October 1946. On Orthodox halachic evaluations of Reform marriages, see Norman E. Frimer and Dov I. Frimer, "Reform Marriages in Contemporary Halakhic Responsa," *Tradition*, 21, no. 3 (1984), pp. 7–39.
39   Rosh Hashanah sermon of Leo Teitz, New Hope Congregation(?), September 1942.
40   See AJA, MS, n. 83.
41   See AJA, MS, n. 85.
42   See Correspondence file, Susan Freudenthal to Robert Katz, 6 January 1951; sisterhood minutes, Fall 1966.
43   On Baeck in Cincinnati, see Leonard Baker, *Days of Sorrow and Pain* (New York, 1978), pp. 248, 326–329; Wolfgang Hamburger, "Teacher in Berlin and Cincinnati," *Leo Baeck Institute Year Book*, 2 (1957), pp. 27–34; Michael A. Meyer, "A Centennial History," in *Hebrew Union College-Jewish Institute of Religion at One Hundred Years*, ed. Samuel A. Karff (Cincinnati, 1975), pp. 219–220, 239. Baeck had also been previously suggested as High Holiday preacher at New Hope, but this suggestion was not approved. See MB, 20 August 1948. The man most responsible for advocating Baeck's involvement in New Hope's activities was president Fred Mott, who, though fully Orthodox himself, was, like Baeck, a Berliner with strong ties to and remembrances of Berlin Jewry. A dignified lawyer who had served briefly as a judge in Berlin, Mott possessed an abiding appreciation for general German and German Jewish culture and hence did not rule out cooperation and association with Reformer Baeck. See the bulletins that Mott edited in the late 1940s and early 1950s. In anticipation of the 1959 dedication of the New Hope building, Mott in 1958 returned from Berlin with a piece of a brick from Berlin's Adas Jeshurun Synagogue, which he then arranged to have placed in New Hope's cornerstone.
44   Leo Teitz to New Hope president and the board, March–April(?) 1950. Also see his letter to Mott 16 January 1950, which noted his feeling that he had been deliberately omitted from the speaker's committee preparing for the dedication.
45   See my taped interview with Prof. Petuchowski, 7 March 1983. Also see the letter of Petuchowski to Rev. Rabenstein, 5 September 1961, explaining why he had walked out suddenly in the middle of Sabbath services – the noise was so loud that he could no longer hear the Torah reading. "But I did expect a higher standard of decorum in a congregation which is one of the all too few surviving heirs of the Torah im Derekh Erets school, and of that type of German Orthodoxy to which I had been accustomed in my childhood." Despite New Hope's formal dedication to quiet and dignified services, noise during the services plagued the congregation continually and the minutes contain frequent complaints and discussions of the subject. See also Petuchowski's letter to President Ernst Kahn, 15 September 1967, which

recorded his astonishment that a suggestion he had made to Kahn – that for decorum's sake the congregation institute the *spirit* of Samson R. Hirsch's *Synagogen-Ordnung fuer die Synagogue der Israelitischen Religionsegesellschaft* in Frankfurt a. M. 1847 – was going to be introduced in actual *letter*. Kahn had published the decrees in the September Bulletin of 1967 and announced their adoption, but Petuchowski felt that Hirsch's *Ordnungen* for *derech-eretz* and decorum should be emulated but not in an unchanged or unrevised form. See Jakob J. Petuchowski, *Prayerbook Reform in Europe* (New York, 1968), chap. 6, "Order and Decorum," pp. 105–128, esp. pp. 123–124 on Hirsch's rules.

46   See the acceptance speech of Ernst Kahn, 3 May 1964. Also see MB, 10 June, 5 May 1965, and 1 May 1966. The first congregational *seder* was held in the spring of 1966, the first dinner-dance in the spring of 1966, the first breakfast *minyan* in October 1967, the first *ongei shabbat* programs in the fall of 1968, and the first New Year's Eve party, 31 December 1968.

47   MB, Fall 1966; no more specific date is given.

48   One can trace the evolution of the debate between the traditionalists and the liberals in the minutes and correspondence file. See MB, 10 August 1966, 6 August 1967, and 5 May, and August 1968. See Minutes of the Executive Committee, 13 July, 19 July, 2 August, 9 September 1967; 21 May, 5 June 1968. Also see Werner Coppel to Rev. Rabenstein, 26 July 1968; and AJA, MS, n. 94.

49   On Petuchowski's historical assessment of the *piyutim*, which initially were intended to revitalize services but which, according to him, over the centuries became a yoke even to the Orthodox, let alone to German Reformers in the nineteenth century, see his *Prayerbook Reform*, pp. 27–30. Furthermore, some Orthodox members recall his poking fun at the "Sabbath belt," which could be linked to a house key so as to allow the wearer to avoid violating the prohibition against carrying it on the Sabbath while enabling him to open and close his house door. They remember as well his criticism of a *halacha* that would seem to permit carrying an umbrella on a Jewish holiday but not its use.

50   Apology of Jakob J. Petuchowski to Rev. Rabenstein, March 1973.

51   See Bernard Rabenstein's letter to the board, "An Autopsy of a Speech," March 1973. See also AJA, MS, n. 97.

52   Ernst Kahn to the New Hope membership, 10 March 1968.

53   Jakob J. Petuchowski to President Jerry Schottenfels, 2 July 1975. Prof. Petuchowski let his membership lapse the following year, although his wife Dr. Elizabeth Petuchowski maintained her own membership. He does, however, still attend synagogue services occasionally.

54   This was true even in New Hope's early years. See Leo Teitz's complaint that many members only attend services on the first day of Rosh Hashana, not bothering to request another day off from their employers as they do for their personal vacations. Bulletin, September 1947.

55   Taped interview with Prof. Petuchowski, 7 March 1983.

56   With the exception of New Hope and the *Sephardic* Beth Shalom, all Or-
     thodox synagogues in Cincinnati were founded by East European Jews.
57   The biography of Rabbi Silver by Aaron Rakeffet-Rothkoff, *The Silver Era
     in American Jewish Orthodoxy* (Jerusalem, 1981), is very useful, especially in
     the way it places Silver in the broader context of American Jewish Ortho-
     doxy. Nevertheless, it is far too uncritical and leaves very much unsaid,
     especially with regard to Rabbi Silver's relationship to Cincinnati's Orthodox
     Jewish community. On Rabbi Silver, see Samuel H. Schmidt, taped inter-
     view by Stanley F. Chyet et al., 15 April 1964, AJA tape 209; *Der Morgen
     Journal* special edition on Rabbi Silver, 14 April 1948; also the Yiddish
     pamphlet, "Siyum Hagadol and the 20th Anniversary of the Cincinnati Vaad
     Hoir," 1950. Note the variant spellings of Vaad Hoir, including Vaad Ha-
     ir, Vaad Hoier, and Vaad Ho-ir. Also see Schulzinger, *Tale of a Litvak*, p.
     265.
58   See MB, 8 October 1939; 12, 27 July, 26 October 1941; 11 October 1942;
     16 July 1943; 13 December 1955; 6 May 1956.
59   On the founding of the Vaad Hoir, see the "Constitution of the Vaad Hoier,"
     AJA, microfilm 855; Rakeffet-Rothkoff, *The Silver Era*, pp. 79–81, 90–91.
     The constituent members of the Vaad in 1940 are listed in *Every Friday*, 19
     July 1940. Silver's centralized authority in the Vaad reached almost the
     farcical. The 1931 Vaad constitution declared in one article that the "Vaad
     Hoier shall be subject to the exclusive authority of the Aggudath Horab-
     bonim, the highest Rabbinical organization of the United States and Can-
     ada." When he wrote this, Silver was not yet *Rav* of the Cincinnati Vaad,
     but he sought to ensure that the Vaad would be subject to the Agudath
     Harabbonim of which he was president. When he shortly thereafter became
     Rav of the Cincinnati Vaad, the thrust of this article made Silver's Vaad
     subject to Silver's Agudath Harabbonim. Rabbi Eliezer Silver of Cincinnati
     was accountable to Rabbi Eliezer Silver, "Chief Rabbi of the United States
     and Canada," as he liked to be called.
        Not all agreed to join the Vaad, the most prominent dissenter being Rabbi
     Betzalel Epstein of the Agudas Israel (Golf Manor) Synagogue, who had his
     own *kashrut* supervision and who viewed Rabbi Silver's enterprise as en-
     croachment. See *The Silver Era*, p. 90. Silver jealously guarded his hegemony
     and was known to have made life very difficult for some of the Orthodox
     rabbis who came to Cincinnati to officiate at other synagogues, including
     Bernard Greenfield of Ohav Shalom, Asher Reichel of the defunct Young
     Israel, Bernard Kalchman of the Yad Harutzim (North Avondale) Syn-
     agogue, and even his own associate in the Vaad, Rabbi Leib Potashnik, who
     ultimately became rabbi of the Beth Hamidrash Hagadol. Silver was espe-
     cially unsympathetic to congregations wanting English-speaking rabbis and
     he expressed similar reservations while a rabbi in Springfield, Massachusetts.
     See *The Silver Era*, pp. 74–75.
        One of Rabbi Silver's most outspoken supporters was Samuel M.
     Schmidt, editor of *Every Friday*, who later, at Silver's request, became Eu-

ropean delegate of the Agudath Harabbonim for the religious rehabilitation of Jews in Europe. See the Schmidt tape, AJA, no. 209, which describes his relationship with Rabbi Silver; see also Schmidt's letter to Pincus Schoen, AJA microfilm 855, 19 December 1948. On Schmidt and Silver, consult *The Silver Era*, pp. 189–192, 198–199, 226–227, 247; also Schmidt's autobiographical assessment in the final issue of *Every Friday*, 13 August 1965; and Schulzinger, *Tale of a Litvak*, p. 265ff.

60 A few New Hope members, particularly the presidents – Leo Teitz, Fred Mott, Eugene Hilb – all enjoyed positive relationships with him. Leo Teitz enjoyed enormously his *daf yomi* Talmud class with Rabbi Silver. See AJA, MS, n. 143.

61 The money raised was used to support Rabbi Silver and some of his multifarious causes. He was known to be extraordinarily generous, to the point of neglecting his own family needs at times. Admirers of Rabbi Silver therefore tried to protect him to some extent. Cash gifts from Cincinnati Jews were often placed in a trust; otherwise, Rabbi Silver would be likely to give the money away for worthy causes. See *The Silver Era*, p. 252.

62 MB, 30 November 1941; 11 January, 12 April 1942; 15 February 1943; 23 October 1949; 13 December 1955; December 1961.

63 New Hope Bulletin, 1 April 1950.

64 The broad theme of German–East European Jewish mutual perceptions and interactions in prior eras in Europe and in America has received renewed attention of late. See Steven E. Aschheim, *Brothers and Strangers: The East European Jew in German and German-Jewish Consciousness, 1800–1923* (Madison, 1982) and the review of it by Ismar Schorsch, *Judaism*, 33 (Winter, 1984); Jack Wertheimer, *Unwelcome Strangers: East European Jews in Imperial Germany* (New York, 1987); Selma Berrol, "Germans versus Russians: An Update," *American Jewish History*, 73 (1983), pp. 142–156, which takes to task Moses Rischin, *The Promised City* (New York, 1964), for minimizing the real tensions between the two groups in the book's chapter, "Germans versus Russians." See Rischin's acerbic yet justifiable rejoinder in the same *AJH* issue, pp. 193–198. The interchange between them continued in their respective communications to the editor in *American Jewish History*, 73 (1984), pp. 481–484. See also Zosa Szajkowski, "The Yahudi and the Immigrant: A Reappraisal," *American Jewish Historical Quarterly*, 63 (September 1973), pp. 13–44; Maxwell Whiteman, "Western Impact on East European Jews: A Philadelphia Fragment," in *Immigrants and Religion in Urban American*, ed. Randell M. Miller and Thomas D. Marzik (Philadelphia, 1977), pp. 117–137; Michael A. Meyer, "German Jewish Identity in Nineteenth Century America," unpublished MS, February 1983, p. 29; Abraham J. Karp, "The Making of Americans: German-Russian Jewish Confrontation," in *Contemporary Jewry: Studies in Honor of Moshe Davis*, ed. Geoffrey Wigoder (Jerusalem, 1984), pp. 45–64. See also Naomi W. Cohen, *Encounter with Emancipation: The German Jews in the United States, 1830–1914* (Philadelphia, 1984), pp. 302, 324–329; Schulzinger, *Tale of a Litvak*, p. 236ff.

On the general theme as it pertains specifically to the German Jewish refugees of the 1930s, see Carlebach, "German Jewish Immigration," p. 365; Grebler, "German-Jewish Immigrants to the United States," pp. 96, 108–111; Stock, "Washington Heights' 'Fourth Reich,' " p. 581; Anton Kuk, "These Are the Refugees," *Jewish Frontier*, 7 (1940), pp. 7–11; Max Gruenewald, "Forgotten German Jew," *Ten Years: American Federation of Jews from Central Europe, 1941–1951*, pp. 16–19.

With respect to local Cincinnati German–East European feelings and tensions, see one German Jewish immigrant's disgust with intra-Jewish ethnic separations, which she claims she felt while still in Europe. At any rate, German Lotte Kwiatek married an East European. See AJA, MS, n. 151.

65 AJA, MS, n. 152.

66 On East Europeans joining New Hope as members and their reasons, see AJA, MS, n. 154.

67 On Aaron Rabenstein, see AJA, MS, n. 157.

68 MB, March, May 1972; also, AJA, MS, n. 159.

69 Not all Germans were happy with their presence by any means. Previously angered by Aaron Rabenstein's *yeshiva* antics, and generally unhappy with the religious direction in which New Hope seemed to be heading, Jakob J. Petuchowski observed in his 2 July 1975 letter of resignation from the synagogue board: "Perhaps New Hope will survive a while longer as another synagogue of Polish Jewish orthodoxy. I wish it well, but it is not quite my cup of tea." It was not quite "the cup of tea" of most other German members.

70 In the mid to late 1940s, some of the younger New Hope members in their late teens or early twenties enjoyed going to the Young Israel, originally situated in the basement of Rabbi Silver's Knesset Israel. It featured a more modern service, English sermons, and communal singing and was populated by social peers of Orthodox East European origin. Eric Teitz, Ernst Frankel, and George Auman, for example, found the *ongei shabbat* programs and socializing quite appealing; Eric, in fact, became president of the strong college group known as Sinai, which was centered at the Young Israel. These younger German Jews with American army experience under their belts had become acclimated to a new synagogue service style of Americanized East European *minhag*. Leo Teitz was none too happy with his son's participation in the Young Israel, particularly on Friday nights. See AJA, MS, n. 165.

71 For an insightful theory as to the process of ethnicization in general, see Sarna, "From Immigrants to Ethnics."

72 Lloyd P. Gartner, "The Midpassage of American Jewry, 1929–1945," *The Fifth Annual Rabbi Louis Feinberg Memorial Lecture in Judaic Studies*, University of Cincinnati, Judaic Studies Program, 13 May 1982, p. 8. Although it does not make this exact point, Gartner's analysis is relevant here.

73 See Arthur A. Goren, *The American Jews* (Cambridge, 1982), pp. 66–67, 78–79. Exceptions include the *Sephardim* from Greece, Turkey, and Syria and the Persians who arrived during the twentieth century. Ibid., p. 104. On

the Sephardim, see Sklare, *America's Jews*, pp. 13–14; Joseph A. D. Sutton, *Magic Carpet: Aleppo-in-Flatbush* (New York, 1979); Abraham D. Lavender, "The Sephardic Revival in the United States: A Case of Ethnic Revival in a Minority-within-a-Minority," *The Journal of Ethnic Studies*, 3 (1975), pp. 21–31; Marc D. Angel, "The Sephardim of the United States; An Exploratory Study," *American Jewish Year Book*, 74 (1973), pp. 77–138, and his more recent *La America: The Sephardic Experience in America* (Philadelphia, 1982).

74 The old notions of monolithic and unilinear assimilation of all immigrant groups and the inevitable dissolution of all their ethnic ties popularized by Robert F. Park have long been modified and even abandoned. See Robert F. Park and Herbert A. Miller, *Old World Traits Transplanted* (New York, 1921). Ethnicity and, for the purposes of this essay, ethnic religion persist. See Nathan Glazer and Patrick Moynihan, *Beyond the Melting Pot*, 3d ed. (Cambridge, 1970); Rudolph J. Vecoli, "Ethnicity: A Neglected Dimension of American History," in *The State of American History*, ed. Herbert J. Bass (Chicago, 1970), pp. 70–89; Joshua Fishman, ed., *Language Loyalty in the United States* (The Hague, 1966); Joan H. Rollins, *Hidden Minorities: The Persistence of Ethnicity in American Life* (Washington, D.C., 1981); Herbert J. Gans, "Symbolic Ethnicity: The Future of Ethnic Groups and Culture in America," in *On the Making of Americans: Essays in Honor of David Riesman*, eds. Herbert J. Gans, Nathan Glazer, Joseph R. Gusfield, and Christopher Jencks (Philadelphia, 1979), pp. 193–220; see Chaim I. Waxman's discussion of "straight line" ethnicity and the problematics of Gans's "symbolic ethnicity" in his *America's Jews in Transition* (Philadelphia, 1983), pp. 225–236; Yisrael Ellman, "The Ethnic Awakening in the United States and Its Influence on Jews," *Ethnicity*, 4 (1977), pp. 133–155, esp. 139–149. On a negative forecast for Jews, see Harold Abramson, "The Religio-Ethnic Factor and American Experience: Another Look at the Three Generations Hypothesis," *Ethnicity*, 2 (1975), pp. 163–177. See also the sources cited in n. 2.

10

Conflict over Reforms: The Case of Congregation Beth Elohim, Charleston, South Carolina

ROBERT LIBERLES

The Reformed Society of Israelites

Established in 1749, Congregation Beth Elohim in Charleston, South Carolina, was one of America's oldest and largest congregations. Of the estimated 2,500 Jews in the United States in 1800, there were 500 Jews in Charleston and 1,000 in South Carolina. By the 1820s the Charleston Jewish community had begun to stagnate; nevertheless, during the third decade of the nineteenth century, Charleston became significant in the religious history of American Jewry.[1]

In 1824, a segment of the membership of Congregation Beth Elohim submitted a petition to the Adjunta (Board of Directors) of that institution, calling for reforms in the synagogue service. When the board refused to consider the petition, the reformed group proceeded to organize a separate society to further its cause.[2] This study is about the history of the Reformed Society and the process that led to the adoption of religious reforms within the larger congregation.

Why did the impulse toward reform in America originate in Charleston? Early writers suggested that the dictatorial nature of Beth Elohim, whose constitution was patterned after that of Congregation Bevis Marks in London, was inappropriate for the American scene in which Jews enjoyed civil and religious freedom.[3] Indeed, Charleston was more restrictive than other communities,[4] but this fact became relevant only after religious discontent had arisen. The autocracy of the congregational leadership does not explain the drive for religious change.

Some historians have imposed on the events in Charleston their own understanding of the forces behind the later growth of American Reform.[5] Hence, several writers have argued that the Charleston Reformers were heavily influenced by developments in Germany.[6] True, the

274

The setting of the Beth Elohim controversy. From the Darmstadter Photo Collection in the Jewish Museum, New York.

Charleston Reformers vaguely knew of those early efforts.[7] They may have conceived of the idea of religious change because of news from Germany, but of the content of those efforts they knew little, and their proposals for change differed greatly from the issues in Germany. Nothing in the initial petition dealt with the liturgical changes that were hotly debated in Germany, and the antirabbinism of the Charleston group preceded anything comparable in Germany by two decades.

A very different set of interpretations was put forth in 1964 by Lou H. Silberman, who offered several explanations for the emergence of a reform tendency in Charleston in the 1820s.[8] Silberman called attention to religious divisions within the Protestant community of Charleston just seven years prior to the formation of the Reformed Society. Between 1815 and 1817, members of the First Independent Church of Charleston argued over the religious views of one of its pastors, Anthony Forster, and in the end decided upon a split within the church. In 1819, Forster was succeeded by a Unitarian, Samuel Gilman, who later became an important link to the Jewish Reformers as indicated by his sympathetic account of the society's founding in the *North American Review* in 1826. Silberman suggested that the Protestant schism provided the model for Jewish Reformers.

In discussing the adamant antirabbinism that permeated the society's

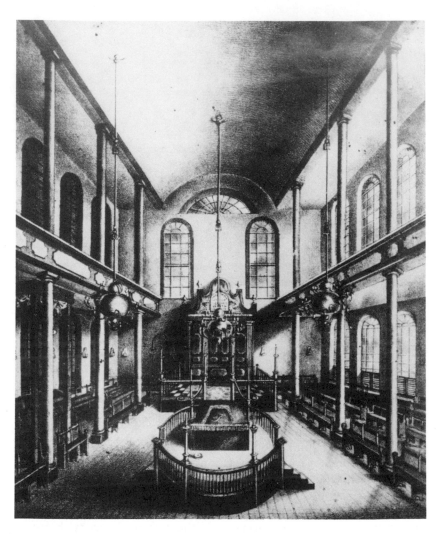

The interior of Beth Elohim in the 1820s. From the Darmstadter Photo Collection in the Jewish Museum, New York.

polemical literature, Silberman traced the background of the society's leader and spokesman, Isaac Harby, to eighteenth-century England, where there existed a group of "friends and sympathizers of the Karaite Sect." This group had, according to Jakob Petuchowski, been influenced by the antirabbinic stance that had developed within some Sephardi communities of former Marrano Jews, most notably in seventeenth-century Amsterdam.[9] Basing his claim on Petuchowski, Silberman argued that the line of influence that had started with Amsterdam Jewry, and continued through eighteenth-century London, proceeded on to nineteenth-century Charleston.

Silberman's suggestion that the earlier Christian schism served as a model for Jewish reforms and that Gilman encouraged the Jews is quite plausible. Gilman was a sympathetic observer of the events and an acquaintance of Harby's. Yet, Protestant influence, like that of the Jewish Reformers in Europe, although it perhaps explains how Charleston's Jews were able to conceive of the idea of religious reform, does not explain what prompted the Jewish Reformers to act.

The suggestion that Charleston's antirabbinism derived from Marrano antecedents is speculative. However, the problem is not just lack of evidence. What influence could this vague connection with the English upbringing of Harby's father possibly have? The founding of the Reformed Society was an event engaged in by more than forty members and, indeed, antirabbinism appeared frequently as a motif in the society's documents written by various hands. By the nineteenth century, antirabbinism was a common theme, and Silberman himself correctly suggested that its presence in Charleston could easily have been derived from the extensive and antirabbinical references in Enlightenment literature.[10]

In explaining the events in Charleston and why American Reform Judaism originated there, most writers offer some social or economic description of the members of the Reformed Society. However, the inconsistency of these descriptions is revealing. One writer has stated that "the petition was signed by men who represented the intellect of the community," whereas another has asserted that they were the "well-to-do" of the community. Still another writer offers a synthesis of some of these views, referring to the founders as "American Jewish intellectuals, cultured and wordly-wise."[11]

These interpretations seem to reflect certain suppositions concerning the participants in reform efforts, rather than the results of a systematic analysis of the society's founding membership. Such an analysis, based on occupational information, is presented below. Table 1 lists the names and occupations (when this could be determined)[12] of the forty-three men who signed the constitution of the Reformed Society of Israelites, which was adopted on February 15, 1825.

Charles Reznikoff has already correctly noted that the economic position of the members ranged from customhouse weigher to owner of a

Table 1. *The founding members of the Reformed Society*

Name	Place of birth	Place of death	Date of death	Occupation
1. Aaron Phillips	Germany	Charleston	1834	Grocer
2. Samuel Hyams	England	Louisiana	1843	Jailor, court crier
3. Isaac Harby	Charleston	New York City	1828	Newspaper editor, political leader
4. Isaac N. Cardozo				Customhouse weigher
5. David N. Carvalho				Merchant, later city judge in Philadelphia
6. David C. Levy				Merchant, bank director, member, Board of Health
7. Hayman Levy				Merchant, bank director
8. Jacob Lazarus				n.i.a.
9. Michael Lazarus		South Carolina	1862	Steamship co., political leader
10. Isaac Mordechai	Charleston	Charleston	1846	Merchant
11. Levy M. Harby				Officer in the U.S. Navy
12. Henry J. Harby	South Carolina	Charleston	1851	City blacksmith, Board of Health
13. Thomas W. Mordechai				n.i.a.
14. Emanuel Levy	Charleston	Charleston	1865	Merchant or planter
15. Jacob Hertz	Germany	Charleston	1846	Merchant
16. E.P. Cohen				n.i.a.
17. Abraham Moise	South Carolina	South Carolina	1869	Attorney, justice of the peace, city magistrate
18. Philip Philips			1834	Lawyer, legislator
19. Jacob A. Cohen				n.i.a.
20. I.C. Moses		New Haven	1834	Justice of the peace
21. T.S. Moise				Artist
22. I.S. Tobias				n.i.a.
23. Jacob Harris	Holland	Charleston	1837	Merchant

Table 1. *(cont.)*

Name	Place of birth	Place of death	Date of death	Occupation
24. Jacob Moise		Left Charleston	1837	Merchant
25. Barnard Levy			1869	n.i.a.
26. Morris Goldsmith	England	Charleston	1861	Deputy U.S. marshal
27. Henry M. Hyams	England	New Orleans (left Charleston 1828)	1852	In Louisiana: banker & lieutenant governor
28. George Lyon	England	Charleston	1844	Watchmaker
29. Solomon Levy			1839	n.i.a.
30. Lyon Levy	England	Charleston	1835	State treasurer
31. Phillip Benjamin				Shopkeeper
32. Abraham Seixas	New York	Charleston	1834	Accountant
33. Levy I. Abrahams				n.i.a.
34. Henry Goldsmith				Deputy registrar in equity
35. Jacob Moses		New York	1854	n.i.a.
36. Joseph H. Goldsmith				Clerk
37. Moses Simon				n.i.a.
38. Isaac Moise		Charleston		Merchant, soldier
39. Abraham C. Labat				n.i.a.
40. M.K. Hyams				Justice of the peace
41. Myer Jacobs		South Carolina		Bank officer
42. Isaac Soria				n.i.a.
43. Samuel Sampson				Warden of Georgetown

Note: n.i.a. = no information available.

steamship company. It is not surprising, then, that writers who looked at wealth alone had difficulty characterizing the status of the society's membership. However, religious controversy is often predicated not on different economic levels, but on conflicting social positions.

Occupational information was available on thirty-one of the forty-three members. Of these, eleven held various elected or appointed posts and at least six others were civil employees. Two of the remaining members were actively involved in politics – Michael Lazarus and Isaac Harby. Lazarus owned a steamship company; Harby was a newspaper editor who wrote regularly on national issues.[13] Almost all of the remaining members on whom information is available were either bank directors or merchants. In sum, although the others either were not involved or not sufficiently active to be noted in community histories, at least nineteen of the forty-three signers of the Reformed Society Constitution were actively involved in civil or political matters.[14] These included the state treasurer, the deputy U.S. marshal, a future lieutenant governor of Louisiana, a future city judge in Philadelphia, a member of the legislature, magistrates, justices of the peace, public commissioners, and a number of civil servants.

Before building an interpretation on our results, we must ask if this degree of political activism was at all a noteworthy phenomenon. A comparison of this kind with the general Jewish population is not possible, but we can examine for contrast the very Adjunta, or Board of Directors, of Congregation Beth Elohim that had rejected the society's petition in 1824 (see Table 2).

Information was available on fourteen out of twenty-five board members; of these five fell in the political categories used above; and of these, one, Lyon Levy, became a founding member of the Reformed Society. A comparison of the two tables yields the following results:

	Sample size	Information available	Politically involved
Reformed Society Founders	43	31 (73%)	19
Adjunta	25	14 (56%)	5

Thus, the number of politically involved in relation to the total sample yields this comparison:

	Percentage of membership	Percentage of information available
Reformed Society	44	61
Adjunta	20	36

Finally, let us recall that we have been comparing the *membership* of the Reformed Society with the *leadership* of Congregation Beth Elohim – a comparison ostensibly favorable to the latter, since it would be natural

Table 2. *The Adjunta of Congregation Beth Elohim (1820)*

Name	Place of Birth	Place of Death	Date of Death	Occupation
1. Abraham Alexander	England	Charleston	1844	n.i.a.
2. David Cardoza	New York	Charleston	1835	Lumber measurer or teacher
3. Moses Cohen				n.i.a.
4. Philip Cohen	South Carolina	Charleston	1866	Broker & merchant
5. Emanuel De La Motta	West Indies		1821	Merchant, state politics, Board of Health
6. Jacob DeLeon				n.i.a.
7. Hyam Harris				n.i.a.
8. Nathan Hart	Germany	Charleston	1840	Merchant, constable, political leader
9. S.M. Hart	South Carolina	Charleston	1880	Merchant
10. H.M. Hertz				n.i.a.
11. Solomon Hyams	Ireland	Charleston	1837	Merchant
12. Joseph Joseph	South Carolina			Shopkeeper
13. Jacob Lazarus				n.i.a.
14. Marks Lazarus	Charleston	Charleston	1835	n.i.a.
15. Lyon Levy	England	Charleston	1835	State treasurer
16. Moses C. Levy	Poland	Charleston	1839	Merchant
17. Simon Levy				n.i.a.
18. Isaac Lyons				Planter
19. Abraham Lipman				n.i.a.
20. Simon Mairs	Germany	Charleston	1833	Liquor store
21. Aaron Moise	Santa Domingo	Charleston	1852	Accountant
22. Isaiah Moses	Germany	Charleston	1857	Planter
23. Lyon Moses	Amsterdam	Charleston	1821	n.i.a.
24. Myer Moses		New York	1833	Economist, bank director & legislator
25. Samuel Simons				n.i.a.

Note: n.i.a. = no information available.

to assume that synagogue leaders would also be more active in local politics. A similar examination of the officers of the Reformed Society and its corresponding committee in 1825 shows that six of nine individuals in leadership positions were known to be politically active. Therefore, the membership of the Reformed Society of Israelites was far more involved in the political life of Charleston than even the governing body of Beth Elohim.

Apparently the contrast between the two groups is even greater. Solomon Breibart has attained the following results by comparing the age composition of both groups: "In 1825, the average age of 22 members of the Society was 32 years; the average age of 16 of the 25 members of the Beth Elohim Adjunta in 1820 was about 62."[15] It appears, that the membership of the society derived from a younger generation, which was breaking new ground for the position of Jews in American society.

Our quantified investigation has informed us that Jews active in public life in Charleston, South Carolina, in the 1820s were motivated to withdraw from the established Jewish congregation and to form a congregation of their own – a Reform synagogue. The constitution of the Reformed Society gives us some indication of the motives of the founding members.

> Deeming it a truth well established from history, that the great cause of many of the calamities with which mankind have been so often visited, resulted from a blind observance of the ceremonial law. . . . It is therefore a fundamental principle of this institution, to cultivate and promote true piety as the first great object of our Holy Religion.[16]

We can infer that these men feared further "calamities" toward the Jewish people, and also that Jews were not altogether guiltless in provoking antisemitism. Isaac Harby made the point explicitly in his discourse celebrating the first anniversary of the founding of the society: "But my respected friends, your feelings must not be entirely engrossed with the sufferings and the valour and the patience of your Jewish brethren. You must also take view of their *follies* and their *vices*, which invited the oppression of tyrants, and gave colour to the calumnies of monks."[17]

The constitutional paragraph is somewhat ambiguous as to whether these Charleston Jews felt threatened by actual occurrences of antisemitism or whether they were concerned about the possibility that history might repeat itself once again on American shores. The Jews of Charleston had reached a level of equality almost unknown in the history of the Jewish people in the diaspora. They served in elected offices and in civil service positions, sure proof of their ascent toward equality. Another thirty years elapsed before the Jews of England attained this status, and even longer in Germany. If the Jews of Charleston felt insecure, their anxiety can only be understood in the light of history.

Indeed, all three published anniversary addresses indicate that the leaders of the Reformed Society were very much aware of the uniqueness of their position. Harby made the point in his first discourse:

> Let us take a rapid glance at the history of our people since the destruction of the temple, and view the contrast the Jews of the United States now exhibit in opposition to the Jews of Europe – the contrast between a once powerful people, scattered by the Almighty's anger, and bowed in the dust, and humiliated into ignorance by the petty tyrants of the earth – and the freeborn Jew, the citizen of these enlightened States, raising once more the brow of manhood and proud equality![18]

Abraham Moise, in the discourse the following year, stated in a similar vein: "It was the imperious suggestion of conscience which led the Puritans across the Atlantic to such religious freedom in a nation of savages, and to lay one of the cornerstones to the political existence of a people, whose civil liberty has no parallel in the history of the world."[19]

However, the discourses also reveal that the threat motivating the reformers was as much contemporary as it was historical. For example, Moise stated in his address: "When our principles shall have permanently settled throughout the United States – when the modern Jew shall be regarded as a citizen of the world . . . when all distinctions in society shall be lost in one general effort to be virtually considered a part of 'God's chosen race,' then shall we indeed boast of moral triumphs."[20]

Throughout the documents there is a juxtaposition of the unique opportunities provided in America with an awareness that all was not yet well. Thus Isaac Cardozo could speak on the one hand of "the rapid spread of amelioration speedily producing such a state of things as will leave little to be desired for the cause of human right or the advancement of human virtue and intelligence", and yet begin the concluding paragraph of his discourse with the remark: "Whilst touching on the subject of the purity and freedom which should pervade all our institutions, we cannot refrain from alluding to that feeling of intolerance which still in some degree exists against the principles of Judaism."[21] The sense of insecurity clearly permeating these addresses by Charleston Reformers reflects their anxiety that even in America, Judaism was still not completely tolerated.

What was the source of this insecurity? Three pieces of evidence support the claim that this apprehension derived from the "Jew Bill" controversy raging at that very time in nearby Maryland. The Reformers did not refer directly to the controversy, but they certainly did refer to a current sense of intolerance.

First, the Jew Bill itself was concerned with the question of whether or not Jews could hold elective office in the State of Maryland. Here was a matter of political rights that Charleston Jewry had succeeded in actualizing more than any other Jewish community in America at that time. Arguments against passage of the Jew Bill included claims that Jews were a separate people unwilling to integrate with Marylanders and that, in fact, Jews themselves were not even interested in the bill or the rights involved.[22] Failure to permit Jews in Maryland to hold elective office could certainly be perceived as a threat to Jews in a nearby state who did hold elective office. In fact, this very question was being debated simultaneously even closer to Charleston – in North Carolina. That debate, however, did not arouse the same excitement as the controversy in Maryland.[23]

Second, let us consider the chronology of the controversy. The Jew Bill, which sought to remove existing disabilities, was first defeated in 1819. It passed the House of Deputies in 1822, but had to be passed by the next legislature as well. The issue was of great significance in the elections of 1823. Thomas Kennedy, the major spokesman for the bill, was defeated in those elections, and the bill was defeated by the new legislature.[24] It was finally passed in January 1826, but the Reformed Society had already been organized in 1824 – not long after the bill's second defeat in the Maryland legislature.

The third reason for drawing a causal link between the Jew Bill controversy and the establishment of the Reformed Society in Charleston is that evidence exists to demonstrate that the controversy was being watched far beyond the borders of Maryland, and certainly in Charleston. A number of newspapers issued editorials in favor of the bill, including papers from Mississippi, Virginia, Philadelphia, and New York and the Charleston *Southern Patriot*. An editorial of 1819 in the *National Intelligence*, published in Washington, predicted that the next step in Maryland would be the designation of an established church. In February 1824, the *Southern Patriot* printed two extracts from the *Baltimore American* reporting on the controversy.[25]

The references cited above from the three anniversary addresses demonstrate in part just how conscious the Charleston Reformers were of the political status attained by America's Jews. Let there be no mistake: Political references in these addresses were not merely passing comments in an otherwise religious context. These were documents by men who thought, reflected, and acted upon political questions – men such as Isaac Harby, who was a newspaper editor and political activist, and Abraham Moise, who delivered the second discourse and was a lawyer, a justice of the peace (1827–1840), and then a magistrate (1842–1859).

The Maryland Jew Bill controversy precipitated the Reform initiative in Charleston, but it is important to recognize that the controversy was not the primary cause of those events. It would be speculative to claim a greater role for the controversy; it would also be superfluous. American Reform Judaism originated in Charleston because the integration of its Jewry had reached the political plane. The Jew Bill, and especially its several setacks, reminded Charleston Jewry that its position was not yet fully secured.

The contrast between the status of the Jews in Charleston and that in Maryland can teach us something fundamental about the subsequent growth of Reform in America. Reform prospered primarily in two countries: in Germany, where emancipation was accomplished only through a long and frustrating struggle; and in America, where considerable opportunities were openly available. Despite the impression that Reform dominated the Jewish communities of Germany, it was in the atmosphere of freedom and opportunity that Reform actually found its most conducive environment. Significantly, the fact that the drive for Reform in America originated in Charleston and not in Maryland illustrates the importance of opportunity, and not restrictions and disabilities, for the growth of American Reform Judaism.

The subsequent history of the Reformed Society is not well documented. In fact, reconstructing the most basic facts poses a serious challenge. What was the scope of the society's activities? In 1826 the society initiated a building campaign to establish a second congregation in Charleston. In 1830 it issued a prayerbook for Sabbath services,[26] but the elementary question of whether the society conducted its own services has been a matter of doubt. None of the early sources refer to services sponsored by the society. Yet, later sources do state that the society conducted religious services, and Barnett Elzas has provided this summary: "Parts of the service were recited both in Hebrew and English. An English discourse formed part of the morning service. There was instrumental music and the congregation worshipped with uncovered heads. David Nunez Caravalho was the volunteer "Reader", and the Society met in Seyle's Masonic Hall on Meeting Street."[27] Apparently these services were initiated some time after 1826. In 1826 Samuel Gilman stated explicitly in the *North American Review* that the Reformers still hoped to avoid the establishment of a separate congregation.[28]

A second area of confusion concerning the brief history of the society is the date of its dissolution. In 1833, the society terminated its building campaign and returned the funds that had been contributed. Since nothing is known of later society activities, it has been assumed that the society fully disbanded in 1833. That, however, may not have been the case.

When Elzas published the list of signatures on the society's constitution, he included annotations by the society's last president, Abraham Moise, that indicated the deaths and resignations of a number of the members. Elzas wondered about the date of Moise's entries, but we can easily determine that these annotations were written later than 1833, the presumed date of the society's demise. Several of the deaths occurred in 1834, and one in 1837. Also the list of resignations include several officers of the society as of 1833. Alone, Moise's annotations are insufficient evidence, although it would be rather curious to mark "dead" next to the names of the members at least four years after the society had been dissolved.

Additional evidence can be found in Article 12 of Beth Elohim's revised constitution of 1837:

> No Israelite[s] shall combine for the purpose of erecting another Synagogue within five miles of Charleston – nor shall any member or members of this Congregation be permitted to become members of any Society, in which has been adopted, or shall be adopted, innovations in our Sacred Religion, alterations in the form of worship, as practised heretofore, or changes in the Mosaical or Rabbinical Laws.[29]

It should also be noted that the Reformers claimed in their legal plea discussed below that the Reformed Society "had been dissolved and their place of worship abandoned, before July, 1840." This certainly does not imply a date of dissolution as early as 1833.[30]

Taken together, these pieces of evidence imply that the society continued to exist even after its decision in 1833 to abandon its building campaign. By the end of the decade, its members had resumed their original objective, to influence the nature of religious worship in Congregation Beth Elohim itself. The conflict over religious reforms now became an internal dispute within the larger congregation. The Reformed Society of Israelites was important in American Jewish history because it represented the first effort to introduce synagogue reform in America. Its significance was enhanced in 1840, when Congregation Beth Elohim adopted a number of the society's proposals and became America's first Reform Synagogue.

Reforms in the Synagogue

Between 1840 and 1842 Congregation Beth Elohim adopted several proposals for religious reform, thus becoming the first Reform Congregation in America. Rabbinical leadership for the new reform initiative came from Gustav Poznanski, who had been appointed *hazan* of the congregation in 1836.[31] The first of the proposals for reform came in the spring of 1840 when, following the destruction of the old synagogue by fire in 1838, a number of members urged that an organ be installed in the new edifice then being completed for use during Sabbath services. The trustees voted against the proposal four to one, but agreed to bring the matter before a congregational meeting.

Much to the surprise of the traditional party, Gustav Poznanski, the congregation's spiritual leader, let it be known that he favored using the organ, despite the fact that he had pledged his strict observance of both "Rabbinical and Mosaical laws."[32] The organ was approved by a vote of forty-six to forty. Shortly after the new building was dedicated and the organ installed, a group of almost forty opponents withdrew from the congregation and established Congregation Shearith Israel.[33]

In November 1840, Beth Elohim adopted a number of revisions in its constitution. Among these was an expansion of the number of trustees from five to seven. One of the new positions was assumed by Abraham Moise, former president of the Reformed Society.

During the course of the next two years, the congregation attempted to solidify a position of religious change, while encouraging the traditional sector to resign its membership. The innovations involved eliminating some prayers while increasing the role of English in the services. Among the constitutional changes of November 1840 was a regulation imposing an annual fine of $100 on all members who affiliated or prayed in another synagogue in the city. The trustees also threatened the burial rights of those affiliated with the new congregation.[34]

Even after the Orthodox secession, no consensus existed within Beth Elohim on the question of religious change. In May 1842, an opponent of further change was elected to the board. In January 1843, a proposal to further increase the role of English in the service was withdrawn after much opposition was expressed.[35] When, in April 1843, Poznanski preached a sermon calling for the abolition of the Second Days of the Festivals, a majority of the trustees objected both to the proposal and to Poznanski's sermon on the subject in the synagogue. Poznanski responded by discontinuing his sermons until a consensus could be reached within the congregation. The trustees referred the matter to a congregational meeting, and the last shreds of congregational harmony rapidly disintegrated.

An alliance was subsequently formed between the orthodox seceders and a party still within the synagogue to attempt to revoke the reforms already introduced.[36] Petitions were forwarded to the president who, however, refused to convene a meeting of the trustees. Eventually meetings were held, without the presence of the president. Decisions were reached, and the seceders reinstated. By May 1843, the matter was in court, with reformers arguing that it was unconstitutional to reinstate the Orthodox seceders.

The synagogue's minute books attest to the bitter divisions within the congregation. On June 27, 1843, a general meeting was held without the president, and resolutions were passed to stop the playing of the organ on Sabbaths and festivals so that the congregation could be reunited.[37] Subsequently the president, who was outnumbered on the board, refused to allow the trustees to conduct meetings in the synagogue building. The minutes record his statement that, if they wanted to get in, "they could break in." Indeed, a case of forced entry was reported on July 1, 1843, although apparently perpetrated by the supporters of reform.[38] Later that summer, the congregation was unable to conduct services on the fast day of the Ninth of Ab because the synagogue's vice-president refused to open the building. By the end of August, a truce was reached between the two parties, with a decision that each party would conduct services on alternating weeks.[39] The conflict was subsequently brought to trial. A court decision in 1844 and an appeal in January 1846 both decided against the traditionalists, so that the Reformist control of the congregation was upheld.

What factors enabled the Reformers to attain a majority of votes in the early 1840s? Of course, intangible factors played some role. Reform had been discussed in Charleston for some sixteen years, and initial resistance must have weakened for the congregation to have reached its decision in favor of innovation. In fact, Isaac Harby had commented in 1826 that "the Jews born in Carolina are mostly of our way of thinking on the subject of worship, and act from a tender regard for the opinions and feelings of their parents in not joining the society."[40] When the question arose again in 1840, it was no longer necessary for reformers to secede from the congregation. Poznanski's stance in favor of the organ must also have helped to swing the vote, which passed by the narrow margin of forty-six to forty.

In evaluating these developments, we must also assess the role played by the Reformed Society, or at least its former members. The two legal documents submitted to the courts are contradictory on this point. The

Orthodox stated in their statement of 1843 that several members of the society "who had never been in the Synagogue for 15 years" returned to the congregation just prior to the vote on the organ, "with a settled purpose and intention to change the existing Institutions and Ceremonial of the Synagogue." Their statement also indicates that Abraham Moise, former president of the society, was readmitted to Beth Elohim in October, 1840 – just before the constitutional changes were adopted in November. Moise was then elected as a trustee when two new positions were created.[41] The Reform Party denied that former society members had returned to the congregation just prior to the organ vote, but admitted that nine or ten of them did reenter the congregation in September 1840. That was in time to vote on the constitutional changes.[42]

An examination of the minute books indicates the Reform Party's version to be mostly correct and, in fact, rather understated. Since the petition calling for the introduction of an organ included at least seven signatures of former society members, clearly some former members of the society had already rejoined the congregation. It is striking that there was an active enrollment of new members in July, the month of the organ vote, but none of the seventeen names that I recorded as joining on July 14 and 25 were society members.

The Reformers offered only a weak denial of the Orthodox charge that supporters of reform had affiliated just prior to the crucial votes. Yet, on the basis of the congregational minute books, it can be demonstrated that the opposite was true: The majority of new members who enrolled in July 1840, just prior to the organ vote, voted against the use of the organ. The four members elected on July 14 were split in their votes; but of the thirteen members elected on July 25, one day before the general meeting, seven voted against the organ, three in favor, and three were not tallied. The count, disregarding all members admitted during the month of July, would have read forty-one in favor and thirty-one against the organ. A number of new members did join subsequent to the organ vote, especially on October 4; in fact, Abraham Moise, the leader of the society, rejoined just in time to be elected a trustee.

According to this evidence, it is far more difficult to define the importance of the Reformed Society in the decisions that were reached. Moise's annotations suggest that the majority of society members had resigned, and the petition to introduce the organ indicates that some subsequently rejoined the congregation. Another sector of eight to ten members had remained outside the congregation, only to rejoin after the first significant victory had been attained. This would indicate that the Reformed Society had maintained some level of organization, perhaps only a casual one, continually until the events of 1840. Finally, Moise's immediate election indicates that he was still the acknowledged leader of the Reformers.

In sum, the decisions to introduce a program of reform into Congregation Beth Elohim were aided by the return of some society members to the congregation, the support given by the congregation's rabbi, and the esteem of the community for some supporters of reform, such as Moise. Finally, the timing of the votes in favor of reform was hastened by the destruction of the synagogue in 1838. In Charleston, as in so many communities in Germany during this period, construction of a new synagogue edifice raised fundamental questions of religious direction, and the organ petition was submitted just as construction neared completion.

The Conflict in Court

It was not unusual at mid-nineteenth century for a religious conflict in America to end up as a civil court case. The traditional Jewish reluctance to bring internal religious matters before civil authorities gave way during this period of religious controversy. Both in Europe and in America, one side or another often turned to an outside power to break a deadlock or to reverse the status quo. In England, the West London Synagogue, where the Board of Deputies long denied its rights to conduct weddings, eventually was so empowered by a special act of Parliament. In Berlin, Hamburg, Frankfurt, Breslau, and every other German community that witnessed conflict between Reform and Orthodox parties, the civil authorities were petitioned or initiated their own intervention. Indeed, religious affairs in Europe were clearly supervised by the governments, and Jewish affairs and conflicts were no exception. In Germany, for example, tensions were all the greater because, until the late nineteenth century, the right to establish congregations and to appoint rabbis was severely restricted and closely supervised.

The American context was different. American Jews were free to establish additional congregations and to appoint rabbis of their choice. In America, when Jews sought an outside authority to settle a dispute, such conflicts were not brought to the government, but to the courts, as civil suits contesting ownership of congregational property. During the same period that the Charleston case was being tried, at least two other synagogue disputes were simultaneously before the courts.[43]

In the Charleston case the congregation's president, Abraham Ottolengui, charged that the Orthodox members of Shearith Israel had been illegally readmitted to membership in Beth Elohim and that decisions reached at a subsequent congregational meeting, in which some religious innovations including the organ were revoked, were, therefore, not binding. The legal question hinged on whether the trustees, who were responsible for admitting members, could be convened without the president's approval. The court upheld the president's prerogative to convene the trustees and thereby disallowed the readmission of the Orthodox members.

In the course of deliberations in 1843, the judge refused to admit as evidence the traditionalists' claims that the religious nature of the congregation as prescribed in the constitution had been altered by the decisions for reform, and especially by the introduction of the organ. This position might be understood as an attempt by the courts to remain outside the specifically religious nature of the conflict, but, in fact, the subsequent appeal decision of 1846 stated a quite clear position on the question of religious reforms:

> It is not practicable to frame laws in such a way as to make them, by their arbitrary and controlling influence, preserve, in perpetuity, the primitive identity of social and religious institutions.
>
> The granite promontory in the deep may stand firm and unchanged amidst the waves and storms that beat upon it, but human institutions cannot withstand the agitations of free, active and progressive opinion. Whilst laws are stationary, things are progressive. Any system of laws that should be made without the principle of expansibility, that would, in some measure, accommodate them to the progression of events, would have within it the seeds of mischief and violence.[44]

In disallowing the Orthodox claims, the appeals judge did not hesitate to take sides on the religious dispute in question. Concerning the claim that the organ violated the Sephardi ritual as prescribed in the constitution, the judge argued:

> I suppose it might be admitted that in its origin, such a ritual was practiced without the aid of instrument accompaniment – but to suppose that the exact kind of music that was to be used in all future time had been fixed and agreed upon by the Jewish worshippers who obtained this charter would be to attribute to them an impracticable undertaking. That such music was not used, is certain; but that it might not, in the progress of human events, be adopted, would be an attempt to anticipate the decision of posterity on matters that must be affected by the progress of art, and the general tone of society – which could not be controlled by arbitrary limitation.[45]

Thus, the Charleston court case of 1843–1846 resulted not only in a decision in favor of the Reformers, but in a clear public testimony in support of reform by the appeal judges. Whether or not the decision was fair is ultimately irrelevant – congregationalism *was* a solution available in American society for settling religious disputes. Unlike the religious disagreements in Europe, those in America did not have to be resolved within a unified community. Nor is it important to claim that the views of the judges were themselves of considerable influence, although they seem to have curtailed any further attempts at this time to unify the congregations and to moderate reforms.[46] However, those views *do* provide an indication of how sympathetically American society could respond to the Reform cause.

To return to our point of departure, the events in Charleston from 1824 to 1846 demonstrate how conducive America was for the progress of religious reform. Developments in Germany were largely irrelevant for what started as a reaction by lay leaders to historical circumstances. The case of Charleston provides additional empirical evidence for the argument that religious reform in America was indigenous to the American scene.[47]

Of course, *American Judaism* did not become *Reform Judaism*, but we must also recognize to what extent American Jewry reached a consensus on the question of religious change. Not long after the founding of Congregation Shearith Israel in Charleston, its president reported in the pages of *The Occident* this description of the services the Orthodox party conducted on alternate weeks in the synagogue of Beth Elohim:

> The responses are made by the whole congregation audibly. The tunes to the psalms are the same as with the other congregations, and conducted by a well-instructed choir of gentlemen, the ladies chiming in good harmony with the members generally, producing a regular and pleasing effect, far different to what it was formerly . . . .
>
> In addition to the service, the Rev. Mr. Rosenfeldt reads a prayer in English for the government, and has recently commenced, what we understand he contemplates continuing with on every Sabbath, a discourse or sermon also in the English language.[48]

One group of Charleston Jews enjoying the rather unique benefits of American freedom showed the first impulse toward religious change in the 1820s. By the 1840s, even in the midst of controversy, most Jews in Charleston seemed to think that America had provided a new setting for Jews as well as for Judaism.

NOTES

I wish to express my appreciation to Dr. Abraham Peck and Mrs. Fannie Zelcer of the American Jewish Archives for their kind assistance, and to Solomon Breibart of Charleston, South Carolina, for his careful reading of the manuscript and for a number of helpful suggestions.

1 Charles Reznikoff and Uriah Z. Engleman, *The Jews of Charleston* (Philadelphia, 1950), pp. 11, 17, 66–69.

2 The fullest accounts of these events are in Barnett A. Elzas, *The Jews of South Carolina* (Philadelphia, 1905), pp. 147–165; and Reznikoff and Engelman, *Jews of Charleston*, pp. 113–148. The text of the petition is in L. C. Moise, *Biography of Isaac Harby* (n.p., 1931), pp. 52–92.

3 Elzas, *Jews of South Carolina*, pp. 147–155; Moise, *Harby*, pp. 33–34.

4 See the excerpts in Elzas, *Jews of South Carolina*, pp. 152–153.

5 The subsequent development of Reform Judaism in America was closely intertwined with the work of such leading rabbis as Isaac Mayer Wise, David Einhorn, Samuel Hirsch, and others – all immigrants from Germany. As a result, conditions that made America fertile ground for an enthusiastic response to this largely imported leadership were obscured until the appearance of Leon Jick's work on the American synagogue, in which he developed an alternative formulation that explained the growth of Reform in America in terms of increasing affluence and acculturation. This chapter shares the assumption that Reform Judaism developed and prospered in America because of historical forces characteristic of the American context. Leon A. Jick, *The Americanization of the Synagogue, 1820–1870* (Hanover, N.H., 1976).

6 Both Elzas and David Philipson made this claim: Barnett A. Elzas, ed., *The Sabbath Service and Miscellaneous Prayers Adopted by the Reformed Society of Israelites*, repr. (New York, 1916), Editor's Preface, n.p.; and David Philipson, *The Reform Movement in Judaism* (New York, 1906), p. 461. But Elzas did not assert German influence in his essay, *The Reformed Society of Israelites* of the same year, nor in his *Jews of South Carolina*. Philipson also contradicted himself. See p. 464.

7 Moise, *Harby*, p. 58.

8 Lou H. Silberman, *American Impact: Judaism in the United States in the Early Nineteenth Century* (Syracuse University, 1964). The lecture was published without pagination.

9 Jakob Petuchowski, *The Theology of Haham David Nieto*, rev. (New York, 1970), pp. xvi–xvii.

10 For the broader picture, see S. Ettinger, "Jews and Judaism as seen by the English Deists of the 18th Century" (Hebrew), *Zion*, 29 (1964), pp. 182–207; and Arthur Hertzberg, *The French Enlightenment and the Jews* (New York, 1968).

11 Elzas, *Jews of South Carolina*, p. 157; Morris U. Schappes, *A Documentary History of the Jews of the United States* (New York, 1971), p. 171; Joseph L. Blau and Salo W. Baron, eds., *The Jews of the United States, 1790–1840, A*

Documentary History, vol. 2 (New York, 1963), p. 658, n. 138; and Reznikoff, *Jews of Charleston*, pp. 124, 132.

12   The list of signatures is found in Barnett A. Elzas, *The Reformed Society of Israelites* (New York, 1916), p. 43. Political activities are noted especially in Elzas, *Jews of South Carolina* and Reznikoff, *Jews of Charleston*. Occupational information is available in these studies as well as the following files from the American Jewish Archives, Cincinnati: Charleston, S.C., Death Notices, 1786–1905/Vital Statistics; Charleston, S.C., Free Population List, 1850.

13   On Harby's writing, see Moise, *Harby*, especially pp. 1–8 and 24–31. On Lazarus's activities, see Elzas, *South Carolina*, p. 206.

14   Some of those I have identified as appointed officials may have actually been civil servants and vice versa. The listing of such specific identifications is always fraught with a number of difficulties. Several encountered in constructing these tables and in drawing conclusions were (1) conflicting information (for example, one source indicated Emanuel Levy was a dry goods merchant, whereas the 1850 census indicated "planter"); (2) the proper identification of the correct individual (since the records used derive from a different date than the events in question, there is often confusion as to whether the names on the different lists are the same individuals); (3) the political or public involvement indicated did not necessarily derive from the same date as the events we are analyzing (I have made the decision that the political interest was probably already strong at an earlier date).

15   For the list of the society's officers, see Reznikoff, *Jews of Charleston*, p. 132. My gratitude to Solomon Breibart for sharing his findings with me.

16   Moise, *Harby*, p. 61.

17   Ibid., p. 113. Emphasis in original.

18   Ibid., p. 105.

19   Ibid., p. 124.

20   Ibid., p. 126.

21   Ibid., pp. 128, 139.

22   On the Jew Bill controversy, see E. Milton Altfeld, *The Jew's Struggle for Religious and Civil Liberty in Maryland* (Baltimore, 1924); and Edward Etches, "Maryland's 'Jew Bill,' " *American Jewish Historical Quarterly*, 60 (1971), pp. 258–279. On the status of Charleston Jewry, see Reznikoff, *Jews of Charleston*, p. 124.

23   Leon Hühner, "The Struggle for Religious Liberty in North Carolina, with Special Reference to the Jews," *Publications of the American Jewish Historical Society*, 16 (1907), pp. 37–71, especially 51–54.

24   Altfeld, *Jew's Struggle*, pp. 27–34.

25   Ibid., p. 36; Etches, "Jew Bill," p. 268, n. 31. I am grateful to Solomon Breibart for information on the extracts in the *Southern Patriot*. Isaac Harby was the former owner of the *Southern Patriot*, but there is some disagreement as to whether Harby sold his interest in 1817 or 1822. In any case, the publisher in 1824 was J. N. Cardozo. Contrast William L. King, *The News-*

paper Press of Charleston, South Carolina, repr. (New York, 1970), pp. 77–78; and Jacob Nunez Cardozo, *Reminiscences of Charleston* (Charleston, 1866), p. 33.

26 Elzas, *The Sabbath Service*. The two manuscripts of the prayerbook in the American Jewish Archives are dated 1825 and 1826. The "Defendants' Return" discussed below dated the publication itself to 1825, p. 2.

27 Elzas, *Jews of South Carolina*, pp. 160–161.

28 "Harby's Discourse on the Jewish Synagogue," in *North American Review*, 23 (1826), pp. 71–72.

29 "Defendants' Return", p. 3. Malcolm Stern, based on similar reasoning, fixed the date of the society's demise as 1837. Malcolm Stern, "Reforming of Reform Judaism – Past, Present and Future," *American Jewish Historical Quarterly*, 63 (1973), p. 118. The course of events between 1838 and 1843, as well as some valuable information on the earlier period, is documented in the congregational minute books, which are extant only from 1838, and two legal sources pertaining to the court suit discussed below. The traditionalists served as defendants in the case. Their 1843 statement is in the American Jewish Archives: Charleston, S.C. – K. K. Beth Elohim, miscellaneous file. Report of a Law Suit Regarding the Mode of Services used by the Congregation (hereafter "Defendants' Return"). The ruling in favor of the Reformers is in Richardson's Law Reports, vol. 2, 245, a copy of which is in the American Jewish Archives, Charleston, S.C., K. K. Beth Elohim Documents (hereafter "Judge's Report").

30 "Judge's Report," section 248.

31 The fullest published account of these events is Allan Tarshish, "The Charleston Organ Case," *The Jewish Experience in America*, ed. Abraham J. Karp (New York, 1969), vol. 2, pp. 281–315. On Poznanski, see Solomon Breibart, "The Rev. Gustavus Poznanski, First American Reform Minister," published by Kahal Kodosh Beth Elohim (Charleston, S.C., 1979).

32 "Defendants' Return", pp. 3–4. "Judge's Report," section 252.

33 *The Occident*, 1, p. 492.

34 "Defendants' Return," p. 8. The rules governing burial were changed to require that the congregation's *hazan* perform the funeral service, a stipulation unacceptable to the seceders.

35 "Judge's Report," sections 258–259; "Defendants' Return," pp. 12, 14.

36 "Defendants' Return," pp. 20–21.

37 American Jewish Archives, Charleston, S.C. – Congregation Beth Elohim, minute books, pp. 286–289.

38 Ibid., pp. 291, 293–294.

39 Ibid., p. 302.

40 "Harby's Discourse on the Jewish Synagogue," *North American Review*, 23 (1826), p. 74.

41 "Defendants' Return," pp. 5, 8.

42 "Judge's Report," sections 248, 253–255.

43 One of these was the 1850 case described at some length by American Reform

leader Isaac Mayer Wise in his *Reminiscences*, involving the Jews of Albany, where he then served as rabbi. Wise's followers left their strife-torn congregation and, together with Wise, established a new Reform congregation. Isaac Mayer Wise, *Reminiscences*, 2d ed. (New York, 1945), especially pp. 155–175.

44 "Judge's Report," section 270.
45 Ibid., section 272.
46 Two decades later, in the aftermath of the Civil War, the two congregations were once again reunited. Reznikoff, *Jews of Charleston*, p. 163.
47 Jick, *Americanization of the Synagogue*, especially pp. 79–96.
48 *Occident*, 2, pp. 27–28.

11

A Synagogue Center Grows in Brooklyn

DEBORAH DASH MOORE

Sixty-five years after its founding, the Brooklyn Jewish Center stands in the middle of a mixed neighborhood of black Americans and Lubavitch Hasidim. Its imposing facade still dominates its section of the tree-lined boulevard of Eastern Parkway, but the building's interior suffers from neglect. The Orthodox Jews who conduct a day school for boys on the premises are scornful of American society, viewing its blandishments, such as television, as sinful temptations to follow a life-style far removed from Judaism's prescribed way. Yet even they cannot resist the impulse to display to visitors the magnificent synagogue housed within the center. Although they reject the principles of its founders, the current occupants of the Brooklyn Jewish Center marvel at its physical presence. There is irony in the course of history. Never in their wildest dreams did the center's founders imagine that the living testimonial they were building to a vibrant modern amalgam of Judaism and Americanism in the future would serve as an institution furthering the cause of Orthodox separatism in the United States. In truth, the transformation of the Brooklyn Jewish Center speaks more to the persistence of urban patterns of residential succession than to an evaluation of the center's reality.

Any assessment of the significance of the Brooklyn Jewish Center must first look at its origins and historical context, as a product of the postwar era, the response of the first generation of East European Jews born in the United States to the promise and challenge of living as a visible minority group in a relatively open society. The men and women who built the Brooklyn Jewish Center, one of the nation's first synagogue-centers, pioneered in developing an institution to promote a type of American Judaism now recognized as Conservative. With their rabbi, Israel Levinthal, whose life intertwined thoroughly with that of the cen-

297

ter, these energetic men and women institutionalized their vision of a healthy, adjusted Judaism. Fortunately for them, their legacy transcended the walls of their beloved synagogue-center to influence other Jews who live far beyond the reaches of Eastern Parkway. This chapter explores the formative years of the Brooklyn Jewish Center: the genesis of a new institution, the synagogue-center; the forms of its expression of Judaism and Americanism; and the nature of its relationship to other components of Jewish life. The chapter suggests, too, how possibilities emerged for organizational innovation in religious ritual and the sacralization of secular customs. Finally, it tells part of the story, beginning in December 1918, of an important stage in the evolution of American Judaism.

A month after the armistice was signed bringing World War I to a close, thirteen men gathered at the home of Louis Cohen on President Street in the Crown Heights section of Brooklyn to discuss the prospects of establishing a Jewish center for their new neighborhood. Samuel Rottenberg, an ardent advocate of the center idea, explained its attractions to the assembled friends. The center was to be more than a synagogue, for all of the men were members of a synagogue. They came to the meeting on December 29 because they wanted to create a Jewish organization that would answer their needs as successful businessmen, as family men, as committed Jews, and as patriotic Americans. They self-consciously chose to stake out a fresh path in the lush semiurban wilderness of Brooklyn. Confident of their future success, they decided to create a model Jewish center in Brooklyn and to limit membership to those able to afford not less than a $500 membership fee and initial minimum dues of $100 per member. Each man supported Moses Ginsberg's call for organization and pledged to bring in twenty-five members. Agreeing to meet the following week, they elected Louis Cohen as their president.[1]

The next week, with a larger group of family and friends present, discussion about the form of the proposed Jewish center grew more heated. Louis Cohen urged that they adopt the structure of the Jewish Center on Eighty-Sixth Street in Manhattan. Cohen's brother Joseph was president of that innovative synagogue-center, which had begun under the inspiration and leadership of Rabbi Mordecai Kaplan. The Jewish Center was so popular with its members, Cohen averred, that they said they would never move from the neighborhood as long as it existed. He pressed for the membership to be restricted to 100 families who would live not more than the traditional walking distance of five or six blocks from the center. Nonetheless, Cohen was willing to go along with a membership limit of 200 families because he was confident that this number of families could not be found. His ideal center was intimate, accessible, a place where children would be cared for – starting at the age of four – whenever their parents were engaged in activities, whether social or religious, during the day or at night. A Jewish center had to exude *yidishkayt* (Jewish culture) as a home away from home, but it also had to embody American upper–middle–class standards of comfort.

The issue that stirred the most debate revolved less around the complete ideal of a Jewish center – after all, it was hard to argue with Rottenberg's prescription that it "be everything that a man needs in the way of recreation, physical and mental, . . . from his infancy to his old age" – than around its financing. How was membership to be understood: Did one purchase seats as one did on the stock exchange where everyone was equal and the seat was only an idea or did one buy a seat as one bought stocks, and would one sell the seat if one moved so that the investment would not be lost? The Christian model of selling pews seemed to Nathan Friedman to be on the way out in favor of greater democracy. But Rottenberg protested that since they couldn't sit in a circle during services, there had to be front rows and back rows. He favored democracy in the rest of the building, but not in the synagogue. There some would have better seats, and these men should be willing to pay more for the honor. By the time that Cohen smoothed out the disagreement and each man announced his membership pledge, Rottenberg's point of view appeared to have gained the upper hand. Generously, he contributed the largest amount to the fledgling center. Rottenberg's $2,500 pledge outranked Cohen's $1,500 contribution and augured future patterns of leadership.[2]

The sticky issue of membership temporarily resolved, the group turned to the practical problems of building the center. Here the men were in their element, for several had made their fortunes in the real estate and construction trade. After discussing a number of lots on Eastern Parkway, they finally agreed to buy eleven lots between Brooklyn and New York avenues. By the February 10th meeting, the specific features of the proposed center were agreed upon by the men. The building would house a school and kindergarten, a gym and synagogue, as well as dining, social, and directors' rooms. In addition the men wanted to include a library with a reading room; an auditorium that could serve as theater and dance hall, a roof garden, *succah*, and bowling alley; and an apartment for the janitor. The synagogue should be designed to accommodate 800 congregants, the auditorium should seat 1,000, and the dining room should hold 800 patrons. With these specific dimensions agreed upon, the founders of the Brooklyn Jewish Center articulated their ideal in concrete. They planned to build an elegant American Jewish home where the sacred and secular would flourish cheek by jowl as symbolized in the conjunction of *succah* and bowling alley.[3] A building committee was authorized to pursue these goals while a temporary office would be established at 1323 President Street. By March, with the well-known Jewish architect Louis Allen Abramson engaged, the Brooklyn Jewish Center was launched.[4]

By the fall, it was apparent that the pioneers found it easier to reach an accord on the external structure of the center than on its inner spirit. At the October meeting after the High Holidays and a summer break, the more Orthodox leadership of the center resigned. Cohen stepped down as president, and Rottenberg took his place. Nevertheless, Cohen remained an active member of the center and many continued to describe the center's Judaism as Orthodox. But with the ascension of Rottenberg, the leadership moved to invite Israel Levinthal, the rabbi of Temple Petach Tikvah in Brownsville where many of the men were congregants, to serve as rabbi of the infant Brooklyn Jewish Center. Petach Tikvah was a modern Orthodox synagogue. Its young rabbi, the son of the distinguished Orthodox rabbi of Philadelphia, Bernard Levinthal, had recently graduated from the Jewish Theological Seminary. Israel Levinthal already demonstrated at Petach Tikvah an inclination to innovate by introducing a late Friday evening lecture and song service. The more liberal leaders of the Brooklyn Jewish Center found that his blend of American education and Jewish learning, his authentic American Jewish style of preaching, and his moral vision that embraced Jewish and American patriotism reflected their inner ideals. By choosing Levinthal as their rabbi, they specified their blueprints for the spiritual character of the center. Levinthal would devote his life to harmonizing the inner and outer form and substance of the Brooklyn Jewish Center.[5]

When Levinthal accepted a five-year contract at an annual salary of $6,000, which placed him securely in the precincts of the middle class and reflected favorably on the generosity of the leadership, the board rented temporary quarters at 851 Eastern Parkway, several blocks from the construction site. Soon work moved quickly on the physical and spiritual shape of the center. The contractors were efficient and did not work on the Sabbath or any Jewish holidays, thus upholding the religious commitments of the leadership. The latter noted with satisfaction that such adherence to Jewish law did not cost the center any extra money. Levinthal started to prepare a song manual with Rabbi Israel Goldfarb of the New York Kehillah to be used for late Friday night services. He also welcomed the decision to issue a monthly bulletin describing the activities of the center, taking note of important events in the Jewish world, and providing a mouthpiece for the rabbi's comments on topics of interest. The following month of February saw the inaugural issue of the Jewish center bulletin. It demonstrated concretely that the Brooklyn Jewish Center was a reality, a multipurpose Jewish organization that intended to serve as the locale for the growing neighborhood's Jewish life. The donation of the first Sefer Torah by Moe Ginsberg's wife in honor of her son's Bar Mitzvah in March completed the essential equipment of the center.[6]

The center's leadership defined their neighborhood of Crown Heights as bounded by Utica Avenue in the east, separating this upper-middle-class enclave from immigrant Jewish Brownsville, and Bedford Avenue in the west, the block before commercial Flatbush Avenue. The northern boundary ran along Bergen Street, which included the better part of the older Bedford neighborhood; Crown Street in the South, at the edge of the new, undeveloped section of Flatbush, marked the southern edge. The leaders expected that the Brooklyn Jewish Center would draw its membership from within these ninety-nine city blocks, not exactly the five- to six-block radius that Cohen had suggested as desirable. Crown Heights by 1920 was emerging as an affluent Jewish part of Brooklyn, attracting successful business and professional men with young families who purchased the large modern houses on the side streets south of Eastern Parkway. Many of the area's Jewish residents had moved up from older, poorer, and less desirable sections of the borough, especially from its working-class neighbor, Brownsville. They saw themselves as pioneers and developers of a new American Jewish life-style. In fact, several of them would continue to build the neighborhood, substituting modern large apartment buildings for the private homes when the cost of lots reduced the profits on the latter. They were genuine American boosters, as devoted to the growth of their section of the borough as any booster was to his small but promising town. Crown Heights was their American home, and at its heart would stand their Jewish home, the Brooklyn Jewish Center. In doubling the center's membership radius from five to ten blocks, the leadership forsook the Old World immigrant intimacy of tradition for a more grandiose vision of progressive urban solidarity.[7] The reality would represent even more of a compromise with their original plans.

The cornerstone-laying ceremony in June of 1920 expressed in ritual the values of the men who had worked over the past year to build the Brooklyn Jewish Center. It attracted a large crowd of people who comported themselves "in fine decorum and a spirit of reverence." The leaders acknowledged the appropriateness of this response for they felt that those assembled were "witnessing one of the great historic events in the annals of American history." This historic event began with a flag-raising ceremony: first an American flag used by Jewish soldiers in France during the war followed by a Jewish flag. The music followed the same pattern: first the "Star Spangled Banner" played by the Hebrew Orphan Asylum band, and then the "Hatikvah." The ritual, which would become familiar to American Jews over the course of several decades, here appeared to be fresh, innovative, triumphant. The speakers who honored the event with their oratory again blended the American and Jewish components. Judge Abram Elkus, former U.S. Ambassador to Turkey, led off with a speech on the Jewish center movement. After him came Rabbi Simon Finkelstein of Ohab Shalom in Brownsville, one of the leading Orthodox immigrant rabbis, who was a fine scholar. Finkelstein had been an early supporter of the Brooklyn Jewish Center and would continue to be honored by center leaders in the years to come. Following Finkelstein, a secular representative of Brooklyn Jewry, Judge Alex Geismar, spoke on the need to win Jews back to Judaism. He was succeeded by a minister, who extended the hand of interreligious cooperation in civic endeavors. The honor of laying the cornerstone was given to Israel Levinthal's father, Bernard, assisted by Finkelstein and Israel Levinthal. The leadership chose not to auction off the privilege as Jews traditionally had done. They saw a contradiction between raising funds and celebrating a semisacred event and were proud that the fund-raising aspects of the center could be eliminated from a ritual designed to inspire and uplift. The ceremony concluded with an address by the center's rabbi on the ideals of the synagogue and melodies sung by the famous cantor, Josef Rosenblatt. The ritual completed, the members and their guests walked to the center's temporary quarters where they feasted on a lunch lavishly prepared by their wives.[8]

It proved to be more difficult to integrate American norms into traditional Jewish observances than it had been to modify the secular ceremony of laying a cornerstone to reflect Jewish spiritual values. When the leaders met to plan for the High Holiday services of Rosh Hashanah and Yom Kippur in the autumn, they recognized that the victory of the liberal wing the previous year did not remove the necessity of compromise. Although Rottenberg favored mixed seating, enough of the leadership rejected this innovation as violating the spirit and letter of Jewish custom to lead to a temporary compromise: The congregants would be given a choice between mixed seating, in the center rows, or separate seating by sex, women in the right rows and men in the left rows. This compromise satisfied all of the members and was supported by the rabbi.[9] Although supposedly temporary, it turned out to be a permanent solution and suggestive of how such disputes over sacred space would be resolved in the future.

Although the building was incomplete, the opening of the Jewish year found the Brooklyn Jewish Center ready to host the many activities the leaders envisioned. Only a year after its founding, the Brooklyn Jewish Center had provided space for the Bedford Group of Hadassah to meet, and had offered its help to the Brooklyn Federation of Jewish Charities annual fund-raising drive. Now in the fall the center opened a Hebrew school, organized a sisterhood for the married women and youth group for teenagers, and started classes for men and women, children and adults. The decisions were taken by the membership at the monthly meetings. Although membership had grown to over 300 by January 1921, the meetings were well attended. After lessons in communal singing led by the center's musical director, Samuel Goldfarb, the members decided to inaugurate Friday evening lectures and musical services. In March a daily *minyan* was organized at the center. With all of the worship services in place, the leaders began to search for a cantor, eventually choosing Samuel Kantor of Boston over Samuel Rothstein. Each new activity the center sponsored led to the creation of a standing committee. By the time the center building was finished, the committees included building, house, membership, education, bulletin, as well as a *hevra kadisha*. The high level of participation clearly indicated the appeal that the creation of a new Jewish institution had for the founding members. They discovered a challenge worthy of their talents as well as an outlet for their enormous energies, and they were rewarded with a sense of satisfaction in addition to honor and recognition from friends and family whose esteem they valued.[10]

This enthusiasm endured for a third year, at which time the formative years of the Brooklyn Jewish Center drew to a close. By the spring of 1922, the members finished hiring the professional staff to run the center. These included the rabbi and cantor, a physical education director who later became the executive director in charge of the social and recreational programs, a manager for the dining room and a *mashgiach* to supervise the kosher kitchen, a janitor, and office staff. With the opening of the center library and dining room, the main physical features of the center were in place. The center also inaugurated its popular Monday night forum series on January 9, 1922, with a debate on immigration to the United States between Professors Henry Pratt Fairchild and Isaac Hourwich. The forum lecture series reached a large audience, offering a form of adult education that complemented the Columbia University extension courses the center had started the previous year. The series also allowed Levinthal to use sacred time during Sabbath services to address spiritual issues rather than current events. By creating a secular time for discussion of topical matters, the center leadership avoided potential conflict. In addition, the Friday night lectures and musical services provided for the presentation of talks on contemporary Jewish subjects. Thus the Sabbath sermon was reserved for a *dvar Torah*, an interpretation of the weekly portion read from the Torah and the traditional subject for sermons. Finally, in the fall of 1922 the center formalized its leadership by establishing an Associate Board of Directors, which included women. A year later the members elaborated on their hierarchy by creating a Board of Trustees.[11]

The men who conceived of and founded the Brooklyn Jewish Center shared a similar sociocultural background although they often differed over issues of religious observance. Most had grown up in the United States and achieved success in business. A 1925 survey of the center's membership, which had by then reached the 1,000 mark, showed that the largest single group, almost 25 percent, were manufacturers, followed by professionals, mostly lawyers and doctors. Together with merchants, realtors, and building contractors, these occupational categories accounted for over 50 percent of the membership. The leaders considered this membership "truly democratic," despite the absence of the working class, and thought that "with its cosmopolitan complexion" it "does indeed typify American Jewish communal life." Certainly it typified those affluent and upwardly mobile bourgeoisie, committed Jews who were attracted to the synagogue-center.[12]

Ambitious and proud of their worldly accomplishments, they were also devoted to their families and loyal to Judaism. Although not intellectuals – most had only completed grade school – they embraced upper-middle-class cultural norms. They considered themselves patrons of the arts, especially the popular New York culture that would make the city a world capital of the arts. Their enjoyment of music, opera, theater, art museums, and libraries did not involve the sacrifice of Judaism, for these could be appreciated within a Jewish milieu. They designed the center to nourish this milieu, beginning with its physical reality and extending to the many varied programs offered within its walls. As Joseph Krinsky saw it in 1925, the men who built the center intended to "create cultural values as Jews and as Americans," whose fruits "should be a harmonious blending of what we have brought to this country as descendants of the Sages and what we have acquired here in our schools and universities and in the daily practice of free and enlightened citizenship."[13] Significantly, Krinsky described himself and his peers as descendants of "the Sages" and not of poverty-stricken Jewish immigrants from Eastern Europe.

To achieve their ends, the center leadership encouraged a broad eclecticism in center programs. Topics of the Monday night forum in 1925 covered the World Court, capital punishment, the British Labour Party, bigotry, the child labor amendment, marriage, and divorce, and even included Rosika Schwimmer on "the anti-feminism of Bolshevism." The Yiddish and Hebrew lecturers, Hayim Zhitlowsky, Shmuel Niger, Meyer Berlin, Zvi Masliansky, and Hayim Tchernowitz, among others, similarly touched on a wide spectrum of Jewish subjects. Although the Columbia University extension courses that could be taken for credit offered more consistency, the exceptional popularity of Will Durant's course on philosophy indicates the type of learning and enrichment sought by the members. The class covered Spinoza, Voltaire, Spencer, and Nietzsche in the first term and Bergson, Russell, Santayana, James, and Dewey in the second. Durant must have found his teaching experience to be rewarding because he sent anniversary greetings in 1925 praising the center as a "symbol of American liberty and Jewish genius."[14] The forums, Jewish lectures, and extension classes reveal the extent to which the pursuit of culture was a form of amusement for many. These second-generation Jews were continuing the tradition established by their immigrant parents who had flocked to the lectures offered by settlement houses, the Board of Education, and the Socialist Party in the heady years before World War I. Like their parents, they, too, were creating cultural values, albeit within a middle-class Jewish institution.[15]

The shaping of the spiritual values of the center devolved largely on the shoulders of its rabbi, Israel Levinthal. In fact, it is impossible to imagine the center without him, so completely did he dominate its religious life, giving tone to its ritual and expression to its ideals. Levinthal accepted this task of interpreting Judaism for the American reality and joined his vision of the synagogue–center to that of the leaders. In an early sermon delivered in the basement of the building, before the edifice was completed, Levinthal outlined his rabbinic credo: "Priest, Prophet, and Rabbi." The sermon described the priest as the servant of the congregation, the preacher of the good life, and the pastor looking after personal needs. The rabbi is epitomized in the scholar, while the prophet speaks as the conscience of his people. Levinthal embraced the three roles and rarely spoke of their contradictions.[16]

Although the son of a prominent rabbi and the descendant of rabbis on his mother's side, Levinthal came to the rabbinate only after some difficulty. Born in Vilna, he came to the United States with his parents at the age of three. In Philadelphia, he was influenced by the rabbinic scholars Marcus Jastrow and Solomon Cohen, who inspired him to enter the rabbinate. His parents were not enthusiastic about his pursuing such a career because, among other things, it paid poorly. Nonetheless, Levinthal attended the recently reorganized Jewish Theological Seminary

*What A Member of the Brooklyn
Jewish Center Enjoys:*

The membership fees in the Brooklyn Jewish Center are: $50. per year for
a family; $37.50 a year for single men; $25 a year for single women.

The privileges, besides the use of the beautiful building, are:—

The Forum—
Approximately 60 lectures by notable speakers per year, of which about
fifty are free to members. For the others a slight charge is made.

The Gymnasium—
Entirely free to all members. The activities comprise swimming, basketball,
handball, volley ball, calesthenics, reducing courses for both men and women, health courses, both through physical instruction and lectures, therapeutic treatments, roof garden.

Social Activities:
Clubs within the Center and their various entertainments, including dances
and dinners.

Dramatic Club:
All who wish to join are given dramatic training by a noted actor or director,
and three or four productions are made every year. Instructors during the
past few years have been Moss Hart, now the famous Broadway playwright,
and Benjamin Zemach, noted member of the former Habimah.

The Institute for Jewish Studies For Adults:
Courses: Elementary Hebrew; Intermediate Hebrew; Conversational Hebrew;
Jewish History; Jewish Religion; History of Jewish Literature; The Bible as
Literature; History of Zionism; Contemporary Jewish Life. Classes weekly.
No charge.

The "Brooklyn Jewish Center Review"
Monthly twenty-four page magazine of Jewish interest. Free to all members.

The "Brooklyn Jewish Center Bulletin"
Weekly schedule of activities. Mailed free to members.

The Academy, Hebrew School, Three-Day-a-Week School for Girls and
Kindergartens:
Reduction in fees to all members. Sunday School free to members only.

Bar Mitzvahs and Marriage ceremonies:
Performed by the Rabbi and Cantor of the Center. Reduced rates to members.

THE BROOKLYN JEWISH CENTER, 667 Eastern Parkway, Brooklyn, N.Y.   - DECATUR 2-8200

Membership benefits. Reprinted with permission from the *Brooklyn
Jewish Center Review*, November 1933.

(JTS) as well as enrolling at Columbia. He did well in school although
as a student he married May Bogdanoff, his childhood sweetheart, and
their first daughter was born before he graduated. The year he graduated
he found a position with Congregation B'nai Sholem in south Brooklyn
in 1910. For five years he combined rabbinical duties with law school
studies. Upon passing his bar exam, Levinthal practiced briefly, but gave
it up after eight months despite the better pay. The call to come to Temple
Petach Tikvah, the only English-speaking congregation in Brownsville,
drew him firmly back into the rabbinate.[17]

Levinthal's flirtation with a legal career typified the ambivalence toward the rabbinate characteristic of others of his generation. In addition
to some Reform rabbis who left the pulpit for law, even such a figure
as Mordecai Kaplan toyed with the idea of becoming an insurance sales-
man. The difficulties and dilemmas these men had faced as they strove
to define a meaningful rabbinical role for themselves and their congregants in time receded, overshadowed by their subsequent success. The
model they pioneered in conjunction with the creation of the synagogue-

THE CENTER ACADEMY

of the

BROOKLYN JEWISH CENTER

A PROGRESSIVE SCHOOL FOR THE AMERICAN JEWISH CHILD

Chartered by the University of the State of New York

Sophia Soskin, Principal   Rabbi Israel H. Levinthal, Educational Consultant

Samuel Lemberg, President of Board of Trustees

Daily: 8:45 A.M. to 3:10 P.M.

> The Center Academy is designed to promote the continuous growth and enrichment of the individual child through helping him to orient himself in the basic relationships of living.

Radio Operators at Work

> The child works within the democratic process and is helped to understand and promote it.

Tug-of-War

Reprinted with permission from the *Brooklyn Jewish Center Review*, May 1942.

center became the norm for future generations of rabbis. Yet in the years around World War I it was not clear to anyone, least of all the rabbis, just how it would all turn out. Kaplan left the Jewish Center in a bitter dispute with its membership only a few years after he had helped to

Notable guests at a center dinner: *left to right*, Heinz Liepmann, Albert
Einstein, and Rabbi Israel H. Levinthal. Reprinted with permission from
the *Brooklyn Jewish Center Review*, January 1935.

found the synagogue-center. Judah Magnes, a Reform rabbi who also
struggled with the quandaries surrounding an uncharted rabbinical position, resigned from his third pulpit in seven years for the leadership of
the New York Kehillah. At the time that Levinthal accepted the offer of
twenty-five former congregants to come to the newly organized Brooklyn Jewish Center to serve as its rabbi after five years at Temple Petach
Tikvah, the Kehillah had collapsed and Magnes was on the verge of
abandoning both the rabbinate and the United States. Kaplan subsequently worked out a modus vivendi with the membership of the Society
for the Advancement of Judaism: He accepted no salary in order to
preserve his independent voice and insisted on the title of "leader," not
rabbi. Magnes ultimately found a secular pulpit from which to preach,
the presidency of the Hebrew University in Jerusalem. But Levinthal
managed to pursue his rabbinical ideal from within the Brooklyn Jewish
Center. Although his way was marked by compromise, it did present a
viable alternative in a situation of extremes.[18]

The key to Levinthal's success lay in his personality. He was beloved
by the membership as a warm man of integrity. If he lacked the intellectual brilliance of a Kaplan or the oratorical magnetism of a Magnes,

he compensated by a steady commitment to study and a spontaneous preaching style. While the center was under construction Levinthal applied himself to graduate study, writing a thesis for JTS on the Jewish law of agency. Thus when he began active duties as rabbi for the center, he possessed not only a law degree from New York University but a doctorate from the seminary certifying him as a scholar, not just as a professional. Levinthal devoted thought and care in the preparation of his sermons, which he delivered in an extemporaneous style. He recognized "the element of personality that must be considered, the way the message is presented, the mood of the congregation as well as the mood of the preacher, the delivery, the expression with which the words are clothed."[19] He became a successful preacher, drawing large crowds to his Friday evening sermons. Over the course of his rabbinic career he published four volumes of sermons. Indeed, by the 1930s Levinthal had attracted national attention for his sermons as models of effective preaching. He had been influenced at JTS by Joseph Mayer Ascher, an advocate of a new style of preaching. Ironically, Ascher had returned to the tradition magid's use of material, adapting it for Jews who were unfamiliar with the sources. In 1937 the Seminary recognized Levinthal's accomplishment and invited him to occupy its chair of homiletics while Mordecai Kaplan was on leave teaching at the Hebrew University.[20]

Levinthal developed a theory of preaching that served as the linchpin in his interpretation of the modern rabbi's role. The modern rabbi, he argued, needed to continue to learn Torah because this traditional activity was still expected of him. However, in addition to being learned in scripture, the rabbi was expected, through his sermon, to explain to the masses "what Judaism has to say upon all these manifold vital concerns that affect the life of humanity today."[21] The rabbi's individual opinion counted less than his ability to bring "the impress of Torah" to his discussion of contemporary issues. Levinthal understood "the impress of Torah" as the use of midrashic material. The advantage of using midrash to "clothe your views" was twofold: It gave the rabbi's ideas the stamp of Jewish authority and it enriched the tradition of Torah by contributing to its interpretation. Although when stated this baldly the theory behind the effective sermon sounds manipulative, in truth Levinthal represented a posture of humility. He did not encourage the rabbi to be the bold individualist. He saw the rabbi as one called to his vocation and rejected the notion of the rabbinate as a profession; at the same time, he frowned upon the rabbi as prophetic iconoclast. His understanding of rabbinic leadership pictured the rabbi as a gentle guide, filled with compassion for the human situation as well as sympathy for the conflicting demands made on the individual in the modern era. And he never relinquished the notion that the rabbi should participate in practical Jewish affairs, albeit not at the expense of scholarship.[22]

Levinthal lived up to the demands of the new rabbinic role he had formulated. His sermons reflected his perceptions of the critical problems facing contemporary American Jews and interpreted the solutions in terms of Torah. A typical example was his Rosh Hashanah sermon delivered in September 1933. "A New Deal for Judaism" drew obvious inspiration from Franklin D. Roosevelt's first 100 days and his program of coping with the economic disaster that had engulfed the United States. In the sermon Levinthal called for an "NRA" in American Jewish life because the old deal Jews had given themselves had failed miserably. Levinthal's metaphors, however, stood not just for a National Recovery Administration; each initial represented a synthesis of Jewish moral and political values. The "N" should remind Jews of the nationality of Israel, the sense of responsibility of each Jew for the other, and the cause of Palestine as the symbol of Jewish nationality as well as the sole hope of German Jewry under Hitler. The "R" represented, of course, the religion of Israel and the need to revive Judaism. Finally, the "A" symbolized action, the importance of acting as Jews.[23]

The themes of the New Deal sermon reiterated the major axes of Levinthal's concerns and those of the center membership: American life, the condition of Judaism in America, Zionism as the highest form of Jewish political idealism, and a pragmatic inclination toward social action in the causes of the day as a Jew. His first collection of sermons published in 1928 after almost a decade of preaching at the Brooklyn Jewish Center emphasized the importance of awakening American Jews "to the need of planning and working, of studying and moulding the future of Jewish life in this land and also in that land of Jewish promise – Palestine."[24] Levinthal imagined at the first services held at the magnificent completed synagogue of the Brooklyn Jewish Center that his congregants could produce a generation of Isaacs – of committed Jews born in the United States to American parents. Optimistically, he faced the challenge of the third generation, encouraging his second-generation supporters to "produce another Golden Era for Judaism, just as Spain did in the past."[25] Levinthal here echoed the more profound optimism of such Jewish thinkers as Kaplan and Israel Friedlaender. The path toward American Jewish spiritual greatness lay in religion and education, in building modern Jewish institutions like the Brooklyn Jewish Center – a model for the nation, according to Levinthal – and in renewing ancient Jewish foundations like the home.

Levinthal explicitly identified the Brooklyn Jewish Center as one of the causes of his optimism. The center pointed to the creative potential of American Jews, to the viability of beautifying Judaism in America and making it attractive to young Jews, to the reconciliation of old and new, and to a policy of action. "Our Center," he preached, "aims to teach the Jews of our community, and through them the Jews of all this land, . . . that the Torah is to function here in America as well as in the lands of the old world, . . . that Religion is to be beautified and can be beautified; . . . that we must be doing something concrete and definite to bring back the old strength to our historic Faith."[26] And within the center the synagogue dominated. This was apparent in the architecture, where a spirit of sanctity pervaded even the lobby and social rooms, reflecting Levinthal's ideology. Even as he admitted to sugar-coating heaven with earthly pleasures, Levinthal took pride in his "Seven Day Synagogue" and the number of people who entered its doors. He glorified it as "an heroic" attempt "to save American Jewry from spiritual stagnation."[27] If the synagogue dominated the center, the rabbi reigned over the synagogue.

During the formative years of the center, most of its leaders identified their Judaism as Orthodox, although they were willing to adopt such departures from tradition as mixed seating. Because of his active involvement with the United Synagogue and the emerging Conservative organizations, Levinthal undoubtedly saw the center as charting a new path. Nonetheless, he rarely justified innovations in ideological language and always expressed a willingness to compromise with the center's more traditionalist wing. He supported the compromise on seating and even used it as a model for resolving conflict over the adoption of a new prayerbook in 1947. In a lengthy letter to the Board of Trustees, Levinthal urged that both old and new prayerbooks be available, that he refer to double pages during the service, that the cantor follow the old prayerbook for the *musaf* and refer to the temple sacrifices in the future tense and keep the fire offerings. Levinthal thought the other changes made the new Rabbinical Association prayerbook more accurate, and he favored following it, especially in the English. This compromise did not have to be binding – since all of the board favored adopting the new siddur – but it would keep the peace and avoid having the opposition drag the center to a *Din Torah*.[28] The concern over the dispute entering a rabbinical court indicates the continuing strength of the Orthodox minority and the respect accorded Orthodox institutions. Given his inclination to avoid controversy, Levinthal chose to innovate selectively. Usually this meant introducing new elements into the synagogue service, rather than modifying traditional customs.

Levinthal brought his first major innovation to the Brooklyn Jewish

Center from Temple Petach Tikvah. There he had started to develop a
late Friday evening service structured around a lecture with accompanying songs. As a young man in his twenties, he began to attract crowds
to the synagogue to hear his English lectures. In 1916 he compiled a
book for the Sabbath Eve Service that reflected his experiences at Petach
Tikvah. Four years later with Israel Goldfarb, rabbi of Congregation
Beth Israel Anshe Emeth in Brooklyn and an instructor in *hazanut* at the
seminary, Levinthal prepared and published a small volume entitled *Songs
and Praise for the Sabbath Eve* that was longer and more traditional than
the *Sabbath Eve Service*. Both books attempted to respond to the growing
popularity of late Friday evening lectures while not offending those rabbis
who found postponing the regular Sabbath eve services until after dinner
to be repugnant. Nonetheless, when the volumes were published, they
were boycotted by the Orthodox. Levinthal was caught in a dilemma.
He did not want to change the time of Jewish prayer services, yet he
also did not like the idea of Jews gathering on Friday night to hear a
mere lecture "without giving them at the same time some of the spiritual
benefits derived from public devotion and congregational singing." He
feared that the lectures "robbed of the Sabbath sentiment and the religious
influence, are bound to become secularized, and to fail in their purpose."
Not wanting to supplant the traditional Friday evening service held before
the meal at sundown, Levinthal justified his efforts to supplement this
service by speaking of the transfer of the "singing of the 'Zimiroth' from
the supper table to the Synagogue or Public Forum."[29]

In fact, the late Friday night lecture and musical service, as it was called
for years at the Brooklyn Jewish Center, did represent the shift to a
public place of the previously private, familial celebration of the Sabbath.
The *oneg shabbat* that had traditionally occurred in the home now acquired
a new locale and form. Within the synagogue it became a time for
socializing and discussing the issues of the day, spurred on by the rabbi's
lecture. The intellectual and social aspects were embedded in an abbreviated worship service that began, as a Sabbath service often did, with
the *Ma Tovu*. This was followed by another psalm, and then the *Shema
Yisrael*. However both the *Shema* and the song, *Shalom Aleichem*, which
came next, were printed with music and transliterated Hebrew to allow
even the Jewishly ignorant to participate. The remainder of the service
included traditional Sabbath songs, in Hebrew, with music and transliteration, which were parceled out, two per week, for the four weeks of
the month. The manual also offered responsive reading of psalms in
English, again divided according to the week, and one English song on
a Jewish theme. Special holidays were recognized with distinctive songs
and psalms. After the lecture the service concluded with the *Aleynu*, a

mourner's kaddish, closing hymn, and benediction. At the very end came two patriotic American songs, the national anthem and "America," and the Hatikvah, the Zionist hymn.[30]

This relatively simple service, lacking the central features of a traditional Jewish worship service but including its introductory and concluding sections, consistently drew enormous crowds to the Brooklyn Jewish Center. During its heyday in the 1920s and 1930s, the Friday night lectures and musical services often attracted close to 1,000 people. Its season began after the High Holidays and ended usually before Passover. The creation of an aesthetically appealing and intellectually stimulating ritual spoke to the center's American Jewish constituency. Its novelty disturbed the traditionalists less because it did not involve the radical revision of an existing service. At the Friday night lectures and musical services the marginal Jew and the committed Jew rubbed shoulders. As a semisacred ritual, it allowed for a measure of innovation that would not normally be tolerated within the synagogue.

Levinthal did not carry the burden of lecturing alone, on top of his standard Sabbath sermon. The center often invited well-known figures in the Jewish world to speak. In 1925 this included the writer Maurice Samuel, the Zionist leader Shmarya Levin, the scholar and future chancellor of the Jewish Theological Seminary Louis Finkelstein, the judge Alex Geismar, and rabbis Max Drob, David Yellin, and Israel Goldfarb. The flexibility of the lectures and musical services appears not only in the eclectic list of speakers but in the willingness of the center to invite women and Yiddish lecturers to its innovative platform. In 1926–1927 Anita Mueller-Cohen and Leon Reich, speaking in Yiddish on Polish Jews, addressed center members. By the 1928–1929 season, the center had inaugurated a special service devoted to women. The Friday night lectures and musical services provided women with their first opportunities to participate as equals in the synagogue. Although their involvement never became extensive, it represented an important token of the changing role of women within Judaism and complemented the inclusion of several women on the center's governing board.[31]

The second major innovation proposed by Levinthal and supported by the center directly involved women. In 1936 the Brooklyn Jewish Center inaugurated a consecration service for girls. Although Levinthal, like Kaplan, fathered daughters and not sons, he was not the radical innovator Kaplan was and did not introduce a Bat Mitzvah ceremony for girls parallel to the Bar Mitzvah ritual for boys. However, Levinthal was concerned with the education of Jewish girls and with strengthening their loyalty to Judaism. Thus he embraced the opportunity to institute a ritual to initiate girls into Jewish religious life when it arose. The moment came in the mid-1930s when Levinthal could rely on the opinion of the British Chief Rabbi Joseph Hertz sanctioning a consecration service for girls that had become popular in England and had been adopted by the Orthodox Spanish-Portuguese synagogue in Philadelphia. Levinthal was careful to distinguish the new service from the Reform practice of confirmation. He emphasized that the girls needed to be properly trained in the "religious tenets" and "cultural achievements" of their people. They should be inspired to contribute to "the glory of Israel," albeit largely by their manner of living.[32] The center accordingly set high standards for participation in its consecration service, hoping thereby to move parents to lead their daughters "to the fountains of Jewish learning."[33]

The program of the consecration service, first held on *Shavuot*, 1936, focused on Jewish women in history. The girls' teachers, which included Israel's daughter Helen Levinthal, recognized the importance of providing role models for their students.[34] The eight talks on Jewish women in history clearly overshadowed the three other recitations that, together with two blessings for the Torah, comprised the consecration service. In subsequent years the emphasis remained on the significance of Jewish women within Judaism. This perspective challenged the regnant values of the membership, which supported a five-day-a-week Hebrew school for boys and a three-day-a-week Hebrew school for girls. The consecration service also brought girls into the synagogue as participants rather than as observers, albeit in a ritual that was conducted almost exclusively in English. Finally, the service borrowed some of its trappings from American Christian ceremonies – the girls all wore white and carried flowers – and suggested a mixture of public school graduation and communion. Although it never became as popular as the Friday night lectures and musical services, the consecration service did identify the Jewishly committed elite of the center and rewarded them through recognition. Often the center recruited its teachers from among its consecration graduates.[35]

The consecration service spoke to the inadequacy of the Jewish education offered to the children of center members. Although the center leadership expressed their institutional philosophy by placing Jewish education as the second of a series of concentric circles with the synagogue at the core – followed by youth activities, general education, social affairs, and physical education – the reality struggled to match the ideal. When the center began, classes for children were started and a Hebrew school meeting five days a week quickly became an established fact. Both Levinthal and the leadership disliked the meager fare served up in congregational Sunday schools and so avoided establishing one. However, the

standard supplementary Hebrew school program proved unsatisfactory
to two different constituencies: one that wanted a less rigorous program
and one that wanted a more intensive one. In 1927 the Board of Trustees
agreed to the demands of both groups and authorized the establishment
of a Sunday school and of the Center Academy.[36]

The decision to establish a modern Hebrew day school under congregational auspices in 1927 represented a bold step, one in congruence with
the founding spirit of the Brooklyn Jewish Center itself. The vast majority of American Jews, including New Yorkers, had flocked to the
public schools in the 1920s. Few except for the committed Orthodox
worried excessively about the inadequacies of supplementary Jewish education. Even those educators concerned with fostering a Jewishly
knowledgeable American Jewry supported public education as necessary
for the preservation of a vital American democracy. The scant number
of Jewish day schools and their small enrollments were evidence of these
priorities. In the ten years preceding the establishment of the Center
Academy, only eleven day schools had opened in New York City, making a total of seventeen such schools in the United States, whose enrollment was approximately 4,300 pupils. The day schools, located in
densely populated sections of Brooklyn, were sponsored by voluntary
societies, not by synagogues.[37] In 1924 at a conference on Jewish education, Levinthal pointed to the Hebrew Institute of Boro Park as a model
because it was the first to introduce the *ivrith b'ivrith* method of teaching
Hebrew. Levinthal championed their spoken language method for Hebrew instruction and favored the Hebrew Institute's integration of secular
and religious teaching in contrast to the rigid separation characteristic of
parochial schools or *yeshivot*.[38]

Ultimately, however, the character of the Center Academy, like that
of the Brooklyn Jewish Center itself, reflected the values of the lay men
and women who established the school. Although they shared some
ideals with Levinthal and looked to him for guidance in shaping the
Hebraic part of the curriculum, they also embraced the ideas of progressive education and a vision of American society that included Jews
as integral members. They designed the school's structure and curriculum
to implement this vision, to nurture the new American Jew, the Isaac
who would be the first fruit of the American Judaism embodied in the
center. Such a Jew would be "steeped in Jewish culture yet thoroughly
at home in his American milieu, disciplined yet free, adjusted to the
machine age but saved from its serfdom by a critical eye and a sentient
heart."[39]

In 1932 Fannie Neumann, an organizer of the Center Academy and
head of its Hebrew department, explained the school's genesis to profes-

sional Jewish educators. "To begin with, we were ourselves American born or bred, with a genuine and organic relation to American life," she wrote. "It was, therefore, unthinkable to us that the Jewish education of our children should be treated as something apart from their general American and secular training." Not only were these second-generation Jews secure in their American and Jewish identity, they were also disdainful of the dualism that plagued American Jewish life, typified in "the partition of the child's personality between the public school and the Jewish school, between the home and the street." Knowing all too well "the inner conflicts, the maladjustments, the emotional strains, to which we ourselves were subjected in our childhood," the parent founders of the Center Academy resolved to spare their children this anguish. Their goal was an "integrated personality."[40]

But if the supplementary Hebrew school and the yeshiva were clearly inadequate to bridge the dualism of American Jewish life, the goal of synthesis sought by the founders of the Center Academy was even more complicated.

> We were not only seeking a synthesis of the Jewish and American elements in the education of our children; we were also intensely interested in the newer trends in education theory and practice. The public schools, quite apart from their disintegrating effect on the Jewish personality, seemed to us inadequate on general humanistic grounds. Their overcrowded classrooms, with their formalism and regimentation, their iron-clad curricula, their disproportionate emphasis on the acquisition of facts rather than on the development of native powers – these shortcomings of the public schools were only too patent.

This critique of the public schools in the 1920s during what many historians of education consider the best years of the New York City school system suggests the extent to which the upper-middle-class standing of the Center Academy founders refracted their view of public education. Certainly the schools in Crown Heights and Flatbush did not fit the description offered, although the memory of the public education of their childhood undoubtedly corresponded more closely to the depiction. As upper-middle-class parents, they wanted a private "academy" education for their children similar to that given the sons and daughters of other upper-middle-class Americans. But as devotees of progressive education, they wanted their academy to be run according to the latest educational theories. And as Jews, they wanted to avoid any conflict with a latent Christian environment. Their ideal: "the best available type of general secular instruction; a well balanced Jewish training calculated to impart

Jewish knowledge, Jewish loyalty, and a sense of 'belonging' to a definite historic entity; and finally, a close coordination between the secular and the Jewish work, so that the child's school life might be animated by a single spirit.[41]

The single spirit dominating the school was Hebraic and Zionist, rather than Judaic. The parents all agreed that there was no substitute for Hebrew language instruction as a link with the new Palestine and its pioneering spirit. The drama of agricultural growth, the cultural revival, and national renewal characteristic of Jewish life in Palestine they thought would appeal to an American Jewish child. There was less unanimity regarding the Judaic aspects of the curricula. To avoid too much dissension, the parents split the issue of religion into theological and ceremonial components. They discarded the theological but taught the ritual. Thus the *siddur*, introduced in the fourth grade, was taught as a part of Jewish life, albeit without its central religious ideas. Students were encouraged to understand the ethical significance of prayer, its historical background and the role of the synagogue in promoting the survival of the Jewish people. The holidays received greater attention, especially the customs associated with them. Students learned to conduct a *seder*, built and decorated a *succah*, composed short Purim plays, and eventually mastered the Sabbath service. The founders thought that this compromise should satisfy both the Orthodox and the nonreligious parents. The former could provide religious doctrine in the home and the latter could look forward to adolescence to free their children from religious belief.[42]

The school's strength appeared most vividly in its integrated curricula. Although the original plan of having two teachers in each classroom, one for the Jewish and the other for the secular instruction, was abandoned owing to its expense, the curricula did structure the secular and Jewish learning components into parallel units. Judith Eisenstein, the music teacher at the academy, taught her students Zionist folksongs together with the folksongs of other lands. Because of her knowledge of Hebrew, she also helped the children compose their own songs and led them in festival ceremonies. Marcus Rothkowitz (later Marc Rothko), the art teacher, mounted an equally innovative art program. He encouraged self-expression through art and stimulated the children to paint such diverse Jewish and American subjects as the harbor at Tel Aviv, a Talmud student, and the trees in Prospect Park, or to sculpt both a French dancer and Haman. The art program's success received recognition through an exhibition of students works at the Brooklyn Museum and in galleries on both the West and East Coast. These two models of cultural learning not only integrated Jewish and American components but reflected progressive theories of activity oriented education.[43]

The social science units of study similarly melded Jewish or Zionist themes with American ones. In the first grade Hebrew and secular teachers taught about the family and the neighborhood. In the second grade the theme was transportation, in New York and Palestine. The third grade studied the early settlers and pioneer life, the English in New York and Abraham in Palestine. Bible study as a separate unit appeared in the fourth grade, but there was no study of Talmud or Rashi. By the sixth grade the similarities and contrasts of Jewish and American life received explicit attention. Then students studied early American history up through the Civil War while also examining the period of the monarchy in ancient Israel and the separation into two kingdoms, north and south. The focus returned to contemporary issues by the final, eighth grade. During the early 1940s the theme of "problems of democracy" sent students to search the Bible for its contribution to democratic ideals and to analyze the speeches of Franklin D. Roosevelt. While traditionalist Jews would surely blanche at placing FDR on an equal plane with Biblical heroes, and Zionists would disapprove of endowing American culture with such centrality and sanctity for Jews, the synthesis typified the approach of the Center Academy. The Hebrew studies were distributed throughout the school day, a regular one which began at 8:45 a.m. and ended at 3:15 p.m. In fact, the only subject the school director, Alice Brennan, admitted to failing to integrate was arithmetic.[44]

Although the school suffered chronic financial difficulties – the depression years were not auspicious times to launch an expensive private school – the parents and teachers associated with it considered their experiment a success. Despite its stiff tuition fees, the student body grew until it reached 130 students in the 1940s. The children who graduated acquired, the school's supporters thought, "an inner security which permits them to express themselves freely." Through knowledge of their background and an "appreciation of the beauty and glory that has come down to them through the centuries," the students were prepared to face a "world of unhappiness." They understood Hebrew, which was considered "the key to further study" that would allow them to continue to grow as American Jews.[45] The leaders of the Brooklyn Jewish Center were proud of the Center Academy, but disturbed at its independence. Increasingly, parents were not drawn from the membership and the school, although housed in the center and in an auxiliary building purchased by the center for it on Lincoln Place, did not seem to the board to function as an integral part of the center's educational efforts. Yet when the academy was established, Rottenberg in his annual report hailed it as "the crowning effort" of the center's Hebrew School Department. He was "certain it will point the way and be another example for all communal institutions in America to follow."[46]

In many ways the integrated curriculum of the Center Academy translated into childhood education the point of view inherent in the center's adult educational activities. Both the Columbia University extension courses and later the Institute of Adult Jewish Studies combined Jewish and secular learning, as did the subjects of the popular Monday night forum lectures. The latter introduced Brooklyn Jews to the exponents of the latest issues of the day. Famous political figures, writers, philosophers, and men and women of influence came to the center to speak. Several, like Eleanor Roosevelt, returned. In an age before television, the weekly forum provided a mixture of enlightenment and education that contemporary news shows now find so profitable. And since the center sponsored the forums and did not have to worry about commercial support, Jewish current events received attention. The consistently high level of forum programs drew large audiences for its speakers and set a standard for other synagogue-centers to emulate.[47]

The self-conscious posture of the center's leadership toward their programs ensured a measure of deliberation each time a new activity was adopted. Certain choices were made quickly and easily. The decision to offer adult education courses required little debate. All were convinced of the significance of life-long learning for Jews. But the character and substance of the center's social and recreational activities often sparked dissension. The range of social activities in 1924 included celebrations of Thanksgiving, Hannukah, New Year's Eve, Lincoln's and Washington's birthdays, and Purim as well as a book party for the library, an election eve dinner-dance, and a presentation of Israel Zangwill's play, "The Melting Pot." Recreation centered around the gym with basketball games between the center and the teams of such varied Jewish groups as Young Israel of Williamsburg, Temple Petach Tikvah, the Hebrew Educational Society of Brownsville, the Society for the Advancement of Judaism, and the Brooklyn branch of City College's Menorah Society. The dilemma for the leadership stemmed from their desire to have the spiritual dominate the secular. Although all accepted this goal as laudatory, they often were not sure how to accomplish it. The swimming pool, located in the basement of the center, maintained a separate-sex policy, allocating most of the available hours to men. When the synagogue was used for a forum, because it could accommodate more people than the auditorium, the board voted to require men to wear hats, albeit not without debate.[48]

The tug of war between sacred and secular, Jewish and American, could scarcely be resolved by the center leadership for they were committed to both cultures. When they hired Rubin Tucker as their new cantor in 1943, they were enthralled by the beauty of his voice and his skill in cantorial singing. Yet shortly after his arrival some center members began to encourage Tucker to turn to opera, despite the clause in his contract prohibiting him from engaging in any opera or theater performances. Perhaps the pinnacle of high culture in the eyes of its devotees, which included center members, was the opera. Each year the center ran an annual gala fund-raising night at the Metropolitan Opera House. The opera house ultimately exercised a greater attraction than the sacred setting of the synagogue. Although the tale of "The Jazz Singer" is not strictly analogous, it is suggestive of the cantor's dilemma. Richard Tucker's decision to quit the center after a three-year tenure for the Metropolitan poignantly points to the ambiguities of living wholeheartedly in two civilizations, even under the institutional roof of the synagogue center. When the center agreed to hire a new social director to replace Moss Hart, who had joined the center in 1926 and had created the Center Players, an amatuer theater group, they were not sure if the social problems of the center could be solved.[49] Hart had successfully promoted dramatic productions at the center, not only by the little theater group he established, but also through visits by such professional Jewish troupes as the Habima and Vilna Troupe. Despite the flourishing theater, which continued after Hart moved on to Broadway, Rottenberg lamented in 1929, when he was about to step down after ten years of serving as the center's president, "We have not yet found something that will attract the member to spend his leisure time at the Center when he is not anxious to pray, be lectured to, or be educated."[50]

The difficulty stemmed in part from the shifting composition of the membership. Had the center chosen to be an intimate synagogue-center, limiting membership to several hundred, the socializing would have flowed naturally. But within five years of its founding the center enrolled 1,000 members, and the figures stayed in this bracket for several decades. However, the relatively steady membership numbers disguised a fluidity of actual members. Each year the center lost close to one-third of the membership and approximately an equal number joined. Some of these changes reflected normal migration patterns in and out of the neighborhood, but others suggested to the leadership a failure to integrate new members into the social milieu of the center. Even a long-time active member and vice-president recalled that he had worshiped at the center for several years but traveled to the 92nd Street YM-YWHA in Manhattan to use the gym because he perceived the Brooklyn Jewish Center to be an exclusive group. When he was invited to join the center he was amazed, and the day he and his wife received their membership cards was a big event. Although fees were substantial – in the 1930s they were reduced from $100 to $50 per family, $37 for single men, and $25 for single women – the cost was less restrictive than the tone.[51]

For those who stayed with the center, it became an important social milieu that opened doors into the larger Jewish world in Brooklyn and the United States. The center maintained a steadfast commitment to Zionism from the earliest days when it hosted a mammoth meeting to greet Chaim Weizmann and Albert Einstein. Levinthal participated actively in the Zionist Organization of America, and even hoped to succeed to its presidency in 1938. The center sponsored his visit to Palestine, which allowed him to speak briefly at the dedication ceremonies of the Hebrew University on Mount Scopus. There existed, as well, an overlapping directorate of leaders between the Brooklyn Jewish Center and Brooklyn Eastern Parkway Zionist district. Often men moved from positions of prestige and power within the center to similar positions in the Zionist organization. Others translated success in Jewish politics into a career in American local politics. Louis Gribetz, for example, who edited the *Brooklyn Jewish Center Review* for many years after its debut in 1933, used the center as a springboard to launch a campaign for the City Council in 1937. Some politicians just joined the center because it was "good politics." But for committed Jews like Gribetz, center involvement expressed his central values of what it meant to be an American and a Jew.[52]

Participation in Brooklyn and Jewish politics did not preclude the center pursuing a leadership role in Jewish communal affairs. Levinthal, in particular, strove to assert the center's preeminence throughout the borough and to use its reputation for collective betterment. In the 1920s Levinthal spurred the establishment of a Brooklyn Jewish Ministers Association that would allow Orthodox, Conservative, and Reform rabbis to meet to discuss common problems. In the mid-1930s Levinthal extended the rabbinic role to include labor mediation. The Brooklyn Jewish Ministers Association appointed a committee, headed by Levinthal, to resolve a dispute between the workers and management of Beth Moses Hospital. Its success in getting the hospital to agree to labor's demand to organize probably encouraged the rabbis subsequently to create a Brooklyn Jewish Community Council to fight local antisemitism and "foster mutual understanding among all the people of all races and all creeds."[53] In each of these instances the center strove to be in the midst of communal life, to demonstrate the wider significance of the synagogue in Jewish political affairs, and to nurture a Jewishly responsible leadership. The synagogue-center produced leaders not from the periphery but from the core.

The center's extraordinary success during the first twenty-five years of its existence stemmed from a happy conjunction of people and place. Within a decade of its founding the center produced the synthesis of Judaism and Americanism sought by its founders. Subsequently it proved the centrality of the synagogue to American Jewish life and encouraged the creation of indigenous American Jewish values. Center leaders enjoyed the advantage that came from being in the vanguard. They were among the first Jews with an East European background to taste the rich economic rewards of the American marketplace. Though traditional in behavior and committed to Jewish survival, they eschewed dogmatism, as much from a lack of theological commitment as from an American-bred pragmatism. Thus they were able to recruit some of the best and brightest rising Jewish talents to conduct their art and music classes, give their lectures, supervise their social and recreational activity, before secular American society became sufficiently liberal to welcome these people's creative energies. Center leaders succeeded with their first try at matchmaking and found a rabbi whose spiritual vision, Jewish dedication, personal wealth, and enormous energy complemented the American and Jewish ethos of the members. The leadership encouraged Levinthal to innovate selectively and avoid controversy, so as to produce that harmony they fervently believed existed between Jewish and American norms and ideals. The resulting stability in the leadership provided the balanced framework for the introduction of successful experiments. The forum series brought many of the most prominent figures in American life to Brooklyn's Eastern Parkway, thereby enriching both the audience and lecturer, each discovering aspects of a partly unknown world. The university classes and Jewish studies institute made concrete the traditional understanding of life-long learning even as they widened the interpretation of its content and method. The popularity and profitability of the kosher dining room augured the time when *kashrut* would indeed become fashionable, not behavior to be scorned as superstitious. The social and recreational activities, the modifications of ritual, the introduction of women's participation within the synagogue, the political action – all would become standard features of synagogue-centers in the affluent suburbs of post–World War II America.

From these features it appears that the Brooklyn Jewish Center was a model of the contemporary synagogue-center, anticipating many of its institutional attributes. However, such a view – which was the one held by the leadership – obscures the extent to which the center perhaps represented more an ideal, than an actual model. Its very pioneering character as the first major attempt in a new, affluent Jewish neighborhood to establish an American Jewish institution drew to it the most ambitious and dedicated individuals, as well as professional talent scarcely tapped by other organizations. Lacking rivals, the center attracted the most ambitious from the growing Jewish population that would make Brooklyn the heart of the traditional Jewish world in the United States. The feature that clearly illustrated the center's uniqueness, the Center Academy, found no followers. Neither the widespread affluence of American Jews in the decades after World War II nor a rising acceptance of the legitimacy of Jewish day schools led other synagogue-centers to attempt to duplicate the daring undertaking of the Center Academy. They did not have the professional resources, the commitment, and the money to sponsor such a day school, settling instead for modest programs of supplementary Jewish education. That the center leaders saw the academy as their crowning achievement speaks to the breadth of their vision of American society and the depth of their commitment to Jewish life.

Ironically, the very forces that contributed to the success of the center during its first three decades fed its gradual decline in the 1960s. The very America that enabled the early generation of center members to rise economically, aspire spiritually, and acquire the knowledge to create a synagogue-center led to its demise. The success of the center's constituency and the social mobility of other groups who moved into Crown Heights in the years after World War II dispersed the center's membership. Forsaking Brooklyn, they moved out further on Long Island, moved up to Manhattan's expensive neighborhoods, or moved down to Florida to retire. Without such men and women as those who had built the institution, endowing it with the best they had to offer, the Brooklyn Jewish Center gradually lost its special character. Without the Jewish community of Crown Heights as soil in which to grow, the center could no longer serve as a focal point for Brooklyn Jewish life. Its very strengths – rooted in the neighborhood, a flower of the community it served – made it particularly vulnerable to the changing environment. However, the early years do herald the history of American Judaism in the post–World War II era, especially the institutional structure of the synagogue-center in which was embedded the amalgam of Jewish American core values. Despite tensions and ambiguities, the Brooklyn Jewish Center achieved the balance that committed Americans and Jews desired.

NOTES

I am grateful for Arthur Goren's constructive criticism and insightful reading of the essay, Sarah Schulman's careful research, Batya Siskind's efficient typing, and the generous support of the Memorial Foundation for Jewish Culture. I am indebted also to Lewis Kramer for his willingness to share his memories of the Brooklyn Jewish Center and to facilitate my examination of synagogue records.

1   Minutes of the Brooklyn Jewish Center, 29 December 1918.

2   Ibid., 5 January 1919.

3   Ibid., 10 February 1919. For brief biographies of several of the builders, see Leon Wexelstein, *Building Up Greater Brooklyn* (New York, 1925).

4   Minutes of the Brooklyn Jewish Center (hereafter Minutes), 11 March 1919. Subsequently the leadership quarreled with Abramson. Their case against Abramson went into arbitration with both sides accepting the decision to take the center's offer of an additional $3,000, making Abramson's total fee $15,000 rather than 5 percent of cost, as first proposed. Ibid., 27 March 1922.

5   Minutes, 14 October 1919. Joseph Kaye, "The Making of a Rabbi," *Brooklyn Jewish Center Review* (February 1938), p. 7. On the center's Orthodox Judaism see, for example, Sammuel H. Klein, "The Center and Its Youth," *The Brooklyn Jewish Center Annual*, vol. 1, ed. Louis Gribetz (1925), p. 13.

6   Minutes, 14 October, 11 November 1919; 5 January, 9 February, 8 March 1920.

7   Minutes, 19 November 1919. For the growth of Brooklyn neighborhoods and their character see my book, *At Home in America* (New York: Columbia University Press, 1981), chaps. 2 and 3.

8   Quotes and description from the Minutes, 14 June 1920.

9   Minutes, 15 July 1920.

10 Minutes, 20 September, 11 October, 8 November, 27 December 1920; 11, 24 January 1921. For a summary of the events in the first three years see the Dedication Number of *Jewish Center Bulletin* (December 31, 1922).

11 *Jewish Center Bulletin*, 9 January, 9 May, 13 June, 26 September, 15 October 1922; 7 March, 18 October 1923.

12 *The Brooklyn Jewish Center Annual*, ed. Louis J. Gribetz (New York, 1925), p. 12.

13 Joseph Krinsky, "The Function of the Center," *The Brooklyn Jewish Center Annual* (New York, 1925), p. 8.

14 Harry Horwitz, "Educational Activities," *The Brooklyn Jewish Center Annual* (New York, 1925), p. 10, see also pp. 14–15, 19–22.

15 On immigrant interest in lectures, see Irving Howe, *World of Our Fathers* (New York, 1976), pp. 238–244, and Stephan F. Brumberg, *Going to America, Going to School* (New York, 1986), pp. 153–173.

16 *Annual of the Brooklyn Jewish Center* (1930), n.p.

17 Kaye, "The Making of a Rabbi," pp. 5–7.

18 On Levinthal, see Kaye, "The Making of a Rabbi," pp. 5–7. On Magnes, see Arthur A. Goren, "Judah L. Magnes: The Wider Pulpit," unpublished essay in possession of the author; and "Introduction," *Dissenter in Zion* (Cambridge, Mass., 1982), p. 28. On Kaplan, see Charles Liebman, "Reconstructionism in American Jewish Life," *American Jewish Year Book*, 71 (1971), pp. 25–39.

19 Israel Levinthal, "Introduction," *Steering or Drifting – Which?* (New York, 1928), p. ix.

20 Kaye, "The Making of a Rabbi," p. 6; *Brooklyn Jewish Center Review* (October 1937), p. 16.

21 Levinthal, "Introduction," p. ix.

22 Israel Levinthal, "The Rabbi in Present-Day Jewish Life," *Brooklyn Jewish Center Review* (April 1936), pp. 16–17; Israel Levinthal, "The Sermon as a Form of Art," *Brooklyn Jewish Center Review* (April 1935) p. 7.

23 Israel Levinthal, "A New Deal for Judaism," *Brooklyn Jewish Center Review* (September 1933), p. 3.

24 Levinthal, "Introduction," p. xi.

25 Israel Levinthal, "What Ails American Jewry? A Diagnosis," *Steering or Drifting – Which?* (New York, 1928), p. 48.

26 Israel Levinthal, "What Is This and Why Is This?" *Steering or Drifting – Which?* (New York, 1928), p. 169.

27 Israel Levinthal, "What Does the Center Stand For?" *The Brooklyn Jewish Center Annual* (New York, 1925), pp. 5–6.

28 Minutes, 5 June 1947.

29 Israel Goldfarb and Israel Levinthal, *Song and Praise for Sabbath Eve* (New York, 1920), n.p.

30 Ibid.

31 *The Brooklyn Jewish Center Annual* (1925), p. 19; Brooklyn Jewish Center, *Second Annual Building Redemption Fund Dinner* (1928), n.p.; Brooklyn Jewish Center, *First Annual Building Redemption Fund Dinner* (1927), p. 23.

32 Israel Levinthal, "Initiating Girls in Jewish Religious Life," *Brooklyn Jewish Center Review* (February 1935), p. 13.

33 *Brooklyn Jewish Center Review* (June 1936), p. 3.

34 In 1939 Helen Levinthal became the first woman to complete the course of rabbinical training at the Jewish Institute of Religion. However, she was not ordained a rabbi and could follow no further in her father's footsteps because of her sex. But she did give a lecture at the Friday evening service. *Brooklyn Jewish Examiner*, 2 June 1939.

35 *Brooklyn Jewish Center Review* (May 1936), p. 16, (June 1936), p. 3.

36 Minutes, 20 September 1920; 3 August 1927, 8 January 1928.

37 Alvin Irwin Schiff, *The Jewish Day School in America* (New York, 1966), pp. 39, 41.

38 *United Synagogue Recorder* (January 1925), p. 22.

39 Fannie Neumann, "A Modern Jewish Experimental School – In Quest of a Synthesis," *Jewish Education*, 4, no. 1, (January-March, 1932), pp. 26–27.

40 Ibid.

41 Ibid. For the character of the New York public schools in the 1920s, see Diane Ravitch, *The Great School Wars* (New York, 1974).

42 Sophia Soskin, "A Notable Anniversary," *Brooklyn Jewish Center Review* (May 1938), p. 7; Irene Bush Steinbach, "Center Academy of the Brooklyn Jewish Center," *Jewish Education*, 20, no. 2 (February 1949), p. 42.

43   Soskin, "A Notable Anniversary," p. 8; Alice Brennan, "Problems of a Progressive Jewish School," *Jewish Education*, 6, no. 3 (October 1934), p. 166.

44   Brennan, "Problems of a Progressive Jewish School," pp. 165–167; Irene Bush Steinbach, "The Progressive Center Academy," *Jewish Education*, 15, no. 1 (May 1945), pp. 9–10.

45   Quotes from Brennan, "Problems of a Progressive Jewish School," p. 167; for an optimistic assessment, see David Rudavsky, "The Brooklyn Jewish Center Academy," *Jewish Education*, 20, no. 1 (November 1948), pp. 49–52, 57.

46   *Second Annual Building Redemption Fund Dinner* (1928), n.p.

47   See Annual Reports, Brooklyn Jewish Center, 1925–1945.

48   Minutes, 4 April, 22 September 1927; *The Jewish Center Bulletin* (July 1952).

49   Minutes, 29 June 1942; Brooklyn Jewish Center, *Second Annual Building Redemption Fund Dinner* (1928), n.p.

50   Brooklyn Jewish Center, *Tenth Anniversary Dinner* (January 1929), n.p.

51   Annual Reports, Brooklyn Jewish Center, 1925–1945; interview with Lewis Kramer, 10 August 1983.

52   Minutes, 2 June 1943; *The Brooklyn Jewish Center Annual* (1925), p. 27; *Brooklyn Jewish Examiner*, 29 May 1931, 22 October 1937, 24 June and 1 July 1938; 29 January 1943, 28 January 1944, 16 May 1947; *Brooklyn Review* 20 April, 18 May 1928; interview with Lewis Kramer, 10 August 1983.

53   *Brooklyn Jewish Examiner*, 8 February, 23 August 1929; 17 February, 3 March 1933; 14 and 28 June, 26 July, 20 September 1935; 22 March, 19 April 1940. Quotation from "Brooklyn Forms Jewish Council," *Brooklyn Jewish Examiner*, 22 March 1940.

12

Choosing a Synagogue: The Social Composition of Two German Congregations in Nineteenth-Century Baltimore

MARSHA L. ROZENBLIT

In 1870, a few disgruntled members of the Baltimore Hebrew Congregation petitioned for the introduction of reforms in the style of synagogue worship so that "religious life of the congregation may not suffer." When the congregation approved the reforms, a minority of twenty furious members sued Baltimore Hebrew for its infractions of ancient Jewish rituals. Although they settled out of court, the traditionalists resigned from the mother congregation.[1] These men, and some of their friends and relatives, founded a new German Orthodox synagogue in April 1871. They designed Congregation Chizuk Amuno to be a place "where our Prayers will be offered in accordance with the orthodox Rituals, the very same manner of worship, as it was inherited to us by our Forefathers."[2]

The establishment of this German Orthodox congregation in 1871, at a time when most German synagogues were rapidly adopting radical reforms, reveals that the religious history of American Jewry is by no means linear. Despite the prevalent notion that virtually all American Jews of German descent had reformed the religious style of their synagogue services by the 1880s,[3] in Baltimore some prosperous German Jews chose to reject reform and retain traditional services.[4] Moreover, among those German Jews who affiliated with the Reform Movement, an old guard continued to demand sensitivity to Jewish tradition as late as the turn of the century.

Scholars have long stressed the important connection between the desire for religious reform and the twin processes of Americanization and upward social mobility among German Jewish immigrants.[5] A study of two German synagogues in Baltimore in the second half of the nineteenth century reveals, however, that although many German Jews did seek Reform as they became prosperous Americans, rising social status and acculturation did not push all of them into the Reform camp. Although many prosperous Jews did choose Reform, the pace of that reform was often slow, and it met with great resistance. Moreover, many Baltimore German Jews who had become wealthy businessmen and had successfully Americanized continued to attend Orthodox religious services. Thus personal preference and individual taste also informed the development of Reform and Orthodox Judaism in America.

In this chapter I adopt a new approach to the question of Jewish religious affiliation. I compare the socioeconomic backgrounds of the members of two Baltimore German synagogues before World War I: Congregation Oheb Shalom, a moderate Reform congregation founded in 1853, and Congregation Chizuk Amuno, an Orthodox congregation that was formed in 1871 and became Conservative after World War II. By the 1890s, Oheb Shalom contained some of the richest Jews in Baltimore, but many of these men resisted further religious change, keeping Oheb Shalom the most traditional of Baltimore's three Reform congregations despite its wealth. On the other hand, the German Jews who founded Chizuk Amuno were just as affluent and just as Americanized as the members of Baltimore's Reform congregations. They had created an Orthodox synagogue because they preferred traditional services.

These two synagogues were chosen for study because of their intrinsic interest and because they possess extant, albeit incomplete, membership records and minute books.[6] Information from sketchy membership rolls was supplemented by data from the Baltimore city directories, which listed occupations, rarely mentioned in membership records, for all subscribers.[7] Information on residence and occupation of members of Oheb Shalom and Chizuk Amuno in several sample years, as well as data from a 1900 control sample of members of the Baltimore Hebrew and Har Sinai congregations,[8] was then subjected to a computer-assisted analysis. This study terminates around the time of World War I, before the entry of prominent Jews of Eastern European origin complicated the picture still further.

Oheb Shalom

On October 31, 1852, several Baltimore German Jews assembled to form a new "Israelite Congregation in the City."[9] These men founded Oheb Shalom, "lover of peace," as Baltimore's fourth congregation, alongside then Orthodox Baltimore Hebrew and Fells Point congregations and radical Reform Har Sinai.[10] Although all of the "official" histories of the congregation argue that the congregation was founded by those who sought moderate reforms,[11] Oheb Shalom behaved like a traditional synagogue in its early years. Only in 1858, when it purchased a site for a synagogue on Hanover and Lombard streets in southwest Baltimore, far from Baltimore Hebrew's east Baltimore location, did Oheb Shalom exhibit its first stirrings toward Reform. Members asked a "Dr. Weiss," undoubtedly Reform Rabbi Isaac Mayer Wise, to preach at the August 13, 1858, inauguration of the new synagogue. They also asked Wise's permission to play the organ, which they had found in the church they had bought as a site for their synagogue, during Sabbath services.[12] The congregation, with its ladies' section, its synagogue honors, and its concern for kosher meat, adopted Wise's prayerbook *Minhag America* at that time.[13]

The synagogue clearly articulated its desire for moderate reform in April 1859 when it hired a rabbi. The man selected was Benjamin Szold, a recent graduate of the Breslau Seminary in Germany. An advocate of reforms conceived in a spirit of affection for Jewish history and tradition, Szold is now regarded as one of the intellectual forebears of the later Conservative Movement.[14] In their April 10 (German) letter offering Szold the position, Oheb Shalom's leaders spelled out the extent to which Oheb Shalom sought to reform Jewish worship. Oheb Shalom, they informed Szold, stood firmly in the middle between Orthodoxy and ultra-Reform. Thus, the congregation used an organ on the Sabbath, had eliminated *piyyutim*, except on the holidays, did the Torah reading without the special chanting, read the Haftarah in German, and had provisionally accepted Wise's prayerbook. Defending these reforms, the leaders argued: "Historical reform is a necessity here in America if the younger generation will be retained and infused with the moving spirit of Judaism. [It is a necessity] especially since Orthodoxy is merely empty words, the holding fast to old forms in the synagogue, in glaring opposition to the desires of the large majority who separate themselves from it."[15]

These men certainly did not seek reform in order to make their Judaism conform to their high social status. Although prosperous enough to pay a five-dollar initiation fee and three dollars in annual dues, Oheb Shalom's founders, all German immigrants in their mid-thirties, were not particularly rich men.[16] Among the original members, only five were merchants who owned their own companies, mostly in the clothing business, ten were just "dry goods dealers" or clothiers, and three were artisans. Among the eighty-nine men who belonged to the congregation between 1853 and 1862 (see Table 1), none were professionals or manufacturers, and only 19.1 percent were merchants who owned their own firms. The majority of early members (61.8 percent) were traders of one sort or another, men who did not own their own firms and who were, in all likelihood, glorified peddlers.

Table 1. *Occupations of members of Congregation Oheb Shalom, 1853–1906 (percent)*

	1853–1862 N = 89	1892 N = 96	1900 N = 102	1906 N = 66
Professionals	0	2.1	5.9	7.6
Manufacturers	0	22.9	43.1	31.8
Merchants with firms	19.1	52.1	32.4	42.4
Merchants, no firm	61.8	13.5	9.8	6.1
Business employees	2.2	8.3	7.8	10.6
Artisans	14.6	1.0	1.0	1.5
Workers	1.1	0	0	0
Peddlers	1.1	0	0	0
Total	100.0	100.0	100.0	100.0

In their choice of occupations, the early members of Oheb Shalom closely resembled the members of Baltimore Hebrew Congregation in 1860.[17] In fact, the 144 members of Orthodox Baltimore Hebrew may have been somewhat wealthier than the members of the new Reform congregation. Only 19 percent of the members of Oheb Shalom owned their own business firms, but 24 percent of the members of Baltimore Hebrew in 1860 did so. Virtually the same percentage of members in both congregations practiced a craft or were workers. In both synagogues, the overwhelming majority of members sold dry goods and clothing. The notion of Rabbi William Rosenau, Oheb Shalom's rabbi from 1892 to 1939, that Oheb Shalom was founded by clothing dealers dissatisfied with their treatment at Baltimore Hebrew, finds no support in the statistics.[18]

Rabbi Adolf Guttmacher, the rabbi of the Baltimore Hebrew Congregation at the end of the century, has suggested that the men who created Oheb Shalom did so simply to have a synagogue near their new homes in southwest Baltimore.[19] Analysis of the residential patterns of the founders of Oheb Shalom does not bear out Guttmacher's argument. Rabbi Guttmacher must have read back into 1853 the situation of the congregation in the post–Civil War decades, when indeed the members did congregate within a few blocks of the synagogue building on West Lombard and Hanover streets. In 1853, however, members of the new congregation lived all over downtown. In this period, there was no "Jewish" concentration in Baltimore (see Map 1). Thus, of the nineteen original members for whom an address can be determined, fifteen lived

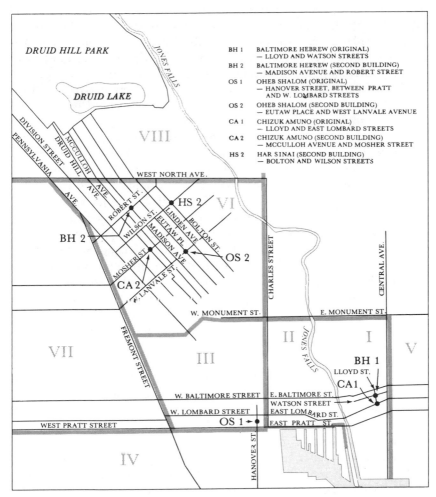

Map 1. Nineteenth-century Baltimore and its German synagogues. Prepared by the Cartographic Services Office, University of Maryland.

in east Baltimore, four of them between Jones Falls and Central Avenue (quadrant I), four east of Central Avenue (quadrant V), and seven between Charles Street and Jones Falls (quadrant II). Only four lived west of Charles Street at all (quadrant III).[20] In fact, in the entire first decade of the synagogue's existence, members continued to live all over the Baltimore downtown area. Although 30 percent of all the members between 1853 and 1862 did live in quadrant III in west Baltimore, 20 percent lived between Charles Street and Jones Falls (quadrant II), 26 percent between Jones Falls and Central Avenue (quadrant I), and 12 percent lived east of Central Avenue altogether. In this period, fully 68 percent of the members of the congregation lived in east Baltimore.

This residential pattern closely resembled that of the members of Baltimore's mother congregation, the Baltimore Hebrew Congregation. In 1860, 78 percent of its members lived east of Charles Street: 40.5 percent between Charles Street and Jones Falls (I), 11.4 percent between the Falls and Central Avenue (II), and 26.1 percent east of Central Avenue (V). In that year, one-fifth of the members resided in west Baltimore. Although members of Baltimore Hebrew were more likely than members of Oheb Shalom to live far east in the city, and members of Oheb Shalom were somewhat more likely to reside in the west, there is insufficient evidence to suggest that Oheb Shalom was originally built to suit the needs of west Baltimore Jews, even rich west Baltimore Jews. The richest members of Oheb Shalom in its first decade avoided living east of Jones Falls, but otherwise scattered in more or less the same pattern as all other members of Oheb Shalom and Baltimore Hebrew congregations.

Of course, even if they lived in east Baltimore, most members of Oheb Shalom lived very close to the synagogue. Whether in east or west Baltimore, about 54 percent of the members lived within ten blocks of Hanover and Lombard streets in southwest Baltimore. In all likelihood, its founders did not consciously create Oheb Shalom as a west Baltimore synagogue, but its location served as a magnet for Jews who increasingly moved there after the Civil War.

In the decades after Benjamin Szold's arrival, Oheb Shalom followed a cautious path of reform. Guided by the traditionalist sensibilities of its rabbi, the congregation introduced reforms to bring order and dignity to the service.[21] Moreover, Oheb Shalom adopted Benjamin Szold's prayerbook, *Avodath Yisroel*, which retained a traditional Hebrew service while eliminating references to the sacrifices or a physical return to Zion.[22] In the 1870s Oheb Shalom hired as teachers for its religious and German school only applicants who observed the Sabbath, denied synagogue functions to anyone who did business on the Sabbath, and encouraged members to close their businesses on Saturday.[23] In 1882 the congregation joined the Reform Union of American Hebrew Congregations, although members vigorously protested the radical Pittsburgh Platform adopted by the Reform Movement in 1886.[24] In 1890, Oheb Shalom also joined the Conservative Jewish Theological Seminary Association.[25]

By the early 1890s the more radical members of the congregation gained the upper hand and managed to impose their desire for more fundamental change on the synagogue. In this period, Oheb Shalom divided over an important issue: whether to hire an English-speaking rabbi. "English-speaking" became a code-word for a rabbi who was

American-trained and more radical than Szold, the traditionalist. Although it was certainly possible that Szold's English, like that of most
of his congregants, was not perfectly eloquent,[26] nevertheless the interest
in an English-speaking rabbi reflected the desire of a large segment of
Oheb Shalom's membership both to Americanize fully and to adopt a
more radical reform posture. An old guard, consisting of supporters of
Szold who wanted to maintain Jewish tradition, protested vigorously for
years.

The origins of the request for an English-speaking rabbi can be traced
to the desire of the congregation to attract a larger and younger membership. In 1882 a group within the congregation began to press for "a
[sic] English [sic] rabbi" in conjunction with Szold. Szold, they thought,
could still handle all religious questions, but another rabbi could give
sermons in English "with which language our children our [sic] only
familiar."[27] In the 1880s Oheb Shalom repeatedly tabled or ignored such
petitions, probably because of the strength of the opposition and fear of
offending the beloved Rabbi Szold.[28]

At the same time, President Isaac Strouse and others felt that the
congregation could gain many more members by leaving the building
on Hanover and West Lombard streets, located in an area that had become
a factory district, and moving uptown to newly fashionable Bolton Hill.
Strouse felt that the congregation could become "a model for American
Israelites" if it moved uptown, built a beautiful new structure, and
modernized.[29]

In 1890–1891 the dual campaigns to move uptown and hire an "English" rabbi reached fever pitch. A group of ninety-seven men sent a
petition to President Strouse on April 7, 1890, insisting that "the future
of our Congregation requires the services of an English speaking rabbi,
in connection with our Rev. Dr. Szold."[30] The April 17 meeting held
to discuss the issue revealed the deep divisions in Oheb Shalom. The
congregation voted unanimously to hire an English-speaking assistant to
Rabbi Szold but took no action on its decision.[31] Probably in deference
to a deeply offended Szold, Oheb Shalom members who desired modernization merely tried to convince the sixty-one-year-old Szold to agree
with their wishes.[32]

Fearing a loss of revenue from resigning members, in October 1891
Strouse finally decided to abandon Szold and arrange for Oheb Shalom
to hire a less traditional rabbi and move uptown. In rather purple prose,
this clothing manufacturer from Germany who served Oheb Shalom as
president for thirty-three years (1879–1912) decried the tide that was
"carrying us on the ruthless rocks" and argued that the congregation
could "weather the gale and rebuild our craft in modern ways." Since,

he believed, the present location and a German-speaking rabbi were "against the wishes of the majority," he urged the congregation to do something "in a business like manner without consideration for our social feelings." Thus he concluded "that an English speaking minister and a new Temple is what we must have" in order to restore Oheb Shalom to its rightful place as the leading congregation in Baltimore.[33] As a result, the congregation unanimously decided to hire an English-speaking rabbi. At the same time they resolved to move uptown.[34] Within a week, and therefore probably as arranged beforehand, Oheb Shalom bought a lot on elegant Eutaw Place, on the corner of Lanvale Avenue. Shortly thereafter many former members resumed their membership in the congregation.[35]

The true desires of Congregation Oheb Shalom in hiring an English-speaking rabbi appeared in the contract that it hammered out with an angry Benjamin Szold. Oheb Shalom forcefully retired Szold as of September 1892 and relegated him to the status of rabbi emeritus, with the right to preach in German once a month. It officially presented the forced retirement as necessary for Szold's sake, because the strenuous demands of the new synagogue required a "younger and more vigorous minister." One significant provision of the contract reveals that what members really wanted was not just a younger man who spoke better English but an American rabbi, a man who would uphold the radical reform positions and perform in the style of American-trained rabbis of the time. The contract stipulated that the congregation would dispense with Szold's services if he advocated "principles or measures" that were "in conflict with those advocated by our rabbi to be hereafter elected, which are calculated to cause dissensions [sic]."[36] Some members may have sought a new-style rabbi for ideological reasons. Others presumably were willing to accept such reform as part of the total "American" package. But whether for theological reasons or to prove their status as prosperous Americans, Oheb Shalom members felt the need to adopt an American posture when they moved uptown.

By the following March, Congregation Oheb Shalom had hired its new "English" rabbi, William Rosenau, a recent Hebrew Union College graduate.[37] The members had now found both the radical reformer and the "American" rabbi that Szold was not. Strouse tried to calm the fears of those members who worried that Rosenau would introduce liturgical changes that they would find un-Jewish and distasteful,[38] but those that feared changes in the services certainly had every reason to fear. Although not an extremist who wanted to move the Sabbath to Sunday, Rosenau stood far to the left of Szold on all issues and used his position to influence a willing congregation in the direction he wanted. His great-granddaughter writes that "the Boss" "was always successful in getting the laymen to implement his plans," overcoming the "extreme conservatism" of some members to introduce more English into the service, along with bare heads and the radical Union Prayerbook. Rosenau, moreover, believed so completely in the vehemently anti-Jewish–nationalist position of the Reform Movement that he later became a founder and leader of the militantly anti-Zionist American Council for Judaism.[39]

Of course, one must ask to what extent the desire to oust Szold and hire the more radical Rosenau was the result of the growing wealth and higher social status of the members of Congregation Oheb Shalom. Certainly the members of this congregation displayed the usual socio-economic patterns of German Jews in the United States. In the decades after the Civil War they experienced rapid and profound upward social mobility, leaving their peddling baskets and pushcarts to become leading clothing manufacturers, department store magnates, and prosperous businessmen, mostly in the clothing, liquor, and tobacco businesses. Few became professionals, but by the turn of the century, none worked as artisans, workers, or peddlers, and very few of the businessmen did not own their own companies. In 1892, for example (see Table 1), almost one-quarter of the members were manufacturers and over half were merchants with their own firms. By 1900, over two-fifths were manu-facturers and one-third were merchants with their own firms. These statistics stand in stark contrast to those from 1853–1862 and reveal the enormous economic success of Oheb Shalom's members. In 1853–1862 only 19.1 percent of them owned their own businesses; by 1892, 75 percent did so.

The majority of these manufacturers or merchants produced or sold clothing or clothing-related items like shoes, hats, and textiles, and thus participated in Baltimore's leading industry, the manufacture of men's ready-to-wear clothing.[40] In 1892, 72 percent of Oheb Shalom's indus-trialists manufactured clothing, and by 1900, 82.7 percent manufactured clothing. Cigar manufacture provided the only other important area for industrial enterprise, accounting for 8 percent of Oheb Shalom's man-ufacturers in 1892 and 13 percent in 1906. In 1892, of all Oheb Shalom's members in commerce, 29.5 percent sold clothing and another 32.9 per-cent sold clothing-related items. The only other commercial area that attracted many of Oheb Shalom's merchants was alcohol, which ac-counted for 11.5 percent of the merchants in 1892.

A few examples of success stories among Oheb Shalom members might be in order. Henry Sonneborn, a man who served Oheb Shalom as vice-president from 1893 to 1912, and as president from 1913 until his death at age ninety-one in 1917, was Oheb Shalom's most prominent clothing manufacturer. Born in 1826 in Breitenbach, Hesse-Nassau, Germany, he and his brother left the fur and cattle business in Germany to come to America in 1849. Working as a peddler among the Germans of Pennsylvania, he saved enough money by 1851 to open a men's clothing store in Fairmont, West Virginia. By 1853 he owned a chain of stores in the Midwest and established his headquarters in Baltimore, where he began to manufacture men's clothing and sell it in the Midwest and South. After the Civil War, with a loan from Johns Hopkins, he developed Henry Sonneborn and Company, an eight-story factory employing 2,500 people located on Pratt and Paca streets in southwest Baltimore, into a national enterprise that could produce three thousand suits a day.[41] Isaac Strouse enjoyed a similar career. He was born in Grombach, Baden, Germany, in 1835 and came to America in 1850. After working as a clerk, he opened a store in Peru, Illinois, and then returned to Baltimore to found Strouse and Brothers, a clothing-manufacturing house.[42] William Schloss, Oheb Shalom's vice-president from 1881 to 1892, was born in Germany in 1861 and also became a clothing manufacturer, the owner of Schloss Brothers and Company, which operated two factories employing 4,000 workers.[43] The sons and grandsons of these men became active members of Oheb Shalom.

Many members of Oheb Shalom had thus become quite wealthy by the end of the nineteenth century. In 1892, members pledged large sums of money for the new synagogue building on exclusive Eutaw Place in upper northwest Baltimore. The list of contributions by 120 members indicates a very prosperous membership. Altogether members pledged $55,650. Three members each pledged over $1,000, twenty members each pledged $1,000, twenty-eight pledged between $500 and $1,000, thirty-three members pledged $250–500, sixteen over $100 but less than $250, nineteen pledged $100, and one member pledged $50. The manufacturers were the richest group in the congregation. Fully 45.4 percent of them donated $1,000 or more to the new synagogue, and 47.4 percent of all donors who gave $1,000 or more were manufacturers. Many merchants who owned their own firms were also quite prosperous; 22 percent donated $1,000 or more, and 30 percent over $400. Merchants without firms, on the other hand, proved to be less prosperous. Over half (53.8 percent) of them pledged the smallest amounts, and most of the rest pledged between $200 and $600 each. Business employees and artisans, nine men altogether, were only able to pledge in the smallest categories.

It could easily be argued that Oheb Shalom's desire for a more radical reform rabbi derived from the enormous financial success of its members. Many contemporary observers certainly thought so. Aaron Friedenwald of Orthodox Chizuk Amuno wrote to his son Harry in 1887 to tell him:

Table 2. *Occupations of Oheb Shalom members who petitioned for an "English" rabbi compared to overall occupational distribution in 1892 (percent)*

	Petitioners N = 52	All members N = 96
Professionals	1.9	2.1
Manufacturers	19.2	22.9
Merchants with firm	61.5	52.1
Merchants, no firm	9.6	13.5
Business employees	7.7	8.3
Artisans	0	1.0
Total	100.0	100.0

"Reform in America is pretty much what the wholesale clothing dealers want it to be."[44] Henrietta Szold, daughter of Rabbi Szold, upset with those at the synagogue who desired radical changes, observed bitterly in a letter to her friend Harry Friedenwald that it was the extreme radicals, "who . . . it must be remembered, are wealthy," who were responsible for the distasteful changes.[45]

That the richest members of Oheb Shalom were the vanguard pressing for change was simply not the case, however, The congregation split on this issue, and the split did not bear a direct relationship to wealth, as the richest members of the congregation placed themselves on both sides of the issue. Personal preference and individual taste, not wealth, led members to support either Szold or an "English" rabbi.

A look at the occupational distribution of the men who signed the petition against Szold (Table 2)[46] does not indicate that wealth necessarily induced members of the congregation to oppose the traditional rabbi. The two groups of wealthier members, manufacturers and merchants with firms, divided on the issue. Merchants with firms were proportionately more likely to vote for an English-speaking rabbi than their numbers would warrant, but manufacturers, the richest group in the synagogue, were proportionately less likely to do so. Thus 23 percent of all members were manufacturers, but only 19 percent of the petition signers were manufacturers. On the other hand, 52 percent of all members were merchants with firms, but 62 percent of all those who signed the petition were merchants with firms. Business employees, a relatively poor sector of the congregation, and professionals, a relatively prosperous group, could be found proportionately in both camps. Merchants without their own firms tended not to sign the petition.

Moreover, although those who petitioned for an American rabbi included many of the richest men in Oheb Shalom, many equally rich men did not seek a new-style rabbi. It is true that a majority of those who pledged the largest amounts to the new synagogue in 1892 did petition for an "English" rabbi. Eleven of the nineteen men who pledged $1,000 each, and seventeen of the twenty-eight men who pledged between $500 and $1,000 signed the 1890 petition. Still, those who signed the petition donated altogether $27,150, slightly less than the $28,500 pledged by those members who did not sign. The three largest donors did not sign the petition for an "English" rabbi, and only one of them could not do so because he served as an officer of the congregation. Furthermore, those who donated the smallest amounts in 1892 also divided on the issue. Thus wealth alone was no guarantee that a synagogue member favored more reforms, and many of the least prosperous hoped to radicalize the synagogue.

According to contemporaries and later versions of events, the old guard that opposed Rosenau and reform was actually old, holding on to tradition for nostalgic reasons, unconcerned that a younger generation might not share its views.[47] Perhaps many of the old guard were indeed old, but age was not a determining factor in the controversy over a new rabbi. The membership of Oheb Shalom in 1892 still contained thirteen men who had been members of the congregation between 1853 and 1862. These men divided evenly on the issue of ousting Rabbi Szold. Despite their age, six of these men petitioned for a new-style rabbi, and seven did not do so. Interestingly, those who sought change were by far the least rich of the old-timers, donating a total of $2,650 to the new synagogue, in contrast to $6,750 donated by the seven old members who did not sign the petition. Thus neither age nor wealth was the sole determining factor in the issue of more radical reform for Oheb Shalom.

Richer members of Oheb Shalom did have a decisive voice, however, in the other congregational concern of 1892, the move uptown to newly fashionable upper northwest Baltimore (quadrant VI), to Bolton Hill, the area around elegant Eutaw Place, with its large, fine homes for the truly rich and such fancy streets as Madison and Linden avenues and Bolton and McCulloh streets.[48] President Strouse argued that Oheb Shalom had to move uptown or it would lose members who now disliked attending services in the factory and business district in which the old building was located.[49] Baltimore's German Jewish community, he assumed, was fast moving uptown, and the synagogue must relocate to retain and gain members.

Table 3. *Residential distribution of Oheb Shalom members, 1853–1906 (percent)*

		1853–1862 N = 84	1892 N = 104	1900 N = 135	1906 N = 87
Quadrant					
I	Jones Falls to Central Avenue	20.2	0	0	0
II	Jones Falls to Charles Street	26.2	1.0	0	0
III	Charles Street to Fremont Avenue	29.8	26.0	3.7	0
IV	South of Pratt Street	9.5	1.0	0.7	0
V	East of Central Avenue	11.9	5.8	1.5	0
VI	Upper northwest to North Avenue	2.4	46.2	69.6	72.4
VII	West of Fremont Avenue	0	19.2	4.4	1.1
VIII	Northwest of North Avenue	0	1.0	20.0	26.4
	Total	100.0	100.0	100.0	100.0

In fact, however, in 1892 just under half of the members of Oheb Shalom lived uptown, and half continued to live downtown, all in west Baltimore (see Table 3 and Map 1), about one-quarter of them between Charles and Fremont streets (quadrant III) and about one-fifth west of Fremont Street (quadrant VII). Certainly after Oheb Shalom moved to Eutaw Place, it served as a magnet for members (including Rabbi Szold himself). By 1906 virtually all of Oheb Shalom's members lived in upper northwest, about three-quarters of them below North Avenue, and about one-quarter above North Avenue in the area first annexed by the city in 1888, southeast of Druid Hill Park.[50]

In 1892, therefore, Oheb Shalom did not have to move uptown simply because most of its members had done so. As a Reform congregation it was under no obligation to move within walking distance of its members, half of whom now lived over a mile away. It appears that it was the leaders of Oheb Shalom who wanted a new synagogue uptown, because they – and the majority of the richest members of Oheb Shalom – had already moved there, and they wanted their synagogue close at hand. In 1892 only 46.2 percent of all members lived in quadrant VI, but 66.7 percent of the manufacturers and 52 percent of the merchants with firms already had moved into the large, beautiful townhouses in this area of the city. Henry Sonneborn, for example, moved to Eutaw Place as early as 1878. Isaac Strouse still lived on Hollins Avenue in west Baltimore, but all of his sons lived on Eutaw Place or nearby.[51] On the other hand, less prosperous merchants without firms and business employees still resided downtown. Only 26 percent of all members lived in quadrant III, but 46.2 percent of the merchants without firms lived there. After the richer members decided to move the congregation uptown, the less prosperous members moved uptown to join the new cluster of German Jews in the city.

In any case, after Rosenau's arrival and the construction of a truly elegant new synagogue on Eutaw Place,[52] Oheb Shalom began to reform its style of worship more thoroughly. Led by Rosenau and the newly retitled Divine Services Committee, the congregation proceeded to institute reforms for greater decorum that bleached away the traditional flavor of services at Oheb Shalom. Most of the reforms of the 1890s called for more English, less congregational participation, and more performance by rabbi and cantor.[53]

Despite these changes, in the years before Szold's death in 1902, Oheb Shalom remained much more traditional than its sister congregations on Bolton Hill. Writing in 1953, Louis Cahn recalled that when he was a boy in 1903, many members of his congregation were still observant, walking to the synagogue if they still lived far away, observing the dietary laws, not eating bread for eight days on Passover, wearing hats in the synagogue, and fasting all day on Yom Kippur. Cahn noted that at that time the synagogue had felt more "orthodox" in ritual.[54] Oheb Shalom had the richest membership of any synagogue in Baltimore, but the pace of its reform lagged behind that of the other congregations. In the first decade after Rosenau's arrival, an old guard managed to resist many of the changes that the new rabbi and his followers sought, much to the chagrin of President Strouse, who feared that such traditionalism retarded synagogue growth.[55]

After Szold's death in July 1902 the pace of reform quickened. Immediately, the congregation ceased paying dues to the Jewish Theological Seminary.[56] Two years later, Rabbi Rosenau urged the congregation to discontinue the use of Szold's prayerbook, *Avodath Yisroel*, and adopt the new radical *Union Prayerbook*. Arguing that the English in the Szold-Jastrow *siddur* was filled with Germanisms and "Hebraic literalisms," Rosenau insisted that the old prayers may have answered the needs "of a period of transition," but a new generation had to pray out of a new book.[57] President Strouse agreed, mostly because he thought that such reforms would generate more members and more money.[58]

In 1906 Oheb Shalom traditionalists lost their last-ditch effort to stem

Congregation Oheb Shalom on Eutaw Place and Lanvale Avenue at the turn of the century. Courtesy of the Maryland Jewish Historical Society, Baltimore.

the tide of reform and prevent the congregation from adopting the new *Union Prayerbook*. On April 19, 1906, Oheb Shalom, at an exceptionally well-attended congregational meeting, voted fifty-five to thirty-seven to adopt the *Union Prayerbook*.[59] Thus fourteen years after Baltimore Hebrew Congregation adopted the *Union Prayerbook*,[60] Oheb Shalom became a full-fledged Reform congregation. Despite the hope of Strouse and Rosenau, Oheb Shalom experienced no mass infusion of new mem-

Table 4. *Occupations of those who voted for and against adopting the* Union Prayerbook, *Oheb Shalom, 1906 (percent)*

	For N = 41	Against N = 25	1906, Overall N = 66
Professionals	4.9	12.0	7.6
Manufacturers	34.1	28.0	31.8
Merchants with firm	36.6	52.0	42.4
Merchants, no firm	9.8	0	6.1
Business employees	14.6	4.0	10.6
Artisans	0	4.0	1.5
Total	100.0	100.0	100.0

did it witness any mass defection. Its traditionalists simply had no place else to go.

As in the controversy over hiring an "English" rabbi, the positions in the *Union Prayerbook* controversy did not clearly depend on wealth. The issue deeply divided Oheb Shalom: 59.8 percent voted to adopt the prayerbook, and 40.2 percent opposed. The proponents of radical change were not only the rich, and the opponents were not only the less prosperous.[61] Manufacturers, the richest group in the congregation, seemed only slightly more likely to vote for the *Union Prayerbook* than their numbers would warrant (see Table 4). On the other hand, merchants with their own firms, the other wealthy group, tended to vote against the prayerbook. Forty-two percent of members were merchants who owned their own companies, but 36.6 percent of those who voted yes and 52 percent of those who voted no were wealthy merchants. Surprisingly, professionals (N = 5) tended to oppose the new book, and business employees (N = 7) overwhelmingly favored it. Among clerks, the least prosperous group of members, 85.7 percent voted for the new prayerbook. Less prosperous merchants without firms also solidly supported the radical change. Thus wealthy and middle-class members voted on both sides of the issue.

By the end of World War I Oheb Shalom had become a mainstream Reform congregation, indistinguishable from its fellow Reform congregations on Bolton Hill. In 1918 it quietly approved the Central Conference of American Rabbis' condemnation of the Balfour Declaration and adopted the newly revised *Union Prayerbook*.[62]

Chizuk Amuno

Oheb Shalom followed the path of reform traveled by German synagogues in America, albeit at a much slower pace, thanks to its cadre of traditionalists. The history of Chizuk Amuno Congregation, on the other hand, demonstrates how some upwardly mobile Americanized German Jews did not follow this path at all, choosing instead to maintain Orthodox synagogue worship. These men may not have been as rich as the members of Oheb Shalom, but they were prosperous Baltimore businessmen, enjoying the same level of prosperity as the members of the Baltimore Hebrew Congregation, from which they had seceded in 1871 when the mother congregation embarked on a path of radical reform. By no means recent immigrants or more bound to their German homes, these men apparently chose religious Orthodoxy – at least in the synagogue – because they preferred a conservative religious style.

On April 2, 1871, the men who had tried to sue Baltimore Hebrew when it sought religious reform met at the call of Jonas Friedenwald, a prominent businessman, to establish an Orthodox synagogue.[63] Proud of this effort, and in less-than-perfect English, Secretary Henry S. Hartogensis reminded the new congregation six months later that "We have shown the world that the old roots of our holy religion notwithstanding which a great many want and are seeking to destroy have not died away yet but started again." Interspersing his speech with biblical prooftexts in Hebrew, Hartogensis declared that he foresaw a great future for the congregation, whose name meant "strengthening of the faith," for "abundant peace have they who love thy law."[64]

The earliest available constitution (1876) of Congregation Chizuk Amuno (spelled Chizuk Amoono, Chizack Amoonu, Chizack Amuno, and a variety of other ways), reflected the firm commitment of its founders to a totally Orthodox style of worship and their desire to prevent reform in the synagogue. The constitution not only prohibited any alterations to the services without the unanimous consent of the entire membership, but also stipulated that if any member so much as offered a motion to introduce ritual change, "he shall ipso facto forfeit his membership." Moreover, no member could hold office in the congregation if he "publicly violates the Sabbath or Hollidays [sic]."[65]

The concerns of the congregation in the first decade of its existence – when it had about forty members – reflected its Orthodox position. Not only did Secretary Hartogensis pepper the minutes with Hebrew words and phrases, but the Board of Trustees regularly discussed such issues as forming a kosher slaughtering board in Baltimore, finding a scribe to repair the Torah, supporting a communal Mikveh, and whether the cushions on the benches in the new synagogue, located on Lloyd and East Lombard streets in east Baltimore, contained a mixture of fibers that rendered them ritually impure.[66] When they hired a rabbi in 1876, they found one perfectly suited to their needs, a man born in America who had received his rabbinical training in the modern Orthodox seminary of Rabbi Esriel Hildesheimer in Berlin. Rabbi Henry Schneeberger, who also had a bachelor's and master's degree from Columbia University, actively participated in the Union of Orthodox Jewish Congregations and in the Jewish Theological Seminary Association, which he helped found in 1886.[67]

The curriculum in Chizuk Amuno's religious school derived from the congregation's firm commitment to religious Orthodoxy and not from romantic yearnings for small-town German roots. Thus, unlike the school at Oheb Shalom, the school at Chizuk Amuno did not teach German. The curriculum emphasized Hebrew language, prayers, Bible translations, and Jewish history and customs, and stipulated that "the English language is to be used in the translation and in conversation with the pupils."[68] This curriculum did not replicate traditional *cheder* learning, but it did emphasize the fundamentals of the Jewish tradition.

The initial members of Congregation Chizuk Amuno had already Americanized. Their commitment to English-language instruction in the religious school certainly reveals their sense of belonging in America and their attachment to American culture. Hiring an American-born rabbi also resulted from their sense that theirs was an American synagogue. Moreover, from its inception in 1871 Chizuk Amuno recorded its minutes in English, whereas Reform Oheb Shalom kept its minutes in German until 1880. Orthodoxy for these men was by no means the result of a lower level of assimilation into American society.

Was their attachment to Orthodoxy, however, the result of a lower level of economic prosperity than in the Reform congregations in Baltimore? Nothing about the occupations of Chizuk Amuno members would indicate that they did not enjoy the same economic success as all other German Jews in America (see Table 5). In 1871 about two-fifths of the original members were merchants who owned their own companies, two-fifths were traders of one sort or another, and one-fifth were artisans. Two-thirds of these men were in the clothing business, and 43.8 percent owned their own firms. This occupational distribution is strikingly similar to that of the members of the Baltimore Hebrew Congregation in 1860. In that year, 24 percent of the members of the mother congregation were merchants who owned their own firms, and 53 percent were merchants who did not.[69] Allowing for the prosperity of the

Table 5. *Occupations of members of Chizuk Amuno, 1871–1906 (percent)*

	1871 N = 16	1889 N = 26	1896 N = 42	1900 N = 73	1906–1911 N = 98
Professionals	0	7.7	11.9	15.1	11.2
Manufacturers	0	19.2	26.2	21.9	33.7
Merchants with firm	37.5	30.8	19.0	15.1	19.4
Merchants, no firm	37.5	11.5	19.0	27.4	15.3
Business employees	6.3	15.4	16.7	17.8	15.3
Artisans	18.8	15.4	7.1	2.7	5.1
Total	100.0	100.0	100.0	100.0	100.0

post–Civil War years to generate more merchants with firms, probably those who seceded from Baltimore Hebrew practiced exactly the same occupations and enjoyed the same level of wealth as those in the reforming congregation from which they seceded.

The original members of Chizuk Amuno did differ from the members of Oheb Shalom in their choice of residence: All of them lived in east Baltimore. In 1871, 30 percent of the Chizuk Amuno founders lived in quadrant I, between Jones Falls and Central Avenue, 60 percent in quadrant II, between Charles Street and Jones Falls, and 10 percent east of Central Avenue altogether. Many members of Oheb Shalom, on the other hand, already lived in west Baltimore. In their proclivity to an east Baltimore address, members of Chizuk Amuno also differed from members of the Baltimore Hebrew Congregation, 21.7 percent of whom had already moved to west Baltimore by 1860. Their residence in east Baltimore certainly explains why members of Chizuk Amuno bought a site for their new synagogue on Lloyd and East Lombard streets, only a block away from Baltimore Hebrew's Lloyd and Watson Street location.

The founders of Chizuk Amuno did not found their synagogue because of great economic distance between themselves and those who fancied a more Reform style of worship. To be sure, differences did exist in the level of wealth of members of Oheb Shalom and Chizuk Amuno. Oheb Shalom was the richer synagogue. In 1869, dues at Oheb Shalom ran $40 a year whereas dues at Chizuk Amuno in 1876 came to $10.[70] In 1870, Oheb Shalom rented its pews for $50 to $25 and single seats for $13 to $6. Chizuk Amuno rented seats in 1876 for $6 to $3 for the High Holidays.[71] The rabbi of Oheb Shalom received a higher salary than the rabbi at Chizuk Amuno. In 1873 Oheb Shalom raised Benjamin Szold's salary to $4,500, but, in 1876, Rabbi Schneeberger at Chizuk Amuno only received $1,200 a year, a modest amount, which the synagogue raised to $1,400 in 1882. By 1908 Oheb Shalom was able to pay Rabbi Rosenau $7,000 a year.[72]

Members of Oheb Shalom possessed more wealth than the members of Chizuk Amuno, but the members of the latter, whose numbers grew significantly, to about 120 by the 1890s, were by no means poor. About three-quarters of Oheb Shalom's members in the late nineteenth and early twentieth century owned their companies, but almost half (47 percent) of the members of Chizuk Amuno did so as well. The members of Chizuk Amuno experienced the same kind of social mobility after the Civil War as did the members of Oheb Shalom (compare Tables 1 and 5). The percentage of manufacturers among Chizuk Amuno's membership rose just as dramatically as it did at Oheb Shalom, so that by the turn of the century both congregations contained roughly similar and large proportions of manufacturers, the result of a marked increase in the number of industrialists in the Baltimore German Jewish community. At Oheb Shalom for example, the percentage of manufacturers grew from none in 1853–1862 to 31.8 percent in 1906. Similarly at Chizuk Amuno, the percentage of manufacturers grew from none in 1871 to 33.7 percent between 1906 and 1911. Like Oheb Shalom, Chizuk Amuno shared in the de-proletarianization of the entire German Jewish community in the post–Civil War years. In both congregations the percentage of artisans declined considerably. In 1871, 18.8 percent of Chizuk Amuno members practiced a craft; by 1906–1911 only 5.1 percent did so. Finally, at Chizuk Amuno, just as at Oheb Shalom, the percentage of members who pursued careers as merchants but did not own their own companies declined in the decades before World War I. In 1871, 37.5 percent of the members of the Orthodox congregation were merchants without firms, but by 1906–1911 only 15.3 percent fit into this category.

A few flesh-and-blood examples of the careers of Chizuk Amuno members will illustrate that they experienced the same sort of financial success as members of Baltimore's Reform congregations. Michael S. Levy, who served as vice-president and president of Chizuk Amuno for many years, was Chizuk Amuno's most prominent industrialist. Born in Mur-Goslin, Posen, Germany in 1836, he began to manufacture straw hats in Baltimore when he was eighteen and built M.S. Levy and Sons into one of the largest industrial concerns in the city. Max Skutch, born in Kriegshaben, near Augsburg, Bavaria, in 1850, began his American career as a clerk, but soon became a partner in Henry Sonneborn and Company, clothing manufacturers. Joseph Friedenwald, son of Chizuk Amuno's founder Jonas Friedenwald, was born in Altenbusek, Hesse-Darmstadt, in 1827, at first associated himself with his brother-in-law's wholesale clothing firm, Wiesenfeld and Company, and then owned his own company, Crown Cork and Seal. Finally, Philip Herzberg, born in 1822 in Klingenberg a/Main, Bavaria, came to Baltimore in 1840 and established Philip Herzberg and Company, a wholesale and retail clothing establishment.[73]

Some Chizuk Amuno members did experience a somewhat different mobility pattern than the members of Oheb Shalom. In the first place, a much larger share of its members pursued careers as business employees in the early twentieth century. Indeed, in the early 1900s just under a tenth of Oheb Shalom's members worked as clerks or managers (Table 1), but between 15 percent and 18 percent of Chizuk Amuno's members did so (Table 5); this percentage reflects almost triple the proportion of clerks among the 1871 founders. Moreover, Chizuk Amuno's members practiced mercantile careers far less often than members of Oheb Shalom. Whereas the percentage of merchants who owned their own firm increased at Oheb Shalom, the percentage of such merchants decreased at Chizuk Amuno, from 37.5 percent in 1871 to 15.1 percent in 1900. In 1900 twice as many Oheb Shalom members were merchants with firms as Chizuk Amuno members.

Another major difference in the occupational distribution of members of the two congregations lay in area of concentration. Indeed, the differences in occupation between the two congregations in the 1880s and 1890s could lead one to deduce that many people joined one synagogue or the other because they wanted to worship together with people in the same line of work in order to make business contacts in temple. This division by area of specialization was especially pronounced among the manufacturers. As if the synagogue served as a board of trade, the large-scale men's clothing manufacturers – the Sonneborns, the Strouses, the Strausses – all affiliated with Oheb Shalom, whereas the industrialists at Chizuk Amuno tended not to produce men's clothing. In 1892, for example, at Oheb Shalom 72 percent of the manufacturers produced clothing and 4.0 percent related items, whereas at Chizuk Amuno in 1896, 21.3 percent of the manufacturers produced clothing and 21.4 percent produced related items. Members of Chizuk Amuno concentrated more heavily in the garment industry with the passage of time. In 1889, only a third of Chizuk Amuno manufacturers produced garments or related goods. By 1906 members of Chizuk Amuno produced clothing as often as members of Oheb Shalom.

The importance of business contacts as a factor in synagogue affiliation can be seen among the merchants as well. Both congregations contained many clothing-store owners, but Oheb Shalom seems to have been the home of Baltimore's Jewish shoe-store owners. In 1906, for example,

21.9 percent of those in commerce had shoe stores, compared with only 5.7 percent at Chizuk Amuno. On the other hand, 14.3 percent of Chizuk Amuno's merchants sold hats, but none of the merchants at Oheb Shalom were in the hat business.

Chizuk Amuno may have contained fewer rich merchants and many more middle-class clerks than Oheb Shalom, but it boasted a far higher percentage of professionals, mostly doctors and lawyers, than did the Reform synagogue. That percentage increased notably at the end of the century, from 7.7 percent in 1889 to 15.1 percent in 1900 (Table 5). At Oheb Shalom the percentage of professionals only grew from 2.1 percent of all members in 1892 to 7.6 percent in 1906 (Table 1). The presence of so many professionals at Orthodox Chizuk Amuno is an important indicator that religious Orthodoxy was by no means related to low social status or lack of Americanization. These doctors and lawyers had certainly received an American education, and some of them, especially the Friedenwalds, possessed great wealth, but they preferred Orthodox services. Normally, increased professionalization among Jews is associated with decreased religious observance, yet Chizuk Amuno, an Orthodox congregation, proved attractive to Jewish professionals who preferred traditional worship.

Chizuk Amuno's professionals, men like architect Louis Levi, born in 1868, or lawyer Moses Meyer, born in 1879, were native Baltimoreans.[74] The most prominent professionals at Chizuk Amuno were the Friedenwald physicians. Their prominence in synagogue affairs led many to call Chizuk Amuno the "Friedenwald shul."[75] Jonas Friedenwald, the family scion, and been born in Altenbusek, Hesse-Darmstadt, in 1802, and arrived penniless in Baltimore with his family in 1832. He achieved rapid success in business. In 1854 he retired, a wealthy man, and until his death in 1893 at the age of 91 he devoted himself to Chizuk Amuno, always giving it money for its special needs.[76] His son, Aaron, born in Baltimore in 1836, rejected a career in the family businesses in order to become a doctor and professor of ophthalmology.[77] Aaron's sons Harry, Julius, and Edgar Friedenwald, and his grandson Jonas, also became prominent physicians in Baltimore.[78]

Aaron Friedenwald, like his father before him, was an observant Jew. During two years of study in Europe in the early 1860s, his letters home, written in English to his father and German to his mother, reveal that he kept kosher but did not fully observe the Sabbath, disliked assimilated Berlin Jews, and greatly admired German Orthodox leader Samson Raphael Hirsch. The latter's synagogue service, he noted, "is near the same as in the Lloyd Street Congregation [Baltimore Hebrew, then still Orthodox], being freed from the confusion so often attending orthodox worship, by the presence of an excellent choir."[79] As a doctor in Baltimore, he returned to full observance of the Sabbath. Letters to his children at the end of the nineteenth century repeatedly discuss the problems of obtaining kosher food and not being able to write to them on the Sabbath. In 1898, for example, he wrote to his children during an ocean voyage: "I have enlarged my menu. I get, besides fruit, as on the last voyage, baked potatoes, baked apples, and a cup of coffee. It is a feast for a king; that is, when a king is at sea and is of the Davidian dynasty."[80] Friedenwald mixed easily and frequently in non-Jewish circles and felt a fierce pride in his traditional Jewish life-style. Critical of reformers and of the unbending Orthodox, this man who served Chizuk Amuno as president for many years considered himself a Conservative Jew, and helped found the Jewish Theological Seminary Association. He also played an active role in Orthodox circles and in the American Zionist movement.[81]

Harry Friedenwald, his eldest son, a professor of ophthalmology at the University of Maryland, served as one of the leaders of American Zionism in the early twentieth century.[82] At the same time, he remained an observant Jew. Eschewing what he regarded as the overly strict Orthodoxy of such German Orthodox leaders as Esriel Hildesheimer,[83] Friedenwald vehemently opposed innovations at Chizuk Amuno in the 1920s and especially after World War II. He urged his Chizuk Amuno not to celebrate "the 75th anniversary of our congregation by reversing the judgment of our founders, under which our Congregation has thriven."[84] Friedenwald felt warm and emotional bonds to the Jewish tradition and the Jewish people. Writing to William Rosenau in 1926, he criticized the Reform Movement for its deadly dogmas and philosophies. He reminded Rosenau: "You and I love many Jewish ceremonies but it is not because of their religious or spiritual messages, it is because of associations that are dear to us."[85]

Religious reform, then, in the Baltimore German Jewish community did not result simply from Americanization or increased wealth. Indeed, a comparison of the members of four German congregations on Bolton Hill in 1900 – one Orthodox and three Reform – reveals striking similarities in occupational preference (Table 6).[86] Members of Orthodox Chizuk Amuno, for example, were just as likely as members of the Reform Baltimore Hebrew and Har Sinai congregations to pursue careers in the professions, manufacturing, or as merchants who did not own their own firms, although they were less likely to be merchants with their own firms. Moreover, the occupational differences that did exist among these four congregations did not necessarily give rise to differences in religious preference. Oheb Shalom, for example, the richest congre-

Table 6. *Occupations of members of Oheb Shalom, Chizuk Amuno, Baltimore Hebrew, and Har Sinai congregations in 1900 (percent)*

	Oheb Shalom N = 102	Chizuk Amuno N = 73	Baltimore Hebrew N = 145	Har Sinai N = 111
Professionals	5.9	15.1	14.5	13.5
Manufacturers	43.1	21.9	18.6	23.4
Merchants with firm	32.4	15.1	30.3	35.1
Merchants, no firm	9.8	27.4	21.4	15.3
Business employees	7.8	17.8	13.1	11.7
Artisans	1.0	2.7	2.1	0.9
Total	100.0	100.0	100.0	100.0

gation with by far the highest proportion of manufacturers and the smallest number of merchants who did not own their own companies, still retained a traditional flavor in 1900. Har Sinai, the synagogue with the most concern for ideological reform, contained members who practiced more or less the same occupations as the members of Reform Baltimore Hebrew and Orthodox Chizuk Amuno.

The only differences in occupation among the four German congregations were in the kinds of goods members produced or sold. It would appear that people joined a certain synagogue to pray with people in a similar line of work. Oheb Shalom, as we have seen, contained Baltimore's clothing manufacturers, and few clothing manufacturers or even dealers belonged to Har Sinai. In 1900, fully 39.9 percent of all Oheb Shalom members produced clothing, textiles, shoes, or hats, compared with 17.8 percent for Chizuk Amuno, 12.4 percent for Baltimore Hebrew, and 10.8 percent for Har Sinai. Although about a quarter of all members at Oheb Shalom, Chizuk Amuno, and Baltimore Hebrew sold clothing or related items, only 16.2 percent of the members of Har Sinai did so. The members of all these congregation came from similar backgrounds; some simply chose to be Orthodox and others Reform.

Before the mid-1890s, Oheb Shalom and Chizuk Amuno members did differ in one very important respect: They lived in different parts of Baltimore. It will be recalled that by 1892 about half of Oheb Shalom's members lived in upper northwest Baltimore, about a quarter between Charles and Fremont avenues, and a fifth west of Fremont Avenue in west Baltimore. Virtually none still resided in east Baltimore. Many members of Chizuk Amuno, on the other hand, still lived in east Bal-

Table 7. *Residential distribution of Chizuk Amuno members, 1871–1906 (percent)*

		1871 N = 20	1889 N = 30	1896 N = 44	1900 N = 111	1906–1911 N = 109
Quadrant						
I	Jones Falls to Central Avenue	30.0	30.0	11.4	2.7	2.8
II	Jones Falls to Charles Street	60.0	10.0	0	5.6	1.8
III	Charles Street to Fremont Avenue	0	20.0	13.6	3.6	4.6
IV	South of Pratt Street	0	3.3	0	0	0
V	East of Central Avenue	10.0	26.7	18.2	3.6	7.3
VI	Upper Northwest to North Avenue	0	10.0	36.4	63.1	46.8
VII	West of Fremont Avenue	0	0	18.2	7.2	7.3
VIII	Northwest of North Avenue	0	0	2.3	18.9	29.4
	Total	100.0	100.0	100.0	100.0	100.0

timore in 1889 (see Table 7), and only a few had already moved into the upper northwest (quadrant VI). Indeed, in 1889, two-thirds of all Chizuk Amuno members still lived east of Charles Street, with over one-quarter of them living in quadrant V, east of Central Avenue, where already a large community of Russian Jews had begun to settle in the 1880s.[87] Very few lived far from Chizuk Amuno itself in the western parts of downtown Baltimore, where a large number of Oheb Shalom members resided. Thus in 1889 about 43 percent of all Chizuk Amuno members lived within a half-mile of the synagogue in east Baltimore, and another 27 percent lived between eleven and twenty blocks away.

Preference for east Baltimore did not derive from the fact that Chizuk Amuno members were too poor to move uptown but rather from the genuineness of their religious orthodoxy. As long as Chizuk Amuno was located on Lloyd and East Lombard streets, most members continued to live in east Baltimore so that they could walk to the synagogue on the Sabbath, even though it was no longer fashionable to live in that part of town. The wealthiest members of the congregation were only slightly more likely than others to live over a mile away. In 1889, about 30 percent of Chizuk Amuno members lived a mile or more away from the synagogue; 40 percent of the five manufacturers lived over a mile away, and 28.6 percent of the merchants with firms did so. The willingness to ride was not related to occupation.

The fact that Chizuk Amuno's members lived in east Baltimore for religious and not financial reasons is amply demonstrated by their very rapid movement into northwest Baltimore after the congregation moved to McCulloh and Mosher streets in 1895. By 1896, only one year later, over a third of the members had already moved to northwest Baltimore, led by the richest members: professionals, manufacturers, and merchants who owned their own firms. In that year, therefore, almost half of Chizuk Amuno's members did live over a mile from the synagogue. The situation was remedied by 1900, however, when virtually all of Chizuk Amuno's members lived in quadrant VI (63.1 percent) or quadrant VIII (18.9 percent), so that 82 percent lived in upper northwest Baltimore and only 6 percent lived over a mile away. Chizuk Amuno members had always had enough money to buy homes uptown, but had delayed doing so until their synagogue, to which they had to live near for religious reasons, moved uptown. Members of Orthodox Chizuk Amuno formed an integral part of the affluent German Jewish community uptown, distant from their poor East European co-religionists in east Baltimore.

By 1900, then, virtually the entire Baltimore German Jewish community lived uptown, on the fancy new avenues of upper northwest Baltimore. They belonged either to the three Reform congregations or the two Orthodox congregations there. They formed one community, and had created a gilded ghetto on Bolton Hill. Indeed, contrary to the expectations of many sociologists, these German Jews lived in a more densely Jewish neighborhood when they had become rich than they ever had as impoverished new immigrants. Virtually all of these men lived next door to one another on the six major avenues of the area: on Eutaw Place, Madison Avenue, Linden Avenue, McCulloh Street, Bolton Street, Druid Hill Avenue, and their extensions in the Annex (see Map).

In 1900 about two-thirds of the members of Oheb Shalom, Chizuk Amuno, Baltimore Hebrew, and Har Sinai resided in quadrant VI, and about one-fifth in quadrant VIII, in the Annex, with a scattered few still downtown or in west Baltimore. The overwhelming majority of members of all four synagogues lived on the above-named six streets, almost all above Mosher Street, and almost none lived on the cross-streets of the area. In Oheb Shalom, for example, 92.6 percent of those who lived

Congregation Chizuk Amuno at the turn of the century, located at McCulloh and Mosher streets. Courtesy of the Chizuk Amuno Congregation.

in quadrant VI in 1900 resided on six streets. One-third of them owned homes on elegant Eutaw Place. Such an address appealed particularly to Oheb Shalom's manufacturers, 58.8 percent of whom owned large homes here. Members of Chizuk Amuno, somewhat less wealthy, but still an integral part of Baltimore's affluent German Jewish community, also resided on these streets (84.4 percent), even if fewer of them lived on fashionable Eutaw Place and more of them lived further west, on Druid Hill Avenue, Division Street, and Pennsylvania Avenue, near Baltimore's black community, which lived west of Druid Hill Avenue.[88] The men who lived west of Druid Hill Avenue tended to be the least prosperous of Chizuk Amuno's members: business employees and merchants without firms. The rich at Chizuk Amuno lived on McCulloh Street.

The members of Baltimore Hebrew and Har Sinai congregations owned homes on exactly the same streets, north of Mosher Street. About one-quarter of the members of both synagogues lived on elegant Eutaw Place, a number higher than at Chizuk Amuno (14.3 percent) and lower than at Oheb Shalom. In both congregations, virtually all the members who lived in quadrant VI lived on the major avenues, with few on the side streets, and like the members of Chizuk Amuno substantial numbers of Baltimore Hebrew and Har Sinai members lived on Druid Hill Avenue, closer to Baltimore's blacks than the members of Oheb Shalom. In these synagogues, the wealthiest members – manufacturers and merchants who owned their own companies – concentrated on Eutaw Place, and less prosperous members lived on such streets as Druid Hill Avenue and West North Avenue. At Har Sinai, the manufacturers shunned Eutaw Place, home of Oheb Shalom's industrialists, for Madison Avenue.

The members of this Baltimore German Jewish community not only lived on Bolton Hill next door to one another, but also formed one social set and thus married and befriended each other irrespective of their "religious" affiliation. Henrietta, the daughter of Henry Sonneborn, one of Oheb Shalom's leading clothing manufacturers, for example, married Charles Hutzler, son of the owner of Hutzler's Department Store and a staunch Har Sinai member. Henry Sonneborn's nephew Rudolph became a protégé of Aaron Friedenwald of Chizuk Amuno. Harry Friedenwald shared a life-long friendship with Henrietta Szold, the daughter of Rabbi Benjamin Szold of Oheb Shalom, with whom he had studied as a young man. Harry himself married Birdie Stein, the daughter of Samuel Stein, a clothing merchant and banker who served for a time as president of the Baltimore Hebrew Congregation, although grandfather Jonas Friedenwald insisted that the wedding take place at Chizuk Amuno.[89]

Moreover, members of one congregation – even officers and trustees – frequently belonged to the other synagogues, so that some members of Reform Oheb Shalom often also paid dues to Orthodox Chizuk Amuno and other congregations. Such a situation certainly confuses any socioeconomic analysis. A few examples will suffice. Henry Sonneborn, a member of Oheb Shalom since 1858 and the largest donor in 1892, retained his Baltimore Hebrew membership through the 1860s and was also a member of Chizuk Amuno at the turn of the century. Similarly, various members the Hecht family belonged to both synagogues in 1906. Silas Fleischer became an active member in both Oheb Shalom and Chizuk Amuno. Julius Schloss, the youngest son of the Oheb Shalom Schlosses, belonged to Orthodox Shearith Israel. Many members of Chizuk Amuno, like Aaron Friedenwald and Henry Hartogensis, also belonged to Shearith Israel, either because they lived closer to it or because they preferred its more traditional style. Max Skutch on the other hand belonged both to Chizuk Amuno and Baltimore Hebrew.[90]

By the turn of the century, Baltimore's German Jews formed an integrated community despite differences in religious preference. They were separated by miles – actual as well as emotional – from Baltimore's East European Jewish community, almost all of whom lived in east Baltimore, and who worked in the factories owned by the Sonneborns, Schlosses, and other wealthy German Jews.[91] Only much later could they join the German Jews in the synagogue, first at Chizuk Amuno,[92] and then at the Reform congregations.

In Baltimore, and presumably in other cities as well, German Jews affiliated with Reform or Orthodox congregations, not because their pocketbooks dictated it, but because of personal preference, because they wanted to join a synagogue in which they could make business contacts, or because their relatives had already joined and urged them to do so. Indeed, a very high percentage of the members of the two congregations studied here had relatives in the congregation. At Oheb Shalom 56.1 percent of the members in all sample years combined had relatives in the congregation. The percentage increased from 48 percent in the period from 1853 to 1862 to 63 percent in 1906. At Chizuk Amuno in 1871, 27.3 percent of the members had relatives in the synagogue; by 1906–1911 the figure had risen to 57.4 percent. Needless to say, the number of people with relatives in the same congregation was probably higher than these statistics, based on people with the same surnames, indicate.

German Jews in Baltimore, like German Jews elsewhere in America, succeeded in Americanizing rapidly and in rising in social status and wealth. Some of them translated that success into a quest for Reform in Judaism. Others did not, preferring merely to Americanize the service in their synagogues without detracting from its traditional content and its traditional flavor. This American brand of German Orthodoxy did not possess any strong ideological justifications. It did not try to explain in a theoretical way why Jews should continue to worship in the Orthodox pattern. This matter-of-fact American Orthodoxy may have helped set the stage for the later development of the Conservative Movement, a movement that also wanted to Americanize the synagogue without detracting from its traditional nature.

NOTES

1 Adolf Guttmacher, *A History of the Baltimore Hebrew Congregation Nidchei Israel, 1830–1905* (Baltimore, 1906), pp. 42–44; Isaac M. Fein, *The Making of an American Jewish Community: The History of Baltimore Jewry from 1773 to 1920* (Philadelphia, 1971), pp. 49, 116.
2 Chizuk Amuno, Minute Book 1871–1880, special meeting, 2 April 1871, p. 1; Guttmacher, *Baltimore Hebrew*, p. 45; Henry W. Schneeberger, "Chizzuk Amoonah Congregation," p. 67 in *The Jews of Baltimore: An Historical Summary of Their Progress and Status as Citizens of Baltimore from Early Days to*

the Year Nineteen Hundred and Ten, ed. Isidor Blum (Baltimore and Washington, 1910).

3   Leon A. Jick, *The Americanization of the Synagogue, 1820–1870* (Hanover, N.H., 1976), p. 174; Nathan Glazer, *American Judaism*, 2d. rev. ed. (Chicago and London, 1972), p. 38.

4   In addition, in 1879 another group of German Jews founded a second Orthodox congregation, Shearith Israel. See Rev. Dr. S. Schaffer, "Sketch of the History of the Shearith Israel Congregation," p. 62 in Blum, *Jews of Baltimore*; Arnold Blumberg, *A History of Congregation Shearith Israel of Baltimore on the Threshold of a Century* (n.p., n.d., probably after 1970).

5   See especially Jick, *Americanization of the Synagogue*, pp. 78–81, 86, 93–96, 174–81, 183; and Moshe Davis, *The Emergence of Conservative Judaism: The Historical School in 19th Century America* (Philadelphia, 1963 [1965]), p. 152.

6   Congregation Chizuk Amuno possesses good membership records – which, unfortunately, provide only names and addresses – for 1871, 1889–1894, 1896, 1906–1911, and 1910–1913. These records are located in the archives of the congregation, in its present location on Stevenson Road in Baltimore. Oheb Shalom did not keep its membership records from the pre–World War I period. I created a list of members for 1853–1862 from the names of new members recorded in the synagogue minutes, located in the congregational archives in Oheb Shalom's present location on Park Heights Avenue. I was able to determine synagogue membership in 1892 from a list of those who donated money to the new temple in that year. This list, which represents virtually all members, had been placed for safekeeping in a copper box in the foundation stone and is now in the archives. I generated a 1906 sample from the names of those who voted in the controversial *Union Prayerbook* issue, recorded in the synagogue minutes. Finally, I used the official list of members of both synagogues provided in *The Elite Hebrew Dictionary of Baltimore City, 1900* (Baltimore, 1899), pp. 85–89 and 102–107, to create a 1900 sample. Minute books for Oheb Shalom are complete for the entire period from 1853 to the present. Unfortunately, Chizuk Amuno's minute books are only available for 1871–1880, and since 1920.

7   The Baltimore city directories were prepared by John W. Woods for most of the period between 1856 and 1883, and by R. L. Polk Company after 1887. For 1853–1856 I used *Matchett's Baltimore Director*. Because I already knew the addresses, I rarely had problems with multiple names in the city directories. Owing to their prosperity, most of these men could be located in the directories.

8   *Elite Hebrew Dictionary*, pp. 74–82 and 93–100. The sample represents the entire membership in that year.

9   Oheb Shalom Minute Book 1853–1862 (English translation), p. 1. At some point someone translated the German minute books into English.

10 For a history of the congregations see Fein, *Making of an American Jewish Community*; Guttmacher, *Baltimore Hebrew*; and Abraham Shusterman, *The*

Legacy of a Liberal: The Miracle of Har Sinai as It Is Recounted in the One Hundred and Fifth Anniversary (Baltimore, 1967).

11 See, for example, Louis F. Cahn, *The History of Oheb Shalom, 1853–1953* (Baltimore, 1953), pp. 15–16; William Rosenau, "Oheb Shalom Congregation," p. 65 in Blum, *Jews of Baltimore*; Fein, *Making of an American Jewish Community*, p. 66.

12 Oheb Shalom Minute Book 1853–1862 (English translation), pp. 66, 69; Cahn, *Oheb Shalom*, pp. 23, 66.

13 Oheb Shalom Minute Book 1853–1862 (English translation), pp. 69, 73, 78, 88, 104, 117.

14 Ibid., p. 99; Cahn, *Oheb Shalom*, pp. 27–29. On Szold, see Alexandra Lee Levin, *The Szolds of Lombard Street: A Baltimore Family 1859–1910* (Philadelphia, 1960), pp. 3–23; Marvin Lowenthal, *Henrietta Szold: Life and Letters* (1942; reprint, Westport, Conn., 1975), pp. 2–8; Fein, *Making of an American Jewish Community*, pp. 89–91; Davis, *Conservative Judaism*. Unfortunately, no serious scholarly study of this interesting and important rabbi exists.

15 American Jewish Archives, Benjamin Szold Collection, box 1897. Translation mine.

16 On fees and dues, see Oheb Shalom Minute Book 1853–1862 (English translation), pp. 2, 20. On ages, see biographical sketches of original members in Cahn, *Oheb Shalom*, pp. 17–20. Economic information from analysis of membership records.

17 Information on Baltimore Hebrew members derived from membership lists of Baltimore Hebrew, 1860, in Guttmacher, *Baltimore Hebrew*, pp. 38–39, traced in the *Baltimore City Directory*, 1860.

18 Cahn, *Oheb Shalom*, pp. 15–16.

19 Guttmacher, *Baltimore Hebrew*, p. 36.

20 The quadrants referred to here were created by me to facilitate analysis. They do not represent an official division of the city.

21 Oheb Shalom Minute Book 1853–1862 (English translation), meeting, 3 June 1860, p. 126; 15 March 1861, pp. 142–143; Oheb Shalom Minute Book 1867–1880 (English translation), meeting, 3 January 1869, pp. 41–42; 6 June 1869, p. 49; meeting, 3 November 1879, p. 262; Oheb Shalom Minute Book 1881–1893, congregational meeting, 17 August 1884, pp. 127–128.

22 Benjamin Szold, *Avodath Yisroel: The Order of Prayer for the Israelitish Divine Service on Every Day of the Year, Revised and Translated by Benjamin Szold* (Baltimore, 1865); Idem, *Avodath Yisroel; Israelitisches Gebetbuch für den Oeffentlichen Gottesdienst im ganzen Jahre*, 2d ed. (Baltimore, 1871); Benjamin Szold and Marcus Jastrow, *Avodath Yisroel; Israelitish Prayerbook for all the Public Services of the Year. Originally Arranged by Rev. Dr. Benjamin Szold*, 2d. ed. (Hebrew and German), revised by Revs. Drs. M. Jastrow and H. Hochheimer, Hebrew and English edition by M. Jastrow (Philadelphia, 1873).

23 Oheb Shalom Minute Book 1867–1881 (English translation), congregational meeting, 6 April 1873, p. 157; congregational meeting, 4 May 1874, pp.

185–186; meeting 6 September 1874, p. 195; meeting, 3 November 1879, p. 262; congregational meeting, 5 October 1880, n.p.

24 Oheb Shalom only joined the UAHC after years of discussion. See Oheb Shalom Minute Book 1867–1881 (English translation), meeting, 1 July 1874, p. 193; congregational meeting, 16 May 1875, p. 202; Oheb Shalom Minute Book 1881–1893, congregational meeting, 8 January 1882, p. 30; annual meeting, 3 October 1882, p. 69. On the Pittsburgh Platform see congregational meeting, 5 October 1886, pp. 177–178, 181; congregational meeting, 4 October 1887, p. 199.

25 Oheb Shalom Minute Book 1881–1893, congregational meeting, 15 May 1890, p. 240.

26 See congregational complaints about the way he read notices: Oheb Shalom Minute Book 1881–1893, meeting, 2 April 1882, p. 42; meeting, 14 May 1882, p. 45. Certainly congregational officers also did not know perfect English. Their English speeches preserved in the minutes contain numerous errors in grammar and spelling and sound like German.

27 Oheb Shalom Minute Book 1881–1893, annual meeting, 3 October 1882, p. 72.

28 Ibid., congregational meeting, 30 May 1883, pp. 92–93; congregational meeting, 6 May 1888, p. 206; meeting, 6 June 1889, p. 223.

29 Oheb Shalom Minute Book 1881–1893, congregational meeting, 6 October 1885, pp. 155–157; congregational meeting, 14 October 1887, pp. 195–196; congregational meeting, 2 October 1888, pp. 212–213.

30 Oheb Shalom Archives, file, "Petition for an English Speaking Rabbi."

31 Oheb Shalom Minute Book 1881–1893, special congregational meeting, 17 April 1890, p. 239.

32 Ibid., congregational meeting, 7 October 1890, pp. 244–246, 249; special congregational meeting, 31 May 1891, p. 255; meeting 30 June 1891, p. 257; meeting, 6 July 1891, p. 257; meeting, 1 September 1891, p. 260.

33 Ibid., congregational meeting, 6 October 1891, pp. 264–265.

34 Ibid., pp. 267–268.

35 Ibid., special congregational meeting, 15 October 1891, p. 270; meeting, 30 October 1891, p. 271.

36 Ibid., congregational meeting, 30 November 1891, pp. 273–274. Rosenau argued that Szold retired because of ill-health; see Blum, *Jews of Baltimore*, p. 66.

37 Oheb Shalom Minute book 1881–1893, congregational meeting, 6 March 1892, p. 279.

38 Ibid., congregational meeting, 4 October 1892, p. 290.

39 On Rosenau see American Jewish Archives, Biographies, "Biographical Study Written by Rosenau's Great-granddaughter, Ms. Sally Korkis, Cincinnati, Ohio, 1982"; Cahn, *Oheb Shalom*, pp. 47–49. On his role in the American Council for Judaism, see American Jewish Archives, ms. coll. 41, William Rosenau Papers, series A, box 1, file 1/4.

40 On Baltimore's clothing industry see Charles Hirschfeld, *Baltimore, 1870–*

1900: Studies in Social History, Johns Hopkins University Studies in Historical and Political Science 59, no. 2 (Baltimore, 1941), pp. 41–46; Sherry H. Olson, *Baltimore: The Building of an American City* (Baltimore and London, 1980), pp. 175–176; Edward K. Muller and Paul A. Groves, "The Changing Location of the Clothing Industry: A Link to the Social Geography of Baltimore in the Nineteenth Century," *Maryland Historical Magazine*, 71, no. 3 (Fall 1976), pp. 404–408, 411, 413, 416.

41 American Jewish Archives, Biographies, "Biography of Henry Sonneborn," by Henry Sonneborn, Jr., 1977, pp. 1–10; Blum, *Jews of Baltimore*, p. 165; Hirschfeld, *Baltimore*, p. 42; Olson, *Baltimore*, p. 282.

42 Blum, *Jews of Baltimore*, p. 169.

43 Ibid., pp. 187, 190.

44 Aaron Friedenwald to son Harry, 26 June 1887, in Harry Friedenwald, *Life, Letters, and Addresses of Aaron Friedenwald M.D.* (Baltimore, 1906), p. 126.

45 Henrietta Szold to Harry Friedenwald, 2 January 1888, in Lowenthal, *Henrietta Szold*, p. 29.

46 I traced the petitioners for an "English" rabbi in the 1892 list of donors to the new temple. The donor list included virtually all members of Oheb Shalom at that time.

47 William Rosenau, *A Brief History of Congregation Oheb Shalom, Baltimore, Maryland Covering Third Quarter of a Century 1903–1928* (Baltimore, 1928), p. 32; Cahn, *Oheb Shalom*, p. 42.

48 On the elegance of Bolton Hill and Eutaw Place, see Olson, *Baltimore*, pp. 167, 271–272, 303; John Dorsey and James D. Dilts, *A Guide to Baltimore Architecture*, 2d rev. ed. (Centreville, Md., 1981), pp. 183–187; J. Thomas Scharf, *History of Baltimore City and County*, vol. 1 (1881; reprint, Baltimore, 1971), p. 281.

49 On the development of the western part of downtown as a factory and business district, see Olson, *Baltimore*, pp. 172–173, 247; Dorsey and Dilts, *Guide to Baltimore*, p. 93; Muller and Groves, "The Changing Location," pp. 413–414; Edward K. Muller and Paul A. Groves, "The Emergence of Industrial Districts in Mid–Nineteenth Century Baltimore," *Geographical Review*, vol. 69 (1979), p. 175.

50 On the Annex, see Olson, *Baltimore*, pp. 209, 217–219.

51 American Jewish Archives, Henry Sonneborn Biography, p. 7. Strouses' addresses from subscribers' list, 1892, Oheb Shalom.

52 For a description of the Eutaw Place Temple itself, see Dorsey and Dilts, *Guide to Baltimore*, p. 186. See also the photograph included here. The building now serves as a Masonic hall.

53 For example, see Oheb Shalom Minute Book 1881–1893, meeting, 31 May 1893, pp. 303–304; meeting, 13 August 1893, p. 308. See also meeting, 14 August 1892, p. 285; meeting, 31 October 1892, pp. 293–294.

54 Cahn, *Oheb Shalom*, pp. 41–42.

55 For examples see Oheb Shalom Minute Book 1893–1897, meeting, 3 February 1894, p. 35; meeting, 19 May 1894, p. 54; meeting, 29 May 1894, pp.

57–59; meeting, 28 February 1895, p. 133; Oheb Shalom Minute Book 1897–1902, congregational meeting, 24 November 1897, pp. 5–6; congregational meeting, 19 September 1898, p. 67; meeting, 30 November 1898, pp. 82–83; meeting, 24 June 1902, p. 349; Oheb Shalom Minute Book 1902–1905, meeting, 2 September 1902, p. 3; Oheb Shalom Minute Book 1893–1897, congregational meeting, 4 October 1894, pp. 83–86; congregational meeting, 1 October 1895, p. 180.

56   Annual financial reports beginning in 1902 made no mention of JTS dues. See Oheb Shalom Minute Book 1902–1905, congregational meeting, 21 October 1902, p. 21; congregational meeting, 20 October 1903, p. 103; congregational meeting, 18 October 1904, pp. 178, 186.

57   Oheb Shalom Minute Book 1902–1905, annual meeting, 18 October 1904, p. 186; Letter of Rosenau to congregation, congregational meeting, 18 October 1905, pp. 24–25. See also Rosenau, *A Brief History*, p. 20.

58   Oheb Shalom Minute Book 1905–1913, congregational meeting, 18 October 1905, pp. 6–8, 11.

59   Oheb Shalom Minute Book 1905–1913, congregational meeting, 19 April 1906, pp. 56–57. Ninety of the 157 congregational members attended the meeting. On the number of members, see annual meeting, 18 October 1905, p. 8.

60   Baltimore Hebrew Congregation adopted the *Union Prayerbook* in 1892. See Guttmacher, *Baltimore Hebrew*, p. 50.

61   Names of voters on each side recorded in Oheb Shalom Minute Book 1905–1913, congregational meeting, 19 April 1906, pp. 56–57, and traced in the *Elite Hebrew Dictionary* and *Baltimore City Directory*.

62   Oheb Shalom Minute Book 1916–1920, meeting, 27 August 1918, n.p.; congregational meeting, 12 November 1918, n.p.

63   Chizuk Amuno Minute Book 1871–1880, meeting, 2 April 1871, p. 1.

64   Ibid., congregational meeting, 15 October 1871, p. 20.

65   Ibid., congregational meeting, 16 July 1876; Article II, section 2 of Constitution, p. 172; Article IV, section 8, p. 173. I have chosen to use the current spelling adopted by the congregation.

66   Ibid., congregational meeting, 7 January 1872, p. 27; meeting, 4 February 1872, p. 28; congregational meeting, 15 February 1872, p. 29; meeting, 7 April 1872, p. 32; meeting, 1 December 1872, p. 54; meeting, 2 February 1873, p. 59; meeting, 28 November 1875, p. 148; meeting, 5 December 1875, p. 149; meeting, 30 December 1876, p. 204; meeting, 4 November 1877, p. 244.

67   *Encyclopedia Judaica*, vol. 14, 982.

68   Chizuk Amuno Minute Book 1871–1880, school commissioners' meeting, 14 October 1877, pp. 242–243.

69   Calculations for Baltimore Hebrew members' occupations and addresses based on names provided in Guttmacher, *Baltimore Hebrew*, pp. 38–39, traced in the *Baltimore City Directory*.

70   Oheb Shalom Minute Book 1867–1880 (English translation), meeting, 27

June 1869, p. 50; Chizuk Amuno Minute Book 1871–1880, congregational meeting, 16 July 1876, p. 176.

71 Oheb Shalom Minute Book 1867–1880 (English translation), meeting, 18 September 1870, p. 91; Chizuk Amuno Minute Book 1871–1880, meeting, 17 August 1876, p. 181.

72 Oheb Shalom Minute Book 1867–1881, meeting, 20 November 1873, pp. 173–174; Chizuk Amuno Minute Book 1871–1880, meeting, 30 August 1876, p. 183; Chizuk Amuno Minute Book Abstracts, meeting, 4 June 1882, p. 25; Oheb Shalom Minute Book 1905–1913, congregational meeting, 31 December 1908, p. 243. Unfortunately, Chizuk Amuno Minute Books were not available from 1880 until the 1920s, so it is impossible to compare Rosenau's salary with Schneeberger's in the early twentieth century.

73 Blum, *Jews of Baltimore*, pp. 153, 161, 195, 225.

74 Ibid., pp. 235, 269.

75 Alexandra Lee Levin, *Vision: A Biography of Harry Friedenwald* (Philadelphia, 1964), pp. 34, 337.

76 Harry Friedenwald, *Life, Letters, Addresses*, pp. 16–21; Levin, *Vision*, p. 111. On Jonas Friedenwald's gifts to Chizuk Amuno, see, for example, Chizuk Amuno Minute Book 1871–1880, meeting, 23 April 1871, p. 4; meeting, 5 May 1872, p. 37; congregational meeting, 2 January 1876, p. 154; congregational meeting, 30 August 1876, p. 183; meeting, 2 June 1878, p. 268.

77 Friedenwald, *Life, Letters, Addresses*, pp. 22–34, 59, 75–76, 83–88, 108–116.

78 Levin, *Vision*.

79 American Jewish Archives, Harry Friedenwald Papers, microfilm reel 440, Aaron Friedenwald to Jonas Friedenwald, 19 October 1860; 4 December 1860; Aaron Friedenwald's diary, 1860; see also Aaron to Jonas, 28 May 1860, in Friedenwald, *Life, Letters, Addresses*, pp. 34–35, 49.

80 Letter from Aaron Friedenwald, 26 April 1898, in Friedenwald, *Life, Letters, Addresses*, p. 169; See also American Jewish Archives, Harry Friedenwald Papers, microfilm 440, letters from Aaron Friedenwald, 25 March 1864; 8 August 1879; 31 July, 1, 2 August 1882.

81 Friedenwald, *Life, Letters, Addresses*, pp. 93–94, 118–124; Aaron to Harry, 21 September 1887, p. 130; 28 December 1887, p. 137; 10 January 1888, pp. 138–140; 17 December 1888, p. 147; 26 June 1889, p. 151. See also Aaron to his children, 25 June 1895, p. 160; "A Trip to Palestine, address to the YMHA, New York, 25 February 1899," pp. 318–337.

82 Levin, *Vision*.

83 Ibid., pp. 62–66.

84 As quoted in ibid., p. 399. See also p. 337.

85 Harry Friedenwald to Rosenau, 2 October 1926, American Jewish Archives, William Rosenau Papers, ms. coll. 44, file 1/15. See also, Harry S. Friedenwald, "The Survival of the Jew," in *Reverend Doctor Schepschel Schaffer, Twenty-five Years of Activity in the Cause of Orthodox Judaism, 1893-1918* (Baltimore, 1918) n.p.

86 Information on members of the Baltimore Hebrew Congregation and Har Sinai Congregation is from the *Elite Hebrew Dictionary* and the *Baltimore City Directory*, 1900.

87 Fein, *Making of an American Jewish Community*, p. 159; Olson, *Baltimore*, pp. 279, 291.

88 At the turn of the century, Baltimore's prosperous blacks lived in the northwest, near St. Mary's Seminary around Pennsylvania Avenue and Dolphin Street, Druid Hill Avenue, and the side streets of Bolton Hill. See Olson, *Baltimore*, pp. 233–235, 273–277.

89 American Jewish Archives, Biography of Henry Sonneborn; *Elite Hebrew Dictionary*, p. 5; Lowenthal, *Henrietta Szold*, p. 26; Levin, *Vision*, pp. 39–40, 49, 134, 140, 148, 194, 242, 358, 365, 396, 398.

90 Information on overlapping membership from membership records, and *Elite Hebrew Dictionary* listings in 1900 of members of all the German synagogues; Guttmacher, *Baltimore Hebrew*, pp. 38–39. See also Blum, *Jews of Baltimore*, pp. 189, 281, 243. On Fleischer's activity at Oheb Shalom, see minutes. On Aaron Friedenwald's attachment to Shearith Israel, see Friedenwald, *Life, Letters, Addresses*, p. 93; Levin, *Vision*, pp. 39, 140; Rev. Dr. S. Schaffer, "Sketch of the History of the Shearith Israel Congregation," p. 62. It is possible that Aaron Friedenwald did not attend Chizuk Amuno services because he simply did not like Rabbi Schneeberger. See Bertha Friedenwald to children, 1 August 1882, American Jewish Archives, Harry Friedenwald Papers, microfilm 440, in which she says, "What a torment the lecture of Dr. Schneeberger must have been last Saturday, the man has neither sense nor pity."

91 Muller and Groves, "The Changing Location," pp. 411–420. Unfortunately, this article never refers to the fact that all the "Russians" and "Germans" mentioned were Jews. See also Olson, *Baltimore*, p. 280; Fein, *Making of an American Jewish Community*, pp. 165–173.

92 Chizuk Amuno Minute Books in the 1920s show the presence of wealthy Eastern European Jews.

13

The Debate over Mixed Seating in the American Synagogue

JONATHAN D. SARNA

"Pues have never yet found an historian," John M. Neale complained, when he undertook to survey the subject of church seating for the Cambridge Camden Society in 1842.[1] To a large extent, the same situation prevails today in connection with "pues" in the American synagogue. Although it is common knowledge that American synagogue seating patterns have changed greatly over time – sometimes following acrimonious, even violent disputes – the subject as a whole remains unstudied, seemingly too arcane for historians to bother with.[2] Seating patterns, however, actually reflect down-to-earth social realities, and are richly deserving of study. Behind wearisome debates over how sanctuary seats should be arranged and allocated lie fundamental disagreements over the kinds of social and religious values that the synagogue should project and the relationship between the synagogue and the larger society that surrounds it. As we shall see, where people sit reveals much about what they believe.

The necessarily limited study of seating patterns that follows focuses only on the most important and controversial seating innovation in the American synagogue: mixed (family) seating. Other innovations – seats that no longer face east,[3] pulpits moved from center to front,[4] free (unassigned) seating, closed-off pew ends, and the like – require separate treatment. As we shall see, mixed seating is a ramified and multifaceted issue that clearly reflects the impact of American values on synagogue life, for it pits family unity, sexual equality, and modernity against the accepted Jewish legal (*halachic*) practice of sexual separation in prayer. Discussions surrounding this innovation form part of a larger Jewish debate over Americanization, and should really be viewed in the overall context of ritual reform.[5] By itself, however, the seating issue has taken on a symbolic quality. It serves not only as a focus on the changing nature of the American synagogue, but also on the changing nature of the larger society – American and Jewish – in which the synagogue is set.

I

The extent to which men and women were separated in the synagogues of antiquity has been disputed. There can, however, be no doubt that separate seating of one form or another characterized Jewish worship from early medieval times onward. The idea that men and women should worship apart prevailed in many Christian churches no less than in synagogues – although the latter more frequently demanded a physical barrier between the sexes – and separate seating remained standard practice in much of Europe down to the contemporary period.[6]

In 1845, the Reform Congregation of Berlin abolished the separate women's gallery in the synagogue and the traditional *mechitsa* (partition) between men and women. Although mandating "the seating of men and women on the same floor," the congregation continued to preserve the principle of sexual separation during worship: Men occupied the left side of the auditorium, women the right.[7] As late as the early twentieth century, the Hamburg temple, the cradle of German Reform, refused a donation of one million marks from the American banker Henry Budge, who had returned to settle in Hamburg following his father's death, because the sum was conditional on "men and women sitting together" in the new edifice. To Dr. Jacob Sonderling, then rabbi of the temple, that idea was shocking. "In the Hamburg Temple," he reports, "men and women remained separated up to the last moment."[8]

Mixed synagogue seating, or to use the more common nineteenth-century term, "family seating," first developed in Reform Jewish circles in the United States. Rabbi Isaac Mayer Wise, the leading nineteenth-century exponent of American Reform, took personal credit for this particular innovation, claiming to have introduced Jewry's first family pews "in 1850 [*sic*] ... in the temple of Albany."[9] Wise, however, did not *invent* family seating. To understand what he did do, and why, requires first a brief digression into the history of church seating in America.

The earliest New England churches and meetinghouses, following the then-traditional British practice, separated men, women, and children in worship. Men and women sat on opposite sides of a central aisle, and children, also divided according to sex, sat in the back or upstairs. As John Demos points out, "Family relationships were effectively discounted, or at least submerged, in this particular context ... the family

The consecration of an ornate new synagogue prior to the advent of mixed seating. Note the women's gallery. From the Darmstadter Photo Collection in the Jewish Museum, New York.

community and the religious community were fundamentally distinct."[10] Churches sought to underscore the role of the individual as the basic unit in matters of faith and prayer. "God's minister," according to Patricia Tracy, "superseded the role of any other agent; each heart was supposed to be unprotected against the thunder of the Gospel."[11]

Beginning in the mid-eighteenth century, church seating patterns began to change. Families at first won permission to sit together in church on a voluntary basis, and subsequently family seating became the norm.[12] Outside of New England, the history of church seating has not been written, and the pattern may have been more diverse. Missouri Synod Lutherans, for example, maintained separate seating in their churches (which were heavily influenced by German practice) down to at least the end of the nineteenth century. For the most part, however, the family pew won rapid and widespread acceptance in church circles, and Americans, forgetting that there were other possibilities, came to believe that "the family that prays together stays together."[13]

The overwhelming move to adopt family seating stems from great changes in the history of the family that have been amply detailed elsewhere. The growing differentiation between home and work saw families take on a new symbolic role, termed by Demos "the family as refuge," the image being that of family members clustering together for protection against the evils of anomic industrial society. Fear of family breakdown naturally led to a host of new rituals and forms (including the cult of domesticity) designed to "strengthen the family" against the menacing forces threatening to rend it asunder.[14] The family pew was one of these new forms. By raising the family's status over that of the single individual, and by symbolically linking family values to religious values, the family pew demonstrated, as separate seating did not, that the church stood behind the family structure one hundred percent. Family burial plots,[15] which came into vogue at about the same time as family pews, carried the same message of family togetherness on into eternity.

Whether Rabbi Isaac Mayer Wise appreciated the symbolic significance of family pews when he introduced them in 1851 cannot be known. His biographer waxes enthusiastic about how the new system, "enable[d] families to worship together and to have the warmth of togetherness . . . in the deepest and most sacred of moments,"[16] but Wise himself never said anything of the sort. Instead, as he related the story, family pews became a feature of Congregation Anshe Emeth in Albany almost as an afterthought.

Wise had first come to Albany in 1846 to serve as the rabbi of Congregation Beth El. He was a new immigrant, twenty-seven years old, and thoroughly inexperienced, but he dreamed great dreams and displayed boundless energy. Before long he introduced a series of reforms. Like most early reforms, Wise's aimed mainly at improving decorum and effecting changes in the liturgy. He abolished the sale of synagogue honors, forbade standing during the Torah reading, eliminated various medieval liturgical poems (*piyyutim*), introduced German and English hymns into the service, initiated the confirmation ceremony, and organized a mixed choir.[17] But his effort to effect Berlin-style changes in synagogue seating to make room for the choir ("I suggested to apportion the seats anew, and to set apart half of the floor, as well as of the gallery, for the women") raised a howl of protest and got nowhere, and even within the mixed choir "the girls objected strenuously to sitting among the men."[18] Wise never even raised the issue of family pews.

A series of tangled disputes between Wise and his president, Louis Spanier, led to Wise's dismissal from Beth El Congregation two days before Rosh Hashanah in 1850. Wise considered his firing illegal, and on the advice of counsel took his place as usual on New Year's morning. As he made ready to remove the Torah from the ark, Louis Spanier took the law into his own hands and lashed out at him. The assault knocked off the rabbi's hat, wounded his pride, and precipitated a general melee that the police had to be called out to quell. The next day, Wise held Rosh Hashanah services at his home. The day after that, he was invited to a meeting consisting of "prominent members of the congregation together with a large number of young men,"[19] where a new congregation, Anshe Emeth, came into being with Wise as its rabbi. Anshe Emeth dedicated its new building, formerly a Baptist church, on October 3, 1851. Wise served the congregation there until 1854, when he journeyed west to Cincinnati to assume his life-long position at Bene Yeshurun.[20]

Anshe Emeth is usually credited with being the first synagogue with mixed seating in the world. As Wise relates the circumstances in his *Reminiscences*: "American Judaism is indebted to the Anshe Emeth congregation of Albany for one important reform; viz., family pews. The church-building had family pews, and the congregation resolved unanimously to retain them. This innovation was imitated later in all American reform congregations. This was an important step, which was severely condemned at the time."[21] According to this account, and it is the only substantial one we have, family pews entered Judaism for pragmatic reasons: Members voted to make do with the (costly) building they had bought, and not to expend additional funds to convert its American-style family pews into a more traditional Jewish seating arrangement. Had members considered this a particularly momentous action on their part, they would surely have called attention to it in their consecration proceedings, and Isaac Mayer Wise would have said something on the subject in his dedication sermon. Nothing at all was said, however, and only the sharp eye of Isaac Leeser detected in the description of the synagogue "another reform of the Doctor's, one by no means to be commended." Far from being "severely condemned at the time," the reform seems otherwise to have been uniformly ignored.[22] Pragmatic reforms aimed at improving decorum and bringing the synagogue more closely into harmony with the prevailing American Christian pattern were nothing new, even if this particular reform had not previously been introduced. Nor was there any organized opposition to Wise within his own congregation to generate adverse publicity against him. The "loud remonstrations of all orthodoxy," which Wise purported to remember, actually came later. Anshe Emeth's family pews met with scarcely a murmur.[23]

The introduction of family seating at New York's Temple Emanu-El in 1854 attracted no more notice. When Emanu-El was established in 1845, the very year of the Berlin seating reform, its sanctuary provided for separate seating, women behind the men, in one room. The move to family pews took place, as at Anshe Emeth, when the congregation moved into a new building (the Twelfth Street Synagogue), a former church, and there found enclosed family pews already set up.[24] Although they had no known ideological basis for introducing mixed seating, members presumably found the thought of families worshiping together as a unit in the American fashion far more appealing than the thought of introducing separate seating where none had been before. Convenience triumphed, and justifications followed.

II

Ideological defenses of mixed seating, when they came, concentrated not on family worship, an American innovation, but rather on an older, European, and more widely contended Jewish issue of the day: women's status in the synagogue. Rabbis versed in the polemics of Reform Judaism in Germany felt more at home in this debate, having argued about the status of women at the rabbinical conferences in Frankfurt (1845) and Breslau (1846),[25] and they viewed the principle involved as a much more important one than mixed seating, which they had never before seen, and which seemed to them at the time to be just another case of following in the ways of the Gentiles.[26] As a result, the same basic arguments that justified the abolition of the gallery and "separate but equal" seating in Germany came to be used to justify mixed family seating in the United States. Critical differences between these two new seating patterns proved less important in the long run than the fact that Jews and non-Jews on both sides of the Atlantic came to view the debate over the synagogue seating of women as a debate over the synagogue status of women, and they followed it with interest.

The status of women in the synagogue, and in Judaism in general, attracted considerable attention in early America, much of it negative. As early as 1744, Dr. Alexander Hamilton, a Scottish-born physician, compared the women's gallery in New York's Shearith Israel to a "hen coop." Dr. Philip Milledoler, later president of Rutgers, told a meeting of the American Society for Evangelizing the Jews in 1816 that the "female character" among Jews "holds a station far inferior to that which it was intended to occupy by the God of nature." *The Western Monthly Review*, describing "The Present State of the Jews" in 1829, found that "the Jewess of these days is treated as an inferior being." That was putting it mildly, according to James Gordon Bennett, editor of the *New York Herald*. After visiting Shearith Israel, on Yom Kippur 1836, he attacked the status of women in Judaism as one of the most lamentable features in the entire religion – and one that Jesus improved:

> The great error of the Jews is the degradation in which their religion places woman. In the services of religion, she is separated and huddled into a gallery like beautiful crockery ware, while the men perform the ceremonies below. It was the author of Christianity that brought her out of this Egyptian bondage, and put her on an equality with the other sex in civil and religious rites. Hence, have sprung all the civilization, refinement, intelligence and genius of Europe. The Hebrew prays "I thank thee, Lord, that I am not a woman" – the Christian – "I praise thee, Lord, that I and my wife are immortal."[27]

There were, of course, other, more positive images of American Jewish women available, including not a few works of apologetica penned by Jews themselves. These explained the traditional rationale behind Jewish laws on women and enumerated long lists of Jewish women "heroes" from the biblical period onward.[28] Literary treatments of Jewish women also offered occasional positive images, usually of noble, alluringly exotic, Semitic maidens, who functioned more as "erotic dream figures," manifestations of romantic ideals, than anything else.[29] Still, to many Americans, Judaism's "mistreatment" of "the weaker sex" was an established fact: evidence of Judaism's "Oriental" and "primitive" character, in stark contrast to "modern" Christianity. By visibly changing the position of women in the synagogue, Jews sought to undermine this fact, to buttress their claims to modernity, and to fend off the embarrassing Christian charges that they had otherwise to face. In abolishing the women's gallery, synagogue leaders thus sought to elevate not only the status of women in Judaism, but also the status of Judaism itself.

The first Jewish leader in America to stress the relationship between changes in synagogue seating and changes in the status of Jewish women seems to have been Rabbi David Einhorn, who immigrated to America in 1855 and rapidly came to dominate the radical wing of the nascent Reform Movement. Einhorn had agitated for "the complete religious equality of woman with man" at the 1846 Breslau Reform Rabbinical Conference, where he declared it his "mission to make legal declaration of the equal religious obligation and justification of women in as far as this is possible."[30] Within the first few years of his tenure at Temple Har Sinai in Baltimore, he endeavored to put this principle into effect, abolishing what he called the "gallery-cage," and bringing women down to share the same floor as men, though apparently not, at first, the same pews.[31]

In discussing the women's issue in *Sinai*, his German-language magazine, Einhorn characteristically stressed the higher "principle" behind his action, in this case abandonment of what he considered to be misguided Oriental rabbinic strictures against women, and a return to what he identified as the more proper biblical lesson of sexual equality. Gallery seating, he sneered, originally stemmed from unseemly acts of levity that marred the celebration of *simchat bet hashoeva* (the water-drawing festival) in temple times. Since staid Occidental modes of worship held forth no similar dangers to modesty, the gallery could be dispensed with. Although clearly less comfortable with the proprieties of completely mixed seating, Einhorn nevertheless allowed that when a husband sat next to his wife and children nothing untoward could be expected. The essential principle, he repeated, was "religious equalization of women." Everything else connected with seating reforms was of secondary importance.[32]

Einhorn's rationale for mixed seating won wide acceptance, perhaps because it offered a specifically Jewish as well as ethically motivated reason to adopt an American practice, and also perhaps because it made a virtue out of what many were coming to see as a practical necessity. Whatever the case, family seating spread. Chicago Sinai, ideologically linked to its Baltimore namesake, never had a gallery and wrote into its basic propositions (1859) that "in the public worship of the congregation, there should be no discrimination made in favor of the male and against female worshipers."[33] A year later, in San Francisco, Rabbi Elkan Cohn, newly appointed to Congregation Emanu-El, introduced mixed seating as one of his first acts, complaining, as he did so, that Judaism "excluded women from so many privileges to which they are justly entitled."[34] The next fifteen years saw mixed seating develop at a rapid pace. In some cases, proponents exclusively stressed women's inequality and the bad image it projected. Rabbi Raphael D'C Lewin, for example, denounced separate seating as "a relic of the Dark Ages."[35] More frequently, pragmatic considerations – purchase of a new synagogue building (perhaps a church containing pews), the need to use the gallery for a choir, the inability of women in the gallery to hear what was going on, or the "undignified" appearance presented by a synagogue where the gallery was far more crowded than the main sanctuary below – worked hand in hand with ideological factors in bringing about reform.[36] In at least one case, Sherith Israel in San Francisco, mixed seating came about because, as the minutes report, "the existing custom of separating the sexes during Divine Services is a cause of annoyance and disturbance in our devotion."[37] Whatever the real reason, however, most synagogues eventually came to justify mixed seating on the basis of women's equality. Isaac Mayer Wise led the way, quite misleadingly retrojecting the women's issue back into his Albany reforms:

> The Jewish woman had been treated almost as a stranger in the synagogue; she had been kept at a distance, and had been excluded from all participation in the life of the congregation, had been relegated to the gallery, even as was the negro in Southern churches. The emancipation of the Jewish woman was begun in Albany, by having the Jewish girls sing in the choir, and this beginning was reinforced by the introduction of family pews.[38]

Although mixed seating looked like an imitation of gentile practices, no proponent of Reform would admit that it was. In seeking to modernize Judaism, Reform leaders always insisted that they were strengthening the faith and preventing defections to Christianity; assimilation was as much anathema to them as to their opponents. Knowing how sensitive they were on this issue, critics of mixed seating regularly coupled their references to the innovation with terms like "Gentile fashion," "semblance of a church," and "Christian."[39] They knew that such charges struck home.

Otherwise, traditionalists generally contented themselves to defend their time-honored practices on the basis of Jewish legal precedents and religious prooftexts, chief among them the Talmudic discussion of temple seating practices in Tractate Sukkah 51b. "This is the direct and forcible language of the Talmud," the learned Laemmlein Buttenwieser insisted after quoting his source at length, "and on it we are content to rest our case without further argument."[40]

Proponents of change naturally put forward different interpretations of these texts.[41] Even those most eager to introduce reforms still continued to seek the legitimacy that textual roots provided. The never-ending textual arguments, however, are less important than the fact that the two sides in the seating controversy unwittingly talked past one another. Proponents defended mixed seating as a test of Judaism's ability to meet modernity's challenge to Jewish survival. Opponents defended traditional seating as a test of Judaism's ability to parry modernity's threats to Jewish distinctiveness. Although the two sides seemed only to be debating about laws and practices, the words they used and the passions behind them indicate that the central arguments really reached deeper. Ultimately, they touched on the most basic values – traditional ones and Enlightenment ones – that each side held dear.

III

The first synagogues to introduce mixed seating did so on a consensus basis. Anshe Emeth in Albany, Emanu-El in New York, Keneseth Israel in Philadelphia, Sinai in Chicago, and others had chosen the path of reform early on, and clearly identified themselves as alternative congregations, designed for those who felt dissatisfied with the prevailing traditional congregations to which most affiliated American Jews belonged. As we have seen, however, mixed seating quickly spread from fringe to mainstream, with more and more synagogues adopting it. This, of course, led to a breakdown in consensus and to many an internal synagogue dispute. In Cleveland's Congregation Tifereth Israel (now The Temple), the decision in favor of mixed seating (1861) "resulted in severing the connection of several of the old members," as well as in the resignation of the congregation's twenty-seven-year-old and highly precocious treasurer and Sunday school superintendent, Benjamin Franklin Peixotto.[42] In Cincinnati, a few years later, a similar dispute wracked Temple Bene Israel, with similar results.[43] Disputes over mixed seating have continued to splinter synagogues down to the present day.

One of the most historically interesting clashes over mixed seating took place at the venerable B'nai Jeshurun synagogue in New York City in 1875. The dispute eventually reached civil court – one of comparatively few such cases to do so – and involved many of the leading rabbis of the period. It serves as a valuable case study of the whole mixed seating issue as it developed in, disrupted, and ultimately split an individual congregation.

B'nai Jeshurun was the second synagogue founded in New York City (1825) and has proudly boasted of being New York's "oldest Ashkenazic

Congregation." From its founding, it followed the path of traditional Judaism, maintaining close ties with the Great Synagogue in London. It grew steadily, various schisms notwithstanding. From 1825 to 1850, its membership increased fivefold to nearly 150, and during the same period its financial condition strengthened appreciably. An even more dynamic period of growth began in 1849 when it elected Rabbi Morris J. Raphall, then rabbi and preacher of England's Birmingham Hebrew Congregation, to serve as its "Lecturer and Preacher." Raphall's salary reputedly was "the most munificent salary received by any preacher in the country" – an investment that handsomely paid off. As America's first "glamour rabbi," he attracted large numbers of new members to the congregation and won B'nai Jeshurun a position of high regard both in the Jewish and the non-Jewish communities. This position was enhanced in 1851 when the congregation dedicated its magnificent new edifice, the Greene Street Synagogue.[44]

As so often the case, the new situation at B'nai Jeshurun created pressures for ritual reform. Decorum became the watchword as trustees worried more and more about the image projected by the congregation to the world at large. In 1851 and again in 1856 the interests of decorum ("that high standing of respectability which the world has a right to expect and which should correspond with this noble edifice") motivated changes in the distribution of synagogue honors, and in the method of announcing synagogue offerings.[45] Subsequent changes affected the saying of the priestly blessing, henceforward to be repeated "without singing and chanting," and of the Mourner's Kaddish, which mourners were instructed to recite "in unison with the Reader." The institution of a choir, and the introduction of special attire for the cantor and rabbi underlined B'nai Jeshurun's transformation into a showpiece synagogue with a performance-oriented ritual: a move that the congregation's new membership, new building, and new community status had made inevitable.[46]

Once begun, the pressure for reform at B'nai Jeshurun did not so easily abate. The needs and desires of members, coupled with contemporary trends favoring liberalization in synagogues and churches, motivated board members to initiate discussion of seating changes (abolition of the gallery and mixed pews) as early as 1862. At the rabbi's urging, they were not followed up. In 1868, following the death of Rabbi Raphall, the trustees formed a joint committee on ritual, charged with investigating a wide range of possible "improvements" to the synagogue service, alterations in the "internal arrangement of the Synagogue," being only one of them. As a first step, the reader's desk was moved from its traditional place at the center of the synagogue to the front, a move that three years earlier had been voted down. In 1869, the board introduced a confirmation ceremony. Some sixty-three other changes also came up for consideration that year: Most dealt with abolition of liturgical poems (*piyyutim*); a few went further, suggesting such things as doing away with the priestly blessing and ending the traditional calling up of seven men to the Torah. After consultation with their new rabbi, Dr. Henry Vidaver, and with Rabbi Jonas Bondi, editor of the *Hebrew Leader*, both of whom evaluated the proposed changes from the perspective of Jewish law, many of these changes, though not the most radical ones, were put into effect.[47]

In November 1871, the congregation took another step along the road to reform. It voted fifty to thirty-one to include women in the choir. Although sanctioned by Rabbi Vidaver, and widely practiced elsewhere, this move by one of America's oldest and most distinguished congregations generated considerable controversy. In spite of Rabbi Vidaver's insistence that Jewish law had not been breached, everyone realized that a mixed choir involved a more substantial departure from Jewish tradition than had previously been allowed. The choir was subsequently abandoned, "as it was found impracticable without an organ," but further steps in the direction of reform seemed inevitable.[48] Nobody should have been surprised when, on November 8, 1874, four months after Rabbi Vidaver had left the congregation for a more lucrative position in San Francisco, B'nai Jeshurun's members met to consider "the propriety of altering the present seats into Pews and also to add an Organ to the Choir."[49]

In reviewing the many changes that took place during this trying period in B'nai Jeshurun's history, Rabbi Israel Goldstein stressed the uncertainty of the congregation, the inner struggle between competing values that pulled members simultaneously in two directions, toward tradition and toward change: "The Congregation's decisions were made and unmade, amidst turbulent sentiment. Many of the members threatened to resign if the changes were not introduced. Others threatened to resign if the changes were introduced. Questions were repeatedly resubmitted and reconsidered, and the sentiment shifted as each faction in turn gained ascendancy."[50]

Even those most favoring change in congregational ritual aimed to stay within the bounds of "our established [Jewish] laws." They wanted the bountiful benefits that they thought reform would bring without sacrificing the comforting legitimacy that they knew tradition provided. Ideally, they somehow sought to be both Orthodox and modern at the same time, enjoying the benefits of both positions, and satisfying everyone.[51]

Although all members of B'nai Jeshurun may have prayed for this Utopia, younger and newer members nevertheless spearheaded the movement for change. One wishes that available evidence on this point were more substantial. Still, of the identifiable members who signed the petition calling for a special congregational meeting to consider instituting family pews and an organ, all five were members of ten years' standing or less (two additional signers cannot be identified). The fact that Joseph Aden, a member of B'nai Jeshurun, laid special stress on his being sixty-two years old when he declared himself in favor of the proposed changes – as if most reformers were far younger – offers additional corroborative evidence.[52]

Reforms in the 1870s all over the American Jewish community stemmed, at least in part, from fears that the young, American-born children of Central European immigrants were being lost to Judaism. Many Jews worried for their faith's future survival. Some foresaw a merger with Unitarianism. Young William Rosenblatt, in an article entitled "The Jews: What They Are Coming To" printed in the widely read *Galaxy*, openly predicted impending doom: "Of that ancient people only the history of their perils and their sufferings will remain."[53] Although various Jews resigned themselves to this "inevitable" fate, others looked to reforms that promised to win the young people back. When, as at B'nai Jeshurun, younger members took upon themselves the initiative to bring about change, their elders usually agreed to support them. They feared, as B'nai Jeshurun's president, Moses Strasburger, candidly admitted, that without changes the congregation would "become disbanded."[54]

Support for reform was by no means unanimous at B'nai Jeshurun: At the tumultuous special meeting called to discuss the question, fifty five members voted for seating changes and installation of an organ, thirty members remained opposed. The majority viewed the changes they sanctioned as permissible and necessary next steps in the long process of internal transformation that had been going on for a quarter of a century. They believed that by modernizing B'nai Jeshurun – bringing it into harmony "with the requirements of modern taste and culture" – they were saving it for the next generation.[55] The minority, which had grown increasingly restive as the pace of reform quickened, viewed the same changes as confirming evidence of the congregation's final abandonment of Jewish law and tradition. They wondered aloud if the reforms would have been promulgated had an "orthodox lecturer" stood at the congregation's helm.[56]

Opponents of change at B'nai Jeshurun rallied around Israel J. Salomon, son of Jonas Salomon, one of B'nai Jeshurun's earliest members

(1827) and its second sexton. Back in 1844, when he was but twenty-five years old, Israel Salomon had helped lead the young, anti-establishment forces, who successfully fought the reigning leadership oligarchy at B'nai Jeshurun in a battle over voting rights that ended with the formation of Congregation Shaarey Tefilah – a rare case of leaders withdrawing from a synagogue leaving dissidents behind.[57] Salomon subsequently rose to become president (*parnass*) of B'nai Jeshurun for an unprecented eight-year term (1860–1868). The years following, however, saw him grow increasingly disenchanted, both with his congregation's reforms, especially its mixed choir, and with its leadership.[58] The decision to introduce mixed seating, accompanied as it was by an acrimonious debate, induced him to pursue his claims in court. He had gone that route in an earlier day, when he cloaked himself in the mantle of democracy and youth. He now returned to the fray, less concerned about democracy, but clad instead in the shining armor of a warrior for Orthodoxy.

The case of *Israel J. Solomon* [sic] v. *The Congregation B'nai Jeshurun, and others*[59] focused widespread attention on the mixed seating issue (Salomon did not challenge the congregation's decision to install an organ),[60] and followed a pattern that became characteristic of most court cases of this sort.[61] On the surface, the case dealt with extraneous issues: "the rights and franchises of a pew owner" and the "powers of trustees of a religious corporation to manage the temporal affairs of the church." Affidavits and testimony nevertheless dealt largely with the institution of mixed seating, and offered contradictory testimony regarding its legitimacy. The decision of the judge returned to the original legal questions and added to them principles related to state intervention in church affairs.

In his complaint, Israel Salomon charged that the decision of the congregation in favor of "a mingling of the sexes during divine worship" – a practice that, perhaps in a bid for support from purity crusaders, he termed "immodest" and "unchaste" – unlawfully deprived him of seats that he had purchased, and also violated the original constitution of the synagogue that mandated worship "according to the rites, customs and usages of the German and Polish Jews." He backed up his case with affidavits from Jerucham Kantrowitz, an Orthodox Jewish New York bookseller (whose claim to be "an ordained minister of the Jewish persuasion" was later challenged in court); Rabbi Abraham J. Ash, rabbi of the Beth Hamedrash Hagodol; Rev. Dr. Henry W. Schneeberger, minister of Congregation Poel Zedek; Rev. Samuel M. Isaacs, minister of Congregation Shaarey Tefilah; and various others, including one signed by sixty New York Jews. All attested to the fact that what Isaacs termed "the promiscuous seating of sexes during divine worship" violated German-Polish practice.

The congregation, for its part, claimed that the changes voted on were legal, well within the power of the trustees to implement, and not harmful to the plaintiff's rights. It then observed that many previous changes had been made in the congregation's ritual over the years without being challenged, and that "throughout the civilized world" it had become customary "for the male and female members to sit together during worship"; such actions were thus neither unprecedented nor immoral. As further evidence, it offered testimony from Rabbi Gustav Gottheil of Temple Emanu-El, who told the court that the "unified appearance of a household before God tends to enhance devotion," and similar testimonials from Rabbi David Einhorn of Temple Beth El, Rabbi Henry Vidaver, formerly of B'nai Jeshurun, and Rabbi Isaac Mayer Wise, who specifically said that family seating "is not antagonistic to the teachings of the Holy Scripture and the Talmud." Various laymen swore in addition that they supported family seating, and that they had heard Salomon say that his real intention was to destroy the congregation.

Judge Larremore decided against Salomon and for the congregation. On the question of pew rights, he determined that purchase only implied acquisition of an easement subject to B'nai Jeshurun's rules and regulations – and these, of course, could be changed. As to whether mixed seating violated "a cardinal principle of the faith professed by this society," Larremore, noting "the opposing affidavits," withheld judgment. Like most other American judges put in the difficult position of ruling on questions of ecclesiastical law, he demurred, leaving the matter instead "where it properly belongs, to the judicature of the church." That did not necessarily mean the full church membership, for Larremore ruled, on the basis of a recent state law, that "the trustees of the Society B'nai Jeshurun had a legal right to make the alterations in questions [on their own], without any action on the part of said society."[62] But since the congregation *had* sanctioned the change at a general meeting, the decision certainly had "binding and conclusive" force, and Salomon's request for an injunction was accordingly denied. After a temporary stay of the case was vacated on appeal, Salomon succumbed to the inevitable and discontinued his action.[63]

Larremore's decision evoked various responses. Some saw it as a victory for congregational autonomy and church–state separation. America, unlike Europe, would not allow an orthodox minority to use the law to enforce its will on the majority. Others, especially non-Jews, rejoiced over "the good done to Judaism" by the judge's ruling, seeing it as a victory for the forces of "modernity" that were demanding that Judaism improve its treatment of women. *The Jewish Messenger* responded in this case that "separation of the sexes in divine services is not . . . opposed to modern civilization" and "not associated with a sentiment of disrespect for woman [*sic*]," but to no avail. Still others lamented that an internal Jewish matter had been brought to a secular court in the first place: "The dispute should have been settled within the synagogue, by mutual concession and an amicable adjustment."[64]

At B'nai Jeshurun, meanwhile, the judge's decision resulted in the resignation of over thirty members – those who had from the beginning been opposed to the reforms. New members joined, however, and in 1877 the congregation hired a new rabbi: Henry Jacobs. Although changes continued during the first years of his tenure, mostly designed to improve decorum and abbreviate the service, he gradually steered the congregation toward the emerging middle road in American Judaism. By the twentieth century, B'nai Jeshurun was firmly entrenched in the Conservative camp.[65]

The B'nai Jeshurun experience illustrates the major issues raised by mixed seating controversies from the late nineteenth century onward. For supporters, the proposed seating change translated into terms like family togetherness, women's equality, conformity to local norms, a modern, progressive image, and saving the youth – values that most Jews viewed positively. For opponents, the same change implied abandonment of tradition, violation of Jewish law, assimilation, Christianization, and promiscuity – consequences that most Jews viewed with horror. Pulled simultaneously in two directions that both seemed right – directions that reflected opposing views on modernity – many of those seeking compromise in the middle took solace in assurances from their leaders that Judaism and mixed seating were fully compatible. Rabbinic arguments and the adoption of mixed seating in synagogue after synagogue made the case for the "Jewishness" of the practice that much more compelling. Feeling reassured that they could reconcile modernity and tradition and still have mixed seating, majorities at congregations like B'nai Jeshurun opted for change. Minorities opposed to the change, meanwhile, found in separate seating a visible and defensible issue around which they could rally. Separate seating imparted just that sense of detached protest against modernity that, supporters felt, Judaism needed to express in order to survive. By exhibiting their reverence for tradition through the basic spatial arrangement of the synagogue, traditionalists made their point of disagreement with innovators plain for all to see. In time, "separate seating" and "mixed seating" became shorthand statements, visible expressions of differences on a host of more fundamental issues that lay beneath the surface.

IV

Mixed seating generally ceased to be a controversial issue in Reform Judaism after the 1870s. By 1890, Isaac Mayer Wise, who was in a position to know, wrote that "today *no* synagogue is built in this country without family pews."[66] Applied to Reform temples, the statement seems to be correct. Orthodox synagogues, of course, continued to separate men and women, and this remained true in the new Orthodox "showpiece" congregations erected, particularly in New York, in the wake of large-scale East European Jewish immigration.[67] In 1895, a proposal for mixed seating did agitate the nation's leading Sephardic Synagogue, Shearith Israel, but the trustees unanimously voted it down. They resolved that in the new synagogue, then under construction, seating would remain, "men in the auditorium and women in the galleries as in the present synagogue." Ninety-six women submitted a resolution supporting the maintenance of this "time-honored custom."[68]

Over the next two decades, debates over mixed seating took place at a good many other modern Orthodox synagogues, especially those that sought to cater to young people. But for the most part – Congregation Mount Sinai of Central Harlem, founded in 1904, being a noteworthy exception – separate seating held. Modernity in these congregations came to mean decorum, use of the English language, and weekly sermons. Proposed seating reforms, by their nature far more divisive, were effectively tabled.[69]

Between the two world wars, the issue of mixed seating arose again, this time in the rapidly growing Conservative Movement. Living in what Marshall Sklare has identified as "areas of third settlement" – younger, more aware of surrounding non-Jewish and Reform Jewish practices, and more worried about the Jewishness of their children – Conservative Jews sought a form of worship that would be "traditional and at the same time modern." Gallery seating for women was not what they had in mind. It violated the American norm of family seating. It ran counter to modern views on the position of women. And it proved dysfunctional to synagogue life, since in America, Jewish women played an increasingly important part in all religious activities, and felt discriminated against by the gallery. Seating reforms thus ranked high on the Conservative Jewish agenda.[70]

At the synagogue of the Conservative Movement's Jewish Theological Seminary, Solomon Schechter, its president, had already in the first decade of the twentieth century established the principle of "separation" rather than "invisibility" (i.e., a physical barrier). This conformed both to his understanding of Jewish law, and to the practice "in orthodox synagogues . . . in England." Somewhat later, his successor, Cyrus Adler, claimed that the seminary's practice of "separate but equal" seating did "not afford a precedent for the general synagogue because the Seminary synagogue was really built for Seminary students and at the time it was planned, it was not supposed that women would attend the services there." It appears, however, that he was mistaken.[71]

In 1921, the question of "whether family pews would be a departure from traditional Judaism" came before the Rabbinical Assembly's [Conservative Jewish] Committee on the Interpretation of Jewish Law. Professor Louis Ginzberg, chairman of the committee, responded that gallery seating was unnecessary, but that "the separation of the sexes is a Jewish custom well established for about 2000 years, and must not be taken lightly."[72] The "separate but equal" seating pattern that Ginzberg and Schechter (like David Einhorn) advocated failed to satisfy proponents of family togetherness in worship, and most Conservative synagogues introduced mixed seating instead, in some cases preserving sexually segregated areas in the synagogue for those who wanted them ("compromise seating").[73] In 1947, Ginzberg himself told a congregation in Baltimore that if "continued separation of family units during services presents a great danger to its spiritual welfare, the minority ought to yield to the spiritual need of the majority."[74] Privately he admitted that "when you live long enough in America you realize that the status of womanhood had changed so much that separating women from men has become obsolete."[75] By 1955, according to Marshall Sklare, mixed seating featured in "the overwhelming majority of Conservative synagogues," and served "as the most commonly accepted yardstick for differentiating Conservatism from Orthodoxy."[76]

Although recognized Orthodox leaders did indeed tout mixed seating as the "great divide" – the action that put a congregation beyond the pale of Orthodox tradition – many members of Orthodox congregations apparently disagreed. Congregations that both professed to be Orthodox and employed rabbis who graduated from Orthodox rabbinical seminaries still introduced family pews, defending them in one case, on the basis of the "spirit, traditions and procedure of Orthodox Judaism," and in another on the pragmatic grounds that they would "be inviting to the younger members."[77] One source claims that in 1961 there existed "perhaps 250 Orthodox synagogues where family seating is practiced."[78] A different estimate, from 1954, holds that "90% of the graduates of the Chicago Hebrew Theological Institution, which is Orthodox, and 50% of the graduates of the Yeshiva, the Orthodox institution in New York, have positions where family seating or optional family seating prevails." How accurate either estimate was remains unclear, but at least according to one (perhaps biased) observer family seating had "definitely become a form and tradition of Orthodox Israelites adopted and practiced by an overwhelming number of Orthodox Synagogues." Certainly rabbis who served mixed-seating congregations continued to belong to the Orthodox Rabbinical Council of America without fear of expulsion.[79]

Synagogue practices notwithstanding, Yeshiva University continuously opposed mixed seating. It nominally revoked the ordination of its graduates if they continued to serve mixed-seating congregations after having been warned to leave them. The only temporary justification allowing a graduate to accept a mixed-seating position was if Yeshiva's then president, Bernard Revel, felt that "an able, diplomatic man" could bring the errant congregation "back to the fold."[80] Although in some cases this happened, and in others the rabbi resigned after failing, an apparently substantial but undetermined number of Yeshiva University graduates, torn between piety and prosperity, or influenced by American conditions, made peace with mixed seating. In a few cases, they later defended the practice's orthodoxy in court.

Court proceedings dealing with the mixed-seating problem were, as we know from the B'nai Jeshurun affair, nothing new. A series of cases in the 1950s,[81] however, had the effect of solidifying Orthodoxy's position on the issue, while undermining the comfortable arguments of those who insisted that mixed seating and Jewish tradition could be made compatible. Leading Orthodox spokesmen, in concert with the Union of Orthodox Jewish Congregations of America and the Rabbinical Council of America, so vigorously insisted that mixed seating violated *halachah*, that those who supported the opposite position realized that they were clinging to a view that no institutionalized brand of Orthodoxy would agree to legitimate.

Three cases received particular attention. The first involved Congregation Adath Israel in Cincinnati. Founded by Polish Jews in 1853, and for many years the leading non–Reform synagogue in the city, Adath Israel harbored a range of traditional Jews and had for many years walked a tightrope between the Conservative and Orthodox movements. The synagogue's constitution proclaimed adherence to the "forms and traditions of Orthodox Israelites."[82] At the same time, the synagogue belonged to the Conservative, United Synagogues of America. Fishel J. Goldfeder, Adath Israel's rabbi, boasted both an Orthodox and a Conservative training. Members sought to appeal to those with Orthodox leanings and Conservative leanings at one and the same time.

Separate seating of some form or other had been the rule at Adath Israel since its inception. At least since 1896, "separate but equal" seating had been deemed sufficient: "Men sit on one side and the women sit on

Congregation Adath Israel after the introduction of mixed seating.
Courtesy of Congregation Adath Israel, Cincinnati.

the other side of the first floor of the Synagogue without any curtain or
any partition between them."[83] In 1923, apparently in reaction to liberalization moves in many Conservative synagogues, members voted an
amendment to their constitution: "that no family pews be established
nor may men remove their hats during services; that no organ be used
during services; that no female choir be permitted so long as ten (10)
members in good standing object thereto."[84]

Beginning in 1952, however, the congregation, which had been expanding rapidly, began to be agitated by demands for optional family
seating, many of them from younger members. The board of trustees,
with the blessing of Rabbi Goldfeder, voted 17–9 in favor of optional
family seating on December 30, 1953, and a congregational meeting
subsequently ratified the action by a vote of 289–100.[85]

Opponents claimed that mixed seating violated the synagogue's constitution. They pointed out that more than the necessary ten members
objected to family seating, and besides, they insisted that family seating
contravened the "forms and traditions of Orthodox Israelites." They,
therefore, moved to block the action, and by mutual agreement finally

submitted their dispute to a private court. A three-judge panel ("each side to the controversy shall select one Judge of its own choosing and the third Judge shall be selected by agreement of the counsel for both sides") was given binding authority to decide the case.[86]

The court proceedings brought to the fore the deep divisions within Adath Israel that had long simmered beneath the surface. As the judges noted in their decision, "Some witnesses contended that the . . . Synagogue is strictly Orthodox; some said that it is liberal Orthodox, and others believed that it is a Conservative synagogue."[87] Supporters of mixed seating argued, on the one hand, that the congregation was Conservative, since it lacked a formal *mechitsah* (partition), employed a microphone, and confirmed women, and on the other hand, that mixed seating accorded "with the forms and traditions of Orthodox Israelites," as defined by their rabbi. By contrast, opponents of mixed seating argued that the congregation was Orthodox, notwithstanding earlier reforms, and that mixed seating would cause Adath Israel "to lose its status as a proper place of worship."[88] Testimony from leading figures in Orthodox and Conservative Judaism put forth diverging views on mixed seating's *halachic* status, and on the meaning of "Orthodoxy" to different kinds of Jews.

In their decision, Judge Chase M. Davies and Rabbi Joseph P. Sternstein (the third judge, Mr. Sol Goodman, dissented) refused to consider these *halachic* issues at all. Having been instructed to "resolve the controversy involved in the synagogue on a legal basis," they first ruled the 1923 amendment outlawing family pews "not a valid and presently effective amendment to the Constitution and By-Laws of the congregation," since improper procedures had accompanied its adoption. On the more important question of whether family seating violated Orthodox "forms and traditions," the judges, on the basis of American precedents, decided that the issue

> presents a religious question over which a Court of law, and this private Court, which has been instructed to follow legal principles, has no right, power, or jurisdiction. To hold otherwise would be an assumption by this private Court of monitorship of the religious faith of the members of the congregation, since under federal and state Constitutions, there can be no disturbance of or limitation to the power and right of the congregants to exercise that freedom of conscience which is the basis of our liberty.[89]

Given the fact that the board of trustees, the majority of the members and the rabbi all supported "optional family seating," the judges ruled the practice valid. They took pains to point out, however, that as an opinion of a private court, theirs "should not be considered, or cited, as authority in any other case."[90]

In closing, the judges expressed the hope that their decision would "result in a harmonious and unified worship of God by all members of the congregation."[91] That, however, did not come about. Instead, many of the members who had always considered Adath Israel to be Orthodox and opposed mixed seating, withdrew and joined other synagogues. Those who remained at Adath Israel became more closely aligned with the Conservative Movement and referred to themselves increasingly as Conservative Jews. The seating controversy thus unwittingly served as a vehicle for clarifying both religious identity and ideology. By taking a stand on one issue, people expressed their views on a host of other issues as well.

Davis v. Scher,[92] the second mixed-seating case, concerned Congregation Beth Tefilas Moses, an avowedly Orthodox Jewish congregation in Mt. Clemens, Michigan, which voted to introduce family seating into its sanctuary in 1955. Baruch Litvin, a businessman who belonged to the congregation and was cordially disliked by many of its members, took up the battle against this decision,[93] basing himself on an established American legal principle: "A majority of a church congregation may not institute a practice within the church fundamentally opposed to the doctrine to which the church property is dedicated, as against a minority of the congregation who adhere to the established doctrine and practice."[94] Litvin's attorneys, supported by the Union of Orthodox Jewish Congregations, introduced a great deal of evidence to support the claim that mixed seating was "clearly violative of the established Orthodox Jewish law and practice" and argued that if mixed seating were introduced, the Orthodox minority would have to worship elsewhere, "deprived of the right of the use of their property . . . by the majority group contrary to law." The congregation, by contrast, argued that the dispute involved only "doctrinal and ecclesiastical matters," not property rights, and that "it would be inconsistent with complete religious liberty for the court to assume . . . jurisdiction."[95] Despite court urging, the congregation's lawyers refused to cross-examine witnesses or to introduce any testimony of their own in defense of mixed seating, for fear that this would weaken their argument. They did not believe that the secular courtroom was the proper forum for Jewish doctrinal debates.

Lower courts sided with the congregation and refused to become involved, arguing that Congregation Beth Tefilas Moses' majority voice had the power to rule. The Michigan Supreme Court, however, unanimously reversed this decision and accepted the minority's claims. It stressed that "because of defendants' calculated risk of not offering proofs, no dispute exists as to the teaching of Orthodox Judaism as to mixed seating." By the laws governing implied trusts, therefore, the congregation's majority was denied the power to carry property dedicated for use by Orthodox Jews "to the support of a new and conflicting doctrine." "A change of views on religious subjects," the court ruled, did not require those who still held to older views to surrender property originally conveyed to them.[96]

The third case, *Katz v. Singerman*,[97] had much that was seemingly in common with *Davis v. Scher*. Congregation Chevra Thilim of New Orleans voted in 1957 to introduce family pews, and a minority, led by Harry Katz, went to court to thwart the move. Like Baruch Litvin, Katz argued for minority rights, particularly since the Chevra Thilim charter explicitly included "the worship of God according to the orthodox Polish Jewish ritual" as one of its "objects and purposes," and the congregation had accepted the donation of a building upon the stipulation that it "shall only be used as a place of Jewish worship according to the strict ancient and orthodox forms and ceremonies."[98] The issue to be determined by the court was "whether the practice of mixed or family seating in Chevra Thilim Synagogue is contrary to and inconsistent with the 'orthodox Polish Jewish Ritual' and 'Jewish worship according to the strict ancient and orthodox forms and ceremonies,' and therefore in violation of the trust and donation . . . and also the Charter of the Congregation."[99]

Where *Katz v. Singerman* differed was in the strategy employed by defendants. They introduced considerable testimony in support of mixed seating, including evidence supplied by Rabbi Jacob Agus, ordained at Yeshiva University, as well as twenty-seven affidavits testifying that mixed seating "is not contrary to Orthodox Jewish forms and ceremonies."[100] Seventy-five affidavits, and a host of formidable witnesses from across the Orthodox spectrum opposed this testimony, offering abundant evidence in support of separate seating. The court was left to decide who understood Jewish law better.

Lower courts, impressed by the plaintiff's legal display and by the strong pro–Orthodox language employed in the original charter, decided in Katz's favor. The Supreme Court of Louisiana, however, in a decision similar to that rendered in the Adath Israel affair, decided differently. Given the "well-settled rule of law that courts will not interfere with the ecclesiastical questions involving differences of opinion as to religious conduct,"[101] and the famous Supreme Court decision in *Watson v. Jones* (1872), which held that "[i]n such cases where there is a schism which leads to a separation into distinct and conflicting bodies, the rights of such bodies to the use of the property must be determined by the ordinary principles which govern voluntary associations,"[102] the court decided that

Chevra Thilim's board of directors alone had the "authority to ascertain and interpret the meaning of 'orthodox Polish Jewish Ritual.' " The fact that Chevra Thilim's rabbi agreed with the board and favored mixed seating held "great weight" with the court, which also cited precedents based on church–state separation and the principle that "churches must in their very nature 'grow with society.' "[103] "This case differs from the case of *Davis v. Scher*," the judges insisted, "for there the evidence was all on one side." Here, with two sides offering conflicting testimony as to what the phrase "orthodox forms and ceremonies" means, the court, following abundant precedent, left the matter for the congregation to decide.[104]

From the point of view of law, *Katz v. Singerman* dealt a severe blow to Orthodoxy, since it made it highly difficult for an Orthodox minority to overturn in court any majority decision, even one found unacceptable in terms of *halacha*. From another point of view, however, the case, like *Davis v. Scher* and the Adath Israel case, actually strengthened Orthodoxy, for it gave publicity to the movement's views and established in the popular mind the fact that "true" Orthodoxy and separate seating went hand in hand. Orthodox Jewish publications denominated those who defended the orthodoxy of mixed seating as "Conservative Jews," and ridiculed "mixed-seating Orthodoxy" as a contradiction in terms.[105] Those who did define modern Orthodox in terms of mixed seating found themselves increasingly isolated. In some cases, congregations that once considered themselves modern Orthodox moved, after adopting mixed seating, firmly into the ranks of the Conservative Movement.[106] In other cases, particularly in congregations served by rabbis from Hebrew Theological College in Chicago, modern Orthodox congregations began to worship under the label of traditional Judaism.[107]

Exceptions notwithstanding, mixed seating, even more than when Marshall Sklare first made the observation, symbolized by the third quarter of the twentieth century that which differentiated Orthodoxy from Jewry's other branches.[108] The symbol that had first signified family togetherness and later came to represent women's equality and religious modernity, had finally evolved into a denominational boundary. Around it American Jews defined where they stood religiously and what values they held most dear.[109]

NOTES

I am grateful to Rochelle Elstein, Barry Feldman, Robert Shapiro, and Barbara E. Ullman for bringing valuable materials to my attention; to Professors Benny Kraut, Jacob R. Marcus, Michael A. Meyer, Jeffrey S.

Gurock, Robert Handy, Chava Weissler, Jack Wertheimer, and Lance J. Sussman, for commenting on earlier drafts of this chapter; and to the Memorial Foundation for Jewish Culture for its ongoing support of my work.

1   John M. Neale, *The History of Pews*, 2d ed. (Cambridge, England, 1842), p. 3.

2   The best available materials on synagogue seating have been prepared by parties in legal disputes; see Baruch Litvin, ed., *The Sanctity of the Synagogue* (New York, 1959); and the special issue of *Conservative Judaism*, 11 (Fall, 1956), devoted to the Adath Israel affair.

3   For two responsa on this issue, see Bernhard Felsenthal, "Muss Man Sich Beim Beten Nach Osten Wenden?" *Sinai*, 6 (May, 1861), pp. 110–111; and Shaul Yedidyah Shochet, *Tiferet Yedidya*, vol. 2 (St. Louis, 1920), pp. 26–32. See also Franz Landsberger, "The Sacred Direction in Synagogue and Church," *Hebrew Union College Annual*, 28 (1957), pp. 181–203.

4   See Jacob Agus, "Mixed Pews in Jewish Tradition," *Conservative Judaism*, 11 (Fall, 1956), pp. 35–36; and Rachel Wischnitzer, *Synagogue Architecture in the United States* (Philadelphia, 1955), p. 60.

5   For various perspectives, see Leon A. Jick, *The Americanization of the Synagogue 1820–1870* (Hanover, N.H., 1976); Moshe Davis, *The Emergence of Conservative Judaism* (Philadelphia, 1965); Nathan Glazer, *American Judaism*, 2d ed. (Chicago, 1972); and Allan Tarshish, "The Rise of American Judaism" (Ph.D. diss., Hebrew Union College, 1938).

6   Ismar Elbogen, *Hatefilah Beyisrael* (Tel Aviv, 1972), pp. 350–352; Andrew Seager, "The Architecture of the Dura and Sardis Synagogues," in *The Synagogue*, ed. Joseph Gutmann (New York, 1975), pp.156–158, 178 nn. 35–36; Salo W. Baron, *The Jewish Community*, vol. 2 (Philadelphia, 1945), p. 140; Samuel Kraus, *Korot Bate Hatefilah Beyisrael* (New York: Histadrut Ivrit, 1955), pp. 239–240; *Encyclopedia Judaica*, 11, pp. 134–135; Shaye J. D. Cohen, "Women in the Synagogues of Antiquity," *Conservative Judaism*, 34 (November-December, 1980), pp. 23–29; J. Charles Cox, *Bench-Ends in English Churches* (London, n.d.), pp. 17–27.

7   David Philipson, *The Reform Movement in Judaism* (New York, 1931), p. 245. A similar seating arrangement may have been in effect as early as 1815 in the Reform congregation that met at the home of Jacob Herz-Beer in Berlin. See Nahum N. Glatzer, "On an Unpublished Letter of Isaak Markus Jost," *Leo Baeck Institute Year Book*, 22 (1977), opposite p. 132. I owe this reference to Professor Michael A. Meyer.

8   Jacob Sonderling, "Five Gates – Casual Notes for an Autobiography," *American Jewish Archives*, 16 (November 1964), p. 109. On Budge, see Cyrus Adler, *Jacob H. Schiff: His Life and Letters*, vol. 1 (Garden City, N.J., 1929), pp. 7–8. Rebekah Kohut reports in 1929 that "everywhere in Europe, except in the Reform Temples of Paris and London, men and women still worship separately." *As I Know Them* (New York, 1929), p. 119.

9   *American Israelite*, 37 (27 November 1890), p. 4.

388 *Jonathan D. Sarna*

10 John Demos, "Images of the American Family, Then and Now," in *Changing Images of the Family*, ed. Virginia Tufte and Barbara Myerhoff (New Haven, 1979), p. 48; Cox, *Bench-Ends*, pp. 17–19; Robert J. Dinkin, "Seating the Meeting House in Early Massachusetts," *New England Quarterly*, 43 (1970), pp. 450–464; Peter Benes and Philip D. Zimmerman, *New England Meeting House and Church, 1630–1850* (Boston, 1979), pp. 55–56; Wischnitzer, *Synagogue Architecture*, 12.

11 Patricia J. Tracy, *Jonathan Edwards, Pastor* (New York, 1980), p. 128. For a similar contemporary argument, see Morris Max, "Mixed Pews," *Conservative Judaism*, 11 (Fall 1956), p. 70.

12 Dinkin, "Seating the Meeting House," p. 456; Tracy, *Jonathan Edwards, Pastor*, p. 244 n. 9.

13 Alan Graebner, *Uncertain Saints* (Westport, Conn., 1975), p. 17; "Pews," *The American Quarterly Church Review*, 13 (July 1860), pp. 288–289. See Jacob Agus's discussion of the 1885 mixed-seating controversy in Grace Methodist Church of Dayton, Ohio, in Agus, "Mixed Pews in Jewish Tradition," p. 41.

14 Demos, "Images of the American Family," pp. 43–60, esp. p. 49; Carl N. Degler, *At Odds: Women and the Family in America from the Revolution to the Present* (Oxford, 1980), p. 9; and Carl N. Degler, "Women and the Family," in *The Past Before Us*, ed. Michael Kammen (Ithaca, 1980), esp. p. 317.

15 Hyman B. Grinstein, *The Rise of the Jewish Community of New York* (Philadelphia, 1945), pp. 317–318; see Kenneth L. Ames, "Ideologies in Stone: Meanings in Victorian Gravestones," *Journal of Popular Culture*, 14 (1981), pp. 641–656.

16 James G. Heller, *Isaac M. Wise: His Life, Work and Thought* (New York, 1965), p. 214.

17 Heller, *Wise*, pp. 124–183; Naphtali J. Rubinger, "Dismissal in Albany," *American Jewish Archives*, 24 (November 1972), pp. 161–162.

18 Isaac M. Wise, *Reminiscences* (1901; 2d ed., New York, 1945), pp. 116–117.

19 Wise, *Reminiscences*, p. 172.

20 Rubinger, "Dismissal in Albany," pp. 160–183; Heller, *Wise*, pp. 184–234. On the conversion of churches into synagogues, a phenomenon little known in Europe, see Wischnitzer, *Synagogue Architecture*, pp. 61–62. Apparently, Wise did not introduce mixed pews immediately upon his arrival in Cincinnati. They only came to Bene Yeshurun in 1866 when the congregation moved into the Plum Street temple. See James Heller, *As Yesterday When It Is Past* (Cincinnati, 1942), p. 114.

21 Wise, *Reminiscences*, p. 212.

22 *Occident*, 9 (December, 1851), p. 477; *Asmonean*, 10 October 1851, p. 226; 17 October 1851, p. 240; see 21 November 1851, p. 53; 19 December 1851, p. 83.

23 *American Israelite*, 15 November 1872, p. 8; 27 November 1890, p. 4. Naphtali J. Rubinger, "Albany Jewry of the Nineteenth Century: Historic Roots and Communal Evolution" (Ph.D. diss., Yeshiva University, 1970),

p. 120, notes other occasions when Wise retrospectively exaggerated the extent of the opposition against him. Such efforts aimed at creating a personal "hero myth" are common; see Frank J. Sulloway, *Freud, Biologist of the Mind* (New York, 1979), pp. 445–495; Joseph Campbell, *The Hero With A Thousand Faces* (Princeton, 1968).

24 Myer Stern, *The Rise and Progress of Reform Judaism* (New York, 1895), p. 14; *New Era*, 4 (1874), p. 126; Grinstein, *Jewish Community of New York*, p. 267; see also Leopold Mayer's description of Emanu-El in 1850, in Morris U. Schappes, *A Documentary History of the Jews in the United States, 1654–1875* (New York, 1971), p. 308.

25 Philipson, *Reform Movement*, pp. 183–184, 219–220; see Kaufmann Kohler, *Jewish Theology* (New York, 1918), pp. 472–473.

26 See *Sinai*, 6 (August 1861), pp. 205–207. For a sociological perspective on the German debate in terms of "identity formation and boundary maintenance," see David Ellenson, "The Role of Reform in selected German-Jewish Orthodox Responsa: A Sociological Analysis," *Hebrew Union College Annual*, 53 (1982), pp. 357–380.

27 Alexander Hamilton, *Itinerarium*, quoted in David and Tamar De Sola Pool, *An Old Faith in the New World* (New York, 1955), p. 453; *Religious Intelligencer*, 1 (1817), p. 556; *Western Monthly Review*, 2 (January 1829), p. 440; *New York Herald*, 22 September 1836. For other negative notices, see Joseph S. C. F. Frey, *The Converted Jew* (Boston, 1815), p. 15; *The Jew at Home and Abroad* (Philadelphia, 1845), p. 65; Joseph L. Blau and Salo W. Baron, *The Jews of the United States, 1790–1840: A Documentary History*, vol. 3 (New York, 1963), pp. 677–680; and Lydia M. Child, *The History of the Condition of Women in Various Ages and Nations*, vol. 1 (Boston, 1835), p. 20. Cf. I. J. Benjamin's Jewish critique (1859) in his *Three Years in America*, vol. 1, transl. Charles Reznikoff (Philadelphia, 1956), pp. 85–89; and see more broadly Joan Jacobs Brumberg, *Mission for Life* (New York, 1984), pp. 79–106.

28 *New York Herald*, 28 September 1836; *Sunday Times and Noah's Weekly Messenger* (New York), 7 July 1850, 26 January 1851; James Parton, *Topics of the Times* (Boston, 1871), pp. 299, 308. The leading Jewish apologia, imported from England, was Grace Aguilar, *The Women of Israel*, 2 vols. (New York, 1851). For a modern analogue, see Lucy Davidowicz, *The Jewish Presence* (New York, 1978), pp. 46–57.

29 Louise Abbie Mayo, "The Ambivalent Image: The Perception of the Jew in Nineteenth Century America" (Ph.D. diss., City University of New York, 1977), pp. 93–104.

30 Philipson, *Reform Movement*, p. 220.

31 *Sinai*, 3 (1858), p. 824; Isaac M. Fein, *The Making of an American Jewish Community* (Philadelphia, 1971), p. 113.

32 *Sinai*, 3 (1858), pp. 818–824; 6 (1861), pp. 205–207.

33 Bernhard Felsenthal, *The Beginnings of the Chicago Sinai Congregation* (Chicago, 1898), p. 23.

34   *Occident*, 18 (1860), p. 154; Fred Rosenbaum, *Architects of Reform* (Berkeley, 1980), p. 26.
35   *New Era*, 1 (February 1871), p. 193.
36   Jerome W. Grollman, "The Emergence of Reform Judaism in the United States" (Ord. thesis, Hebrew Union College, 1948), pp. 18, 43 passim; *A History of Congregation Beth El, Detroit, Mich., 1850–1900* (Detroit, 1900), pp. 26–28; Jonathan D. Sarna, "Innovation and Consolidation: Phases in the History of Temple Mishkan Israel," *Jews in New Haven*, vol. 3, ed. Barry E. Herman and Werner S. Hirsch (New Haven, 1981), p. 102; Edward N. Calisch, *The Light Burns On* (Richmond, 1941), p. 25; Frank J. Adler, *Roots in a Moving Stream* (Kansas City, 1972), p. 22; Isidor Blum, *The Jews of Baltimore*, 1910), p. 23; *New Era*, 5 (1875), p. 4; Solomon Breibart, "The Synagogue of Kahal Kadosh Beth Elohim, Charleston," *South Carolina Historical Magazine*, 80 (July 1979), p. 228 – all describe the adoption of mixed seating in other nineteenth-century American Reform congregations. For the situation at the more traditional congregation Sherith Israel of San Francisco in the 1870s, see Norton B. Stern, "An Orthodox Rabbi and a Reforming Congregation in Nineteenth Century San Francisco," *Western States Jewish Historical Quarterly*, 15 (April 1983), pp. 275–281.
37   Quoted in Grollman, *Emergence of Reform Judaism*, p. 89.
38   Wise, *Reminiscences*, p. 212.
39   *Occident*, 13 (1855), p. 417; 21 (1863), p. 345; 21 (1864), p. 500.
40   *Occident*, 21 (1863), p. 407. On Buttenwieser, see A. Z. Friedman, *Tub Taam*, 2d ed. (New York, 1904), introduction.
41   E.g., *American Israelite*, 13 December 1878, p. 4.
42   *Occident*, 19 (1861), pp. 87–88; Lloyd P. Gartner, *History of the Jews in Cleveland* (Cleveland, 1978), pp. 39–41. Peixotto nevertheless admitted to Leeser that "my private conviction[s] rather favor the mingling of both sexes in the synagogue." Peixotto to Leeser, 16 November 1859, microfilm 200, American Jewish Archives. I owe this reference to Prof. Lance Sussman.
43   *Occident*, 21 (1864), pp. 501–510.
44   Israel Goldstein, *A Century of Judaism in New York: B'nai Jeshurun, 1825–1925* (New York, 1930), pp. 51–113; see also Grinstein, *Jewish Community of New York*; Moshe Davis, "The Synagogue in American Judaism: A Study of Congregation B'nai Jeshurun, New York City," in *Two Generations in Perspective*, ed. Harry Schneiderman (New York, 1957), pp. 210–235, translated and revised in Moshe Davis, *Beit Yisrael Be-Amerikah* (Jerusalem, 1970), pp. 1–24. On Raphall, see Bertram W. Korn, *Eventful Years and Experiences* (Cincinnati, 1954), pp. 40–41.
45   Goldstein, *B'nai Jeshurun*, p. 126.
46   Ibid., pp. 126–129; see Jonathan D. Sarna, ed., *People Walk on Their Heads: Moses Weinberger's Jews and Judaism in New York* (New York, 1981), pp. 12–14.

47 Goldstein, *B'nai Jeshurun*, pp. 128, 153–156; *Answers to Questions Propounded by the Ritual Committee on the Subject of the Improvements Intended to Be Introduced in the Synagogue Service of the Cong. "B'nai Jeshurun"* (New York, 1869); Minutes of Congregation B'nai Jeshurun, 1865–1875, Congregation B'nai Jeshurun Papers, microfilm 493c, American Jewish Archives, Cincinnati, Ohio.

48 Goldstein, *B'nai Jeshurun*, p. 156; Nahum Streisand, *Lilmod Latoim Binah* (New York, 1872); *Jewish Messenger*, 16 July 1875.

49 B'nai Jeshurun Minutes, 8 November 1874.

50 Goldstein, *B'nai Jeshurun*, p. 157.

51 Ibid., p. 155; *Answers to Questions*, p. 1; cf. *New Era*, 1 (1870), p. 36, for an attack on this phenomenon.

52 *B'nai Jeshurun Minutes*, 8 November 1874, as correlated with the "Register of Congregational Membership," in Goldstein, *B'nai Jeshurun*, pp. 404–436; *Jewish Messenger*, 16 July 1875, p. 6.

53 William M. Rosenblatt, "The Jews: What They Are Coming To," *Galaxy*, 13 (January 1872), p. 60; *New Era*, 4 (1874), pp. 14, 513; for a similar later argument (1922), see Aaron Rothkoff, *Bernard Revel* (Philadelphia, 1972), p. 111.

54 *Jewish Messenger*, 16 July 1875, p. 6.

55 *Jewish Times*, 21 May 1875, p. 184.

56 *Jewish Messenger*, 21 May 1875, p. 21.

57 All major accounts of this episode are incomplete and flawed: Goldstein, *B'nai Jeshurun*, pp. 91–92; Simon Cohen, *Shaarey Tefila: Its Hundred Years* (New York, 1945), pp. 3–6; E. Yechiel Simon, "Samuel Myer Isaacs: A 19th Century Minister in New York City" (D.H.L. diss., Yeshiva University, 1974), pp. 34–37; and Leo Hershkowitz, " 'Those Ignorant Immigrants' and the B'nai Jeshurun Schism," *American Jewish History*, 70 (December 1980), pp. 168–175. Valuable information found in the *New York Herald* and the *Voice of Jacob* (England) has been overlooked.

58 Minutes of the Board of Trustees, 8 October 1872, 16 March 1873, B'nai Jeshurun Papers, microfilm 493d.

59 49 Howard's 263 (N.Y.); see *Jewish Messenger*, 16 July 1875, pp. 5–6 for a more complete report of the case. Unless otherwise stated, my discussion of this case is based on these sources.

60 The classic organ case in America involved Congregation Beth Elohim in Charleston back in 1840; see Allan Tarshish, "The Charleston Organ Case," *American Jewish Historical Quarterly*, 54 (1965), pp. 411–449.

61 Bernard J. Meislin, *Jewish Law in American Tribunals* (New York, 1976), esp. pp. 132–141.

62 An 1866 case, *Rossman v. Jewish Congregation Anshi Chesed*, was decided differently on the basis of an older law; see *Jewish Messenger*, 13 April 1866, p. 5.

63 Minutes of the Board of Trustees, 12 July 1875, 3 August 1875, B'nai Jeshurun Papers; Goldstein, *B'nai Jeshurun*, p. 158.

64 Quotations are from *Jewish Messenger*, 20 August 1875, 16 July 1875; see also 23 July 1875–10 September 1875; *Jewish Times*, 16 July 1875; *New Era*, 5 (1875), pp. 517–518.

65 Goldstein, *B'nai Jeshurun*, pp. 159–164. The B'nai Jeshurun decision soon influenced its neighbor congregation Shaarey Tefilah. It adopted mixed seating in 1880. See Cohen, *Shaarey Tefila*, pp. 31–33.

66 *American Israelite*, 37 (November 27, 1890), p. 4, italics added. See Gustav Gottheil, "The Jewish Reformation," *American Journal of Theology*, 6 (April 1902), p. 279.

67 Jo Renee Fine and Gerald R. Wolfe, *The Synagogues of New York's Lower East Side* (New York, 1978).

68 Pool, *An Old Faith*, p. 100.

69 Jeffrey S. Gurock, *When Harlem Was Jewish* (New York, 1979), p. 117; see also Chapter 1 in this volume.

70 Marshall Sklare, *Conservative Judaism* (1955; 2d. ed., New York, 1972), pp. 85–90.

71 Solomon Schechter to Mayer Sulzberger, 14 June 1907, Solomon Solis-Cohen Archives, Philadelphia, Pa.; Cyrus Adler to Morris Teller, 24 September 1916, in *Cyrus Adler: Selected Letters*, vol. 1, ed. Ira Robinson (Philadelphia, 1985), p. 319. See Bernard Leventhal to Mayer Sulzberger, 13 June 1907, Solis-Cohen Archives.

72 *United Synagogue Recorder*, 1 (July 1921), p. 8.

73 The Cleveland Jewish Center case of 1927, involving Rabbi Solomon Goldman (*Katz v. Goldman*, 33 Ohio App. 150), drew particular notice. The Ohio Supreme Court ruled in Goldman's favor, refusing to invalidate the changes that he introduced. See Aaron Rakeffet-Rothkoff, *The Silver Era in American Jewish Orthodoxy* (New York, 1981), pp. 112–114, 121 n. 14, 326–347; Jacob J. Weinstein, *Solomon Goldman: A Rabbi's Rabbi* (New York, 1973), pp. 12–17.

74 *Conservative Judaism*, 11 (Fall 1956), p. 39; Eli Ginzberg, *Keeper of the Law: Louis Ginzberg* (Philadelphia, 1966), pp. 229–230.

75 Sonderling, "Five Gates," p. 115.

76 Sklare, *Conservative Judaism*, p. 88; see Rothkoff, *Bernard Revel*, p. 111; and Norman Lamm, "Separate Pews in the Synagogue [1959]," in *A Treasury of Tradition*, ed. Norman Lamm and Walter S. Wurzberger (New York, 1967), pp. 243–267.

77 *Katz v. Singerman*, 241 Louisiana 154 (1961); Rothkoff, *Bernard Revel*, p. 164.

78 *Katz v. Singerman*, 241 Louisiana 150.

79 "Opinion in Kahila Kodesh Adath Israel Congregation Matter" (Cincinnati, 1954, mimeographed), p. 42, Louis Bernstein, *Challenge and Mission: The Emergence of the English Speaking Orthodox Rabbinate* (New York, 1982), pp. 20–21, 36, 46–49, 138–141.

80 Rothkoff, *Bernard Revel*, p. 164.

81 For the legal background, see Meislin, *Jewish Law in American Tribunals*; and W. E. Shipley, *Change of Denominational Relations or Fundamental Doctrines by Majority Faction of Independent or Congregational Church as Ground for Award of Property to Minority*, 15 ALR 3d 297 (1967). The Supreme Court's ruling in *Presbyterian Church in the United States v. Mary Elizabeth Blue Hull Memorial Presbyterian Church*, 393 U.S. 440 (1969) resolved several important legal questions bearing on mixed seating disputes; see Paul G. Kauper, "Church Autonomy and the First Amendment: The Presbyterian Church Case," in *Church and State: The Supreme Court and the First Amendment*, ed. Philip B. Kurland (Chicago, 1975), pp. 67–98.

82 "Opinion in Adath Israel Matter," p. 4. In what follows, I cite this version; a slightly abbreviated and variant version of the decision may be found in *Conservative Judaism*, 11 (Fall 1956), pp. 1–31.

83 "Opinion in Adath Israel Matter," p. 12. David Philipson found this seating pattern when he preached at Adath Israel's dedication in 1927. He predicted that "ere long the women will sit with their husbands and children." *My Life as an American Jew* (Cincinnati, 1941), p. 378.

84 Philipson, *My Life as an American Jew*, p. 8.

85 Ibid., pp. 8–12.

86 Ibid., pp. 1–3. On the use of arbitration in cases of this sort, see Jerold S. Auerbach, *Justice without Law?* (New York, 1983), pp. 69–94.

87 Auerbach, *Justice without Law?* p. 63.

88 Ibid., p. 30; *Conservative Judaism*, 11 (Fall 1956), p. 44.

89 *Opinion in Adath Israel Matter*, pp. 43–66; quotations from pp. 47, 45, 66.

90 Ibid., p. 59.

91 Ibid., p. 67.

92 The case is reported in 356 Michigan 291, and is described in great detail, with documents, in Litvin, *Sanctity of the Synagogue*. Much of what follows is based on this volume. See also Bernstein, *Challenge and Mission*, pp. 138–141.

93 Litvin, *Sanctity of the Synagogue*, pp. 11–17.

94 Ibid., p. 378.

95 Ibid., pp. 382, 412, 408.

96 Ibid., pp. 407–418 reproduces the entire Michigan Supreme Court decision; quotations are from pp. 417, 415.

97 The case is reported in 241 Louisiana 103. For early documents, see Litvin, *Sanctity of the Synagogue*, pp. 61–77; see also Bernstein, *Challenge and Mission*, pp. 138–140.

98 *Katz v. Singerman*, pp. 107, 109.

99 Ibid., p. 114.

100 Ibid., pp. 136–149. Agus's testimony resembled that which he gave in the Adath Israel matter; see *Conservative Judaism*, 11 (1956), pp. 32–41.

101 *Katz v. Singerman*, 116 quoting *Katz v. Goldman*, above n. 73.

102 *Katz v. Singerman*, 118; cf. *Watson v. Jones* 13 Wall. 679, 20 L ed. 666 (1872).

103   *Katz v. Singerman*, pp. 131, 134.
104   Ibid., p. 151. Shipley, *Change of Denominational Relations*, pp. 324, 331, overlooks this critical point.
105   E.g., Litvin, *Sanctity of the Synagogue*, p. 73.
106   See Isaac Klein's letter in *Conservative Judaism*, 11 (Winter 1957), p. 34.
107   E.g., Joseph P. Schultz, ed., *Mid-America's Promise: A Profile of Kansas City Jewry* (Kansas City, 1982), p. 42.
108   Cf. Alan J. Yuter, "Mehizah, Midrash and Modernity: A Study in Religious Rhetoric," *Judaism*, 28 (1979), pp. 147–159; Samuel Heilman, *Synagogue Life* (Chicago, 1976), p. 28. Charles Liebman, "Orthodoxy in American Jewish Life," *Aspects of the Religious Behavior of American Jews* (reprinted from *American Jewish Year Book*, 66; New York, 1974), p. 146, notes "some 30 synagogues" which once had mixed seating and, since 1955, have installed *mechitsot* – no doubt to maintain their Orthodox affiliation.
109   In a conversation with me, Prof. Sefton D. Temkin quotes a colleague of his as pointing out that whereas American Orthodoxy defined itself in terms of opposition to mixed seating, British Orthodoxy did so in terms of opposition to the mixed choir, German Orthodoxy in terms of opposition to the organ, and Hungarian Orthodoxy in terms of opposition to the raised, forward pulpit. A comparative study elucidating these differences would be of inestimable value.

14

Music in the American Synagogue: A Case Study from Houston

KAY KAUFMAN SHELEMAY

Around 4 p.m. on Thursday, June 16, 1870, people began to gather outside the Masonic Temple on Main Street in Houston, Texas. They formed a colorful procession nearly 1,000 strong: firemen in bright red and blue uniforms, civic association members waving emblems and banners, civilians in elegant dress. Led by Schmidt's Brass Band and escorted by marshals on horseback, they marched to a grandstand erected at Franklin Avenue and Crawford Street and looked on as a large stone was unloaded from a wagon. With prayers, speeches, and hymns, the assembly dedicated the cornerstone for a new "Hebrew Temple of Worship," Congregation Beth Israel.[1] It is no coincidence that the ceremony marking the ground breaking for Congregation Beth Israel's first permanent building was also a musical event, for music has always been central to synagogue life.

This chapter examines musical traditions in the American synagogue through a case study of a major Reform synagogue of the urban Southwest. Founded[2] less than twenty years after the Allen brothers bought land on Buffalo Bayou, which they named after General Sam Houston,[3] Beth Israel is the oldest synagogue in Texas. Its unbroken continuity and extensive archives[4] enable us to discuss in considerable detail musical activities throughout its history.

The approach here differs from previous discussions of synagogue music by moving beyond the liturgical context to explore musical activity within the social and educational domains.[5] A number of studies have treated cantors, composers, and liturgical music.[6] However, these discussions have tended to overlook the synagogue's role as the preeminent social institution in American Jewish life, a reality that has generated a rich array of musical activities, both sacred and secular, that merit investigation.

The following discussion traces the history of Beth Israel's musical life in the liturgical, educational, and social spheres separately, setting forth the course of events within each area before exploring the implications of their frequent interaction and interdependence in the conclusion. By so doing, it is possible to arrive at a more richly textured perspective on both the nature of music in the American synagogue and its role in synagogue life.

Music in the Context of Worship

Liturgical music at Beth Israel was always shaped by synagogue rituals. Until the mid–1860s, Beth Israel worshipers employed an Orthodox Ashkenazic liturgy. Subsequently, a debate over liturgical custom culminated in the adoption of Isaac Mayer Wise's *Minhag America* in 1867 (2A, 7/7/1867). By the early 1890s, the board of trustees once again began a search for a new prayerbook, adopting the *Union Prayer Book* in 1899 (2C,5/7/1899). This liturgy was used through its various editions until the *Gates of Prayer* was formally introduced in January 1976.[7]

As each new prayerbook was adopted, changes were made in the musical content of the service. During the early years, when an Orthodox liturgy was observed, individual members were assigned to chant different parts of the service (2B, 8/31/1869). Congregational participation was then dictated by tradition, but also necessitated by the dearth of qualified clergymen available at the time, especially in Houston's isolated location.[8] However, the role of the congregation in liturgical performance underwent a major transition after 1867, when a choir was founded.

Founding a Choir

Shortly after the debate began concerning *Minhag America*, a choir was formed at Beth Israel (2A, 11/18/1868). From the beginning, the choir contained both men and women and comprised mainly non-Jewish singers from the Houston community. By 1871, board minutes mention regular appropriations for choir expenses, which included fees for a musical director, expenses for copying music, and payments for professional soloists (2A, 6/24/1871); by 1874, the musical director also began serving as organist (2A, 2/15/1874). That the choir soon became an important part of worship is attested by the frequent enthusiastic acknowledgments and occasional complaints concerning its performance (2B, 9/24/1874).

Although the choir was instituted without the controversy that attended other changes in liturgical performance, there was intermittent

Table 1. *Hymnals used in Beth Israel worship, c. 1930*

Hymns, Psalms, and Prayers in English and German. Edited by Isaac M. Wise (and others). Cincinnati: Bloch and Company, 1868.

Israelitsche Tempel-Gesänge; Hymnen für Sabbath-und-Fest-Tage, mit deutschen und englischen Text. Edited by Otto Lob. Chicago: E. Rubovits, 1896.

Jewish Hymns, for Sabbath-Schools and Families (English and German). Edited by Simon Hecht. New York: Bloch Printing Company, 1896. (originally published 1878)

Kol Zimrah, A Hymn Book for Temples and Sabbath Schools. Edited by Morris Goldstein. Cincinnati: n.p., 1885.

Sefer An'im Zemirot. Liederlust für israelitische Elementarschulen. Edited by Abraham Treu. Münster: n.p., 1882?

Songs of Juda: Hymns, Psalms, and Anthems. Edited by C. Otto Weber. New York: Bloch Publishing Company, 1905.

The Jewish Song Book for Synagogue, School, and Home. Composed and arranged by A. Z. Idelsohn. Cincinnti: The composer, 1928. (Subsequent editions in 1929, 1938)

The Voice of Prayer and Praise. Kol Rinnah we-Todah. Edited by Francis L. Cohen. London: Greenberg and Company, 1899. (Originally published in 1889)

Zemirot u-Teffilot Yisrael. A Synagogue Hymnal for Sabbath and Festivals. Edited by Max Halpern. Boston: Boston Music Company, 1915.

---

concern that more Jewish singers should be used and that the congregation should be encouraged to participate in the liturgy (2B, 12/14/1873; 2A, 5/11/1879; S1, 6/3/1888). No explicit information is given in archival sources concerning what music the choir sang, other than references to an unidentified hymnal. It probably used Isaac Mayer Wise's *Hymns, Psalms, and Prayers*, the likely companion to *Minhag America*, as well as other editions of the period (see Table 1).[9] Requests from the choir director for additional music in 1894 and 1900 suggest that musical resources were limited (S1, 10/28/1894).

Most of the repertory sung by the Beth Israel choir was in the four-part harmonic style widely used in American Reform congregations in the late nineteenth and early twentieth centuries. The choir evidently always sang in this fashion: Speaking at a special board meeting called to inquire into the "very bad shape" of the choir, the director "explained it was entirely on account of not having a sufficient number of voices for harmonizing, having but *one* soprano and *no* tenor" (S1, 7/19/1894).

We are able to compile far more detailed information concerning the status of the choir, its members, administration, and repertory by the last years of the century. A request was received from the choir for more rehearsal time than usual during the summer of 1900 since there was "new and difficult music to be learned in connection with the *Union Prayer Book* recently adopted" (S1, 6/24/1900). Only six months later, the ritual committee again requested an appropriation for new music since "the choir has but one set of music for the *Union Prayer Book* for Sabbath Services and it is therefore getting very monotonous for the Congregation" (S1, 11/23/1900).

Written records of musical programs from regular or holiday services either did not exist or have not survived. However, programs from two special services held around the turn of the century provide colorful examples of the type of music performed. A Chanukah service sponsored by B'nai B'rith on December 23, 1900, combined readings from the prayer book with a series of instrumental and vocal selections well known at that time (see Table 2). Particularly noteworthy is the participation of Beth Israel school children and several Jewish musicians. A memorial service for community leader Leo M. Levi held on January 31, 1904, included passages from the *Union Prayer Book* as well as classical musical selections deemed appropriate for the occasion, such as "Funeral March" by Chopin and by Mendelssohn, and Baumbauch's "Life and Immortality."

After the transition to the *Union Prayer Book* was made and the repertory stabilized in 1902, the choir consisted of a professional quartet of non-Jewish musicians so dissatisfied with their $15.00 monthly salary that they attempted to strike (S1, 10/26/1902). Choir personnel changed frequently in the first decade of the century, and by 1911, concern was again expressed that the director should "educate a number of coreligionists to sing as chorus in our choir and to eventually become soloists" (S2, 6/11/1911).

By 1920, the choir was supported by a budget surpassed only by the rabbi's salary. In 1921 the first efforts were made to found a children's choir, which remained a part of religious school activities until the present (S3,5/1/1921). In 1922 Portia Spencer was appointed choir director, a post she was to hold until 1960, concurrently serving her own church, Trinity Episcopal (B, 106/1). For most of her tenure, the choir consisted of a mixed quartet expanded on High Holidays to a double quartet; almost without exception, the singers were not Jewish.[10] This arrangement remained until 1974, when members were once again invited to join (B, 120/12). In 1983–1984, Beth Israel's choir had six professional soloists and a contingent of eight volunteers.

Until 1868, members of Beth Israel had played an active role in liturgical performance; however, the establishment of a choir at the synagogue drastically reduced the level of lay participation. The introduction

Table 2. *Chanucah-B'nai Brith Service held at Temple Beth Israel*

DECEMBER 23rd, 1900	TEBETH 1ST, 5601

Organ Accompanist, Mr. W. Hodgkins

1. Union Prayer Book 231–237

2. Violin Solo   Cavatine   (Raff)   Miss Mabel Lipper

3. Essay   EMMA LAZARUS   Mrs. I. G. Gerson

4. Flute Solos   a. Simple Aveux   (Thomas)
   b. Serenatus   (Braga)
   Mr. Harold Raphael

5. Prayer Book 238–240

6. The Lighting of the Candles and Singing of the Chanucah Hymn
   by the School Children of the Beth Israel Congregation

7. a. Chanucah Prayer   (Prayer Book, Minhag America, 17–19)
   b. A Lecture to B'nai Brith   I.O.B.B. Handbook, 33–39

8. Song   Berceuse from Jocelyn   (Godard)
   Miss Burgheim (Violin Obligato Mr. B. B. Schram)

9. Prayer Book 48–51

10. Violin Solo   Largo   (Handel)   Mr. B. B. Schram

11. Address   The Independent Order of B'nai Brith
    Mr. M. Malevintsky

12. Song   Thou'rt Passing Hence   (Sullivan)
    Mr. A.M. Downie

13. The Jewish Societies of Houston

14. Violin Solo   Romanza   (Becker)   Miss Mabel Lipper

15. Benediction   The Rabbi

of a new prayerbook along with an unfamiliar musical repertory must have prevented the congregation from participating in the service. However, non-Jewish musicians, particularly those of Protestant backgrounds accustomed to choral singing in worship, were available to fill the void. One can only hypothesize that this format became so well established that by the time the congregants were again familiar with the service and its musical content, there was little incentive for them to participate.

Liturgical music at Beth Israel became a domain for professionals, and subsequent attempts to encourage congregational participation were largely unsuccessful. Certainly there were Jewish musicians in the community; the program reproduced in Table 2 suggests that several congregants were accomplished amateurs. However, their participation was limited mainly to instrumental or choral selections. Only when innovative liturgies were introduced in the late 1960s were individual Beth Israel members drawn back into the sphere of liturgical music.

The Beth Israel Organ

Although specifics of the Beth Israel organ controversy do not survive in the same detail as do those that took place in Germany some half-century before,[11] there was apparently considerable resistance to the organ on both religious and aesthetic grounds. Discussion concerning acquisition of an organ began in 1868 (2A, 9/6/1868), funds were appropriated for its purchase three years later (2B, 6/24/1871), and an instrument was evidently incorporated into Beth Israel worship late in 1873 (2B, 10/5/1873). Many entries in the minute books provide no details concerning the new organ, but they leave little doubt about its poor condition and the need for frequent repairs.

In 1901, the "Ladies of the Congregation" held a bazaar to raise money for the "Pipe Organ Account" (S1, 4/28/1901; 2C,5/5/1901), and a new pipe organ was subsequently consecrated on Friday evening, January 10, 1902. With the exception of an arrangement of the Kol Nidre and several hymns, the program for this occasion was primarily drawn from well-known oratorios such as Mendelssohn's "Elijah" and Haydn's "Creation." In 1927, the congregation purchased a Pilcher organ, which was moved in 1967 to the new building on North Braeswood, where it is still in use.[12]

From the time of its adoption, the organ played an important role in Beth Israel's ritual life, enforcing silence at the beginning of the ritual and becoming an integral part of worship. Indeed, a primer on temple etiquette published in 1971 states that "When the organ music begins, the service has started. All conversation should stop" (B, 117/15).

The organ repertory has traditionally been the responsibility of the organist. As with all other early Beth Israel appointments, there was considerable turnover until Anthony Rahe assumed the position from 1930 through 1973. Rahe, who also served during this period at the Trinity Episcopal Church and at Settegast-Kopf Funeral Home, acquired knowledge of Jewish liturgy and music in 1920 when he moved to Texas and became organist at Temple B'nai Israel in Galveston under Rabbi

Henry Cohen.[13] Mr. Rahe's career exemplifies the close and cordial relations between many churches and synagogues in Texas, which extend to sharing principals on the music staff. Indeed, Thomas J. Crow, the current Beth Israel organist and choir director, also serves as organist and choirmaster for St. Mark's Episcopal Church.

Despite the broad experience of Rahe and Crow in Christian liturgy, both maintain a separate repertory for the synagogue. Anthony Rahe recalls: "I used mostly things that had Jewish melody or were written by a Jewish composer. I stuck to the religious part of it. I mean, some organists, they'll play anything else from other composers to show off, but I never did that. I always used music that was traditionally from the liturgy."[14]

Other instruments have occasionally been used to accompany the liturgy at Beth Israel. The flute and violin were used for special or commemorative services early in the century (see Table 2), but in more recent years, instrumental music has also been used occasionally for High Holiday services, including a cello rendition of the Kol Nidre (B, 122/26). On another occasion, a string quartet played during the Memorial Service on Yom Kippur "to add to the majesty and beauty of the Great White Fast" (B, 115/4).

Most discussions acknowledge the impact of Christian models upon American Judaism. However, despite the sharing of important musical personnel such as choir directors and organists, the influence of Houston's churches are not immediately obvious in Beth Israel's musical life. Melodies and hymns of Christian origin are, of course, contained in many hymnals; however, almost without exception these collections were compiled by Jews. The use of Christian musicians seems to have had less impact on the Beth Israel repertory than might have been anticipated [15]

The Musical Repertory

The musical content of Beth Israel services has remained fairly stable since the adoption of the *Union Prayer Book*. Organist Anthony Rahe remembers his forty-three year association with Beth Israel as a period of musical stability: "There wasn't too much change then. It was pretty quiet. Different composers would come along with another service and we'd add those things to our repertory. We used the *Union Hymnal*, and then they got the *Songster*... after we got out to the new Temple."[16] In addition to the *Union Hymnal* in its three editions and the *Songster*, other hymnals were used during Rahe's years as organist (see Table 1).

Except for Mr. Rahe's personal files, no record exists of musical repertory performed at Beth Israel until the late 1970s. From that time, choir room files preserve "Weekly Service Music Outlines," which provide the names of composers and selections used on specific Sabbaths; nearly complete records exist for repertory performed in 1977 and from 1982 to 1984, with partial listings for 1978 to 1981. A comparison of works (reconstructed by Mr. Rahe) performed between 1930 and 1973 with those programmed between 1977 and 1984 provides evidence of a rather predictable rate of change in the repertory. During Mr. Rahe's tenure, the repertory consisted primarily of European Jewish composers born in the mid-to-late-nineteenth century. In contrast, repertory exclusively used after 1977 drew primarily upon individuals composing for the American synagogue. Since 1977, more "classic Jewish composers" such as Sulzer, Birnbaum, and Rossi have also been added to supplement compositions of Kaiser, Lewandowski, Schalit, Freed, and Helfman already in the repertory. This modest shift toward more traditional composers in recent years has been noticed by individuals in the Houston community: "In the modern Reform, whether it's Temple Emanu El or Beth Israel, they have gone back to the traditional music more and more. They're doing Sulzer . . . they've picked up where somebody who didn't know left off long ago."[17]

Some new repertory introduced since 1973 was necessitated by the addition of a cantorial soloist. A concerted effort has been made to incorporate new compositions entering the mainstream of the Reform Movement, and Beth Israel recently began to commission works from well-known composers such as George Kleinsinger (1979) and Ben Steinberg (1982). Composers Bonia Shur and Michael Isaacson visited Beth Israel and conducted their compositions in special services held in 1980 and 1983, respectively.

Although the organ and accompanied choral selections dominate the musical portion of the Beth Israel liturgy, congregational participation has been encouraged in recent years. However, the architecture of the main sanctuary has obstructed such participation. As one member stated,

> Congregational singing . . . was never very strong here. Our sanctuary is so large that it's inhibiting for people to join in . . . they're not sure when to join in. It's a very formal atmosphere. People don't sing that much . . . they have a very limited repertory of hymns, and even when they do the same things over and over, they don't join in that much in the big hall. Now, in the chapel where people are closer together, you notice an instantaneous change.[18]

A small corpus of melodies from the *Songster* are used regularly in the liturgy. (These are summarized in Table 3.) The biblical portion is read

Table 3. *Frequently performed selections from* The Union Songster, *1977–1984*

Union Songster number	Title	Composer
8	"Adon Olam"	(traditional) E. Gerovitch
112	"Lecha Dodi"	(traditional) L. Lewandowski
288	"Barchu"	S. Sulzer and E. Werner
291	"Shema"	S. Sulzer
303A	"U'Anachnu"	S. Sulzer
305	"Kiddush"	After Lewandowski
314A	"Sh'u Sharim"	L. Lewandowski
318	"Baruch Shenatan"	S. Sulzer and H. Coopersmith
320	"Shema/Lacha Adonay"	S. Sulzer
320A	"L'haw Adonay"	G. Ephros
322	"Hodo Al Eretz"	S. Naumbourg and H. Coopersmith

aloud, not chanted. Organ preludes and postludes also vary from week to week, at the discretion of the organist; on some occasions, classics of the organ repertory have been used.[19] Most often, however, the organist improvises, either on a traditional melody or one of his own composition.[20] Occasionally, on interfaith Sabbaths or Thanksgiving, secular American hymns like "America the Beautiful" are performed.[21]

In addition to the regular repertory used for Sabbath and holiday services, a number of special services have been held in the last twenty years. Temple bulletins record a first presentation of Ernest Bloch's *Sacred Service* in 1963 to mark the golden anniversary of National Sisterhood (B, 109/38); the service was repeated in 1972 and 1976. More recently, services have been devoted to the works of individual composers, such as Salomone Rossi in 1977 and Max Janowski in 1978. Occasionally, a service is planned for other special purposes, such as "A Musical Sermon" presented in June 1979, which sought to "exhibit the changing Jewish style through the centuries" (B, 126/10). For this concert, works by Salomone Rossi, F. Mendelssohn Bartholdy, Abraham Ellstein, and Max Janowski were selected to represent the "late Renaissance, the Romantic Era, contemporary choral modes, and a contemporary cantorial piece," respectively.

Although much of the music composed for the synagogue can be termed "innovative" in its time, an active and explicit concern with liturgical innovation first appears at Beth Israel in the early 1960s. Mem–

bers of the Ritual and Music Committee in this period examined and digested "newer experiments in ritual, liturgy, and the conduct of worship by visits to nearby temples and churches"; the committee also discussed and evaluated "published material dealing with practices now evolving in religious circles throughout America" (B1, 1963). Innovations were deliberately integrated into Beth Israel rituals and congregational reactions to changes were elicited (B1, 1966). Through subsequent years, one can trace generally positive responses to the experimentation. Only a few innovations – such as performances by the Lyric Quartette at the Yom Kippur Memorial Service – were eliminated because of negative response (RMC, 2/15/1971).

Early creative services drew upon resources of the Institute of Creative Judaism, which published materials written primarily by Hebrew Union College students and graduates. In the mid–1970s, Beth Israel members began to compose their own services. At the invitation of Rabbi Samuel Karff, Debbie Friedman began to perform her own folk-rock compositions accompanied by guitar, such as the Chanukah Cantata (B, 125/8).[22] By the early 1980s, creative services were an established part of the Beth Israel liturgical cycle and were acknowledged as such in the annual president's report (B, 127/17).

In seeking an overview of the forces that guided Beth Israel's musical activity in the liturgical domain, we find that the power rested primarily with individuals, wielded by outside musical specialists (organists, choir directors) from the late 1860s. Only since 1973 has an inside musical specialist, the cantor, been a factor in selecting repertory or determining performance practice.

Rabbis who have occupied the pulpit since 1900 have also had an impact on liturgical music. Rabbi Barnston, who arrived in 1900, was active in the arts and spoke frequently about music. Born and educated in England, he was probably responsible for the introduction of a considerable number of English compositions into Beth Israel's repertory.[23]

Barnston's successor, Rabbi Hyman Judah Schachtel, played an active role in the musical life of the congregation, presenting a series of well-attended "music-book lectures" (B1, 106/12), and composing music for Beth Israel liturgy and special events. Schachtel often selected music for the Beth Israel service:

> Dr. Schachtel would pick out certain hymns and had the words printed on sheets which the congregation sang from. "Praise to the Living God" was one, plus several different renditions of "Adon Olam." There was a Ritual Committee, but usually

whenever there was a certain selection to be used, Schachtel asked for it, suggested it.[24]

Schachtel's successor, Rabbi Samuel Karff, likewise has participated in incorporating new musical materials into the worship experience.

Although the members of Beth Israel had relatively less impact on musical change between 1870 and 1970, many of the innovations of the last decade are in direct response to membership desires. In the spring of 1973, the Ritual and Music Committee conducted a congregational survey that addressed, among other issues, the musical content of the liturgy. In response to this questionnaire, 47 percent of those surveyed said they desired more music in the liturgy, 45 percent wanted to hire a cantor, and 36 percent wished to have an all-musical service periodically. The committee concluded that the survey reflected the realities of Beth Israel's changing membership: "Half the people want the format left exactly as it is and half want it changed. This is the crux of our problem" (RMC, 5/21/1973).

A reason frequently cited by knowledgeable Beth Israelites for musical change is the migration of more traditional Jews from the Northeast to the Sunbelt, as well as a more general trend toward tradition within the larger Reform Movement.[25]

Music in the House of Meeting

Beyond the liturgical arena, music has played an important role in Beth Israel social life. The major annual social event in the late nineteenth century was the annual Purim Ball, which featured music and elaborate masquerades held to raise money for a variety of causes (S1, 3/22/1885; S1, 2/22/1891).

By the end of the century, Chanukah emerged as an increasingly important holiday in the liturgical calendar. At the annual Chanukah celebration in 1898, musical selections by Rossini ("Quis est Homo"), Millard ("Father Hear Us"), Randegger ("Save Me O God"), and Greiner ("Adon Olom") were featured. At the end of the formal program, the rabbi announced that dancing would next take place in the adjoining Montefiore Hall: "The young folks took immediate advantage of the opportunity and before the wellfilled audience had entirely vacated the Temple, the strains of music and tip of toe could be heard in the hall adjoining. . . . The finale of the Chanukah feast was concluded with rejoicing and merriment" (*Lone Star Lodge Minutes*, 210).

The frequency of these events and the enthusiastic response they elicited is made clear by a new synagogue policy in 1901 that disallowed dancing in the temple hall to prevent "misuse" of the building (2C, 11/3/1901).

Other than occasional information about musical events held by various synagogue organizations, detailed calendars of Beth Israel's musical events survive only after 1954, when congregational bulletins were systematically preserved and bound into volumes annually. The bulletins indicate that three main types of musical events took place: (1) holiday celebrations with elaborate musical programs, (2) dances, and (3) concerts and musical revues.

The holiday celebrations with musical content were without exception held on Purim and Chanukah. Purim activities from 1954 up to the present included carnivals, dances, and operettas, and Chanukah was celebrated with concerts of holiday songs and dances. These occasions were advertised to attract a wide cross section of temple members, who were invited to "join in the delightful Chanukah songs and recall the great spirit of the Maccabees with your family" (B, 106/8). Many of the events featured sing-a-longs, and there were clear efforts by the late 1960s to include members as participants.

Like the nineteenth-century Purim Ball, the dance in the mid-twentieth century remained an important mechanism for bringing together all groups within the temple social structure. Bulletins since 1954 mention dances of every conceivable theme organized for all age groups. The youth attended dance lessons, sports dances, confirmation dances, and sock hops. New members were wooed and past leadership honored at a variety of dance functions. The sisterhood and brotherhood sponsored dances with themes including "golden galas" and "Hawaiian luaus." The Couples Club may have had the most inventive dance themes: a "bring-your-worst-wedding-gift dance," a "sweetheart dance," a "calories don't count party," and a "western dance." In total, forty-three dance events were announced in the bulletin between 1958 and 1984.

Concerts and musical revues represent a third type of musical event frequently held at Beth Israel. Approximately forty-four concerts, reviews, or programs with substantial musical content were advertised in the bulletins since 1954. Many events contained musical repertory without explicit Jewish content, such as a piano concerto with orchestra (2/23/1974) and an offering of operatic selections by Cantor and Mrs. Arturo Sergei (5/4/1974). Important organizational meetings such as sisterhood luncheons often included a musical program; a spoof on "Mame" performed on September 15, 1969 is a typical example. Other concerts had sacred content: Beth Israel's choir participated on May 7, 1967, in "Operation Understanding" an ecumenical "Festival of Worship Music," at which they presented the "historical development of worship music from shofar to guitar" (B, 113/35). On April 1, 1984, Beth Israel Cantor Robert Gerber took part in the "First Annual Houston Cantorial Concert," a performance by five Houston area cantors held to benefit their respective cantorial schools and the Jewish Community Center School of Music.[26]

The most complex musical events have been a series of six fully staged musical reviews presented by the Beth Israel Sisterhood since 1974 as its primary fund-raising vehicle. Beth Israel members serve as cast and crew for a production supplied and directed by Jerome H. Cargill Productions from New York. The event is chaired by a sisterhood member and all work on the production is done by volunteers; only a professional orchestra is hired.[27] To date, all have been two-act musical reviews with numbers linked by a loose theme such as a carnival, variety show, or circus.

The reviews have varied in content, but all have in some manner addressed the concerns of a typical member of Beth Israel as a Jewish Houstonian, Texan, and American. Most productions reaffirm these roles through contrast or parody. For example, the 1984 "Carnival Tonight" presented a series of skits portraying the Orient, Haiti, Brazil, and Spain, ending with a finale of American patriotic songs sung before a stage-size replica of the American flag. Previous reviews, such as "Hello Texas" in 1981, featured musical skits parodying stereotypical elements of Texas life (cowboys, cowgirls), as well as a comic number called "Country Cantor." Although the scripts for these shows are provided by the producers, the sisterhood committee selects the show from a number of alternatives and then makes changes to customize the content to the Beth Israel audience.

Most Beth Israel musical events are multifunctional – they serve social and expressive purposes and almost always raise money. The significance of the synagogue musical event as a fund-raiser cannot be overemphasized. Although the content shifts to reflect different musical tastes, the same motivation behind the sisterhood fund-raisers in the 1980s have generated events throughout Beth Israel's history. One program survives from a concert held on April 8, 1907, to raise money for the building fund; it contained a mixture of sacred and secular compositions ranging from portions of the synagogue service to excerpts by Rossini and Wagner.

Thus Beth Israel is the locus of many musical events that extend far beyond the boundaries of liturgy or even Jewish content. These events are advertised in synagogue publications such as the bulletin and are a primary focus of member activity. Although the content of the dances and musical reviews may not always be related to Jewish religious tradition, they are integrally tied to the identities and self-images of Beth

Israel members as Jews. The sheer numbers that plan and participate in these events and the frequency of their occurrence are testimony to their important role in Beth Israel musical life.

Music and Education

Ever since the inauguration of musical activity in the spring of 1864 "for the purpose of instilling the principles of our religion into the minds of the Hebrew children" (2B, 10/27/1878), ample evidence exists of such activity in Beth Israel's school. An organ was purchased in 1878 for the exclusive use of the school (2B, 10/27/1878), and the budget for events such as the annual Sabbath school picnic included music expenses (2C, 5/5/1891). Singing was officially introduced into the Sabbath school curriculum in 1896 for performance at a children's service and was termed a "pleasing innovation" (S1, 8/23/1896). From Beth Israel's earliest years to the present, children have been taught music intended to help them participate in the synagogue service: "Pupils are making good progress in learning to sing Hebrew responses with the object of introducing them at the services in the Temple on Sabbaths and ordinary Holidays" (S1, 8/22/1897).

Throughout the first half of the twentieth century, music continued to be a focal point of the educational program and, as in other musical activities, the rabbi played an important role. Dr. H. Barnstein once recommended that a vocal class be organized (S2, 3/26/1916); it subsequently performed on May 6, 1916. Other musical activities proliferated over the years, including a "club activity program" in the Sunday school curriculum that featured music (B,102/1). By 1967, the music curriculum had become "an integral part of [the] school" (B, 114/5).

In 1968, Beth Israel started a day school. Rapid expansion put pressure on the music program, and in 1970 "a paid music teacher" was hired to "do rhythms and teach Nursery School songs of both a secular as well as Jewish nature" (B, 116/38). In 1978, composer-performer Debbie Friedman was engaged to direct music at the day school as well as to "enrich" other Beth Israel programs (B, 125/5). The Beth Israel cantor, Robert Gerber, also played an active role after his arrival in 1983 and was charged with redesigning the school music curriculum.[28] Music has been integrated into the Beth Israel Day School and regular religious school programs to the extent that a list of objectives for student chapel experience includes singing a selected group of prayers to both traditional and new melodies.[29]

By the mid-twentieth century, musical education was no longer restricted to children. The adult education curriculum included courses on music for the synagogue (B, 123/28; B, 130/3), and special programs with folk singing were featured at weekend singles retreats (B, 126/3).

Music also became an increasingly important focus of Beth Israel youth group activity. Among the first events scheduled when a chapter of Federated Temple Youth was founded at Beth Israel (BIFTY) in the summer of 1958 was Thursday evening South American dancing lessons; one of the first items requested by the youth committee was a jukebox (B1, 1958).

Creative activity in the domain of music for worship became an increasingly important aspect of youth activities. By the late 1960s, BIFTY was sponsoring Sabbath services at Beth Israel with nontraditional content, including dance:

> There was singing, that musical declaration of a pure and simple faith, "I Believe," preceded by the Sh'ma. Later, the Adoration became a lusty, joyous affirmation of God as the chorus of singers responded to guitar player Sammy Jacobson. . . . There was dancing. To the stirring strains of "Eli, Eli," four young girls moved gracefully across the altar, speaking with their bodies the prayerful words of this haunting melody. (B, 115/17)

Rabbi Schachtel encouraged the intense interest in creative worship among temple youth (B, 116/8). Eventually, BIFTY activity contributed to the establishment of alternative services on the High Holidays. That these services have now entered the Beth Israel mainstream is confirmed by the performance of Debbie Friedman's guitar-accompanied confirmation service in 1983 and 1984. The Beth Israel liturgy increasingly reflects the strong, creative thrust of BIFTY musical activity.

Conclusion

A recent study has suggested that the American synagogue is "the institutional center of Jewish life," with an official public image based upon religious activity while in actuality supporting the activities of "folk religion."[30] The preceding survey of music in Beth Israel's history supports this perspective and confirms that worship is only part of the complex of activities that make up the American synagogue today. Correspondingly, liturgical music is at the core of Beth Israel's image, but remains only one of several domains of musical activity that at different times in Beth Israel's history have either existed independently or interacted closely. Musical life at Beth Israel comprises varied and often distinct activities in different areas surrounding the "official" arena of liturgical music. Diverging from standard liturgical content are the growing number of special services for diverse occasions. Closely related, yet emphatically nonliturgical, are the elaborate musical events for Purim and Chanukah. A special domain of musical activity is that incorporated in the educational curriculum for members of all ages. Dance events, yet another type of musical activity, serve to define and reinforce peer groups within the Temple social structure. In addition, Beth Israel holds concerts and musical reviews of largely secular content.

Sometimes, musical events in different domains are interconnected. For example, in the last twenty years, musical innovations in the educational and social domains have directly shaped the music used in the liturgy. Special services, particularly interfaith worship, often provide a context for interaction between liturgical and secular music.

There is little doubt that these diverse musical activities are an integral part of congregational life. The public concern with planning these functions as well as the enthusiastic official praise for successful carnivals, concerts, and dances testifies to the leadership's recognition of and concern with these many manifestations of "folk culture." Music in the secular domains is no less distinctively Beth Israel's own than that in the liturgy. The early twentieth-century shift from the musical elaboration of Purim to Chanukah is a tacit acknowledgment by Beth Israelites of the importance of the Christmas season in the American calendar. The changing themes of temple dances over the years reflect Beth Israel's response to the changing currents in American popular culture. Future research must look beyond the domain of liturgical music if it is to fully evaluate the broad role of music in the synagogue.

The diverse musical life at Beth Israel further serves to define and mediate different aspects of the Beth Israel members' identity: the religious self, the communal self, the social self, and the patriotic self. Identities are complex, and musical activities within synagogue life are both reflective and expressive of that reality. That the frequently elaborated Houston-Texas-Jewish identity is not ephemeral fashion but a deep part of Beth Israel's heritage seems clear; studies in other regions may help refine our understanding of how the synagogue serves as a mediator of different identities.[31] Particularly in concerts and musical reviews we find that the multiple identities of the typical Beth Israel member intersect: Reform Jew, Texan, and American. The importance and significance of musical events like "Hello Houston" are not so much that they raise money for sisterhood activities as that they mediate and in many ways reconcile the contradictions in each Beth Israelite's identity. Many members can attend and enjoy musical revues because these events address, at least in part, the very special perspective that Jews living in Houston, Texas, share.

This discussion of music within the history of Congregation Beth Israel raises many questions that cannot be answered in a single case study. Is Beth Israel atypical in the sheer volume of musical activity it has generated? One scholar has suggested that the local synagogue tradition is essentially a personal tradition dependent upon the particular rabbi, cantor, or other factors of a given time and place.[32] Certainly we have seen ample evidence of autonomous choir directors and organists, as well as a series of Beth Israel rabbis who were unusually sensitive to and supportive of music. Yet one must also consider that much of Beth Israel's musical development is not idiosyncratic, but reflects the character of the American synagogue in general, and the Reform Movement in particular. Studies of other synagogues may help us distinguish the personal and local from the universal.

This study has only been able to touch on the role of individuals and groups in generating musical life and events in the synagogue; indeed, Beth Israel is fully representative of the "culture of organizations" identified as an increasingly significant aspect of American Jewish life since World War II.[33] There appears to be a clear division in musical activities and status between the professional and volunteer musician as well as gender-specific roles. In general, male professionals have controlled most activity related to liturgical music, whereas female volunteers have traditionally dominated musical activity in the educational and social domains. But this pattern is already in transition, particularly in the Reform Movement, where women now comprise a majority training for the cantorate.

A central issue, and one with which we can conclude, is the role of change in American synagogue music, as demonstrated in this case study. We have seen slow and somewhat predictable changes in the liturgical repertory at Beth Israel over the years; only recently has enthusiastic acceptance of creative liturgy spurred the incorporation of diverse musical styles into the service. Yet change, even that of recent years, does not always indicate a movement away from tradition. The last decade has also seen the arrival of a cantor, the revival of traditional nineteenth-century musical repertory, and the integration of a regular music curriculum into the expanding day school.

Discussions of synagogue music in the past have often been preoccupied with tracing continuity, while ignoring or disparaging change.[34] The case of Beth Israel suggests that both have continually interacted to shape a complex and multilayered musical tradition.

NOTES

I would like to thank the staff at Congregation Beth Israel for their enthusiastic cooperation. Cantor Robert Gerber, Executive Director Doris Markoff, Librarian Lorraine Lessey, and Building Manager Irving Berk devoted many hours to help me locate materials and gather information that could easily have been overlooked. Former Beth Israel Organist Anthony Rahe provided details concerning Beth Israel's musical life that were otherwise unavailable. I greatly appreciate the advice provided by the staff at the Houston Metropolitan Research Center under the guidance of its head, Dorothy Glasser. In addition, Morris Berman, Thomas Crow, Cantor Irving Dean, Abram Geller, Lillian E. Kaufman, Raymond R. Kaufman, Mrs. G. Lipper, Rabbi Carole L. Meyers, Kenneth Midlo, Rabbi Hyman Judah Schachtel, Celia Siegel, and Cantor George Wagner provided a wealth of information in interviews.

1   *Daily Houston Telegraph*, 17 June 1870.
2   The Beth Israel charter was approved on 28 December 1859, but the synagogue was founded earlier, and 1854 is celebrated as the year of founding. A copy of the original charter is enclosed in Beth Israel Board Minutes 1922–1942, p. 91; the original has evidently been lost.
3   David G. McComb, *Houston: A History*, rev. ed. (Austin, 1981), pp. 11–12.
4   Extant records date from 1861, beginning with minutes of both regular and annual congregational meetings; minutes of the board of trustees are preserved from 1866. These and other organizations' minute books, financial records, committee reports, correspondence, clippings, and miscellany were transferred to the Houston Metropolitan Research Center of the Houston Public Library in 1977, where they have been cataloged and are available for research purposes. Most materials dating from the 1920s, also cataloged in 1977, remain at Beth Israel. Abbreviations for various archival resources cited are as follows:

2A	Minutes of regular and annual meetings (1861–1889), 496 pp.
2B	Minutes of regular meetings of the board of trustees (1866–1884), 282 pp.
2C	Minutes and reports of annual and regular meetings (1890–1907), 132 pp.
S1	Minutes of regular and special meetings of the board of trustees (1884–1907), 364 pp.
S2	Minutes of annual assemblies and regular board meetings (1907–1922), 288 pp.
S3	Minutes of meetings of the board of trustees (December 1920–December 1921), 7 pp.
S4	Board minutes (1922–1942), n.p.
B1	Minutes of the regular meetings of the board of trustees (1957–1974, missing 1966–1968, 1969)
AMC	Occasional minutes of ritual and music committee, 1948–1984
B	Congregation Beth Israel Bulletin (1954–1984)

Interviews with Houstonians are cited by name and date of interview unless anonymity was requested.

5   This study approaches music in the synagogue according to a model often employed by Jewish Houstonians, who perceive the synagogue as a "house of worship, a house of meeting, and a house of study." Judge Norman W. Black, "An Invitation" (to attend adult education series, 1977–1978), B,123/22. This perspective of synagogue life closely resembles that in the midwestern synagogue, where involvement was expressed through worship, participation in adult religious study, and social interaction with peers. See Marshall Sklare and Joseph Greenblum, *Jewish Identity on the Suburban Frontier*, 2d ed. (Chicago and London, 1979), p. 179.

6   For studies of music in the liturgical context, see A. Z. Idelsohn, "Synagogue Music Past and Present," *Central Conference of American Rabbis Yearbook*, 33 (1923); A. W. Binder, "A History of American Jewish Hymnody," in *A. W. Binder: His Life and Work*, ed. Irene Heskes (New York, 1965), pp. 255–269; Albert Weisser, *The Modern Renaissance of Jewish Music. Events and Figures, Eastern Europe and America* (New York, 1983); and Eric Werner, *A Voice Still Heard. The Sacred Songs of the Ashkenazic Jews* (University Park, Pa., and London, 1976).

7   *Minhag America. The Daily Prayers* was first published in 1857 and then revised in 1866 and 1872. The *Union Prayer Book* was first published in 1895, with subsequent editions in 1918 and 1940. For details of the complicated history of the various editions, see Lou H. Silberman, "The Union Prayer Book: A Study in Liturgical Development," in *Retrospect and Prospect*, ed. Bertram Wallace Korn (New York, 1965), pp. 46–80; Lawrence A. Hoffman, "The Language of Survival in American Reform Liturgy," *CCAR Journal*, 24, no. 3 (Summer 1977), pp. 87–106; and Central Conference of American Rabbis, *Gates of Prayer, The New Union Prayerbook* (New York, 1975).

8   Only in 1900 did Beth Israel achieve continuity in rabbinical appointments. Rev. Dr. H. Barnstein of London, England, was elected minister as of 1 January 1900 (2C, 12/18/1899) and served until 1943; a name change to Barnston first appears in congregational records around 1920 (S2, 3/28/1920). Barnston was succeeded by Dr. Hyman Judah Schachtel in 1943, and Schachtel by Samuel Egal Karff in 1975. Beth Israel hired opera singer Arturo Sergei as cantor in 1973 (B1, 6/20/1973) and welcomed its first invested cantor, Robert Gerber, in June 1983 (B, 129/18).

9   Table 1 is compiled from the records of Anthony Rahe, Beth Israel organist from 1930 to 1973; see the discussion under "A Local Organ Controversy" for further information. Also see Eric Werner, *A Voice Still Heard* (University Park, Pa., and London, 1976), p. 235.

10 Interview with Anthony Rahe, 23 July 1984.

11 The organ was first introduced into the German synagogue at Seesen, and later at the Neue Israelitische Tempel-Verein (New Israelite Temple Society) in Hamburg during the first two decades of the nineteenth century. For details of the ensuing controversy, see W. Gunther Plaut, *The Rise of Reform Judaism* (New York, 1963), pp. 34–42, 166–169; and Werner, *A Voice Still Heard*, pp. 194–198.

12 Interview with Anthony Rahe, 23 July 1984.

13   Henry Cohen became rabbi of Congregation B'nai Israel in 1888, and served for sixty-two years. He wrote about the history of Jews in Texas, notably in "Early Jewish Settlements in Texas," in *One Hundred Years of Jewry in Texas* (Dallas, 1936). For further information about his life and contribution, see Anne Nathan Cohen, *Henry Isaac Cohen. The Man Who Stayed in Texas* (New York, 1941).
14   Interview with Anthony Rahe, 23 July 1984.
15   Specific evidence of Christian influences on Beth Israel's ritual or musical life is scattered and superficial: A long-ago comment states that Beth Israel religious school students are making "progress in all classes except Catechism" (S1, 12/28/1890), and some more recent remarks refer to "Sukos Vesper Services" (B, 115/4, 177/24).
16   Interview with Anthony Rahe, 23 July 1984. *Songster* refers to *The Union Songster, Songs and Prayers for Jewish Youth* (New York, 1960).
17   Morris Berman, July 1984.
18   Anonymous, July 1984.
19   Weekly Service Music Outline, 2 June 1978. These have included "Concerto in G Major" by Antonie Soler and "Chaconne in G Minor" by Louis Couperin Le Grand.
20   Interview with Thomas Crow, 10 March 1984.
21   Weekly Service Music Outline, 30 November 1979.
22   Composed by Friedman in 1973 at the request of Samuel Karff while he was still rabbi at Sinai Congregation in Chicago, the Chanukah Cantata was first performed at Beth Israel in 1975. Friedman also wrote a confirmation service that was performed in 1983 and 1984.
23   These included the hymnal, *The Voice of Prayer and Praise*, and works by English composers Marcus Hast, Israel L. Mombach, Charles K. Salaman, and Hayyim Wasserzug.
24   Interview with Anthony Rahe, 23 July 1984.
25   Anonymous, summer 1984.
26   *The Message of Congregation Beth Yeshurun*, vol. 2, no. 29, 30 March 1984.
27   Interview with Celia Siegel, 10 March 1984.
28   Interview with Robert Gerber, 11 July 1984.
29   Mimeographed sheet provided by Kenneth Midlo, 24 July 1984.
30   Charles S. Liebman, "The Religion of American Jews," in *The Jew in American Society*, ed. Marshall Sklare (New York, 1974), p. 245.
31   It may prove fruitful to investigate whether there are any clear regional preferences for particular musical content in liturgy. This possibility was raised by A. W. Binder, who mentioned that *Minhag America* was accepted primarily by congregations in western and southern cities. See "A History of American Jewish Hymnody," p. 262.
32   Werner, *A Voice Still Heard*, p. 235.

33 Jacob Neusner, *American Judaism. Adventure in Modernity* (Englewood Cliffs, N.J., 1971).

34 Judith Eisenstein's recent article is indicative of a growing interest in change. See "The Chant in the Changing American Synagogue," *Proceedings of the World Congress of Jewish Music* (Jerusalem, 1978).

Index

Aaron Wise Industrial School, 214
Abrahams, Abraham I., 2
Abrahams, Jacob, 38
Abrahamson, Louis Allen, 300
acculturation, 43–4, 88; of children and grandchildren, 66–7; and relation to synagogue, 47, 51–2, 60, 64
acculturation levels, 181; and synagogue relocation, 185, 186; and synagogue structure and function, 201–2
activities (synagogue), 220; at Brooklyn Jewish Center, 303, 304–5; of sisterhoods, 215–16, 218; synagogue purpose reflected in, 197
Aden, Joseph, 375
Adler, Cyrus, 380
Adler, Felix, 94
Adler, Liebman, 8
Adler, Samuel, 11, 94
administration (synagogue): decision-making in, 185–6; in Sephardic synagogue, 157; see also governance (synagogue)
adult education, xii, 125, 138, 173, 197; in Brooklyn Jewish Center, 303–4, 305, 319; music in (Beth Israel, Houston), 408–9
affiliation, 328; reasons for, 26; multiple, 354; patterns of, in Conservative synagogues, 116–17
Agudath Ha-Rabbonim (Union of Orthodox Rabbis of the United States and Canada), 55, 60, 78n69, 271n59
Agus, Jacob, 385
Ahawath Chesed Shaar Hashomayim Sisterhood, 209
Albany, N.Y., xii, 177; Congregation Anshe Emeth, 366, 367, 368, 372; Congregation Beth El, 366–7; Temple Israel, 173
Alhadeff, Solomon, 155
alienation, 40, 135
aliyot, see Torah honors (aliyot)
Alliance Israélite Universelle, 153
Almeleh, Jacob, 158, 161
America, La (newspaper), 154
American Council for Judaism, 101, 102, 335
American Federation of Jews from Central Europe, 264n12

American Jewess, 207, 210–11
American Jewish Committee, 95
American Jewish Congress, 95
American Jewish Yearbook, 24, 102
American Judaism, 292, 298; dualism of, 316; impact of Christianity on, 401
American Reform Judaism, see Reform Judaism
American Orthodoxy, 63, 64–8, 259; 355; defined in terms of opposition to mixed seating, 394n109; dissatisfaction with, 124–5
American rite, 9, 46
Americanization, x, xi–xii, xiii, 11, 20, 43–44; and Conservative Movement, 117, 118; and East European congregations, 48–54, 56, 58; education for, 172; ethnic-religious ambiguities and, 245, 246, 248, 251, 258; in governance, 16; and Jewishness, 179, 180; Jewish refugees and, 64–5, 67; Orthodoxy and, 38, 45, 46; and religious reform, 9–10, 327–8, 333, 334, 344, 348, 349, 355, 363–4; and Sephardic Synagogue, 157, 158, 160, 162, 163
Amsterdam Jewry, 277
Angel, Sadick, 155
antirabbinism, 275–7
antisemitism, 99, 282–4
anti-Zionism, 335
architects, 49, 191, 192
architecture, xiii, 24, 105, 114, 127, 147n35, 181, 186, 199, 202; of Brooklyn Jewish center, 311; and congregtional participation, 402
Arian, Shraga (Philip), 175, 176
art, synagogue, 147n35
articles of incorporation, 44
arts, patronage of, 304; see also culture
Arzt, Max, 128
Ascher, Joseph Mayer, 309
Ash, Abraham Joseph, 13–14, 376
Ashkenazic Jews, xi, 6–7, 41, 71n16, 72n20, 153, 372–3; in Sephardic synagogue, 167; migration to U.S., 231; ritual of, 235; see also German rite (minhag Ashkenaz)
assimilation, 9, 60, 99, 241, 371, 378; Americanized Orthodoxy and, 63; cultural, 13, 172; economics of, 57;